D0427486

Western Balkans

Richard Plunkett
Vesna Maric, Jeanne Oliver

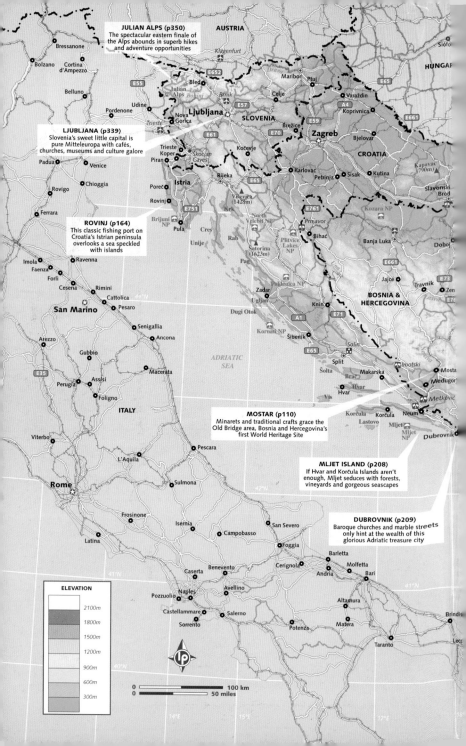

JULIAN ALPS (p350)
The spectacular eastern finale of the Alps abounds in superb hikes and adventure opportunities

LJUBLJANA (p339)
Slovenia's sweet little capital is pure Mitteleuropa with cafés, churches, museums and culture galore

ROVINJ (p164)
This classic fishing port on Croatia's Istrian peninsula overlooks a sea speckled with islands

MOSTAR (p110)
Minarets and traditional crafts grace the Old Bridge area, Bosnia and Hercegovina's first World Heritage Site

MLJET ISLAND (p208)
If Hvar and Korčula Islands aren't enough, Mljet seduces with forests, vineyards and gorgeous seascapes

DUBROVNIK (p209)
Baroque churches and marble streets only hint at the wealth of this glorious Adriatic treasure city

ELEVATION

	2100m
	1800m
	1500m
	1200m
	900m
	600m
	300m

0   100 km
0   50 miles

ADRIATIC SEA

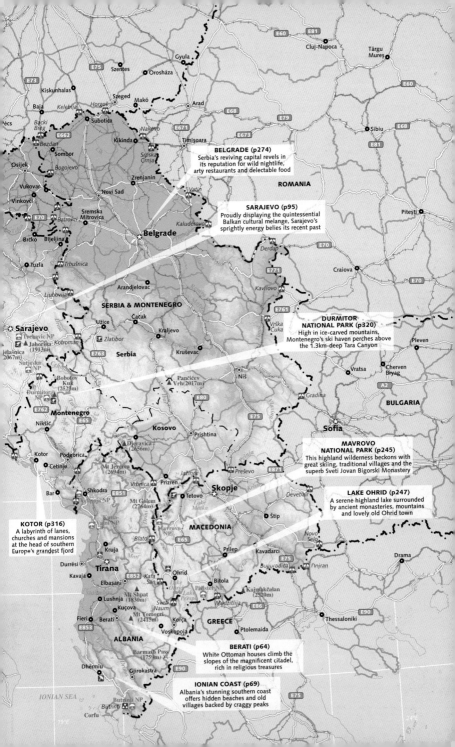

BELGRADE (p274)
Serbia's reviving capital revels in its reputation for wild nightlife, arty restaurants and delectable food

SARAJEVO (p95)
Proudly displaying the quintessential Balkan cultural melange, Sarajevo's sprightly energy belies its recent past

DURMITOR NATIONAL PARK (p320)
High in ice-carved mountains, Montenegro's ski haven perches above the 1.3km-deep Tara Canyon

MAVROVO NATIONAL PARK (p245)
This highland wilderness beckons with great skiing, traditional villages and the superb Sveti Jovan Bigorski Monastery

LAKE OHRID (p247)
A serene highland lake surrounded by ancient monasteries, mountains and lovely old Ohrid town

KOTOR (p316)
A labyrinth of lanes, churches and mansions at the head of southern Europe's grandest fjord

BERATI (p64)
White Ottoman houses climb the slopes of the magnificent citadel, rich in religious treasures

IONIAN COAST (p69)
Albania's stunning southern coast offers hidden beaches and old villages backed by craggy peaks

Destination Western Balkans

Croatia's fabulous coast and Slovenia's Alpine splendours are already making an impression on the world tourism scene, but there's much more to discover in the countries of the Western Balkans. This compact region of six republics (with two more possibly on the way) offers ski resorts, beaches, castles, bazaars and café cultures barely known to outsiders. After the tumultuous 1990s, Albania and the former Yugoslavia are ready to welcome visitors again. Compared with neighbouring Italy and Greece the region is great value, and you aren't bustled along with zillions of holidaymakers competing for the same restaurant table or patch of beach.

The region's ethnic complexity is renowned, and we'd argue that despite its recent history this is far from a bad thing. The colourful frescoes and hallowed icons of Orthodox monasteries, the pencil-like minarets of Ottoman mosques and the splendour of medieval Catholic churches share common ground. And while there is a wealth of traditional life and culture to savour, new scenes keep evolving, such as the techno clubs of raffish Tirana and the riverside bars of reviving Belgrade. Ironically enough, while some parts of the region are pressing for independence, their newly independent neighbours are making their way into a federation with the EU. But let's drop the politics – everyone in the Western Balkans has had enough of it. Just enjoy the wine, the evening strolls through town squares, the walks on pine-capped islands, and find your own freedom here.

PAUL DAVID HELLAND

City Life

Watch men playing chess outside Skenderija (p99) in Sarajevo, Bosnia and Hercegovina, and see if you can pick their next move

OTHER HIGHLIGHTS

- Serbia's Belgrade (p274) has wild nightlife and boisterous restaurants, all watched over by the massive Kalemegdan Citadel.

- As well as galleries, museums and café culture, Ljubljana (p339), in Slovenia, has the counter-cultural Metelkova centre.

- The museum-rich capital of Croatia, Zagreb (p148) has baroque architecture, outdoor cafés and a series of parks.

Check out the baroque architecture of the Cathedral of the Assumption of the Virgin (p211), in Dubrovnik's Old Town, Croatia

See how the apartment buildings of Tirana (p54), in Albania, have been redecorated

Natural Wonders

Walk the wooden footbridges through the beautifully damp Plitvice Lakes National Park (p191), a World Heritage site in Croatia

MARTIN MOOS

GRANT DIX

Climb the Alps in Slovenia's Triglav National Park (p357), the perfect starting point for an adventure into the natural wonders of the Western Balkans

PATRICK HORTON

Ski in Montenegro's Durmitor National Park (p320), dominated by the rounded mass of the 'Bear' (Međed)

OTHER HIGHLIGHTS

- Macedonia's Lake Ohrid (p247), overlooked by the marvellous church of Sveti Naum, is the deepest in the Balkans.
- Mavrovo National Park (p245) in Macedonia has great skiing, traditional villages and the splendid Sveti Jovan Bigorski monastery.

History & Culture

Peek inside Belgrade's mighty Sveti Marko church (p281), final resting place of Emperor Dušan, ruler of Serbia during its 'Golden Age'

Gaze up at the tightly-tiered Ottoman-era villas in the three old quarters of Berati (p64), Albania

OTHER HIGHLIGHTS

- Spanning the Neretva River, the rebuilt Old Bridge (Stari Most) area of Mostar (p111) is Bosnia's first World Heritage site.

Compare old and new along the waterfront of Durrësi (p60), Albania

Sand & Sea

Relax on Croatia's tranquil Mljet Island (p208)

OTHER HIGHLIGHTS

- Rovinj (p164), on Croatia's Istrian Peninsula, has an unspoiled fishing port and pleasant views of the offshore islands.
- Croatia's striking Dalmatian coast (p187) is the place to be if you want to be on, under or near the water.

Marvel at the view of Kotor Fjord, the largest fjord in southern Europe, from the beautiful Old Town of Kotor (p316), in Montenegro

PATRICK HORTON

Get away from it all at Drymades (p70), one of the white-sand beaches near Dhërmiu on Albania's Ionian Coast

RAFAEL ESTEFAN

Contents

Regional Map Contents

Slovenia
p330

Croatia
pp138-9

Bosnia and
Hercegovina
p88

Serbia and
Montenegro
p268

Macedonia
p232

Albania
p42

The Authors

RICHARD PLUNKETT Coordinating Author, Albania, Macedonia

Richard grew up on a vineyard in southern Australia, and has a peculiar fascination for wines made from obscure varieties. Albanian Kallmet and Macedonian Vranec more than satisfied his curiosity. Richard has written for Lonely Planet on a gaggle of postcommunist countries, including Uzbekistan, Armenia and Turkmenistan, and enjoys visiting cities with vast plazas suitable for May Day tank parades. He also writes freelance articles and stories and is battling away at a degree in international relations.

Life on the Road

Without sounding too much like an obscure-destination travel snob, I love going places that I'd never dreamed I'd go to. Travelling to a sturdy old monastery topped with gleaming domes, or to a beach with rocky islets within swimming distance, are the kind of trips that make me grin in a happy, stupid kind of way. The easiest thing about travelling in this region is that no matter how unpronounceable the destination (Mljet? Jajce? Krk??) it isn't hard to find a comfy, cosy bed that won't trigger hysteria when the credit-card statement comes. After a night of weird local drinks at a lunatic bar where Shakira battles Pink Floyd on the playlist, a warm room with a frilly duvet and a hot shower is sweet comfort.

VESNA MARIC Bosnia & Hercegovina, Serbia & Montenegro

Vesna was born in Mostar, Bosnia and Hercegovina and moved to Britain at the age of 16. Her love for all things Balkan has never subsided, although it has sometimes manifested itself as frustration. Returning to Bosnia and Hercegovina and Serbia and Montenegro as a travel writer for this book deepened her love for (and some frustration towards) the region. Vesna has written magazine articles, produced radio features and worked on short films.

LONELY PLANET AUTHORS

Why is our travel information the best in the world? It's simple: our authors are independent, dedicated travellers. They don't research using just the Internet or phone, and they don't take freebies in exchange for positive coverage. They travel widely, to all the popular spots and off the beaten track. They personally visit thousands of hotels, restaurants, cafés, bars, galleries, palaces, museums and more – and they take pride in getting all the details right, and telling it how it is. For more, see the authors section on www.lonelyplanet.com.

JEANNE OLIVER
Croatia, Slovenia

Jeanne has been visiting and writing about Croatia and Slovenia since 1996, shortly after the new countries were 'born'. Travelling these countries by bus, boat, train and car, she's swum in the Adriatic, hiked on trails and stuffed her backpack full of local cheese, homemade brandy and a handful of recipes to keep her going until the next trip. She's looking forward to eventually visiting every one of Croatia's islands, especially now that she's finally figured out how to decipher the Jadrolinija schedule.

Getting Started

According to experts like us, travelling in the Western Balkans is dead easy. And that statement is almost entirely true! Visiting Slovenia and Croatia is no more difficult than going to Germany or Italy. Bosnia, Serbia and Montenegro, and Macedonia are less expensive; they feature lots of signs in Cyrillic alphabets, but are still easy to visit. Albania is more challenging: the capital Tirana is in the middle of a building boom, and many roads are either in dreadful shape or being rebuilt, though some of the main arteries have been finished. All around the region there are ATMs from which you can withdraw money from your account at home, and Internet cafés where you can check your email. Lots of new hotels and restaurants have opened in recent years, and there are many more on the way. If you are visiting in July and August it is useful to book accommodation ahead, particularly on Croatia's popular Dalmatian coast. The conflicts of the 1990s are well and truly over and the region is safe to visit, though it pays to check on current events in Kosovo before you venture there.

WHEN TO GO

The Western Balkans has a surprisingly consistent weather pattern for a region of its size. The high season for tourism runs from May until September. Croatia and Slovenia are the only countries where the sheer volume of visitors can be a hassle at the height of the season in July and August, though the main coastal resorts in Albania and Montenegro get fairly busy as well. The best time to visit is either side of the summer peak: May, June and September stand out, when it's not too hot, too crowded or overbooked anywhere. The ski season runs from late November until March.

See the Climate Charts (p388) for more information.

Travelling out of season can result in some real bargains in accommodation, although many places where tourism is the main industry all but close down during the low season. Also, bear in mind that the mountains have very cold winters. Winter is quite cold everywhere except for the Adriatic coast.

DON'T LEAVE HOME WITHOUT...

- Appropriate luggage: a travel pack (combined backpack/shoulder bag) with zip-away straps; a big zip bag with a wide shoulder strap; or a suitcase with wheels (though these can be awkward on cobblestone streets)
- Sunscreen, which can be rather expensive here
- Light cotton clothes between June and September, plus a light jacket or sweater for the mountain regions
- A coat, thick socks and a rainproof jacket if travelling during winter
- A Swiss army knife (just don't put it in your hand luggage before boarding a plane) to slice up local cheeses and pop corks on wines bought at the supermarket
- An iPod, to block out the sometimes overwhelming Balkan turbofolk music
- Ladies, bring your most lurid eye shadow for dress-ups à la Belgrade's Silicon Valley (see p287)

COSTS & MONEY

There's a quite a wide variation in average travel expenses across the Western Balkans. The further north and west you go, the more expensive it is. Slovenia is the most expensive country, and Croatia isn't far behind. Prices are steadily rising in the most popular resorts and cities. Serbia and Montenegro and Bosnia and Hercegovina are moderately priced, especially outside Belgrade and Sarajevo, while Macedonia (with the exception of Skopje) and Albania are quite budget friendly – certainly comparable to Turkey. Even so, don't expect to live royally on a few dollars a day.

Trying to give daily budgets isn't easy. Backpackers staying in hostels and eating cheaply can expect to spend around €40 per day, but will spend more in cities such as Zagreb, Belgrade and Ljubljana. Those wanting to have a more comfortable trip (staying in midrange accommodation and eating at decent restaurants most of the time) will probably spend between €70 and €100. In the countryside you'll be able to get by on far less, but in big cities during the high season you'll need more, especially if you're visiting a lot of museums and sights.

As long as you have an ATM card, you need not worry about money in any decent-sized town. All major credit and debit cards are accepted by ATMs, including those on the Cirrus/Maestro platform. Travellers cheques used to be a good backup, but are less so now. They may be the safest way to carry a lot of money, but they can often be an utter pain to change; bank staff are usually unfamiliar with them, so if there's a big business hotel with an in-house bank, try there. Having €100 in cash tucked away in a safe place is the best insurance – enough to land a cheapish hotel room, a meal and a ride to a working ATM the next day. Many currencies are difficult or impossible to exchange outside of the country in which they are used. It's best to change the local currency into euros or dollars before leaving.

READING UP
Books

The Fall of Yugoslavia by Misha Glenny is one of the more easy-to-read tomes on the ex-Yugoslav wars. Though not without critics, Glenny spells out the details with verve and clarity.

Explaining Yugoslavia by John Allcock does just that: this scholarly book pulls together historical, cultural and political analysis of the highest order to reach some surprising conclusions.

Ismail Kadare has written serious works as well as the light, funny *The File on H*, about two Irish academics who stumble into local politics. Highly recommended for anyone who fears Balkan literature may be boring.

Black Lamb & Grey Falcon by Rebecca West is a sprawling, poetic account of travels through Bosnia, Serbia, Kosovo, Croatia and Albania in the 1930s and 1940s. West shows her prejudices quite clearly, but she's an incredible reporter.

Through the Embers of Chaos by Dervla Murphy is widely available and gives terrific background information on the region. Murphy bicycles through the region and describes the 'decade of decay' beautifully, but her strident interjections can be quite irritating.

Historian Noel Malcolm takes on the near-impossible task of setting out disputed histories clearly in *Bosnia: A Short History* and *Kosovo: A Short History* – they're not light reads (warning: neither is particularly short) but they are authoritative.

WESTERN BALKANS WORLD HERITAGE LIST

This list of sites deemed 'world heritage' by Unesco includes some – but not all – of the most remarkable attractions of the region. In 2005 Bosnia and Hercegovina's Mostar and Albania's Gjirokastra joined the register of the world's most precious cultural and natural treasures. For more information see http://whc.unesco.org.

Albania

■ Ancient ruins of Butrinti (p72)
■ Museum-City of Gjirokastra (p73)

Bosnia & Hercegovina

■ Old Bridge (Stari Most) area of Mostar (p111)

Croatia

■ Dubrovnik's Old Town (p211)
■ Plitvice Lakes National Park (p191)
■ Poreč's Euphrasian Basilica (p163)
■ Šibenik's Cathedral of St James
■ Split's historic centre with Diocletian's Palace (p195)
■ Trogir's Old Town (p200)

Macedonia

■ Ohrid and its lake (p247)

Serbia & Montenegro

■ Dečani Monastery (p307)
■ Durmitor National Park (p320)
■ Kotor and its gulf (p316)
■ Stari Ras and Sopoćani Monastery (p301)
■ Studenica Monastery (p302)

Slovenia

■ Škocjan Caves (Rakov Škocjan, p362)

Websites

There's a vast amount of information on the Web about the Western Balkans, which is useful whether you're planning a full two-month tour from Maribor to Bitola or a weekend in Dubrovnik. The following are recommended:

Hostels.com (www.hostels.com/en/easterneurope.html) This site has a list of most hostels and budget accommodation in the region, as well as ratings and a lot of photos.

In Your Pocket (www.inyourpocket.com) This publishing firm gives information on Albania and Croatia and publishes frequently updated pocket guides to Zagreb, Zadar and Tirana.

Rail Europe (www.raileurope.com) Tonnes of information on routes, prices and timetables for the whole region, bar Albania, is available on this website.

Thorn Tree (http://thorntree.lonelyplanet.com) Lonely Planet's travellers' bulletin board has a wealth of information on the region – the Eastern Europe and the Caucasus branch covers the Western Balkans. Post a query and online experts generally give a quick reply.

Virtual Tourist (www.virtualtourist.com) This covers virtually the entire world, including all of the Western Balkans, with reviews, forums, photos and tips from travellers and amateur experts. It's slightly difficult to navigate, but with patience and a healthy scepticism it yields a lot of information.

FESTIVALS & EVENTS

Western Balkan cities and towns come alive during festivals, and while you may need to book accommodation in advance it's a great time to visit. See each of the country chapters for details on local festivals. Following is a selection of our favourites.

Ljubljana Summer Festival (early July–late August) This annual celebration of music, opera, street theatre and dance is now in its fifth decade. It's held at venues around Slovenia's capital, but is centred on the open-air Križanke theatre (p344).

Exit Festival (July) The biggest rock concert in the Serbian summer draws top international rock and techno performers to Novi Sad (p293).

Galičnik Wedding Festival (mid-July) Over the second weekend in July this rustic village in Mavrovo National Park, Macedonia hosts a very popular festival of traditional, wildly romantic weddings. Tissues a must (p246).

Baščaršijske Noči (Baščaršija Nights; July) This festival in the heart of Sarajevo encompasses everything from dance to pop music, traditional folk music and theatre (p103).

International Carnival of Rijeka (January or February) Croatia's wildest carnival falls before the Lenten fast, with concerts, parties, balls and grotesque parades (p181).

RESPONSIBLE TRAVEL

Litter in national parks, nature reserves and picnic spots can be quite severe, especially in the southern parts of the Western Balkans. Do remember to pack up your litter, and let's hope it starts a trend. Minimise the waste you must carry out by taking minimal packaging and no more food than you need. Don't use detergents or toothpaste (even if they are biodegradable) in or near natural water sources. When camping in the wild (checking first to see that it's allowed), bury human waste in holes at least 15cm deep and at least 100m from any nearby water.

When visiting mosques and *tekkes* (shrines or monasteries), wear conservative clothes which cover arms and legs, and take off your shoes

---

CONDUCT IN THE WESTERN BALKANS

There's nothing really unusual about the customs of the region that might cause you to stumble into a major faux pas, but here are a few tips to make the locals like you even more.

The Balkan and/or Mediterranean idea of time is something that superefficient global professionals might chafe against. If you're here for work, expect to mix business with pleasure. Cafés are not places for a quick caffeine refill, but somewhere to laze for an hour or three. Conversations about every aspect of your family and your marital status are a sign of friendly interest, not nosiness. If you go into a shop, a cheerful hello in the local lingo is appreciated, rather than just making a beeline for the display racks.

Spouting forth with your theory on the fall of communism and the Yugoslav wars of the 1990s probably won't win you many friends. You may have all the facts at your fingertips, but in many cases the reaction to an opinionated dissertation will be a politely strained silence or a sharpish retort along the lines of 'You weren't here, you can't possibly know'. Asking people about their experiences in the conflicts will inevitably bring up some interesting anecdotes but perhaps also some horrendous memories.

Alcohol tends to flow fairly freely in the Christian parts of the region, less so in Muslim areas (where the habit of drinking endless cups of coffee risks caffeine overload). Being high-spirited is fine, being totally rotten isn't, especially for women. If people start spouting nationalist rhetoric after a few shots of firewater, it's your turn to be diplomatically polite.

and socks before you enter. Women should cover their hair. Don't walk around in front of people if they are praying. When visiting Orthodox churches and monasteries, it is customary to buy a few candles and light them; it's an ancient tradition and it generates a bit of income for the custodians.

If you go diving on the Adriatic coast, try to protect the environment you're visiting by not taking souvenirs, not standing on or touching corals (contact can kill them) and following the instructions of your diving guide.

Itineraries

CLASSIC ROUTES

THE ESSENTIAL TOUR   Two Weeks

Start in Slovenia with a cheap flight into **Ljubljana** (p339). Explore this charming capital before heading into the **Julian Alps** (p350) and the divine scenery around **Lake Bled** (p351). Whether you like adventure sports or quiet strolls, Slovenia's mountains have much to offer. Head south to dip your toes into Croatia's dramatic **Dalmatian coast** (p187). Take a ferry across to the jet-setters' island of choice, **Hvar** (p203), before heading to the architectural splendours of **Dubrovnik** (p209). You might want to detour into Bosnia to visit the cultural treasures of **Mostar** (p110), Bosnia's first World Heritage–listed city, where the Neretva River has been hurdled by the famous Old Bridge. From Dubrovnik it's a short hop south to Montenegro's dramatic **Bay of Kotor** (p316), where you can stay in the walled port towns of **Herceg Novi** (p319) or **Kotor** (p316). Next is a classic Balkan train journey over the Dinaric Alps into the rolling hills of Serbia and the party capital of the Balkans, **Belgrade** (p274), with riverboat party palaces, restaurants and nightclubs, plus a fine array of museums and galleries. For a taste of Serbia's Orthodox Christian heritage, take a detour to the vineyards and monasteries of **Fruška Gora** (p294). A train ride through the fields of Slavonia brings you to **Zagreb** (p148), great for strolls through plazas, parks and elegant streets.

This is a great trip for any first-time visitor to the Western Balkans, taking in the highlights of four countries. It begins in Slovenia, heads along the coast of Croatia with a detour into Bosnia, then into Montenegro. Here you turn north to the region's biggest city, Belgrade, and stop at Zagreb on the way back to Slovenia.

WORLD HERITAGE SIGHTS (PLUS EXTRAS)   One Month

Start in Corfu and catch a ferry across to Saranda in Albania to visit the ruins of **Butrinti** (p72), then head on to the Ottoman-era hill town of **Gjirokastra** (p73). Culture and history buffs will also enjoy **Berati** (p64), arguably Albania's finest Ottoman town, and the mountain town of **Kruja** (p63), near Tirana. Take a bus into Macedonia to explore the churches of **Ohrid** (p247), and maybe the Baba Arabati *tekke* (shrine) at **Tetovo** (p243). From Ohrid head north into Kosovo via Skopje. The **Dečani Monastery** (p307) in Kosovo is a Serbian cultural treasure. From here it's just a short trip to Novi Pazar and the Serbian Orthodox monastery of **Studenica** (p302). From Novi Pazar travel to Montenegro and the spectacular **Durmitor National Park** (p320), and it's just a short hop down to pretty **Kotor** (p316) on the gulf of the same name. Montenegro's old capital at **Cetinje** (p310) is also worth a visit. Heading up the Adriatic coast into Croatia, **Dubrovnik's Old Town** (p211) is probably the most famous World Heritage site in the region. Dubrovnik is also a jumping-off point for the island of **Hvar** (p203). The centre of Hvar town is quite incredible. From Dubrovnik take a detour to **Mostar** (p110) in Bosnia, then head up the Dalmatian coast to **Split** (p192), with its historic centre and the ruins of Diocletian's Palace. The old town of **Trogir** (p200) is very close to Split. Further north and a little inland there's the rugged **Plitvice Lakes National Park** (p191). Then head to the Istria region and the enormous Euphrasian Basilica at **Poreč** (p161). From Poreč it's not far to Slovenia's limestone **Škocjan Caves** (p363) and **Lake Bled** (p351).

This route has a peculiar start – from package tour heaven in Corfu straight into Albania – and takes in Orthodox monasteries, Catholic churches, lake towns, walled port cities, old Ottoman-era towns plus a couple of the region's best national parks and natural attractions.

ROADS LESS TRAVELLED

HERITAGE & TRADITIONS   Three to Four Weeks

Start in Thessaloniki and take a train to **Skopje** (p236), the Macedonian capital. Explore the Ottoman bazaar, the city's churches and monasteries, and take a trip to **Šuto Orizari** (p238), Europe's biggest Roma settlement. Swing south on a detour to **Ohrid** (p247), the ancient Macedonian cultural centre. Head north to **Prishtina** (p304) in Kosovo, capital of this largely Albanian-populated UN protectorate. The **Dečani Monastery** (p307) near Peja is one of the treasures of the Serbian Orthodox Church. In the Muslim corner of Serbia near Novi Pazar, is the grand monastery of **Studenica** (p302). Head for Montenegro, one part of the Balkans where people of different faiths have always seemed to get along. **Kotor** (p316) is a divine port town, and **Ulcinj** (p314), near the Albanian border, is a well-integrated Christian-Muslim community. Head up to **Dubrovnik** (p209), Croatia's Adriatic jewel, then inland to Hercegovina's peculiar pilgrimage town of **Međugorje** (p119) and the reviving town of **Mostar** (p110). **Sarajevo** (p95), the heart of the Balkan conundrum, is close by with churches, mosques and synagogues. Move on to **Banja Luka** (p125), the capital of Bosnia's Republika Srpska region. Head north to Croatia's museum-rich capital, **Zagreb** (p148). A side trip to **Samobor** (p158) offers a taste of Croatian village life. The coastal towns of Istria are becoming well known but inland gems like **Motovun** (p178) and **Pazin** (p177) move at a slower pace. Heading into Slovenia, **Piran** (p366) is as charming a port as you'll find; from the graceful capital, **Ljubljana** (p339), it's easy to take trips into the **Julian Alps** (p350) and old craft centres like **Kropa** (p355).

This trip emphasises the cultural and historic treasures of the Western Balkans – a taste of each of the region's main cultures, faiths and traditions. There's also a lot of spectacular scenery along the way, plus many authentic B&Bs to get a further insight into the Austro-Hungarian-Orthodox-Ottoman influences that underpin the region's sensibilities.

THE WILD SIDE
One Month

Slovenia's **Triglav National Park** (p357) covers almost all of the **Julian Alps** (p350) and is the perfect starting point for an adventure into the natural wonders of the Western Balkans. Slovenia's Karst region has some rare sights, including the gorge of **Rakov Škocjan** (p362), the **Križna Cave** (p363) and the **Škocjan Caves** (p363). Moving south into Croatia, Pula is the stepping-off point to **Brijuni National Park** (p177). The **Plitvice Lakes National Park** (p191) near Zadar is a must, but take time to venture into the **Kornati Islands** (p189). **Makarska** (p200), on the Adriatic, is a great base for hiking up Mt Biokovo. Further south, check out the national park on **Mljet Island** (p208). Most of Bosnia's national parks are still off limits because of land mines, so head on to Montenegro's **Bay of Kotor** (p316) and the **Lake Skadar National Park** (p309). Montenegro's best nature reserve is **Durmitor National Park** (p320), which has a ski resort and is dotted with lakes. Another highlight there is rafting through the immense **Tara Canyon** (p320). Serbia's rugged **Kopaonik National Park** (p299) can be reached from the southern city of Novi Pazar, and is also Serbia's biggest ski resort. Kosovo's nature reserves and parks are in a similar state to Bosnia's – it would be unwise to explore them for now. Most of Albania's national parks are inaccessible, so aim for Macedonia's **Lake Matka** (p243) near Skopje, which has some fantastic hiking. Macedonia's two best national parks are **Mavrovo National Park** (p245) in the west, with skiing, miles of forest and the rocky slopes of Mt Korab, and **Pelister National Park** (p252) in the southwest, with old villages, treks to highland lakes and rare fauna.

This tour emphasises the natural wonders of the Western Balkans, from Alpine hikes to white-water rafting to skiing. Kick off in Slovenia and make your way down through the heart of the region all the way to Macedonia, enjoying as many thrills and spills as you can handle (don't forget the travel insurance).

TAILORED TRIPS

THE 'ARE WE THERE YET?' TOUR WITH KIDS

Any of the itineraries listed in this section would be suitable for children, just at a slower pace. An alternative strategy might be to pick a central base and do short trips from there. These suggestions centre on seaside holidays. There are quite a few direct flights into Croatian coastal cities like Split, Zadar and Dubrovnik, and there are lots of apartment rentals along the Dalmatian coast. The island of **Mljet** (p208) is a tranquil retreat ideal for a family holiday, and other islands such as **Korčula** (p205), **Krk** (p183) and **Rab** (p184) are suitable as well. An expedition to the **Plitvice Lakes National Park** (p191) is an easy day trip from underrated **Zadar** (p187).

Montenegro's coast packs a lot of variety into a small area. **Kotor** (p316) and **Herceg Novi** (p319) grace the spectacular Bay of Kotor, while **Budva** (p311) and **Ulcinj** (p314), further south, have decent beaches. It's easy to make excursions up to **Cetinje** (p310) and **Durmitor National Park** (p320).

Albania is a child-friendly country but the broken pavements and rustic roads might be too much of a strain. Still, if the kids don't mind a bit of adventure then the Ionian Coast port of **Saranda** (p71) might be fun – it's just a short ferry ride from Corfu.

THE ADRIATIC

This tour is for people who do like to be beside the seaside, and highlights some of the lesser-known beaches and resorts. Start off in Corfu and catch a ferry across to Saranda in Albania. The little resort of **Ksamili** (p73), south of Saranda, has fine beaches and views over to Corfu. Heading north along the Ionian Coast there is a fabulous beach at **Dhërmiu** (p70), though facilities are much simpler than in Croatia or Montenegro. Crossing into Montenegro aim for **Ulcinj** (p314) and **Budva** (p311).

Croatia's seaside resorts are booming but there are still plenty of lesser-known spots. **Cavtat** (p215) is a good alternative to Dubrovnik. **Mljet Island** (p208) and **Korčula Island** (p205) are more laid-back than Hvar. **Brela** (p202), near Makarska, has 6km of pebbly beach. Further north, underrated **Zadar** (p187) is a base to visit the gorgeous Kornati Islands, **Rab Island** (p184) has dozens of tiny coves and beaches, and for a touch of class there's **Opatija** (p182), near Rijeka. On the Istrian Peninsula there are plenty of camping grounds around **Pula** (p166). Slovenia's seaside resorts are normally quite busy, but **Izola** (p366), near Piran, is quieter than most.

Snapshots

CURRENT EVENTS

Democracy and capitalism have taken over: Serbia and Montenegro was the last country to throw off communist-style rule when Slobodan Milošević was finally wrenched out of office in 2001. Although voting irregularities still occur in some countries, a return to dictatorship is unlikely anywhere in the region. Economically the picture is more mixed. The wars of the 1990s set Bosnia and Hercegovina and Serbia and Montenegro back at least a decade, and like Macedonia they are making only a stuttering recovery. Slovenia and Croatia were always the wealthiest parts of the region, and their export-oriented businesses have slotted easily into the capitalist system. Albania has probably the fastest-growing economy, though that's partly because it is developing from such a low base. Millions of people from the region work elsewhere in Europe and further abroad, and the remittances they send home are a vital part of local economies.

The big questions are whether Kosovo and Montenegro make the shift to full independence, and whether the region will be able to join the EU. Slovenia signed up to the club in 2004, but the other countries are lagging behind. Croatia was accepted for negotiations towards membership in October 2005 and Macedonia may join by the end of the decade. The danger is that if countries such as Bosnia and Hercegovina and Macedonia don't join, ethnic tensions might build up again and trigger more conflicts. It would be wrong to assume that the hatreds and suspicions behind the 1990s wars have disappeared. Many Serbians feel there's a Muslim conspiracy against their countrymen in Kosovo and Bosnia and Hercegovina, the main communities in Macedonia are still edgy, and Kosovo's Serb and Roma communities live with sporadic violence and harassment.

The greatest potential for a flare-up is in Kosovo. The majority Albanian population is increasingly unhappy about the UN protectorate they've been living under since 1999. The UN believes that Kosovo won't be ready for independence until minority rights are assured and a good proportion of the Serb minority return. It's a slightly dreamy ideal. Most of the Serbs that left don't want to live under Albanian rule, and there isn't much incentive to return to a territory with a moribund economy. Kosovo's economy remains in tatters partly because the final status of the region hasn't been settled – catch-22! Serbia's government will greet Kosovo's independence with extreme displeasure, to say the least. The good news, perhaps, is that the big international players are well aware of the dangers of letting the region tip back into aggression, and in the meantime ordinary people in former trouble spots go about their lives unthreatened by war.

The Southeast European Times (www.setimes.com) covers all the serious stuff: economics, politics and analysis plus exchange rates. It's handy in case local politics boils over…

Homeland Calling: Exile Patriotism and the Balkan Wars by Paul Hockenos explores the fascinating stories of émigrés who involved themselves in the wars back 'home'.

HISTORY

The Western Balkans is the product of a complex history, to put it mildly. The region hasn't been controlled by one government since the Roman Empire. Farming first came to the area around 6000 BC, and was well established by 4000 BC. By 700 BC the local population was growing as

TIMELINE	1000 BC	400 BC
	Illyrians settle in the Western Balkans	Greek colonies founded along Adriatic coast

---

WHAT'S IN A NAME?

It wasn't easy thinking up a title for this book. *Former Yugoslavia and Albania* was technically true, but dull and somewhat passé. *Slovenia, Croatia, Serbia & Montenegro, Bosnia & Hercegovina, Macedonia, Albania and potentially Kosovo/Kosova* would have run all over the front cover and the next page as well. So how about *Western Balkans*? The problem with this title was that Slovenes don't see themselves as Balkan, and many Croatians aren't wild about being called Balkan either. A politically correct title would have had Southeastern Europe in it, but *Southeastern Europe – The Western Half* doesn't really work. Then there was an idea for *The Eastern Adriatic*, but Macedonia doesn't have a coast. Ideas about southern Slavic states plus Albanian entities came and went. One wit suggested *Greater [insert country here] and the Occupied Territories*; some classicists suggested *Illyria*; and meanwhile the deadline for a title whizzed by. Stumped, we went back to *Western Balkans*. It's not perfect. The word Balkan is Turkish in origin (it means Mountain), which suggests the former Ottoman Empire's European territories. This does not include Croatia and Slovenia, or the heart of Montenegro either. So the title could have been *Western Balkans, Croatia, Slovenia, and Old Montenegro*. The good thing about *Western Balkans* is that most people around the world sort of know where we're talking about. More or less the former Yugoslavia and Albania, but not Bulgaria and Romania. We apologise to anyone aggrieved by the title.

---

increasing amounts of iron tools, horses and chariots helped to spread trade routes. By the time Celtic tribes drove south and mixed with the native Illyrian and Thracian tribes, there were Greek colonies along the coast of Albania and Croatia. The Roman Empire introduced decent roads and vineyards, and built towns and fortresses all over the region. Even so, there remained pockets in the mountains of northern Albania where the Illyrian tribes largely managed their own affairs. The first division of the region can be dated to AD 395, when the Emperor Theodosius split the Roman Empire into an eastern, Greek-influenced half ruled from Byzantium (later Constantinople) and a western, Latin-influenced half ruled from Rome. This division laid down the first fault line between the western and eastern churches, even before the original Serbs and Croats had settled in. The Roman Empire was weakened by economic crises and plagues around the time it was divided, and invading 'barbarians' repeatedly plundered the region.

The Slavs

The Avar, Goth and Hun invasions weakened the Roman defences along the Danube so much that the Slav tribes (farmers and herders originally from eastern Ukraine) were able to move south of the river during the 5th and 6th centuries. Then, in the 9th century, Christian monks such as Cyril and Methodius began to evangelise the Slavs; the earliest Christian communities had been mostly eliminated by the barbarian invasions. Cyril and Methodius developed the first Slavic alphabet, called Glagolitic, and translated Christian scriptures. One of Methodius' students based in Bulgaria developed another alphabet, called Cyrillic, based on Byzantine Greek letters. This gradually replaced Glagolitic over several centuries, and eventually became the alphabet of the Serbian and Macedonian languages.

Another divide in Western Balkan history occurred in the same era that Cyril and Methodius were sharpening their quills. The Franks took

---

AD 272

Emperor Constantine the Great born in Niš, Serbia; converts to Christianity on deathbed

5th & 6th centuries

Slav tribes cross south of the Danube River

over the northwest of the region and the Croats and Slovenes came under Western European cultural influence. The first independent Croatian kingdom appeared under Ban Tomislav in 924. In the rest of the region the Byzantine Empire was weakening militarily but still held a great deal of cultural influence. The first Serb principality was established under the Byzantine umbrella around 850, but it wasn't until the 12th century that Stefan I Nemanja established the first fully independent Serbian kingdom. His son Stefan II built Serbia into a stable nation, recognised as independent by the pope but still with religious ties to the Orthodox Church in Constantinople. Many of Serbia's great religious artworks date from this time, as artists combined the strict formulas of Byzantine iconography styles with local influences. The greatest Serbian ruler was Stefan Dušan (r 1331–55), who was crowned at Skopje and established the Serbian Orthodox Patriarchate at Peč in western Kosovo.

The Turks Arrive

The Seljuk Turks swept out of central Asia into the Byzantine heartland of Anatolia in the 11th century. Their successors, the Ottomans, established a base in Europe in 1354, and over the next century they steadily increased their European territories. The early Turkish sultans lived in shifting military camps for up to nine months of the year, and had the best-paid, most professional and most sober army in Europe. The Ottoman 'victory' (more of a draw in fact) over the Serbs at Kosovo Polje in 1389 completed the separation of the southern Slavs; the Catholic Slovenes and Croats remained beyond Turkish rule, while the Orthodox Serbs and Macedonians were now under it. The Turks had conquered almost the entire region by 1500, and continuing raids in the 16th and 17th centuries prompted the Slovenes to abandon the lowlands for safer areas, and to fortify their churches in the Julian Alps. The core of Montenegro remained independent under a dynasty of prince-bishops from their mountain stronghold at Cetinje.

Over time, some communities in Bosnia, Albania and Kosovo adopted Islam. The reasons for the conversion are complex. In Bosnia there had been an independent Christian sect called the Bogomils, and it seems that some Bogomils adopted Islam as a way of preserving their independence. For Albanians, conversion to Islam occurred more gradually and in more of a piecemeal fashion. A famous Albanian poet once said that the true religion of Albania is simply being Albanian. As late as 1900 there were families in central Albania who had Muslim names in their outside lives as they came into contact with Muslim government authorities, but used Christian names at home. In the mountainous north, some Albanian tribes remained Catholic while their traditional rivals embraced Islam. Many Roma communities also converted to Islam.

The Ottoman Turks encouraged the association between people and religion under the *millet* (roughly, 'national') system, where local laws were decided through religious authorities. Muslims answered to mullahs, Jews to rabbis, and Christians to priests. Serbs kept the dream of independence alive through romanticising the *hajduks* (bandits) who had taken to the hills to raid Turkish caravans, and through endless variations in epic poems retelling the betrayals which led to the end of their empire

The London-based Bosnian Institute has a good website for Bosnian history (one of the founders was historian Noel Malcolm). Follow the links from www.bosnia.org.uk.

Ban Tomislav unites first Croatian kingdom

European Christianity divides between Catholic and Orthodox churches at the 1389 battle of Kosovo Polje. Some Serbs moved to the shifting frontier region between the Catholic Austrians and the Turks, which more or less coincides with the modern border between Bosnia and Croatia. This stark mountain region became known as Krajina, which means 'borderland'. The Serbs of Krajina were under constant pressure to convert to Catholicism, another theme in Serbian identity.

By 1700 the Turkish Empire was lagging behind the other great European powers. The Austrians pushed south and reconquered Croatia, and began eyeing territory further south.

Nikola Tesla, the brilliant Serbian inventor, was working on a 'death beam' when he died, the plans for which mysteriously disappeared.

Divide & Conquer

The history of the Western Balkans in the 19th and 20th centuries is even more complicated. For more information on history in this period, see the country chapters. In broad strokes, the 19th century saw the bloody decline of Turkish power and the emergence of competing nationalisms. Pan-Slavism – the idea of uniting the Croatians, Serbians and Slovenians under one flag – initially took off in Slovenia. The Croatian Bishop Josip Strossmayer was a strong proponent of Pan-Slavism, and founded the Yugoslav Academy of Arts & Sciences in 1867. An independent Serbian kingdom gradually emerged over the 19th century, expanding from its early base around Belgrade. The Austro-Hungarian empire claimed Bosnia and Hercegovina in 1878, and competition between Serbia, Greece and Bulgaria for the remaining Ottoman territories in Albania, Macedonia and northern Greece was intense. The first Balkan War, in 1912, pushed the Turks back to Constantinople, but the Greeks, Serbs and Bulgarians soon began fighting each other. The conflict continued into WWI, and devastated much of Albania and Macedonia. After WWI the Pan-Slav dream was fulfilled in the Kingdom of the Serbs, Croats and Slovenes, renamed Yugoslavia in 1929. Albania also emerged as an independent state, ruled by the self-proclaimed king, Zog. Both countries were largely rural, Ruritanian dictatorships with very little industry. Neither regime was able to resist the Italian and German invasions during WWII.

In 1934, 12-year-old Jan Yoors ran away from home, joining a Roma clan. His books *The Gypsies*, *Crossing* and *The Heroic Present* explain Roma life.

Something like 10% of the region's population perished during WWII, as fascist Croatian Ustaše fought communists and Serbs, the Germans fought communists and royalist Četniks, and Albanian factions fought the Germans, the Italians and each other. The Germans had installed the far-right Croatian Ustaše party as leaders of the Independent State of Croatia, which included modern Croatia, Bosnia and Hercegovina and parts of Serbia and Slovenia. The Ustaše's brutality towards Serbs in particular shocked even the Nazis. The Yugoslav communist party under Josip Broz Tito and the Albanian communist party under Enver Hoxha took power at the end of the war and dispatched most of their rivals by the bullet or sent them to prison camps.

Communism

Yugoslavia and Albania were the only countries in Europe where communists took power without the assistance of the USSR's Red Army. This gave the communist party leaders an unusual amount of freedom compared to the other new communist regimes in Eastern Europe. The Yugoslav communist party was quick to collectivise agriculture, but by

1346–55	1389
Peak of Serbian Golden Age under Tsar Stefan Dušan	Serbs fight Turks at Kosovo Polje; exact events unclear since

the late 1940s they faced stagnant growth and dwindling popularity. Fed up with interference from Moscow, Tito broke with Stalin in 1948. The collectivisation of land was reversed in 1953, and within a year most peasants had returned to farming independently. The reforms were successful and the economy was booming in the late 1950s. Albania's leader, Enver Hoxha, looked on Yugoslavia's reforms with utter distaste, and kept true to the hard-line Stalinist path. The Albanian communist party controlled every aspect of society – religion was banned during a Chinese-style cultural revolution in the late 1960s – and the country became a kind of communist hermit kingdom.

After WWII Soviet leader Stalin wanted Yugoslavia, Bulgaria and Albania to be united into one communist federation. The Bulgarian leadership scuppered the idea.

Almost uniquely, Yugoslavs were able to travel freely to Western countries as well as in the Eastern Bloc. In the 1960s Yugoslavia's brand of socialism, with self-management principles, contributed to a struggle developing between the republics within it. Richer republics such as Croatia wanted more power devolved to the republics, while Serbia's communist leaders wanted more centralised control. The Albanian majority in Kosovo started to protest against Serbian control in the 1960s, which began the long cycle of riots, violence and repression that lasted until the UN took control of the territory in 1999. There was a saying that the end of the Yugoslav dream would begin in Kosovo and end in Kosovo, which turned out to be sadly true.

After Tito's death in 1980 the federal presidency rotated annually among the eight members of the State Presidency. The economy stalled as foreign debt mounted, and rivalries between the constituent republics grew. Serbian communist party boss Slobodan Milošević exploited the tensions by playing up disturbances between Serbs and Kosovar Albanians in Kosovo, and this allowed him to consolidate his power base.

Berlin wasn't the only divided city in Cold War Europe: after losing Gorizia to Italy, Tito built Nova Gorica on the Slovenian side of the border.

Things Fall Apart

As the democracy movement swept Eastern Europe, tensions grew between the central powers in Belgrade dominated by Milošević and the pro-democracy, pro-independence forces in the republics. Slovenia declared independence in 1991, and after a short war became the first republic to break free of Yugoslavia. Croatia soon followed, but the Serbs of the mountainous Krajina region set up their own state. Macedonia became independent without much trouble, but when Bosnia and Hercegovina followed suit the country fell into a brutal civil war between the three main communities: Bosniaks, Serbs and Croats. The war continued until 1995 and cost 200,000 lives. The Dayton Peace Accords divided the country into a federation, awarding 49% to the Serbs and 51% to a Croat-Muslim federation. In the same year the newly strengthened Croatian army conquered the breakaway Serbs' regions. Meanwhile, in rump Yugoslavia (Serbia and Montenegro) the worst hyperinflation in history occurred between 1993 and 1995, when prices grew by five quadrillion percent – which is a number five with 15 zeroes after it. In Albania the communist regime was kicked out in 1992, and the country descended into a kind of free-market vacuum where anything was possible. Peasants stole animals and equipment from the old collective farms, people pillaged factories for building materials, and gangsters ruled major port towns. It all came to a head in 1997, when the collapse

Emir Kusturica's film *When Father was Away on Business* addresses Tito's brutal rule. Malik believes his father is away on business. The truth is much darker…

1443–68	1520–66
Skanderbeg defends Albania against Ottoman Turks	Height of Ottoman Empire under Suleyman the Magnificent

of pyramid banking schemes set off a violent uprising. The international community stepped in and Albania has since made a rather successful recovery, going from being a failed state to an up-and-coming potential EU candidate. In Kosovo, rebel Albanians began a guerrilla campaign against Serb forces in 1996, which eventually triggered NATO intervention in 1999. The territory has been under UN control ever since. Serbian strongman Slobodan Milošević was finally pushed out of power in 2001. The war in Kosovo had spilled over into Macedonia, where around a quarter of the population is ethnic Albanian. An accord promising more self-government for Albanian areas helped to restore peace. By 2002 the region was at last mostly peaceful, though there are still fears for future stability in Kosovo and Macedonia.

Thousands of ex-Yugoslavs pay 'homage' to Tito at www.titoville.com. The site includes songs, speeches, portraits, medals and honours, biographies of his many mistresses and Tito jokes.

PEOPLE

Only 60 years ago the Western Balkans was an overwhelmingly agricultural region with a couple of smallish cities. These days most people live in cities, but the ties to rural traditions are strong. Many men still like to brew homemade spirits in the suburbs, while women preserve fruits and make condiments the old-fashioned way. A certain amount of nostalgia for the certainties of life under communism remains, particularly among older people in poorer parts of the former Yugoslavia.

It's still a fairly macho culture. Men smoke and chat in cafés on Saturday mornings while women do the grocery shopping. Younger people are as hip to the latest hair products and MP3 downloads as anywhere in the world, but gender roles at home are quite traditional.

Unhappy with the conflicts during the break-up of Yugoslavia, the villagers of Vevčani in Macedonia voted to declare their home an independent republic in 1991.

Millions of ex-Yugoslavs and Albanians work in Western Europe and hundreds of thousands have emigrated permanently. Just about everyone in the region has an uncle or a cousin who has left for Canada, Switzerland or Australia. The wars of the 1990s and high unemployment sparked another wave of departures. Not surprisingly, very few migrants have moved into the region, except for people returning from exile or work overseas. Illegal migrants have used the region as a final staging post for the journey into the wealthier parts of Europe, but there has been a crackdown on this in recent years.

RELIGION

The film No Man's Land sees a Serb and a Bosnian soldier trapped in a trench. More complications occur when the media and UN blunder in.

If there's one defining characteristic of the Western Balkans, it's the diversity of faiths. Belgrade once had a Tibetan-style Buddhist temple, built by Kalmyks from southern Russia. Even among those who only celebrate religious rituals at weddings and funerals, most align themselves with their ancestral faith. The most religious area of the Western Balkans is probably Kosovo, while Slovenia and Albania are perhaps the least religious. Precise figures are almost impossible to pin down, but out of a total population of about 26.8 million people in the Western Balkans, roughly 37% are Orthodox, 25% are Catholic, 25% are Muslim and about 13% belong to other faiths or profess no religion.

The biggest Orthodox Church in the Western Balkans is the Serbian Orthodox Church, with adherents in Serbia, Montenegro, Bosnia and Croatia. The Macedonian Orthodox Church split from the Serbian church as recently as 1967, and has the allegiance of about 66% of the

1808	1815
The term 'Balkans' invented by a German geographer	Serbia wins de facto independence

Macedonian population. The Albanian Orthodox Church, also a 20th-century creation, is followed by about 20% of Albanians, mostly in the southern half of the country.

Croatia and Slovenia are predominantly Catholic, as are the Hungarians of Serbia's Vojvodina region. About 12% of Albanians in both Albania and Kosovo are Catholic too – Mother Teresa of Calcutta was born into an ethnic Albanian family in Skopje, Macedonia.

The Muslim population is divided into a number of groups. The two biggest groups are the Sunni Muslims of Bosnia and Hercegovina and southern Serbia who speak Slavic dialects, and the Albanians of Kosovo, Albania and Macedonia. There is also a small Turkish Muslim community, mostly in old Ottoman towns such as Prizren in Kosovo and Bitola in Macedonia. There are a number of smaller Muslim groups such as the Bektashi, who have their world headquarters in Tirana. Bektashi Muslims hold the Prophet Mohammed's son-in-law Ali in particular esteem, and usually allow members to drink alcohol. Roughly 15% of the people of Albania follow the Bektashi sect.

There is a smallish number of Protestants in the region, mostly ethnic Hungarians in Serbia's Vojvodina region. The majority of the Jewish population was murdered by the Third Reich in the 1940s, though one happy exception was Albania, where the small Jewish population actually grew during WWII as Jewish people sought refuge there. Many abandoned synagogues are falling into disrepair.

Sarajevo Rose: A Balkan Jewish Notebook by Stephen Schwartz traces the remnants of a lost Jewish world, which intermingled with the other faiths of the region.

ARTS
Literature
The oldest form of Western Balkan literature, if literature is the right word, is the tradition of epic poetry which survives in the Dinaric Range from Croatia to Albania. The country bards who memorise vast verse epics work in a tradition dating back before Homer. In Serbia, Bosnia and Hercegovina and Croatia the poems are recited to the accompaniment of the *gusle*, a one-stringed lute. Epic poetry was the most important way of recording historical events and figures for centuries: the 1389 battle of Kosovo Polje features in Serbian epic poetry, and some historians believe the heroic myths associated with the battle (which was more or less a draw) came from the epic poetry tradition. Serbian epic poetry was first written down by the 19th-century writer and linguist Vuk Karadžić, whose works were brought to a wider audience through translations by Goethe and Walter Scott.

The Culture of Lies by Croatian dissident Dubravka Ugrešić mercilessly examines the little dictators and macho blather of the 1990s.

Contemporary Albanian author Ismail Kadare wrote a short, humorous book about the epic poetry tradition in *The File on H*. Kadare is Albania's most famous novelist, and a perennial candidate for a Nobel prize for literature. He won the inaugural Man Booker International Prize in 2005.

Other famous authors from the region include the Bosnian Ivo Andrić, who won the Nobel prize for literature in 1961 for works such as *Bridge over the Drina*. Milovan Djilas of Montenegro was a senior figure in the early days of Yugoslav communism who was on the verge of becoming president in 1954 when he was suddenly expelled from the party. His book *The New Class: An Analysis of the Communist System* landed him in

1878	1912
Serbia and Montenegro recognised as fully independent; Austro-Hungarian empire takes over Bosnia and Hercegovina	First Balkan War begins; Albania declares independence

jail for arguing that communist regimes had created a small, exploitative class of senior party leaders rather than an egalitarian utopia. It created a sensation when it was first published in 1955. A later book, *Conversations With Stalin*, is a classic reportage-style book on Djilas' meetings with the Soviet dictator in the 1940s, and also led to jail time.

Architecture

The region's architecture is as varied as its history. The Roman amphitheatre at Pula in Croatia is one of the best preserved in the world, while the Euphrasian Basilica at Poreč earned a World Heritage listing for its preservation of Byzantine and classical elements dating back to the 4th century. Croatia's Adriatic coast has many Venetian-influenced buildings, while Slovenia's architecture shows links with Austria. Serbia's Vojvodina region has Hungarian-influenced elements, particularly in the Art Nouveau buildings in Novi Sad. The Turkish influence in mosques, *madrassas* (colleges for learning the Koran), *hammams* (public baths) and domestic architecture spreads from Macedonia to Albania, Serbia and Bosnia and Hercegovina. Berati in Albania has a particularly fine set of Ottoman-era neighbourhoods. Sarajevo and Mostar in Bosnia and Hercegovina have a delightful mix of Ottoman-style structures, Orthodox churches and Habsburg-era public buildings. Baroque and Gothic architecture mostly appears in Slovenia and Croatia. These two countries also have a strong legacy of Romanesque architecture, continuing long after this style had been supplanted by Gothic design in other parts of Europe.

Religious buildings have often been singled out in the Western Balkans conflicts. Hundreds of mosques, churches and monasteries have been vandalised or destroyed, as recently as 2004 in Kosovo.

The Western Balkans also has an unmistakable communist influence – it's not much appreciated now but one day architecture critics may be raving about Skopje's magnificent ensemble of 1960s concrete and praising the clean lines of Podgorica's apartment blocks. The weirdest communist building in the Western Balkans must be the Pyramid in Tirana, Albania, built as a museum and shrine to dictator Enver Hoxha.

Music

Candidates for the oldest living musical traditions in the Western Balkans are the old Slavonic hymns of the Serbian Orthodox Church and southern Albania's polyphonic singing. Croatia's four-voice *klapa* music is another unusual a capella tradition. The various Islamic dervish orders have traditions of religious chants on mystical themes. One regional curiosity is *blehmuzika*, Serbian brass music influenced by Turkish and Austrian military music. It's often played by Roma bands at weddings and funerals. Other folk traditions include Macedonian *gajda* (bagpipe) tunes, accompanied by drums, and Serbian peasant dances led by bagpipes, flutes and fiddles. Kosovar folk music bears the influence of Ottoman military marching songs, with careening flutes over the thudding beat of goatskin drums. Bosnia's traditional music is *sevdah*, a melancholy form sometimes described as the Bosnian blues. Slovenian folk music features accordions and flutes made of wood, clay and reeds, and central European rhythms such as the polka and waltz are popular.

Brenda Brkusic's *Freedom from Despair* is a riveting film that mixes documentary footage with reenactments to tell the story of Croatia's struggle against ex-Yugoslavia.

Dozens of Tirana's grey Stalinist buildings have been painted in vibrant colours –one has appeared on the cover of *Art in America* magazine.

1918	1941
Kingdom of Serbs, Croats and Slovenes formed; renamed Yugoslavia in 1929	Hitler invades; Croatian fascists take power in puppet state

Strangely enough, pop music is one link from the old Yugoslav federation that hasn't been broken. Female popstresses with voluminous blonde hair and enough make-up to camouflage a commando battalion are preferred over their (sometimes) more toned-down international counterparts. Popular Serbian, Croatian and Bosnian artists have a bigger audience than imports from other European countries throughout the former federation – 'from Triglav to the Vardar', to quote an old Yugoslav anthem. The videos are often celebrations of big hair and vaguely saucy themes that remind visitors of the glory days of 1980s videos. 'Turbo-folk', pop music mixed with folk, is popular everywhere. Hip-hop is also building a strong following all over the region, with skinny white kids in leisure suits throwing shapes and dissing rivals seemingly everywhere – Eminem has a lot to answer for. More challenging types of music also have a strong base among the substantial urban bohemian community. Internationally, the best-known alternative band from the region would be the Slovenian veteran industrial collective Laibach, who released an album in 1990 of nothing but different versions of the Rolling Stones' *Sympathy for the Devil*.

Visual Arts

Serbian and Macedonian medieval architecture is mostly on a provincial scale compared with Orthodox Christian centres such as Kiev and Moscow, but in fresco painting local artists rivalled anything produced in the Orthodox world. Many of the classic frescoes painted in churches and monasteries from the 10th to the 14th centuries were hidden by whitewash applied by the new Turkish rulers (which inadvertently helped to preserve them), and obscured by dense layers of smoke and candle residue. The frescoes in the churches of Sveti Pantelejmon near Skopje and Sveti Kliment in Ohrid display a skill for expression that predates the Italian Renaissance by 150 years. Albania also has a largely unknown tradition of fine Orthodox art, exemplified by the icon painter Onufri, who has a museum dedicated to his colourful, expressive work in Berati.

In the 20th century one important Yugoslav art movement was Zenitism, from the word 'zenith', which fused French and Russian intellectualism with Balkan passion. Belgrade's Museum of Contemporary Art has a particularly fine collection of Zenitist works which are now back on display – the gallery was purged of works by non-Serbian artists by a Milošević appointee in the 1990s.

Socialist realist art (art dedicated to glorifying the worker and the achievements of communism) had only a brief heyday in Yugoslavia, where artists were allowed to return to their own styles in the early 1950s, but it lasted right up until the early 1990s in Albania. Tirana's National Art Gallery has a salon devoted to socialist realist works.

In sculpture, the best-known artist from the region is Ivan Meštrović, born into a poor farming family in Croatia in 1883. He taught himself to read from the Bible, and went on to create some of the finest examples of religious sculpture since the Renaissance. Though he emigrated to the USA, around 60 of his works are scattered around the former Yugoslavia, including the *Monument to the Unknown Hero* in Belgrade.

> Tirana-born, Paris-based artist Anri Sala is revitalising the video art scene with entrancing, engaging works (often dealing with the boundaries of language).

1945	1967
Tito forms new socialist Yugoslavia	Albanian cultural revolution attacks all religions

ENVIRONMENT

While reasonably heavily populated, the natural environment of the Western Balkans has some outstanding wilderness areas with wildlife in numbers rarely seen elsewhere in Europe. The area around the borders of Albania, Montenegro and Kosovo is one of the least touched alpine regions on the continent. Rural populations have been falling over the past 60 years, and while this suggests there may be less pressure on the terrestrial environment there has also been a shift towards industry-scale logging and mechanised farming.

The wars of the 1990s had a mixed impact on the environment. Wolves were reported to be roaming into parts of Croatia's Dalmatia region, where they hadn't been seen in decades, as the conflict in the Serb-populated Krajina region caused farmers to desert the land and un-protected herds of livestock presented an unusual feeding opportunity. The planting of land mines has meant that regions of Bosnia, Croatia and Kosovo have become de facto wilderness areas. But the growth in city populations as a result of refugee movements (and the postcommunist freedom to leave collective farms in Albania) has put urban environments under tremendous strain. For tips on lessening your impact when visiting sensitive environmental areas, see Responsible Travel (p18).

The Neue Slowenische Kunst (New Slovenian Art) movement (www .nskstate.com) offers a challenge to totalitarianism which spans theatre, music and the visual arts.

The Land

A wide belt of mountains parallel to the Adriatic coast covers about 60% of the region; it's often made of limestone and has long valleys, dramatic gorges, vast cave systems and oddities such as disappearing rivers. The Dinaric Range along Croatia's coast has partly sunk into the sea, creating an incredibly convoluted network of islands, peninsulas and bays. A knot of fault lines in the southern part of the Western Balkans sometimes causes shattering earthquakes, such as the 1963 quake, which demolished Macedonia's capital, Skopje. The region's highest mountain is Triglav (2864m) in Slovenia's Julian Alps, while the second highest is Korab (2751m) on the border of Albania and Macedonia. The Pannonian plain along the Sava and Danube Rivers in Croatia and in northern Serbia was the floor of an ancient sea up to 2.5 million years ago, and has rich sediments up to 150m deep.

Having sex on a Croatian beach can earn you 30 days in jail – compared to up to three years behind bars in Italy.

For information on national parks in the region, see the individual country chapters.

Wildlife

The Western Balkans is a refuge for many of the larger mammals that were almost eliminated from Western Europe 150 years ago. The rugged forests of the Dinaric Range from Slovenia to Albania shelter wolves, red deer, roe deer, lynx, chamois, wild boar and brown bears. Wolves, in particular, are sometimes targeted for eradication campaigns because of their impact on livestock. The forests of the region are roughly divided into a conifer zone, beginning between 1500m and 2000m, and including silver fir, spruce and black pine; broad-leaved beech forests, which occur lower down; and a huge variety of oak species below this again. Birds of prey found in the region include griffon falcons, kestrels and peregrine falcons. The great lakes of Ohrid and Prespa in the far south of the region are havens for Dalmatian pelicans, herons and spoonbills.

1978	1989
Albania breaks with China and achieves near-total isolation	Slobodan Milošević abolishes Kosovo's autonomy

The more populated shores of the Adriatic coast have endangered populations of golden jackals, red foxes and badgers, while bigger predators such as wolves and brown bears have largely been eradicated. Classic Mediterranean species such as junipers, heaths and olive trees grow well in the high summer temperatures of this area. The Adriatic shore also used to be home to the endangered Mediterranean monk seal, which grows up to 3.5m long in adulthood, but a recent comprehensive survey of habitats along the Albanian and Croatian coasts suggests they may no longer inhabit the region. Monk seals prefer isolated caves and tend to desert their young if disturbed. On a happier note, the number of bottlenose dolphins seems to be growing again in Croatia's Gulf of Kvarner.

The Pannonian plains of northern Bosnia, northern Serbia and Croatia's Slavonia region are mostly devoted to agriculture, but still have pockets of broad-leaved temperate forest. The banks of the Danube and Sava Rivers have riverine forests of alder, ash and willow. The grasslands are inhabited by hares and rabbits, while raptor birds such as goshawks hunt them from the skies.

Environmental Issues

The Western Balkans was almost entirely agricultural until after WWII, when communist party central planners decreed rapid industrialisation on a massive scale. As in other communist-controlled regions, the damage caused by industrial waste wasn't recognised for many years, and pollution from lignite (brown coal) power plants and other industries is still the biggest environmental concern today. Albania's communist party members had a particular liking for seriously big industrial plants. The humungous Steel of the Party metallurgical plant in Elbasani emitted so much filth that it poisoned the surrounding valley and made agriculture impossible. Towns and cities all over the Western Balkans have problems with air, soil and water poisoned by messy industrial plants.

Albania's authorities also tried to tame the natural landscape to their grand visions. Thousands of hectares of hillsides were terraced in a campaign to turn the hills into fields, with predictable results for soil erosion. The Yugoslav authorities, though, could be surprisingly sensitive to environmental issues; nomadic sheep- and goat-herding was banned in 1951 by the Law on Soil Erosion, which was hugely unpopular at the time. Tito's regime also created a network of national parks and protected areas.

Air pollution is a concern in cities such as Belgrade, as it is in most big cities around the world. The worst place for air pollution in the region is Prishtina in Kosovo. Here the lignite-burning power plants at Obiliq on the city's outskirts were built only to supplement power supplies from Serbia. However, when Kosovo became a UN protectorate, it was farewell to Serbian electricity. The power plants now work full time to supply the city's needs, and a bad cough in Kosovo has become known as an 'Obiliq cough'.

Refugee movements and an exodus from rural areas have caused rapid and unplanned urban growth in cities like Sarajevo, Tuzla, Belgrade, Prishtina and Tirana, with all the attendant problems relating to sewage, waste disposal and water supply. Sewage outflows in some coastal resorts is also a problem, particularly in the summer when volumes literally surge.

The Albanian Green Party website (www .tegjelberit.org) has information in both Albanian and English. There's a quarterly newspaper accessible through the site.

1991	1992
Slovenia, Croatia and Macedonia declare independence; wars in Croatia and Bosnia and Hercegovina begin	Communists lose power in Albania

The disappearance of communist rule has caused some damage in parts of the region. In Albania, uncontrolled logging has become a problem in a country where such activities would previously have earned the culprits a life sentence in the chrome mines. There was also once a complete ban on fishing for trout on the Albanian side of Lake Ohrid, as this was a special privilege of the party elite. When the party fell from power, uncontrolled fishing took off with a vengeance, threatening an already endangered species.

The Dalmatian coast faces a host of environmental challenges but Sunce, a Split-based environmental organisation, has risen to the occasion. Track its efforts at www.sunce-st.org.

The wars of the 1990s caused environmental damage, though it's churlish to compare this to the human cost. The NATO bombing campaign against Serbian forces in 1999 used shells tipped with superhard armour-piercing depleted uranium (which can vaporise on impact and form airborne particles), and there is estimated to be 10 tonnes of this by-product of the nuclear industry scattered over Kosovo. NATO also blew up dozens of petrochemical plants, chemical factories and oil refineries, with wildly unpredictable environmental consequences. One of the worst examples was the destruction of two chemical plants at Pančevo, northeast of Belgrade, which released huge amounts of ethylene-dichloride, mercury, polychlorinated biphenyl and other toxic chemicals and metals into the environment.

FOOD & DRINK

The cuisines of the Western Balkans mix and match Mediterranean, central European and Turkish influences, making use of the wealth of superb produce from this agriculturally rich region. When locals eat out, it usually means Italian food (pizza and pasta are practically local dishes) and hefty servings of lamb, chicken or fish. There is a legion of local cheeses barely known outside the immediate area, and an excellent range of fresh fruits in season: grapes, cherries, apples, peaches, pears, plums, melons, figs and quinces. In the colder regions cabbages, walnuts and root vegetables such as turnips are used. Local dishes tend to be fairly simple, relying on abundant quality produce to present tasty meals. Eating hours across the region are much the same as the rest of Europe. There are many local terms for restaurants and eateries, from Croatian *gostionica* (restaurant) to Albanian *byrektorë* (bakeries selling *burek*, stuffed filo pastry); see the country chapters for details.

The Best of Croatian Cooking by Liliana Pavicic and Gordana Perker Mosher is just what it says it is.

Staples & Specialities

Burek or *byrek* sold in bakeries is the classic Western Balkans breakfast snack and is usually eaten with yogurt. *Bureks* have a range of fillings including cheese, meat, potato and mushrooms. Appetizers include locally smoked hams, pickled vegetables and feta-style cheeses. For lunch and dinner, the most common restaurant dishes are various types of grilled meats – the most famous being *ćevapčići* (grilled spicy kebabs) and *ražnjiči* (shish kebab, called *qebap* in Albanian areas), found all over the region. Kebabs are often served with spongy Turkish-style bread and sliced onions. Stews are popular, often cooked slowly over an open fire, with favourites such as *bosanski lonac* (Bosnian stew of cabbage and meat). Croatia offers an array of fish stews. Goulash made with paprika is a hearty dish found in regions bordering Hungary. Coastal Croatia, Albania, Montenegro and the littoral of Slovenia have seafoods such as

FLAVOURS TO SAVOUR

Had any *ajvar* with a glass of *salep* lately? Here are a few regional rarities to watch out for:

Ajvar Macedonia's national relish, made from red peppers, aubergine, paprika, olive oil, onion and garlic.

Hurmasica A Bosnian dessert made from filo pastry with cream and lemon.

Jukvi A breakfast pancake made from semolina, which is cooked and dried and then recooked with water and milk.

Kajmak A dairy dish made from clotted cream, ranging from buttery when fresh to like a soft cheese when matured. Very popular in Serbia – incredibly rich and strangely addictive.

Krema snežna rezina Sweet cream slices that quickly disappear from the shelves of bakeries at Slovenia's Lake Bled.

Kukurec A rather fearsome dish made from sheep intestines stuffed with chopped liver.

Raca Pig's head or knuckles, fried in herbs and served cold in slices. A real man's food.

Riblji paprikaš A spicy Slavonian fish stew flavoured with paprika.

Salep A drink made from powdered wild orchid root and hot milk, quite hard to find.

Sheqerpare Balls of sweet dough baked in butter, popular in Kosovo and Albania.

Tartufe Truffles from the hinterland of Croatia's Istrian Peninsula, sold sliced or prepared into oils and pasta sauces.

Tufahija Apples filled with walnuts and almonds, doused in syrup, dusted with cinnamon and topped with *kajmak*.

---

shellfish, scampi, calamari and fish stews with sea bass, bream and hake. Salads with diced cucumber and tomato drizzled in olive oil and sprinkled with herbs accompany many main meals.

Drinks

Every country has its favourite locally made beer (*pivo* or *piva* in Slavic languages, *birra* or *birrë* in Albanian), challenged on the shelves by major international brews such as Heineken and Fosters. Two local beers worth looking out for are Karlovačko *pivo* from Karlovac in Croatia and Nikšićko *pivo* from Montenegro. Most beers are lagers, though there are some dark stouts and ales available. In the harder stuff, there is an incredible array of spirits called *rakija* in Slavic tongues and *raki* in Albanian, which is usually distilled from grapes but also comes in a range of varieties made from or flavoured by other fruits, including mulberries, pears, strawberries, cherries and apples, and also walnuts. The alcohol content is generally between 40% and 70%, so not surprisingly it's drunk from special little glasses. Macedonia's local variant is *žolta* (yellow) *rakija* with wheat added during a secondary fermentation – even more than most *rakijas*, it kicks like a mad mule. The most common fruit *rakija* is made from plums, and is variously called *šljivovica* (Croatia, Bosnia and Hercegovina, Serbia and Montenegro) or *slivovka* (Slovenia). This is the national drink in Serbia, where something like 70% of the plum harvest goes into its production. The drink appears at any excuse for a celebration, from Christmas to birthdays to anniversaries. Albania's liquor of note is Skënderbeu *konjak*, a surprisingly smooth and subtle brandy. The region also has a range of herbal liqueurs, from Albania's very curious Fernet to Serbia and Croatia's rather medicinal-tasting *pelinkovac*.

The region produces a huge array of wines, from 10L plastic containers of basic country plonk to refined whites and reds matured in oak. Slovenia alone has something like 400 wine producers, most with less than 10 hectares of vineyards. Slovenian wines are fairly similar to northern Italian and Austrian wines, with an emphasis on aromatic dry whites.

California's popular wine grape Zinfandel descends from the ancient Croatian varietal Crljenak, which now exists in such small numbers that no pure Crljenak is made.

1997	1999
Revolution and anarchy in Albania	Kosovo becomes UN protectorate after NATO anti-Serbian bombing campaign

Many Slovenian towns have a *vinoteka* (wine shop) selling local varieties such as Sipon, Traminec and Beli Pinot as well as better-known varietals such as Merlot and Cabernet Sauvignon. The late harvest or *izbor* dessert wines are more expensive but can be spectacular.

Croatia's wine producers are divided into the inland Slavonia region, where 93% of wines are whites, and the coastal Dalmatian area, where 70% of wines are reds. Graševina, a gentle golden-hued white similar to Riesling, is the most widely grown variety in Slavonia. The Dalmatian coast wineries are increasingly growing Merlot and Cabernet Sauvignon, but some unusual varieties grown here include Plavac Mali from the Dubrovnik region, which produces dense bunches of blue-skinned berries. One crisp, cleansing Dalmatian white is Pošip.

The rest of the region is lagging behind in producing fine wines. Vineyards are mostly geared towards the mass production of cheap wines, and while there's been a slow switch from low-quality, high-yielding varieties to premium local and French varieties, the local industries still have a long way to go. Macedonia has vast vineyards but production is dominated by one company, Tikveš. It makes the popular table wine T'ga za Jug, named after a famous poem *Longing For The South*. Boutique wine producers such as Bovin are just beginning to appear in Macedonia's vineyard heartland in the Kavadarci-Negotino region. Serbia's workhorse red grape is Prokupac, a dense, robust red with high sugar levels, often blended with French varieties such as Gamay and Merlot. In Serbia the Fruška Gora region is a major wine producer, and a very pretty one. One rich, earthy red variety, which repays cellaring, is Vranec (Macedonia) or Vranac (Montenegro). Fine wines from Hercegovina include Žilavka (white) and Blatina (red). Albania's wine industry is fairly small, but offers some real curiosities such as red Kallmet from the northern Shkodra region.

> Serbs sometimes call a dose of potent *rakija* 'a glass of chat', and back it up with the old saying 'Without *rakija* there is no conversation'.

Besides alcohol, coffee is the main social lubricant. The Ottoman aristocracy introduced the caffeine habit in the 16th century, and coffee houses have been pillars of local communities ever since. Turkish-style coffee is traditionally the most popular, though Italian- and Austrian-style brews are probably more popular now in the big cities. Turkish coffee is prepared by heating finely ground coffee beans and water slowly for 15 to 20 minutes. In Serbia, Kosovo and Albania the custom is to mix sugar with the coffee powder and water as well. The coffee is then served in a small cup with the obligatory layer of froth on top, plus a glass of water and perhaps a biscuit or piece of Turkish delight as well.

Vegetarians & Vegans

There are lots of vegetarian options in home recipes, but most restaurants tend to serve meat dishes. There are some delicious Turkish-style vegetable dishes to be had, such as roast peppers and aubergines, cauliflower moussaka and vegetarian *bureks*. Many entrées are vegetarian as well. On the other hand, vegetarian soups are sometimes flavoured with smoked ham. Many traditional and top-end restaurants will have several vegetarian dishes, but generally vegetarians will fare better in summer. In winter there may be little on offer besides nuts, chips and omelettes. Pure vegans will struggle at restaurants and may do better shopping at local food markets.

2001	2004
Short war in Macedonia ends with Ohrid Agreement	Slovenia joins EU

Albania

RAFAEL ESTEFANIA

Albania

The mountainous Mediterranean nation of Albania is taking off into a well-earned era of confidence, vitality and decent plumbing. Once known as a shadowy communist prison state, Shqipëria, as the locals call it, is emerging from a hugely difficult transition period. Travel here still has a few rough edges, but enduring bumpy bus rides and scratchy phone lines will be amply repaid with generous hospitality, gorgeous mountain scenery and sights you can savour without any tourist bustle and hustle.

The capital Tirana, once a byword for torpid communism, has reinvented itself into a buzzing young city, which artists have literally redecorated. The old grey Stalinist apartment buildings are vibrant canvases for pastels and primary colours. Tirana's evening *xhiro* (stroll) is becoming the beginning of a night out, rather than the end of the day. In the mountains of the north, castles guard the valleys and proud old tribesmen and women still wear traditional dress, while the south has a wonderful mix of Muslim and Christian shrines, a spectacular coastline along the Ionian Sea and several classical cities hidden in the countryside.

Albania's economy has been booming since the start of the new century, and the country has officially shrugged off its tag as Europe's poorest country (sorry, Moldova). Few visitors find that the challenges of rapid development (ripped-up footpaths and roads being relaid) impede their enjoyment of a country beginning to appreciate a period of hard-won prosperity and freedom.

FAST FACTS

- **Area** 28,748 sq km
- **Capital** Tirana
- **Currency** lek; €1 = 122 lek; US$1= 101 lek; UK£1 = 178 lek; A$1 = 77 lek; ¥100 = 91 lek; NZ$1 = 71 lek
- **Famous for** being 'mysterious', concrete bunkers, unique language
- **Key phrases** *tungjatjeta/allo* (hello), *lamtumirë* (goodbye)
- **Official language** Albanian
- **Population** 3.56 million
- **Telephone codes** country code ☎ 355; international access code ☎ 00
- **Visas** no visa needed for citizens of the EU, Australia, New Zealand, the US and Canada; see p82 for details

HIGHLIGHTS

- The wild colour schemes and all-hours café culture of **Tirana** (p52)
- Skanderbeg's spectacular **castle** (p63) at Kruja; perched against a mountain wall of rock with views over the Adriatic Sea
- The sunny 'museum city' of **Berati** (p64) and its gorgeous citadel
- The south's dramatic Ionian Coast, from the beaches of **Dhërmiu** (p70) to the jungly ruins of **Butrinti** (p72)
- The city-turned-village of **Voskopoja** (p76), deep in the southern highlands

ITINERARIES

- **One week** Spend two days in Tirana, checking out museums, markets and the burgeoning dining and nightlife scenes. Take a day trip out to Kruja for magnificent views out over the Adriatic Sea, as well as some intriguing museums and a cute little bazaar. Then hop on a bus or *furgon* (minibus) to Berati, Albania's loveliest Ottoman-era town, for two days of tramping around the town's old quarters. Next, make your way to Saranda by the sea and do a day trip to the wonderful jungly ruins of Butrinti.
- **Two weeks** Spend three days in Tirana with a day trip to Kruja, then head to Durrësi for the excellent Archaeological Museum and seaside bar-restaurants. From Durrësi take a trip to the ruins of Apollonia near Fieri. After this, spend two days at Berati, maybe with a day trip up to Mt Tomorri. Catch a bus down to Vlora, and head on to Llogaraja Pass if you like mountain scenery, or to the beaches at Dhërmiu, Vuno or Himara on the Ionian Coast if the sea is more your thing. Check

out Saranda and Butrinti, then cruise up to Gjirokastra to explore another Ottoman-era town. Next comes adventure on the stunning road to Korça – not an easy ride but an unforgettable one. Korça has a lovely museum and the old village of Voskopoja is a wonderful day trip. At the end of it all, head back to Tirana for some R and R.

CLIMATE & WHEN TO GO

Coastal Albania has a pleasant Mediterranean climate. In Tirana and other inland towns on the plains there is plenty of rainfall during the winter, but temperatures below freezing are rare. The high mountains often experience heavy snow between

---

HOW MUCH?

- **Shot of mulberry raki (a local spirit)** 100 lek
- **Bunker-shaped ashtrays (great souvenirs!)** 500 lek
- **Short taxi ride** 300 lek
- **Loaf of bread** 50 lek
- **Fërgesë Tiranë (traditional Tirana dish)** 300 lek

LONELY PLANET INDEX

- **Litre of petrol** 100 lek
- **Litre of bottled water** 50 lek
- **Tirana beer** 150 lek
- **Souvenir T-shirt** 800 lek
- **Street snack (byrek)** 30 lek

A SHORT LESSON ON ALBANIAN GRAMMAR

One of the more complicated things about Albania is that there are two common ways of spelling place names. The 'proper' name of Albania's most beautiful Ottoman town is Berati, but road signs and many maps show 'Berat'. The difference is because in Albanian grammar, the definite form is 'Berati', meaning 'the Berati', while the indefinite form, eg 'to Berati', changes the spelling to 'Berat'. So when a road sign reads 'Berat – 25km', it means 'to Berati – 25km'. Make sense? We hope so. In this book, we have used the definite form for place names, even when it goes against the usual foreign usage. 'Durrës' is nearly always used on maps printed outside the country rather than 'Durrësi'. Names ending in 'i' and 'u' lose that letter in the indefinite form, eg Durrësi becomes Durrës and Dhërmiu – Dhërmi; names ending in 'a' change to ë, eg Tirana – Tiranë and Saranda – Sarandë, and names ending in 'ra' change to 'ër', eg Shkodra – Shkodër and Gjirokastra – Gjirokastër. Apologies for any confusion, we're just trying to be consistent.

ALBANIA

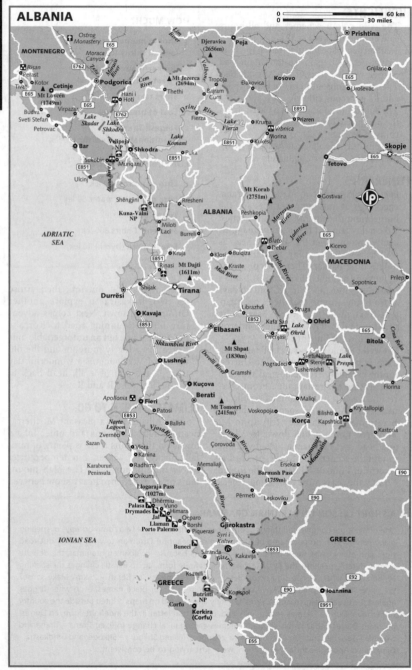

ALBANIA

| 0 | 60 km |
| 0 | 30 miles |

MONTENEGRO

Ostrog Monastery E65
Risan
Perast
Kotor
Tivar
Cetinje
Mt Lovćen (1749m)
E65
Budva
Sveti Stefan
Petrovac
Virpazar
E762
Moraca Canyon
Zeta River
Morača River
Podgorica
Hani i Hoti
Cem River
Lake Skadar
Lake Shkodra
E762

Lim River
Djeravica (2656m)
Peja
Prishtina

Mt Jezerca (2694m)
Tropoja
Thethi
Bajram Curri
Vjosë
Đakovica
Kosovo
Gnjilane
E65
Uroševac

Bar
Sukobin
E851
Muriqani
Ulcinj

Drini River
Fierza
Lake Komani
Lake Fierza
Kruma
Morina
Vrbnica
Prizren
Kukësi
Skopje
E65
Tetovo
Gostivar

Velipojë NP
Shkodra
E851
Puka

Mt Korab (2751m)

Marrowska River
Jadovska River
E65
Kicevo

ADRIATIC SEA

Shëngjini
Lezha
Rresheni
ALBANIA
Peshkopia
Blato
Debar
Drini River
MACEDONIA

Kuna-Vaini NP
Miloti
Laci
Burreli
Klosi
Bulqiza
Kraste
Mati River

Sopotnica
Prilep

Kruja
Rinasi
Mt Dajti (1611m)
Shijak
Tirana
Durrësi

Librazhdi
Struga
Ohrid
E65
Bitola
Crna Reka

Kavaja
Elbasani
Shkumbini River
Mt Shpat (1830m)
Devolli River
Kafa San
Lake Ohrid
Prenjasi

Lushnja
Gramshi
Sveti Naum
Stenje
Lake Prespa
Pogradeci
Tushëmishti
Florina

Apollonia
Fieri
Patosi
E853
Ballshi
Kuçova
Berati
Mt Tomorri (2415m)
Voskopoja
Maliqi
Bilishti
Krystallopigi
Korça
Kapshtica
Kastoria

Narta Lagoon
Zvernëci
Sazan
Vjosa River
Çorovoda
Osumi River
Erseka
Grammoz Mountains

Vlora
Kanina
Memaliaj
Radhima
Orikumi
Karaburun Peninsula
Këlcyra
Barmash Pass (1759m)
Leskoviku
E90
E90

Llogaraja Pass (1027m)
Dhërmiu
Palasa
Vuno
Drymades
Himara
Jali
Qeparo
Llaman
Borshi
Porto Palermo
Piqerasi
Drinos River
Përmeti
Gjirokastra
Syri i Kalter
GREECE
E90

IONIAN SEA
Buneci
Kakavija
E853

Ksamili
Saranda
Bistrica
E92
Ioannina

GREECE
Butrinti NP
Konispol
E90
E951
Corfu
Kerkira (Corfu)

E55

November and March, and towns such as Korça become icy. Roads and tracks to mountain villages can be blocked by snow for months.

In the summer Tirana swelters, especially in August when temperatures reach the high 30s, and even in the mountain towns the mercury frequently rises to 40°C. The temperatures on the coast are milder. See Climate Charts, p388.

The best time to visit Albania is spring or autumn, particularly May and September, when you can sightsee in the mild sunshine.

HISTORY

Albanians call their country Shqipëria (pronounced something like *schip*-ree-ya), and trace their roots to the ancient tribal Illyrians. The Albanian language is descended from Illyrian, making it a rare survivor of the Slavic and Roman influx and a European linguistic oddity on a par with Basque. The Illyrians occupied the Western Balkans during the 2nd millennium BC. They built substantial fortified cities, mastered silver and copper mining and became adept at sailing the Mediterranean. The Greeks arrived in the 7th century BC to establish self-governing colonies at Epidamnos (now Durrësi), Apollonia and Butrinti.

In the second half of the 3rd century BC, an expanding Illyrian kingdom based at Shkodra came into conflict with Rome, which sent a fleet of 200 vessels against Queen Teuta (who ruled over the Illyrian Ardiaean kingdom) in 228 BC. A long war resulted in the extension of Roman control over modern-day Albania by 167 BC, after the capture of the last stronghold of the Ardiaean king Genti – the Rozafa fortress in Shkodra.

Under the Romans, Illyria enjoyed peace and prosperity, though the large agricultural estates were worked by slave labour. Like the Greeks, the Illyrians preserved their own language and traditions despite centuries of Roman rule. The main trade route between Rome and Constantinople, the Via Egnatia, ran from Durrësi to Thessaloniki.

When the Roman Empire was divided in AD 395, Illyria fell within the Eastern Roman Empire, later known as the Byzantine Empire. Invasions by migrating peoples – Visigoths, Huns, Ostrogoths and Slavs – continued through the 5th and 6th centuries. The Illyrian language survived in the mountains of northern Albania and the adjacent areas of Kosovo and Montenegro. The populace slowly replaced the old gods with the new Christian faith championed by the Emperor Constantine the Great. Three early Byzantine emperors – Anastasius I, Justin I and Justinian I – were of Illyrian origin.

In 1344 Albania was annexed by Serbia, but after the defeat of Serbia by the Turks in 1389 the whole region was open to Ottoman attack. The Venetians occupied some coastal towns, and from 1443 to 1468 the national hero Skanderbeg (Gjergj Kastrioti) led Albanian resistance to the Turks from his castle at Kruja. Skanderbeg won all 25 battles he fought against the Turks, and even Sultan Mehmet-Fatih, the conqueror of Constantinople, could not take Kruja. The Ottomans finally overwhelmed Albanian resistance in 1479, 26 years after they had captured Constantinople. Albanians proudly assert that Skanderbeg's resistance saved Europe from Ottoman conquest, because their courageous ancestors engaged the attentions of the Ottoman army during one of its strongest periods of conquest. After the conquest many Catholic Albanians moved to southern Italy, particularly to the Catanzaro Mountains of Calabria and the region around Palermo in Sicily. Their descendents are called the Arberesh. Today there is a community of something like 100,000 people who speak an Albanian dialect called Tosca in southern Italy.

Meanwhile, back in Albania, the Ottomans settled into a long, largely economically stagnant rule, which lasted until 1912. The Albanian clan chieftains of the mountains largely ran their own affairs, except for paying taxes to the imperial treasury. Gradually, a majority of Albanians converted to Islam, doing so partly because Christians were levied with extra taxes and because Christian families sometimes had to send one of their sons to join the sultan's special army of converts, the Janissaries. Later in the Ottoman era some administrators actively pushed for conversions to Islam, especially in the more easily controlled coastal plains. Some northern tribes such as the Shoshi and Mirdite remained Catholic, while in the south the religious mix eventually stabilised at around 50% Orthodox Christian and 50% Muslim.

In 1878 the Albanian League at Prizren, which is in present-day Kosovo (Kosova to Albanians), began a struggle for autonomy that was put down by the Turkish army in 1881. Not initially successful on the battlefield, the new Albanians nationalists were more successful in the cultural field, sparking the Rilindja Kombétare (National Renaissance) movement of great poets and writers. The Rilindja leaders quickly realised that one of the keys to building unity among Albanians would be a common script for their language. Previously Albanian had been written in Arabic, Greek and Latin scripts, depending on the faith of the writer. A couple of unique Albanian scripts briefly appeared in the 19th century – the Elbasani script and Beitha Kukju – but weren't widely adopted. In 1909 a conference of writers and intellectuals agreed on adopting a common Latin alphabet, which is used today.

Further uprisings between 1910 and 1912 culminated in a proclamation of independence and the formation of a provisional government led by Ismail Qemali at Vlora in 1912. These achievements were severely compromised when Kosovo, roughly one-third of Albania, was ceded to Serbia in 1913. The Great Powers tried to install a young German prince, William of Weld, as ruler of the rump Albania, but he was never accepted and returned home after six months. With the outbreak of WWI, Albania was occupied in succession by the armies of Greece, Serbia, France, Italy and Austria-Hungary. The country suffered appalling damage, and essentially broke into warring statelets.

In 1920 the capital city was moved from Durrësi to less-vulnerable Tirana. A government under the Orthodox priest Fan Noli helped to stabilise the country, but in 1924 Noli was overthrown by the Interior Minister, Ahmed Bey Zogu. A warlord of the northern Mati tribe, Zogu declared himself King Zog I in 1928, and cooperated extensively with Italy in developing the country. This soon became something of a mixed blessing: the Italians helped develop Tirana from a smallish country town into something like a capital city, but as Albania's debts to Italy stacked up the country increasingly became a de facto Italian colony. Settlers from Italy began moving to the more fertile southern parts of the country,

and Italian advisors increasingly took over the day-to-day running of the country.

During Zog's rule, serfdom was gradually abolished, schools were established and the country's rudimentary infrastructure was vastly improved. Zog himself became a rather eccentric character who played poker relentlessly, hoarded gold and jewels and smoked as many as 150 cigarettes a day. After an assassination attempt in 1931 he became fearful of being poisoned (not by nicotine, evidently) and installed his mother as head of the royal kitchens. In some assassination attempts he actually managed to shoot back. The Great Depression pushed Albania's shaky finances into complete submission to the Italian government. King Zog occasionally managed to get back at the Italians by selling them inaccessible forests and sending them the bill for his lavish wardrobe.

In April 1939, when Mussolini ordered an invasion of Albania, Zogu fled to Britain with his young wife Queen Geraldine and newborn son Leka. He used gold looted from the Albanian treasury to rent a floor at London's Ritz Hotel. In light of the communist regime that followed, Albanians look back on King Zog's reign with some fondness. The first uprising against fascism in Europe occurred in Albania in November 1939, and sparked a long-running fight against the occupiers.

The Rise of Communism

On 8 November 1941 the Albanian communist party was founded with Enver Hoxha as first secretary, a position he held until his death in April 1985 (see opposite). The communists led the resistance against the Italians and, after 1943, against the Germans, ultimately tying down 15 combined German-Italian divisions.

After the fighting had died down, the communists consolidated power. In January 1946 the People's Republic of Albania was proclaimed, with Hoxha as president and 'Supreme Comrade'.

In September 1948 Albania broke off relations with Yugoslavia, which had hoped to incorporate the country into the Yugoslav Federation. Instead, Albania allied itself with Stalin's USSR and put into effect a series of Soviet-style economic plans. The US and Britain tried to overthrow the regime by sending in Albanians trained in guerrilla warfare, but they were betrayed by the British spy Kim Philby, captured and killed.

Albania collaborated closely with the USSR until 1960, when Nikita Khrushchev demanded that a submarine base be set up at Vlora. Breaking off diplomatic relations with the USSR in 1961, the country reoriented itself towards the People's Republic of China. The shift also allowed Hoxha to purge some of his rivals in the party on the grounds of being spies for the Soviet Union, just as he had after the split with Yugoslavia.

From 1966 to 1967 Albania experienced a brutal Chinese-style cultural revolution. Administrative workers were suddenly transferred to remote areas, younger cadres were placed in leading positions, churches and mosques were sacked and destroyed, and the collectivisation of agriculture was completed.

COMRADE ENVER

Enver Hoxha (pronounced hoe-dja) ruled Albania for 40 years, until his death in 1985. The old cliché about ruling with an iron first would be an understatement on his time in power. An idea of his popularity can be gauged by the reaction after the communist regime had fallen. Every single public image of the self-styled Supreme Comrade was destroyed. Huge ENVER letters spelled out in stones on mountains and hillsides all over the country were painstakingly removed. People ripped down the portraits they had to hang on their walls and smashed them. Some even sought out his endless volumes of theory and doctrine to use as toilet paper.

Enver Hoxha was born into a middle-class family in Gjirokastra in 1908. He attended a French school in Korça and later the American school in Tirana (the latter being something of an embarrassment to official biographers). In 1930 he won a scholarship to study in France, where he picked up a taste for natty French fashion and hard-line communism, writing articles for communist newspapers under the pseudonym Loulou. He returned to Albania in 1936 and became one of seven committee members at the founding of the Albanian communist party in 1941. In WWII Hoxha managed to put himself in control of an increasingly capable guerrilla army, which had 70,000 members by 1944. After the war he began to purge every possible rival through show trials, executions and forced labour camps, and consolidated his grip on power. Partly because of the country's poor communications system, the Party of Labour of Albania (Partia e Punës së Shqipërisë, or PPSh) developed a massive secret police force called the Sigurimi to control the populace. They would intrude into every corner of life. The regime denied Albanians freedom of expression, religion and movement. People could be sentenced to 10 years working in chrome mines for listening to foreign radio broadcasts. A strong admirer of Stalin, Hoxha rejected the USSR's relative relaxation after the dictator's death and became a hard-line defender of Stalinism. Hoxha broke with the USSR in 1961, and took the opportunity to purge rivals he accused of being 'revisionists'. Albania then developed close ties with Mao Tse-tung's China. After Mao's death in 1976, Hoxha felt that China, too, was following a revisionist path, and relations withered by 1978. By then, Hoxha had assessed Eurocommunism, Yugoslav communism, Chinese communism and Soviet communism and found them all to be revisionist errors. Meanwhile his personality cult grew – by 1979 his official title had become 'Comrade-Chairman–Prime Minister–Foreign Minister–Minister of War–Commander in Chief of the People's Army'. In 1980 he engineered the downfall of his long-time deputy Mehmet Shehu, who was driven to suicide. The regime accused Shehu of being a spy for the USA, the UK and Yugoslavia – simultaneously. Hoxha then crept into a kind of retirement in his villa in the Blloku district of central Tirana, an area that no ordinary Albanian was allowed to see. He died in 1985, and was briefly honoured by an entire museum dedicated to his life and works: the Pyramid building in Tirana, which opened in 1988 (it was turned in a conference centre four years later).

Anyone wishing for a sample of the sort of turgid prose Albanians were forced to learn can look up some of Hoxha's writings at www.marxists.org/reference/archive/hoxha/. A taste of it can be deduced from this title: 'Reject the Revisionist Thesis of the XX Congress of the Communist Party of the Soviet Union and the Anti-Marxist Stand of Khrushchev's Group! Uphold Marxism-Leninism!' For more information, check the curiously unironic www.pksh.org for speeches, photos and more.

Following the Soviet invasion of Czechoslovakia in 1968, Albania left the Warsaw Pact and followed a self-reliant defence policy. Some 700,000 igloo-shaped concrete bunkers (see 'The Bunkers' boxed text below), conceived of by Hoxha, serve as a reminder of this. The communist party authorities drained the malarial swamps of the central coastal plains, built some major hydroelectric schemes, raised the literacy level and laid down the country's railway lines.

With the death of Mao Tse-tung in 1976 and the changes that followed in China after 1978, Albania's unique relationship with China also came to an end, and the country was left isolated and without allies. The break with China stunted the economy, and food shortages became more common.

Post-Hoxha

Hoxha died in April 1985 and his long-time associate Ramiz Alia took over the leadership. Restrictions loosened half a notch, but the whole system was increasingly falling apart. In the interests of stability, the regime perfected the art of doing nothing, and doing it slowly. Meanwhile, people were no longer bothering to work on the collective farms, which led to food shortages in the cities, and industries began to fail as spare parts ran out. The party leadership promised reform, but remained paralysed.

In June 1990, inspired by the changes that were occurring elsewhere in Eastern Europe, some 4500 Albanians took refuge in Western embassies in Tirana. After a brief confrontation with the police and the Sigurimi (secret police) these people were allowed to board ships for Brindisi in Italy, where they were granted political asylum.

After student demonstrations were held in December 1990, the government agreed to allow opposition parties. The Democratic Party, led by heart surgeon Sali Berisha, was formed. Further demonstrations produced new concessions, including the promise of free elections and independent trade unions. The government announced a reform programme and party hard liners were purged.

THE BUNKERS

On the hillsides, beaches and generally most surfaces in Albania, you will notice small concrete domes looking down on you through their rectangular slits. Meet the bunkers: Enver Hoxha's paranoid concrete legacy, built from 1950 to 1985. Made out of concrete and iron and weighing five tonnes, these hard little mushroomlike creations are almost impossible to destroy, since they were built to repel the threat of foreign invasion and can resist full tank assault. The Supreme Comrade hired a chief engineer to design a super-resistant bunker. The engineer then had to vouch for his creation's strength by standing inside it while it was bombarded by a tank. The shell-shocked man emerged unscathed and the bunkers were built; the estimated number of these concrete gun posts is 700,000 – one for every four Albanians at the time. The plan was for every able-bodied Albanian man to be able to defend his country from a bunker. Around Gjirokastra and Lake Ohrid you can make out some of the grand strategy behind the arrangement of the bunkers, where they spread in rows radiating out from once-permanently manned big bunkers.

Some observers see a link between the communist-era bunkers and the medieval-era *kulla* stone defensive towers, built by families to protect themselves in regions affected by blood feuds. Otherwise their sheer ubiquity says a lot about the mindset of the previous regime. There are so many bunkers around Albania that after a while you barely notice them. They're just a part of a huge legacy of military and security hardware, which includes mysterious tunnels, underground armaments factories, nuclear bunkers under every apartment building (the nuclear bunkers under Tirana built for the leadership are rumoured to be enormous) and nasty surprises like the 16 tonnes of chemical weapons rediscovered at a military base close to Tirana in 2005.

Today the bunkers are the bane of farmers and builders across the country. They are expensive to remove and very hard to destroy. It took one man three months of weekend and after-hours work to demolish one by hand in order to make room for a garage. In places people have tried to decorate them as mushrooms, and have converted larger command bunkers into barns. They do have one modern use. Quite a few Albanians will admit to losing their virginity in the security of a bunker.

In early March 1991, as the election date approached, some 20,000 Albanians fled the country's crumbling economy. They set out from Vlora to Brindisi by ship, creating a crisis for the Italian government, which had begun to view them as economic refugees. Most were eventually allowed to stay.

The March 1992 elections ended 47 years of communist rule. After the resignation of Alia, parliament elected Sali Berisha president in April. In September 1992 former president Alia was placed under house arrest after he wrote articles critical of the Democratic government. In August 1993 the leader of the Socialist Party, Fatos Nano, was also arrested on corruption charges.

During this time Albania switched from a tightly controlled communist regime to an rambunctious free-market free-for-all. A huge smuggling racket sprang up bringing stolen Mercedes-Benzes into the country, and some former collective farms were converted into marijuana plantations. The port of Vlora became a major crossing point for illegal immigrants from Asia and the Middle East into Italy. A huge population shift took place as collective farms were broken up and reclaimed by former landowners. People who had been forced to move to these collectives by the communist party were forced to leave again. Tirana's population tripled as people who were now able to freely move to the city joined internal exiles driven off the old collective farms.

A severe crisis developed in late 1996, when private pyramid investment schemes – which were actually legal at the time – inevitably collapsed. Around 70% of Albanians lost their savings, in total over US$1 billion, resulting in nationwide disturbances and riots. Elections were called, and the victorious Socialist Party under Nano – who had been freed from prison by the rampaging mob – was able to restore some degree of security and investor confidence. But the new wave of violence had destroyed many of the remaining industries from the communist era. Towns where the whole working population had been employed by one mine or factory were left destitute as the economy collapsed again.

In spring 1999 Albania faced a crisis of a different sort. This time it was the influx of 465,000 refugees from neighbouring Kosovo during the NATO bombing and the Serbian ethnic-cleansing campaign. While this put a tremendous strain on resources, the net effect was, in fact, positive. Substantial amounts of international aid money poured in, the service sector grew and inflation declined to single digits. The security situation stabilised and many of the more colourful business activities were shut down.

Since 2002 the country has at last found itself in an economic revival, with large amounts of money being poured into construction projects and infrastructure renewal. Wages have doubled since 1998. It is estimated that around one million out of a population of 3.5 million are working abroad. Remittances from these workers have become crucial to the economy.

The construction boom hasn't been without its problems, however, and the array of ugly concrete apartments and hotels has despoiled the coastline around Durrësi. Corruption also remains a real issue, and the political parties represent rival blocs of business interests as much as they do an ideology. There's still a lingering desire in the electorate for 'strong' leaders, perhaps an echo of the old personality cult of Enver Hoxha. Albanians were very happy to see their kin in Kosovo break free of Serbia in 1999, but there doesn't seem to be much of a groundswell to unify with the territory.

Albanian politics and the economy have become relatively stable, but there's still a long way to go. While new roads are being built and apartment blocks are springing up there are still some seriously poor regions. It is estimated that around 30% of the population lives in poverty, and this figure rises to as much as 50% in the northeastern mountains. Still, as one person said, the worst day today is better than the best day under the communists.

PEOPLE

In July 2005 the population was estimated to be 3,563,112, of which approximately 95% is Albanian, 3% Greek and 2% 'other' – comprising Vlachs, Roma, Serbs and Bulgarians. The Vlach are an old ethnic group in the Balkans, whose name is supposed to originate from the Greek word *vlach* (shepherd). The Vlach language is related to Romanian, and Vlachs are historically a trading community, who are by now well integrated into all of the Balkan societies.

ALBANIA

One of the best things about Albania is its people, who are kind, helpful and unquestioningly generous. Most speak more than one foreign language: Italian is almost a second language in the north and centre, as well as the north coast of the country, and Greek is widespread in the southern regions where the Greek minority is concentrated along the Drinos River. You can rely on the majority of young people to speak English, but learning a few words of the unique Albanian language will delight your hosts. Note that Albanians shake their heads sideways to say yes *(po)* and usually nod and 'tsk' to say no *(jo)*. The Shkumbini River forms a boundary between the Gheg cultural region of the north and the Tosk region in the south. The people in these regions still vary in dialect, musical culture and traditional dress, though the differences are often overstated by outsiders.

RELIGION

Albanians are 70% Muslim, 20% Christian Orthodox and 10% Catholic, but in most cases this is merely nominal. Religion was ruthlessly stamped out by the 1967 cultural revolution, when all mosques and churches were taken over by the state. By 1990 only about 5% of Albania's religious buildings were left intact. The 1976 constitution banned 'fascist, religious, warmongerish, antisocialist propaganda and activity'. Despite the fact that the people are now free to practise their faith, Albania remains a very secular society and it is difficult to assess how many followers each faith has. Intermarriage between people of different faiths is quite common.

The Muslim faith has a branch called 'Bektashism', similar to Sufism, and its world headquarters were in Albania from 1925 to 1945. Rather than mosques, the Bektashi followers go to *teqe* (templelike buildings without a minaret, sometimes housed in former churches). *Teqes* are usually found in mountain towns or on hilltops in towns where they were built to escape persecution, and you will no doubt come across at least one of them. Most Bektashis live in the southern half of the country.

ARTS
Visual Arts
The art scene in Albania is slowly on the rise. One of the first 'signs of art' that will strike you are the multicoloured buildings of Tirana, a project organised by the capital's mayor Edi Rama, himself a painter.

There are still some remnants of socialist realism, with paintings and sculptures adorning the walls and gardens of galleries and museums, although many were destroyed after the fall of the communist government as a reflex against the old regime.

One of the most delicious Albanian art treats is to be found in Berati's Onufri Museum (p66). Onufri was the most outstanding Albanian icon painter of the 16th and 17th centuries and his work is noted for its unique intensity of colour, using natural dyes that are as fresh now as the day he painted with them.

Music
Polyphony, the blending of several independent vocal or instrumental parts, is a southern Albanian tradition dating from ancient Illyrian times. Peasant choirs perform in a variety of styles, and the songs, usually with an epic-lyrical or historical theme, may be dramatic to the point of yodelling, or slow and sober, with alternate male and female voices combining in harmony. Instrumental polyphonic *kabas* (a sedate style, led by a clarinet or violin alongside accordions and lutes) are played by small Roma ensembles. Musical improvisation is accompanied by dancing at colourful village weddings. One well-known group, which often tours outside Albania, is the Lela Family of Përmeti.

An outstanding recording of traditional Albanian music is the CD *Albania, Vocal and Instrumental Polyphony* in the series 'Le Chant du Monde' (produced by the Musée de l'Homme, Paris).

Literature
There is no substantial body of Albanian literature before the 19th century besides some Catholic religious works. The Ottomans banned the teaching of Albanian in schools, fearing the spread of anti-Turkish propaganda. The adoption of a standardised orthography in 1908, when the literary wing of the Rilindja (Renaissance) movement rose together with the Albanian national movement, led to Albanian independence in 1912. A group of romantic patriotic writers at Shkodra, including Migjeni (1911–38) and Martin Çamaj (1925–92), wrote epics

THE KANUNS

The traditional Albanian *kanuns* (codes) consist of hundreds of articles covering every aspect of daily life: work, marriage, births, deaths, family organisation, property questions, inheritances and gender roles. Many people in northern Albania still live by their strict laws. There are three main codes still in practice today: the Kanun of Lek Dukagjini, the Kanun of Skanderbeg and the Kanun of the Mountains. The most popular version is that of Lek Dukagjini, the chief of the most powerful clan in 15th-century Albania. The *kanuns* were passed down through oral traditions, and weren't written down until the late 19th century. Many claim that the *kanuns* have their origins in the laws and customs of the pre-Roman Illyrian tribes.

The most important things in life, according to the *kanuns*, are honour (personal and family) and hospitality. If these two are disrespected by any individual, the family of the person responsible can become involved in the dreadful cycle of killing known as the blood feud or *gjakmarrja*. 'An offence to honour is not paid for with property, but by the spilling of blood or by a magnanimous pardon (through the mediation of good friends)' states the *Kanuni i Lek Dukagjinit* (The Code of Lek Dukagjini, by Lek Dukagjini, Shtjefen Gjecov and Leonard Fox). Only men are involved in blood feuds, and it is their duty to avenge the life and honour of their clan or *fis* by 'taking blood' (murdering) a male member of the clan who originally committed murder against their family. In centuries past, the cycles of killings of families 'in blood' could go on for generations. Blood feuds were outlawed under the communist regime, but in the chaos and poverty of the immediate postcommunist era, blood feuds made a comeback with a vengeance, so to speak. In the mid-90s something like 2700 families were targets of blood feuds, though one NGO estimates this number had fallen to 670 families by 2005. Some of these families have lived in armed isolation for 10 years trying to avoid revenge attacks. Modern blood feuds rarely follow the strict laws of the *kanuns*, and often descend into relentless violence where even women and children are killed. The prominent activist Emin Spahia of the Reconciliation Missionaries group had helped to negotiate the end of hundreds of blood feuds until he was himself murdered in Shkodra in 2004.

In the traditions of the *kanuns*, reconciliation is possible through mediation between the families in conflict. Usually, the mediators are respected village elders, and after an agreement has been reached to end the feud (usually through a financial payment or land sharing, or by taking a *besa* – a sacred oath) the families seal their peace by eating a 'Meal of Blood' prepared by the murderer's family. Hospitality is so important in these parts of Albania that the guest 'takes on a godlike status' according to the anthropologist Kauhiko Yamamoto. There are 38 articles giving instructions on how to treat a guest – an abundance of food, drink and comfort is at his or her disposal, and it is also the host's duty to avenge the murder of his guest, should this happen during their visit.

and historical novels. Poetry that drew on the great tradition of oral epic poetry was the most popular literary form during the Rilindja period.

Perhaps the most interesting writer of the interwar period was Fan Noli (1880–1965). Educated as a priest in the USA, Noli became premier of Albania's Democratic government until it was overthrown in 1924, when he returned to head the Albanian Orthodox Church in America. Although many of his books have religious themes, the introductions he wrote to his own translations of Cervantes, Ibsen, Omar Khayyám and Shakespeare established him as Albania's foremost literary critic.

The only Albanian writer who is widely read outside Albania is the contemporary Ismail Kadare (1936–). His books are not only enriching literary works, but are also a great source of information on Albanian traditions, history and social events. They exquisitely capture the atmosphere of the country's towns, as in the lyrical descriptions of Kadare's birthplace Gjirokastra in *Chronicle in Stone* (1971), where wartime experiences are seen through the eyes of a boy. *Broken April* (1990), set in the northern highlands before the 1939 Italian invasion, describes the life of a village boy who is next in line in the desperate cycle of blood vendettas (see boxed text, above). One of

Kadare's lighter, more accessible works is *The File on H*, the tale of two Irish academics who go searching for traditional epic poets in northern Albania in the 1930s, and stumble into local politics.

Cinema

With its turbulent historical events, Albania has provided the backdrop for some interesting celluloid moments. Many of the films which were made during the communist era have only recently been screened on Albanian TV again – not because of the turgid socialist themes so much but because there was an unofficial ban on anything which portrayed the greatness of Enver Hoxha, which they almost invariably did. Filmgoers in the West have had the opportunity to see Gjergj Xhuvani's comedy *Slogans* (2001), based on the autobiographical short story by Ylljet Alicka, *Slogans of Stone* (well known in Albania), a satirical account of life during communist times.

Another film worth seeing is *Lamerica* (1995), a brilliant and stark look at Albanian postcommunist culture. Woven loosely around a plot about a couple of Italian scam artists, and Albanians seeking to escape to Bari, Italy, the essence of the film is the unshakeable dignity of the ordinary Albanian in the face of adversity.

Renowned Brazilian director Walter Salles (*Central Station*) adapted Ismail Kadare's novel *Broken April* and, having kept the novel's main theme, moved the action to Brazil in *Behind the Sun* (2001).

ENVIRONMENT
The Land

More than three-quarters of Albania is made up of mountains and hills. There are three zones: a coastal plain, a mountainous region and an interior plain in the south. The coastal plain extends approximately 200km from north to south and up to 50km inland. The 2000m-high forested mountain spine, which stretches the entire length of Albania, culminates at Mt Jezerca (2694m) in the north, near the Serbian border. The country's highest peak is Mt Korab (2751m), on the border with Macedonia. The interior plain is alluvial, with seasonal precipitation. It is poorly drained and therefore alternately arid or flooded and is often as inhospitable as the mountains.

Albania has suffered some devastating earthquakes, including the one that struck in 1979, leaving at least 100,000 people homeless.

The longest river in Albania is the Drini River (285km), which starts at Lake Ohrid. In the north the Drini flows into the Buna River, which connects Lake Shkodra to the sea. The Ionian littoral, especially the 'Riviera of Flowers' stretching from Vlora to Saranda, offers magnificent scenery from the highest peak in this region, the Llogaraja Pass (1027m). Forests cover 40% of the land, and the many olive trees, citrus plantations and vineyards give Albania a Mediterranean air. One of Enver Hoxha's bolder schemes was to turn the hills into fields, and all over the country you can see the result of backbreaking labour where entire ranges of hills have been terraced. In some places this seems to have successfully established new orchards and olive groves, but in other places the terracing has unleashed appalling soil erosion.

Wildlife

Albania's territory is rich in flora with beech trees and oak, and patches of rare Macedonian pine *(Pinus peuce)* in the lower regions. Birch, pine and fir cover the mountain sides until they reach 2000m, above which all is barren. Forests cover an estimated 36% of the country, much of it in the isolated northern highlands and close to the Greek border. Bears, deer and wild boar inhabit these isolated forests, but they have been pushed out of regions closer to settlements by widespread summer grazing and by the Albanian penchant for hunting, particularly during the lawless 1990s. Likewise, the koran trout population of Lake Ohrid has fallen dramatically due to illegal fishing since the fall of communism.

The endangered loggerhead turtle nests on isolated beaches on the Ionian Coast and on the Karaburun Peninsula, where Mediterranean monk seals may also have colonies.

There are several wetland sites at the mouths of the Buna, Drini and Mati Rivers in the north and at the Karavasta Lagoon south of Durrësi, with many interesting and rare birds (white pelicans, and whiteheaded ducks, among others) to spot for those with a keen pair of binoculars. The Albanian portion of Lake Prespa is another important haven for birdlife.

National Parks

Most of Albania's national parks and nature reserves, although theoretically protected areas, are not really protected by anything but their remoteness, and tree felling and hunting still take place. There are no hiking maps of the national parks, nor are there generally any hotels or camping grounds. The only place that does have accommodation is the Llogaraja Pass (p69), where you can also go for shorter hikes. Mt Tomorri near Berati is another national park becoming popular with hikers. The Karaburun Peninsula near Vlora is a nature reserve protected largely by its isolation.

Independent camping is not advisable as the mountains are almost completely uninhabited and have no mobile-phone coverage; in case of an injury, help would be impossible to find.

Environmental Issues

Since the collapse of communism, during which time there were around 500 cars in the country, the number of roaring automobiles has risen drastically to around 500,000, many of which are Mercedes-Benzes stolen from Western Europe. There used to be huge caryards full of illegally acquired vehicles around the ports of Vlora and Durrësi, but these have been shut down in recent years. There's a story about an Albanian foreign minister on an official visit to Greece whose Mercedes was impounded at the border after it was found to be stolen. As a consequence of the explosion in vehicle numbers, air pollution in Tirana especially has become a problem.

Illegal logging and fishing was beginning to reach epidemic proportions during the 1990s, but the authorities are now clamping down on the problem.

There is a saddening amount of rubbish littering roadsides, beaches and picnic spots everywhere. This seems to be result both of novelties like plastic bags, which don't degrade, and of a reaction against the harsh communist-era rules on littering. Albanians are, however, doing their bit to improve these conditions and there is considerable Western investment in aiding this process.

FOOD & DRINK

Albanian cuisine is mainly dominated by delicious roast lamb in the mountains and fresh fish and seafood dishes near the coast. The local ingredients tend to be organic by default – few farmers can afford pesticides and agroindustrial meat factories are rare. Offal, veal escalopes, *biftek* (beef loin), *qebaps* (kebabs) and *qoftë* (meat balls) are also very popular. *Fërgesë Tiranë* is a traditional Tirana dish of offal, eggs and tomatoes cooked in an earthenware pot. The regional cuisine of Korça is particularly varied and rich (in flavours as well as oils and fats); the Tirana restaurant Serenata (p57) is a famous exponent of this style.

Italian cuisine can be found everywhere. Most Albanians can't afford to eat out much, and when they do they prefer the food of their Adriatic neighbour. For vegetarians there are some delicious Turkish-style vegetable dishes to be had too, such as roast peppers and aubergines, and cauliflower moussaka. Plenty of *kos* (yogurt) is served in restaurants to accompany any dish. There are also lots of *byrek* (stuffed filo pastry) stands selling both vegetarian and meat-filled varieties.

Albanians do not eat desserts after their meal, but they do drink a shot of *raki* (a local spirit) before they tuck into their food, as an apéritif. *Raki* is very popular and there are two main types in Albania: grape *raki* (the most common), and *mani raki* (mulberry). Ask for homemade if possible *(raki ë bërë në shtëpi)*. If *raki* is not your cup of tea, try Rilindja wine, either a sweet white (Tokai) or a medium-bodied red (Merlot). Wine aficionados should seek out the native red varietal Kallmet. Skënderbeu *konjak* (cognac) is the national aperitif, and it's very good indeed.

There are some issues with the quality of milk of Albania. The country's cows are susceptible to brucellosis and tuberculosis, and not all milk is properly pasteurised. It would be sensible to stick to imported UHT milk.

Eat Your Words

Many cafés and restaurants in Tirana and the big cities have menus in English, but here's a list of common menu items in Albanian:

akullore	ice cream
birrë	beer
bukë	bread
çaj	tea
djathë	cheese

domate	tomato
fasule	beans
fruta deti	seafood
gjalpë	butter
kafe	coffee
kos	yogurt
leng	juice
mish lope/kau	beef
mish qingji	lamb
mish viçi	veal
mollë	apple
paidhaqe	grilled lamb ribs
patate të skuqura	french fries
patëllxhan	eggplant
peshk	fish
pije freskuese	soft drinks
portokall	orange
pulë	chicken
qumësht	milk
sallam	sausage
sallatë	salad
speca	peppers
sufllaqe	souvlaki
troftë	trout
ujë	water
ujë i gazuar	sparkling mineral water
verë	wine

ALBANIAN ADDRESSES

Albania hasn't yet developed much of a need for things like postcodes, street signs or street numbers. People usually direct you to places by saying things like 'Turn left at the green building near the old bus depot and it's the third house past Sali's café on the right.' This works fine for locals, but visitors won't know that the old bus depot is now a furniture store, and have no idea which of the cafés is owned by Sali. This can make finding a particular house a bit like one of the contests on *The Amazing Race*.

The country has a distinctive address system. An example might read, rr Elbasanit, Pall 18, Shk 3, Ap 6. Decoded, rr means *rruga* or street, Pall or sometimes just 'P' means *pallati* or building, Shk means *shkallë* or entrance (there may be several) and Ap means apartment. You may also see the word *përballë* on an address – this means 'in front of', usually referring to some (hopefully) obvious landmark.

In this chapter we've used the abbreviations 'rr' for *rruga* and 'blvd' for *bulevardi*.

TIRANA

☎ 04 / pop 700,000

Tirana is like a cross between Naples and Istanbul with a touch of Minsk: shady boulevards with elegant 1930s Italian architecture, communist monuments, trendy bars, street markets, parks, handsome mosques, rows of moneychangers and fun nightlife. The city has grown rapidly since the end of communism – from around 250,000 people to an estimated 700,000. New neighbourhoods of unplanned housing have sprung up all around the city, and the authorities are struggling to build enough new roads, pipes and power lines to integrate them. Since 2000 the energetic mayor Edi Rama has cleared out a lot of the wilder excesses of the 1990s, restoring the central Parku Rinia, cleaning up the Lana River and installing street lights. Tirana is still very much a work in progress, and the endless rebuilding causes nuisances such as blocked streets and ripped-up footpaths. There's plenty to see and explore on foot (just watch your step), and the city's varied dining and nightlife scene won't strain your finances.

HISTORY

Founded by a Turkish pasha (military governor) in 1614, Tirana developed into a craft centre with a lively bazaar. In 1920 the city was made the capital of Albania as those in power decided it was better to rule the country from its centre rather than from Durrësi, the more vulnerable capital on the coast. Diplomats bemoaned the move to what was then a dusty country town, but the Italians soon built handsome ministry buildings and laid out the main boulevards. The city was severely damaged in the liberation battle in 1944, and the new communist regime knocked down a lot of the remains of the old country town to make space for vast plazas. There's been another building boom in the last decade, with many new apartment buildings going up, and new roads and highways being built on the outskirts.

ORIENTATION

Tirana revolves around the busy central Sheshi Skënderbej (Skanderbeg Sq) from where various streets and boulevards radiate out

TIRANA

0 500 m
0 0.3 miles

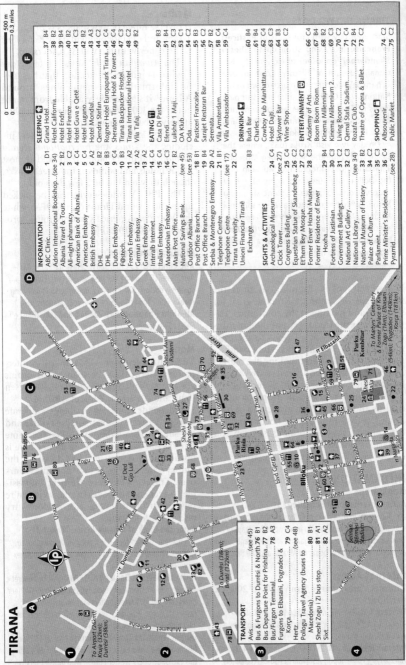

INFORMATION
ABC Clinic	1 D1
Adrion International Bookshop	(see 34)
Albania Travel & Tours	2 B2
All-night pharmacy	3 C2
American Bank of Albania	4 C4
American Embassy	5 C4
British Embassy	6 A2
DHL	7 B2
DHL	8 B3
Dutch Embassy	9 C4
F@stech	10 B3
French Embassy	11 A2
German Embassy	12 A2
Greek Embassy	13 A2
Interalb Internet	14 C4
Italian Embassy	15 C4
Macedonian Embassy	16 C3
Main Post Office	17 B2
National Savings Bank	(see 45)
Outdoor Albania	18 B1
Post Office Branch	19 B4
Post Office Branch	20 A2
Serbia & Montenegro Embassy	21 B1
Telephone Centre	(see 17)
Telephone Centre	22 C4
Tirana University	
Unioni Financiar Tiranë Exchange	23 B3

SIGHTS & ACTIVITIES
Archaeological Museum	24 C4
Clock Tower	(see 27)
Congress Building	25 C4
Equestrian Statue of Skanderbeg	26 C2
Et'hem Bey Mosque	27 C2
Former Enver Hoxha Museum	28 C3
Former Residence of Enver Hoxha	29 B4
Fortress of Justinian	30 C3
Government Buildings	31 C2
National Art Gallery	32 C2
National Library	(see 34)
National Museum of History	33 B2
Palace of Culture	34 C2
Parliament	35 C3
Prime Minister's Residence	36 C4
Pyramid	(see 28)

SLEEPING
Grand Hotel	37 B4
Hotel California	38 B2
Hotel Endri	39 B4
Hotel Firenze	40 B2
Hotel Guva e Qetë	41 C3
Hotel Lugano	42 B2
Hotel Mondial	43 A3
Qendra Stefan	44 C2
Rogner Hotel Europapark Tirana	45 C4
Sheraton Tirana Hotel & Towers	46 C4
Tirana Backpacker Hostel	47 C3
Tirana International Hotel	48 C2
Vila Tafaj	49 B2

EATING
Casa Di Pasta	50 B3
Efendi	51 B4
Lulishte 1 Maji	52 C3
OA Klub	53 C1
Oda	54 C2
Pasticeri Francaise	55 B3
Sarajet Restoran Bar	56 B2
Serenata	57 B2
Vila Amsterdam	58 C4
Vila Ambassador	59 C4

DRINKING
Buda Bar	60 B4
Charles	61 B4
Cowboy Pub Manhattan	62 C3
Hotel Dajti	63 B3
Skytower Bar	64 B2
Wine Shop	65 C2

ENTERTAINMENT
Academy of Arts	66 C4
Boom Boom Room	67 B4
Kinema Millennium	68 B2
Kinema Millennium 2	69 C2
Living Room	70 C2
Qemal Stafa Stadium	71 B4
Rozafa Club	72 B4
Theatre of Opera & Ballet	73 C2

SHOPPING
Albsouvenir	74 C2
Public Market	75 C2

TRANSPORT
Avis	(see 45)
Bus & Furgons to Durrësi & North	76 B1
Bus Departure Point for Prishtina	77 B2
Bus/Furgon Terminal	78 A3
Furgons to Elbasani, Pogradeci & Korça	79 C4
Hertz	(see 48)
Pollogu Travel Agency (buses to Macedonia)	80 B1
Sheshi Zogu i Zi bus stop	81 A1
Sixt	82 A2

ALBANIA

TIRANA IN TWO DAYS

Start your day with croissants in **Pasticeri Francaise** (p57) and stroll up to **Sheshi Skënderbej** (opposite) to explore the National Museum of History. Look around Et'hem Bey Mosque and march down to the National Art Gallery. Admire the stunning views of Tirana at sunset as you wine and dine at the **Skytower Bar** (p59). Drink and party in the trendy **Blloku** (p56) area.

On day two visit **Kruja** (p63), where the castle walls hide the Skanderbeg Museum, a fascinating Ethnographic Museum and the Dollma *teqe* (Bektashi temple), full of history. Don't forget to do some shopping at the lovely bazaar and have a traditional Albanian lunch in one of its small restaurants. Back in Tirana, dinner at **Villa Ambassador** (p57) is obligatory for a diverse, mouth-watering menu.

---

like wheel spokes. Running south is the shady blvd Dëshmorët e Kombit, great for strolling and looking at the communist relics and near the trendy part of Blloku. Running north, blvd Zogu I leads to the busy train and bus station where bus conductors shout out their destinations like market sellers. Most sights and services are within a few minutes' walk of Sheshi Skënderbej.

All incoming buses will drop you off at the bus and train station at the end of blvd Zogu I, a five-minute walk north from the city centre. *Furgons* (minibuses) drop you at various points around the city, but it's easy to grab a taxi to your destination.

INFORMATION
Bookshops
Adrion International Bookshop (☎ 235 242; ☺ 9am-9pm) In the Palace of Culture on the right-hand side, this bookshop has Penguin literary classics, maps of Tirana and Albania, foreign magazines and newspapers, and an excellent selection of books on Albania and the Balkans.

Internet Access
Internet cafés charge from 150 to 200 lek per hour.
F@stech (☎ 251 947; rr Brigada e VIII; ☺ 8.30am-11pm) A 1st-floor joint, with high stools bringing you up to your walled-in screen.
Interalb Internet (☎ 251 747; rr Dëshmorët e 4 Shkurtit Pall 25/1; ☺ 8am-10pm) Just plain not-so-old computers.

Media
A diverse range of newspapers is printed in Tirana and the independent daily *Koha Jonë* is the paper with the widest readership.

The *Albanian Daily News* is a fairly dry English-language publication that has useful information on happenings around Albania. It's generally available from major hotels for 300 lek, or you can read it online at www.albaniannews.com.

Foreign newspapers and magazines, including the *Times*, the *International Herald Tribune* and the *Economist*, are sold at most major hotels and some central street kiosks, though they tend to be a few days old.

The BBC World Service can be picked up in and around Tirana on 103.9FM, while the Voice of America's mainly music programme is on 107.4FM.

Medical Services
ABC Clinic (☎ 234 105; 360 rr Qemal Stafa; ☺ 8am-4pm Mon-Fri) Opposite the New School, with English-speaking doctors, ABC offers a range of services including regular (€50) and emergency (€80) consultations.
All-night Pharmacy (☎ 222 241; blvd Zogu I) Just off Sheshi Skënderbej.

Money
Tirana has plenty of ATMs linked to international networks. The main ATM chains are Tirana Bank, Pro Credit Bank, Raiffeisen Bank and American Bank of Albania.

Independent money exchangers operate directly in front of the main post office and on Sheshi Skënderbej and offer the same rates as the banks. Changing money here is not illegal or dangerous, but do count the money you receive before handing yours over. Travellers cheques are near impossible to exchange outside Tirana, so if you're relying on them (our advice is, don't) try one of the following:
American Bank of Albania (rr Ismail Qemali 27; ☺ 9.30am-3.30pm Mon-Fri) A reliable, secure place to cash your travellers cheques (2% commission). The Amex representative.
National Savings Bank (☎ 235 035; blvd Dëshmorët e Kombit; ☺ 10.30am-5pm Mon-Fri) Located in the Rogner Hotel Europapark Tirana, it offers MasterCard advances, cashes US dollar, euro and sterling travellers cheques for 1% commission and exchanges cash.
Unioni Financiar Tiranë Exchange (☎ 234 979; rr Dëshmorët e 4 Shkurtit) Just south of the main post office, this exchange offers Western Union wire transfer services.

Post

DHL (DHLAlbania@tia-co.al.dhl.com) rr Ded Gjo Luli (☎ 227 667; fax 233 934; rr Ded Gjo Luli 6); rr Dëshmorët e 4 Shkurtit (☎ 232 816; fax 257 294; rr Dëshmorët e 4 Shkurtit 7/1) The international courier service has two offices in Tirana.

Main post office (☎ 228 262; Sheshi Çameria; ☉ 8am-8pm Mon-Fri) On a street jutting west from Sheshi Skënderbeg. There are branch post offices on blvd Zogu I and on rr Muhamet Gjollesha.

Telephone

There's a telephone office at the main post office.

Telephone centre (blvd Zogu I) This other telephone office is about 400m north of Sheshi Skënderbeg, on the right-hand side.

Tourist Information

Tirana does not have an official tourist office, but travel agencies (below) can help.

Tirana in Your Pocket (www.inyourpocket.com) tells you what's hot, and is available at bookshops and some of the larger kiosks for 400 lek.

Another useful reference is *Tirana: The Practical Guide and map of Tirana* with telephone numbers and addresses for everything from hospitals to embassies, though some of the entries are only in Albanian. This is also available at the main hotels and bookshops for 200 lek.

Travel Agencies

Travel agencies and airlines of all descriptions and destinations abound on rr Mine Peza. Nearly all sell tickets to leave Albania but there are very few internal tour agencies – in addition, not all operators speak English.

Albania Travel & Tours (☎ 232 983; fax 244 401; rr Durrësit 102; ☉ 8am-8pm Mon-Fri, 8am-2pm Sat & Sun) A good place to arrange ferry tickets from Durrësi (see p403), and/or book private rooms, or possibly tours around the country.

Outdoor Albania (☎ 272 075; www.outdooralbania .com; rr Siri Kodra 42/1; ☉ 8am-8pm Mon-Fri) Excellent trailblazing adventure tour agency offering trekking, ski touring, sea and white-water kayaking, paragliding and more. Outdoor Albania organises stays in village houses, and also runs the groovy OA Klub restaurant-bar in Tirana.

DANGERS & ANNOYANCES

Beware the potholes! Tirana's streets are badly lit during the night so arm yourself with a pocket torch to light your way around, but watch out for the potholes during the day too. Some of these monsters are over a metre deep so you could incur serious injury. There are occasional power cuts in the city – another reason for carrying a pocket torch. Crossing the street is not for the faint-hearted either – don't assume the traffic automatically stops at a red light.

SIGHTS

Sheshi Skënderbej is the best place to start witnessing the daily goings-on, as kids in orange plastic cars zip past your ankles, and real cars zoom around the **equestrian statue of Skanderbeg** on the southern side of the square. If you stop to examine Skanderbeg's emblematic goat's head helmet, the minaret of the 1789–1823 **Et'hem Bey Mosque** (Sheshi Skënderbej) will catch your eye on the left. The small and elegant mosque is one of the oldest buildings left in the city, spared from destruction during the atheism campaign of the late '60s because of its status as a cultural monument. Take your shoes off and go inside to take a look at the beautifully painted dome. Behind it is the tall **Clock Tower** (Kulla e Sahatit; ☎ 243 292; rr Luigi Gurakqi; admission free; ☉ 9am-1pm & 4-6pm Mon, Wed & Sat), which you can climb to watch the square, with its colourful Ferris wheel entertaining the tiny Tiranans.

On the northwestern side of the square, beside the 15-storey Tirana International Hotel, is the **National Museum of History** (Muzeu Historik Kombëtar; Sheshi Skënderbej; admission 50 lek; ☉ 9am-1pm & 5-7pm Tue-Sat, 9am-noon Sun), the largest museum in Albania, which holds most of the country's archaeological treasures and a replica of Skanderbeg's massive sword. There's a sombre gallery devoted to the miseries of the communist era on the top floor, including a full-scale model of a prison cell. Do take a guide (there are English-, French- and Italian-speaking guides) around the museum, as most of the information is in Albanian; it's common to tip the guide 100 or 200 lek. The fantastic **mosaic mural** entitled *Albania* adorning the museum's façade shows Albanians victorious and proud from Illyrian times through to WWII. A golden statue of Enver Hoxha once stood in front of the museum.

If you are an archaeological glutton, there is an extensive collection to be seen in the **Archaeological Museum** (Muzeu Arkeologik; Sheshi

Nënë Tereza; admission 200 lek; 10.30am-2.30pm Mon-Fri), close to the main Tirana University.

To the east of Sheshi Skënderbeg is the white stone **Palace of Culture** (Pallate Kulturës; Sheshi Skënderbej), which has a theatre, shops and art galleries. Construction of the palace began as a gift from the Soviet people in 1960 and was completed in 1966, after the 1961 Soviet-Albanian split. The entrance to the **National Library** is on the south side of the building.

Stroll down the spacious tree-lined blvd Dëshmorët e Kombit to Tirana's **National Art Gallery** (Galeria Kombëtare e Arteve; blvd Dëshmorët e Kombit; admission 100 lek; 9am-1pm & 5-8pm Tue-Sun), where the garden is adorned with statues of proud partisans. See the astonishing exhibition of icons inside by Onufri, the renowned 16th-century master of colour. One hall features socialist realist paintings with names like the *Giants of Metallurgy*. There is also a room adjacent to the gallery space where you can see busts of Mother Teresa (who had Albanian ancestry) and Enver Hoxha, among others. Temporary exhibitions are on the ground floor.

If you turn up rr Murat Toptani you pass the 6m-high walls of the **Fortress of Justinian** (rr Murat Toptani), the last remnants of a Byzantine-era castle. The **Parliament** (rr Punëtorët e Rilindjes) building is just a little further on. Head back to blvd Dëshmorët e Kombit and take a break at the Hotel Dajti (p58) for a whiff of 1930s-Italian-meets-communism and feel transported to a different time in this tranquil building with soft armchairs and low chandeliers as the sunlight peeks through the ochre drapes. The Dajti was sold by the government in 2005, and will probably soon be another luxury hotel.

Further down on the left, after crossing the bridge over the tiny Lana River, you'll see the sloping white-marble and glass walls of the 1988 **Pyramid** (former Enver Hoxha Museum; blvd Dëshmorët e Kombit), designed by Hoxha's daughter and son-in-law. Now used as a disco and conference centre, the building never really took off as a museum, but does very well as a slide for children. Nearby is the **Prime Minister's Residence** (blvd Dëshmorët e Kombit), from where Enver Hoxha and cronies would stand and view military parades from the 2nd-floor balcony.

Another creation of the dictator's daughter and son-in-law is the square **Congress Building** (blvd Dëshmorët e Kombit), just a little down the boulevard. Follow rr Ismail Qemali, two streets north of the Congress Building, and enter the once totally forbidden but now totally trendy **Blloku** area, the former communist party elite hang-out. When it was first opened to the general public in 1991, Albanians flocked to see the style in which their 'proletarian' leaders lived. If we are to judge by the **former residence of Enver Hoxha** (cnr rr Dëshmorët e 4 Shkurtit & rr Ismail Qemali), a three-storey pastel-coloured house, they lived like the Western suburban bourgeoisie.

If you fancy a break from the city buzz, head southeast a couple of blocks to the lush **Parku Kombëtar** (National Park), with a *teatri veror* (open-air theatre) and an artificial lake, where Tiranans get fit, breathe some fresh air, or spend a romantic moment or two.

SLEEPING

Tirana's accommodation is improving and there are a few good budget options as well as some quality midrange and more pricey top-end places to lay your head.

Budget

Tirana Backpacker Hostel (068 216 7357, 068 222 2304; tiranabackpacker@hotmail.com; rr Elbasanit 85; dm €12) Albania's first hostel opened in 2005 in a villa close to the city centre. It has 18 beds in three rooms and two shared bathrooms. It has some big balconies, a garden, a kitchen for guests to use and friendly, helpful young managers. Prices are 20% lower from November to May.

Qendra Stefan (Stephen Center; /fax 245 924; stefan@icc-al.org; rr Hoxha Tahsim 1; s/d €30/50) This bright, airy little hotel is American owned and is a safe, friendly refuge. The downstairs café is a popular expat hang-out, and has free wi-fi access in case you brought a laptop with you. The rooms have great bathrooms and comfy beds. The very helpful staff make it a delightful base in Tirana.

Hotel Endri (244 168, 229 334; Pall 27, fl 3, apt 30, rr Vaso Pasha 27; r €18) Good value and located where all the action is, in Blloku. The 'hotel' is basically a couple of clean rooms in a building next to the owner Petrit Alikaj's apartment. This friendly little lodge has nice bathrooms and excellent showers.

Hotel Guva e Qetë (235 491/40; fax 222 228; rr Murat Toptani 25; s €24-32, d €32-40, q €48) This little lodge has a central location with some nicely renovated rooms and some less appealing older rooms. The newer rooms are spacious with TVs and brand-new bathrooms. The managers don't speak any English, but at least it's clean and central.

Midrange

Hotel Mondial (☎ 232 372; www.hotelmondial.com.al; rr Muhamet Gjollesha; s/d €80/100) Though situated about 1km away from Sheshi Skënderbej, the Mondial gets lots of reports of good service and excellent food at its Italian restaurant. The rooms are very pleasant and there are lots of original artworks decorating the place. The rooftop swimming pool is just the cherry on top.

Vila Tafaj (☎ 227 581; vilatafaj@abissnet.com.al; rr Mine Peza; s €40-50, d €60-70; ✿) This handsome little boutique hotel in an ornate 1930s villa has a lovely garden at the back with draping vines and wisteria, and canaries twittering in cages. All the rooms have minibar and satellite TV.

Hotel California (☎ /fax 253 191/2; california@ albmail.com; rr Mihal Duri 2/1; s/d €50/70) Lyrically named and thankfully nothing like the song, the rooms here are clean with comfy beds, TVs, telephones and sparkling bathrooms. The rooms on the 5th floor have great views over the city from the balconies. Laundry service is free.

Hotel Lugano (☎ /fax 222 023; rr Mihal Duri 34; r €50) The newly renovated rooms have heavy red drapes on the windows, good beds, and some, though not all, have kitsch marble-copy bathrooms that may give you a shock in the morning. It's opposite Hotel California.

Hotel Firenze (☎ 249 099; firenzehotel@albania online.net; blvd Zogu I 72; s/d €50/70; P ✿) This cheerfully colourful little hotel between the railway station and Sheshi Skënderbej has seven rooms with TV and minibar, and a nice little restaurant serving Italian and Albanian food.

Top End

Rogner Hotel Europapark Tirana (☎ 235 035; www .rogner.com; blvd Dëshmorët e Kombit; s €180-210, d €220-250, ste €320-350; ✿) With an unbeatable location in the heart of the city, the Rogner is a peaceful oasis with a big garden, free Internet access in every room (if you have your own laptop), banks and travel agencies. The hotel rooms are spacious and very

comfortable, and the restaurant has tasty international cuisine. Drink into the night on the cool terrace. Amex, Visa and MasterCard accepted.

Sheraton Tirana Hotel & Towers (☎ 274 707; www.starwoodhotels.com; Sheshi Italia; r €180, ste €273-384) This is an impressive new upper-end business hotel, whose blank mirrored glass and monumental frame might be a nod to the country's totalitarian past. Services and facilities match the prices.

Tirana International Hotel (☎ 234 185; www .tirana-international.com; Sheshi Skënderbej; s/d €110/130, ste €157-270) Originally the Soviet-built Hotel Tirana, the modern incarnation is just as imposing but far more comfortable. Fine artworks decorate the lobby, and the sleek, luxurious rooms have great views of the busy square.

Grand Hotel (☎ 253 220; grandhotel@icc-al.org; rr Ismail Qemali 11; s/d €120/160, ste €220; ✿) A smaller upmarket hotel in the heart of trendy Blloku. The rooms are a teensy bit dated (the suites and the restaurant look like a set from *Goodfellas*) but perfectly comfortable. The hotel also has a sauna.

EATING

If you thought that cuisine in Tirana's restaurants might be monotonous or that eating out would be a downmarket experience, you were wrong. The buzzing central street of Blloku, rr Dëshmorët e 4 Shkurtit, is the top spot for cafés, bars and restaurants.

Pasticeri Francaise (☎ 251 336; rr Dëshmorët e 4 Shkurtit 1; breakfast 150 lek; ◷ 8am-10pm) One of the few breakfast spots in Tirana, this French-owned place has red walls and high ceilings, and small lamps light individual tables giving it an ooh-la-la feeling!

Villa Ambassador (☎ 068 202 4293; rr Themistokli Gërmenji; meals 1000 lek; ◷ noon-11.30pm) A smart atmosphere, fantastic service and tasty Albanian dishes for carnivores and vegetarians alike. The former East German embassy has evolved into one of Tirana's best food choices.

Serenata (☎ 273 088; rr Mihal Duri 7; meals 1500-2000 lek; ◷ 9am-midnight) One of Tirana's best places for regional Albanian cuisine, Serenata specialises in Korçan food, which consists of meat dishes like oven-baked liver, veal and wild boar, and vegetarian delicacies. It also serves some interesting local wines and *rakis* from Korça. This

ALBANIA

place is traditionally decorated and has gentle Korçan music *(serenata)* tinkling from the speakers.

Casa di Pasta (☎ 251 157; Parku Rinia; meals 700 lek; ☺ 8am-midnight) The delightfully weird Disneyesque structure called the Taivan Kompleksi (Taiwan Complex) in Parku Rinia houses this excellent Italian restaurant and a café called Le Café open the same hours. Case di Pasta has terrific pizzas for around 500 lek and entrées such as salmon with rocket for 400 lek. The terrace is a popular spot to watch international football matches on a big screen erected outside.

Lulishte 1 Maji (☎ 230 151; rr Punëtorët e Rilindjes; mains 500 lek; ☺ 8am-late) This complex offers several different kitchens (Chinese, Turkish, Mexican, Italian), lots of tables under umbrellas in the spacious shaded garden, and even a playground for kids. The Turkish food is particularly good, with filling *pides* (a bit like a pizza or calzone) for 400 lek. It also has live music some nights.

OA Klub (☎ 272 075; rr Siri Kodra 42/1; mains 400 lek; ☺ 8am-11pm) This laid-back, arty little café/bar/restaurant is in a slightly out-of-the-way location, but well worth hunting out for its ever-changing array of vegetarian meals, cool little garden under citrus trees and nice lounges upstairs. It's very close to a hotel called the Alpin.

Oda (☎ 249 541; rr Luigj Gurakuqi; meals around 500 lek; ☺ noon-late) A cute little traditional Albanian restaurant run by artist Paskal Prifti, with tasty home cooking, and an array of powerful *rakis* and fragrant homemade wines. Mr Prifti is a fan of traditional Albanian polyphonic singing and sometimes has friends drop by to sing the old melodies. The restaurant is on an alley just off the street near Sheshi Avni Rustemi.

Efendi (☎ 246 624; rr Sami Frashëri 20; meals around 2500 lek; ☺ 11am-11pm) Quite expensive by local standards, the Ottoman cuisine served here by a chef who worked in Turkey is utterly superb. The selection of mezes is tremendous: puréed eggplant, spicy beans and mushrooms and rich kebabs. Main courses cost around 1000 to 1200 lek, entrées around 400 lek. The décor is simple but the food is sumptuous – a great place to blow the budget.

Vila Amsterdam (☎ 267 439; rr Asim Zeneli 9; meals 600 lek; ☺ 7am-11pm) This cheerful pizzeria, bar and restaurant across the street from the Dutch embassy has a charming little garden where you can sit and devour pizzas and pasta, and enjoy good service.

Sarajet Restoran Bar (☎ 243 038; rr Abdi Toptani 7; meals 600 lek; ☺ 9am-11pm) This restaurant serves fairly typical Italian fare, but what makes it special is the fine Ottoman-era villa it occupies. It once belonged to the wealthy Toptani family. The ground floor has been 'modernised' but the private dining rooms on the first floor retain many original features.

DRINKING

Tirana has a vibrant, fast-changing bar and café scene, with a particular concentration around the corner of Ismail Qemali and Dëshmorët e 4 Shkurtit in Blloku.

Cowboy Pub Manhattan (☎ 253 822; rr Dëshmorët e 4 Shkurtit, Pall 7/1; ☺ 8am-late) Popular with expats and trendy young locals alike, this oddly named pub has a prime location in the heart of Blloku. A Bitburger beer costs 300 lek and comes with a small bowl of crisps. A good selection of tunes plays through a hefty sound system.

Charles (☎ 253 754; rr Pjeter Bogdani 5; ☺ 8am-late) Charles is a consistently popular bar with Tirana's students because of its ever-varying music: jazz, blues, orchestral and rock on different nights of the week. Charles has a very pleasant, relaxed vibe – fashionable but not pretentious.

Buda Bar (☎ 068 205 8825; rr Ismail Qemali; ☺ 9am-late) All about a relaxed atmosphere with subdued lighting, incense burning, chaise longues and armchairs abounding with cushions.

Wine Shop (☎ 264 347; rr Hoxha Tahsim; ☺ 8am-11pm) Popular with a more mature clientele, this cosy little bar just past Qendra Stefan offers wines from all parts of Albania and a goodly selection of vintages from Europe, plus tasty cheese platters and nibbles.

Hotel Dajti (☎ 251 031; blvd Dëshmorët e Kombit 6; ☺ 9am-midnight) The Hotel Dajti has just been sold and will probably become an up-market hotel in the future. In the meantime, this is Tirana's most evocative remaining communist-era relic, and it's well worth visiting the bar on the ground floor to soak up the atmosphere of hushed intrigue. A large splash of Skënderbeu cognac costs just 100 lek. Apparently there are crawl spaces between each floor of the hotel where spies could listen in on foreign guests. The small terrace in the front is a great place for a break in the shade, too.

Skytower Bar (☎ 221 666; Sky Tower, rr Dëshmorët e 4 Shkurtit; ☼ 9am-11pm) Spectacular city views from the revolving bar/restaurant and the breezy terrace on top of one of the highest buildings in town. It's more notable for the views and the décor than the food (mains 500 lek), but a swish joint nonetheless.

ENTERTAINMENT

There is a good choice of entertainment options in Tirana, in the form of bars, clubs, cinema, performances and exhibitions. For the low-down on events and exhibitions, check out the monthly leaflet *ARTirana* (a free supplement to *Gazeta Shqiptare*), which contains English, French, Italian and Albanian summaries of the cultural events currently showing in town.

Cinemas

Kinema Millennium (☎ 248 647; rr e Kavajës; admission 200-500 lek) The best cinema in Tirana, the Millennium shows recent box-office hits (earlier shows are cheaper).

Kinema Millennium 2 (☎ 253 654; rr Murat Toptani; admission 200-500 lek) A second location nearby shows art-house productions and boasts a lovely garden bar. All films are shown in the original language with Albanian subtitles.

Live Music

Qemal Stafa Stadium (Sheshi Italia) Next to the university, this stadium often hosts pop concerts and other musical events. Look out for street banners bearing details of upcoming events. Football matches are held here every Saturday and Sunday afternoon.

Boom Boom Room (☎ 243 702; rr Gjin Bue Shpata; ☼ 7pm-2am) This place has a smoky jazz crowd, live performances most evenings and a lively atmosphere.

Theatre of Opera & Ballet (☎ 224 753; Sheshi Skënderbej; admission from 300 lek; ☼ performances from 7pm, from 6pm winter) Check the listings and posters outside this theatre for performances. You can usually buy tickets half an hour before the show for 200 lek.

Academy of Arts (☎ 257 237; Sheshi Nënë Tereza) Classical music performances take place throughout the year in this building opposite the Archaeological Museum. Prices vary according to the programme.

Nightclubs

Rozafa Club (rr Ismail Qemali; ☼ 8pm-late) Next door to the Buda Bar, this club is the place to dance till dawn. House, hard House and techno dominate the DJ repertoire.

Living Room (☎ 242 481; rr Punëtorët e Rilindjes; ☼ 24hr) One of the hippest places to drink and dance in Tirana, with an eclectic mix of tunes (Latin, funk, jazz, House, etc), DJ and an up-for-it, fun crowd. It has cool lampshades, '70s armchairs and sofas for you to lounge on when you're danced (or drunk) off your feet. It's a pink-and-yellow building across the street from the parliament.

SHOPPING

There are a few good souvenir shops along rr Luigj Gurakuqi between Sheshi Skënderbej and Sheshi Avni Rustemi, plus a couple more on rr Barrikadave, including a communist-relic tourist kiosk evocatively named **Albsouvenir** (rr Barrikadave). Most of them sell the same things: Albanian flags, carved wooden plates, beaten copper plates, pistols and knives (not a great hit with airline security these days), as well as traditional textiles and some very funky T-shirts.

Public market (Pazari i Ri; Sheshi Avni Rustemi; ☼ 7am-8pm) Tirana's eclectic market, north of the Sheshi Avni Rustemi roundabout several blocks east of the Clock Tower, is largest on Thursday and Sunday. The fruit market is right on the square, then there's a collection of butchers and cheese shops, and further on there are stalls selling carved wooden trays, small boxes, wall hangings and bone necklaces, though many just sell cheap house supplies for the locals.

GETTING THERE & AWAY
Air

Nënë Tereza (Mother Teresa) Airport (surely the only airport named after a nun?), also known as Rinas Airport, is at Rinasi, 26km northwest of Tirana. It is currently being modernised and a new passenger terminal opened in 2005. The unruly queues for passport control are followed immediately by an unruly queue to pay the €10 visa fee. There are currency exchange counters and car-hire offices at the airport.

For a list of airlines flying from Albania to other parts of the Western Balkans, see p83.

ALBANIA

Bus

The public transport system is quite confusing because it's impossible to pin down exactly where all the buses and *furgons* leave from. Some of the traditional bus and *furgon* depots have been shifted because of building projects, and have ended up in temporary digs in unlikely parts of town (such as an abandoned factory somewhere off rr Durrësit). Generally, buses and *furgons* going north (Kruja, Lezha, Shkodra) leave and drop you off next to the train station. If you are arriving from the south, your bus/*furgon* will drop you at Sheshi Zogu i Zi – the intersection of the ring road (Unaza) and rr Durrësit. *Furgons* to Korça, Pogradeci and Elbasani leave from a stand by Qemal Stafa stadium. If you want to take a bus or *furgon* anywhere else in the south, the departure points are in a complete state of flux. The easiest is just to jump in a taxi and say *'Dua të shkoj në* (Berat, Vlorë, wherever)', meaning 'I want to go to (Berati, Vlora, wherever)'. Taxi drivers always know the latest departure points.

The following table will give you an idea of distances and average costs involved for departures from Tirana. *Furgons* are usually 40% to 50% more expensive than buses.

Destination	Cost	Duration	Distance
Berati	250 lek	2½hr	122km
Durrësi	100 lek	1hr	38km
Elbasani	300 lek	1½hr	54km
Fieri	260 lek	3hr	113km
Gjirokastra	700 lek	7hr	232km
Korça	700 lek	4hr	181km
Kruja	150 lek	¾hr	32km
Kukësi	1000 lek	8hr	208km
Pogradeci	600 lek	3½hr	150km
Saranda	800 lek	8hr	284km
Shkodra	300 lek	2½hr	116km
Vlora	300 lek	4hr	147km

Note that both buses and *furgons* normally leave when full. Pay the driver or conductor on the bus.

For information on buses arriving in Tirana from other countries in the Western Balkans, see under Land, p83.

Car & Motorcycle

For the brave few, there are car-hire companies at the airport, and here are some major car-hire companies in Tirana:

Avis (☎ 235 011; Rogner Hotel Europapark, blvd Dëshmorët e Kombit)
Hertz (☎ 255 028; Tirana Hotel International, Sheshi Skënderbej)
Sixt (☎ 259 020; rr e Kavajës 116)

Train

The run-down train station is at the northern end of blvd Zogu I. Albania's trains range from sort-of OK to very decrepit. Eight trains daily go to Durrësi (55 lek, one hour, 36km). Trains also depart for Elbasani (160 lek, four hours, three daily), Pogradeci (245 lek, seven hours, twice daily), Shkodra (150 lek, 3½ hours, twice daily) and Vlora (210 lek, 5½ hours, twice daily).

GETTING AROUND
To/From the Airport

The airport is 26km from Tirana. The only public transport to Tirana is a very irregular bus for airport workers (50 lek), but taxis ply the route. The fee should be settled before you hop in – the going rate is €20. You can avoid haggling the minute you arrive in Albania by arranging for a hotel to send someone to collect you. Given the state of traffic in Tirana, and particularly in this direction (it's via the main highway out of town), give yourself a little extra time to get out to the airport when you're leaving.

Car & Motorcycle

Some of the major hotels offer guarded parking; others have parking available out front.

Taxi

Taxi stands dot the city and charge 400 lek for a ride inside Tirana (600 lek at night). Make sure you reach an agreement with the driver before setting off. **Radio Taxi** (☎ 377 777), with 24-hour service, is particularly reliable.

CENTRAL ALBANIA

DURRËSI
☎ 052 / pop 85,000

Durrësi is an ancient city and Albania's old capital. It has a 10km-long built-up beach stretching south where families play football, and people stroll and cool down in the shallow waters of the Adriatic. The town

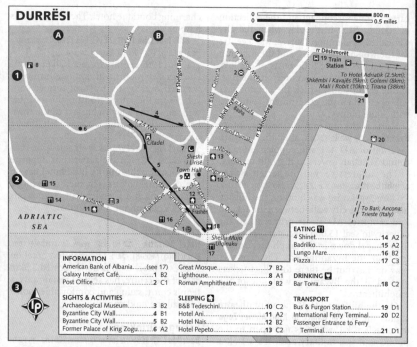

DURRËSI

0 — 800 m
0 — 0.5 miles

INFORMATION		Great Mosque	7	B2
American Bank of Albania	(see 17)	Lighthouse	8	A1
Galaxy Internet Café	1 B2	Roman Amphitheatre	9	B2
Post Office	2 C1			

SIGHTS & ACTIVITIES		SLEEPING		
Archaeological Museum	3 B2	B&B Tedeschini	10	C2
Byzantine City Wall	4 B1	Hotel Ani	11	A2
Byzantine City Wall	5 B2	Hotel Nais	12	B2
Former Palace of King Zogu	6 A2	Hotel Pepeto	13	C2

EATING		
4 Shinet	14	A2
Badrilko	15	A2
Lungo Mare	16	B2
Piazza	17	C3

DRINKING		
Bar Torra	18	C2

TRANSPORT		
Bus & Furgon Station	19	D1
International Ferry Terminal	20	D2
Passenger Entrance to Ferry		
Terminal	21	D1

authorities have built a boardwalk along the beach and added some Disney-style streetlights, but the city's beaches are something of a lesson in unplanned development. An outbreak of skin infections among swimmers in 2005 suggests all is not well with the water quality. Away from the sea, Durrësi is a relaxed, amiable port with some gracious early-20th-century buildings, interesting ancient remains, an excellent museum and a clutch of very good bars and restaurants. Good bus and train connections make Durrësi a great base for exploration of archaeological sites such as Apollonia, and it's a quieter alternative to the capital.

Orientation

The town centre is easily covered on foot. In the centre, the **Great Mosque** (Xhamia e Madhe Durrësi; Sheshi i Lirisë) serves as a point of orientation: the archaeological attractions are immediately around it, and the train and bus stations plus the harbour are to the northeast. Durrësi's main *xhiro* (evening stroll) goes from this square down rr Tregtare to Sheshi Mujo Ulqinaku, so there are

lots of cafés along this street. The palace of King Ahmet Zogu and the lighthouse are to the west, on the ridge.

Information

The **post office** (blvd Kryesor) is one block west of the train and bus stations. There are quite a few ATMs around town, including a branch of the **American Bank of Albania** (Sheshi Mujo Ulqinaku); **Galaxy Internet** (rr Taulantia; per hr 200 lek) is near the bank.

Dea Lines (☎ 30 386; dealines@dealines.com; rr Tregtare 102; ☼ 9am-6pm) is a trustworthy travel agency in the middle of town with up-to-date information on ferries and flights from nearby Nënë Tereza Airport.

Sights

The **Archaeological Museum** (Muzeu Arkeologik; rr Taulantia; admission 200 lek; ☼ 9.30am-12.30pm & 5-7pm Tue-Sun) on the waterfront is very well laid out and has an impressive collection of artefacts from the Greek, Hellenistic and Roman periods on the ground floor. Highlights include engraved Roman funeral stelae (memorial stones), some big carved stone sarcophagi and the collection of statues. Back in the day when the city was called Epidamnos, Durrësi was a centre for the worship of Venus, and the museum has a cabinet full of little busts of the love goddess. There's a collection from the Byzantine era upstairs, which the curator says will open when the government comes up with some money.

North of the museum are the 6th-century **Byzantine city walls**, built after the Visigoth invasion of AD 481 and supplemented by round Venetian towers in the 14th century. The impressive but neglected **Roman amphitheatre** (rruga e Kalasë; admission 100 lek; ☺ 10am-5pm Mon-Sat) was built on the hillside just inside the city walls between the 1st and 2nd centuries AD; in its prime it had the capacity to seat 15,000 spectators. There's a little chapel down in the amphitheatre dating from the Byzantine era. The caretaker may or may not be there to collect tickets around at the Byzantine wall side of the amphitheatre.

On the hilltop west of the amphitheatre stands the **former palace of King Ahmet Zogu** (rr Anastas Durrsaku), which is not open to the public as it is a military area. It's a 1.5km walk to the top of the hill, but the views of the bay make it well worth the climb. A **lighthouse** (rr Anastas Durrsaku) stands on the next hill from where you can enjoy the royal views and check out the bunker constellation (see p46).

Sleeping

Durrësi has a variety of accommodation in the city itself and many, many hotels line the long beaches of Shkëmbi i Kavajës, Golemi and Mali i Robit. Most of these hotels cater to local holidaymakers and ethnic kin from Kosovo and Macedonia.

IN TOWN

Hotel Pepeto (☎ 24 190; fax 26 346; rr Mbreti Monun 3; s/d €30/40; ✵) A homely, well-run guesthouse just off the square fronting the mosque. The rooms are decent and quiet, with good showers, minibar and TV. There's a spacious, groovy lounge with big couches and a bar downstairs, and the hotel offers free laundry service.

Hotel Nais (☎ 30 375; fax 24 940; rr Naim Frashëri; s/d €30/40) Perched by the city walls, this refurbished 1930s building is now a

charming boutique hotel. The comfy rooms have balconies.

B&B Tedeschini (☎ 24 343, 068 224 6303; ipmcrsp@ icc.al.eu.org; Dom Nikoll Kaçorri 5; s/d €15/30) This gracious 19th-century former Italian consulate has airy rooms with antique furniture, watched over by portraits of former consuls. From the square fronting the mosque, walk down the alley right next to the town hall, take the first right, a quick left, then a quick right.

Hotel Ani (☎ 24 288; fax 30 478; rr Taulantia; s €40-80, d €50-90; ✵) On the waterfront opposite the museum, this quirky little hotel has an eye-catching colour scheme, sparklingly clean rooms and friendly staff. The rooms have TV, telephone and minibar.

THE COAST

Hotel Adriatik (☎ 60 850; www.adriatikhotel.com; Plazhi Illiria; r €65-81; ✵) The grandest hotel on Durrësi's beaches, this hotel, located 2.5km east of the centre, has several restaurants, a tennis court, sauna and comfortable rooms with all the mod cons.

Eating & Drinking

Badriklo (☎ 25 560; rr Taulantia; mains 500 lek; ☺ 9am-11pm) This restaurant on the landward side of rr Taulantia may lack sea views but it has the best pizzas in Durrësi, good service and a lively terrace bar.

4 Shinet (☎ 25 429; rr Taulantia; meals 600 lek ☺ 9am-11pm) Right by the sea at the end of rr Taulantia, the 'Four Seasons' is popular with young professionals looking for fresh sea air, good tunes and tasty light meals such as pasta and pizza.

Lungo Mare (☎ 35 835; rr Taulantia; meals 700-1500 lek; ☺ 11am-10pm) This restaurant is on the 1st floor of a two-towered pale green apartment building between Bar Torra and the museum. It's renowned locally for fine seafood; fish dishes are priced by weight, and start at 700 lek for smallish portions.

Piazza (☎ 069 209 4887; Sheshi Mujo Ulqinaku; meals 800-1000 lek; ☺ 9am-midnight) Situated above a branch of the American Bank of Albania opposite the Bar Torra, Piazza offers excellent Italian cuisine and a terrace overlooking the city. The antipasto platter (500 lek) is practically a meal in itself. Piazza also has a good array of wines and icy cold beer.

Bar Torra (Sheshi Mujo Ulqinaku; ☺ 8am-midnight) Housed inside a fortified Venetian tower, this was one of the first private cafés in Albania, opened by a team of local artists. There's a roof terrace for cheap alfresco eating (order a panini for 100 lek) or drinking coffee, cocktails or beer under the stars.

Getting There & Away

Albania's 720km railway network centres on Durrësi. There are eight trains a day to Tirana (55 lek, one hour), two to Shkodra (150 lek, 3½ hours) via Lezha, three to Pogradeci (245 lek, 6¾ hours) via Elbasani, and two to Vlora (210 lek, five hours) via Fieri. The station is beside the Tirana highway, conveniently close to central Durrësi.

Furgons (150 lek, one hour) and buses (100 lek, one hour) to Tirana leave from beside the train station whenever they're full, and service elsewhere is frequent as well.

Numerous travel agencies along rr Durrësit handle ferry bookings. All offer much the same service (see p403). International ferries leave from the terminal south of the train station.

KRUJA

☎ 0511 / pop 17,400

Kruja's impressive beauty starts on the approach from Tirana, up the winding road, into the grey rocky mountains. The fields stretch around you, and soon you can make out the houses seated in the lap of the mountain, and the ancient castle jutting out on one side. Kruja is a magnificent day trip from Tirana, and the best place for souvenir shopping in the country: the bazaar hides antique gems and quality traditional ware, such as beautifully embroidered traditional tablecloths, copper coffeepots and plates, and hand-woven *qilims* (rugs). You can also see women hand weaving these rugs at the bazaar.

As you get off the bus a statue of Skanderbeg (Gjergj Kastrioti, 1405–68) wielding his mighty sword greets you, with the sharp mountain profiles as his backdrop. In fact, this hill-top town attained its greatest fame between 1443 and 1468 when national hero Skanderbeg made Kruja his seat of government. At a young age, Kastrioti, the son of an Albanian prince, was handed over as a hostage to the Turks, who converted him to Islam and gave him a military education at Edirne in Turkey. There he became known as Iskander (after Alexander the Great) and

Sultan Murat II promoted him to the rank of *bey* (governor), thus the name Skanderbeg.

In 1443 the Turks suffered a defeat at the hands of the Hungarians at Niš in present-day Serbia and Montenegro, which gave the nationally minded Skanderbeg the opportunity he had been waiting for to abandon the Ottoman army and Islam and rally his fellow Albanians against the Turks. Among the 13 Turkish invasions he subsequently repulsed was that led by his former commander Murat II in 1450. Pope Calixtus III named Skanderbeg the 'captain general of the Holy See' and Venice formed an alliance with him. The Turks besieged Kruja four times. Though beaten back in 1450, 1466 and 1467, they took control of Kruja in 1478 (after Skanderbeg's death) and Albanian resistance was suppressed.

The main sight in Kruja is the splendid **castle** and its peculiar **Skanderbeg Museum** (admission 200 lek; ☺ 8am-1pm & 3-8pm). Designed by Enver Hoxha's daughter and son-in-law, it mainly displays replicas of armour and paintings depicting Skanderbeg's struggle against the Ottomans. The museum is something of a secular shrine, and takes itself very seriously indeed with giant statues and dramatic battle murals. There's a fantastic view from the terrace at the top.

The **Ethnographic Museum** (☎ 22 225; admission 100 lek; ☺ 8am-1pm & 3-8pm), opposite the Skanderbeg Museum, is certainly one of the most interesting experiences in Kruja. Set in an original 19th-century house that used to belong to the affluent Toptani family, you can see the level of luxury and self-sufficiency maintained in the household with the production of necessities such as food, drink, leather and weapons, and their very own steam bath. The English-speaking guide will explain everything in detail; it's polite to tip him 100 or 200 lek.

Dollma teqe is a small place of worship for the Bektashi branch of Islam (see p48), and maintained by successive generations of the Dollma family since 1789. It was resurrected after the fall of the communist regime and is now functioning again.

Hotel Panorama (☎ 30 92; Bazaar; s/d €10/15; ⌘) has eight simple rooms, TVs and a small restaurant. It's just opposite the entrance to the bazaar.

Kruja is 32km from Tirana. A cab from Kruja to Tirana and back with two hours' waiting time costs around 4000 lek while a *furgon* will cost 200 lek.

MT DAJTI NATIONAL PARK

Mt Dajti (1611m) is a national park visible from Tirana, 25km to the east. It is the most accessible mountain in the country and many Tiranans go there on the weekends to escape the city rush and have a spit-roast lamb lunch. There is a checkpoint about 15km from Tirana which levies a park admission fee of 100 lek for cars with up to three passengers, or 200 lek for those with four or more passengers. Put your sturdy shoes on for a gentle hike in the lovely, shady beech and pine forests and have a coffee and enjoy the spectacular views from the wide terrace of the **Panorama Restaurant** (☎ 361 124; meals 800 lek; ☼ 9am-11pm), the most popular spot on Dajti. There are several other restaurants along the road to the Panorama. The very top of the mountain is a restricted zone with military communication aerials.

The only downside is that there is no public transport to the mountain, so unless you have private transport you will have to get a taxi from the city; the ride takes about 45 minutes, and you can arrange to phone the driver to pick you up when you want to go back. The taxi ride shouldn't set you back more than 700 lek each way. The road to Dajti starts on rr Qemal Stafa in Tirana.

APOLLONIA

The ruined city of ancient **Apollonia** (admission 700 lek; ☼ 9am-5pm) is 12km west of Fieri (Fier), itself 89km south of Durrësi. It's set on rolling hills among olive groves, and the views of the plains below stretch for miles.

See the picturesque 3rd-century BC **House of Mosaics**, and examine the elegant pillars on the façade of the city's 2nd-century AD administrative centre. The Byzantine church of St Mary is a jewel with fascinating gargoyles on the outside pillars. In the church garden there are artefacts displayed, although they are labelled only in Albanian.

Apollonia was founded by Corinthian Greeks in 588 BC and quickly grew into an important city-state, which minted its own currency. Under the Romans the city became a great cultural centre with a famous school of philosophy. Julius Caesar

rewarded Apollonia with the title 'free city' for supporting him against Pompey the Great during the civil war in the 1st century BC, and sent his nephew Octavius, the future Emperor Augustus, to complete his studies here. After a series of military disasters, the population moved southward into present-day Vlora, and by the 5th century only a small village with its own bishop remained at Apollonia.

Fieri is a drab agroindustrial centre with a couple of not particularly friendly hotels. It's better to visit Apollonia on a day trip Tirana or Durrësi. The lack of public transport to Apollonia means that you will have to get a bus/*furgon*/train to the nearest town, Fieri. There's a bus from Durrësi (200 lek, 1½ hours), and from Tirana (300 lek, two hours). Once in Fieri, you will have to get a taxi; you should expect to be charged around 2500 lek for a return journey (30 minutes each way) and an hour's waiting time.

BERATI

☎ 062 / pop 47,700

Berati (Berat) is one of Albania's most beautiful towns and thanks to being the second 'museum city' in the country, its churches and mosques were spared destruction during the atheist campaign. The handsome Ottoman-era villas in the three old quarters of Gorica, Kalasa and Mangalem give Berati the name 'the town of a thousand windows'. The old quarters are lovely ensembles of whitewashed walls, tiled roofs and old stone walls guarding courtyards shaded by grapevines. Around the town, olive and cherry trees decorate the gentler slopes, while pine woods stand on the steeper inclines. However, this being Albania, the centre of town and the newer outlying areas along the river flats are blocks of rectilinear concrete. In the best Albanian tradition of religious cooperation, an elegant mosque with a pencil minaret is partnered on the main square by a large new Orthodox church.

In the 3rd century BC an Illyrian fortress called Antipatrea was built here on the site of an earlier settlement. The Byzantines strengthened the hill-top fortifications in the 5th and 6th centuries, as did the Bulgarians 400 years later. The Serbs, who occupied the citadel in 1345, renamed it Beligrad, or 'White City', and there is speculation that

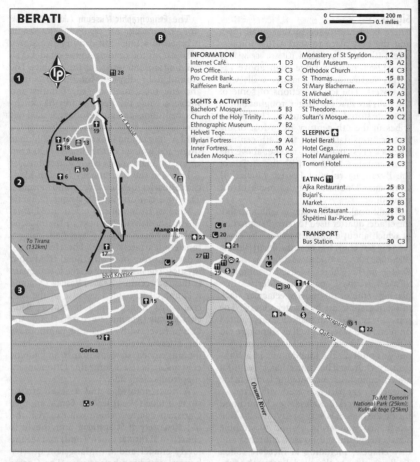

BERATI

| 0 | 200 m |
| 0 | 0.1 miles |

INFORMATION	
Internet Café	1 D3
Post Office	2 C3
Pro Credit Bank	3 C3
Raiffeisen Bank	4 C3

SIGHTS & ACTIVITIES	
Bachelors' Mosque	5 B3
Church of the Holy Trinity	6 A2
Ethnographic Museum	7 B2
Helveti Teqe	8 C2
Illyrian Fortress	9 A4
Inner Fortress	10 A2
Leaden Mosque	11 C3

Monastery of St Spyridon	12 A3
Onufri Museum	13 A2
Orthodox Church	14 C3
St Thomas	15 B3
St Mary Blachernae	16 A2
St Michael	17 A3
St Nicholas	18 A2
St Theodore	19 A1
Sultan's Mosque	20 C2

SLEEPING	
Hotel Berati	21 C3
Hotel Gega	22 D3
Hotel Mangalemi	23 B3
Tomorri Hotel	24 C3

EATING	
Ajka Restaurant	25 B3
Bujari's	26 C3
Market	27 B3
Nova Restaurant	28 B1
Shpëtimi Bar-Piceri	29 C3

TRANSPORT	
Bus Station	30 C3

Kalasa

Mangalem

To Tirana (132km)

blvd Kryesor

Gorica

rr e Skrapartit

rr Qafoku

Osumi River

To Mt Tomorri National Park (25km); Kulmak teqe (25km)

this is where the town's name came from. In 1450 the Ottoman Turks took Berati. After a period of decline, the town began to thrive in the 18th and 19th centuries as a crafts centre specialising in woodcarving. For a brief time in 1944 Berati was the capital of liberated Albania.

Information

Berati is another one of those towns where street signs are nonexistent and street names are mere rumours. Luckily, the locals are very friendly and will direct you to the right place if you look lost.

There are two ATMs in town: one at the Raiffeisen Bank across from the Tomorri Hotel, and another at Pro Credit Bank

about 200m away. The post office is on rr e Kalasë.

Albanien Reisen (☎ 069 268 1308; info@regio-berater.de) is a local tourist information centre and travel agency run by a German-Albanian husband and wife team who can organise accommodation in a traditional Berati house, tours to Mt Tomorri National Park and trips way off the beaten track to local waterfalls, villages and other sites. If you can't email or phone in advance, any hotel can help you track down co-owner Martin Heusinger.

A simple, functional no-name **Internet café** (rr e Skrapartit; per hr 100 lek; ⏰ 9am-10pm) is on the ground floor of an apartment block near the Hotel Gega.

Sights

There is plenty to see in this small town and the best place to start is the impressive 14th-century **Kalasa** (Citadel; admission 50 lek; 24hr) along a ridge high above the gorge, surrounded by massive walls with 24 towers. The lower sections of some of the walls are made of bigger, rougher blocks that date from fortifications built by Illyrian tribes in the 4th century BC. Most of the fortifications dates from the 14th century: there's a cross made of bricks set above the main entrance archway with the initials of the Byzantine ruler of Epirus, Michael II Comnenas Doukas, who did much of the rebuilding.

Traditionally a Christian neighbourhood, the citadel quarter used to have 20 churches, of which about a dozen remain. The quarter's biggest church is now the **Onufri Museum** (Muzeu Onufri; 32 248; admission 200 lek; 9am-2pm Mon-Fri), in the Church of the Dormition of St Mary (Kisha Fjetja e Shën Mërisë), displaying some of the most spectacular work in iconographic art by master Onufri. The museum is filled with magical icons painted on metal and wood, as well as some rare old tapestries. The church itself dates from 1797, but was built on the foundations of a 10th-century church. The centre has a beautiful gilded iconostasis and hanging lamps made of ostrich eggs partly covered with silver.

The 10-hectare Kalasa neighbourhood inside the citadel is very pretty, and it's well worth just wandering around to stumble across delightful old houses, churches and tiny chapels, including **St Theodore** (Shën Todher), close to the citadel gates; the substantial **Church of the Holy Trinity** (Kisha Shën Triades), below the upper fortress; and the little chapels of **St Mary Blachernae** (Shën Mëri Vllaherna) and **St Nicholas** (Shënkolli). Some of the churches date back to the 13th century, but it's a bit hit and miss if they'll be open. The staff at the Onufri Museum can help in tracking down caretakers and keys. The views from the walls over the rest of Berati and the Osumi valley are quite spectacular. The highest point of the citadel is occupied by the **Inner Fortress**. It's quite an exhausting slog up to the Kalasa from town, so you might want to take a taxi up to the citadel gates. Perched on a cliff ledge below the citadel is the artfully positioned little chapel of **St Michael** (Shën Mihell).

The **Ethnographic Museum** (Muzeu Etnografik; 32 224; admission 200 lek; 9am-4pm Mon-Fri) is based in a fine 18th-century two-storey villa just off the road up to the citadel. The building is as interesting as the exhibits. The ground floor displays traditional clothes and the tools used by silversmiths and weavers, while the upper storey has kitchens, bedrooms and guest rooms decked out in traditional style. Check out the *mafil*, a kind of mezzanine looking into the lounge where the women of the house could keep an eye on male guests being entertained.

Down in the traditionally Muslim Mangalem quarter there are three grand mosques. The 14th-century **Sultan's Mosque** (Xhamië e Mbretit) is one of the oldest in Albania. There is a **Helveti teqe** next to the mosque with a richly decorated prayer hall – unfortunately it's rarely open. The Helvetis are a dervish order or brotherhood of Muslim mystics. The big mosque on the town square is the 16th-century **Leaden Mosque** (Xhamië e Plumbit), so named because of the lead coating its domes. The 19th-century **Bachelors' Mosque** (Xhamië e Beqarëvet) is by the Osumi River, with enchanting paintings on the external walls. The mosque was built for unmarried shop assistants and junior craftsmen; there are some fine Ottoman-era shopfronts alongside.

A new footbridge and a seven-arched stone bridge (1780) lead to **Gorica**, another Christian quarter, where you can visit the old **Monastery of St Spyridon** and the little church of **St Thomas** (Shën Tomi) and see the lovely citadel and the Mangalem-quarter houses stretching before you. The Gorica quarter is tucked under a steep hillside and never sees the sun in the winter. If you feel energetic you can climb up to the remains of an old **Illyrian fortress** in the woods above Gorica.

Sleeping & Eating

Tomorri Hotel (34 462; fax 34 602; Central Sq; s/d €30/50) A tower-block hotel with nice, clean rooms overlooking either the citadel or the mountains. There's a good rooftop café and pizzeria with great views over the town. The hotel is on the main square by the bus station.

Hotel Berati (36 953; rr Veli Zaloshnja; s/d €18/30) This traditional-style building is just off rr e Kalasë, hemmed in by modern buildings.

THE AUTHOR'S CHOICE

Hotel Mangalemi (Hotel Tomi; ☎ 32 093, 068 242 9803; rr e Kalasë; s/d €12/24) For our money this is the best budget B&B in Albania. Run by the affable Tomi Mio (it's also called Hotel Tomi locally) and his family, the hotel has a great bar and restaurant on the ground floor and a clutch of warm, cosy rooms upstairs, plus a terrace with great views across Berati over to Mt Tomorri. Kind hospitality, tasty food, decent plumbing – does it get any better? It's on the street up to the Kalasa from the main square.

The hotel offers nine pleasant rooms and a cosy little restaurant.

Hotel Gega (☎ 34 429, 069 208 7181; rr e Skrapartit; r €20) This communist-era hotel has been renovated, so the rooms are rather small and plain but quite comfortable. The restaurant on the ground floor has a certain socialist grandeur.

Ajka Restaurant (☎ 34 034; Gorica; meals 800 lek; ☺ 9am-late) This substantial restaurant is run by an Armenian family whose ancestors settled in Albania early in the 20th century. The restaurant has a lovely setting above the Osumi River, looking over the houses of the Mangalem quarter. Pizzas cost around 400 lek, and a substantial mixed meze platter costs 500 lek. It also serves grilled dishes and ice cream.

Bujari's (meals 200 lek; ☺ 9am-9pm) In the *markati* (market) area between the two main roads in the lower town you might be able to find this simple café with wonderful home-style meals. The restaurant doesn't have a menu, just a selection of daily offerings. There's no sign, so look for a single-storey light-blue building in the lane behind the Shpëtimi Bar-Piceri.

Nova Restaurant (Kalasa; meals 700 lek; ☺ 10am-11pm) Succulent shish kebabs with generous salad portions on a sunny terrace overlooking the citadel. It's north of the citadel entrance.

Shpëtimi Bar-Piceri (rr Margarita Tutulani; pizzas 400 lek; ☺ 9am-10pm) Shpëtimi is a cheerful modern place with good pizzas.

Getting There & Away

Buses and *furgons* run between Tirana and Berati (250 lek, 2½ to three hours). From Tirana, they leave from rr e Kavajës, and go every hour on the hour until 3pm. In Berati, all buses depart and arrive at the bus station next to the Leaden Mosque. *Furgons* leave when full (roughly one an hour) for Tirana until about 4pm. There are nine buses a day to Vlora (250 lek, 2½ hours), one bus at 7am to Gjirokastra (350 lek, five hours) and one at 8am to Saranda (400 lek, six hours).

Around Berati

Mt Tomorri National Park is Albania's biggest nature reserve. The mountain is some 20km long and 6km wide, and its highest peak of 2415m is almost always covered in snow. Tomorri has been a holy mountain since pagan times, and is the Albanian equivalent of Mt Olympus. On the southern peak of the mountain is an important Bektashi shrine, the **Kulmak teqe**, with the grave of the Bektashi saint Abaz Aliu. The roads up to the mountain are pretty hairy, and require a 4WD and an experienced guide. Contact Albanien Reisen (p65) for information on getting to the park.

SOUTHERN ALBANIA

Stunning views of sharp, snowcapped mountain peaks, wide green valleys zigzagged by rivers, and inviting white beach crescents touching the gentle blue sea make southern Albania the most visually exciting part of the country.

VLORA

☎ 033 / pop 71,200

One of Albania's major ports, the Mediterranean port of Vlora (the ancient Aulon) is set on a fine bay. It's a bustling little city with a long palm-lined avenue stretching across the centre of town towards the seafront and the beaches. There isn't a great deal to see or do in the city itself. The beaches around the town are muddy and grubby, but the coves and little beaches along the rocky shore of Uji i Ftohtë nearby are charming. Vlora has the sense of a work-in-progress to it: there are lots of shiny new buildings going up, but just a block away from the main road the town turns into ramshackle neighbourhoods of concrete connected by potholed dirt tracks. The city was one of Albania's wilder towns during the 1990s – the 1997 revolution after the collapse of the pyramid schemes started here, and it took several years for the authorities to crack down on local gangs. Vlora's main claim to fame is that it was the place where Albanian independence was proclaimed in 1912.

Information

Everything you'll need in Vlora is on rr Sadik Zotaj, which runs across the centre of the city. A small room with half a dozen computers passes for an **Internet café** (rr Sadik Zotaj; per hr 200 lek; ⊗ 9am-noon) halfway up the long avenue. There are several banks with ATMs along rr Sadik Zotaj, and the main post office and its three branches and telephone centres are also dotted along the avenue.

The helpful **Colombo Travel & Tours** (☎ 27 659; www.colomboalb.com; Hotel Sazani, Sheshi i Flamurit; ⊗ 8am-7pm), on the ground floor of the Hotel Sazani, sells ferry tickets for Brindisi in Italy and organises yacht tours to the Karaburun Peninsula and Sazan Island for 1000 lek per person with a minimum of five people.

Sights

At the top end of Zotaj (away from the harbour) is **Sheshi i Flamurit** (Flag Sq). The magnificently socialist realist **Independence Monument** (Sheshi i Flamurit) stands proud against the sky, representing the key figures in the movement for Albania's sovereignty, with a statue of a flag bearer on the top of the monument hoisting the double-headed eagle into the blue.

Opposite the Independence Monument is the **Historical Museum** (Sheshi i Flamurit; admission 100 lek; ⊗ 9am-2pm & 7-9pm Tue-Sun), housed in what was originally the town hall, with artefacts showing the history of the Vlora area up until recent times. Next to the Historical Museum is the **Ethnological Museum** (Sheshi i Flamurit; admission 100 lek; ⊗ 9am-2pm Tue-Sun), in a house which saw the establishment of the Labëria Patriotic Club, a major player in Albania's movement for independence. Walk down towards the **Muradi Mosque** (rr Sadik Zotaj), a small, elegant structure in red and white stone with a modest minaret, whose exquisite design is attributed to one of the greatest Ottoman architects, Sinan Pasha. Further down and by the harbour is the **Museum of Independence** (rr sadik zotaj; admission 100 lek; ⊗ 9am-noon & 5-8pm), with plenty of old ministerial ornaments, photographs

and maps, all recording Albania's road to sovereignty.

The hill overlooking the town is topped by the Bektashi shrine of **Kuzum Baba**, with a fantastic view over the Bay of Vlora and the Narta Lagoon. If that view isn't enough, head about 4km southeast of the city – either on the road from Kuzum Baba or from Uji i Ftohtë, where the buses stop (near the post office) – to **Kanina Castle** (Kalaja e Kaninës), first fortified in the 4th century BC and remodelled over the centuries by the Romans, Byzantines, Normans and Ottomans.

The beaches close to the port aren't terribly nice, so jump on a bus or take a taxi to **Uji i Ftohtë** (which means 'cold water'). The bus stops at the Uji i Ftohtë's post office, from where you can take a taxi or walk to several small beaches scattered along two or three kilometres. There are several villas which used to belong to the Party of Labour of Albania (PPSh) hierarchy along this stretch of coast, some of which are being renovated into hotels while others lie spookily derelict. The little beaches here are semiprivatised and you will be asked to hire a chaise longue and umbrella for 100 lek per person. Each beach has several bars and cafés. The water along here is very clean, but it's a bit of shame the road runs so close to the sea.

About 6km north of Vlora is the Narta Lagoon, with salt pans on the landward side separated by a dyke from a calm expanse of water closer to the sea. The lagoon attracts water birds in their thousands. The **Monastery of St Mary** (Shën Mëri) occupies a wooded island reached by a wooden boardwalk from the village of Zvernëci, about 10km from Vlora. The main church is a modest little country construction with some battered frescoes, but it's a very peaceful spot. There's a festival here on 15 August with much feasting and dancing. The road out to Zvernëci passes through some of the Vlora neighbourhoods that harboured illegal immigrants during the 1990s – speedboats laden with Kurds, Chinese and marijuana used to zip across the 75km Straits of Otranto to Italy almost nightly.

Sleeping & Eating

Palma (☎ 29 320; Uji i Ftohtë beach; per person €8) Seated on top of a hill with views of the Bay of Vlora to die for, this former workers' camp still gives off a whiff of socialist idealism. Encircled by gorgeous gardens, this is the best budget choice. It has basic double and triple rooms with run-down bathrooms.

Hotel New York (☎ 25 648; www.hotelnewyork -al.com; Uji I Ftohtë beach; s/d €30/50, ste €70-120) Situated near the road tunnel, this hotel has great views across the Bay of Vlora to Sazan Island. The tiled rooms are airy and tidy, and the cheaper suites have balconies while the larger ones have a lounge room as well. There's a bright, modern restaurant here with Italian meals for around 1300 lek. The hotel also has a swimming pool.

Hotel Tozo (☎ 23 819; rr Sadik Zotaj; s/d €20/40; 🞰) Just off Zotaj about halfway between the bus station and the port behind a small park, this friendly and comfortable little hotel has luxurious beds in large rooms, good bathrooms, air-conditioning and TVs.

Hotel Vlora International (☎ 24 408; rr Sadik Zotaj; s & d €50) By the port at the end of rr Sadik Zotaj, this is the biggest hotel in town with modern, comfortable rooms and a good restaurant downstairs.

Kobolira (☎ 068 220 4430; Skela Beach; mains 340-400 lek; 🕑 9am-11pm) For traditional Vloran baked fish (tavë peshku), this is your place.

Riciola (☎ 069 255 3469; Skela Beach; mains 400 lek, fresh fish around 1000 lek; 🕑 9am-11pm) Good fish dishes and seafood pasta in a convivial local atmosphere.

Getting There & Away

It's easy getting to Vlora from Tirana (bus/ furgon 300/400 lek, three hours) and Durrësi (bus/furgon 300/400 lek, three hours), with buses and furgons whizzing back and forth in the morning hours. Buses from Vlora to Saranda (500 lek, six hours) and on to Gjirokastra (700 lek, 5½ hours) leave at 6am, 7am, 1pm and 2pm. There are also buses every hour till 3pm to Berati (250 lek, two hours) In Vlora, the bus terminus is easily spotted near the Muradi Mosque.

There are two ferries daily (but only one on Sunday) to Brindisi, with Skenderbeg Lines (€40, 4½ hours) and the Agoudimos Line (€40, seven hours). Both have one class only. Book tickets through Colombo Travel & Tours (opposite).

Getting Around

There are municipal buses to Uji i Ftohtë every 20 minutes (15 lek, 15 minutes) from

8am to 6pm, which run from the Muradi Mosque along rr Sadik Zotaj out to the Uji i Ftohtë post office. There are usually taxis at the terminus which can take you to a beach or hotel further along.

IONIAN COAST

Maritime Albania's greatest gift is the coast between the Llogaraja Pass and Saranda, a dramatic meeting of steep, cloud-shrouded mountains plunging into a deep sea. Ethnic Greek and Albanian villages cling to ridges and hillsides, eking a living from olive groves and orchards. The road along the coast is being improved but it still has some rough stretches. At the moment most accommodation is in village houses, but you get the feeling that this area is just about to be discovered. Club Mediteranee is said to be eyeing a beach near Saranda.

GETTING THERE & AROUND

Buses go regularly between Vlora and Saranda via Himara and stop at the Llogaraja Pass and Dhërmiu on the way. Ask the conductor when you get on to let you off at your destination. At Llogaraja, the best place to be dropped off is at the Tourist Village, 1km from the summit.

Public transport on the Vlora–Saranda road is hit and miss: there are quite a few furgons in the busy summer months but not many at other times of the year. Furgons run from 7am between Saranda, Himara and Vlora (Saranda–Himara and Himara–Vlora each 300 lek and three hours on a winding road). From Himara furgons leave from the seafront at the end of the promenade. A furgon passes through from Saranda on the way to Vlora at around 8.30am; wait for it by the Hotel Gjiçali. Going from village to village along the Ionian Coast by public transport is a time-consuming business, so many travellers take the risk of hitchhiking, or throw away any notion of a schedule and take as much time as it takes.

In July and August there are usually two ferries a week going to Corfu (one way €25, around three hours) that stop in Saranda, though these depend entirely on demand.

Llogaraja Pass (National Park)

The road going south from Vlora climbs up to the Llogaraja Pass, over 1000m high, for some of Albania's most spectacular scenery

ALBANIA

and delicious spit-roast lamb. If you are going to Dhërmi or Himara, this is the road you will take. From it you will see clouds descending onto the mountain, steep hillsides crashing into the sea below, shepherds on the plains guiding their herds, and thick forests where deer, wild boar and wolves roam. The local name for these mountains is Malet e Vetetimes, which means 'thunder mountains'. Despite its uncreative name, the **Tourist Village** (Fshati Turistik; ☎ 068 212 8640; per chalet 8000 lek) is the best place to sleep if you decide to stay and breathe the fresh air in Llogaraja. Wooden chalets with modern amenities, fresh food and pure spring water house up to four people.

Dhërmiu & Around

As you zigzag down the mountain from the Llogaraja Pass, the immaculate white crescent beaches and the azure waters lure you from below. The first beach along the coast is **Palasa**, around the alluvial fan at the foot of the pass. There are no hotels here yet, so if you have your own transport it's a wonderfully isolated spot to visit. **Dhërmiu** (Dhërmi) has several comfortable hotels and a beautiful long beach, and is a popular summer destination among locals and expats. This ethnic Greek village saw most of its inhabitants take Greek passports and head south in the 1990s, and now the village is mostly inhabited by a small population of elderly people outside of the tourist season. People have started to return to the village in the warmer months to rent out rooms to visitors, while others rent out houses in their entirety. The whitewashed church of St Mary (Shën Mëri) stands on the hill above the village. The beach is about 2km below the Vlora–Saranda road. The bus stop is in the village on the mountain road and you have to make your own way down to the beach, which is an easy 10-minute walk downhill (not so easy on the way back though).

Right on the beach is the **Hotel Dhërmi** (☎ 069 207 4000; Dhërmiu Beach; r 6000 lek), with rooms that all look onto the sea. The bathrooms are sparkling clean and the hotel restaurant serves excellent fish courses for 500 lek. Prices drop to around 4000 lek outside of July and August, down to 2500 lek in winter.

The **Hotel Riviera** (☎ 068 263 3333; Dhërmiu Beach; r 4000-6000 lek; ⚄) is fairly simple lodge

with six rooms with TV, minibar and a little private stretch of beach.

Also on the beach, barely 10m from the sea, is the **Hotel 2000** (☎ 068 225 7164; Dhërmiu Beach; r 8000 lek), with beach umbrellas and lounges just out the front door. The rooms are simple but comfortable, with TV, minibar and views onto the Ionian. The restaurant serves Greek and Italian cuisine. The prices drop by about half outside of July and August.

A half-hour walk through some olive groves brings you to **Drymades**, a quieter option, with a white virgin beach stretching before you. You can stay in a bungalow, camp or simply sleep under the stars on the beach. To get to Drymades, turn off the asphalted road going down into Dhërmiu at the sign indicating 1200m to Drymades Beach. **Drymades Hotel** (☎ 068 228 5637; per bungalow 4000 lek) is a constellation of bungalows under the shade of pine trees, a step away from the blue sea. Each can house two or three people, although the interiors are a little shabby. There's a bar and restaurant in the shade, plus a beach bar with a straw roof.

Jal Beach is an isolated spot 3km from the charming roadside village of **Vuno**, which is 8km along from Dhërmiu. There are a couple of simple hotels (around €25 per person) and camping sites here. Some of the villagers in Vuno also rent out rooms in the summer.

Himara & Around
☎ 0393 / pop 4500

This sleepy town has tremendous potential as a holiday spot, with fine beaches, a couple of Greek tavernas and some nice hotels. Unfortunately, the beaches are marred by half-demolished concrete buildings and a disturbing amount of litter – strolling past rusting car wrecks and a tidal line of plastic may not be quite what you'd expected in a beach. Hopefully the government can find the money to clean up the shoreline. There are two sections to the town: the handsome old town is up on the hill and the seaside fishing village where boats from Corfu dock in summer is about 1km away. The port is at the western end of the town beach, with outdoor cafés along a promenade. To the east is a small headland and another beach.

Himara has a number of hotels, and quite a few villagers rent out rooms.

Near the port, the **Hotel Manol Kolagji** (☎ 27 01, 068 230 5107; s/d €25/50) has 10 rooms with kitchenettes, TV and plain, simple décor. There's a restaurant here as well.

Likoka (☎ 27 45, 068 226 3608; s/d €20/40) is a white, circular hotel at the far end of the beach (towards Saranda) with spacious rooms and light balconies for alfresco breakfasts overlooking the sea. Eat fish, pizza or pasta on the veranda of the hotel restaurant for 450 lek.

On the headland between the beaches, right by the sea, is the **Hotel Gjiçali** (☎ 26 57, 068 244 5832; s/d €20/40). The downstairs café is very pleasant, but the rooms are simple to the point of being stark – a single bare light bulb and plain white walls. Still, you can't get closer to the ocean.

One good beach near Himara is Llaman, 2km away, which has the **Llaman Beach Bar-Restaurant** (☎ 069 241 2172; pizzas around 400 lek; ☯ Jul-Sep). It serves pizza, cold beer and grilled fish on a shaded terrace right on the beach.

Heading towards Saranda the next sight is **Porto Palermo**, a bay with a submarine base at one end (off limits) and a large castle on a peninsula in the middle. The castle was built by Ali Pasha Tepelena in the 19th century on the foundations of an older fortress. The road then passes the village of **Qeparo**, another semideserted village perched above a nice beach, then the road passes through **Borshi**, where a rushing mountain stream passes under a roadside café. Below the village there's a fertile plain with a 3km-long beach – the warmest spot in Albania, apparently. The owners of Borshi's café can help people find accommodation in village houses. Next along is the village of Piquerasi, and after 4km there's a turn-off to **Buneci** beach, which has a couple of restaurants. The road then climbs over a pass and loops around behind the mountains before reaching Saranda.

SARANDA
☎ 0852 / pop 12,000
Horseshoe-shaped Saranda is a stone's throw from the Greek island of Corfu (27km) and a good point to cross into Albania from Greece and vice versa. Its houses descend from the hillsides, small boats bob on the blue sea, people stroll up and down the relaxing promenade and the town boasts around 290 sunny days a year. An early monastery dedicated to 40 saints (Ayii Saranda) gave Saranda its name. The town was called Porto Edda for a period in the 1940s, after Mussolini's daughter. At present it is half holiday destination, half building site. The number of buildings in various stages of construction (active and dormant) is phenomenal, and new neighbourhoods of apartments and hotels are spreading along the coast either side of the town. Saranda's beaches are quite modest, but the town has a charmingly relaxed atmosphere anyway.

Most of Saranda's attractions are a little outside of the town itself. Nearby are the mesmerising ancient archaeological site of Butrinti, the hypnotic Blue Eye Spring, and some lovely beaches at Ksamili village where you can dip and refresh after a day of exploring.

Orientation & Information
There are four main streets, which arc around Saranda's bay. There are three banks with ATMs along the sea road (rr 1 Maji) and the next street inland (rr Skënderbeu). Buses to Butrinti leave from rr 8 Nëntori, which is the next street uphill from rr Skënderbeu, while the bus station is on rr Lefter Talo, uphill from rr 8 Nëntori. There's one main street linking the four called rr Vangjel Pando, where taxis wait for customers. Most of the restaurants, bars and cafés are around this street and along the seafront.

The **post office** (☎ 23 45; rr Skënderbeu) is near the bus stand. Cardphones abound while mobile-phone users can pick up Greek transmitters as well as Albanian ones. Mobile phones have the annoying habit of switching inexplicably between the Albanian and Greek networks, depending on where you're standing. To find an Internet café, head up the street along the sea (rr 1 Maji) towards the port, and look for a blue petrol station on a roundabout. Hang a hard right and there's a coffeeless **Internet Café** (rr Skënderbeu; per hr 150 lek) in the shops above the petrol station. With luck there will be a terminal free of adolescents playing Counterstrike.

Sleeping & Eating
Accommodation prices in Saranda vary a lot according to the season: prices rise by

ALBANIA

about 20% on those given here in the busiest periods of July and August, and drop by 30% during the winter season. The rates are always negotiable, no matter what time of the year. Most of the 60-odd hotels in and around Saranda are in the one-star category, and charge similar prices to the Hotel Kaonia and Hotel Ari.

There are many more bars, cafés and restaurants around the centre of town than we've listed here, as well as several *byrek* joints. With the current building boom, there are certain to be more still.

Hotel Kaonia (☎ 26 00/8; rr 1 Maji; s/d €20/40) A lovely, small hotel on the seafront with great beds, power showers, TVs and sea views. It's right in the centre of town (walk down the steps to the shore and take a right) and the owners are very affable.

Hotel Butrinti (☎ 55 92; www.butrintihotel.com; rr Butrinti; s €90, d €90-100, ste €135-210; ✕ ♥) This hotel, on the opposite side of the bay from the port, styles itself as five star, when it's more of a three-star hotel, but it's very nice nonetheless. The spacious modern rooms have satellite TVs, and the hotel has a fitness centre. The restaurant serves very acceptable Italian cuisine for about 1500 lek per meal, and has an indoor section and great views from the tables on the terrace. The hotel accepts Visa.

Hotel Palma (☎ 29 29, 069 232 7261; rr Mithat Hoxha; s/d €20/30, apt €120; ♥) Right next to the port, this new hotel has a spacious restaurant downstairs, and handsome rooms in blue and white with great views over the bay – plus a disco!

Hotel Ari (☎ 27 65, 069 231 3536; rr 1 Maji; s/d €20/40) Next door to the Kaonia, the Ari has similar standards, though the rooms are a little smaller. The rooms facing the bay have balconies.

Zhupa Restaurant (rr 1 Maji; meals 400-800 lek; ♥ 9am-last customer) This is a friendly little eatery just past the Hotel Ari serving Greek, Albanian and Italian dishes. Pastas cost around 200 lek, steaks around 500 lek while fish dishes depend on weight – 800 lek is a medium-sized meal.

Limani Café-Bar (rr 1 Maji; meals around 600 lek; ♥ 8am-midnight) A series of open-air pavilions set between two little harbours in the middle of the seafront promenade, serving very good pizzas amid many potted plants.

Kalaja e Lekurësit (☎ 55 32; Lekurës; meals around 1500 lek; ♥ 9am-midnight) This restaurant is situated inside the Lekurës castle above Saranda and serves traditional Albanian cuisine (grills and fish) plus Italian dishes. The views over Saranda, Corfu and the Butrinti Lagoon are tremendous. A taxi up to the castle costs about 300 lek.

Getting There & Away
BOAT
There are usually three boats a day to Corfu, depending on demand. The two ferry companies are **Petrakis Lines** (☎ 0030-2661 038 690; petrakis@hol.gr; 9 Eleftherious Venizelou, New Port, Corfu, Greece) and **Finikas Lines** (☎ 60 57; finikaslines@yahoo .com; rr Mithat Hoxha). A one-way ticket to Corfu costs €17.50 (euro only; you can change money at any of Saranda's banks), while coming from Corfu costs €15 (there's a €2.50 port tax charged leaving Saranda). At the time of writing, boats left at 9.30am, 11am and 2pm. Finikas Lines have an office just above the port, but for the Petrakis boat you buy a ticket downstairs in the cute little terminal building. In July and August there are boats which stop at Saranda on the way to Himara, usually twice a week.

BUS
There are regular buses nine times a day between 7am and 6pm to Butrinti via Ksamili (50 lek, about 40 minutes). They leave from the street just below the bus station (rr 8 Nëntori).

There are buses to Tirana (1000 lek, eight hours) at 5am, 6.30am, 8.30am, 9.30am and 10.30am; to Gjirokastra (300 lek, 1½ hours) at 6am and 8.15am; and one bus to Durrësi (900 lek, seven hours) at 2.30pm. There are two or three services a week to Korça (1000 lek, eight hours). There are also *furgons* to Gjirokastra (one hour, 500 lek) and Vlora (six hours, 600 lek) via Himara, usually leaving between 7am and 9.30am.

TAXI
A taxi to the Greek border at Kakavija will cost 3500 lek while a cab to the border near Konispoli will cost around 3000 lek.

Around Saranda
The ancient ruins of **Butrinti** (Butrint; ☎ 0732-46 00; admission 700 lek; ♥ 8am-7.30pm), 18km south of Saranda, are renowned for their size and

beauty. They are in a fantastic natural setting, part of a 29-sq-km national park; set aside at least three hours to lose yourself and thoroughly explore this fascinating place.

Although the site had been inhabited long before, Greeks from Corfu settled on the hill in Butrinti (Buthrotum) in the 6th century BC. Within a century Butrinti had become a fortified trading city with an acropolis. The lower town began to develop in the 3rd century BC, and many large stone buildings had already been built by the time the Romans took over in 167 BC. Butrinti's prosperity continued throughout the Roman period and the Byzantines made it an ecclesiastical centre. The city subsequently went into decline, and it was abandoned until 1927 when Italian archaeologists arrived.

As you enter the site the path leads to the right, to Butrinti's 3rd-century-BC **Greek theatre**, secluded in the forest below the acropolis. Also in use during the Roman period, the theatre could seat about 2500 people. Close by are the small **public baths**, with geometric mosaics, which are unfortunately buried under the sand and cannot be seen. You are allowed to make a small hole to peek at the mosaics, but don't touch them, and do cover it up again.

Deeper in the forest is a wall covered with crisp Greek inscriptions, and a 6th-century palaeo-Christian **baptistry** decorated with colourful mosaics of animals and birds, again under the sand. Beyond are the impressive arches of the 6th-century **basilica**, built over many years. A massive **Cyclopean wall** dating back to the 4th century BC is further on. Over one gate is a splendid relief of a lion killing a bull, symbolic of a protective force vanquishing assailants.

The top of the hill is where the **acropolis** once was; there's now a castle here, which is closed, but you can have a look around the courtyard. The view of the city from above gives you a good idea of its layout. You can enjoy the views of Lake Butrinti from the courtyard and see the Vivari Channel which connects it to the Straits of Corfu.

There are nine buses a day from Saranda to Butrinti (50 lek, about 40 minutes) via Ksamili. A cab to Butrinti from Saranda will cost around 2000 lek and you can usually negotiate to get there and back and see the Blue Eye Spring for 4000 lek.

The **Blue Eye Spring** (Syri i Kalter), about 15km east of Saranda, is a hypnotic pool of deep-blue water surrounded by electric-blue edges like the iris of an eye. It feeds the Bistrica River and its depth is still unknown. This is the perfect picnic spot, under the shade of the oak trees. You can also check out the 12th-century monastery of **Mesopotami** en route, perched on a little hill by the Bistrica.

A better bathing alternative to Saranda's beaches is **Ksamili**, 17km south, with four small, dreamy islands within swimming distance and a couple of beachside bars and restaurants open in the summer. Ksamili was founded in 1973 as a model communist collective. Tourist developers have big plans for it, and a couple of hotels were being built at the time of research.

GJIROKASTRA

☎ 084 / pop 24,500

Austere old Gjirokastra watches over the Drinos valley beneath it from its rocky perch. It's sometimes called the city of a thousand steps, and you'll see why when you tackle the steep cobbled streets that wind between solid grey stone houses and mansions roofed in slate. Spend a day absorbing the life of the labyrinthine streets of the old town and, for an architectural feast, check out the unique houses and the dark castle overlooking the town.

Gjirokastra's Greek name, Argyrokastro, means Silver Castle. The town was well established and prosperous by the 13th century, but declined after the arrival of the Turks in 1417. The 17th century brought about improvement and the town became a major trading centre with a flourishing bazaar where embroidery, felt, silk and its white cheese (which is still famous today) were traded. One of the Ottoman Empire's most prominent individuals, Ali Pasha Tepelena, seized the town in the early 19th century and strengthened the citadel.

Gjirokastra was the birthplace of former dictator Enver Hoxha who awarded it the status of 'museum city'. Thanks to this, special care was taken to retain its traditional architecture during the communist era; the modern city in the basin below the old town was built during that time. Gjirokastra's other famous son is writer Ismail Kadare, who set the novel *Chronicle in Stone* in his home town. Today, a large student population studying at the local university helps to enliven the place.

Information

The main street of the old town has little besides some small cafés – most businesses are down in the new town – though there is a branch of Raiffeisen Bank with an ATM near the courthouse. The main street in the new town, blvd 18 Shtatori, has banks, a post office and pizzerias. There are a couple of Internet cafés on the street around the uphill side of the football stadium, just off 18 Shtatori.

Sights

Gjirokastra's **19th-century houses** were mostly built between 1800 and 1830. Most have three storeys: the lower floors are used for storage and the upper floors for living quarters, some with lavishly decorated rooms, especially those for receiving guests. The neighbourhoods with these classic Ottoman houses encircle the castle. The houses are fiercely expensive to maintain, and some are sadly falling into disrepair. About 10 of the 400-odd legally protected houses have collapsed in the last five years. The local Ethnographic Museum is being moved to a particularly fine mansion up past the Hotel Kalemi on the road up to the Këculla Bar-Restaurant.

The splendidly gloomy **castle** (Old Town; admission 100 lek; 8am-noon & 4-7pm) is the city's dominant feature. There are two gates into the fortress: one at the end of the ridge and one in the middle of its northern flank. Built from the 6th century AD onwards, this brooding giant was used as a prison by King Zogu, then the Nazis, then the communists until 1971, when it became a museum. The prison is on top of the highest point of castle; turn left when you enter from the gate in the middle of the castle's flank and pick your way up the stairs to have a look. This gate is also the entry to a display of tanks in the main gallery of the fortress. There isn't much lighting, and the silhouettes of cannons in the gloom are quite striking. Outside, the shell of a 1957 **US military jet** is a bizarre addition to the ramparts of the castle. The communist party used to explain that it was a spy plane that had been forced down and captured. In fact it was a training jet from a NATO base in Italy which had run into mechanical trouble and made an emergency landing in Albania.

There's a quaint old **Orthodox church** on the tip of the ridge in front of the castle, which is worth a look if churches interest you.

If the mountains around town look inviting, jump on a local bus to Këlcyra and Përmeti (300 lek, 1½ hours). The route up the Vjosa valley is nothing short of breathtaking. There are regular *furgons* between Gjirokastra and Përmeti until about 5pm.

Sleeping & Eating

Hotel Kalemi (/fax 67 260; draguak@yahoo.com; Lagja Palorto; r incl breakfast 4000 lek) Somewhere between a hotel and a museum, this is the most authentic experience of old Albania, with carved wood ceilings and stone fireplaces in the 1st-floor rooms. The breakfast is delicious.

Guest House Haxhi Kotoni (35 26; Lagja Palorto 8, rr Bashkim Kokona; s/d incl breakfast 1500/2000 lek) This guesthouse has small but clean and comfy double rooms with TV and heating.

Hotel Çajupi (Sheshi Çerçiz Topulli; r 600-2000 lek) This is one of the hotels located by the main square of the old town that seem to be just clinging on. It has a couple of renovated rooms with en suite bathroom for 2000 lek and some grim, unrenovated ones with shared bathrooms for 600 to 800 lek.

Fantazia Bar-Restaurant (66 991; Pazar i Vjetër; meals 800 lek; 11am-midnight) This modern café-bar-restaurant just past the courthouse in the upper town has a fantastic view over the new town from the tables on the terrace. The restaurant serves Italian food.

Këculla Bar-Restaurant (069 214 6265; Lagja Palorto; meals 700 lek; 11am-midnight) If you want spectacular views of the castle and town with your dinner, walk uphill to the radio towers and dine in this friendly restaurant. Lamb and chicken grills cost 400 lek. It's quite a steep walk up to the restaurant (about 15 minutes from the Hotel Kalemi), so nonathletic types should consider a taxi from the upper town (150 lek).

Cueva de Toro Bar (Lagja 18 Shtatori; 10am-late Mon-Sat) For something different, head down to the new town to the Cueva de Toro, on the road around the downhill side of the football stadium. The interior has been rendered into a bizarre cave. The sound system pumps out the latest from Top Radio, Albania's hippest station.

Getting There & Around

Buses to and from Gjirokastra stop on the main highway, 1.5km from the old town. Taxis can take you into town for about 200 lek. A taxi between the new town and the old town (which saves a lot of hard walking) costs 150 lek. In the upper town there's a taxi rank on the main square, Sheshi Çerçiz Topulli. Buses to Tirana (1000 lek, eight hours) are fairly frequent. There are four a day to Saranda (300 lek, 1½ hours) and one to Korça (700 lek, seven hours), which takes the spectacular route through Përmeti and Erseka. You'll need to take a taxi to get to the Greek border at Kakavija (1500 lek, 30 minutes).

KORÇA

☎ 082 / pop 62,200

Korça prides itself as being one of the most 'civilised' places in Albania, and while it's a friendly, easygoing place there's isn't a great deal to see or do. There is a busy market by the bus station where goats get sold and carried off like handbags, and where you can buy everything, from fruit, vegetables and livestock to CDs and cassettes of pumping music. There are several banks and Internet cafés along the main street (blvd Republika). The main reason to visit Korça is to tackle the dramatic route along the Greek border down to Gjirokastra or to explore the city-turned-village of Voskopoja.

Sights

The **Museum of Albanian Medieval Art** (Muzeu i Artit Mesjetar; ☎ 43 022; rr Stefan Luarasi; admission 200 lek; ☉ 10am-3pm Mon-Fri) is a treasury of religious art collected from churches sacked during Albania's cultural revolution. The main gallery has an astonishing array of icons from the 13th to the 19th centuries alongside silver bible covers, grails, crucifixes and two complete carved iconostases. Another gallery has early Christian stone carvings from Butrinti, Apollonia and other sites. The museum was opened in 1980 on the site of an Orthodox cathedral dynamited in 1968 during the cultural revolution. The museum is a bit hard to find. Facing the new Orthodox Cathedral, head left for two blocks left along blvd Republika, then turn right and head 150m or so uphill into the warren of the old town, and look for the imposing white Episcopal Residence on a little square;

the museum is in the light brown three-storey building next to the bishop's house.

The other big sight (literally) in Korça is the new **Orthodox Cathedral** (blvd Republika), a striking confection in pink, blue and brown. From the Hotel Grand head up blvd Shën Gjergji (the main shopping strip) and you can't possibly miss it.

Sleeping

Hotel Gold (☎ 46 894; rr Kiço Golniku 5; s/d 1888/2830 lek) This is the best budget option in town, with clean rooms, TVs and heating, and en suite bathrooms. Follow the signs for 800m from the avenue leading from the bus stop to the main square.

Hotel Grand (☎ 43 168; www.grandhotelkorca.com; Central Sq; s/d/ste €21/34/44) Around the corner from the bus station, this is a comfortable hotel with a grandiose reception area and large plants. The rooms are spacious, the beds good and the bathrooms have shower curtains – a rarity in Albania. The helpful staff, particularly the young manager, can arrange trips to nearby villages and sights. The hotel has a good restaurant and a bar.

Hotel Turizëm Behar Koçibelli (☎ 43 532, 068 239 3395; Central Sq; s/d €15/25) This hotel is one half of the old Hotel Turist – the other half being the Hotel Grand, which rather overshadows it. Still, it's not bad, and the rooms are comfortable and clean.

Eating

Restaurant Alfa (☎ 44 385; blvd Shën Gjergji; mains 400-500 lek; ☉ 9am-midnight Mon-Sat) Located off the main square, this restaurant has a tasty Greek menu and a good atmosphere.

Vasport (☎ 50 388; rr Naim Frashëri; mains around 500-600 lek; ☉ 9am-midnight) Opposite the cathedral with a popular bar on the ground and 1st floors, this restaurant has a rustic feel, decent meat and good wine.

Shtëpia Voskopojare (☎ 42 784; rr Stefan Luarasi; mains 600 lek; ☉ 10am-11pm) Just behind the Orthodox Cathedral, this bar-restaurant with a startling orange and burnt-red exterior has a charming dining room, a good selection of Albanian and Macedonian wines, and well-prepared steaks and local specialities; the name means 'Voskopojan household'.

Getting There & Away

Buses and *furgons* all congregate at the official bus station, a block away from the

ALBANIA

main square near the market. Arriving *furgons* will normally drop their passengers off on the main square as well. *Furgons* to Tirana (500 lek, four hours) via Pogradeci (100 lek, one hour) depart when full. There are buses to Tirana (300 lek, six hours). There are three *furgon*s a day to Voskopoja (80 lek, 40 minutes) at 8am, 10am and 1.15pm, and three buses a week to Gjirokastra (300 lek, around seven hours) on the awesome Korça–Gjirokastra road.

For Greece there are three buses daily to Thessaloniki (€19, seven hours) and four a week to Athens (€30, 16 hours) at noon on Sunday, Monday, Thursday and Friday. Go to the ticket office in the street behind the Grand Hotel to book your seat.

Note: you can take a *furgon* to the border at Kapshtica for around 300 to 400 lek, but a Greek taxi from the Albanian–Greek border to Florina or Kastoria alone will cost you a minimum of €30. There are only two or three inconveniently timed local buses daily linking the Greek border village of Krystallopigi with Florina, and none to Kastoria. The direct international bus from Korça is by far the best option; the trip to either Florina or Kastoria takes about two hours.

Around Korça
VOSKOPOJA
Around 1750 Voskopoja was the biggest city in the Balkans, with a population of 35,000 and 24 churches. Today this village, 21km from Korça, has a population of a couple of hundred (roughly half Muslim Albanian and half Orthodox Vlach) after repeated sackings and lootings as recently as WWII. There are piles of grey rubble around the village that hint at the scale of the town when it was at its peak, before Ali Pasha Telepena sacked it in 1788. Eight churches remain, including **St Michael** (Shën Mihali), **St Nicholas** (Shënkolli) and **St Athanasius** (Shën Athanasi), scattered between old stone houses and around neighbouring fields. Some of the church murals painted by the Zografi brothers Konstantin and Athanas are still in superb condition. About 2km out of town, up a dirt track across the river, the Monastery of St Prodhomi nestles in the woods. It is mostly in ruins, but the walk to it is very pretty. There are plans to establish a ski resort near the village (it's at

an altitude of 1160m), but for now it's best enjoyed for its lovely highland setting and wealth of monuments.

The delightful little **Hotel Pashuta** (☎ 068 266 4374; s/d €10/20) has four rooms, three with bathrooms. It's on the far side of the village from the Korça road, over a little bridge – anyone in town can direct you to it. Breakfast costs €4. Ask if they'll prepare the traditional Vlach meal of *pitau* (layers of thin pastry filled with leeks).

The handsome **Hotel Akademia Voskopoja** (☎ 068 256 9435; s/d €18/42) is about 1.5km out of Voskopoja on the way to the Monastery of St Prodhomi. It's a former communist hotel and has been comprehensively renovated. The manager is keen and helpful. There's a lovely garden with tables set out on the lawn and a good restaurant. It's a bit of a surprise to find such a nice place in such an isolated spot.

From Voskopoja there are *furgon*s to Korça (80 lek, 30 minutes) at 7am, 8am and 11am. Otherwise it's easy to hire a taxi for a day trip from Korça.

KORÇA–GJIROKASTRA ROAD
The **road to Gjirokastra** is worth the bumps and aches for its stunning scenery and raw isolation. After the highland town of Erseka, about one hour south of Korça, the road begins to climb into the wild pine forests along the edge of the Grammoz mountains and crosses the Barmash Pass (1759m). There's a small hotel called the **Jorgos** (☎ 0821-2700; r €20) about 45 minutes south of Erseka, with a restaurant. After the village of Leskoviku the road descends into the spectacular narrow valley of the Vjosa River to Përmeti. The region around Këlcyra downstream is sometimes called the Tibet of Albania. Following the gorge of the Vjosa, the road then turns up the Drinos valley to Gjirokastra. There are buses three times a week in either direction between Korça and Gjirokastra (700 lek, around seven hours).

NORTHERN ALBANIA

The northern Albanian landscape has rich wildlife, swamps and lagoons around Shkodra and Lezha, and high, unforgiving mountains in the northeast (named the

Accursed Mountains, Bjeshkët e Namuna, in Albanian). Visits to the region still involve some element of risk due to continuing instability in the neighbouring area. The main road corridor from Tirana to the border with Serbia and Montenegro (the area where Shkodra and Lezha are located) is generally fine.

SHKODRA

☎ 022 / pop 91,300

Shkodra (Shkodër), the traditional centre of the Gheg cultural region, is one of the oldest cities in Europe. Rozafa Fortress is beautiful and the Marubi permanent photography exhibition is fascinating. The city is quite run down and hasn't had the sort of economic rebirth that other Albanian cities have enjoyed. The tatty grey apartment buildings only serve to lend it a rather sombre air. Most travellers just pass through on the way between Tirana and Ulcinj in Montenegro.

As the Ottoman Empire declined in the late 18th century, Shkodra became the centre of a semi-independent *pashalik* (region governed by a pasha, an Ottoman high official), which led to a blossoming of commerce and crafts. In 1913 Montenegro attempted to annex Shkodra (it succeeded in taking Ulcinj), a move not approved of by the international community, and the town changed hands often during WWI. Badly damaged by the 1979 earthquake, Shkodra was subsequently repaired and is Albania's fourth-largest town. The communist-era Hotel Rozafa in the town centre is a dump but it makes a good landmark – restaurants, transport to Montenegro and most of the town's sights are close by.

Information

There's a **Tirana Bank ATM** (rr 13 Dhjetori) next to the Hotel Colosseo, and a buzzing Internet café called **ArtCom** (☎ 068 212 3599; rr Çajupi; per hr 150 lek; 9am-11pm) on the street behind the Hotel Rozafa.

Sights

Two kilometres southwest of Shkodra, near the southern end of Lake Shkodra, is **Rozafa Fortress**, founded by the Illyrians in antiquity and rebuilt much later by the Venetians and Turks. The fortress derives its name from a woman named Rozafa, who was allegedly walled into the ramparts as an offering to the gods so that the construction would stand. The story goes that Rozafa asked that two holes be left in the stonework so that she could continue to suckle her baby. Nursing women still come to the fortress to smear their breasts with milky water taken from a spring here. There are marvellous views from the highest point. The castle is about 3km south of the city centre and the walk there from the town centre takes you through some very poor neighbourhoods, so it would be better to take a taxi.

Hidden inside a building that looks like a block of flats, the **Marubi Permanent Photo Exhibition** (rr Muhamet Gjollesha; admission free; 9am-1pm) boasts fantastic photography by the Marubi 'dynasty', Albania's first and foremost photographers. The first-ever photograph taken in Albania is here, taken by Pjetër Marubi in 1858. The exhibition shows fascinating portraits, places and events, including a young Enver Hoxha giving a speech while he was still in local government in Gjirokastra. Not only is this a rare insight into what things looked like in old Albania, it is also a collection of mighty fine photographs. To get there, go northeast of the clock tower into Çlirimi street, and Muhamet Gjollesha street darts off to the right. As the building is unmarked, you may have to ask for directions.

Sleeping & Eating

Hotel Colosseo (☎ 47 513; hotelcolosseo@hotmail.com; rr 13 Dhjetori; s/d €50/60, ste €60-70;) Shkodra's best hotel has 14 rooms with balconies, satellite TV and possibly the best plumbing in northern Albania. There's a café-bar downstairs where the local nouveau riche hang out.

Mondial Hotel (☎ 40 194; hotelrestaurantmondial@hotmail.com; rr 13 Dhjetori; s/d €50/60, ste €80-110) The standard rooms are a little small at this new hotel above a popular local restaurant, but the suites have two bedrooms, two bathrooms, a living room and a spa!

Hotel Kaduku (☎ 42 216; rr Vasil Shanto; r €20) This simple hotel is on the roundabout next to the Hotel Rozafa. The old wing is very basic but the new wing next to it is quite good, with new bathrooms. There's no sign for the hotel, so look for the brick building on the roundabout with 'hotel' painted on the wall. No English is spoken here.

ALBANIA

Getting There & Away

There are frequent *furgons* to and from Tirana (300 lek, 2½ hours), leaving Tirana from the Zogu i Zi terminal and dropping you off in the centre of Shkodra. From Shkodra, *furgons* depart from the main road near Rozafa Castle.

There are also regular *furgons* between Shkodra and Ulcinj (Ulqini in Albanian) in Montenegro (one way €8, around 40 minutes). The 17km road between the two towns has been fixed up, and while a bit narrow it is vastly superior to its previous incarnation. *Furgons* leave from outside the Hotel Rozafa. The length of the trip depends on how busy the border at Muroqani is. Don't forget the €10 fee to enter or leave Albania. The road to Han i Hotit on the way to Podgorica was in poorer shape at the time of research, and there were no *furgons* going straight through. A taxi to this border costs about €15.

LEZHA

☎ 0215 / pop 13,500

This quiet little town was home to one of Albania's most significant historic moments: it's the place where Gjergj Kastrioti, Skanderbeg (see p43), brought the Albanian clan heads to unite against their common enemy, the Ottomans. He was buried here in 1468, in Lezha's cathedral. The Ottomans ravaged his tomb some years later, and turned the cathedral into a mosque.

You can see **Skanderbeg's memorial tomb**, with the double-headed eagle flag stretched behind a bronze bust of the man himself, in the remains of the cathedral.

Perhaps the most interesting reason for coming to Lezha is outside the town: **Hotel i Gjuetisë** (☎ 069 217 0898; Ishulli i Lezhës; r 2000 lek, mains 500 lek), a hunting lodge built by Mussolini's son-in-law Count Ciano set in a quiet wetland park rich with flora and rare birds. To get to Hotel i Gjuetisë you will have to take a taxi, which shouldn't set you back more than 500 lek.

There are also a couple of hotels at Shëngjini, a quiet fishing village about 7km north of Lezha. **Hotel President** (☎ 068 222 2802; dritan1@supereva.it; s/d €20/30) is a simple little place with a small restaurant and modern, clean rooms.

Furgons from Tirana to Shkodra stop at Lezha (200 lek, 1½ hours).

ALBANIA DIRECTORY

ACCOMMODATION

The accommodation reviews in this chapter are listed in order of preference. Albania's budget accommodation is usually decent and clean; breakfast is often included in the price. Midrange hotels are a notch up, with telephones and a touch of glamour to the rooms. Top-end hotels are on a par with modern European hotels in terms of comfort and facilities. Most top-end places offer satellite TV and Internet access, and some have swimming pools.

Accommodation has undergone a rapid transformation in Albania, with the opening of lots of new, custom-built, private hotels to replace the run-down state ones. Another positive development for visitors is the conversion of homes or villas into so-called private hotels. For budget travellers, these are without doubt the best way to go. Outside of Tirana, Durrësi and Saranda the choice of lodgings is limited, but there's usually a good hotel or B&B in most price categories. It's worth noting that tourism is just starting to take off in Albania, and the accommodation scene is developing quite rapidly. The local hotel booking company **Albania-hotel.com** (www.albania-hotel.com) is a reliable resource for finding out about new lodgings; the company does a good job assessing recently opened hotels.

PRACTICALITIES

- *Albanian Daily News* is a local English-language newspaper, mostly only available in Tirana. Some of the 18 or so Albanian-language newspapers and news magazines are owned by political parties.

- The national TV and radio broadcaster is RTSh, augmented by dozens of regional radio stations and a growing number of national and regional TV stations. Top Radio is the country's hippest FM station.

- Albania uses standard European electricity (220V to 240V/50Hz to 60Hz).

- The system used for measurements and weights is metric.

You can often find unofficial accommodation in private homes by asking around. Camping is possible in the southern area and sometimes on the deserted beaches.

ACTIVITIES

Swimming is great all along the Adriatic and Ionian Coasts. You can go bird-watching around Lezha (opposite) and hiking in Mt Dajti National Park (p64). Hiking and adventure sports are really in their infancy in Albania, and the national leaders are the enthusiastic young team at Outdoor Albania (p55). Albanien Reisen (p65) has tours to off-the-beaten track areas around Berati, including to Mt Tomorri National Park.

BOOKS

For a helpful list of Albanian words and phrases check out the *Mediterranean Europe Phrasebook* from Lonely Planet, while *Colloquial Albanian* (1994) by Isa Zymberi is a good teach-yourself language course, accompanied by a cassette.

The Albanians – A Modern History (1999), by Miranda Vickers, is a comprehensive and very readable history of Albania from the time of Ottoman rule to the restoration of democracy after 1990.

James Pettifer's *Albania and Kosovo Blue Guide* (2001) is a thoroughly informed source for answering any questions on Albanian history and a good guide of things to see.

Albania – From Anarchy to a Balkan Identity (1999) by Miranda Vickers and James Pettifer covers the tumultuous 1990s in great detail, while managing to convey a sense of the confusion Albania faced as it shed its communist past.

Biografi (1993) by New Zealander Lloyd Jones is a rather arresting story set in post-1990 Albania, and is a semifactual account of the writer's quest for the alleged double of former communist dictator Enver Hoxha.

Rumpalla – Rummaging Through Albania (2002) by Peter Lucas is a personal account by an American journalist of Albanian descent detailing several visits to Albania before and after the revolution.

The Best of Albanian Cooking (1999) by Klementina Hysa and R John Hysa is one of scant few books on Albanian cuisine and contains a wide range of family recipes.

High Albania (published in 1909 and reprinted in 2000), written by Albania's 'honorary citizen' Edith Durham, recounts the author's travels in northern Albania in the early 20th century.

Albania – The Bradt Travel Guide (2004) by Gillian Gloyer is a thorough guide to the whole country, though like any travel guide published during an economic transformation, it can't be completely up to date.

BUSINESS HOURS

Most offices open at 8am and close around 5pm. Shops usually open at 8am and close around 7pm, though some close for a siesta from noon to 4pm, opening again from 4pm to 8pm. Banking hours are shorter (generally 9am to 2.30pm). Restaurants are normally open from 8.30am to 11pm, and bars from 8.30am to midnight or later.

COURSES

The **Tirana University** (Map p53; ☎ 228 402; http://pages.albaniaonline.net/ut/unitirana_en/default_en.htm; Sheshi Nënë Tereza, Tirana) runs a summer-school programme in Albanian language and culture in August. The registration fee is US$100.

DANGERS & ANNOYANCES

Many prejudices regarding dangers surround Albania, but the country is now safe for travel. Some Serbs and Macedonians love to tell stories of bloodcurdling danger if you say you're going to Albania. First of all, the myth that travellers stumble into Albanian blood feuds isn't true. Poverty is a problem, but not this hoary old custom. It pays to be cautious about travelling without a local guide to Bajram Curri and Tropoja in the far north. There are reports of people being held up at gunpoint in isolated corners of northern Albania, though these are becoming rare. There may still be land mines near the northern border with Kosovo around Bajram Curri.

Otherwise, personal safety in Albania is very good. The number of people walking around central Tirana late on a summer evening shows that the locals are confident about safety. There isn't a hard-core drinking culture here so it's almost unheard of to be bailed up by drunks after dark. Take the usual precautions about avoiding rowdy demonstrations, and beware of pickpockets on crowded city buses. The most serious risk is on the roads – Albania has a high traffic accident rate. Other dangers are the ripped-up pavements, ditches and missing manhole covers – watch your step!

There have been a couple of reports of *furgon* drivers ripping off travellers who've just entered Albania from Montenegro. They've been charged up to €50 for the ride from Shkodra to Tirana. The real price is 300 lek, or about €2.30.

As Albania was closed for so long, black travellers may encounter some curious stares; in fact most visitors to Albania can expect a certain amount of curiosity.

There are risks in drinking tap water or local milk; plenty of bottled water and imported UHT milk is available. The standard of health care in Albania is variable: local hospitals and clinics are understaffed and underfunded, but pharmacies are good.

DISABLED TRAVELLERS

There are few special facilities for travellers in wheelchairs. However, there are toilets that cater to people with disabilities in the Tirana International Hotel (p57) and the Rogner Hotel Europapark Tirana (p57).

EMBASSIES & CONSULATES

There are no Australian, New Zealand or Irish embassies in Albania, and vice versa.

Albanian Embassies & Consulates

There's a full list on the website of the **Albanian Ministry of Foreign Affairs** (www.mfa.gov.al). Following are some of the main addresses for Albanian embassies:

Canada (☎ 613-236 4114; embassyrepublicofalbania@
on.albn.com; 130 Albert St, Suite 302, ON K1P 5G4, Ottawa)
France (☎ 01 47 23 31 00; ambasade.albanie@wanadoo
.fr; 57 ave Marceau, Paris 75116)
Germany (☎ 030-259 3040; kanzlei@botschaft-alba
nien.de; Friedrichstrasse 231, D-10 969, Berlin)
Greece (☎ 21 0723 4412; albem@ath.forthner.gr;
Vekiareli 7, GR-15237 Athens)
Italy (☎ 6 8621 4475; fax 6 8621 6005; Via Asmara 5,
00199 Rome)
Macedonia (☎ 2-614 636; ambshqip@mt.net.mk;
ul HT Karpoš 94A, 1000 Skopje)
Netherlands (☎ 70 427 2101; embalba@xs4all.nl;
Anna Paulownastraat 09b, 2518 BD, The Hague)
Serbia and Montenegro (☎ 11-306 5350; fax 11-665
439; Bulevar Mira 25A, Belgrade)
UK (☎ 020-7828 8897; fax 020-7828 8869; 24 Bucking-
ham Gate, 2nd fl, London SW1 E6LB)
USA (☎ 202-223 4942; albaniaemb@aol.com; 2100 S St
NW, Washington DC 20008)

Embassies & Consulates in Albania

The following embassies and consulates are in Tirana (area code ☎ 04):

France (☎ 234 250; ambcrtir@mail.adanet.com.al;
rr Skënderbej 14)
Germany (☎ 232 048; www.tirana.diplo.de;
rr Skënderbej 8)
Greece (Map p53; ☎ 223 959; grembtir@albnet.net;
rr Frederik Shiroka 3)
Italy (Map p53; ☎ 234 045; www.ambitalia-tirana
.com; rr Lek Dukagjini)
Macedonia (Map p53; ☎ 233 036; macambas@albnet
.net; rr Lek Dukagjini 2)
Netherlands (Map p53; ☎ 240 828; www.netherlands
embassytirana.com; rr Asim Zeneli 10)
Serbia and Montenegro (Map p53; ☎ 223 042;
ambatira@icc-al.org; rr Skënderbej Pall 8/3 Shk 2)
UK (Map p53; ☎ 234 973; www.uk.al; rr Skënderbej 12)
USA (Map p53; ☎ 247 285; www.usemb-tirana.rpo.at; rr
Elbasanit 103)

HOLIDAYS

Albania respects the holy days of four different faiths and sects, which makes for a busy religious and secular holiday schedule. The dates of the Muslim religious holidays of Bajram i Madh (the 'big feast' at the end of the fasting month of Ramadan) and Bajram i Vogël (the 'little feast' commemorating the prophet Ibrahim's willingness to sacrifice his son Ismail to God) fall 11 or 12 days earlier every year. Over the next couple of years Bajram i Vogël falls in December, while Bajram i Madh falls in October. See p131 for precise dates. In addition, the Catholic and Orthodox Easter (Pashkët) dates only rarely fall on the same day. Following are the main holidays:
New Year's Day 1 January
Summer Day 14 March
Nevruz 22 March
Catholic Easter March, April or May
Orthodox Easter March, April or May
May Day 1 May
Mother Teresa Day 19 October
Bajram i Madh October
Independence Day 28 November
Liberation Day 29 November
Bajram i Vogël December
Christmas Day 25 December

LANGUAGE

Albanian (Shqip) is an Indo-European language, a descendent of ancient Illyrian, with a number of Turkish, Latin, Slavonic and (modern) Greek words, although it constitutes a linguistic branch of its own. It has 36 characters (including nine diagraphs or double letters, eg ll and dh). It shares certain grammatical features with Romance languages such as Romanian, but it's fair to say the Albanian language is a world unto itself. Most of the vocabulary sounds completely unfamiliar at first.

The core words of the main dialects of Albanian – Tosk and Gheg – were the same, but the grammar was slightly different. For example the word 'working' was *punuar* in Tosk but *punue* in Gheg. A unified form of Albanian was established in 1972 and is now taught wherever Albanians live.

Most Albanian place names have two forms as the definite article is a suffix. An example of this is *bulevardi* (the boulevard), as opposed to *bulevard* (a boulevard). See also the boxed text, p41. In this chapter we use the definite form, the one most commonly used in English.

Many Albanians speak Italian, thanks to Italian TV broadcasts which can be picked up along the populated coast. During the communist period people grew skilled at rewiring their TVs to overcome the Albanian government's attempts to block Italian channels.

Quite a few people in the south also speak Greek, and younger people are learning English.

See the Language chapter on p413 for pronunciation guidelines and useful words and phrases.

MONEY

Albanian banknotes come in denominations of 100, 200, 500 and 1000 lek. There are five, 10, 20 and 50 lek coins. Since 1997, all notes issued are smaller and contain a sophisticated watermark to prevent forgery. In 1964 the currency was revalued 10 times; prices on occasion may still be quoted at the old rate (3000 lek instead of 300).

Everything in Albania can be paid for with lek but most of the hotel prices are quoted in US dollars or euros, both of which are readily accepted.

ATMs

In the last year or so ATMs connected to the major international networks have appeared in towns and cities everywhere,

which makes travel here much easier. The main networks are Raiffeisen Bank, American Bank of Albania, Pro Credit Bank and Tirana Bank.

Credit Cards

Credit cards are accepted only in the larger hotels and travel agencies, and in only a handful of establishments outside Tirana. Major banks can offer credit-card advances.

Moneychangers

Travellers cheques are about as practical and useful here as a dead albatross, though you can change them at Rogner Hotel Europapark Tirana and at major banks in Tirana. Some banks will change US-dollar travellers cheques into US cash without commission. Travellers cheques (euro and US dollar) can be used at a few top-end hotels, but cash is preferred everywhere.

Every town has its free currency market, which usually operates on the street in front of the main post office or state bank. Such transactions are not dangerous or illegal and it all takes place quite openly, but do make sure you count the money twice before tendering yours. The advantages are that you get a good rate and avoid the 1% bank commission. There are currency-exchange businesses in major towns, usually open 8am to 6pm and closed on Sundays.

US dollars and euros are the favourite foreign currencies. You will not be able to change Albanian lek outside of the country, so exchange them or spend them before you leave.

POST

Outside of main towns there are few public mail boxes, but there is an increasing number of modern post offices springing up around the country where you can hand in your mail directly. Sending a postcard overseas costs around 40 to 80 lek, while a letter costs 80 to 160 lek. The postal system is fairly rudimentary – there are no postcodes, for example – and does not enjoy a reputation for efficiency. Don't rely on sending or receiving parcels through Albapost.

TELEPHONE & FAX

Long-distance telephone calls made from main post offices are cheap, costing about 90 lek a minute to Italy. Calls to the USA cost

230 lek per minute. Calls from private phone offices are horribly expensive though – 800 lek per minute to Australia. Unfortunately there are no cheap Internet phone offices, or at least none where you can hear the person at the other end of the line. Hopefully this will change soon. Faxing can be done from the main post office in Tirana for the same cost as phone calls, or from major hotels, though they will charge more. Albania's country phone code is ☎ 355. For domestic directory enquiries call ☎ 124; international directory assistance is ☎ 12.

Mobile Phones

There are two established mobile phone providers (Vodafone and AMC), and a third company, Eagle Mobile, has been granted a licence. Nearly all areas of the country are covered, though the networks can become congested and, after all, it is quite a mountainous nation. The tariffs are quite high. Check that a roaming agreement exists with your home service provider. Numbers begin with ☎ 068 or ☎ 069 (Eagle Mobile's prefix is not yet known). To call an Albanian mobile number from abroad, dial ☎ 355 then either ☎ 68 or ☎ 69 (ie drop the 0).

Phonecards

Phonecards are available from the post office in versions of 50 units (560 lek), 100 units (980 lek) and 200 units (1800 lek). It's quite common to buy some phonecard time from men waiting around public phones: you use one of their cards, then they check how much credit you've used up and you pay them. Be wary of kids trying to sell you phonecards – sometimes they have no credit left on them.

TOURIST INFORMATION

There are no tourist information offices in Albania, but hotel receptionists or travel agencies will help you with directions. You can buy city maps of Tirana in bookshops and larger kiosks in the capital, but in most

---

EMERGENCY NUMBERS

- Ambulance ☎ 127
- Fire ☎ 128
- Police ☎ 129

---

of the other towns they're unobtainable. In addition, many streets lack signs and the buildings have no numbers marked on them! Some streets don't seem to have any name at all. However, you will find that most of the towns are small enough for you to get around without them.

VISAS

No visa is required by citizens of EU countries or nationals of Australia, Canada, New Zealand, Japan, South Korea, Norway, South Africa or the USA. Travellers from other countries should check with an Albanian embassy (p80) for appropriate visa requirements. Citizens of all countries – even those entering visa-free – will be required to pay an 'entry tax' at the border. The entry tax for all visitors is €10. Israeli citizens pay €30.

Upon arrival you will fill in an arrival and departure card. Keep the departure card, which will be stamped, with your passport and present it when you leave.

WOMEN TRAVELLERS

Albania is quite a safe country for women travellers, but it is important to be aware of the fact that outside Tirana it is mainly men who go out and sit in bars and cafés in the evenings, and women generally stay at home. While they are not threatening, it may feel strange to be the only woman in a bar, so it is advisable to travel in pairs if possible, and dress conservatively.

TRANSPORT IN ALBANIA

This section covers transport connections between Albania and the other countries in this book, eg Serbia and Montenegro and Macedonia. For information on getting to Albania from further abroad, see the Transport chapter.

GETTING THERE & AWAY
Air

Albania's only international airport, and in fact the only one with any regular passenger flights, is Nënë Tereza Airport (aka Mother Teresa Airport and more commonly Rinas Airport), 26km northwest of Tirana. There are no domestic flights within Albania, and the selection of flights within the region is limited to Ljubljana in Slovenia and Prishtina

ALBANIA

in Kosovo. The following airlines fly to and from Albania within the Western Balkans:

Ada Air (airline code ZY; ☎ 02-256 111; www.adaair .com; hub Tirana)

Adria Airways (airline code JP; ☎ 02-228 483; www .adria.si; hub Ljubljana)

Albanian Airlines (airline code LV; ☎ 02-235 162, 233 494; www.flyalbanian.com; hub Tirana)

Land

For information on travelling to and from Greece, see Transport (p402). There are no passenger trains into Albania, so the options are buses, *furgons* or taxi to a border and picking up transport on the other side.

BORDER CROSSINGS
Kosovo

The best crossing for travellers is at Morina/ Vrbnica between Kukësi and Prizren, though there is another rather isolated one at Prushi. There are still occasional reports of trouble in the border area, though nothing like as bad it as once was. Travellers on the through-buses to Prishtina should have no problems.

Macedonia

The two best crossings are on Lake Ohrid. The southern crossing is at Tushëmishti/ Sveti Naum, 29km south of Ohrid; the northern crossing is at Qafa e Thanës/Kafa San, between Struga and Pogradeci. If you are taking a bus to/from Macedonia (Tirana–Struga–Tetovo), use the Qafa e Thanës/Kafa San crossing. The Tushëmishti/Sveti Naum crossing is most commonly crossed on foot, as taxis from Pogradeci will drop you off just before the Macedonian border.

There are two smaller border crossings at Blato, 5km northwest of Debar, and at Stenje on the western shore of Lake Prespa. There is no public transport on these routes.

Serbia & Montenegro

At the time of writing there are two border crossings, one is at Han i Hotit (between

Shkodra and Podgorica) and another at Muriqani/Sukobin between Ulcinj and Shkodra. There are no regular buses from Tirana to cities in Serbia and Montenegro, but there are *furgons* between Shkodra and Ulcinj (one way €8, around 40 minutes) on a nicely rebuilt stretch of road; see p78 for details.

BUS
Kosovo

Buses to Prishtina depart daily from beside the Tirana International Hotel on Sheshi Skënderbeg at 6pm (€30, 12 hours).

Macedonia

There are buses from Tirana via Struga (€10, five hours) to Tetovo (€15, seven to eight hours), but not to Skopje. The **Pollogu travel agency** (Map p53; ☎ 04-23 500, 069 209 4906; Pall 103 blvd Zogu I) sells tickets for the Macedonian bus company Polet, which has services at 9am and 9pm daily from the bus stand next to the train station. The Pollogu office is a little hard to find – it's upstairs in a modern apartment building at the top end of Zogu I – in 2005 the entrance was between a jewellery shop and kids' clothing store.

In July and August there are additional services to ethnic Albanian towns in Macedonia from Durrësi.

CAR & MOTORCYCLE
Macedonia

The busiest route to Macedonia is from Tirana to Struga Tirana via Qafa e Thanës/Kafa San, and there are sometimes delays because of trucks. The route around the southern end of Lake Ohrid via Tushëmishti/Sveti Naum is quieter and delays are much less common.

GETTING AROUND
Bicycle

Although many Albanians cycle short distances, cycling through the country is not recommended, especially if you're unfamiliar with the abysmal driving on Albanian roads. Many roads are not paved and there are no cycling paths anywhere in the country.

Bus

Most Albanians travel around their country in private *furgons* or larger buses. These run fairly frequently throughout the day between Tirana and Durrësi (38km) and other towns north and south. Buses to Tirana depart from towns all around Albania at the crack of dawn. Pay the conductor on board; the fares are low (eg Tirana–Durrësi costs 100 lek). Tickets are rarely issued.

City buses operate in Tirana, Durrësi and Shkodra (pay the conductor). Watch your possessions on crowded city buses.

Car & Motorcycle

Albania has only acquired an official road traffic code in recent years and most motorists have only learned to drive in the last 10 years. During the communist era car ownership required a permit from the government, which in 45 years issued precisely two to nonparty members. As a result, the government found it unnecessary to invest in new roads. Nowadays the road infrastructure is improving but it's still more akin to India than Europe. There are decent roads from the Macedonian border to Durrësi and Tirana, and north from these cities to Shkodra, but the main roads leading south are still being expanded. Highway signage is bad – there are hardly any signs in central Tirana showing the route to Durrësi, for example. Plus, there are a lot of roadworks going on to accommodate the explosive growth in vehicle numbers. In short, it's a really, really hard place to drive, and local driving habits are best described as free-spirited. Off the main routes a 4WD is a necessity. Driving at night is particularly hazardous, and driving on mountain 'roads' in winter is a whole new field of extreme sport. There is no national automobile association in Albania as yet.

DRIVING LICENCE
Foreign drivers' licences are permitted but it is recommended to have an International Driving Permit as well. Car-hire agencies usually require that you have held a full licence for one year.

FUEL & SPARE PARTS
There are plenty of petrol stations in the cities and increasing numbers in the country. Unleaded fuel is available along all major highways, but fill up before driving into the mountainous regions. A litre of unleaded petrol costs 120 lek, while diesel costs 85 lek. There isn't yet a highly developed network of mechanics and repair shops capable of sourcing parts for all types of vehicles.

HIRE
Car hire is fairly new to Albania, but given the driving conditions detailed above we wouldn't recommend it unless you have a lot of experience with similar conditions.

ROAD RULES
Drinking and driving is forbidden, and there is zero tolerance for blood alcohol readings. Both motorcyclists and passengers must wear helmets. Speed limits are as low as 30km/h in built-up areas and 35km/h on the edges of built-up areas.

Local Transport

Most Albanians travel around in private *furgons* or larger buses. Bus/*furgon* activity starts at the crack of dawn and usually ceases by 2pm. Fares are low and tickets are rarely issued. Shared *furgons* leave when they are full or almost full. They usually cost more than the bus, but they're still cheap. On intercity *furgons* people usually pay the driver or assistant en route, but on suburban trips they pay when they get out.

Train

Prior to 1948 Albania had only a few minor military and mining industry railway lines, but the communist party built up a limited rail network. Today, however, nobody who can afford other types of transport takes the train, even though train fares are seriously cheap. The carriages are almost invariably in poor condition (a lot of the rolling stock was vandalised in the 1990s) and journeys proceed at a pace best described as leisurely. That said, they are something of an adventure. The line between Pogradeci and Tirana is rather attractive, especially when it crawls along the shores of Lake Ohrid. There is only one class of travel, and there is no reservation system. Ticket offices generally open 10 minutes before a train is due to depart.

Daily passenger trains leave Tirana for Shkodra (120 lek, 3½ hours), Fier (175 lek, 4¼ hours), Vlora (210 lek, 5½ hours) and Pogradeci (245 lek, seven hours). Eight trains a day also make the trip between Tirana and Durrësi (50 lek, 1½ hours).

There is no official Albanian Railways (HSh, Hekurudha e Shqipërise) website, but there's an informative unofficial one at www .angelfire.com/ak/hekurudha/.

Bosnia & Hercegovina

DAN HERRICK

Bosnia & Hercegovina

More than a decade after Bosnia and Hercegovina was only heard of in international news as a conflict area, this 'most easterly point of the West and the most westerly point of the East' is now trying to get itself back on the world's travel maps. The Bosnia and Hercegovina of today manages to combine the great outdoors and age-old glories of cultural diversity with modern global cultural trends in its race to catch up with the rest of Europe.

Bosnia and Hercegovina has been fought over and colonised more times than it's worth counting, but the 500-year Ottoman rule and a relatively short-lived Austro-Hungarian presence have left a lasting imprint on the country. Sarajevo has a melange of shady nooks in the glittering Baščaršija bazaar, from where the nearby peaks of the Catholic Cathedral, Orthodox Church and the domed roof of the Old Temple (Stari Hram) Synagogue can be seen looking up to the heavens alongside numerous minarets. Trendy youth frequent the fashionable bars and clubs, while the older population drinks steaming black coffees sweetened by Turkish delight.

Mostar's Old Bridge has sprung back up over the racy Neretva River, and tanned young things are once again hurling themselves in it, keeping the tourists amused. The heart-stopping whirls of the Una and Neretva Rivers are rafted by the brave and the screaming. The tiny Jajce (literally 'little egg') has capricious waterfalls in the town centre; Hercegovina's cascading Kravice is like a miniature Niagara (or so the locals like to think). Fluorescent two-in-one Jesus and Mary pictures, life-size popes and fashionable bottles of holy water keep the pilgrims safe in the popular village of Međugorje.

All these things are once again rousing the travellers' interest in this forgotten country: a fusion of nature and nightlife, served up against a diverse cultural background.

FAST FACTS

- **Area** 51,129 sq km
- **Capital** Sarajevo
- **Currency** KM; €1 = 1.96KM; US$1= 1.63KM; UK£1 = 2.85KM; A$1 = 1.23KM; ¥100 = 1.48KM; NZ$1 = 1.14KM
- **Famous for** 1984 Winter Olympics, the bridge at Mostar
- **Key phrases** *Zdravo* (hello), *hvala* (thanks), *molim* (please), *doviđenja* (goodbye)
- **Official languages** Bosnian, Croatian and Serbian
- **Population** 3.99 million (estimate)
- **Telephone codes** country code ☎ 387; international access code ☎ 00
- **Visas** not required for most visitors, see p132

HIGHLIGHTS

- The capital **Sarajevo** (p95), where you can enjoy a magnificent *ćevap*, admire grand mosques, churches and synagogues while bargaining over a copper pot or some leather goods in the old Baščaršija bazaar
- The newly rebuilt **Old Bridge** (Stari Most; p111) of Mostar, with dizzying views of the speedy Neretva River below
- The site of the Virgin Mary epiphanies, **Međugorje** (p119), where you can buy your grandma a new pink rosary and your niece a Virgin Mary pencil case
- The hasty waterfalls in the town centre of **Jajce** (p124), and the compelling medieval remains here
- Rafting on the twists of the **Una River** (p128) amidst towering gorges near Bihać

ITINERARIES

- **One week to 10 days** Arrive in Mostar from coastal Croatia and spend the day roaming the Old Town; take a day trip to Blagaj, Međugorje and/or the Kravice waterfalls for a refreshing swim before wandering north to Sarajevo. You could easily spend three or four days in Sarajevo, but day-trip options include Jajce, Travnik or exploring the mountains around Sarajevo along with the locals. Alternatively, have a picnic at the mouth of the Bosna River (Vrelo Bosne) just outside the capital. If you arrive from Zagreb, then start this itinerary in Sarajevo.
- **Two weeks** Adding to the above, visitors can spend more time exploring Hercegovina, spending a day hiking in Podveležje, checking out the medieval necropolis at Radimlja, or visiting Trebinje, before heading to Bihać for some white-water rafting. Extra days in Sarajevo are always a plus, and if you choose to head on to Serbia and Montenegro, do so via Banja Luka.

CLIMATE & WHEN TO GO

Bosnia and Hercegovina has a mix of Mediterranean and central European climates (see Climate Charts p388). Bosnia is hot in summer but chilly in winter, especially at higher elevations where snowfall can last until April. Hercegovina has a Mediterranean climate with scorching summers (40°C) and mild, windy winters.

The best time to visit is spring or summer; skiers should come between December and

---

WARNING: LAND MINES

There are hundreds of thousands of mines and unexploded ordnance here, not only in the country but also around suburbs and in war-damaged buildings.

Sarajevo's **Mine Action Centre** (Map p97; ☎ 033-209 762; www.bhmac.org; Zmaja od Bosne 8; ⏱ 8am-4pm Mon-Fri) has valuable mine-awareness information.

Outside city centres the golden rule is to stick to asphalt and concrete surfaces. Don't enter war-damaged buildings, avoid areas that look abandoned, and never go to places where you don't see the locals go.

February. There's no need to worry about a seasonal crush of tourists just yet.

HISTORY
Early History

Bosnia has been a cultural cocktail from the beginning. People from all over the world, including Italy, Spain, parts of Africa, Asia Minor, Syria, Egypt and Palestine have at various times populated the areas of Dalmatia and Bosnia and Hercegovina. The region's ancient inhabitants were Illyrians, who were followed by the Romans in 9 AD. The Romans first settled around the mineral springs at Ilidža (p110), near Sarajevo.

HOW MUCH?

- **Short taxi ride** 5KM
- **Internet access per hour** 3KM
- **Coffee** 1KM
- **Slug of šljivovica (plum brandy)** 1.50KM
- **Movie ticket** 3KM

LP INDEX

- **Litre of petrol** 1.56KM
- **Litre of water** 2KM
- **Half-litre of beer** 2KM
- **Souvenir Bosnian coffee set** from 25KM
- **Street snack (burek)** 2KM

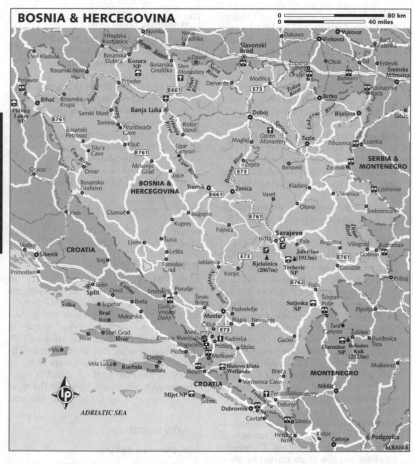

When the Roman Empire was divided in AD 395, the Drina River, today the border between Bosnia and Hercegovina and Serbia and Montenegro, became the line that divided the Western Roman Empire from Byzantium.

The Slavs arrived in the late 6th and early 7th centuries. Bosnia's medieval history is a much debated and politically sensitive subject, mainly because different groups have frequently tried to claim authenticity and territorial rights on the basis of their interpretation of the country's religious make-up before the arrival of the Turks. During this period (1180–1463) Bosnia and Hercegovina became one of the most powerful states in the Western Balkans, and gained control over large parts of the Dalmatian coast.

The first Turkish raids came in 1383, and by 1463 Bosnia was a Turkish province with Sarajevo as its capital. Hercegovina is named after Herceg (Duke) Stjepan Vukčić, who ruled the southern part of the present republic from his mountain-top castle at Blagaj (p117), near Mostar, until the Turks deposed him in 1482.

Ottoman & Austro-Hungarian Empires

Over the next 400 years Bosnia and Hercegovina was completely assimilated into the Ottoman Empire and became the boundary between the Islamic and Christian worlds.

The Islamicisation of Bosnia and Hercegovina largely took place in initial 150 years of Turkish rule. The general idea was that people converted voluntarily over a number of generations. Orthodox and Catholic Christians continued to practise their religions although under certain constraints.

As the influence of the Ottoman Empire declined in the 19th century, the Turks strengthened their hold on Bosnia and Hercegovina as a bulwark against attack. Sparked by the newly born idea of nationhood, the South Slavs (Serbs, Croats, Slovenes, Bosniaks, Montenegrins and Macedonians) rose against their Turkish occupiers in 1875 and 1876.

In 1878 Russia inflicted a crushing defeat on Turkey in a war over Bulgaria, and it was decided at the Congress of Berlin in the same year that Austria-Hungary would occupy Bosnia and Hercegovina.

The Austro-Hungarians developed the country's infrastructure, building roads, railways and bridges. Coal mining and forestry became booming industries and agriculture was dragged, kicking and screaming, into the 20th century. Ivo Andrić's *Bridge over the Drina* describes this process of change as it took place in the town of Višegrad.

But political unrest was on the rise. Previously, Bosnian Muslims, Catholics and Orthodox Christians had differentiated themselves in terms of religion only, and identified with people of the same faith in other countries despite their nationality. But with the rise of nationalism in the mid-19th century, Bosnia's Catholic and Orthodox population started to identify with neighbouring Croatia or Serbia respectively. At the same time, resentment against foreign occupation intensified and young people across the sectarian divide began cooperating, working against the Austro-Hungarians, thus giving birth to the idea of 'Yugoslavism'. Assassination attempts became all the rage. On 28 June 1914 a young Bosnian Serb called Gavrilo Princip shot the Archduke Franz Ferdinand and his wife in Sarajevo. One month later Austria declared war on Serbia. The rest, as they say, is history. Old WWI alliances are still alive in the Balkans today, with the Russians and French being seen as pro-Serb and the Austrians and Germans pro-Croat.

Unification, Communism & Political Tension

After WWI Bosnia and Hercegovina was absorbed into the Kingdom of Serbs, Croats and Slovenes, with the Serbian King Alexander as its head of state. During this time the seeds were already being sown for the conflict that would claim the lives of many at the end of the 20th century: the dominant Serbs were keen centralists, while the Croats and Bosnian Muslims tried to preserve their separate identities within the new kingdom.

Over the next 10 years politics within the kingdom became riddled with strife. Frequent arguments peppered with insults and nonparliamentary behaviour interrupted political debate. It all culminated in 1929 when a Montenegrin deputy, annoyed by interruptions to his speech, pulled out a gun and shot several of his colleagues. Following this, King Alexander clamped down on political opposition. He also renamed the kingdom 'Yugoslavia'. No-one was happy with the new regime. With the support of fascist Italy, the Croats, under the leadership of Ante Pavelić's Ustaše movement, started plotting for Croatian independence. After Yugoslavia's capitulation to Germany in 1941, Bosnia and Hercegovina was annexed by the newly created fascist Croatian state. The Ustaše mimicked the Nazis in persecuting and murdering Croatia's and Bosnia's Jewish population, and added to this its own persecution of the Serbs.

The Serbs responded with two very different resistance movements. The first was the Četniks led by the royalist Draža Mihajlović; the second was the Communist Partisans headed by Josip Broz Tito. The two groups, supported by local peasants, managed to put up quite an effective resistance to the Germans, but long-term cooperation was impossible due to their very different ideologies and plans for the future of the country. In the meantime the fascist Croatian Ustaša started to attack Bosnia's Muslim population, while a separate group of Bosnian Muslims – loyal to the Nazis – began to commit atrocities against Bosnia's Serb population, with the aim of gaining some kind of autonomy for the country. By the end of the war it seemed that everyone was against everyone else, and the only movement that seemed to offer a real alternative was the Communist Partisan party.

Post-WWII, Bosnia and Hercegovina was granted republic status within Tito's Yugoslavia. After Tito fell out with Stalin in 1954 and the country allied itself with Egypt and India to create the so-called 'nonaligned movement', constraints on religious practices were eased but the problem of nationality was ever present. Bosnia's Muslims had to declare themselves to be either Serbs or Croats until 1971, when 'Muslim' was declared to be a nationality unto itself.

During the 1960s Bosnia was one of the least developed republics of Yugoslavia (along with Kosovo) until it was given a much-needed boost when Sarajevo hosted the 1984 Winter Olympics.

Tito was in many ways the glue that held Yugoslavia together, and his death in 1980 exposed a corrupt and crumbling political system. By 1988 Yugoslavia's debt amounted to $33 billion. These circumstances created a fertile breeding ground for nationalists and demagogues.

The infamous appearance in 1990 of a then relatively unknown politician, Slobodan Milošević, on a field outside Kosovo's capital, Prishtina, celebrating the 600th anniversary of the battle of Kosovo Polje, marked a new era. The battle had separated the southern Slavs, placing Serbs and Macedonians under Turkish rule. Roaring references to the times of the Ottoman occupation added fuel to the blaze of new-and-improved Serbian nationalism. The Croatian leader, Franjo Tudjman, called for Croatia's independence. Demands for a looser Yugoslav confederation fell on deaf ears in Milošević's government.

In 1990 and 1991 Slovenia and Croatia were each plunged into a war with the Serb-controlled Yugoslav People's Army. Nationalist sentiment quickly caught on in neighbouring Bosnia and Hercegovina. In the republic's first free elections in November 1990, the communists were easily defeated by nationalist parties. Bosnian Croats joined forces with the Muslims and on 15 October 1991 declared independence from Yugoslavia. Serb parliamentarians wanted none of this and withdrew to set up their own government at Pale, 20km east of Sarajevo. Bosnia and Hercegovina was recognised internationally and was admit-

ted to the UN, but internal talks between the parties broke down.

The 1990s Conflict

One day after Sarajevo came under siege by Serb paramilitaries, Bosnia was recognised as an independent state (6 April 1992) by the international community and entered the UN. Bosnian Serb forces began a campaign of brutal ethnic cleansing, expelling Muslims from northern and eastern Bosnia and Hercegovina to create a 300km corridor joining Serb ethnic areas in the west of Bosnia and Hercegovina with Serbia proper. This is what is now known as Republika Srpska (RS; Serb Republic), with Banja Luka as its administrative centre.

In western Hercegovina the local, predominantly Croat, population armed itself (with the help of neighbouring Croatia) and, joining forces with the territorial defence army of the Bosnian government, managed to successfully fight the Serbs in some areas. Out of this military cooperation a political cooperation between Bosnia and Croatia was born, and the Bosnian president (and leader of the Bosnian Muslims) Alija Izetbegović signed a formal military alliance with Franjo Tuđman in June 1992.

The West's reaction to the increasingly bloody war in Bosnia was confused and erratic. Pictures of concentration camp victims found in northern Bosnia in August 1992 finally brought home the extent to which Bosnian Muslims in particular were being mistreated.

In response to this the UN authorised the use of force to ensure the delivery of humanitarian aid, and 7500 UN troops were sent to Bosnia and Hercegovina. However, this UN Protection Force (Unprofor) was notoriously impotent. In early 1993 fighting broke out between Muslims and Croats, and the war acquired a 'second front'. The Croat expulsion of Muslims from Mostar's west bank to the east culminated in the destruction of Mostar's historic bridge in 1993 by Croat army forces.

In 1994 Western forces began to react to what was taking place in Bosnia and, even as fighting between Muslims and Croats intensified, NATO began to take action against the Bosnian Serbs. A Serbian mortar attack on a Sarajevo market in

February 1994 left 68 dead, and US fighters belatedly began enforcing the no-fly zone over Bosnia and Hercegovina by shooting down four Serb aircraft. When NATO air strikes aimed at protecting Bosnian 'safe areas' were finally authorised, the Serbs captured 300 Unprofor peacekeepers and chained them to potential targets to keep the planes away.

In July 1995 Unprofor's futility was highlighted when Bosnian Serbs, led by the infamous Ratko Mladić, attacked the 'safe area' of Srebrenica, slaughtering an estimated 7500 Muslim men as they fled through the forest.

The end of Bosnian Serb military dominance was near as European leaders loudly called for action. Croatia renewed its own internal offensive, expelling Serbs from the Krajina region of Croatia in August 1995. At least 150,000 of these moved to the Serb-held areas of northern Bosnia.

Following another Serb mortar attack on a market in Sarajevo which killed 37 and wounded 88 people, a swift shift took place in UN and NATO politics. An ultimatum was handed to Mladić to remove his forces from around Sarajevo. Naturally, he refused, but two weeks of NATO air strikes in September 1995 proved more persuasive. US president Bill Clinton's proposal for a peace conference in Dayton, Ohio, USA was accepted soon after.

The Dayton Agreement

The Dayton Agreement stipulated that the country would retain its prewar external boundaries, but would be composed of two parts, or 'entities'. The Federation of Bosnia & Hercegovina (the Muslim and Croat portion) would administer 51% of the country, which included Sarajevo; the RS was allotted 49%.

The agreement emphasised the rights of refugees (1.2 million abroad, and one million displaced within Bosnia and Hercegovina itself) to return to their prewar homes.

A NATO-led peace implementation force was established and named the Stabilisation Force (SFOR). Its current mandate has no definite time limit.

After Dayton

Threatened sanctions forced the wartime Bosnian Serb leader Radovan Karadžić to

THE TWO ENTITIES OF BOSNIA & HERCEGOVINA

step down from the RS presidency in July 1996. Biljana Plavšić, his successor, moved the RS capital to her own power-base of Banja Luka in January 1998.

A new, relatively liberal Bosnian Serb prime minister Milorad Dodik pushed several Dayton-compliant measures through the RS parliament, including common passports, a common licence plate and a new common currency called the convertible mark. Dodik lasted until November 2000, when he failed to be re-elected. Despite his efforts, reforms continue to stall and nationalism in RS is rife.

The Dayton Agreement also emphasised the powers of the Hague-based International Court of Justice and authorised NATO to arrest indicted war criminals. Minor, and a few major, players have been arrested (among them Biljana Plavšić) but the two most-wanted war criminals – Bosnian Serb leader Radovan Karadžić and his military henchman Ratko Mladić – remain at large at the time of writing. Several SFOR hunts for them have ended in embarrassing failure, and while High Prosecutor Carla Del Ponte made confident claims that they would be arrested during 2005, no progress has been made so far.

The presidency of the republic rotates between a Croat, a Bosniak (Muslim) and a Serb leader, but the current president, Adnan Terzić of the Muslim Party of Democratic Action (SDA), will be the first to serve a four-year mandate. The responsibilities of the presidency lie largely in international affairs. In the 2002 elections voter turnout was low and nationalist parties continued to wield their influence. There is general dissatisfaction with the economic state of the country. Terzić has promised to improve socioeconomic conditions in Bosnia, which would help bring the country closer to EU integration.

Paddy Ashdown, former leader of the UK's Liberal Democrat party, stepped down as high representative of the international community in late 2005.

Bosnia and Hercegovina today remains divided along ethnic lines, but tensions have ebbed. More people are now crossing between the RS and the Federation and many refugees are returning home.

PEOPLE

According to the 1991 census, Bosnia and Hercegovina's prewar population stood at around 4.5 million. Today it is estimated at just fewer than four million. No subsequent census has been taken but massive population shifts have changed the size of many cities as ethnic groups from previously mixed populations have moved. The population of Banja Luka, for example, has grown by over 100,000 since the start of the war, as it absorbed many Croatian Serb refugees. Initially Sarajevo and Mostar shrank, although the former has been growing again.

Serbs, Croats and Bosnian Muslims are all Southern Slavs of the same ethnic stock. Physically they are indistinguishable. The prewar population was mixed and intermarriage was common in the cities, but the country's ethnic divisions have changed since the war. Ethnic cleansing has promoted homogeneity not only in rural but in urban areas too. The Croats are dominant in western and southern Hercegovina, Muslims in Sarajevo and central Bosnia and Hercegovina, and Serbs in the north and east (generally in RS).

Inhabitants are known as Bosnian Serbs, Bosnian Croats and Bosniaks.

Relations between the three groups are getting better, and many refugees are returning to their original homes, although just as many are selling up and settling permanently in their place of refuge. The periodic outbreaks of violence seen in the early postwar years are now almost nonexistent, but politically there is little cooperation.

RELIGION

The division of Europe between Catholicism and Orthodox Christianity created a fault line straight through Bosnia and Hercegovina. The west fell under the aegis of Rome and became Roman Catholic while the east looked to Constantinople and the Orthodox Church.

In between was the Bosnian Church (see below), the nature of which has only begun to surface in the last decade.

At the end of the 15th century Spain and Portugal evicted its Jews. Many of these were offered a home by the Turks in Bosnia and Hercegovina, adding a fourth religion to the country.

Today, about 40% of the population is Muslim, 31% is Orthodox, 15% Roman Catholic, 4% Protestant and 10% other

---

THE BOSNIAN CHURCH

During communist times, historians connected the Bosnian Church with Bogumils, a heretical movement founded by a Bulgarian priest called Bogumil in the 10th century. Later on this theory was increasingly discarded, as differing evidence was discovered. The Bosnian Church followed the main Christian beliefs and rituals, such as holding the cross to be a sacred symbol, holding mass and reading psalms (all of which were refused by the Bogumils). The main element of the Bosnian Church is believed to have been monastic life. The monasteries also doubled as inns for guests and travellers. Entire families were permitted to join the monks and thus the division between monastic and ordinary life was blurred. The Bosnian Church monasteries had a strong hierarchical structure with the *djed* (literally 'grandfather') being at the top. Next followed the *starac* (elder) and the *strojnik* (steward). In its heyday the Bosnian Church had considerable power, but with the arrival of the Ottoman Turks many of its adherents converted to Islam, probably in a trade-off to retain civil privileges. The catacombs in Jajce (see p124) are an interesting and unique example of a Bosnian Church temple.

religions. Most Bosnian Serbs are Orthodox and most Bosnian Croats are Catholic.

Across Bosnia and Hercegovina, churches and mosques are being built (or rebuilt) at lightning speed. This is more symptomatic of strong nationalism than religious devotion, since most people are fairly secular.

ARTS

Sarajevo, in the old Yugoslavia, was the cultural capital of the federation, but the wars of the 1990s put an end to that as artists fled back to their home republics or emigrated. Consequently, the arts scene in the country has taken a massive blow from which it has yet to recover. Počitelj (p117) housed an artists' colony for years and some artists are starting to return.

Literature

Bosnia's best-known writer is Ivo Andrić (1892–1975), winner of the 1961 Nobel prize for literature. His novels The Travnik Chronicles and Bridge over the Drina, both written during WWII, are fictional histories dealing with the intermingling of Islamic, Catholic and Orthodox communities in the small Bosnian towns of Travnik and Višegrad.

Another important Bosnian writer is Meša Selimović (1910–82) whose novel Death and The Dervish is a melancholy account of life in Bosnia during the Ottomans and the relationship between man and God.

Going back in time a little, and requiring some Bosnian language skills, is one of Bosnia's literary gems, Ljetopis (Chronicle) by Mula Mustafa Bašeskija (1731–1809). Bašeskija wrote in a version of Turkish spoken by officials in Bosnia at the time, recording events of Sarajevo life over a period of 50 years, starting at the age of 25 and continuing until his death. It is an amazing amalgam of historical data, with weather conditions, diseases and bizarre events, as well as charming stories of local characters and unhappy love stories. Most space was dedicated to lists of the dead and the circumstances of their deaths. The author Meša Selimović used some of Bašeskija's episodes to set the background to his novel The Fortress.

Bosnia's most remarkable poet is Mak Dizdar (1917–71). Born in Stolac (p118) his best poetry was inspired by the Bosnian medieval tombstones, stećci. Francis Jones, translator of other former Yugoslav poets, translated Dizdar's most important and linguistically demanding collection, The Stone Sleeper, into English.

Aleksandar Hemon is a contemporary Bosnian writer who lives in America and writes in English. He went to America on a visit in 1991 and stayed there when the war in his country broke out. His work has been acclaimed in the English-speaking world and his writing style, perhaps a little ambitiously, compared to Nabokov's. His witty and intelligent books The Question of Bruno and Nowhere Man both deal with the life of a Bosnian in America.

Two other contemporaries are Miljenko Jergović and Semezdin Mehmedinović whose brilliant collections of short stories in Sarajevo Marlboro and poems and essays in Sarajevo Blues deal with the subject of the Sarajevo siege.

A wartime journal often compared to Anne Frank's Diary is Zlata's Diary. Written by a young girl, Zlata Filipović, in 1993 Sarajevo, and published in France, the book quickly became an international bestseller. A theatre adaptation was staged in the UK in 2004.

Buybook publishing house and a number of other small publishers in Sarajevo are giving a voice to new Bosnian writers, who are increasingly starting to look away from the subject of war.

Cinema

Bosnia and Hercegovina has done well with film. Danis Tanović won an Oscar in 2002 for his film No Man's Land. The film portrays the relationship between two soldiers, one Muslim, one Serb, caught alone in the same trench while Sarajevo was under siege. Another well-respected Bosnian film about the siege is The Perfect Circle (1997), whose protagonist is a poet. The early films of Sarajevo-born Emir Kusturica, such as When Father was Away on Business and Do You Remember Dolly Bell? deal with fraught family life in 1980s Bosnia and rank among the director's best.

Craft

Sarajevo and Mostar have many private galleries and Sarajevo has a first-class regional public gallery. The work of the artists who stayed on during the war has obviously been influenced by their traumatic experiences.

The craft industry is well developed with artisans working in copper and brass to produce ornamental or practical items, and in gold and silver for jewellery. All these items can be found in the lanes of Kujundžiluk (p114) in Mostar, and Baščaršija (p98) in Sarajevo.

Music

Traditional Bosnian music is called *sevdah* and has been described as the 'Bosnian Blues.' Sung in a heart-wrenching vocal, the lyrics are always about unhappy love. Safet Isović is regarded as the king of traditional *sevdah*. A contemporary band called Mostar Sevdah Reunion is a collection of five musicians from Mostar, most of whom left the city during the war and who recently reunited and recorded several *sevdah* albums.

Pop and rock music has always been successful in Bosnia and Hercegovina, and the music industry is flourishing. Cheap folk albums are also produced at an amazing rate. Recently, hip-hop has taken hold in the country. The local Eminem is a singer called Edo Maajka who raps about wartime and postwar Bosnia.

Jazz is very popular in Bosnia and Hercegovina, particularly in Sarajevo, where live music jazz clubs and bars attract decent crowds. An interesting fusion of traditional Bosnian music and jazz is the Edin Bosnić Quartet's *Bosnian Suite*.

ENVIRONMENT
The Land

Bosnia and Hercegovina is a mountainous country of 51,129 sq km in the central Balkans. Only 8% of the land is below 150m and 30 mountain peaks rise between 1700m and 2386m. Just a toe of land connects it to the sea through Croatia.

The arid south gives way to a central mountainous core, which descends again to the green rolling hills of the north and flatlands of the northeast that form the southern tip of the Hungarian plain.

Limestone forms much of the uplands, creating distinctive scenery with light-grey craggy hills and caves. The rivers shine green and possess a clarity to them that's unusual elsewhere in Europe; they are also part of the country's wealth given their potential for electricity generation. Most of them flow north into the Sava River; only the Neretva River cuts south from Jablanica through the Dinaric Alps to Ploče on the Adriatic Sea.

Wildlife

About half of the country, mostly the north, is covered in forest, with beech at lower altitude giving way to fir trees higher up. Wildlife lives mainly in these forests and includes rabbits, foxes, weasels, otters, wild sheep, ibex, deer, lynxes, eagles, hawks and vultures. At higher altitudes there are bears and wolves.

National Parks

There are two main national parks. Sutjeska still has remnants of a Unesco-protected primeval forest going back 20,000 years, while the Hutovo Blato wetlands are a prime sanctuary for migratory birds.

Environmental Issues

Mines and unexploded ordnance put much of the country around the former battle zones out of reach, but with local guides visits are quite feasible. These leftovers from war, the infrastructure damage, air pollution from metallurgical plants and rubbish disposal are significant environmental problems for Bosnia and Hercegovina.

FOOD & DRINK
Staples & Specialities

Bosnia's Turkish heritage is savoured in grilled meats such as *ćevapčići* (minced lamb or beef), *šnicla* (steak) or *kotleti* (rack of veal). Often accompanying these is a half-loaf of spongy *somun* bread.

Stews are popular, often cooked slowly over an open fire, with favourites such as *bosanski lonac* (Bosnian stew of cabbage and meat) or *dinstana teletina sa povrćem* (veal and vegetable stew).

Burek (stuffed filo pastry) sold in *pekara* (bakery shops) is a filling substitute for a missed breakfast and comes either filled with *sir* (cheese), *meso* (meat) or *krompiruša* (potato).

The ubiquitous pizza and pasta props up the national cuisine and fish is also readily available, especially trout from various fish farms on the nation's rivers.

For sugar-soaked desserts, try baklava or *tufahije* (an apple cake topped with walnuts and whipped cream). Many cities make good cheese; feta-like Travnik cheese is especially well known.

Fine wines from Hercegovina include Žilavka (white) and Blatina (red). These are best sampled in regional wineries; Međugorje has some fine offerings. A meal can always be washed down with a shot of *šljivovica* (plum brandy) or *loza* (grape brandy).

Where to Eat & Drink

In the larger towns and cities there are plenty of small cafés and restaurants offering mostly traditional Bosnian food. In Mostar's Old Town and Sarajevo's Baščaršija, every other establishment seems to be a place offering *ćevapčići;* you just have to follow your nose to find the nearest. Similar snack places can also be found around bus stations.

There are fewer restaurants in the ski resorts as the hotels capture their clients with half- and full-board accommodation.

Alcohol is readily available, even in Muslim areas, and there are enough bars to make a good pub crawl in Mostar, Banja Luka and Sarajevo.

Coffee is, however, the main social lubricant; people meet to sip their Bosnian coffee, smoke, play cards or just talk the world into some sort of order. The coffee is served in a *ldezva* (long-handled small brass pot), from which the precious black liquid is carefully decanted into *fildžan* (thimble-sized cups). Two lumps of sugar are usually added, or the lump is dipped into the coffee and nibbled. A piece of Turkish delight and a glass of water are also sometimes served with the coffee.

Vegetarians & Vegans

The emphasis on meat in the diet means that vegetarians and vegans are hard done by. Vegetarian restaurants are a rarity: only one restaurant in Sarajevo, the Karuzo (p105), offers a meatless menu. Many traditional and top-end restaurants will have several vegetarian dishes, although a vegan would have great trouble following a strict diet when eating out. Snacks for vegetarians are *sirnica* (cheese pie) or *zeljanica* (spinach pie), and for full-blown meals there are stewed beans or courgette dishes.

SARAJEVO

☎ 033 / pop 602,500

Sarajevo is like a kid's pocket after a quick spree at the Woolworth's pick'n'mix counter: it's got bits of everything. Mosques (in abundance), churches (quite a few), an Ottoman bazaar area (only one), wide Austro-Hungarian streets and classy buildings (lots), and grey socialist blocks (yep). But most of all, Sarajevo has tons of character and a kicking spirit. Once famous for being 'Europe's Jerusalem', the place where the world's three main religions sent their prayers upwards in harmony, Sarajevo suffered immense physical and psychological damage during its three-year siege (1992–95). Its citizens went without food, water, electricity and heating for much of that time, but walking down the streets of this animated city now, you'd think it was all a bad dream. Here and there a pockmarked building and a city park graveyard remind of the war.

The Baščaršija bazaar is at the heart of the city, an ancient trading place with small shops, coffee-drinking dens and endless souvenir choices. Moving further away the Ottoman traces disappear and the city takes on its other guise, that of a nostalgic Austro-Hungarian bride left standing at the altar. Surrounding the city's mosques and churches are countless colourful restaurants, bars, cafés, museums and galleries, all testament to the various colonisers that left their heritage behind. The city is bisected by a tiny, feeble river, the banks of which teem with cafés and sun-seeking Sarajevans.

HISTORY

While the region had its attractions for those who populated prehistory, it wasn't until the Romans arrived that Sarajevo gained a significant mention on the pages of history. Their legions, always on the lookout for a new bathhouse, founded the settlement Aquae Sulphurae around the sulphur springs at Ilidža (p110).

Sarajevo then slipped back into obscurity until the Turks arrived in the mid-15th century and their governors set up house and stayed until 1878. The city became an important market and stopping place on the east–west trading routes. It was during this time that the city gained its name, originating from the Arabic word *saray*, which means 'resting place'.

The 'on the go' Austro-Hungarians replaced the fading Ottoman Empire, bringing railways that connected Sarajevo and its outlook to the West. Sarajevo had street lighting before Vienna, as there were doubts about the safety of electricity and it was deemed wiser to try it out in the colonies first. WWI famously has its roots in Sarajevo, where a young Serb, Gavrilo Princip, shot Archduke Franz Ferdinand in protest against the Austro-Hungarian empire. This happened on the Latin Bridge, known as Princip's Bridge for many years, until in 1993 it was changed back to its pre-WWI name. Princip was then declared to be a terrorist and (allegedly) his famous footprints were removed from the spot where he is meant to have stood.

Seventy years after the assassination, in 1984, Sarajevo attracted world attention by hosting the 14th Winter Olympic Games. Then from 1992 to 1995 the infamous siege of the city grabbed the headlines and horrified the world. Ratko Mladić, the Bosnian Serb commander, is reported to have said, 'Shoot at slow intervals until I order you to stop. Shell them until they can't sleep, don't stop until they are on the edge of madness.'

Sarajevo's heritage of six centuries was pounded into rubble and its only access to the outside world was via an 800m tunnel under the airport. Over 10,500 Sarajevans died and 50,000 were wounded by Bosnian Serb sniper fire and shelling. The endless new graveyards near Koševo stadium (Map p97) are a silent record of those terrible years.

ORIENTATION

Sarajevo nestles in a wide valley created by the Miljacka River. The distant mountains of Jahorina and Bjelašnica, host to the 1984 Olympics, flank the city to the south.

STREET ADDRESSES

At the end of a number of addresses in this chapter, you'll notice the letters 'bb' instead of a street number. This shorthand, which stands for *bez broja* (without a number) is used by businesses and other non-residential institutions, indicating that it's an official place without a street number.

SARAJEVO IN TWO DAYS

The only way to start getting the hang of the city is by getting lost in the streets of **Baščaršija** (p98). Follow your nose to Sarajevo's best *ćevapčići* at the legendary **Željo** (p106) and walk over the river to check out the **Sarajevo Brewery** (p107). Go partying at the **Bar** (p107), where you can have fun under the stars.

Have your breakfast at **Mash** (p106) and appreciate stuff at the **Art Gallery** (p99). Check out the churches and the synagogue and stroll to the **National Museum** (p101). Take a city tour and get ready for a night out starting at the **Zlatna Ribica** (p106), then finish with some smooth sounds at **Clou Jazz Club** (p107), Asian cool in the **Buddha Bar** (p107) or go back in time with old-style Sarajevo club **Sloga** (p107).

From the airport, 6.5km to the southwest, the main road runs up to the suburb of Ilidža, then swings east through Novo Sarajevo. In doing so it passes the yellow Holiday Inn, home to journalists during the war, and becomes the section of road that gained notoriety as 'sniper alley'. The bus and train stations are to the north. Near the town centre the road runs alongside the Miljacka River, before leaving it at Baščaršija, which occupies the east end of town.

If you take a taxi up to Sedrenik on the northeastern side you get a fine view of the city and mountains beyond.

INFORMATION
Bookshops

BuyBook (☎ 716 450; www.buybook.com.ba) Radićeva (Map p97; Radićeva 4; ☑ 9am-10pm Mon-Sat, 10am-6pm Sun); Zelenih Beretki (Map pp100-1; ☎ 712 000; Zelenih Beretki 8; ☑ 9am-10pm Mon-Sat) The Radićeva branch has books on the Balkans and a café. The Zelenih Beretki branch has art book specialists, English newspapers and magazines, and CDs at the Karabit Café (p107).

Šahinpašić (Map pp100-1; ☎ 220 111; www.btcsa hinpasic.com; Mula Mustafe Bašeskije 1; ☑ 9am-8pm Mon-Sat, 10am-2pm Sun) English-language newspapers, magazines, maps and a stack of Lonely Planet guides.

Internet Access

Albatros (Map pp100-1; ☎ 555 483; Sagardžije 27; per hr 3KM; ☑ 9am-midnight)

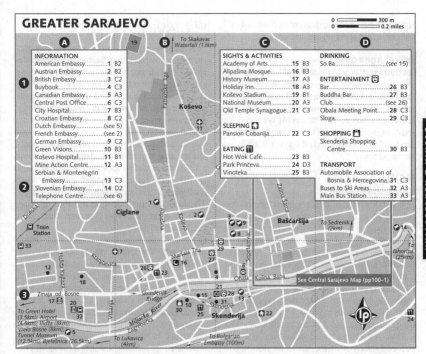

GREATER SARAJEVO

0   300 m
0   0.2 miles

INFORMATION
American Embassy..............**1** B2
Austrian Embassy..............**2** B2
British Embassy..................**3** C2
Buybook..............................**4** C3
Canadian Embassy..............**5** A3
Central Post Office..............**6** C3
City Hospital........................**7** B3
Croatian Embassy................**8** C2
Dutch Embassy..............(see 5)
French Embassy..............(see 2)
German Embassy..................**9** C2
Green Visions.....................**10** B3
Koševo Hospital................**11** B1
Mine Action Centre...........**12** A3
Serbian & Montenegrin
  Embassy.........................**13** C3
Slovenian Embassy............**14** D2
Telephone Centre..........(see 6)

SIGHTS & ACTIVITIES
Academy of Arts...............**15** B3
Alipašina Mosque..............**16** B3
History Museum.................**17** A3
Holiday Inn........................**18** A3
Koševo Stadium.................**19** B1
National Museum...............**20** A3
Old Temple Synagogue...**21** C3

SLEEPING
Pansion Čobanija.............**22** C3

EATING
Hot Wok Café....................**23** B3
Park Prinčeva....................**24** D3
Vinoteka............................**25** B3

DRINKING
So.Ba.............................(see 15)

ENTERTAINMENT
Bar......................................**26** B3
Buddha Bar........................**27** B3
Club...............................(see 26)
Obala Meeting Point........**28** C3
Sloga..................................**29** C3

SHOPPING
Skenderija Shopping
  Centre............................**30** B3

TRANSPORT
Automobile Association of
  Bosnia & Hercegovina..**31** C3
Buses to Ski Areas............**32** A3
Main Bus Station...............**33** A3

BOSNIA & HERCEGOVINA

Koševo
Ciglane
Train Station
Baščaršija
To Skakavac Waterfall (13km)
To Sedrenik (2km)
To Jahorina (25km)
Maršala Tita
Obala Kulina Bana
Skenderija Bridge
Skenderija
Miljacka River
Zmaja od Bosne
To Green Hotel (3.5km); Airport (4.5km); Ilidža (8km); Vrelo Bosne (8km); Tunnel Museum (12.5km); Bjelašnica (26.5km)
To Lukavica (4km)
To Bulgarian Embassy (100m)
See Central Sarajevo Map (pp100–1)

Click (Map pp100-1; ☎ 236 914; Kundurdžiluk 1; per hr 3KM; ☼ 9am-11pm)

Left Luggage

Main bus station (Map p97; Put Života 8; for 3hr 1.50KM, each subsequent hr 0.50KM) Useful while you go into town to look for accommodation.

Media

Oslobođenje (a Sarajevo-based, privately owned daily) and *Dnevni avaz* (the main Muslim daily) are the most popular newspapers in Sarajevo; *Dani* (Sarajevo-based privately owned weekly) is a reliable independent weekly.

Medical Services

Ask your embassy for a list of private doctors. In an emergency, contact one of the following:
Baščaršija Pharmacy (Map pp100-1; ☎ 272 301; Obala Kulina Bana 40; ☼ 24hr)
City Hospital (State Hospital; Map p97; ☎ 291 100; Kranjčevića 12)
Koševo Hospital (Map p97; ☎ 445 522; Gradska Bolnička 25) Ask for the VIP service and take your passport.

Money

ATMs are sprinkled all over the city centre, accepting all varieties of debit cards.
Airport Money Exchange (airport; ☼ 11am-6pm Mon-Sat, noon-7pm Sun) The bureau has an all-card ATM, cashes travellers cheques, transfers money and will give cash advances on your credit card. A financial lifesaver when banks are closed on Sundays.
Turkish Ziraat Bank (Map pp100-1; ☎ 720 209; Ferhadija 10; ☼ 8.30am-8pm Mon-Fri, 9am-noon Sat) Has an all-card ATM and cashes travellers cheques.

Post

Central post office (Map p97; ☎ 650 618; Obala Kulina Bana 8; ☼ 7am-8pm Mon-Sat) Queue at counter 17, which is for post; the others are only for paying bills. There's also a telephone centre here.

Telephone & Fax

Telephone centre (Map p97; ☎ 650 618; Obala Kulina Bana 8; ☼ 7am-8pm) At the central post office.

Tourist Information

Tourist Information Centre (Map pp100-1; ☎ 220 724, 532 606; www.sarajevo-tourism.com; Zelenih Beretki 22a; ☼ 9am-8pm Mon-Fri, 9am-4pm Sat, 10am-2pm

Sun) A great place for books, maps and brochures, and informed answers on the city and the country.

Travel Agencies

Centrotrans (Map pp100–1; ☎ 205 481; ferhadija16@ hotmail.com; Ferhadija 16; ☺ 8am-8pm Mon-Fri, 8am-2pm Sat) Books international bus tickets and is part of the Eurolines trans-Europe bus network.

Relax Tours (Map pp100–1; ☎ /fax 263 190; www .relaxtours.com; Zelenih Beretki 22; ☺ 9am-8pm Mon-Fri, 9am-5pm Sat) Books airline tickets, ferry tickets and accommodation.

SIGHTS

Baščaršija & Around

The mazy streets of Baščaršija are perfect for getting to know Sarajevo's soul. Whatever you decide to buy in the souvenir shops, be it a Bosnia and Hercegovina football shirt or a coffee set, you'll no doubt get into conversation with one of the locals. Watching a craftsman at work can be a great experience, bargaining for some jewellery or a leather bag an even better one, especially if you have no Bosnian and your 'bargainer' no English. The great thing about Baščaršija is that it's relaxed and whatever you do, you can take your time. And, no doubt, the locals will too.

The best place to start exploring is the grandiose Austro-Hungarian **National Library** (Map pp100–1; Obala Kulina Bana bb). This was the building where numerous historical documents, manuscripts and books were archived, all relating to the history of the country. Deliberately targeted by the Serbs for the very reason of being a 'centre' of culture, the library suffered heavy destruction. An incendiary shell fell on the building on 25 August 1992, 100 years after construction began, wiping out much of the country's heritage. Restoration work is slow and many books may be irreplaceable. The library is now graced by a glass-and-steel dome provided by the Austrian government, and every now and then it houses exhibitions and hosts talks.

Nearby is Baščaršija's centre piece, the **Sebilj** (Map pp100–1), a fountain which sits in a small square, surrounded by a colony of pigeons (some even call the square 'Pigeon Square'). This Moorish-style fountain was modelled on a stone fountain in Constantinople (Istanbul). It dates back to 1891 and is the gathering place not only of pigeons

(although they are definitely in the majority) but of Sarajevans of all ages.

A little southeast of the Sebilj is the picturesque 16th-century **Baščaršija mosque** (Map pp100–1; Bravadžiluk), where worshippers pray silently on the outside 'terrace'.

Down an alley accessed from Sarači (near number 73) is **Morića Han** (Map pp100–1). A tavern when Sarajevo was a stopover on the ancient crossroads between East and West, the *han* (an inn and place where merchants and travellers used to sleep) is now a courtyard with cafés and wicker chairs. In the right-hand corner is a carpet shop with plush Persian rugs piled a metre high. The *han* has burnt down a number of times over the years and this reincarnation dates from the 1970s.

Behind Morića Han is the old **Orthodox Church** (Map pp100–1; ☎ 534 783; Mula Mustafe Bašeskije 59), which predates the yellow-and-brown Orthodox Cathedral. Don't miss the **museum** (free admission) inside the church, which showcases Russian, Greek and local icons, tapestries and old manuscripts.

South of here is the **Gazi-Husrevbey Mosque** (Map pp100–1; ☎ 532 144; www.vakuf-gazi.ba; Veliki Mudželiti 21; ☺ 9am-noon, 2.30-4pm & 5.30-7pm). This is one of Sarajevo's most beautiful mosques, with a sunny front square and rows of shoes stacked outside belonging to the faithful. Designed by a Persian, Adžem Esir Ali, a leading architect at the time, the mosque was first built by masons from Dubrovnik in 1531 but has been reconstructed several times since. There's a free guide available between 2.30pm and 4pm. (Note that the mosque is on Sarači, but the address it provides is a little street off Sarači.) Women with headscarves and men with beards move to and fro across the street from the mosque to the **Gazi-Husrevbey madrasa** (Map pp100–1; Sarači), a Muslim place of learning since 1537.

The noisy life of one of Sarajevo's favourite streets can be seen on **Ferhadija**. Newspaper sellers shout the day's headlines, old men sell all sorts of books and magazines, and cake shops display their assets alluringly here.

Away from the mosques, the scenery changes from one of spiritual reverence to consumables-worship at Brusa Bezistan shopping centre (see p107). Unlike your typical shopping mall, this place has real history: the six-domed Bezistan was once upon a time (from 1551) the top place for trading silk coming from Brusa in Asia Minor. Having traversed the Silk Road, the tired tradesmen would rest their feet and hope for profit under the domes, no doubt downing a coffee or two in the meantime.

If you turn right towards Baščeskija street from Ferhadija, you'll enter the **former Jewish quarter**. The Sephardic Jews, fleeing persecution by the Spanish Inquisition in Spain and Portugal, found refuge throughout the Ottoman Empire, and so too in Bosnia and Hercegovina. Also here is the **New Temple Gallery** (Novi Hram Gallery; Map pp100-1; ☎ 233 280; Mula Mustafe Baščeskije 38; admission free), which has interesting displays of historical documents relating to Bosnia and Hercegovina's Jews. Sarajevo's Jews were good tradesmen and blended easily into the city. They built their first place of worship, the **Old Temple Synagogue** (Stari Hram; Map p97; Skenderija), located across the river, in 1581, and this was expanded in 1821 as the community grew.

Back on Ferhadija street you will soon start to leave the Ottoman-style architecture behind and enter the remains of the Austro-Hungarian world. On your right as you walk west you'll see the 19th-century **Catholic Cathedral** (Map pp100-1; Trg Fra Grge Martića) with its neo-Gothic bellowers visible from almost any spot in town. Kids hang out on the cathedral's steps and the late Pope John Paul II served Mass here on his visit to the region in 1997.

Just north of the cathedral is the **Bosniak Institute** (Map pp100-1; ☎ 279 800; www.bosnjackiinstitut .org; Mula Mustafe Baščeskije 21; ☒ 10am-2pm Sat), a relatively new museum dedicated to the history of Bosnia's Muslim population. It has some interesting documents and books by leading Bosniak writers, and newspapers from the beginning of the last century expressing shock and dismay at the assassination of Archduke Franz Ferdinand. Groups can request a free English-language tour.

South again on **Trg Oslobođenja** (Liberation Sq; Map pp100-1), you'll see old men playing chess with empty mortar cases for pieces, and shaking their heads in disbelief at their opponent's ridiculous moves.

Also on this square is the **Orthodox Cathedral** (Saborna Crkva; Map pp100-1; Trg Oslobodjenja), the largest Orthodox church in the city. Built in 1872 in the Byzantine-Serb style, the church is open to visitors most of the (day) time.

A good place to pause is the **Art Gallery** (Map pp100-1; ☎ 266 550; Zelenih Beretki 8; admission 2KM; ☒ noon-2pm Tue-Sat), opposite the Orthodox Cathedral. The sprawling white building also houses the lovely café Karabit (p107), where you can check out the local arty crowd and drink a freshly squeezed juice. The gallery has a comprehensive range of the country's modern and contemporary art and is well worth a visit.

Where Ferhadija reaches its end and meets Maršala Tita street is the **Eternal flame** (Vječna vatra; Map pp100-1; cnr Ferhadija & Maršala Tita), a monument commemorating the victims of WWII.

Walking down Maršala Tita you can do some window shopping or stop in one of the cake shops. A little further west, where Maršala Tita meets Alipašina is **Alipašvina mosque** (Map p97; Maršala Tita), renowned for being a particularly dangerous sniper spot in the recent conflict. Behind the mosque is Skenderija bridge, named after the once grand 1984 Olympic structure **Skenderija** (Map p97; Skenderija). The concrete building, although not a pretty sight, is now a shopping centre and an important landmark in the city.

Walking east along the river after crossing Skenderija bridge, you'll come upon one of Sarajevo's loveliest buildings, the **Academy of Art** (Map p97; Obala Maka Dizdara). Once an evangelical church, this is now the gathering place of the city's arty crowd, with parties and beer drinking going on into the wee hours on the lawns outside. It is possible to go inside and have a coffee in the student bar.

On the other side of the river is the central post office (p97), a beautiful Austro-Hungarian structure, with an elegant and peaceful interior renovated after the war. Next to it is the equally scrumptious **National Theatre** (Map pp100-1; Zelenih Beretki), built in 1899 and designed by the same architect who created the Academy of Art building.

On the fateful day of 28 June 1914, Austrian Archduke Franz Ferdinand and his wife Sophie paused at the National Library (then the town hall) and then rode west along the riverside in an open car to the **Latin Bridge** (Map pp100–1), about 500m south of the National Theatre. It was here that Gavrilo Princip stepped forward to fire his pistol, killing both and sparking off

BOSNIA & HERCEGOVINA

BOSNIA & HERCEGOVINA

CENTRAL SARAJEVO

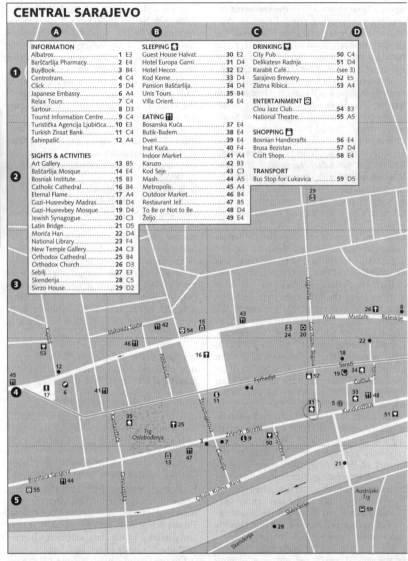

INFORMATION
Albatros.................................1 E3
Baščaršija Pharmacy..............2 E4
BuyBook...............................3 B4
Centrotrans...........................4 C4
Click....................................5 D4
Japanese Embassy..................6 A4
Relax Tours............................7 C4
Sartour.................................8 D3
Tourist Information Centre.......9 C4
Turistička Agencija Ljubičica...10 E3
Turkish Ziraat Bank...............11 C4
Šahinpašić...........................12 A4

SIGHTS & ACTIVITIES
Art Gallery...........................13 B5
Baščaršija Mosque................14 E4
Bosniak Institute...................15 B3
Catholic Cathedral................16 B4
Eternal Flame.......................17 A4
Gazi-Husrevbey Madras........18 D4
Gazi-Husrevbey Mosque.......19 D4
Jewish Synagogue.................20 C3
Latin Bridge.........................21 D5
Morića Han..........................22 D4
National Library....................23 F4
New Temple Gallery..............24 C3
Orthodox Cathedral..............25 B4
Orthodox Church..................26 D3
Sebilj..................................27 E3
Skenderija...........................28 C5
Svrzo House.........................29 D2

SLEEPING
Guest House Halvat...............30 E2
Hotel Europa Garni...............31 D4
Hotel Hecco.........................32 E2
Kod Keme............................33 D4
Pansion Baščaršija................34 D4
Unis Tours............................35 B4
Villa Orient..........................36 E4

EATING
Bosanska Kuća......................37 E4
Butik-Badem.........................38 E4
Dveri....................................39 E4
Inat Kuća..............................40 F4
Indoor Market.......................41 A4
Karuzo..................................42 B3
Kod Seje...............................43 C3
Mash...................................44 A5
Metropolis............................45 A4
Outdoor Market....................46 B4
Restaurant Jež......................47 B5
To Be or Not to Be...............48 D4
Željo....................................49 E4

DRINKING
City Pub...............................50 C4
Delikatesn Radnja.................51 D4
Karabit Café......................(see 3)
Sarajevo Brewery..................52 E5
Zlatna Ribica........................53 A4

ENTERTAINMENT
Clou Jazz Club......................54 B3
National Theatre...................55 A5

SHOPPING
Bosnian Handicrafts..............56 E4
Brusa Bezistan......................57 D4
Craft Shops..........................58 E4

TRANSPORT
Bus Stop for Lukavica...........59 D5

a war by the Austro-Hungarians against Serbia, which in turn, through a series of European alliances, led to WWI.

The elegant stone Latin Bridge has been repaired and the bit of pavement bearing Princip's footprints may now be replaced – it was removed during the recent war when Princip (a Bosnian Serb) was denounced as a terrorist in 1993. There are also plans to place a bust of the archduke here, and to open a museum at the north side of the bridge.

If you go uphill across the river from the National Library, you'll come upon the **Alifakovac cemetery**, a place for great views of the city.

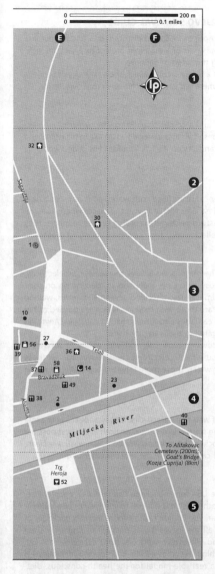

SARAJEVO ROSES

All around town, but particularly along Fer-hadija, pay attention to **Sarajevo roses** on the pavements. These are skeletal handlike indentations of mortar shells and many are symbolically filled in with hard red paint, particularly those where the death toll was very high. Often you will see a series of brass plaques giving the names of those killed by that particular shell.

---

away, including the bedding. That's why the rooms may seem a little bare. There's a useful explanatory brochure in English.

Goat's Bridge

A considerable walk east along the Miljacka River from Baščaršija is **Goat's Bridge**, an elegant arch from where pilgrims to Mecca once began their long journey. It's an 8km walk from the city centre and good for spending the day away from the crowds, or for a decent bike ride.

Novo Sarajevo

The Zmaja od Bosne road, the stretch between the city and the airport, was infamously dubbed 'sniper alley' during the siege of Sarajevo. This was because Serb snipers, who were hiding in the surrounding hills, shot civilians like clay pigeons as they crossed the street on their way to try to get water or go to work.

The bright-yellow and brown **Holiday Inn** (Map p97; Zmaja Od Bosne 4; ☎ 288 000; holiday@bih.net.ba) was the wartime home to international journalists, as it was the city's only functioning hotel. The side facing Sniper's Alley was heavily damaged, but the hotel has since been given a facelift. An important landmark in the city, the Holiday Inn was dubbed 'egg-sunny-side-up' during the winter days when snow would cover up most of the façade, leaving only a few circles of yellow peeking out.

Across from the Holiday Inn is the **National Museum** (Map p97; ☎ 668 026; www.zemaljskimuzej.ba; Zmaja od Bosne 3; adult/concession 5/1KM; ☒ 10am-2pm Tue-Sun, to 7pm Wed in summer). An impressive Romanesque building, the museum is a good place to catch up on the country's history, and displays include items from the Neolithic era; Roman findings;

North of Baščaršija is **Svrzo House** (Map pp100-1; ☎ 535 264; Glodžina 8; admission 2KM; ☒ 10am-5pm Tue-Sat, 10am-1pm Sun), a display of the lifestyle of a well-to-do, 18th-century Muslim family. The owners lived in the house until 1952, when it was passed over to the city as a museum. Turkish homemakers were a tidy lot and everything not in use was put

BOSNIA & HERCEGOVINA

HOW TO GET MORE OUT OF A WAR: SARAJEVO SURVIVAL GUIDE

Written in Sarajevo, between April of 1992 and April of 1993, and distributed in trade paperback by Workman Press of New York, this manuscript is part of a multifold project by FAMA, an independent production company, triggered during the siege of Sarajevo.

Sarajevo Survival Guide is a chronicle, a part of a future archive which shows the city of Sarajevo not as a victim but as a place of experiment, where wit can still achieve victory over terror.

The Modern Sarajevan Male

He has accreditation [ID], weapons, a good car, and a complete uniform. The owner of a bullet-proof vest is regarded with respect. One who doesn't wear a uniform has an axe in his right hand for cutting down trees, and a series of [water] canisters on his left shoulder. His image would be complete with a mask against poison gas.

The Modern Sarajevan Female

She cuts wood, carries humanitarian aid, smaller canisters filled with water, does not visit a hairdresser nor a cosmetician. She is slim, and runs fast. Girls regularly visit the places where humanitarian aid is being distributed. They know the best aid-packages according to their numbers. They get up early to get water, visit cemeteries to collect wood, and greet new young refugees.

Water

Water shortages may last for days, or weeks. The reasons are always the same – no electricity, or an act of terror. Then the search starts…Those who carry water do so, depending on their strength and the number of canisters, several times a day, travelling several kilometres, waiting in a line for at least three hours. The lucky ones are those with bicycles, which are pushed rather than driven. The same with the owners of baby carriages and former market carriages. Anything that rolls will do, for everything is easier than carrying the water by hand.

One of the ways to find water is by using dowsing rods. Life, and your ability to survive, is very much about natural talents. In this case you pit your electromagnetic waves against those of the water. Gifted magicians are searching for water. Those more talented and skilful can even advise you how deep you should dig.

Sleeping

Sleeping is entirely conditioned by the arrival of water and electricity. If they appear at the same time, the shock is complete. The race against time starts – in order to use both in the best possible way. It doesn't matter that it is two or five o'clock in the morning. We cook, we wash, we clean, we take baths. Sometimes even a loaf of bread can be baked, the most wonderful gift.

Eating

By additions and with a lot of imagination, one USA lunch package can feed five people. Rice, macaroni and bread are often eaten together – otherwise it is difficult to survive. For one resident of Sarajevo, during the first seven months of war, you couldn't count more than six packages of humanitarian aid…In spring, summer and fall, all the leaves it was possible to find were used as ingredients – from parks, gardens, fields, and hills which were not [too] dangerous to visit. Combined with rice, and well seasoned, everything becomes edible. Each person in Sarajevo is very close to [being] an ideal macrobiotician, a real role-model for the health-conscious, diet-troubled West.

A war cookbook emerged spontaneously, as a survival bestseller. Recipes spread throughout the city very quickly. People are healthy, in spite of everything, for no-one eats animal fat any more, nor meat, nor cheese–meals are made without eggs, without milk, onions, meat, vegetables. We eat a precious mix of wild imagination.

(The entire Sarajevo Survival Guide is available in Sarajevo bookshops.)

Bosniak, Croat and Serb traditional wear; and the Jewish Haggadah – the holy codex brought here by Sephardic Jews. Some parts of the museum are still closed. The relaxing gardens behind the museum contain a botanical collection.

The adjacent **History Museum** (Map p97; ☎ 210 418; Zmaja od Bosne 5; admission 5KM; ☻ 9am-2pm Mon-Fri, 9am-1pm Sat & Sun) adds more recent history, displaying old photographs of Bosnia and Hercegovina. The outstanding item is a room of harrowing exhibits from the 1990s war; many are personal belongings that bear some imprint of the siege.

Butmir

A tunnel was dug from the garage of a house during the war, and led to the suburb of Dobrinje. It took Sarajevans to the relative safety of the Igman mountain, which was not in the hands of the Serbian army. It was for many a lifeline to the outside world, and is considered to be an inanimate 'war hero'. Now the **Tunnel Museum** (☎ 628 591; Tuneli 1; admission 5KM; ☻ 9am-5pm winter, to 7pm summer), displays 25m of the original 800m that ran underground. You can take a look inside and imagine what it must have been like, and then see the video (mostly reconstruction, inside the museum house) of how the Sarajevans passed through the claustrophobic tunnel. Also displayed here are various bits of Bosnian Army memorabilia.

Most people you meet in Sarajevo will have probably gone through the tunnel at some point and could tell you a personal account of their experience (although some are, understandably, not so keen on talking about it). The museum is on the far (southwestern) side of the airport in the neighbourhood of Butmir and any taxi driver will take you there from the Ilidža tram terminal. The fare should come to around 5KM.

Koševo

Another powerful reminder of the severity of the Sarajevo siege is the new cemetery by the Koševo stadium, with a sea of white tombstones, all victims of the 1992–95 siege.

TOURS

The people to show you the wild side of Bosnia and Hercegovina are at **Green Visions**

(Map p97; ☎ 717 290; www.greenvisions.ba; Radnička bb; ☻ 9am-5pm Mon-Fri). An active and innovative ecotourism organisation that works in promoting and preserving the country's pristine upland environment, Green Visions runs hiking treks, mountain-biking and rafting events, as well as visits to traditional Bosnian villages. It takes zero risks with mines, and operates in places that were never areas of conflict. A great and safe way of getting to know the off-the-beaten-track parts of the country.

The Tourist Information Centre has a list of city tour guides; **Sartour** (Map pp100-1; ☎ 238 680, 061 800 263; www.sartour-hostel-sarajevo.ba; Mula Mustafe Bašeskije 63; ☻ 9am-7pm Nov-Apr, 7am-8pm May-Oct) and **Turistička Agencija Ljubičica** (Map pp100-1; ☎ 232 109, 061 131 813; www.hostelljubicica .com; Mula Mustafe Bašeskije 65; ☻ 8am-10pm winter, 7am-11pm summer) also run city tours.

FESTIVALS & EVENTS

Sarajevo has some good festivals; the Tourist Information Centre has a monthly Programme of Cultural Events. Also check the **Sarajevo arts** (www.sarajevoarts.ba) website. Following is a selection of local festivals:

Baščaršijske Noći (Baščaršija Nights) Basically an excuse to put on and enjoy a whole range of international events covering dance, music and street theatre. It's in July.

Futura This annual festival of electronic music has been held in October; check with the Tourist Information Centre for future dates.

International Theatre Festival (MESS) October.

International Jazz Festival (www.jazzfest.ba) November.

Sarajevo Film Festival (www.sff.ba; Aug) The most notable festival in town. It presents new commercial releases and art-house movies. The atmosphere is always great.

SLEEPING

There are some good, comfortable and affordable sleeping options here. Numerous private rooms, cosy and affordable *pansions* (*pensions* or guesthouses) and expensive hotels all exist in this relatively small capital. The best choice is the *pansions*, with hosts who'll take you in like a long-lost family member. Accommodation agencies in Sarajevo are a flourishing business, especially with the growing influx of visitors to the city. Through them you can find private homes whose owners rent out rooms or apartments of varying sizes and quality. Some agencies also have their own hostels. Always look before you 'buy', and make sure the agency gives you a receipt. Recommended agencies:

Relax Tours (Map pp100-1; ☎ /fax 263 190; www.relax tours.com; Zelenih Beretki 22; r 50KM; ⊗ 9am-8pm Mon-Fri, 9am-5pm Sat) Books hotel rooms including ski hotels.

Unis Tours (Map pp100-1; ☎ 667 229; www.unis-tours .ba in Bosnian; Ferhadija 16; s/d 42/74KM; ⊗ 9am-8pm Mon-Fri, 9am-5pm Sat) Books central rooms and accepts Visa and MasterCard.

Budget

The helpful and hospitable 'would you like a coffee?' **Turistička Agencija Ljubičica** (Map pp100-1; ☎ 232 109, 061 131 813; www.hostelljubicica.com; Mula Mustafe Bašeskije 65; hostel r from €8-16, private r €6-20; ⊗ 8am-10pm winter, 7am-11pm summer) has a nearby hostel or can arrange private rooms. By arrangement it collects from the airport or stations.

Pansion Baščaršija (Map pp100-1; ☎ 232 185; Veliki Ćurčiluk 41; s/d 60/100KM) You'll probably hear the owners playing the guitar and singing, metres before you get to the door of this small *pension*. Slap bang in the centre of Baščaršija, your hosts are a father and son who have been in the business for decades. The rooms have wood-laminate walls, comfortable beds and a cosy atmosphere, and you can tell your hosts care. Bathrooms are shared.

Kod Keme (Map pp100-1; ☎ 531 140; Mali Ćurčiluk 15; s/d from 50/70KM) A private house in a quiet backstreet just south of the Gazi-Husrevbey Mosque. The rooms are white and simply decorated and the 1st floor ones feel a bit like something out of a convent – but in a good way. The Bosnian-Aussie owner speaks excellent English.

Green Hotel (☎ 639 701; www.green.co.ba; Ustanička bb, Ilidža; s/d/tr 45/70.2/105KM) For those who work out, this tidy cheapie (4km from the city centre) comes with a free fully equipped gym and sauna. The tram terminus is a 150m jog away, then there's a 20-minute ride into Baščaršija – or you could run all the way.

Midrange

Pansion Čobanija (Map p97; ☎ 441 749; fax 203 937; Čobanija 29; s/d 80/120KM) If you get tired of sightseeing and partying, you can spend the evening relaxing on the sofas in this *pansion*'s big lounge and watch a bit of telly. (But that's not what you're here for, get out and party.) The rooms are all different, light

and fresh. Consider 202 with its neo-Art Deco mirrored furniture.

Hotel Hecco (Map pp100-1; ☎ 273 730; Medresa 1; s/d/tr 70/100/140KM; P ☐) A spanking new hotel that will leave you out of breath after the mighty walk uphill from the centre. It's designed in what seem like the colours and lines of Mondrian, with water features and even a miniature garden in the reception area. The rooms are fresh and clean and the staff friendly.

Top End

Villa Orient (Map pp100-1; ☎ 232 754; orient@bih.net. ba; Oprkanj 6; s/d 150/200KM; ☐) Running water is relaxingly audible outside this Ottoman building in the heart of Baščaršija. The reception area is flashy and adorned with paintings of one of Bosnia's best artists, Mersad Berber, but the rooms feel a little 'deflated' and their sparkle a tad faded. There's a free fitness centre, Internet (3KM per hour) and a coffee bar open until midnight, with a lovely garden. Oprkanj is a tiny street off Telali.

Hotel Europa Garni (Map pp100-1; ☎ 232 855; www .europa-garni.ba; Vladislava Skarića 3; s/d 183/286KM; P) Fantastic views of Baščaršija's profile from the hotel terrace (and some rooms). The rooms are spacious and, if you're driving, the private parking is useful and that may well tip the balance in this hotel's favour. Once an extension of the 'real' Hotel Europa which is now a war ruin, this place has some modern adaptations including wheelchair access.

EATING

The eating-out scene is well established in Sarajevo. At the snack or quick-lunch

---

THE AUTHOR'S CHOICE

Inat Kuća (Spite House; Map pp100-1; ☎ 447 867; Velika Alifakovac 1; meals 7-10KM) This is one of the loveliest places in Sarajevo, not only because the food is great, but because it's in a gorgeous wooden Ottoman house. The story goes that the restaurant was once on the other side of the river but when the authorities wanted to demolish it during construction of the town hall, the owner insisted it be rebuilt here – piece by piece. Hence the name, Spite House. This is the ideal spot to try *sarma* (pickled cabbage leaves stuffed with minced meat) and *Begova čorba* (Bey's soup). In warm weather the riverside terrace is *the* spot for a bit of afternoon relaxation and reading.

---

level there are *ćevabdžinicas* (places selling *ćevapčići*) and *buregdžinicas* (places selling *burek*); some of the fancy expensive ones are no better than the hole-in-the-wall variety. A bit more upmarket, and aimed at the tourist, are a string of restaurants offering Bosnian cuisine with a little more variety. The top-notch restaurants attract the international clients (there are a lot of them) with international cuisines. The majority of eateries are in the centre, in Baščaršija, and up from the river on the south side.

Restaurants are open from 8am to 11pm unless otherwise mentioned.

Restaurants

Hot Wok Café (Map p97; ☎ 203 322; Maršala Tita 12; www.hotwokcaffe.com; meals 10-15KM; ☻ 8am-midnight) The only Thai restaurant in town, and it's a good one at that. The small space is draped in modern Asian furnishings in the style of the once-ultrafashionable Buddha Bar décor, the Thai chef prepares food in an open-plan kitchen, tables and chairs are high and the food delicious. Whoever wrote the menu was a real comedian – names for dishes with puns on the word 'wok' are endless with sizzlers like 'Moonwoker' and 'Prawn Net Wok' (and the bizarre, and wok-less, 'Noodles Eat Your Heart Out'). There's also a good choice of cocktails.

To Be or Not to Be (Map pp100-1; ☎ 233 205; Čizmedžiluk 5; meals 4-8KM; ☻ 11am-11pm) A tiny place decorated in traditional Bosnian style with wooden stairs leading to another tiny

room, here there are grills, generous salads and tangy seafood dishes to be consumed. The name actually has the 'Not to Be' bit crossed out, dating back to the war years when, according to the owners, not surviving was not an option. Čizmedžiluk is a small street off Ćurčiluk Veliki.

Dveri (Map pp100-1; ☎ 537 020; Prote Baković bb; meals 5-12KM; ☻ 11am-4pm & 7-11pm; ✗) A small, small restaurant, so hidden you might never find it. But if you do, it's well worth eating in what looks like someone's kitchen laid out to expect family guests. Watch your food being prepared from a bench and in- hale the pungent smells of garlic and chillies which, incidentally, also hang all around you. The speciality is Macedonian polenta, a wedge of polenta flavoured with garlic and cream and speckled with ham. Yum.

Bosanska Kuća (Map pp100-1; ☎ 237 320; Bravadžiluk 3; meals 6-9KM; ☻ 24hr) 'Come eat,' says the waiter in national costume, invit- ing you into a restaurant promoting Bos- nian tradition in food and setting. This snappy joint makes choosing easier with its colour-picture menu – maybe a kebab, some grilled fish, or stuffed peppers or aubergines for vegetarians.

Metropolis (Map pp100-1; ☎ 203 315; Maršala Tita 21; meals 7-15KM; ☻ 8am-midnight) Peach walls, little round tables, soft music and plenty of chatter. This restaurant and a café (no alcohol) is a very popular spot with the lo- cals. The menu is mainly pasta based and you can choose to have spaghetti, linguini, penne or macaroni with your sauce of choice. Great cakes too.

Park Prinčeva (Map p97; ☎ 222 708; Iza Hidra 7; meals 7-15KM; ☻ 9am-late) The restaurant for a romantic liaison: tables overlook the twin- kling lights of Sarajevo way down below, velvet music tinkles from the keys of the white piano, and there's *Begova čorba* (Bey's soup; a Bosnian aphrodisiac) on the menu. During the day the restaurant has the best views of the town from its terrace.

Karuzo (Map pp100-1; ☎ 444 467; Mehmeda Spahe bb; meals 6-18KM; ☻ noon-3pm & 6-11pm Mon-Fri, 6- 11pm Sat) It's a rare thing in this country, a meatless menu in a restaurant, not to men- tion a sushi menu. But here you have it. The place is tiny and only 18 can sit together at one time. It's a good idea to book, as it's popular. The owner takes a personal inter- est in your order and cooks it himself.

BOSNIA & HERCEGOVINA

Vinoteka (Map p97; ☎ 214 996; Skenderija 12; meals 14-20KM; ⏰ 11am-3pm & 7-11pm, bar to 1am) A rather upmarket two-floor restaurant and wine bar that specialises in various European cooking schools. This is where the expats come to lunch and dine, as do important people and businesspeople. The menu changes weekly, uses only fresh ingredients and is not too pricey if you want to treat yourself.

Restaurant Jež (Map pp100-1; ☎ 650 312; Zelenih Beretki 14; meals 16-20KM; ⏰ 5pm-late) The name means 'hedgehog', which doesn't feature on the menu of this swish underground restaurant. The entrance is down an alley opposite the Orthodox Cathedral. Go past the old BMW motorcycle, down the stairs, through the antiques arcade, and you're there. The cuisine is typical Bosnian tinged with international extras and the warm seafood salad is worth a try. While you're waiting count the grandmother clocks on the wall. Do they all chime together?

Mash (Map pp100-1; ☎ 308 616; Branilaca Sarajeva; meals 3-14KM; ⏰ 7.30am-1am Mon-Thu, to 3am Fri, 9am-3am Sat, 10am-midnight Sun) On the first floor of an unimpressive looking building, the interior of this fashionable bar is a cool place for a proper breakfast. Sandwiches, snacks and a few veggie dishes (such as veg fajitas) are good to get your stomach out of the nauseous pits of another-late-night.

Quick Eats

Even fast food is enjoyed slowly and quietly in Sarajevo. *Burek* stuffed with meat, cheese, potato or spinach is scoffed sitting down in a *buregdžinica*, accompanied by a fridge-cold yogurt, and the *ćevapi* (small, rolled pieces of spiced, minced lamb meat) are gobbled in a *ćevabdžinica* or on a park bench. Even though there are more quick-eat joints than you can ever sample (not that you'd want to) the following two are city legends.

Željo (Map pp100-1; Bravadžiluk bb; meals 6-8KM) For the best *ćevapčići*, come here. This place is about as famous as Baščaršija itself, and many will say that you haven't been to Sarajevo till you've eaten here. And it's true. The *ćevapčići* are succulent, the *lepinja* bread divine, and for an extra boost, try adding fresh onions to the combination. You might not have any friends later, though.

Kod Seje (Map pp100-1; Mula Mustafe Bašeskije bb; ⏰ 8am-10pm; meals 3-5KM) Just behind the cathedral, the place itself is as basic as it gets, but the *burek* is prepared *ispod sača*, which means that it's baked under hot coals, in a covered tray. You can see the method as you wait. Combine it with a cool yogurt for the ultimate Bosnian fast-food experience.

Butik-Badem (Map pp100-1; ☎ 533 135; Abadžiluk 12) This health-food shop, just downhill from the cobbled square in Baščaršija, has alternative snacks, from yummy chocolate-coated pistachios to fruit bars and nuts.

Self-Catering

Markale market (Map pp100-1; Mula Mustafe Bašeskije; ⏰ 7am-5pm Mon-Sat, to 2pm Sun) This market, behind the cathedral, overflows with fruit and vegetables.

Town market (Map pp100-1; ⏰ 7am-5pm Mon-Sat, to 2pm Sun) This small market off Ferhadija mostly sells fresh dairy products and eggs.

DRINKING

Drinking places turn over rapidly in this city: go away for a few months and there'll be somewhere new and the favourite of last month will have closed. As in most of the Balkans, the line that divides the café from the bar is thin.

Mash (left) is a quiet daytime kitten that turns into a party animal at night, and Sarajevo's youth gets mashed, dancing the night away. It's also a good place for breakfast.

So.Ba (Map p97; ☎ 210 369; Obala Maka Dizdara 3; ⏰ 9am-10pm Mon-Sat, noon-10pm Sun) Inside the Academy of Arts, with thick smoke, pumping music and lots of art students getting into the party mood. There is an Internet café upstairs.

Zlatna Ribica (Map pp100-1; ☎ 215 369; Kaptol 5; ⏰ 9am-late) A quiet place to start the evening, or just enjoy a drink. You will certainly be entertained by the décor in this bar: sewing machine parts, baroque bric-a-brac, *fin-de-siècle* Paris and Vienna, and perhaps a little Art Deco get on smashingly on the walls. The lighting is warm, and there are newspapers in English for the passing tourist. Drinks come with a side plate of complimentary nuts, dried figs or, if you're having a coffee, a biscuit, and the *rakija* (brandy) glass has a little glass cap.

City Pub (Map pp100-1; ☎ 299 916; Despićeva bb; meals 6-9KM; ⏰ 8am-late) A daytime café-bar, with Lebanese and Mexican taste ticklers. At night it's a big music and drinking venue with local bands playing blues, jazz or rock most nights. This pub swings, even the bouncers smile.

Karabit Café (Map pp100-1; ☎ 712 010; Zelenih Beretki 8; ☺ 9am-10pm Mon-Sat, 10am-6pm Sun) If you want to see Sarajevo's creative crowd, this is the place to be, and if not, it's still a great place to be. An airy space, freshly squeezed juices and a huge choice of teas; bring (or buy) a book and relax.

BuyBook (Map pp100-1; ☎ 206 545; Radićeva 4; ☺ 9am-10pm Mon-Sat, 10am-6pm Sun) Part of a great bookshop (see p96), where you can find titles in English and enjoy a good coffee and a good read.

Sarajevo Brewery (Map pp100-1; ☎ 445 430; Trg Heroja 35; meals 8-18KM; ☺ noon-late) Above the river on the south bank stands a large red-and-cream edifice with copper drainpipes that is Sarajevo's famous brewery. Now part of it has been converted into a cavernous bar, all dark stained wood and brass railings. It serves standard Sarajevo beer plus a pleasant dark beer with a caramel aftertaste. When you've had too much (liquid), ride the brass-doored lifts downstairs to the loo.

Delikatesna Radnja (Delicatessen Shop; Map pp100-1; Obala Kulina Bana 10; ☺ 8am-midnight Mon-Sat, 10.30am-midnight Sun) A lively bar on the river bank and a sunny spot during the day, great for relaxing and chatting on the cushioned benches in the front.

ENTERTAINMENT

Check and ask about other jazz clubs around town, they are forever opening and closing.

Nightclubs

Buddha Bar (Map p97; Radićeva bb; ☺ 9pm-late) Three rooms that strive to be a (much) smaller sister to its Parisian counterpart, the décor here is all bamboo and Buddha. The music is good, the atmosphere relaxed and dancing and drinking go on until the wee hours of the morning.

Bar (Map p97; Maršala Tita 7; ☺ 7am-3am) A laid-back club with camouflage and white deck chairs and bolsters under the trees, tropical-lounge style. There is dancing inside and parties on weekends.

Club (Map p97; ☎ 550 550; Maršala Tita 7; ☺ 10am-late) Just around the corner from Bar, inside the large building on the corner of Maršala Tita and Alipašina streets. Inside, take the

first door on the left and then go down the stairs. A 'C' wearing a bowler hat hanging on the building corner is a good indicator of the club's slightly secretive whereabouts. There is DJ music or local bands grooving away in this basement club. There are pizzas (12KM to 25KM) in the restaurant out the back, too.

Sloga (Map p97; Mehmeda Spahe 20; ☺ 6pm-late) If you want to see Sarajevan nightlife pre-1992, this is the place. The three floors cover everything from folky and unplugged sounds to concert space and old Yugo songs that make the punters jump up and down. Drinks are cheap and the atmosphere great – it's one of the city's favourites.

Clou Jazz Club (Map pp100-1; ☎ 061 203 984; Mula Mustafe Bašeskije 5; ☺ 11pm-late) A tiny jazz joint, located in a spooky building that seems like the wrong place for jazz. But fear not and tread bravely down the stairs into the smoky rooms where you can hear local bands plucking, beating, blowing and strumming some good tunes.

Cinemas

Oslobođenje, Sarajevo's daily paper, has daily cinema listings in the 'Kina' column.

Obala Meeting Point (Map p97; ☎ 668 186; Hamdije Kreševljakovića 13; admission from 3KM) Most cinemas show subtitled American blockbusters; this cinema in Skenderija is extra comfortable.

Theatre

National Theatre (Map p97; ☎ 663 647; Obala Kulina Bana 9) This theatre puts on concerts, ballet and plays.

SHOPPING

Baščaršija is the place for souvenirs, especially the craft shops (Map pp100–1) on Bravadžiluk. Check out the special 'war souvenirs' or ashtrays, pens and plant pots made out of mortar cases, empty bullets, etc. There are the more conventional copper coffee sets, jewellery or Oriental shoes, slippers and rugs. Be adventurous and bargain.

Don't miss the *Survival Map* (15KM), a cartoonlike map of wartime Sarajevo, available in bookshops, also produced by FAMA, the group responsible for the *Sarajevo Survival Guide* (see p102).

Brusa Bezistan (Map pp100-1; cnr Ferhadija & Gazi Husrevbegova) This certainly does not look like your typical shopping centre (nor does it hide an IKEA inside) but it's a gorgeous place packed with shops selling clothes, fake designer shades, handiwork, souvenirs and other necessities.

Bosnian Handicrafts (Map pp100-1; in Tuzla ☎ 035-282 554; www.bosnianhandicrafts.com; Ćulhan 1; ☷ 8am-8pm Mon-Fri, 9am-7pm Sat, 10am-4pm Sun) Contribute to a good cause by getting yourself a pair of knitted mitts or slippers from this nonprofit organisation that works with refugees. Located in Baščaršija.

GETTING THERE & AWAY
Air
Sarajevo's international **airport** (☎ 234 841, 289 200; Kurta Schorka 34) is about 6.5km southwest of the town centre. For connections via Sarajevo airport see p132.

Bus
Courtesy of the country's political division, Sarajevo is blessed with two bus stations. Buses to Banja Luka go from both.

Bus schedules do change but the Tourist Information Centre always has an up-to-date schedule.

MAIN BUS STATION
Services from this **station** (Map p97; ☎ 213 100; Put Života 8) serve all places outside the RS as well as Banja Luka.

Frequent buses go to Mostar (one way 9KM, 2½ hours), three to Bihać (27KM, 6½ hours) and two to Banja Luka (23KM, five hours).

For Croatia, three buses run to Zagreb (€30, eight hours), four to Split (€30, eight hours) and one to Dubrovnik (€30, seven hours, 7.15am).

LUKAVICA BUS STATION
This **station** (☎ 057-677 377; Lukavica village) has six buses to Belgrade (20KM, eight hours), four to Podgorica (€10, eight hours) and hourly buses to Banja Luka (18.50KM, five hours).

For the Lukavica terminus take trolleybus 103 from Trg Austrijski (Map pp100–1) to the last stop and walk 150m.

Train
Services from the **train station** (Map p97; ☎ 655 330; Put Života 2) run to Mostar (9KM, three hours, departs 6.20am and 7pm) and Banja Luka (21KM, five hours, departs 10.30am) with international services to Zagreb and Budapest (see p133).

GETTING AROUND
To/From the Airport
A taxi (15KM) is the easiest way to get into town from the airport. A cheaper alternative is to take the taxi to Ilidža (5KM) and transfer to tram No 3 (1.20KM) for Baščaršija.

Car & Motorcycle
Much of Baščaršija is pedestrian and the rest is narrow, making parking either illegal or impossible. The best option is to park to the west and use the tram.

THE ADVANTAGES OF TRAINS

Travellers going to Sarajevo from Mostar should consider the twice-daily train that originates at Ploče on the coast. The best train, involving an early start, leaves the neglected station in Mostar at 7.20am.

Don't expect a big train, maybe a loco and two carriages; you'll probably get a compartment to yourself. There is a buffet service, of sorts, including a range of spirits (which at that hour might be just a tad premature) and coffee.

This is a formidable journey (for the train that is). The first part involves puffing and panting alongside the pea green Neretva River, which, nicely situated in a gorge, has been dammed for electricity. If you ate trout in Mostar, as likely as not it came from one of the fish farms here. Leaving the gorge the train executes a massive U-turn and goes through a series of loops, switchbacks, tunnels and viaducts as it climbs slowly over the Bjelašnica Mountains to Sarajevo.

Another useful train where poor patronage works to the traveller's advantage is the overnight Banja Luka to Belgrade service. It's marginally cheaper than the bus, and takes longer. But which would you prefer? To arrive in Belgrade in the early hours in a cramped bus seat or to travel by train in your own compartment with seating that allows you to stretch right out?

Car-hire agencies at the airport include **Budget** (☎ 427 670), **Hertz** (☎ 235 050), **Avis** (☎ 463 598), **Europcar** (☎ 289 273) and **National** (☎ 893 500). Prices start from about €40 a day, less for longer periods.

Public Transport

An efficient tram network runs east–west between Baščaršija and Ilidža. Tram No 4 from Baščaršija peels off at the main bus station; tram No 1 goes between the main bus station and Ilidža. Buy tickets at kiosks near tram stations (1.20KM; 1.50KM if you buy them from the driver). You can get a daily pass for 5KM from a kiosk. Punch your ticket on board, as there are inspectors about. Bus and trolleybus tickets work the same way.

Taxi

All of Sarajevo's taxis have meters that begin at 2KM and cost about 1KM per kilometre. Call **Radio Taxi** (☎ 1515) or **Yellow Taxi Cab** (☎ 1516).

AROUND SARAJEVO

You can imagine that, as it was chosen to host the Winter Olympics all those years ago, Sarajevo's mountains are as smooth as a ball of ice cream and as varied as Ben & Jerry's flavours. Now, that doesn't mean that you should go up there and start eating snow – but you should head up for a taste of the skiing. Sarajevans are crazy about their skiing, and hotels and *pansions* near ski areas are usually packed. They only accept guests staying for a whole week; the changeover day is Saturday. All accommodation offers a choice of B&B, half or full board; due to this and the effects of the war, restaurants are rather limited, although in season there'll be the ubiquitous *ćevapčići* stands. Many go up for a day's skiing, too.

Other places of interest around Sarajevo are the 100m-tall **Skakavac Waterfalls** located 20 minutes north of the city, and the **Bijambara Caves** near the town of Olovo (around 30 minutes northeast of Sarajevo). The five caves can be seen on guided tours and are believed to be just the beginning of what remains to be discovered inside the mountain. For both of these you will need your own transport unless you join an organised tour through one of the tourist agencies in Sarajevo.

Jahorina
☎ 057
Slightly old-fashioned thanks to there having been no large-scale development here, Jahorina is a gorgeous, simple resort, perfect for relaxing winter sports. The slopes are nearly deserted, and with 20km of runs for alpine and Nordic skiing, you'll feel like the king (or queen) of the hill. Jahorina is in RS, 25km southeast of Sarajevo. The winter season is mid-December to the end of March. Note that all prices could be lower if you are staying for over a week, or if you are in a group.

SLEEPING & EATING

Pansion Sport (☎ 270 333; granzov@paleol.net; r per person 25-55KM; **P**) For those who'd rather be in the Swiss Alps, this is a pleasant Swiss chalet–style guesthouse. It's got a prime position at the base of the ski runs. Rates are dependent on the season and in summer the place is only open on Saturdays and Sundays. Ski-equipment hire is a possibility in the winter.

Hotel Košuta (☎ 270 401; fax 270 400; per person Dec-Feb half board 33-75KM, per person Mar-Nov B&B/ half board/full board 30/33/38KM; **P**) Perfect for skiing as the hotel is just 50m from the ski lift – jump right in there. Košuta is a big, made-for-the-Olympics hotel, some rooms have balconies and the ones at the back have fabulous views.

Hotel Dva Javora (☎ 270 481; fax 270 480; s/d/ tr 70/90/105KM, breakfast/half board/full board extra 5/10/20KM; **P**) This is a brand-new exercise in light-coloured wood and blue furnishings that's open all year. It's very cosy and friendly, in complete contrast to the large impersonal hotels.

Hotel Kristal (☎ 270 430; www.kristal-jahorina .com; winter s/d B&B 75/130, half board 65/150, full board 95/170KM; **P** 🖳) An enlarged mountain-hut of a hotel, the rooms here are comfortable, although not spacious. It is open in summer, when you can bargain those winter prices down. It can be booked out for winter by August.

GETTING THERE & AWAY
There is no public transport for Jahorina and you will need your own wheels, with chains on them during the winter months. The drive could take up to an hour in heavy snow, but the views are beautiful from the road.

BOSNIA & HERCEGOVINA

WARNING

Stay on the groomed ski runs as there are mines in the vicinity of both resorts.

Bjelašnica

☎ 033

This is a more compact area than Jahorina and is within the Federation of Bosnia & Hercegovina. There's only one hotel, but fortunately it's only a few minutes from the skiing action.

Named after old Maršal Tito, the well-equipped **Hotel Maršal** (☎ 279 100; www.hotel-marsal.ba; r summer B&B/half board/full board 65/75/85KM, winter 85/95/105KM; **P** 🖳) has several storeys and commands views over the nearby ski slopes. It will take guests for less than seven days in winter but slaps on a surcharge. Added attractions include a disco with bands in the winter season, excursions to traditional Bosnian villages and transport to Igman, a small nearby skiing field with a lift and ski jump.

There are no buses from central Sarajevo, but there is a minibus from Ilidža that travels to Bjelašnica two times a day (2KM). Ask at the Tourist Information Centre for the times of departure.

Ilidža

This is one of Sarajevo's favourite weekend getaway locations. While its appeal is now limited to the modern man, Ilidža was appealing even in Neolithic times. Evidence of life dating back to 2400 BC to the so-called 'Butmir settlement' has been found here. The Romans, drawn by its healing spas, made this a permanent settlement. The remains of the Roman settlements are near the source of the Bosna River, commonly known as **Vrelo Bosne**. The lush park and wide *aleja* (alley) where Sarajevans jog, stroll or cycle is a beautiful and relaxing area. Get to Ilidža by taking tram 1 from Sarajevo and getting off at the last stop.

HERCEGOVINA

Hercegovina is the country's silent partner, the part that no-one in the West ever mentions, because they can't pronounce it (if you'd like to attempt it, it's *Her-tze-goh-*

vina). But when people say 'Bosnia', what they really mean is Bosnia and Hercegovina, and if the talk is of an arid, Mediterranean landscape, then it's the latter they are talking about. The region is distinct and beautiful, with summers so hot that the fruits of the pomegranate and fig trees sag down towards the parched earth. It is famed for its fine wine, delicious food, fast-flowing rivers, and beautiful towns and cities. Plus the Adriatic coast is only an hour's drive away.

MOSTAR

☎ 036 / pop 94,000

One of the things that most people know about Bosnia and Hercegovina is 'the Old Bridge in Mostar'. And so it's impossible to write an introduction to the city without plunging for the image of the World Heritage-listed stone bridge for inspiration. Before its destruction, and over the bridge's 500-year life, people from the four corners of the earth came to see its beauty; after its destruction curious visitors came to see the fact that it wasn't there any more, and now with the rebuilding of the 'new Old Bridge' in 2004, the magnetic pull of the structure is again gaining strength. And no wonder. Visiting Mostar and seeing the Old Bridge once again span the emerald Neretva River is a great experience.

On each side of the bridge is Mostar's Old Town, a cobbled Ottoman quarter that cradles the city's craftsmen and artists and that has itself had a bit of a face-lift. There are beautiful 16th-century mosques, interesting museums and endless cafés here. The restaurant terraces, dotted on the steep rocky riverbanks, have perfect views of the Old Bridge at sunset and the green rapids of the beautiful Neretva. Stretching further out are old, unchanged neighbourhoods that show Mostar's past lives while the new parts of town bring forth its more recent guises.

Immediately upon entering the city you will notice the war-damaged buildings, although the Old Town is now more or less rebuilt. The city suffered an extreme battering during the '90s conflict, and was among the worst-affected places in the entire country when it came to architectural destruction. Many ruins remain along the former front-line area, which is slowly being rebuilt.

EAST BANK, WEST BANK: MOSTAR'S RECENT HISTORY

In April 1992 Mostar was attacked by Serbian and Montenegrin forces from the surrounding hills. When the heavy bombardment subsided after some six months, fresh trouble was brewing in the injured city. On 9 May 1993 a bitter conflict started between the Croats and Muslims, formerly allied against the Serbian army. The Bosnian Croat forces attacked the Muslims of the city, expelling them from their homes and moving them en masse to detention camps on the east bank of the Neretva River. For two years the conflict continued, with the more powerful Croats pummelling the Muslim side of the city to rubble and strategically destroying the Old Bridge in November 1993. This single event resonated louder than the thousands of dead, and seemed to symbolise the apparent hopelessness of the Bosnian war.

Mostar surfaced in 1995 severely damaged, both physically and spiritually. The once mixed population was divided. Many left the city, and crossing from one side of the town to the other often resulted in revenge beatings. The city resembled Dresden after the end of WWII, and all of its bridges were destroyed.

In the years since, things have gradually improved. Mostar has been largely rebuilt and many refugees have returned to their prewar homes (although others remain where they had fled to during the conflict). Crossing from one part of town to the other is now completely trouble-free, and Mostarians go shopping and strolling as they did before the war. Buildings have been reconstructed and renovated, but there is still a significant amount of ghostlike rubble, particularly along the old front-line area, the Bulevar. The rebuilding of the Old Bridge (Stari Most) has helped to raise the city's spirit, although it will take decades for true reconciliation to take place.

Orientation

Though there are no physical barriers here, Croats live on the western side of the Neretva River and Muslims on the east (though Muslims also control a small strip on the river's west bank). These days people cross freely between these areas, and for travellers there's absolutely no fuss.

Maps are sold at local kiosks and tourist agencies.

Information

INTERNET ACCESS

Cob Net (☎ 555 301; Maršala Tita bb; per hr 1KM; ☾ 8am-10pm) Situated behind Maršala Tita.

Hotel Bristol (☎ 500 100; Mostarskog Bataljona bb; per hr 5KM; ☾ 24hr) There's one Internet computer in the foyer here.

LEFT LUGGAGE

Luggage storage is available in the bus station for 2KM per item per day.

MONEY

Raiffeisen Bank (☎ 398 398; Kralja Tvrtka; ☾ 8am-4.30pm Mon-Fri, to 1pm Sat) Cashes travellers cheques and has an ATM that takes all cards.

Zagrebačka Bank (☎ 312 120; Kardinala Stepinca 18; ☾ 8am-2.30pm Mon-Fri, to noon Sat) Does Western Union transfers, cashes travellers cheques and has an ATM that takes all cards.

POST

Post office (☎ 327 915; Dr Ante Starčevića bb; ☾ 7am-7pm Mon-Fri, to 6pm Sat) Poste-restante mail from window 12 and a bureau de change.

TELEPHONE & FAX

Telephone Centre (☎ 327 915; Dr Ante Starčevića bb; ☾ 7am-8pm Mon-Fri, to 7pm Sat, 8am-noon Sun) Located at the post office.

TOURIST INFORMATION

Tourist Information Centre (☎ 397 350; www .hercegovina.ba; Onešćukova bb; ☾ 9am-9pm) A useful one-stop shop. Sells maps, guidebooks and postcards, and books accommodation, buses, planes and trains.

TRAVEL AGENCIES

Atlas Travel Agency (☎ 326 631; fax 318 771; Kardinala Stepinca bb; ☾ 9am-4pm Mon-Fri, to noon Sat) Books hotels, flights, ferries and arranges car hire; maps available.

Fortuna Travel Agency (☎ 552 197; www.fortuna.ba; Trg Ivana Krndelja 1; ☾ 8am-4.30pm Mon-Fri, 9am-1pm Sat) Sells maps and booklets, books accommodation, and arranges plane and ferry tickets and car hire. It's in the bus station.

Sights

Old Bridge (Stari Most) is the obvious place to start sightseeing. Originally built in 1556 to replace a nearby wooden bridge, it was named 'petrified moon' on account of its

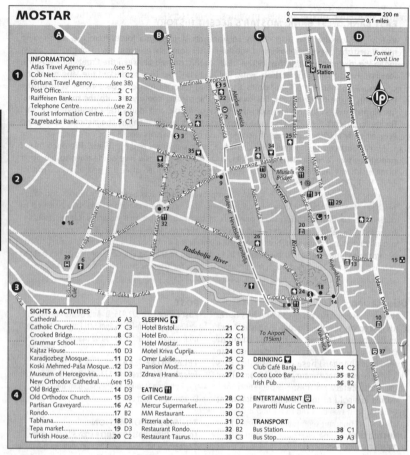

MOSTAR

0   200 m
0   0.1 miles

Former Front Line

INFORMATION
Atlas Travel Agency..................(see 5)
Cob Net.....................................1 C2
Fortuna Travel Agency...........(see 38)
Post Office.................................2 C1
Raiffeisen Bank..........................3 B2
Telephone Centre...................(see 2)
Tourist Information Centre.........4 D3
Zagrebacka Bank.......................5 C1

SIGHTS & ACTIVITIES
Cathedral...................................6 A3
Catholic Church.........................7 C3
Crooked Bridge.........................8 C3
Grammar School........................9 C2
Kajtaz House............................10 D3
Karadjozbeg Mosque...............11 D2
Koski Mehmed-Paša Mosque....12 D3
Museum of Hercegovina...........13 D3
New Orthodox Cathedral.......(see 15)
Old Bridge...............................14 D3
Old Orthodox Church...............15 D3
Partisan Graveyard...................16 A2
Rondo......................................17 B2
Tabhana...................................18 D3
Tepa market.............................19 D3
Turkish House...........................20 C2

SLEEPING
Hotel Bristol.............................21 C2
Hotel Ero..................................22 C1
Hotel Mostar............................23 B1
Motel Kriva Ćuprija...................24 C3
Omer Lakiše..............................25 C2
Pansion Most............................26 C3
Zdrava Hrana............................27 D2

EATING
Grill Centar...............................28 C2
Mercur Supermarket.................29 D2
MM Restaurant.........................30 C2
Pizzeria abc..............................31 D2
Restaurant Rondo.....................32 B2
Restaurant Taurus.....................33 C3

DRINKING
Club Café Banja........................34 C2
Coco Loco Bar..........................35 B2
Irish Pub..................................36 B2

ENTERTAINMENT
Pavarotti Music Centre..............37 D4

TRANSPORT
Bus Station...............................38 C1
Bus Stop...................................39 A3

To Airport (15km)

slender and elegant beauty. Recently rebuilt, the 'new version' resembles the old in minute detail, since the architects and the builders used the original methods traced back to the 16th century (see opposite).

A great time of the year to be here is during the annual diving competition that takes place every July. Young men from all over the country (and all over former Yugoslavia) gather to jump off the bridge into the river 21m below. Before the war the young divers were known as 'the Icaruses of Mostar' and their display of masculinity had a certain pulling power among the girls of the town. In fact, a man was not a real man if he hadn't plunged off the bridge at least once in his life.

During the time when the Old Bridge was destroyed and a wooden bridge stood in its place (1993–2004), the diving competition carried on almost as an act of defiance. The divers jumped off the presumed highest point, replaced by a wooden plank. Now the bridge has been rebuilt, it seems that Mostar's young divers are embracing the tradition with particular frenzy. And while once upon a time boys dove into the freezing Neretva for nothing more than a cigarette or their macho-badge, today's divers are a little more demanding. Hard currency is what they're after, and foreign currency particular. The diving spectacle is a performance and the members of the 'divers' club', housed in one of the towers on the very edge of the bridge, provides the showmen.

Watch the way they do it, it's rather intricate. Two blokes stand around, one of them being the diver and the other 'the hustler' (although they take their roles in turn). One stands on the edge of the bridge, as if preparing to dive, while the other starts clapping his hands maniacally 'to excite the tourists'. Once enough touristy-looking people gather around, the happy clapper collects money from the crowd. They will not dive until they've collected their minimum (the actual figure is still a mystery). The sign that they've gathered enough is when another bloke runs out to the bridge with a kettle of cold water, which the diver will pour on his head to prepare for the shock of the freezing Neretva River. (The river retains its cold temperature even on the hottest of days.) And so on, all day long. You've got to admire them, really.

On each side of the bridge are the **towers of Tara and Helebija**. They stand as architectural anchors to the bridge and as guardians of the crossing. Semicircular Tara, on the west bank, served as a gunpowder and ammunition store during Ottoman times

---

REBUILDING HISTORY

In 1557, at the request of local businessmen, the Turkish architect Hayrudin was employed by Suleyman the Magnificent to build a stone bridge in Mostar. It would replace the suspension bridge which was said to frighten tradesmen as they swung and wobbled their way over the fast-flowing Neretva River.

Mostar's Old Bridge took nine years to build and was opened some time between July and September in 1566. It was built out of local Tenelija stone, which is very pale and appears to change colour depending on the position of the sun and the strength of its rays. Local history contains many myths surrounding the construction of Old Bridge – one of the favourites is that Hayrudin was so afraid that the bridge would collapse once the scaffolding was removed that he fled to the nearby Dervish monastery and never saw the completed structure. By contrast, another story tells how, after the scaffolding had been removed, Hayrudin lay under the bridge for three days, risking his life to prove the structure was stable. Whatever the truth, the bridge stood for 427 years.

The bridge was destroyed in November 1993 and it took more than 10 years for it to be rebuilt. Quite apart from the expectations of Mostar's citizens, the reconstruction challenge was overwhelming. As it was such an important symbol, the new bridge had to be identical to the Old Bridge. It was decided to rebuild it using the 16th-century methods, without the interference of modern building technology. A puzzle presented itself in the old stone-construction work. In ancient times stone was quarried and cut using average measures and the results depended largely on its natural availability. It was assembled onto the centring almost randomly. So although the original bridge was soundly built, it was not regular, and the anomalies created by this method of assembling were at the same time both the real beauty of the bridge and the origin of its complex geometry. In the rebuilding, this random assembly had to be replicated; in order to recreate the shape and the imperfections, each stone had to be cut separately to its own particular shape and planned position.

The same type of stone from the same quarry was used for the rebuilding project. Tenelija stone has good mechanical properties – it is light and resistant to damp and frost. The original blocks that had fallen into the river in 1993 had become unusable by the time they were recovered in 1996. The relatively soft stone had eroded and the metal connections had rusted and created cracks that had rendered it unusable. However, part of the Old Bridge that remained standing after the bridge's destruction – five rows of stone and the whole of the abutment – has been used on the west bank of the Neretva River.

The bombing of the bridge in 1993 was partly a strategic act, but it was also a symbolic destruction of what the bridge represented: beauty, unity and history. Mostar housed Christians, Muslims and Jews alike, but when the bridge was destroyed, it became a divided city. With its reconstruction, the people of Mostar are being reminded of how they used to live, and how they might live again.

and now houses 'the divers' cooperative'; Helebija, on the east bank, housed a dungeon on its lower floors and a guardhouse above. Herceguša, a third tower, stands behind the Tara.

Good spots from which to take photos of the bridge and towers are a small terrace garden amid some art galleries next to 158 Maršala Tita on the eastern bank; the west bank of the Neretva right under the Old Bridge, also a great spot from where to watch the divers plunge; and the top of Kujundžiluk street.

The cobbled street to the east of the bridge is **Kujundžiluk**, part of the Old Town. One of the oldest streets in Mostar, this is the place where *kujunžije* (copper beaters) traditionally work their craft, and the street is named after them. You will also see some wonderful paintings in the artists' studios along the street. It's a lovely place in which to wander a little, and when you hear the sound of hammering on copper (or as some romantically call it 'Mostar's heartbeat'), step into the dark shop and watch the craftsmen at work.

Across the Old Bridge is the other side of the **Old Town**, and its narrow streets are filled with little shops selling Turkish-style souvenirs, and cafés and restaurants. Nearby is the miniature version of the Old Bridge, **Crooked Bridge** (Kriva Ćuprija). It is said to have been the model on which its bigger sister was built. This too is a reconstruction, since the old Ćuprija was destroyed by a flood in 2001. Unfortunately, the new construction does not do justice to the old one; an elegant and frail arch has been replaced by a chunky, clumsy one.

Back in the Old Town, one of the most popular places for a freshly squeezed lemonade, coffee sipping, or *ćevap* eating is the **Tabhana** (Stari Grad bb), formerly a Turkish bath, now a courtyard with lots of bars and restaurants. You will recognise it by the six domes on its roof and by the courtyard full of students and teenagers sunning themselves. If you go under the small arch, you will see that the entire river bank, actually a cliff face, is covered with various cafés and restaurants and that the view of the Old Bridge is the perfect background to your lunch.

On the other side of the Old Bridge, and after Kujundžiluk, is the 1617 **Koski Mehmed-Paša mosque** (Braće Fejića bb). Have a look at the Islamic architecture and wander around both the mosque and the lovely courtyard outside, since this mosque is specially designated for tourist sightseeing. The paintings and the carved woodwork seen inside are an exquisite example of Ottoman art. You can climb up the minaret (2KM) for some amazing views.

The **Tepa market** (Braće Fejića bb; 6.30am-2pm), beyond the mosque, has been going since Turkish times and, judging by some of the characters that work here, it seems that some of the staff date back to that time too. Buy your cherries, figs and watermelons from here in spring and summer; they are fresh and delicious.

Further on is the 350-year-old **Turkish House** (☎ 550 677; Bišćevića 13; admission €1; 9am-3pm Nov-Feb, 8am-8pm Mar-Oct), furnished for the life of a Mostar somebody. The symbolism of the courtyard is intriguing: the ground is decorated with circles of pebbles divided into five sectors denoting the number of times a good Muslim must pray each day. The fountain has 12 spouts for the months, filling four watering pots that symbolise the seasons. Surrounding the fountain are three stone globes, one for the day we were born, the second facing Mecca for the life we lead and the third for death.

Upstairs the rooms are divided into men's and women's quarters. Muslim men had more than one wife and a white cloth draped over a closed door was a signal that the wife was ready to receive her husband. The back room of the house directly overhangs the river.

The lady who looks after the house has a passion for turtles and keeps more than 10 in the courtyard. On a hot day you can refresh yourself with a glass of rose-petal juice, a sweet concoction that'll give you a sugar rush and the energy to chase those turtles.

There is an even older Turkish house called **Kajtaz House** (☎ 550 913; Gaše Ilića 21; admission 2KM; 8am-8pm), behind the Pavarotti Music Centre.

As you leave the Old Town and enter a more modern-looking part, the **Karadjozbeg mosque** (Braće Fejića; admission 2KM; 9am-6pm) will be to your right. Mostar's most important mosque was built in 1557 and its minaret, as well as other parts of the buildings, were heavily damaged during the war. Now completely renovated, the mosque is open to visitors. A man will let you climb the minaret too. Behind the mosque is the old Muslim graveyard, the oldest in town, with beautiful grey *turbe* (tombstones) standing in the grass.

Braće Fejića is the centre of day- and night-life on the east bank of the city. Youngsters sit, drink coffee, smoke, and mouth the words of the songs banging out of the speakers.

Up the hill, above the old Branko-vac neighbourhood, is the site of the **old Orthodox church** (Bjelušine bb). A tiny old chapel which predates the Orthodox church remains here, but cannot be entered. A legend tells of an ingenious priest who managed to save his daughter from the paws of the local *bey* (senior officer of the Ottoman Empire) and build the chapel by tricking the *bey* at his own game. After many refusals, the *bey* promised to let the priest build a church on a piece of ground no larger than the size of the jumper he was wearing. The priest, clever as he was, realised that even though the jumper itself was much too small for a church, the wool out of which it was made would stretch for many metres. And so charming the *bey* with his witty inventiveness, the church was built and his daughter never married the *bey*.

Further south is the Pavarotti Music Centre (p117), a project originally designed and built by the War Child group; the building now hosts many different events. Apart from plays and concerts, the centre's main activity are music- and art-therapy groups for children. War Child is a network of humanitarian organisations who work with children affected by war all over the world.

Heading over to the west bank of the river from Braće Fejića street you will cross the **Musala Bridge** (more commonly known by its former name, Tito's Bridge). Just before you get there, you will see the old Austro-Hungarian-style music school and next to it the public baths, with one of the best bars in town, Club Café Banja (p117), on the top floor. The ruined old Hotel Neretva, on your right, still awaits renewal.

Head west for a few hundred metres, and you will come to the dramatic **former front line**, which now essentially divides the town between Muslims and Croats. It starts at the street behind Hotel Ero, then runs one street west to the main boulevard. Gutted buildings still stand like ghosts, their empty windows gaping like skeletal eye sockets.

The once-stately **Grammar School** (Gimnazija; cnr Nikole Šubića Zrinskog & Bulevar Hrvatskih Branitelja), built in 1896, is now a damaged, yet solid piece of Austro-Hungarian architecture with Moorish flourishes. It was once the most prestigious secondary school in town, and today its floors are divided for teaching in Bosnian and Croatian languages.

In the background stands the **Catholic Church** (Bulevar Hrvatskih Branitelja bb), with an out-of-proportion campanile (bell tower). The original was extended after the war and smacks of 'my campanile is higher than your minaret' one-upmanship. Poor workmanship has meant that it's acquired a lean. Higher up on the hillside is a large white cross that's also a recent addition. Apparently put there to annoy the Muslim population, a local is reported to have said he's grown to like it, because upon seeing it first thing in the morning, he feels like he's woken up in Rio.

The **Museum of Hercegovina** (☎ 551 602; Baja-tova 4; admission 1.50KM; ☒ 9am-2pm Mon-Fri, 10am-noon Sat) is the former house of Džemal Bijedić, ex-head of the Yugoslav government who died in mysterious circumstances in 1978. Now a small museum, dedicated more to Mostar than Bijedić, it has as its prize exhibit a 10-minute film on how Mostar used to be before 1990, with footage of the bridge-diving competition and the actual destruction of the bridge.

At the bottom of the hill below the museum is a telling graveyard where all the headstones share the same date of death.

There are two other sights of interest on the west bank. The first is the **Rondo** roundabout, an area where many dine alfresco. The second is the **Partisan Graveyard** (Kraljice Katarine), a truly socialist monument that was built to commemorate Mostar's Partisans. In socialist Yugoslavia this was the place where young pioneers made their vows to remain faithful to the path of Comrade Tito.

Sleeping

Both **Fortuna Travel Agency** (☎ 552 197; www.fortuna.ba; Trg Ivana Krndelja 1; per person 20-50KM; ☒ 8am-4.30pm Mon-Fri, 9am-1pm Sat) and the local Tourist Information Centre (p111) can book private accommodation.

Motel Kriva Ćuprija (☎ 550 953, 061 135 286; www.motel-mostar.de; Kriva Ćuprija 2; s/d/apt €23/42/45; ☒)

BOSNIA & HERCEGOVINA

As the name suggests, this is right next to the Crooked Bridge. With that lovely sight next to you and a good restaurant (Restaurant Taurus) next door, what else could you need? The rooms are well equipped and comfortable, and some have kitchenettes. Downstairs is a lovely terraced restaurant to have your breakfast at, while gazing at the river. The owner is a returnee from Germany who's happy to help. It's tops.

Hotel Mostar (☎ 322 679; fax 315 693; Kneza Domagoja bb; s/d 53/86KM; P) A good option for a standard hotel, with clean and airy rooms and small bathrooms. Ground- and top-floor rooms have balconies. The restaurant is pleasant with many plants and a choice of local dishes.

Hotel Bristol (☎ 500 100; www.bristol.co.ba; Mostarskog Bataljona bb; s/d 72.50/111KM; ✗ 🖳) Opened in 1904, this fine Austro-Hungarian building was once a legendary gathering place. The Bristol has undergone some significant changes since. Almost completely destroyed in the war and then rebuilt, it is a popular place with the international crowd. The singles are quite cramped, but the doubles a bit better. Specify if you want a room with a balcony, as not all rooms have them. The one computer in the foyer costs 5KM per hour for Internet access.

Pansion Most (☎ 552 528; fax 552 660; Adema Buća 100; s 45-52KM; d 65-75KM; ✗) An eight-room *pansion* on the western edge of the Old Town. Here's your chance to experience Mostar's religious rivalry first hand – the *pansion* is caught between the bells of the gigantic church tower and the call to prayer from the nearby mosque. The rooms are clean, tidy and pleasant and the receptionist speaks excellent English. Internet access is 3KM per hour, and there are maps and brochures available, a currency exchange and a laundry room.

Hotel Ero (☎ 386 777; www.ero.ba; Dr Ante Starčevića bb; s/d 79/136KM; P ✗ 🖳) This has for some years now been a second home to Mostar's UN troops and officials. The bar and restaurant are always buzzing with important (some)bodies. The rooms are bright with cream-coloured walls and white marble, and each has a nice small balcony. There is also wheelchair access.

Omer Lakiše (☎ 551 627; Mladena Balorde 21a; B&B with shared bathroom 20KM) Kind professor Omer (now retired) lets out rooms in his home,

which is hidden away in a quiet street. If you speak French or German, you're in luck because Omer taught both at Mostar's university, but he speaks a bit of English too. There are eight beds in two rooms and homeliness compensates for the shared bathroom and full rooms.

Zdrava Hrana (☎ /fax 551 444; Alikafića 5; per person €15) Set out on three floors, up a hilly street, Zdrava Hrana suits groups better than individual travellers. There are apartments made up of two double bedrooms and a kitchenette, but they have no cooking facilities. You can have a DIY breakfast or order one for 5KM.

Eating

Ćevapi spots are everywhere, of course. In the Old Town, especially the Tabhana area, restaurants dot the river bank and have perfect views of the Old Bridge. Enjoy a traditional coffee with Turkish delight, or a lunch of *šopska salata* (consisting of chopped tomato, cucumber and onion, topped with grated soft white cheese) and fresh trout.

Restaurant Taurus (☎ 212 617; meals 8-15KM; ⏾ 8am-late) An old mill right off Onešćukova, by the Crooked Bridge on the Radobolja River, this place serves some brilliant seafood dishes. The black squid-ink risotto is a treat, as is the shell pasta and, in fact, just about everything on the menu. The terrace looks onto the river and is cool in the summer, and the inside of the restaurant is like a mountain barn with a cosy-looking fireplace.

Pizzeria abc (☎ 194 656; Braće Fejića 45; meals 5-9KM; ⏾ 8am-11pm Mon-Sat, noon-11pm Sun) This is an extension of the most popular cake shop in town. The pasta and 25 varieties of pizza here are highly recommended. Pretend to be one of the locals as you sit on the pavement terrace outside and watch everyone-who's-anyone walk by on their compulsory evening stroll.

Restaurant Rondo (☎ 322 100; cnr Kraljice Katerine & Save Kovačevića; meals 7-14KM; ⏾ 7am-midnight; ✗) On the Rondo roundabout, hence the name, this is a great place to try some really traditional food (or you can go for the Italian options). Tasty recommendations are *buredžike* (yogurt-covered type of *burek*, 3KM), although be prepared for mega-garlic breath; the *zeljanica* (spinach pie, 3KM); the *sirnica* (4KM); or one of the nine soups (2.50KM).

Grill Centar (☎ 061 198 111; Braće Fejića 13; grills 3-4KM; ⏱ 7am-10.30pm) A quick nibble on a *ćevap* with *kajmak* (curdled milk turned to cheese) and a round lump of *lepinja* (a type of pitta bread) and off you go. The wooden benches and tables are for fast-eating customers only, eager to move on and explore the city.

MM Restaurant (☎ 580 192; Mostarskog Bataljona bb; meals 6-12KM; ⏱ 8am-10pm Mon-Sat) A good breakfast spot with ham and eggs (3KM) which will make some feel at home; for vegetarians there are also a few tasty options.

Mercur Supermarket (Maršala Tita bb; ⏱ 7am-10pm) There are plenty of different food goodies for self-caterers here.

Drinking

Mostar has some good bars, and on weekends the partying goes on till the wee hours. The Old Town is lively in the evenings but most bars close around midnight. On the west bank there are clusters of bars in the shopping centre on the Rondo roundabout, and on the long stretch of Kralja Tomislava near the Partisan Graveyard, where there are also fast-food places and games rooms.

Club Café Banja (Mostarskog Bataljona 8; ⏱ 8pm-late, summer only) On the roof terrace of the old baths, this is the hippest place in town and probably the only one where youngsters from the east and west banks come to drink together. The Neretva River cools the air from below, the stars twinkle above, and you might just find yourself lounging on a chaise lounge next to a handsome Mostarian. A real summer idyll.

Coco Loco Bar (☎ 328 004; Kneza Domagoja bb; ⏱ 8am-11pm) This place feels like someone's house, especially on weekends when there's a house party atmosphere with owners-cum-DJs entertaining an animated crowd. Minimal décor and a focus on fun.

Irish Pub (☎ 315 338; Kralja Zvonimira 15b; ⏱ 8am-11pm Sun-Thu, 8am-1am Fri & Sat) If you thought you couldn't have a quiet pint in Mostar, think again. This ersatz Irish pub serves Guinness and Kilkenny Bitter, so sit back and think of Ireland.

Entertainment

Pavarotti Music Centre (☎ 550 750; www.pavarotti musiccentre.com; Maršala Tita 179; ⏱ 9am-10pm) This is the hub of Mostar's cultural activities for young people, with a variety of exhibitions and concerts.

Getting There & Away

Mostar lies on the route between Sarajevo and the coast. Frequent buses run from the **bus station** (☎ 552 025; Trg Ivana Krndelja) to Sarajevo (13.5KM, 2½ hours) Split (17KM, four hours) Dubrovnik (20KM, three hours) and Zagreb (43KM, 9½ hours).

Buses to Međugorje (4KM, 40 minutes) go from the Mostar's main bus station.

The **train station** (☎ 552 198) is upstairs from the bus station. Two daily trains travel to the coast at Ploče and two go to Sarajevo; there is also a daily train to and from Zagreb. See p133 for departure and arrival times.

The airport handles charter flights only.

Around Mostar

About 15km southeast of Mostar is the village of **Blagaj** on the green Buna River. Down at the very end of town, where the river comes gushing out of a towering cliff, is the 16th-century **Tekija** (Dervish monastery; ☎ 573 221; admission 2KM; ⏱ 8am-9pm). Because water is seen as a powerful spiritual element, the Tekija was home to dervishes for centuries. These days they meet here every May. Two wooden tombs in an upper room house the bodies of two Tajik dervishes who arrived with the Turks at the end of the 15th century. You must take your shoes off before entering and women will be given a shawl to cover their head and shoulders with (unless you have one of your own). Downstairs are souvenirs, and the café on the terrace serves traditional coffee with Turkish delight.

Also in Blagaj, on the top of a high hill, is the **Fortress of Herceg Stjepan**. Herceg Stjepan ruled Hum, present-day Hercegovina, in the Middle Ages, and the fortress remains are a magnificent place to climb to for the views of the valley below. Originally an Illyrian settlement, the fortress was in the hands of the Romans, the Bosnians and Hercegovinians, and then the Ottomans. It's an hour's climb up, so if you are attempting it in the summer, start very early in the morning, before it gets too hot.

Buses from the main station go to Blagaj (1.5KM, 30 minutes)

POČITELJ

One of Hercegovina's little gems, this small town is on the road that leads from Mostar to the coast, around 25km south of the city. Heavily damaged during the war, this Ottoman-style beauty has been almost fully restored and the people of Počitelj have returned to their homes. Many of its inhabitants even found Mostar overwhelming when they had to leave their small town, and those who have returned did so because they claim to be unable to find a more beautiful place to live.

In the town you can visit the **Dadži-Alija mosque** and the **Sinan-Ibrahimpaša madrasa**. The beautiful **Clocktower** (Sahat kula), high up on top of the hill in which the town is embedded, is still not reachable due to ruins that remain around it. Wander around Počitelj's little streets and then have a coffee on one of the terraces in the Ottoman surroundings.

Buses from the main station go to Počitelj via Čapljina (4KM, 40 minutes).

KRAVICE WATERFALLS

The 25m cascades that stretch across 100m of hills are a like a (smaller) Niagara Falls and the Adriatic sea rolled into one. You can swim in the pool created by the rushing water. There are a couple of restaurants and cafés just by the water.

There is no public transport from Mostar. If you are driving from Mostar you will turn right at Počitelj, onto the road to Ljubuski. Off the road to Ljubuski, you turn left for Kravice, at a little sign.

HUTOVO BLATO

This is one of the top bird reserves in the country and home to over 250 migratory birds. The Mediterranean marshes of the **Deransko Lake** are said to host around 10,000 feathered friends at a time. Geese, hawks, pheasants and many other creatures make perfect subjects on the **photo safari** (100KM for a group of 15; boat only rented when full), as do the lotus leaves. Check with the office at the reserve for further details on the safari. Fishing is allowed with a permit, and there are plenty of eel and carp. There's no public transport to the park.

PODVELEŽJE

Once only known for its highland sheep rearing, the face of Podveležje was changed forever by one man. He built a little hotel, cooked some good food and took his guests trekking up Mt Velež, one of Hercegovina's highest peaks (1967m). **Motel Sunce** (☎ 560 082; www.hercegovina.ba; r per person from 25KM) is at the centre of all activity. Not only can you eat delicious homemade food in the hotel, you can also take it up into the mountain with you. A guide for a day trip is €30 and lunch is €10 extra. A two-day excursion, which includes taking a horse with you and sleeping under the stars, comes to around €100. Sharing with a group makes the costs less. If you fancy trekking solo, maps are provided. Always remember the mine warning. From July to August you can go medicinal-herb picking.

Pick-up from Mostar's main bus/train station is available. If you are driving, follow the road to Blagaj and watch out for the turn for Podveležje (signs lead to the motel). From Mostar's bus station, take bus 16 all the way to Smajkići village in Podveležje.

STOLAC

After Mostar and Trebinje, Stolac is the smallest of the three Hercegovinian towns hailed for their beauty. It suffered a lot of damage in the recent war, but some impressive buildings still remain, such as the **Church of St Peter and St Paul**, built in 1500, and the **three Ottoman bridges**, Inat Ćuprija, Podgradska Ćuprija, and Begovska Ćuprija, dating from the 15th and 17th centuries.

One of the most fascinating and mysterious historical monuments in the Stolac area, however, is the **necropolis** at Radimlja, containing between 120 and 130 *stećci* (graves and tombstones), belonging to the followers of the medieval Bosnian church (see p92).

There are several *stećci* necropolises throughout the country, and the one at Radimlja is considered to be among the most important for its exquisite stone engravings. It has been interpreted that the engraved symbols represent the profession or rank of the deceased. A riding figure denotes a person who might have got rich as a caravan leader or horse trader. Equally, the enlarged hand on a standing figure and a bow and arrow on the side represents a noble hunter or knight. Some are simply decorative. Radimlja is on the Čapljina road, 3km from Stolac. Buses run from Mostar's main station pretty much all day from 6.30am to 6.20pm (4KM, 1½ hours).

MEĐUGORJE

☎ 036 / pop 4300

Once a nondescript, poor Hercegovinian village, Međugorje became one of the most visited places in the former Yugoslavia when six teenagers claimed that the Holy Virgin spoke to them on 24 June 1981. Since then Međugorje has become a 'global village', with groups of German, French, Korean, Italian and English visitors storming the place regularly, along with the almost-local Irish (there's that many of them!). These Catholic visitors are all here hoping for one thing only: to catch a glimpse of the Virgin Mary at the place she is said to have appeared. Three of the original six teenagers still claim to see the vision daily, while the Virgin Mary only appears for the other three on special days.

Međugorje is awash with souvenir shops selling everything from holy water to fluorescent rosaries, Jesus pencil cases and cross-adorned raincoats. Frankly, it's a sea of kitsch, yet the crowds seem to love it, and even though there are more *pansions* and restaurants per square metre than seems decent, come summertime, they're all packed. (The local wine production can take some credit for that, since the wine from this region is the best in the country.)

The Catholic Church has not officially acknowledged the apparitions (the first in Europe since Lourdes, France, in 1858 and Fatima, Portugal, in 1917).

Međugorje largely escaped the war – some locals attribute this to divine protection but a more likely explanation is that it's an exclusively Croatian area. The conflict zone was as close as 35km away.

Obviously, the Međugorje boom times are around Easter, when the anniversary of the first appearance of the Virgin is celebrated in a parade called the Walk of Peace; the Assumption of the Virgin (15 August); and the Nativity of the Virgin (first Sunday after 8 September).

If accommodation is booked out, Mostar is less than hour away by bus.

Orientation

Međugorje has no street names or numbers. In fact, it's fair to say that there is really only one street, the one stretching for around 500m between the post office and St James' Church. This is where most of the shops,

banks, restaurants and travel agencies are. There are some *pansions* further from the post office but most are dotted along the lanes that reach into the fields and vineyards. Southwest behind the church is Mt Križevac, while Apparition Hill is to the south.

Any of the travel agents can provide a topographical map.

Information

The euro is the favoured foreign currency and is used in most pricing.

Globtour (☎ /fax 651 393, 651 593) Books ferries and runs buses to Split, Dubrovnik and Sarajevo.

Paddy Travel (☎ /fax 651482; paddy@tel.net.ba; ⏰ 9am-3pm Mon-Sat Nov-Mar, to 6pm Mon-Sat Apr-Oct) Books accommodation, changes travellers cheques and organises day trips.

Post office (☎ 651 510; ⏰ 7am-9pm Mon-Sat, 10am-5pm Sun) Internet (per hr 4KM), telephone, postal services and cash advances on credit cards.

Ured Informacija (☎ 651 988; www.medjugorje.hr; ⏰ 9am-6pm) Information office for church schedules and the Virgin Mary monthly message.

Vox Tours (☎ /fax 650 771; ⏰ 9am-5.30pm Mon-Fri, to 2pm Sat) Books airline and ferry tickets, and arranges car hire.

Zagrebačka Bank (☎ 650 862; ⏰ 8am-2.30pm Mon-Fri, to noon Sat) Cashes travellers cheques and has an ATM that accepts all cards.

Sights & Activities

Completed in 1969 before the apparitions began, **St James' Church** is the centre of all religious activity. Prayers, said in many languages, ring from the loudspeakers surrounding the church. A small outside conservatory, behind the church, together with many rows of chairs (both inside and outside of the conservatory) is a pleasant area for prayer.

Following the little path behind the church for around 200m you will reach the **Resurrected Saviour**, also known as the Weeping Knee statue, so called because this gaunt metallic figure of Christ on the Cross oozes liquid at the knee. Pilgrims look on in awe, and bring their rosaries, medallions and small bottles to fill up on the supposedly holy fluid. Indeed something does ooze from a faint crack at the knee, but whether this is a matter of a miracle or some internal plumbing is for the devout and sceptic to debate.

Apparition Hill, where the Virgin was first seen on 24 June 1981, is near Podbrdo hamlet, southwest of town. On the way up, rocks stick out of the red earth like crooked teeth and their sharp edges can be sore on the feet, especially for those going barefoot in the act of penitence. On the way are 14 Stations of the Cross where pilgrims stop to pray. The place of the alleged apparition, part way up the hill, is marked by a statue of the Virgin. Behind her is a blue cross conveying a message of peace. To reach Apparition Hill, take the road curving left (east) from the centre of town, and follow the signs to Podbrdo (1.5km away).

Mt Križevac (Cross Mountain) lies about 2.5km southwest of town. The climb up takes around an hour and, again, the sea of sharp rock challenges the feet. On the top, a white cross awaits, planted there in 1934 to commemorate the 1900th anniversary of Christ's death, or, according to some locals, to keep away the plague that devastated the area at that time. Groups pray together along the 14 Stations of the Cross depicting the suffering of Jesus. The climb is steep and you too can feel the pain. Good shoes are essential unless you're doing it the hard way – in bare feet. No candles please as there's a fire danger.

Refresh at any of the bars at the bottom of the hill.

If trudging up rocky hillsides is not enough activity and you want to go swimming, play tennis or football, or just enjoy a good fitness centre, then the **Circle International** (☎ 651 401; Tromedja bb; admission from €2.50; ☽ 9am-9pm), a sports complex about 2km away on the Mostar road, is the place for all that activity. If your feet have suffered on those rocks, and your face has been burnt by the sun, you can have yourself a pampering session, with massage, spa pools, sauna and a solarium all on offer. It's all your prayers answered.

Sleeping

With 17,000 rooms, Međugorje probably has more accommodation than the rest of Bosnia and Hercegovina combined. As likely as not you'll be sleeping under a cross or image of the Virgin Mary.

Beds are fairly easy to find, except around major holidays. *Pansions* and hotels can fill with large tour groups, so book in advance. Most *pansion* rooms look the same, though they are most expensive around the church. Most friendly proprietors offer the choice

of B&B, half board or full board, and home-made meals are usually complemented with a bottle of *domaće vino* (homemade wine).

The town's few hotels are blander and more expensive than the *pansions*, and the rooms are not much better.

If you thought you could never get the hang of the local language, perhaps the Irish owners of **Paddy Travel** (☎ /fax 651482; paddy@tel .net.ba; r from €15; ☽ 9am-3pm Mon-Sat Nov-Mar, to 6pm Mon-Sat Apr-Oct) can set a good example. Fluent and friendly, they can sort out accommodation for you in a tick, as they have access to 15 of the town's *pansions*.

Over the road from Paddy Travel, **Vox Tours** (☎ 650 771; per person half/full board from €20/26; ☽ 9am-5.30pm Mon-Fri, 9am-2pm Sat) deals with most of the *pansions* in town.

Pansion Stanko Vasilj (☎ 651 042; per person B&B/half board/full board €15/20/25) The owner of this *pansion* happens to be the most famous wine maker in the country. His Žilavka (the local white) has won him many an award. The rooms are airy and clean, and the old-fashioned tavern downstairs is a good place for food and that tasty wine sampling. It's 200m southeast of the bottom of the Mt Križevac trail.

Pansion Park (☎ 651 155; fax 651 494; r B&B/half board/full board €15/22/28) There are two large peach-coloured Alpine chalets with spacious, pleasant rooms and balconies here, fronted by a large garden and seating area. Like most, it's a family-run *pansion* and the hosts are friendly and helpful. There is a large restaurant to cater for those who have opted for half or full board.

Pansion Ivo (☎ 651 973; s/d €12/24) Turning left at the post office if you're coming from the church, you'll probably see Mr Ivo having a coffee and chatting to his mates outside the *pansion*. His is a small house with basic, modern rooms that are good for a couple of nights' stay. There is even a shop opposite if you feel like a snack.

Pansion Zemo (☎ /fax 651 878; www.medugorjetr avel.com/zemo; Kozine district; camp site per person & tent/ B&B/half board €3/9/14; ℗) This is only really good if you have a car, since the 1km walk can be a nightmare in the summer heat. Otherwise, this *pension* is in a nice quiet spot in the village fields, southeast of the church. If you are not into camping you can rent a room, some of which have bathrooms, while others share.

Eating

Međugorje's eating options are good, especially considering it's such a small place. Seafood is tasty and fresh, and the Italian options are decent and mostly *al dente*.

Dubrovnik (☎ 651 472; meals €3-6; ☺ 7am-late) The Dubrovnik has a great outside seating area looking straight onto the churchyard, and a delicious Italian menu. There are good soups, delicious prosciutto and tasty desserts, and even some Guinness if you've had enough of the local wine. Sometimes a bit of partying goes on here, with an accordion getting everybody on the improvised dance floor.

Galija (☎ 651 535; meals €4-5; ☺ 10am-11pm) With a large galley on its roof, Galija's crew in goes for Italian cooking. Recommended is the *risotto alle verdue* (risotto with vegetables and herbs), especially interesting for vegetarians and those who like their risotto more crunchy and less sludgy.

Pizzeria Colombo (pizzas €5-7; ☺ 8am-midnight) Obviously catering to the many Irish pilgrims who flock to Međugorje, this most popular place between the post office and the church has pizza and, Hail Mary!, there's even Guinness. The tap on the bar dispensing this nectar is protected with a rosary to ensure a continual flow of this restorative elixir.

Diskont (☎ 650 780; ☺ 7am-10pm) This is a biggish supermarket, for a small town, about 100m from the post office on the road towards Mostar.

Shopping

If we haven't mentioned enough shopping choices already, here are some more: walking sticks with the image of the Virgin etched on them, jigsaws of the Virgin Mary, priest statues, Christs in snow domes, fluorescent Holy Virgins, pictures of the Virgin and Jesus melding into one as you walk left and right, and pictures of the Virgin and/or Jesus whose eyes follow you around the room. One hundred euro will buy you the vestments to hold your own mass, and €2500 will buy a 1.5m statue of the Virgin Mary, Jesus or the pope.

Meal-themed souvenirs include dried figs, homemade *rakija*, and traditional hand-woven tablecloths. As there is no specific commandment against copyright piracy, there are a number of shops selling very cheap CDs and fake designer sunglasses.

Getting There & Around

Most visitors come to Međugorje from Croatia with **Globtour** (☎ /fax 651 393, 651 593), running buses from Split (18KM, 3½ hours) and Dubrovnik (18KM, three hours) via Mostar. Frequent local buses run to Mostar (4KM, 40 minutes); ask at the post office when the next one will be.

Taxis overcharge a flat fee of €5 to anywhere in the town.

TREBINJE

☎ 059 / pop 30,200

Hailed as Hercegovina's most beautiful town after Mostar, Trebinje is a small place at the southernmost corner of the country, and within spitting distance of Dubrovnik. Leafy squares and a charming old town are cooled by the Trebišnjica River, which in turn is spanned by one of the country's loveliest bridges, the Arslanagić Bridge. The road towards Mostar is a real beauty, with giant mountains looming in the distance, golden fields stretched in between and vast blue skies above. Trebinje can be visited on a day trip from Mostar or Dubrovnik.

Orientation

Trebinje is in RS and therefore all the street signs are strictly in Cyrillic. Perhaps the best way to get your bearings is by looking for the new monastery, overlooking the town from a hill to the south. Arslanagić Bridge is a 15-minute walk east from the centre. Trebinje's central street is Kralja Petra Prvog Oslobodioca and runs north–south through the town. To the west is Desanka Maksimović street, taking you to the old town, and parallel to it is the shady Jovan Dučić square.

Sights

Trebinje is easily walked around and it won't take you more than a couple of hours of very easy-going strolling to see all the sights.

The most important sight is the **Arslanagić Bridge** with its looped arches and smaller decorative half-moon 'incisions'. Built by the Ottomans in 1574, the bridge was an important place of salt trade before the Dubrovnik road was built. It got its name after the rich Ottoman administrator Arslanaga, who collected toll money and built himself a house next to the bridge. The ancient structure has had some trouble staying up in the last 60 years, and not because of its age. Having been damaged in WWII with explosives and surviving the attack, the bridge was completely moved from its original location during the 1960s. The then communist government was building a hydro plant nearby, and managed to completely flood the bridge in the process, inflicting serious damage on the stone. The bridge was removed in 1965. Its stones lay on a site nearby until 1972, when the arches were constructed once again in their original form some metres down the river, closer to the town centre. Fortunately it had better luck in the recent conflict, unlike many other Ottoman buildings in the town.

Trebinje's **old town** sits on the banks of the Trebišnjica River. Its streets are filled with cafés and ancient trees, which throw shade on the hot pavement. The 18th-century Osman-Pasha mosque at the entrance to the old town, destroyed in the war, was recently repaired and is supposed to be functioning again by the time you read this.

The **Jovan Dučić square** nearby is where all of Trebinje hangs out, under the thick leaves of plane trees. Market sellers flog their stuff here in early mornings.

Next to the square is **Jovan Dučić park**, at the end of which you can bear witness to the wonders of socialist realist sculpture and stand in awe of the iron partisans – peasants and workers with a woman as their leader – charging forth in a frozen march.

On the hill south of the town is the **New Orthodox Monastery**, better known as the Hercegovinian Gračanica, since it was built on the model of the Gračanica monastery in Kosovo, a building sacred to many Serbs. Inside this one are the bones of Jovan Dučić, a poet and diplomat born in Trebinje who died in America in 1943, and a man whose work can be said to embody the essence of Serb nationalism. He has had a kind of renaissance in the last 15 years as his nationalist ideas have made him almost a national icon among the Serbs, particularly those in Trebinje. More interesting is the 15th-century **Tvrdoši Monastery** outside town.

If you are journeying between Mostar and Trebinje, you will travel through **Popovo Polje**, a rural region with stunning views and old-fashioned villages that seem to have been forgotten by time.

Sleeping

Hotel Platani (☎ 225 134/5; Svijetni Trg 1; s/d 65/115KM) If you decide to stay the night in Trebinje, this small hotel is a decent option with comfortable rooms and a nice café downstairs.

Eating & Drinking

As in the whole of Bosnia and Hercegovina, places for eating *ćevapi* and *burek* are everywhere. Any of the cafés on Jovan Dučić square or in the old town are a good bet for a decent espresso or cappuccino, as well as a nice traditional coffee.

Pizza Castello (☎ 223 192; Trg Travunije; meals 6.50-7.50KM; ⊗ 7.30am-midnight) A cool terraced pizzeria on the square overlooked by the mosque. A wood-fired oven produces decent pizza, and the zing of the freshly squeezed lemonade is a great energy booster.

Getting There & Away

It's best to visit Trebinje with your own transport, since it is not terribly well connected. Buses go from the **bus station** (☎ 220 466) in the town centre (south); buses to Mostar go three times a day (15KM, four hours), and to Dubrovnik once a day, at 10am (5KM, 30 minutes). From Dubrovnik they go at 1.30pm every day except Sunday.

BOSNIA

TRAVNIK

☎ 030 / 27,500

This small town was once a seat for Turkish viziers (high officials), who would relax here on their plush cushions in the protective shade of the medieval castle and enjoy Travnik's fresh spring-water fish. Later, Travnik produced Bosnia and Hercegovina's Nobel prize–winning writer, Ivo Andrić, who probably wrote his first lyrical lines while gazing at this charming old town. When he became an established writer, Andrić once again turned his attention to his home town, and wrote *The Travnik Chronicles*, a novel in which Travnik is depicted as an international crossroads through the lives of a French and an Austrian ambassador living on the opposite sides of town.

A day trip to Travnik is a treat, and at 90km northwest of Sarajevo, it's easy to get to.

Orientation & Information

Travnik's main street, Bosanska, runs east–west. The **bus station** (☎ 792 761) is off Bosanska on the western end of town, within sight of the **post office** (☎ 547 102; Prnjavor), which can issue MasterCard advances. **Telecent@r** (☎ 518 850; Bosanska 120; per hr 1KM; ☺ 7am–11pm Mon-Sat, 9am–11pm Sun) has Internet access.

Sights

Protectively overlooking the town, the **medieval castle** (☎ 518 140; admission 2KM; ☺ 10am-6pm Apr-Nov) was built in the 15th century to hold the Turks at bay. It never had its moment of glory (or, more likely, failure), because the Bosnian state was already collapsing and its defenders surrendered. The Turks strengthened the fortifications and the castle remains largely intact today. To get here, turn left on Bosanska before the Many-Coloured Mosque, go through the underpass and then straight up the hill. Cross the high arched bridge over the river and enter via an iron gate. In the winter time it's normally locked, but the keys are held at the anthropological and archaeological **museum** (☎ 518 140; adult/concession 1.50/1KM; ☺ 9am-3pm Mon-Fri, 10am-2pm Sat & Sun). The museum, on two floors off Bosanska, presents an eclectic collection of fossils, minerals, stuffed fauna, and artefacts from the Turkish period.

The museum also has the key, if needed, to the **Ivo Andrić museum** (☎ 518 140; Mustafa Kundić; admission 1.50KM; ☺ 9am-3pm Mon-Fri, 10am-2pm Sat & Sun), upstairs from Restaurant Divan. This small museum claims to be the birthplace of the famed author and it even has a little room with a cot, where baby Andrić must have slept. An entire room is dedicated to various editions and translation of *The Travnik Chronicles*. You can also see pictures of the bespectacled author and his wife receiving his 1961 Nobel prize. Given Andrić's fame, it's most surprising that there's no street or building named after him in his home town. Town council, please take note!

At the eastern end of Bosanska is the gorgeous **Many-Coloured Mosque**. It, like all other mosques with any sense of self-worth, allegedly contains hairs from the Prophet Mohammed's beard. (This, like monasteries owning bits of St John the Baptist's hand, must be the clerical equivalent of Michelin stars.) Built in 1815 on the site of the burnt-down 1757 original, it has an eastern rather than a western minaret and the exterior is painted with trees and grapes in lovely pale colours. The engraved wooden door is heavy and beautiful. Underneath the mosque is a small *bezistan* (old shopping bazaar).

Just east of the mosque is **Plava Voda** (Blue Water), where a rushing mountain stream is crossed by small stone bridges and where fat trout swim, waiting to be served up on someone's plate. This is a favourite summer spot for idling. A number of stalls sell touristy knick-knacks and there are a few restaurants.

Viziers' turbes (tombs) in the town reflect the importance of Travnik as the capital of Bosnia in the 18th and 19th centuries. There are a couple on Bosanska near the Hotel Lipa. Some corporate entity has thoughtfully put up explanatory boards, in English, which provide historical background to the town.

Sleeping & Eating

Hotel Lipa (☎ 511 604; Lažajeva 116; s/d 70/140KM). With the reception desk upholstered with stylish cow-skin patterned material, one wonders whether a lost designer once wandered into the Hotel Lipa. Mind you, that's pretty much it for style here, although the rooms are pretty decent with TVs and new bathrooms. Oh, and the TVs have cable and cable apparently has porn, if that'll lure you.

Pansion Oniks (☎ 512 182; Žitarnica bb; s/d 35/70KM) Behind the café of the same name near the Many-Coloured Mosque, Pansion Oniks is an OK option for a night's stay. Check out that town bypass under the window though, it might be noisy at night.

Restaurant Divan (☎ 818 141, 061 372 365; Mustafa Kundić; meals 8-10KM) Directly below the Ivo Andrić museum, Restaurant Divan is the most popular place in town. The usual Bosnian cuisine is served, and if you like meat, they guarantee theirs is always fresh and tender. And there's cherry pie which locals order by the baking tray to take home. Yes, it's that good. Use your chance to try *Travnički sir*, the famed local cheese made from sheep's milk.

Plava Voda (☎ 618 322; Šumeće 14; meals 4-7.50KM) A great place for escaping the summer heat by the stream and munching on tasty trout.

A nice salad and some cool white Hercegovinian wine go well with the fish.

Getting There & Away

Buses go almost hourly to Sarajevo (11KM, two hours), four go daily to Banja Luka (13KM, three hours) and six to Bihać (21KM, six hours).

JAJCE

☎ 030 / pop 30,000 (estimated)

The 'little egg' town is potentially one of Bosnia's most attractive places. It has a charging 21m waterfall right in the town centre; medieval Bosnian catacombs and church remains; a citadel lining an egg-shaped hill (responsible for Jajce's name); and a plush little hotel. You could pass a couple of days here as happy as Larry, especially if you squeeze in some swimming at the nearby Pliva Lake.

Unfortunately, the town is still being rebuilt following the damage it endured during the war. The main street was still in bandages at the time of research, and the restaurants that used to ply the punters with drink while they sighed over the majestic beauty of the waterfalls are all burnt down. Nevertheless, Jajce is a pretty place for a day or two's relaxing, or a day trip on the way to Banja Luka.

Orientation

Jajce is tiny. The bus station is just outside the town walls. To enter the town, pass through the medieval Travnik gate. On your left immediately after the gate is the stairway to the citadel (the citadel was closed to the public at the time of research). On the way up you will see the medieval catacombs and the remains of the medieval church. The waterfalls are on the right, before the Travnik gate, going through the little park. The town's 'exit gate' is the Banja Luka gate on the opposite side of Travnik gate.

Sights

Jajce was the place where medieval Bosnian kings were crowned, and where in 1943 during the second congress of Avnoj (Antifascist Council of the People's Liberation of Yugoslavia), Bosnia and Hercegovina got its stamp of acceptance into the Yugoslav pack. Tito and his mates probably clinked flasks and gazed at the gorgeous

waterfalls from a nearby cave, resting after making such a big decision. The **waterfalls**, of which there are two, are 21m and 18m long and mark the confluence of the Pliva and Vrbas Rivers. The cool air that rises from the smashing water is refreshing and you can see the waterfalls right from the place where the water drops into the abyss below, or if you feel queasy at the thought, there is a lovely spot on the opposite side, with a little balcony made especially for admiring the view.

Climbing the steps towards the **citadel** you'll come across the remains of the medieval **Church of St Luke**, the tower of which looks just like the one on Dubrovnik's main street, the Placa (Stradun). Next to it are the remains of tombs from the 3rd-century Roman temple dedicated to the god Mitras. Mithraism was a religion with strong similarities to Christianity that flourished in the first few centuries AD, and was the first successful monotheistic religion in the Roman Empire. Imported from Persia, it centred around the god Mitras, who created the world by killing a sacred bull.

A few metres from here are the fascinating **catacombs**. To get in, you must ring the house bell of a woman called Alida who lives in the house opposite and has a key. She charges 1KM and will take you inside and show you around. The catacombs, originally built around 1410 as a place of worship for followers of the Bosnian Church (see p92), are divided into two floors. The underground floor has a Bosnian Church altar characterised by a double cross, and surrounding it are shapes of a sickle moon and sun, symbolising pagan beliefs mixed with Christianity. The catacomb arches are lily-shaped, the emblem of Bosnian kings. The ground floor was intended to be a church but these plans were cut short when the Turks came to town. This mysterious location is said also to have been a place of worship for the Sultan Suleiman Pasha. The idea was to bury nobility here, but for some reason it never happened. The place was neglected and in a really bad shape after the war, but thanks to Alida, who even managed to squeeze money for lighting the place from the local authorities, the catacombs now (almost) get the care they deserve.

The 1KM fee also pays for entering the Bear Tower (Medvjed Kula), a watchtower that got its name thanks to its mega-thick walls (strong as a bear). Again, before Alida took things in hand, the tower was a lovers' den. A bit like the citadel is now.

In the town centre, the Dizdar or Female Mosque, one of the most important in the region, was being reconstructed at the time of research. The Pliva Lake on the town's outskirts is a popular place for swimming.

Sleeping & Eating

There are two hotels in town which also serve food.

Hotel Stari Grad (☎ 654 006; Svetog Luke 3; s/d 80/120KM) Set in a traditional old Jajce house and restored by an absentee landlord, this small hotel has everything your heart could desire (well, almost). Spacious, clean and bright rooms with faux-vintage photos of old Jajce adorn the walls. The comfort extends to the Turkish bath and Finnish sauna downstairs. Snug bathrobes hang on the walls, waiting to give you more pleasure. During the hotel's restoration the builders found remains of an old Turkish bath that used to be just opposite the present one, and preserved it behind plexiglass, so the old bath is visible from the reception/ restaurant area. The restaurant serves traditional Bosnian food and some Italian dishes, starting at 200KM.

Hotel Tourist (☎ 658 151; Kraljice Katarine bb; s/d/tr 47/74/96KM) A large, formerly state-run hotel that has only half picked itself up since its near destruction in the '90s. Literally one half of the hotel is 'old rooms' and the other 'new rooms'. Needless to say, ask for a new room. They have good comfortable beds and nice new bathrooms. Plus the waterfalls are just around the corner.

Getting There & Away

There are four buses to/from Sarajevo (20KM, 3½ hours); and several go to Banja Luka (12KM, 1½ hours).

BANJA LUKA

☎ 051 / pop 200,000

Although never much of a tourist place, Banja Luka is a good stopover on the way to bigger and better things, like Zagreb or Belgrade. The town itself is full of greenery and wide streets for strolling. Since it's the capital of RS, it's a good place to see how things are going for the separatist Serbs.

A 1969 earthquake destroyed about 80% of the town and, as if that wasn't enough, in 1993 local Serbs updated the damage by blowing up all 16 of the city's mosques. The famous Ferhadija mosque (1580), originally built with the ransom money for an Austrian count, is due to be rebuilt but its site is still an empty plot.

Down by the emerald Vrbas River the large 16th-century castle is about the oldest thing around and is host to a summer festival of music, dance and theatre. Outside of town is an interesting ecotourist resort worth a visit if you're in Banja Luka.

Orientation

The main street is Kralja Petra I Karađorđevića (Kralja Petra), named after the great Serbian hero who led the first insurrection against the Turks, and it runs northeast to southwest. The Vrbas River takes much the same route but in a lazy, winding way. Parallel to Kralja Petra on the east side is Veselina Masleše, a strip of cafés and bars, plus stalls selling CDs, videos and the like. The castle is just south of the city centre.

The bus station and nearby train station are about 3km northeast of the centre and the airport is some 25km north.

Information

Only RS-issued phonecards work in Banja Luka so it's better to phone from the post office. There are plenty of ATMs, including one outside the post office.

Cambridge Centar (☎ 221 730; Kralja Petra 103; 9am-9pm Mon-Fri, 9am-5pm Sat) For Englishlanguage magazines and classic literature.

Post office (☎ 211 336; Kralja Petra 93; 7am-8pm Mon-Fri, 7am-6pm Sat) Telephones and MasterCard advances.

Raiffeisen Bank (☎ 222 224; Jevrejska bb; 8.30am-7.30pm Mon-Fri, 8am-2pm Sat) Has an allcard ATM and cashes travellers cheques.

Telegroup (☎ 213 388; Braće Mažar bb; per hr 2.50KM; 8am-11pm Mon-Sat, 10am-10pm Sun) Internet access.

Turistički Savež (☎ 212 323; tursavbl@teol.net; Kralja Petra 75; 8am-5pm Mon-Sat) This small office is somewhat difficult to find. It's down a side alley off Kralja Petra. It has maps and brochures and some staff speak a little English.

Zepter (☎ 211 100; Jevrejska bb; 8am-7pm Mon-Fri, to 1pm Sat) Will change KM to dinars for Serbia.

Sights

Banja Luka's parks and green streets are relaxing places to stroll with the seemingly tireless locals who are outside day and night. The large **castle** dates back to the 16th century but has its origins in Roman times. On the banks of the Vrbas River, the green space in which the castle sits has restaurants overlooking the water. Wandering around the ancient castle, you'll come across the amphitheatre, overgrown with plants, whose benches were burned for fuel during the war. There is a towpath along the Vrbas bank for a nice little walk.

Some decent buildings line Kralja Petra street in the town centre. The **presidential palace**, the **Orthodox cathedral** and the **Republika Srpska Art Gallery** are among the most attractive. Chess maniacs might like to challenge the locals to a game on one of the big chessboards painted on the pavement in Gradski Park, near the post office.

Sleeping

Hotel Bosna (☎ 215 775; info@hotelbosna.com; Kralja Petra 97; s/d old 67/104KM, new 102/144KM; **P**) This grand '70s hotel, right in the heart of things, has a new and an old part. The old bit has attractive dark brown décor and large retro room numbers on the doors. The new part is more fancy-schmancy, with comfortable, airy rooms. A big restaurant, bar and shops downstairs make sure you never leave.

Hotel Vidović (☎ 217 217; fax 211 100; Kozarska 85; s/d 70/81KM; **P** **⊠**) The current location of this hotel is down a leafy road a few kilometres from the centre, but apparently

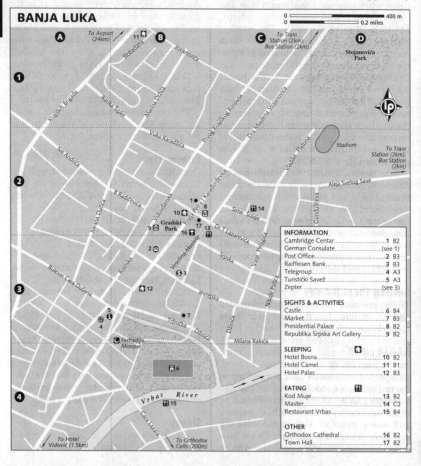

BANJA LUKA

0 — 400 m
0 — 0.2 miles

INFORMATION	
Cambridge Centar	1 B2
German Consulate	(see 1)
Post Office	2 B3
Raiffeisen Bank	3 B3
Telegroup	4 A3
Turistički Savež	5 A3
Zepter	(see 3)

SIGHTS & ACTIVITIES	
Castle	6 B4
Market	7 B3
Presidential Palace	8 B2
Republika Srpska Art Gallery	9 B2

SLEEPING	
Hotel Bosna	10 B2
Hotel Camel	11 B1
Hotel Palas	12 B3

EATING	
Kod Muje	13 B2
Master	14 C2
Restaurant Vrbas	15 B4

OTHER	
Orthodox Cathedral	16 B2
Town Hall	17 B2

there are plans to move to the city centre. They promise to keep prices the same. The rooms are clean and fresh and the secure off-road parking makes this an attractive stop for motoring visitors.

Hotel Palas (☎ 218 723; Kralja Petra 60; www.in ecco.net/palas-sm; s/d/tr from €41/66.70/76.90; P ☒) Look up for the sign or you may be fooled by the pavement cafés that stretch in front of the hotel. Inside, in addition to 'home away from home' rooms, a sauna and fitness centre are available.

Hotel Camel (☎ 319 922; cnr Slobodana & Jovanovića; s/d/tr 68/81/94; P ☒) If a 20-minute walk contributes to your fitness programme, stay here. The rooms are cosy, ochre-coloured, and have doormats with signs of the zodiac for you to wipe your tired feet on.

Eating & Drinking

Veselina Masleše, parallel to Kralja Petra but one block east, has a long strip of cafés, pastry shops and ice-cream vendors.

Restaurant Vrbas (☎ 464 608; Braće Potkornjaka 1; meals 6-11KM; ☼ 7am-11pm; P) Leafy plane trees with humongous trunks shade the terrace of this restaurant by the river's edge. While the Vrbas whooshes past and the waiters move at snail's pace, you can eat your hearty portion and relax.

Kod Muje (☎ 358 492; snacks 2-5KM; ☼ 7am-11pm) This is Bosnia central, with ćevapi and all manner of grilled meats at fantastically cheap prices. Kod Muje is a classic old-style eatery – a wooden cabin with a large terrace – and the owner's wife serves you caringly, as if she were your granny. Although it's in the centre, it can be hard to find. From Kralja Petra strike southeast. With the town hall on your left, cross Veselina Masleše and wander down the lane next to the cinema Kozara.

Master (☎ 317 444; Sime Šolaje 7; meals 8-12KM; ☼ 10am midnight) A sleeping *ranchero* shaded by his sombrero gives this place away amid tower-block buildings. Locals like this place and are getting hooked on the enchiladas, fajitas and Coronas. Unfortunately, there are no *quesadillas* on the menu. A good, though not very authentic, alternative to the meaty Bosnian menus.

Orthodox Celts (☎ 467 700; Stevana Bulajića 12; ☼ 9am-1am) Put up a few posters of Ireland, pull some pints of Guinness, Kilkenny and Harp, and you've got yourself an Irish pub. This lively and often packed bar hides

beneath a suburban house. There's live music several times a week, but it's only rock and roll, no River Dancing. It's south of the Vrbas River, less than half a kilometre from the castle.

Getting There & Away

AIR

The airport, some 25km north of Banja Luka, has flights to Belgrade with JAT. The RS airline Air Srpska has been grounded for some time due to financial problems and is not showing signs of resurrection. A taxi to the airport should cost about 30KM.

BUS

From the **bus station** (☎ 315 865; Prote N. Kostića 38) there are three buses daily to Zagreb (23KM, seven hours), seven to Sarajevo (23KM, five hours) and hourly buses to Belgrade (23KM, seven hours). Four buses run to Bihać (11KM, three hours).

A taxi to the station should cost 5KM.

TRAIN

The **train station** (☎ 300 752; Srpskih Boraca 17) has some useful international connections to Belgrade, coastal Croatia and Zagreb (see p134).

Around Banja Luka

Eco-Centre Lončari (☎ 065 629 128; camping per adult/child/site 3/2/10KM) This is the only holiday resort of its kind in the country. The owner has turned acres of forest and a couple of fields into a place where people can come and put up their tents, barbecue, bathe in the swimming pool, fish in the ponds, and trek in the woods. Fishing is free with camping, but bring your own equipment. He has used only natural and sustainable materials – note the gorgeous sun umbrellas made of hay around the pool. There are plans to build a small hotel on the grounds. It's truly a little paradise.

It's a bit of a hassle to get here without your own transport. You can get a bus to Omarska from Banja Luka and then a taxi for the 15km to the centre. Check by telephoning (there is an English speaker) whether the promised bus service has been organised, which will pick you up from Omarska. If you are driving, follow the road to Omarska until you see the Eco-Centre Lončari signs (on wooden boards).

BIHAĆ

☎ 037 / pop 65,000

If you've come to Bosnia to check out those promises of adrenaline-fuelled adventure, Bihać is the top place. Its reputation as a rafting capital is well deserved and it owes it all to its sapphire-coloured Una River. Try your hand at the whirls, and you're guaranteed tons of fun. Not for the faint-hearted.

Orientation

The usual approach is from Novi Grad on the Croatian border following the Una River southwest through an impressive limestone gorge. The Una River cleaves the town in two, with the town centre on the western side and some expensive hotels and restaurants on the east bank. On this side Bihaćkih Branilaca leads out of town northwards to Novi Grad, and south, past the bus station on Put V Korpusa, to Sarajevo.

Information

Centar (Put V Korpusa 5; per hr 2KM) Internet access.

Post office (☎ 332 332; Bosanska bb; 7am-9pm Mon-Sat, 9am-noon Sun) Poste-restante facilities, MasterCard cash advances.

Raiffeisen Bank (☎ 329 000; Dana Državnosti 5; 8am-6pm Mon-Fri, to 2pm Sat) Cashes travellers cheques and has an ATM that accepts all cards.

Telephone office (☎ 310 055; Bosanska 3; 7am-9pm Mon-Sat, 9am-noon Sun) Opposite the post office.

Tourist office (☎ 222 777; Dr Irfana Ljubijankića 13; 8am-4pm Mon-Fri) A clued-up organisation with its finger on river activities and accommodation possibilities.

Sights

The lofty, stone **captain's tower** on the western side of the river dates from the early 16th century. It was a prison from 1878 to 1959 but now holds a nifty multilevel **museum** (☎ 223 214; admission 1KM; 9am-4pm Mon-Fri, to 2pm Sat) featuring sarcophagi from the Bihać area and the history of the town.

Behind the tower are the remains of the **Church of St Anthony** that was destroyed in WWII. The original St Anthony is now the **Fethya Mosque**, and although not exactly Hagia Sofia, it's worth a look. The church was converted into a mosque by the Turks in the 1530s. At the end of the 17th century the Croats ousted the Turks and built a new St Anthony's. It was never completely finished and war damage has left just a bell tower.

> **WARNING**
>
> Be very aware that the Bihać area was mined during the war. Stick to paths and concreted areas.

Adjacent is a Muslim *turbe* containing the bodies of two martyrs.

Activities

The rafting season usually runs from March to October and the river is higher in spring and autumn. The two main outfits who provide water thrills need about six people to run a trip, but it's always possible to join up with another group. Prices depend upon the length and complexity of the trip. There are two types of rafting experiences: 'extreme' (ie very scary) and 'light' (ie no need to bring a clean pair of pants). The 'extreme' is a four-hour ordeal covering 15km and costs 70KM, and 'light', which suits all ages, is a 10km stretch and costs between 40KM and 50KM. Add between €5 and €15 to that for a postrafting picnic.

Both owners will collect by arrangement from the bus station.

Based at Golubić, 6km from Bihać, **Una Kiro Rafting** (☎/fax 223 760, 061-192 338; www.una-kiro-rafting.com; Muse Čazima Ćatića 1) also offers kayak lessons, equipment and accommodation. Camping is available from €5 per person and there's a free kayak for just messing around in.

Una Rafting (Sport Bjeli; ☎ 223 502, 061 138 853; www.unarafting.com; Klokot, Pecikovići bb), based about 12km from Bihać, offers rafting, kayaking and mountain biking plus accommodation.

For information on fishing, ask at the tourist office.

Sleeping

There's a range of accommodation with the rafting outfits providing camping or basic accommodation, some good *pansions*, and some expensive hotels down on the river which are not worth a look. If the following are full ask the tourist office for some alternatives.

Villa Una (☎/fax 311 393; Bihaćkih Branilaca 20; s/d 50/70KM; **P**) It's central, it's near the river and it's good value for money. What else could you ask for? This is a pristine private home with well-equipped rooms.

Hotel Park (☎ 332 553; fax 331 883; Put V Korpusa bb; s/d unrestored 44/88KM, restored 54/98KM; P) This is the town's big hotel and probably the best bet for value, especially if you go for the unrestored rooms, which are perfectly adequate.

MB Lipovača (☎ 351 620; Dr Irfana Ljubijankića 91; s 32-45KM, d/tr 80/120KM; P) A 2km walk from town, the hotel is well equipped with pleasant rooms, although the cheaper singles are without TV. Catch up on all that holiday reading.

Hut Aduna (☎ 314 304; Put V Korpusa bb; per person 5KM; P) Perfect for your wholesome sporty rafting experience: an under-the-trees camping ground, about 5km out of town between the Una River and the Sunce Hotel. Sites are powered and there's a toilet and shower block.

Eating & Drinking

Sunce (☎ 310 487; Put V Korpusa bb; meals 8-15KM; ☺ 8am-11pm) Try the house speciality, Plata Una, a large plate with various dips and snacks (30KM for two) – very filling. Or you can always go for the trout. The restaurant is large and likes its well-heeled clientele. There are lovely views of the river, islets and an old mill from the big windows.

River Una (☎ 310 014; Džemala Bijedića 12; meals 10-15KM; ☺ 7am-11pm) Another riverside restaurant, with the water at your feet. Recommended are the seafood dishes, but the freshest is always (you guessed it) the trout.

Meno (☎ 311 511; Bihaćkih Branilaca 35; pizzas 5-10KM; ☺ 8am-11pm) Choose any size or topping for your pizza, but choose carefully – you don't want that crispy base getting soggy. This is Bihać's pizza mecca. You can also take away.

Express (☎ 332 380; Bosanska 5; meals 3-5KM; ☺ 7am-10pm) Express by name, express by nature. Choose, point and eat well at this cafeteria near the post office. Choices are hot meals, salads, cakes and drinks.

Samoposluga (☎ 312 601; Bihaćkih Branilaca bb; ☺ 7.30am-10pm Mon-Sat, 8am-3pm Sun) A sizeable supermarket next to Villa Una that should cater to your feed-yourself requirements.

Tasun (Bihaćkih Branilaca bb; ☺ 24hr) If all that rafting has left you yearning for more activity, get yourself down to the town's party location. The music is varied, the punters happy and on weekends, they go on for hours.

Getting There & Away

Bihać is best reached via Banja Luka. Services from the **bus station** (☎ 350 676; Put V Korpusa bb) are somewhat limited with two buses daily to Banja Luka (11KM, three hours), three to Sarajevo (28KM, six hours) and five daily to Zagreb (21KM, 2½ hours).

Trains are still very infrequent and only within the area of Bihać, as much repair work still needs to be done to the infrastructure.

BOSNIA & HERCEGOVINA DIRECTORY

PRACTICALITIES

■ *Oslobođenje* and *Dnevni avaz* are the most popular daily newspapers in Sarajevo; *Dani* is a reliable independent weekly. *Nezavisne novine* is a Banja Luka daily.

■ Most public radio and TV stations are operated by the Bosnian Muslim-Croat and Serb entities; a national public broadcasting service is being developed.

■ Bosnia and Hercegovina uses standard European electricity (220V to 240V/50HZ to 60Hz).

■ The system used for measurements and weights is metric.

ACCOMMODATION

Prices quoted for the summer months are for July to September. Winter prices relate to the ski season, which generally is December to February.

Private accommodation is easy to arrange in Sarajevo and is also possible in Mostar. Elsewhere, ask the local people at markets or shops. Staying in a home is not only cheaper, but also usually very pleasant. As likely as not, your hosts will ply you with coffee, pull out old pictures of Tito (depending on their politics), and regale you with many tales of old Yugoslavia's glorious past.

Sarajevo is well set up for budget accommodation, and as more visitors go to Mostar cheaper accommodation will become more available. Most towns will have *pansions* that are generally slightly humbler than the hotels and more personable through direct contact with the owner. Hotels are everywhere. Some have not changed since the days of their state ownership while some have been privatised and modernised.

Unless otherwise mentioned, breakfast is not included with private accommodation but is for *pansions* and hotels. Also unless stated, all rooms have private bathroom. Most hotels and all but the cheapest *pansions* will have cable TV. Laundrettes have yet to debut in Bosnia and Hercegovina, but *pansions* and hotels will usually do laundry if asked. Prices vary dramatically; expect about 10KM to 20KM a load. Sarajevo has dry-cleaning facilities.

ACTIVITIES

Outdoor activities such as hiking and camping are severely compromised by the presence of mines. However, Jahorina and Bjelašnica, Bosnia and Hercegovina's ski resorts, are again open.

The rafting season runs from March to October. The Una River near Bihać is particularly popular.

Green Visions (Map p97; ☎ /fax 033-207 169; www .greenvisions.ba; Terezija bb) is a Sarajevo ecotourism agency popular with expat workers that runs outdoors trips.

BOOKS

Zoë Brân's *After Yugoslavia*, part of the Lonely Planet Journeys series, follows the author's travels through the former Yugoslavia in the aftermath of the collapse, reflecting on her earlier journey to the region in 1978.

While Rebecca West's mammoth *Black Lamb & Grey Falcon* (published 1941) remains a classic piece of travel writing, its 1937 ending is of no use for understanding what happened next. Noel Malcolm's *Bosnia: A Short History* is a good country-specific complement that brings history more up to date. Misha Glenny's *The Balkans, Nationalism, War, and the Great Powers, 1804–1999*, has some telling pages on the background to the recent war. *Balkan Babel* by Sabrina Ramet is an engaging look at Yugoslavia from Tito to Milošević.

BUSINESS HOURS

Official hours are 8am to 4pm Monday to Friday; banks open Saturday mornings.

Shops are open longer hours (usually from 8am to 6pm), and many open on Sunday. Restaurants are generally open from 11am to midnight Monday to Saturday, and noon to 7pm Sunday. Drinking venues stay open till midnight and clubs operate from 9pm to 2am.

CUSTOMS

Removing your shoes is usual in most households; the host will provide slippers. When greeting acquaintances in Sarajevo or elsewhere in the Federation, it is customary to plant one kiss on each cheek. In the RS, three kisses is the norm.

DANGERS & ANNOYANCES

Bosnia and Hercegovina's greatest danger is that some areas are heavily mined; see p87. Nationalism runs strong in some parts of the country (notably the RS and Croat areas to the south and west), but this should not affect international travellers, who can expect a warm welcome almost everywhere.

DISABLED TRAVELLERS

There has been a concerted effort to make things easier for travellers with disabilities, especially those who use wheelchairs. This is partly in response to those who have been disabled through war and also through rebuilding to Western standards. Smaller hotels won't have lifts. Disabled toilets are still very rare.

EMBASSIES & CONSULATES
Bosnian Embassies & Consulates

Bosnia and Hercegovina has embassies and/ or consulates in the following countries; the website www.mvp.gov.ba contains further listings.

Australia Canberra (☎ 02-6232 4646; fax 02-6232 5554; 6 Beale Crescent, Deakin, ACT 2600)
Canada Ottawa (☎ 613-236 0028; fax 613-236 1139; 130 Albert St, Suite 805, Ottawa, Ontario K1P 5G4)
Croatia Zagreb (☎ 01-48 19 420; fax 01-48 19 418; Pavla Hatza 3, PP27, 10001 Zagreb)
France Paris (☎ 01 42 67 34 22; fax 01 40 53 85 22; 174 Rue de Courcelles, 75017 Paris)
Germany Berlin (☎ 030-814 712 33/5; fax 030-814 712; 31 Ibsenstrasse 14, D-10439); Bonn (☎ 0228-35 00 60; fax 0228-35 00 69; Friedrich-Wilhelm strasse 2, 53113); Munich (☎ 089-982 80 64/5; fax 089-982 80 79; Montsalvat strasse 19, 80804 Munich)

Netherlands The Hague (☎ 070-358 85 05; fax 070-358 43 67; Bezuidenhoutseweg 223, 2594 AL Den Haag)
Slovenia Ljubljana (☎ 01-432 40 42; fax 01-432 22 30; Kolarjeva 26, 1000 Ljubljana)
UK London (☎ 020-7373 0867; 5-7 Lexham Gardens, London W1R 3BF)
USA New York (☎ 212-593 1042; fax 212-751 9019; 866 UN Plaza, Suite 580, New York, NY 10017); Washington DC (☎ 202-337 1500; fax 202-337 1502; 2109 E St NW, Washington, DC 20037)

Embassies & Consulates in Bosnia & Hercegovina

The nearest embassies for Australia, Ireland and New Zealand are found in Belgrade, Ljubljana and Rome respectively. The following countries have representation in Sarajevo (area code 033):

Austria (Map p97; ☎ 279 400; fax 668 339; Džidžikovac 7)
Bulgaria (☎ 668 191; possar@bih.net.ba; Soukbunar 5)
Canada (Map p97; ☎ 222 033; fax 222 004; Grbavička 4/2)
Croatia (Map p97; ☎ 444 331; fax 472 434; Mehmeda Spahe 16)
France (Map p97; ☎ 668 151; fax 212 186; Mehmed-bega K. Lj 18)
Germany (Map p97; ☎ 275 000; fax 652 978; Mejtaš Buka 11-13)
Japan (Map pp100-1; ☎ 209 580; fax 209 583; M.M.Bašeskije 2)
Netherlands (Map p97; ☎ 223 404; fax 223 413; Grbavička 4/1)
Serbia and Montenegro (Map p97; ☎ 260 080; fax 221 469; Obala Maka Dizdara 3a)
Slovenia (Map p97; ☎ 271 260; fax 271 270; Bentbaša 7)
UK (Map p97; ☎ 444 429; britemb@bih.net.ba; Tina Ujevića 8)
USA (Map p97; ☎ 445 700; opabih@pd.state.gov; Alipašina 43)

Germany also has representation in **Banja Luka** (☎ 051-277 949; fax 051-217 113; Kralja Ptra I Karađorđevića 103, Banja Luka).

GAY & LESBIAN TRAVELLERS

Homosexuality is not at all well regarded in Bosnia and Hercegovina, although Sarajevo and Mostar are more tolerant. Homosexuality is legal and the age of consent is 16. There are no public organisations for contact.

HOLIDAYS

Bajram, a twice-yearly Muslim holiday (December and October, see p392 for precise dates), is observed in parts of the Federation. Easter and Christmas are observed but Orthodox and Catholic dates may not coincide.

New Year's Day 1 January
Independence Day 1 March
May Day 1 May
National Statehood Day 25 November

INTERNET RESOURCES

Bosnia and Hercegovina's natural and cultural wonders are talked up at www.bhtourism.ba, which is administered by the Office of the High Representative, itself a good source of news – see www.ohr.int. The website www.insidebosnia.com has news on events and other interesting links. The government website www.mvp.gov.ba gives details on embassies and visas.

LANGUAGE

Notwithstanding different dialects, the people of Bosnia and Hercegovina basically speak the same language. However, that language is referred to as 'Bosnian' in the Muslim parts of the Federation, 'Croatian' in Croat-controlled parts and 'Serbian' in the RS. The Federation uses the Latin alphabet; the RS uses Cyrillic. See the Croatian & Serbian section of the Language chapter (p414).

MAPS

Freytag & Berndt produces a good 1:250,000 road map of Bosnia and Hercegovina. Maps of Mostar, Sarajevo and Banja Luka are readily available from bookshops, kiosks or tourist information centres.

MONEY

The euro is the shadow currency. The convertible mark (KM), Bosnia's currency, is tied to the euro at a rate of 1KM to €0.51129. Many establishments (especially hotels) accept euros (notes only) and sometimes also list their prices in euros. Prices in this chapter conform to quotes of individual businesses.

ATMs are all over the place with MasterCard, Visa and their offshoots being accepted. Visa, MasterCard and Diners Club are readily accepted by larger establishments all over the country.

When changing money, it's best to ask for small bills as shops often are hard-pressed

BOSNIA & HERCEGOVINA

for change. Travellers cheques can be readily changed at Raiffeisen and Zagrebačka Banks, one or both of which have branches in the places mentioned in this chapter.

PHOTOGRAPHY & VIDEO

Photographing military installations (including airports, bridges, checkpoints, troops and bases) and embassies is forbidden. If in doubt, ask before taking any photographs.

POST

Post and telephone offices are usually combined. Poste-restante service is available at all cities included in this book; letters should be addressed to: (Name), Poste Restante, (postcode), Bosnia and Hercegovina.

Postcodes are: Travnik 72270, Banja Luka 78101, Bihać 77000, Međugorje 88266, Mostar 88000. A fee is usually charged when the mail is picked up.

TELEPHONE & FAX

Phonecards, for local or short international calls at public phones, can be purchased at post offices or from street kiosks for 2KM or 5KM.

There's a button labelled 'language' to give you instructions in English. Unfortunately, cards issued in the Serbian, Croatian or Bosnian parts of the country are not interchangeable.

It's cheaper to use the telephone section of post offices for longer calls. Calls to Australia/Britain/North America cost 2.09/1.05/1.05KM. One page of fax to the same destinations costs the same.

Dial ☎ 1201 for the international operator and ☎ 1188 if you need local directory information.

Telephone numbers mentioned in this chapter starting with 061 and 063 are for mobile phones within the Federation and 065 is the mobile code in RS.

EMERGENCY NUMBERS

- Fire ☎ 123
- Medical emergency ☎ 124
- Police ☎ 122
- Roadside emergency ☎ 1282/1288

TOURIST INFORMATION

Bosnia's larger cities, including Sarajevo, Banja Luka, Mostar, Bihać and Međugorje, all have tourist offices. The underemployed staff are generally delighted to see travellers and will dispense maps, brochures and advice.

VISAS

Citizens of the EU and the following countries do not require a visa: Andorra, Australia, Brunei, Canada, Croatia, Japan, Kuwait, Liechtenstein, Macedonia, Malaysia, Monaco, New Zealand, Norway, Qatar, Russia, San Marino, Serbia and Montenegro, Switzerland, the Vatican, Turkey and the USA.

Citizens of all other countries must apply for a visa; forms can be obtained from Bosnia and Hercegovina consular offices. An application for a private visit visa must be accompanied by a letter of invitation from a citizen of the country, while a tourist visa application must be accompanied by a voucher from the tourist agency organising the visit.

The cost of a single entry visa is €31, a multiple-entry visa for up to 90 days €57, and a multiple-entry visa for over 90 days €72. One photograph needs to accompany the application. For a full list and application requirements check the government website www.mvp.gov.ba.

TRANSPORT IN BOSNIA & HERCEGOVINA

This section deals with travel into or out of Bosnia and Hercegovina, and includes general getting around advice and information. For details of travel within the Western Balkans, see the Transport chapter.

GETTING THERE & AWAY
Air

Bosnia and Hercegovina's main airport is at Sarajevo; Mostar has an airport but only receives charter flights. The country's other airport is that of Banja Luka in the RS. The airline Air Srpska was not flying at the time of research due to financial reasons.

Bosnia and Hercegovina is served by a few European airlines such as Austrian Airlines, Alitalia, Lufthansa and Adria Airways, which pick up at intercontinental hubs like London, Milan, Frankfurt and Vienna. No discount airlines fly into Bosnia and Hercegovina but cheap flights to Dubrovnik in Croatia and a bus trip into the country would be worth investigating.

JAT serves **Banja Luka airport** (☎ 051-835 210). The following airlines (Sarajevo phone numbers, are code 033) serve **Sarajevo airport** (☎ 289 100; www.sarajevo-airport.ba):

Adria Airways (airline code JP; ☎ 232 125; www.adria -airways.com; hub Ljubljana)

Austrian Airlines (airline code OS; ☎ 202 059; www .aua.com; hub Vienna)

Croatia Airlines (airline code OU; ☎ 666 123; www .croatiaairlines.hr; hub Zagreb)

JAT (airline code JU; ☎ 259 750; www.jat.com; hub Belgrade)

Lufthansa (code LH; ☎ 278 590; www.lufthansa.com; hub Frankfurt)

Malév Hungarian Airlines (airline code MA; ☎ 473 200; www.malev.hu; hub Budapest)

Scandjet (airline code FLY; ☎ 266 430; www.scandjet .se; hub Gothenburg)

Swiss International Air Lines (airline code LX; ☎ 208 971; www.swiss.com; hub Zurich)

Turkish Airlines (airline code TK; ☎ 666 092; www .turkishairlines.com; hub Istanbul)

Land

A return ticket is cheaper than two single tickets.

BORDER CROSSINGS

There are no problems in crossing any of the borders that Bosnia and Hercegovina shares with Croatia, and Serbia and Montenegro.

If you're travelling by bus, wait inside; a border guard will get on board and check your passport. Sometimes the driver will collect all the passports on board and take them outside to show them to the guards. Don't panic, this is normal. If you are using the train to travel via Croatia (to Budapest, etc), the same procedures apply.

If you are driving, the crossings are usually simply a matter of queuing and showing your passport and car documents.

Croatia

There are several border crossings into Croatia from Bosnia and Hercegovina, but the fastest and least hassle is the crossing at Metković. This is the one that will be used on most bus journeys from the coast

to Mostar or Sarajevo. The points of crossing are: Metković Doljani, Neum, Ivanica, Imotski, Slavonski Brod, Prnjavor, Orašje.

Serbia & Montenegro

If you are coming into Bosnia and Hercegovina from Serbia or Montenegro, make sure you have your police registration documents (your hotel/host is supposed to supply you with these) stating where you have been staying while in the country, as the Serbian & Montenegrin authorities will ask for them and can get slightly tiresome if you can't produce them. (This is not necessary in Bosnia and Hercegovina.) The points of crossing are: Sitnica, Višegrad, Zvornik, Šćepan Polje.

BUS

Well-established bus routes link Bosnia and Hercegovina with its neighbours and Western Europe.

Međugorje, Mostar, Sarajevo and Bihać have bus connections with Split and Dubrovnik on the coast and Zagreb in Croatia.

Sarajevo and Banja Luka have services to Belgrade and Podgorica in Serbia and Montenegro.

Sample routes to Western Europe from Sarajevo are Munich (€54, 16 hours, daily), Amsterdam (€125, 32 hours, Tuesday, Thursday and Saturday) and Brussels (€105, 27 hours, Tuesday and Saturday).

CAR & MOTORCYCLE

Drivers need to ensure that they have Green Card insurance for their vehicle and an International Driving Permit. Fuel is readily available in towns but it's sensible not to get too low, especially at night when stations may be closed. Spares for European-made cars should be readily available and there'll be mechanics in all largish towns.

TRAIN

A daily service connects Ploče (on the Croatian coast) and Zagreb (Croatia) via Mostar, Sarajevo and Banja Luka; another connects Ploče and Sarajevo via Mostar.

Ploče	Mostar	Sarajevo	Banja Luka	Zagreb
5.47am	7.10am	9.34am	3.36pm	7.46pm
10.18am	8.56am	6.41am		
3.50pm	5.20pm	7.39pm		
11.02pm	9.40pm	7.21pm	1.04pm	8.57am

An overnight train runs from Sarajevo to Budapest (€45/65 in 1st/2nd class, 11 hours, 10.25pm). Another overnight train runs from Banja Luka to Belgrade (22.50KM, nine hours, 9.15pm).

GETTING AROUND

Air

Air Srpska and Air Bosna were the only domestic airlines, but due to financial problems they no longer operate. There may be future efforts to resuscitate them.

Bicycle

Only adventurous foreigners cycle out into the countryside, where the roads can be very hilly. Do not venture off established concrete or asphalt surfaces because of the risk of mines. There is a core of cyclists in Sarajevo but, again, they tend to be foreigners.

Bus

Bosnia and Hercegovina's bus network is comprehensive and reliable although some buses verge on the decrepit. Some services between distant towns may be limited. As in other matters the Federation and RS run separate services.

Stowing luggage usually costs up to 2KM per item, depending on the route. Buses usually run on time, although they are slow due to winding roads and occasional stops for drivers and passengers to eat and smoke.

COSTS

Sample fares are 11KM Mostar to Sarajevo, 9KM Sarajevo to Travnik and 11KM from Banja Luka to Bihać.

RESERVATIONS

Reservations aren't really necessary except on international buses or on infrequent long-distance services during holiday times.

Car & Motorcycle

Narrow roads, hills and bends, although through beautiful countryside, make for slow progress by car but for some challenging motorcycling. Kamikaze drivers

pass even on the sharpest of curves. Keep well behind them.

AUTOMOBILE ASSOCIATIONS

Automobile Association of Bosnia & Hercegovina (Map p97; ☎ 033-212 771; www.bihamk.ba; Skenderija 23, 71000 Sarajevo) offers road assistance and towing services for members. A membership costs 35KM per year.

HIRE

Many car-hire places have sprung up, particularly in Sarajevo. Car hire is also available in Banja Luka, Mostar and Međugorje. Prices usually start at €43/€240 for one day/week with unlimited mileage.

Car-hire firms in the Federation do not operate in RS and vice versa.

You'll need a deposit, usually in the form of a credit-card slip, your International Driving Permit and your passport (they'll take a photocopy).

Check the car in the presence of the hirer for existing damage and nonfunctioning items.

ROAD RULES

Driving is on the right, seat belts must be worn and the tolerated level of alcohol in the blood is .05. Speed limits are 60km/h for urban roads and 80km/h for rural roads.

Local Transport

TAXI

Taxis are readily available and cheap, though outside Sarajevo and Banja Luka they may not have (or turn on) meters. If there is no meter, agree on the price before you set off.

Train

There are far fewer trains than buses and they don't necessarily connect with where visitors might go. However, they're more comfortable, there's more to see from them and they can be used as an alternative to the bus for transport between Banja Luka, Sarajevo and Mostar. About 10 daily trains chug out of Sarajevo to minor destinations. Trains from Banja Luka travel locally within the RS.

Croatia

MARTIN MOOS

Croatia

What a difference a decade makes. Only 10 years ago Croatia's principal visitors were peacekeepers and aid workers. Now it's become Europe's latest 'gotta go' destination. Yachts glide up the coast, movie stars discreetly arrange to buy an island or two and no Mediterranean cruise is complete without a stop in Dubrovnik. Trendy travellers are calling it the 'new Greece', the 'new Riviera', the 'new Tuscany', as though the country had recently sprouted from the Mediterranean.

Despite the hype, Croatia's pleasures are more timeless than trendy. Crystalline water laps gently at a 1778km-long coast and no less than 1185 islands. Away from the coast, eight national parks protect pristine forests, karstic mountains, rivers, lakes and waterfalls in a landscape of primeval beauty.

The culture is as varied as the scenery. A parade of Roman, Venetian, Austro-Hungarian and Italian occupiers left Croatia with a unique and slightly schizoid identity. The interior has a strong central-European flavour, evident in the baroque architecture of Zagreb. With its pastel fishing ports and devotion to pasta the coast could be an extension of Italy. In fact it was an extension of Italy for a good part of the last millennium. Yet there's no mistaking Croatia's Slavic soul, especially apparent at festival time when centuries-old songs, dances and costumes animate villages and town squares around the country.

Croatians retain a strong attachment to the land and traditions that nourished the dream of independence for so long. Even as a tide of speculators and developers wash ashore, there is a real commitment to preserving the extraordinary beauty of the coast. Whether the country can hold out against the lure of easy money is an excruciating test of its character. But, so far the signs are promising.

FAST FACTS

- **Area** 56,538 sq km
- **Capital** Zagreb
- **Currency** kuna (KN); €1=7.38KN; US$1=6.16KN; UK£1=10.75KN; A$1=4.63KN; ¥100=5.46KN; NZ$1=4.87KN
- **Famous for** neckties, war, Tito
- **Key phrases** bog (hello); doviđenja (goodbye); hvala (thanks); pardon (sorry)
- **Official language** Croatian
- **Population** 4.5 million
- **Telephone codes** country code ☎ 385; international access code ☎ 00
- **Visas** unnecessary for citizens of the EU, USA, Australia and Canada; see p389 for details

CROATIA

HIGHLIGHTS

- The walled Old Town of **Dubrovnik** (p209) that surrounds luminous marble streets and finely ornamented buildings
- The Venetian architecture and vibrant nightlife of **Hvar town** (p203)
- The colour and spectacle of a *moreška* sword dance in **Korčula** (p208)
- The lakes, coves and island monastery of **Mljet** (p208)
- The cobbled streets and unspoiled fishing port of **Rovinj** (p164)

ITINERARIES

- **One week** After a day in dynamic Zagreb head down to Split for a look at Diocletian's Palace. Then take ferries to Hvar and Korčula. End with three days in Dubrovnik, taking a day trip to Mljet.
- **Two weeks** After two days in Zagreb, head to Rovinj for a three-day stay, taking day trips to Pula and Poreč. Head south to Zadar for a night and then go on to Split for a night. Take ferries to Hvar and Korčula, spending two or three days on each island before ending with three days in Dubrovnik and a day trip to Mljet.

CLIMATE & WHEN TO GO

The climate varies from Mediterranean along the Adriatic coast, with hot, dry summers and mild, rainy winters, to continental inland, with cold winters and warm summers. You can swim in the sea from mid-June until late September. Coastal temperatures are slightly warmer south of Split. The peak tourist season runs from mid-July to the end of August. Prices are highest and accommodation scarcest during this period. See Climate Charts p389 for more.

The best time to be in Croatia is June. The weather is beautiful, the boats and excursions are running often and it's not yet too crowded. May and September are also good, especially if you're interested in hiking.

HISTORY

In 229 BC the Romans began their conquest of the indigenous Illyrians by establishing a colony at Solin (Salona), close to Split in Dalmatia. Emperor Augustus then extended the empire and created the provinces of Illyricum (Dalmatia and Bosnia) and Pannonia (Croatia). In AD 285 Emperor Diocletian decided to retire to his palace fortress in

---

HOW MUCH?

- **Short taxi ride** 50KN
- **Litre of milk** 7KN
- **Loaf of bread** 3.50KN
- **Bottle of house white** 20KN
- **Newspaper** 5KN

LONELY PLANET INDEX

- **Litre of petrol** 8KN
- **Litre of bottled water** 6KN
- **33cl of Karlovačko beer** 10KN
- **Souvenir T-shirt** 75KN
- **Street snack (slice of burek)** 10KN

Split, today the greatest Roman ruin in Eastern Europe. When the empire was divided in 395, what are now known as Slovenia, Croatia and Bosnia and Hercegovina stayed with the Western Roman Empire, while present-day Serbia, Kosovo and Macedonia went to the Eastern Roman Empire, later known as the Byzantine Empire.

Around 625, Slavic tribes migrated from present-day Poland. The Serbian tribe settled in the region that is now southwestern Serbia. The Croatian tribe moved into what is now Croatia and occupied two former Roman provinces: Dalmatian Croatia along the Adriatic, and Pannonian Croatia to the north.

By the early part of the 9th century both settlements had accepted Christianity but the northern Croats fell under Frankish domination while Dalmatian Croats came under the nominal control of the Byzantine Empire. The Dalmatian duke Tomislav united the two groups in 925 in a single kingdom that prospered for nearly 200 years.

Late in the 11th century the throne fell vacant and a series of power struggles weakened central authority and split the kingdom. The northern Croats, unable to agree upon a ruler, united with Hungary in 1102 for protection against the Orthodox Byzantine Empire.

In the 14th century the Turks began pushing into the Balkans, defeating the Serbs in 1389 and the Hungarians in 1526. Northern Croatia turned to the Hapsburgs of Austria for protection against the Turks in 1527 and

CROATIA

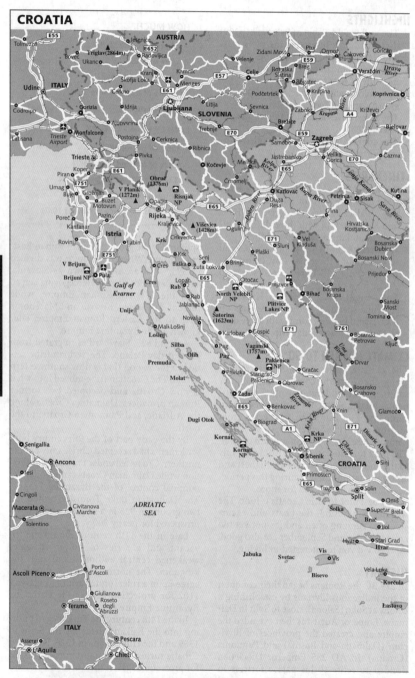

CROATIA

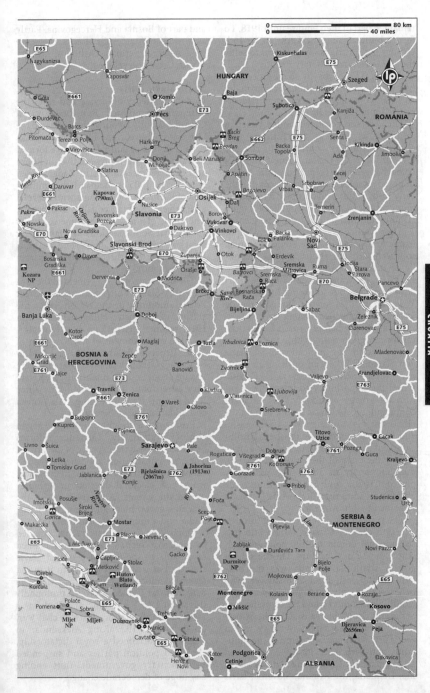

remained part of their empire until 1918. To form a buffer against the Turks, in the 16th century the Austrians invited Serbs to settle the Vojna Krajina (Military Frontier) north of Zadar. The Serbs in the borderlands had an autonomous administration under Austrian control; these areas were reincorporated into Croatia in 1881.

The Adriatic coast fell under Venetian influence as early as the 12th century, although Hungary continued to struggle for control of the region. Some Dalmatian cities changed hands repeatedly until Venice imposed its rule on the Adriatic coast in the early 15th century and occupied it for nearly four centuries. Only the Republic of Ragusa (Dubrovnik) maintained its independence.

After Venice was shattered by Napoleonic France in 1797, the French occupied southern Croatia, abolishing the Republic of Ragusa in 1808. Napoleon merged Dalmatia, Istria and Slovenia into the 'Illyrian Provinces', but following his defeat at Waterloo in 1815, Austria-Hungary moved in to pick up the pieces along the coast.

It wasn't long before Croatia began itching for more autonomy within the Austrian empire and for the unification of Dalmatia and Slavonia. When an uprising in Hungary threatened Austrian rule, Croatia seized the opportunity to intervene in return for greater autonomy. The Croatian commander Josip Jelačić set out to fight the rebels but his campaign was unsuccessful and Croatian hopes were crushed. Disillusionment spread after 1848, and was amplified by the birth of the Austro-Hungarian dual monarchy in 1867. The monarchy placed Croatia and Slavonia within the Hungarian administration, while Dalmatia remained within Austria.

The river of discontent running through late-19th-century Croatia forked into two streams that dominated the political landscape for the next century. On the side of greater south-Slavic unity was the brilliant Bishop Josif Juraf Strossmayer, who believed that only through *Jugoslavenstvo* (south-Slavic unity) could the aspirations of Serbs and Croats be realised. While Strossmayer favoured a Yugoslav entity within the Austro-Hungarian empire, the militantly anti-Serb Ante Starčević envisioned an independent Croatia made up of Slavonia, Dalmatia, the Krajina, Slovenia, Istria and part of Bosnia and Hercegovina. Partly as a result of Starčević's attacks, the sense of a separate Serbian Orthodox identity within Croatia developed.

South Slavic Unity

Under the theory of 'divide and rule', the Hungarian-appointed *Ban* (viceroy) of Croatia blatantly favoured the Serbs and the Orthodox Church, but his strategy backfired. The first organised resistance formed in Dalmatia. Croat representatives in Rijeka and Serb representatives in Zadar joined together in 1905 to demand the unification of Dalmatia and Slavonia with a formal guarantee of Serbian equality as a nation. The spirit of unity mushroomed, and by 1906 Croat-Serb coalitions had taken over local government in Dalmatia and Slavonia, forming a serious threat to the Hungarian power structure.

The outbreak of WWI cemented the idea that only Slavic unity could check Great Power ambitions in the region. After the collapse of the Austro-Hungarian empire in 1918, regional delegations quickly negotiated the establishment of the Kingdom of Serbs, Croats and Slovenes, to be based in Belgrade. Although many Croatians were unsure about Serbian intentions, they were very sure about Italian intentions since Italy lost no time in seizing Pula, Rijeka and Zadar in November 1918.

Problems with the kingdom began almost immediately. Currency reforms benefited Serbs at the expense of the Croats. The new constitution abolished Croatia's Sabor and centralised power in Belgrade, while new electoral districts underrepresented the Croats. A treaty between the Belgrade government and Italy gave Istria, Zadar and a number of islands to Italy.

Opposition to the new regime was led by the Croat Stjepan Radić, who remained favourable to the idea of a united Slavic country but wished to transform it into a federal democracy. His alliance with the Serb Svetpzar Pribićevic proved profoundly threatening to the regime and Radić was assassinated. Exploiting fears of civil war, on 6 January 1929 King Aleksandar in Belgrade proclaimed a royal dictatorship, abolished political parties and suspended parliamentary government, thus ending any hope of democratic change.

Ustaše, Chetnik & Partizans

One day after the proclamation, a Bosnian Croat, Ante Pavelić, set up the Ustaše Croatian Liberation Movement in Zagreb with the stated aim of establishing an independent state by force if necessary. Fearing arrest, he fled to Sofia in Bulgaria and made contact with anti-Serbian Macedonian revolutionaries before fleeing to Italy. There, he established training camps for his organisation under Mussolini's benevolent eye. After organising various disturbances, in 1934 he and the Macedonians succeeded in assassinating King Aleksandar in Marseilles while he was on a state visit. Italy responded by closing down the training camps and imprisoning Pavelić and many of his followers.

When Germany invaded Yugoslavia on 6 April 1941, the exiled Ustaše were quickly installed by the Germans, with the support of the Italians who hoped to see their own territorial aims in Dalmatia realised. They were not disappointed. Pavelić soon agreed to cede a good part of Dalmatia to Italy, which left him with the Lika region southwest of Zagreb and western Hercegovina as his political base.

Within days the Independent State of Croatia (NDH), headed by Pavelić, issued a range of decrees designed to persecute and eliminate the regime's 'enemies', who were mainly Jews, Roma and Serbs. The Ustaše programme called for 'one-third of Serbs killed, one-third expelled and one-third converted to Catholicism', a programme that was carried out with a brutality that appalled even the Nazis. Villages conducted their own personal pogroms against Serbs and extermination camps were set up, most notoriously at Jasenovac (south of Zagreb). The exact number of Serb victims is uncertain and controversial, with Croatian historians tending to minimise the figures and Serbian historians tending to maximise them. The number of Serb deaths range from 60,000 to 600,000, but the most reliable estimates settle somewhere between 80,000 to 120,000, including victims of village pogroms. Whatever the number, it's clear that the NDH and its supporters made a diligent effort to eliminate the entire Serb population.

The Serbs did not quietly accept their fate. Armed resistance to the regime took the form of Serbian 'Chetnik' formations led by General Draza Mihailovic, which began as an antifascist rebellion but soon degenerated into massacres of Croats in eastern Croatia and Bosnia.

Not all Croats supported Pavelić's policies. Josip Broz, known as Maršal Tito, was himself of Croat-Slovene parentage and tens of thousands of Croats fought bravely with his partisans. With their roots in the outlawed Yugoslavian Communist Party, the partisans attracted long-suffering Yugoslav intellectuals, Croats disgusted with Chetnik massacres, Serbs disgusted with Ustaše massacres, and antifascists of all kinds.

Although the Allies initially backed the Serbian Chetniks, it became apparent that the partisans were waging a far more focused and determined fight against the Nazis. With the diplomatic and military support of Churchill and other Allied powers, the partisans controlled much of Croatia by 1943. On 20 October 1944 Tito entered Belgrade with the Red Army and was made prime minister. When Germany surrendered in 1945, Pavelić and the Ustaše fled and the partisans entered Zagreb.

The remnants of the NDH army, desperate to avoid falling into the hands of the partisans, attempted to cross into Austria at Bleiburg. A small British contingent met the 50,000 troops and promised to intern them outside Yugoslavia in exchange for their surrender. It was a trick. The troops were forced into trains that headed back into Yugoslavia where the partisans awaited them. The ensuing massacre claimed the lives of at least 30,000 men (although the exact number is in doubt) and left a permanent stain on the Yugoslav government.

Recent History

Tito's attempt to retain control of the Italian city of Trieste and parts of southern Austria faltered in the face of Allied opposition, but Dalmatia and most of Istria were made a permanent part of postwar Yugoslavia. The good news was that Tito was determined to create a state in which no ethnic group dominated the political landscape. Croatia became one of six republics – Macedonia, Serbia, Montenegro, Bosnia and Hercegovina and Slovenia – in a tightly configured federation. The bad news was that Tito effected this delicate balance by creating a one-party state and rigorously stamping out all opposition, whether nationalist, royalist or religious. The government's hostility to organised religion, particularly the Catholic Church, stemmed from its perception that the Church was complicit in the murderous nationalism that surfaced during WWII.

During the 1960s, the concentration of power in Belgrade became an increasingly testy issue as it became apparent that money from the more prosperous republics of Slovenia and Croatia was being distributed to the poorer republics of Montenegro and Bosnia and Hercegovina. The problem seemed particularly blatant in Croatia, which saw money from its prosperous tourist business on the Adriatic coast flow into Belgrade. At the same time Serbs in Croatia were overrepresented in the government, armed forces and the police, partly because state service offered an opportunity for a chronically disadvantaged population.

In Croatia the unrest reached a crescendo in the 'Croatian Spring' of 1971. Led by reformers within the Communist Party of Croatia, intellectuals and students first called for greater economic autonomy and then constitutional reform to loosen Croatia's ties to Yugoslavia. Tito's eventual crackdown was ferocious. Leaders of the movement were 'purged' – either jailed or expelled from the party. Careers were abruptly terminated; some dissidents chose exile and emigrated to the USA. Serbs viewed the movement as the Ustaše reborn, and jailed reformers blamed the Serbs for their troubles. The stage was set for the later rise of nationalism and war that followed Tito's death in 1980, even though his 1974 constitution afforded the republics more autonomy.

Independence

Tito's habit of borrowing from abroad to flood the country with cheap consumer goods produced an economic crisis after his death. The country was unable to service the interest on its loans and inflation soared. The authority of the central government sank along with the economy, and long-suppressed mistrust among Yugoslavia's ethnic groups resurfaced.

In 1989 severe repression of the Albanian majority in Serbia's Kosovo province sparked renewed fears of Serbian hegemony

and heralded the end of the Yugoslav Federation. With political changes sweeping Eastern Europe, many Croats felt the time had come to end more than four decades of communist rule and attain complete autonomy into the bargain. In the free elections of April 1990 Franjo Tudjman's Croatian Democratic Union (HDZ; Hrvatska Demokratska Zajednica) secured 40% of the vote, to the 30% won by the Communist Party which retained the loyalty of the Serbian community as well as voters in Istria and Rijeka. On 22 December 1990 a new Croatian constitution was promulgated, changing the status of Serbs in Croatia from that of a 'constituent nation' to a national minority.

The constitution's failure to guarantee minority rights, and mass dismissals of Serbs from the public service, stimulated the 600,000-strong ethnic Serb community within Croatia to demand autonomy. In early 1991 Serb extremists within Croatia staged provocations designed to force federal military intervention. A May 1991 referendum (boycotted by the Serbs) produced a 93% vote in favour of independence, but when Croatia declared independence on 25 June 1991, the Serbian enclave of Krajina proclaimed its independence from Croatia.

War & Peace

Under pressure from the EC (now EU), Croatia declared a three-month moratorium on its independence, but heavy fighting broke out in Krajina, Baranja (the area north of the Drava River opposite Osijek) and Slavonia. The 180,000-member, 2000-tank Yugoslav People's Army, dominated by Serbian communists, began to intervene on its own authority in support of Serbian irregulars, under the pretext of halting ethnic violence.

When the Croatian government ordered a blockade of 32 federal military installations in the republic, the Yugoslav navy blockaded the Adriatic coast and laid siege to the strategic town of Vukovar on the Danube. During the summer of 1991, a quarter of Croatia fell to Serbian militias and the Serb-led Yugoslav People's Army.

In early October 1991 the federal army and Montenegrin militia moved against Dubrovnik to protest the blockade of their garrisons in Croatia, and on 7 October the presidential palace in Zagreb was hit by rockets fired by Yugoslav air-force jets in an unsuccessful assassination attempt on President Tudjman. When the three-month moratorium on independence ended Croatia declared full independence.

On 19 November heroic Vukovar finally fell when the army culminated a bloody three-month siege by concentrating 600 tanks and 30,000 soldiers there. During six months of fighting in Croatia 10,000 people died, hundreds of thousands fled and tens of thousands of homes were destroyed.

To fulfil a condition for EC recognition, in December the Croatian Sabor (which was re-established under Tito) belatedly amended its constitution to protect minority groups and human rights.

A UN-brokered ceasefire from 3 January 1992, generally held. The federal army was allowed to withdraw from its bases inside Croatia and tensions diminished.

In January 1992 the EC, succumbing to strong pressure from Germany, recognised Croatia. This was followed three months later by US recognition and in May 1992 Croatia was admitted to the UN.

In January 1993 the Croatian army suddenly launched an offensive in southern Krajina, pushing the Serbs back as much as 24km in some areas and recapturing strategic points. The Krajina Serbs vowed never to accept rule from Zagreb and in June 1993 they voted overwhelmingly to join the Bosnian Serbs (and eventually Greater Serbia).

The self-proclaimed 'Republic of Serbian Krajina' held elections in December 1993, which no international body recognised as legitimate or fair. Meanwhile, continued 'ethnic cleansing' left only about 900 Croats in Krajina out of an original population of 44,000.

While world attention turned to the grim events unfolding in Bosnia and Hercegovina, the Croatian government quietly began procuring arms from abroad. On 1 May 1995 the Croatian army and police entered occupied western Slavonia, east of Zagreb, and seized control of the region within days. The Krajina Serbs responded by shelling Zagreb in an attack that left seven people dead and 130 wounded. As the Croatian military consolidated its hold in western Slavonia, some 15,000 Serbs fled the region, despite assurances from the Croatian government that they were safe from retribution.

Belgrade's silence throughout this campaign showed that the Krajina Serbs had lost the support of their Serbian sponsors, encouraging Croats to forge ahead. On 4 August the military launched a massive assault on the rebel Serb capital of Knin, pummelling it with shells, mortars and bombs. Outnumbered by two to one, the Serb army fled towards northern Bosnia, along with 150,000 civilians whose roots in the Krajina stretched back centuries. The military operation ended in days, but was followed by months of terror. Widespread looting and burning of Serb villages, and attacks upon the few remaining elderly Serbs, seemed designed to ensure the permanence of this huge population shift. Allegations of atrocities caught the attention of the International Criminal Tribunal for the former Yugoslavia at The Hague. Of the two Croatian generals charged with committing crimes against the Serb population, General Gotovina remains at large and General Norac has turned himself in for trial.

The Dayton Accord signed in Paris in December 1995 recognised Croatia's traditional borders and provided for the return of eastern Slavonia, which was effected in January 1998. The transition proceeded relatively smoothly with less violence than was expected, but the two populations still regard each other over a chasm of suspicion and hostility. The Serbs and Croats associate with each other as little as possible and clever political manoeuvering has largely barred Serbs from assuming a meaningful role in municipal government.

Although stability has returned to the country, a key provision of the agreement was the promise by the Croatian government to facilitate the return of Serbian refugees, a promise that is far from being fulfilled. Although the central government in Zagreb has made the return of refugees a priority in accordance with the demands of the international community, its efforts have often been subverted by local authorities intent on maintaining the ethnic purity of their regions. In many cases, Croat refugees from Hercegovina have occupied houses abandoned by their Serb owners. Serbs intending to reclaim their property face a forbidding array of legal impediments in establishing a claim to their former dwellings.

PEOPLE

Croatia has a population of roughly 4.5 million people. Before the war Croatia had a population of nearly five million, of which 78% were Croats and 12% were Serbs. Bosnians, Hungarians, Italians, Czechs, Roma and Albanians made up the remaining 10%. Today Croats constitute 89% of the population, as there was a large influx of Croats from other parts of the former Yugoslavia after the war. Now, slightly less than 5% of the populations are Serb, followed by 0.5% Bosnians and about 0.4% each of Hungarians and Italians. Small communities of Czechs, Roma and Albanians complete the mosaic. Most Serbs live in eastern Croatia (Slavonia) where ethnic tensions between the Serbs and Croats run highest. The largest cities in Croatia are Zagreb (780,000), Split (188,700), Rijeka (144,000), Osijek (114,600) and Zadar (72,700).

Croats are united by a common religion, Catholicism, and a common sense of themselves as European. If you ask a Croat what distinguishes Croatian culture from Bosnian or Serbian culture, the answer is likely to be a variant of 'We are Western and they are Eastern'. Even Croats who bear no particular ill will towards other ethnicities will nonetheless note that their former compatriots in Bosnia and Hercegovina, Macedonia and Serbia and Montenegro eat different food, listen to different music, have different customs and, of course, go to different churches.

Although the shelling of Dubrovnik and the atrocities committed in eastern Slavonia and the Krajina have left a bitter taste in those regions, many Croatians are increasingly open to questioning the conduct of the 'Homeland War'. Self-examining books and articles are a staple of the country's intellectual life but the extradition to The Hague of Croatian generals accused of war crimes remains highly controversial. Initial foot-dragging in cooperating with The Hague tribunal delayed Croatia's bid to join the EU but, as of 2005, Croatia's cooperation was deemed sufficient and the country is negotiating to enter the EU in 2007.

RELIGION

Croats are overwhelmingly Roman Catholic, while virtually all Serbs belong to the Eastern Orthodox Church. In addition to doctrinal differences, Orthodox Christians venerate icons, allow priests to marry and do not accept the authority of the Roman Catholic pope. Long suppressed under communism, Catholicism is undergoing a strong resurgence in Croatia and churches have good attendance on Sunday. The previous pope had visited Croatia several times and religious holidays are scrupulously observed. Muslims make up 1.2% of the population and Protestants 0.4%, with a tiny Jewish population in Zagreb.

ARTS
Visual Arts

Examples of Roman architecture are abundant in Dalmatia where it persisted long after the Gothic style had swept the rest of Europe. In the 13th century the earliest examples of Gothic style appeared, usually still mixed with Romanesque forms. The most stunning work from this period is the portal on Trogir's Cathedral of St Lovro, carved by the master-artisan Radovan. Depicting human figures performing everyday chores was a definite break with traditional Byzantine reliefs of saints and apostles. The Cathedral of the Assumption of the Blessed Virgin Mary (formerly St Stephen's) in Zagreb was the first venture into the Gothic style in northern Croatia.

In independent Ragusa (Dubrovnik) Renaissance art and sculpture flowered. By the second half of the 15th century, Renaissance influences were appearing on late-Gothic structures. The Sponza Palace, formerly the Customs House, is a fine example of this mixed style. By the mid-16th century, Renaissance features began to supplant the Gothic style in the palaces and summer residences built in and around Ragusa by the wealthy nobility. Unfortunately, much was destroyed in the 1667 earthquake and now Dubrovnik is more notable for the mixed Gothic-Romanesque Franciscan monastery, the 15th-century Orlando column and the Onofrio fountain, and the baroque St Blaise's Church and Cathedral of the Assumption of the Virgin.

Northern Croatia is well-known for the baroque style introduced by Jesuit monks in the 17th century. The city of Varaždin was a regional capital in the 17th and 18th centuries and, because of its location, enjoyed a steady interchange of artists, artisans and architects with northern Europe. The combination of wealth and a creatively fertile environment led to it becoming Croatia's foremost city of baroque art.

In Zagreb good examples of the baroque style are found in the Upper Town (Gornji Grad), Kaptol and Gradec. Notice St Catherine's Church and the restored baroque mansions that are now the Croatian History Museum and the Croation Naive Art Museum.

In the 19th century, Dalmatian art stagnated as the region fell prey to political problems, but Zagreb underwent a revival. Vlaho Bukovac (1855–1922) was the most notable painter in the late 19th century. After working in London and Paris, he came to Zagreb in 1892 and produced portraits and paintings on historical themes in a lively style. Early-20th-century painters of note include Miroslav Kraljević (1885–1913) and Josip Račić (1885–1908), but the most internationally recognised artist was the sculptor Ivan Meštrović (1883–1962), who created many masterpieces on Croatian themes. Antun Augustinčić (1900–79) was another internationally recognised sculptor whose *Monument to Peace* is outside New York's UN building.

Postwar artists experimented with abstract expressionism but this period is best remembered for the naive art that began with the 1931 *Zemlja* (Soil) exhibition in Zagreb, which introduced the public to works by Ivan Generalić (1914–92) and other peasant painters. Committed to producing art that could be easily understood and appreciated by ordinary people, Generalić was joined by painters Franjo Mraz and Mirko Virius and sculptor Petar Smajic in a campaign to gain acceptance and recognition for naive art.

The postwar trend to avant-garde art has evolved into installation art, minimalism, conceptualism and video art. On the video scene look for Sanja Ivekovic and Dalibor Martinis. The multimedia works of Andreja Kulunčić and the installations of Sandra Sterle are attracting international notice while the performances of Slaven Tolj could be called 'extreme art'.

Music & Dance

Although Croatia has produced many fine classical musicians and composers, its most original musical contribution lies in its rich tradition of folk music. Croatian folk music itself bears many influences, much of them dating back to the Middle Ages when the Hungarians and the Venetians vied for control of the country. Franz Joseph Haydn (1732–1809) was born near a Croat enclave in Austria and was strongly influenced by Croatian airs. Traditional Croatian music has also influenced modern musicians, most notably the Croatian-American jazz singer Helen Merrill, who recorded Croatian melodies on her album, *Jelena Ana Milcetic aka. Helen Merrill.*

The instrument most often used in Croatian folk music is the *tamburitza*, a three- or five-string mandolin that is plucked or strummed. Introduced by the Turks in the 17th century, the instrument rapidly gained a following in eastern Slavonia and came to be closely identified with Croatian national aspirations.

Tamburitza music survived the Yugoslav period, when it remained the dominant music played at weddings and local festivals. In the 1980s it modernised and many groups began to include electric bass and guitar. First was Zlatni Dukati, who became known for their patriotic music before and during the 1990s war. They were quickly followed by the rock-and-roll influenced Gazde, who are still turning out top-selling CDs.

Vocal music followed the *klapa* tradition. Translated as 'group of people', *klapa* is an outgrowth of church-choir singing. The form is most popular in rural Dalmatia and can involve up to 10 voices singing in harmony about love, tragedy and loss. Traditionally the choirs were all-male but now women have been getting into the act, although there are very few mixed choirs.

Not everyone is listening to folk music of course. Croatian pop is alive and well and you'll hear plenty of it on the radio. Ivo Robić was one of the few Croatian singer-songwriters to gain a following abroad. Doris Dragović has been on the scene for nearly 20 years, while younger stars Severina and Gibonni have wildly enthusiastic fans.

Like the music, Croatian traditional dances are kept alive at local and national festivals. Look for the *drmeš*, a kind of accelerated polka danced by couples in small groups. The *kolo*, a lively Slavic round dance in which men and women alternate in the circle, is accompanied by Roma-style violinists. In Dalmatia, the *poskočica* is also danced by couples creating various patterns.

Literature

The first literary flowering in Croatia took place in Dalmatia and was strongly influenced by the Italian Renaissance. The works of the scholar and poet Marko Marulić (1450–1524), from Split, are still venerated in Croatia. Ivan Gundulić (1589–1638) from Ragusa (Dubrovnik) is widely considered to be the greatest Croatian poet. The plays of Marin Držić (1508–67), especially *Dundo Maroje*, express humanistic Renaissance ideals and are still performed, especially in Dubrovnik.

Croatia's towering literary figure is 20th-century novelist and playwright Miroslav Krleža. Depicting the concerns of a changing Yugoslavia, his most popular novels include *The Return of Philip Latinovicz* (1932), which has been translated into English, and *Banners* (1963–65), a multivolume saga about middle-class Croatian life at the turn of the 20th century.

In poetry, the most towering postwar figure was the lyrical and sometimes satirical Vesna Parun. Although often harassed by the government for her 'decadent and bourgeois' poetry, her *Collected Poems* have reached a new generation who find solace in her vision of wartime folly.

Contemporary writers have been strongly marked by the implications of Croatian independence. Alenka Mirković is a journalist who wrote a powerful memoir of the siege of Vukovar. Goran Tribuson uses the thriller genre to explore the changes in Croatian society after the war. In *O blivion* Pavao Pavličić uses a detective story to explore the problems of collective historical memory.

ENVIRONMENT
The Land

Croatia is half the size of present-day Serbia and Montenegro in area and population. The republic swings around like a boomerang from the Pannonian plains of Slavonia between the Sava, Drava and Danube Rivers, across hilly central Croatia to the Istrian Peninsula, then south through Dalmatia along the rugged Adriatic coast.

The narrow Croatian coastal belt at the foot of the Dinaric Alps is only about 600km long as the crow flies, but it's so indented that the actual length is 1778km. If the 4012km of coastline around the offshore islands is added to the total, the length becomes 5790km. Most of the 'beaches' along this jagged coast consist of slabs of rock sprinkled with naturists. Don't come expecting to find sand, but the waters are sparkling clean, even around large towns.

Croatia's offshore islands are every bit as beautiful as those off the coast of Greece. There are 1185 islands and islets along the tectonically submerged Adriatic coastline, 66 inhabited. The largest are Cres, Krk, Lošinj, Pag and Rab in the north; Dugi Otok in the middle; and Brač, Hvar, Korčula, Mljet and Vis in the south. Most are barren and elongated from northwest to southeast, with high mountains that drop right into the sea.

National Parks

When the Yugoslav Federation collapsed, eight of its finest national parks ended up in Croatia, occupying nearly 10% of the country. Brijuni near Pula is the most carefully cultivated park, with well-preserved Mediterranean holm oak forests. The mountainous Risnjak National Park near Delnice, east of Rijeka, is named after one of its inhabitants – the *ris* (lynx).

Dense forests of beech and black pine in the Paklenica National Park near Zadar are home to a number of endemic insects, reptiles and birds. The abundant plant and animal life, including bears, wolves and deer, in the Plitvice Lakes National Park between Zagreb and Zadar has warranted its inclusion on Unesco's list of World Natural Heritage sites. Both Plitvice Lakes and Krka National Parks (near Šibenik) feature a dramatic series of cascades and incredible turquoise lakes.

The 101 stark and rocky islands of the Kornati Archipelago and National Park make it the largest in the Mediterranean. The island of Mljet near Korčula also contains a forested national park, and the North Velebit National Park includes Croatia's longest mountain range.

Environmental Issues

The lack of heavy industry in Croatia has left the country largely free of industrial pollution, but its forests are under threat from acid rain from neighbouring countries. The dry summers and brisk *maestral* winds pose substantial fire hazards along the coast. The sea along the Adriatic coast is among the world's cleanest especially throughout Istria and the southern Adriatic. Waste disposal is a pressing problem in Croatia, with insufficient and poorly regulated disposal sites.

Wildlife

Deer are plentiful in the dense forests of Risnjak, as well as brown bears, wild cats and *ris* (lynx), from which the national park gets its name. Occasionally a wolf or wild boar may appear but only rarely. Plitvice Lakes National Park, however, is an important refuge for wolves. A rare sea otter is also protected in Plitvice as well as in Krka National Park.

The griffon vulture, with a wing span of 2.6m, has a permanent colony on Cres Island, and Paklenica National Park is rich in peregrine falcons, goshawks, sparrow hawks, buzzards and owls. Krka National Park is an important migration route and winter habitat for marsh birds such as herons, wild duck, geese, cranes, rare golden eagles and short-toed eagles. Kopački Rit swamp near Osijek in eastern Croatia is an extremely important bird refuge, but its status as a visit-worthy place is vague – there are still mines there.

Two venomous snakes are endemic in Paklenica – the nose-horned viper and the European adder – and the nonvenomous leopard snake, four-lined snake, grass snake and snake lizard species can also be found in Krka National Park.

FOOD & DRINK

A restaurant (*restauracija*) or pub may also be called a *gostionica* and a café is known as a *kavana*. Self-service cafeterias are quick, easy and inexpensive, though the quality of the food tends to vary quite a lot. Better restaurants aren't that much more expensive if you choose carefully. The cheapest dishes are pasta and risotto, which can be filling meals. Fish dishes are often charged by weight (from 320KN to 360KN per

kilogram), which makes it difficult to know how much a certain dish will cost but an average portion is about 250g. Some restaurants tack on a 10% cover charge, which is *supposed* to be mentioned on the menu.

Breakfast is included in the price of the hotels in this chapter and usually includes a juice drink, bread, cheese, yogurt, cereal and cold cuts, as well as coffee and tea. No restaurants serve breakfast.

A load of fruit and vegetables from the local market makes a healthy, cheap picnic lunch. There are plenty of supermarkets in Croatia; cheese, cold cuts, bread, wine and milk are readily available and fairly cheap. The person behind the meat counter at supermarkets will make a big cheese or bologna sandwich for you upon request and you only pay the price of the ingredients.

Staples & Specialities

Croatian meals often start with a dish of locally smoked ham or Pag cheese with olives. A Zagreb speciality is *štrukli* (boiled cheesecake), served either plain as a starter or sugared as a dessert. In the north you also might begin with a hearty *Zagorska juha od krumpira* (potato soup Zagorje style) or *manistra od bobića* (beans and fresh maize soup), while coastal folk follow the Italian habit of beginning with a serving of spaghetti or risotto. *Risotto neri* (black risotto) made from squid in its own ink is a particular delicacy.

For a main meal, the Adriatic coast excels in seafood, including scampi (look for *scampi bouzzara*), *prstaci* (shellfish), *lignje* (calamari) and Dalmatian *brodet* (fish stew served with polenta). Istria is known for its *tartufe* (truffles), which frequently appear in risotto or pasta dishes or flavouring meat. The season is from October to January; any other time the chef is using preserved truffles. In Zagreb and in the north you'll find exquisite spit-roasted goose, duck and lamb. Turkey with *mlinci* (baked noodles) is another Zagrebian wonder.

For fast food you can usually snack on *ćevapčići* (spicy beef or pork meatballs), *ražnjiči* (shish kebab), *burek* (a greasy layered pie made with meat) or *sira* (cheese), which is cut on a huge metal tray.

It's customary to have a small glass of brandy before a meal and to accompany the food with one of Croatia's fine wines – there

CROATIA

are about 700 to choose from! Croatians often mix their wine with water, calling it *bevanda*. Croatia is also famous for its *šljivovica* (plum brandies), *travarica* (herbal brandies), *vinjak* (cognacs) and liqueurs, such as maraschino (a cherry liqueur made in Zadar) or herbal *pelinkovac*. Italian-style espresso is popular in Croatia.

Zagreb's Ožujsko *pivo* (beer) is very good but Karlovačko *pivo* from Karlovac is even better. You'll probably want to practise saying *živjeli!* (cheers!).

Vegetarians & Vegans

Outside of Zagreb, vegetarian restaurants are few and far between but Croatia's vegetables are usually locally grown and quite tasty. *Blitva* (swiss chard) is a nutritious side dish often served with potatoes. Pasta, risotto and pizza are often made from scratch and lacto-ovo vegetarians will appreciate Croatia's wide variety of cheese. Look for the sharp lamb's-milk cheese from the island of Pag.

ZAGREB

☎ 01 / pop 780,000

Zagreb is finally coming into its own as an intriguing combination of Eastern and Western Europe. The sober Austro-Hungarian architecture in the town centre houses newly opened boutiques with the latest fashions from France and Italy. Bohemian cafés and sleek cocktail bars enliven the medieval streets of the old Kaptol and Gradec neighbourhoods. The Croatian appreciation of food is divided between its traditional hearty meat and potatoes restaurants and a new smattering of more worldly flavours.

Spreading up from the Sava River, Zagreb sits on the southern slopes of Mt Medvednica and throbs with the energy you would expect from a capital city, but the bustle of business life is interrupted by the long, refreshing stretch of park that bisects the town centre. With simmering nightlife and a wealth of outdoor cafés, packed from the first hint of mild weather, there's no shortage of diversions. Plus, there's an assortment of museums and galleries to explore and a regular concert schedule for the culturally minded.

HISTORY

Medieval Zagreb developed from the 11th to the 13th centuries in the twin villages of Kaptol and Gradec, which make up the city's hilly Old Town. Kaptol grew around St Stephen's Cathedral (now renamed the Cathedral of the Assumption of the Blessed Virgin Mary) and Gradec centred on St Mark's Church. The two hill-top administrations were bitter and often warring rivals until a common threat in the form of Turkish invaders emerged in the 15th century. The two communities merged and became Zagreb, capital of the small portion of Croatia that hadn't fallen to the Turks in the 16th century. As the Turkish threat receded in the 18th century, the town expanded and the population grew. It was the centre of intellectual and political life under the Austro-Hungarian empire and became capital of the Independent State of Croatia in 1941 after the German invasion. The 'independent state' was in fact a Nazi puppet regime in the hands of Ante Pavelić and the Ustaša movement, even though most Zagrebians supported Tito's partisans.

In postwar Yugoslavia Zagreb took second place to Belgrade but continued expanding. The area south of the Sava River developed into a new district, Novi Zagreb, replete with the glum residential blocks that were a hallmark of postwar Eastern European architecture. Zagreb has been capital of Croatia since 1991 when the country became independent.

ORIENTATION

The city is divided into Lower Zagreb, where most shops, restaurants, hotels and businesses are located, and Upper Zagreb, defined by the two hills of Kaptol and Gradec. As you come out of the train station, you'll see a series of parks and pavilions directly in front of you and the twin neo-Gothic towers of the cathedral in Kaptol in the distance. Trg Jelačića, beyond the northern end of the parks, is the main city square of Lower Zagreb. There is a bus that runs from the airport to the bus station (see p158 for details). The bus station is 1km east of the train station. Trams 2 and 6 run from the bus station to the train station, with tram 6 continuing to Trg Jelačića.

ZAGREB IN...

Two Days

Start your day with a stroll through Stross-mayerov trg, Zagreb's oasis of greenery. While you're there, take a look at the **Stross-mayer Gallery of Old Masters** (p153) and then walk on to the town centre, Trg Jelačića. Avoid being hit by a tram as you cross the square, and head up to Kaptol for a look at the centre of Zagreb's (and Croatia's) religious life, the **Cathedral of the Assumption of the Blessed Virgin Mary** (p152). As long as you're 'uptown', pick up some fruit at the **Dolac** (p152) fruit and vegetable market or have lunch at **Kaptol-ska Klet** (p155) and head over to Gradec to check out some churches and museums. Don't miss the **Meštrović Studio** (p152). Try the nightlife along **Tkalčićeva** (p156) and sup at **Baltazar** (p155).

On the second day, make a tour of the Lower Town museums, reserving a good two hours for the **Museum Mimara** (p154), in the western part of the Lower Town. Take tea at **Kazališna Kavana** (p156) and an afternoon break in the **Botanical Gardens** (p154). Early evening is best at **Trg Petra Preradovića** (p156) before dining at one of the many scrumptious Lower Town restaurants and sampling some of Zagreb's nightlife.

INFORMATION

Bookshops

Algoritam (Hotel Dubrovnik, Gajeva) Off Trg Jelačića, Algoritam has a wide selection of books and magazines to choose from in English, French, German, Italian and Croatian.

Emergency

Police station (☎ 45 63 311; Petrinjska 30) Assists foreigners with visa problems.

Internet Access

Art Net Club (☎ 45 58 471; Preradovićeva 25; per hr 20KN; ☽ 9am-11pm) Zagreb's flashiest Internet café, it frequently hosts concerts and performances.
Sublink (☎ 48 11 329; Teslina 12; per hr 20KN; ☽ 9am-10pm Mon-Sat, 3-10pm Sun) It was here first and has a comfortable set up.

Laundry

If you're staying in private accommodation you can usually arrange with the owner to do your laundry, which would be cheaper than the two options listed below. Five kilograms of laundry will cost about 65KN.
Petecin (☎ 48 14 802; Kaptol 11; ☽ 8am-8pm Mon-Fri)
Predom (☎ 46 12 990; Draškovićeva 31; ☽ 7am-7pm Mon-Fri)

Left Luggage

Garderoba bus station (per hr 1.20KN; ☽ 5am-10pm Mon-Sat, 6am-10pm Sun); train station (per day 10KN; ☽ 24hr)

Medical Services

Dental Emergency (☎ 48 28 488; Perkovčeva 3; ☽ 24hr)
KBC Rebro (☎ 23 88 888; Kišpatićeva 12; ☽ 24hr) East of the city, it provides emergency aid.
Pharmacy (☎ 48 16 159; Trg Jelačića 2; ☽ 24hr)

Money

There are ATMs at the bus and train stations and the airport as well as numerous locations around town. Exchange offices at the bus and train stations change money at the bank rate with 1.5% commission. Both the banks in the train station (open 7am to 9pm) and the bus station (open 6am to 8pm) accept travellers cheques.
Atlas travel agency (☎ 48 13 933; Zrinjevac 17) The Amex representative in Zagreb.

Post

Main post office (Branimirova 4; ☽ 24hr Mon-Sat, 1pm-midnight Sun) Holds poste-restante mail. This post office is also the best place to make long-distance telephone calls and send packages.

Tourist Information

Main tourist office (☎ 48 14 051; www.zagreb-touristinfo.hr; Trg Jelačića 11; ☽ 8.30am-8pm Mon-Fri, 9am-5pm Sat, 10am-4pm Sun) Distributes city maps and free leaflets. It also sells the Zagreb Card, which costs 90KN and includes 72 hours of free transport, a 50% discount on museums and a 10% to 15% discount on selected hotels. It can also be purchased online.
National Park Information Office (☎ 46 13 586; Trg Tomislava 19; ☽ 8am-4pm Mon-Fri) Has details on Croatia's national parks.
Tourist office annexe (☎ 49 21 645; Trg Nikole Šubića Zrinjskog 14; ☽ 9am-6pm Mon-Fri) Same services as the main tourist office, but stocks fewer publications.
Zagreb County Tourist Association (☎ 48 73 665; www.tzzz.hr; Preradovićeva 42; ☽ 8am-4pm Mon-Fri) Has information about attractions in the region outside Zagreb.

CROATIA

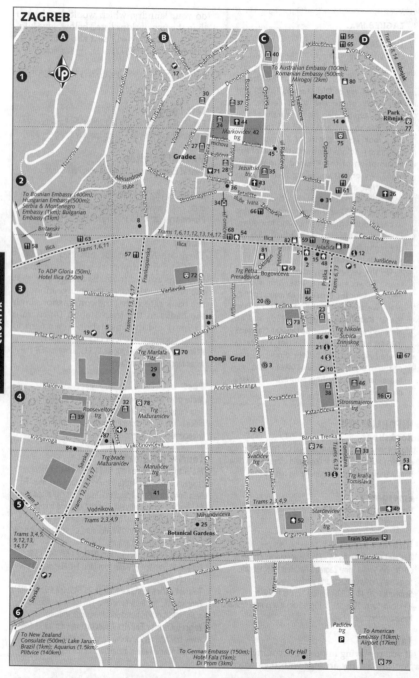

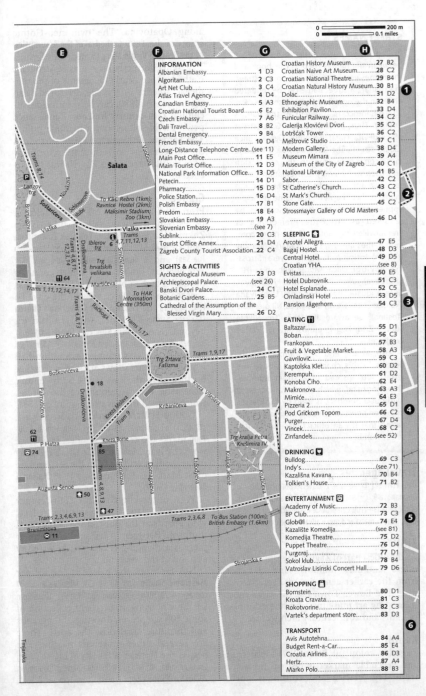

CROATIA

CROATIA

Travel Agencies

Dali Travel (☎ 48 47 472; travelsection@hfhs.hr; Dežmanova 9; ☻ 9am-5pm Mon-Fri) The travel branch of the Croatian YHA. Can provide information on HI hostels throughout Croatia and make advance bookings.

SIGHTS

As the oldest part of Zagreb, the Upper Town offers landmark buildings and churches from the earlier centuries of Zagreb's history. The Lower Town has the city's most interesting art museums and fine examples of 19th- and 20th-century architecture.

Kaptol

Zagreb's colourful **Dolac** (☻ 7am-2pm) fruit and vegetable market is just up the steps from Trg Jelačića and continues north along Opatovina. The twin neo-Gothic spires of the 1899 **Cathedral of the Assumption of the Blessed Virgin Mary** (Katedrala Marijina Uznesenja; formerly known as St Stephen's Cathedral) are nearby. Elements of the medieval cathedral on this site, destroyed by an earthquake in 1880, can be seen inside, including 13th-century frescoes, Renaissance pews, marble altars and a baroque pulpit. The baroque **Archiepiscopal Palace** surrounds the cathedral, as do 16th-century fortifications constructed when Zagreb was threatened by the Turks.

Gradec

From ul Radićeva 5, off Trg Jelačića, a pedestrian walkway called stube Ivana Zakmardija leads to the **Lotrščak Tower** (Kula Lotrščak; ☎ 48 51 768; admission 5KN; ☻ 11am-7pm Tue-Sun) and a **funicular railway** (one way 3KN; ☻ 6.30am-9pm) built in 1888, which connects the Lower and Upper Towns. The tower has a sweeping 360-degree view of the city. To the east is the baroque **St Catherine's Church** (Crkva Svete Katarine), with Jezuitski trg beyond. The **Galerija Klovićevi Dvori** (☎ 48 51 926; Jezuitski trg 4; adult/student 20/10KN; ☻ 11am-7pm Tue-Sun) is Zagreb's premier exhibition hall where superb art shows are staged. Further north and to the east is the 13th-century **Stone Gate**, with a painting of the Virgin, which escaped the devastating fire of 1731.

Gothic **St Mark's Church** (Crkva Svetog Marka; ☎ 48 51 611; Markovićev trg; ☻ 11am-4pm & 5.30-7pm) marks the centre of Gradec. Inside are works by Ivan Meštrović, Croatia's most famous modern sculptor. On the eastern side of St Mark's is the Croatia's 1908 **National Assembly** (Sabor).

West of the church is the 18th-century **Banski Dvori Palace**, the presidential palace, with guards at the door in red ceremonial uniform. Between April and September there is a changing of the guard ceremony at noon at the weekend.

Not far from the palace is the former **Meštrović Studio** (☎ 48 51 123; Mletačka 8; adult/concession 20/10KN; ☻ 10am-6pm Tue-Fri, 10am-2pm Sat), now housing an excellent collection of some 100 sculptures, drawings, lithographs and furniture created by the artist. There are several other museums nearby. The best is the **Museum of the City of Zagreb** (Muzej Grada Zagreba; ☎ 48 51 364; Opatička 20; adult/concession 20/10KN; ☻ 10am-6pm Tue-Fri, 10am-1pm Sat & Sun), with a scale model of old Gradec, atmospheric background music, and interactive exhibits that fascinate kids. Summaries in English and German are in each room of the museum, which is in the former Convent of St Claire (1650). There's also the lively and colourful **Croatian Naive Art Museum** (Hrvatski Muzej Naivne Umjetnosti; ☎ 48 51 911; Ćirilometodska 3; adult/concession 10/5KN; ☒ 10am-6pm Tue-Fri, to 1pm Sat & Sun); the **Croatian Natural History Museum** (Hrvatski Prirodoslovni Muzej; ☎ 48 51 700; Demetrova 1; adult/concession 15/7KN; ☒ 10am-5pm Tue-Fri, to 1pm Sat & Sun), which has a collection of prehistoric tools and bones plus exhibits on the evolution of plant and animal life in Croatia; and the less-than-gripping **Croatian History Museum** (Hrvatski Povijesni Muzej; ☎ 48 51 900; Matoševa 9; temporary exhibitions adult/concession 10/5KN; ☒ 10am-5pm Mon-Fri, to 1pm Sat & Sun)

Lower Town

Zagreb really is a city of museums. There are four in the parks between the train station and Trg Jelačića. The yellow **exhibition pavilion** (1897) across the park from the station presents changing contemporary art exhibitions. The second building north, also in the park, houses the **Strossmayer Gallery of Old Masters** (Strossmayerova Galerija Starih Majstora; ☎ 48 95 115; adult/concession 20/15KN; ☒ 10am-1pm & 5-7pm Tue, 10am-1pm Wed-Sun). When it's closed you can still enter the interior courtyard to see the Baška Slab (1102) from the island of Krk, one of the oldest inscriptions in the Croatian language.

The fascinating **Archaeological Museum** (Arheološki Muzej; ☎ 48 73 101; Trg Nikole Šubića Zrinjskog 19; adult/concession 30/10KN; ☒ 10am-5pm Tue-Fri, to 1pm Sat & Sun) has a wide-ranging display of artefacts from prehistoric times through to the medieval period. The ambient sounds and light put you in a contemplative mood. Behind the museum is a garden of Roman sculpture that is turned into a pleasant open-air café in the summer.

The **Modern Gallery** (Galerija Moderna; ☎ 49 22 368; Andrije Hebranga 1; 10am-6pm Tue-Sat, to 1pm Sun) presents temporary exhibitions that offer

---

A CROATIAN BLOG   *Adapted from Draxblog III (http://draxblog.typepad.com) by Dragan Antulov*

Today Zagreb for the fourth time had a Gay Pride parade. The event wasn't very different from the few previous occasions – around a hundred or so participants, four times more policemen and an unknown number of passers-by shouting all kinds of verbal abuse, mostly elderly people appalled at the prospects of taxpayers' money being spent on such abominations instead of increasing their pensions.

The only difference was in the peculiar absence of males in the parade. This year's event was almost exclusively lesbian-oriented and the organiser was a relatively unknown and obscure feminist group. The reason was because Iskorak, the NGO representing male homosexuals, decided against participation in the event. This created a rift between Iskorak and Kontra, the NGO representing lesbians.

The alliance between Croatian gays and Croatian lesbians – or, to be more precise, alliance between a handful of Zagreb activists claiming to represent Croatian gay and lesbians – is shattered, mostly due to Iskorak leaders finding a Gay Pride event counterproductive in the new social and political climate of today's Croatia. Three years ago gays and lesbians were supposed to give some leftist and liberal credentials to the 'left-centre' government of (Prime Minister) Ivica Račan and show Croatia to be tolerant, progressive and enlightened enough to join the EU, unlike Serbia where the 2001 Gay Pride parade was shattered by skinheads and soccer hooligans. This policy continued under (Prime Minister) Sanader. However, with the prospects of Croatian entry to EU getting dimmer and the rise of Euroscepticism, agressive pushing or even public sympathies for a gay agenda is going to be counterproductive.

Lesbians, on the other hand, have less to worry about, because, for reasons well known to the makers of *Wild Thing* movies, their presence doesn't seem to annoy the average Croatian male as much as the presence of male homosexuals. And since this observation could be applied to a majority of skinheads, soccer hooligans and similar characters, lesbian-only parades are less likely to create as much of a security problem for the Croatian government and City of Zagreb authorities. For that reason alone Croatian lesbians can afford to be more militant in their demands than their male counterparts.

CROATIA

an excellent chance to catch up with the latest in Croatian painting.

West of the Centre

The **Museum Mimara** (Muzej Mimara; ☎ 48 28 100; Rooseveltov trg 5; adult/concession 20/15KN; ☺ 10am-5pm Tue, Wed, Fri & Sat, to 7pm Thu, to 2pm Sun) houses a diverse collection amassed by Ante Topić Mimara and donated to Croatia. Housed in a neo-Renaissance palace, the collection includes icons, glassware, sculpture, Oriental art and works by renowned painters such as Rembrandt, Velázquez, Raphael and Degas.

The neobaroque **Croatian National Theatre** (☎ 48 28 532; Trg Maršala Tita 15; box office ☺ 10am-1pm & 5-7.30pm Mon-Fri, to 1pm Sat, 30min before performances Sun) dates from 1895 and has Ivan Meštrović's sculpture *Fountain of Life* (1905) in front. The **Ethnographic Museum** (Etnografski Muzej; ☎ 48 26 220; Trg Mažuranićev 14; adult/concession 15/10KN; ☺ 10am-6pm Tue-Thu, to 1pm Fri-Sun) has a large collection of Croatian folk costumes, accompanied by English captions. To the south is the Art Nouveau **National Library** (1907). The **Botanical Gardens** (Mihanovićeva; admission free; ☺ 9am-7pm Tue-Sun) is attractive for its plants and landscaping, as well as its restful corners, perfect for a family picnic.

Out of Town

A 20-minute ride north of the city centre on bus 106 from the cathedral takes you to **Mirogoj** (Medvednica; ☺ 6am-10pm), one of the most beautiful cemeteries in Europe. The sculptured and artfully designed tombs lie beyond a majestic arcade topped by a string of cupolas. Don't miss the flower-bedecked tomb of Croatia's last president-dictator, Franjo Tudjman. Some Croats were very sad at his death, some were slightly sad, and some wondered if the international community would have paid Croatia as much for his extradition to the war crimes tribunal at The Hague as they paid Serbia for Milošević.

TOURS

The main tourist office sells tickets for two-hour walking tours (95KN) which operate Monday through Thursday leaving from Trg Jelačića, as well as three-hour bus and walking tours (150KN) that operate Friday through Sunday, leaving from the Arcotel Allegra hotel.

FESTIVALS & EVENTS

During odd-numbered years in April there's the **Zagreb Biennial of Contemporary Music**, Croatia's most important music event. Zagreb also hosts a **festival of animated films** (www.animafest.hr) during even-numbered years in June and a **film festival** (www.zagrebfilmfestival.com) in October. Croatia's largest international fairs are the Zagreb spring (mid-April) and autumn (mid-September) grand trade fairs. In July and August the **Zagreb Summer Festival** presents a cycle of concerts and theatre performances on open stages in the upper town. For a complete listing of Zagreb events, see www.zagreb-convention.hr.

SLEEPING

Budget accommodation is in short supply in Zagreb. An early arrival is recommended, since private room-finding agencies are an attractive alternative and usually refuse telephone bookings. Prices run from about 220KN to 275KN for a double with a shared bathroom and 300KN to 350KN with a private bathroom. Apartments cost at least 380KN per night. There's usually a surcharge for staying only one night. **Evistas** (☎ 48 39 554; fax 48 39 543; evistas@zg.t-com.hr; Augusta Šenoe 28; ☺ 9am-1.30pm & 3-8pm Mon-Fri, 9.30am-5pm Sat) is closest to the train station. **ADP Gloria** (☎ 48 23 567; www.adp-glorija.com in Croatian; Britanski trg 5; ☺ closed Sun), just west of town, is another option for private rooms. **Di Prom** (☎ 65 50 039; fax 65 50 233; Trnsko 25a; ☺ closed Sun) is south of the town centre with rooms in Novi Zagreb.

Lower Town

Arcotel Allegra (☎ 46 96 000; www.arcotel.at/allegra; Branimirova 29; r €136-270; P ⊠ ⊠ ⧉) Billing itself as Zagreb's first 'lifestyle hotel', it's clear that the style of life is quite high here. Your lifestyle, should you choose to accept it, will include ultracontemporary Mediterranean-inspired décor and a fitness centre, plus rooms and accoutrements for your business meetings. The hotel is gay friendly.

Hotel Dubrovnik (☎ 48 73 555; www.hotel-dubrovnik.t-com.hr; Gajeva 1; s/d from €105/162; ⊠) Business travellers love this modern hotel right in the centre of town. Services, rooms and facilities are all first-rate.

Central Hotel (☎ 48 41 122; www.hotel-central.hr; Branimirova 3; s/d €76/100; ⊠) Entirely renovated with modern, plush rooms, this hotel

---

THE AUTHOR'S CHOICE

Hotel Esplanade (☎ 45 66 666; www.regent hotels.com; Mihanovićeva 1; s/d 1875/2025KN; **P** **X** **□**) This six-storey, 215-room hotel was built next to the train station in 1924 to welcome the *Orient Express* crowd in grand style. It's an Art Deco masterpiece replete with walls of swirling marble, immensely wide staircases and wood-panelled elevators. Even if you're not staying at the hotel, take a peek at the magnificent Emerald Ballroom or eat at Zinfandels, the hotel restaurant and one of the finest dining experiences in Croatia.

Rooms vary greatly in size, but all are high-ceilinged and plushly decorated in period upholstery. The best rooms look out at the esplanade in front of the train station. The double-glazed windows mean that you won't be bothered by noise while you contemplate the street scene.

Throughout its history, the hotel has welcomed kings, journalists, artists and politicians, with a coolly professional attention to service. The slightly formal, courtly attitude of the staff blends perfectly with the hotel's style – traditional, classic, unswayed by fads, a bulwark of stability in a frivolous world.

---

represents good value for money, especially given its location across from the train station. The service is coldly efficient.

Pansion Jägerhorn (☎ 48 33 877; www.hotel-pansion-jaegerhorn.hr; Ilica 14; s/d/apt €76/104/125; **X**) The downstairs restaurant is known for serving wild game but there's no wildness in the civilised rooms here. Everything is up to date and well maintained.

Bagaj Hostel (☎ 48 35 865; www.bagaj.hr; Trg Jelačića 1; dm from €14.60, d from €53; **□**) Open from mid-June to mid-September, this new hostel has a fantastic location right in the heart of Zagreb. Rooms are bright, showers are in the hall and Internet access is available for a small fee. You can even hire a bike and a mobile phone at a reasonable rate.

Omladinski Hostel (☎ 48 41 261; fax 48 41 269; Petrinjska 77; per person in 6-/3-bed dm 73/83KN, d 211KN) Some say it's a dump. We prefer to call it an auditory and visual challenge with maintenance issues. Checkout is at 9am. At least it's near the train station.

West of the Centre

Hotel Ilica (☎ 37 77 522; www.hotel-ilica.hr in Croatian; Ilica 102; s/d/tw/apt €55/70/83/118; **P** **X**) For a small hotel, you can't do better than this stylish joint just west of town with comfortable rooms and friendly service. Trams 6, 11 and 12 stop right outside the entrance.

Out of Town

Hotel Fala (☎ /fax 61 94 498; www.hotel-fala-zg.hr; Trnjanske ledine 18; s/d €48/65; **P** **X**) The small rooms have no frills but the price is right and you're not too terribly far from the town centre.

Ravnice Hostel (☎ /fax 23 32 325; www.ravniceyouth-hostel.hr; Ravnice 38d; dm €15; **□**) This is really a delightful option, designed and run by an Australian woman. Comfortable, clean rooms have two, four or 10 beds. Solo female travellers would be most comfortable here. Trams 4, 7, 11 and 12 will take you there.

EATING

As befits an up-and-coming international city, Zagreb presents a fairly wide array of culinary styles. Exotic spices are not part of the Croatian gastronomic vocabulary, but you can't go wrong with fish, pizza, pasta and roasted meats.

Kaptol

Baltazar (☎ 46 66 824; Nova Ves 4; meals from 100KN; 🕙 closed Sun) Duck, lamb, pork, beef and turkey are cooked to perfection here, served with a good choice of local wines.

Kaptolska Klet (☎ 48 14 838; Kaptol 5; meals 75-90KN) This huge and inviting space is comfortable for everyone from solo diners to groups of noisy backpackers. Although famous for its Zagreb specialities such as grilled meats, spit-roasted lamb, duck, pork and veal as well as homemade sausages, it turns out a nice platter of grilled vegetables and a vegetable loaf.

THE AUTHOR'S CHOICE

Boban (☎ 48 11 549; Gajeva 9; mains 30-50KN) This Italian restaurant/bar/café offers sophisticated food at good prices. It has an outdoor terrace and an indoor lounge and terrace that is popular with Zagreb yuppies. Try the gnocchi made from squid ink and topped with salmon sauce.

Pizzeria 2 (☎ 48 17 462; Nova Ves 2; pizzas 28-40KN) Between mouth-watering pizza and a savoury little array of pasta dishes, this place is ground zero for Italian food-lovers on a budget.

Kerempuh (☎ 48 19 000; Kaptol 3; meals from 70KN) Watch the action at the Dolac market below while munching on hearty Zagreb dishes like *sarma* (stuffed cabbage).

You can pick up yummy fresh produce at Dolac (p152)

Gradec

Pod Gričkom Topom (☎ 48 33 607; stube Ivana Zakmardija 5; meals from 90KN) Tucked away by a leafy path below the Upper Town, this restaurant has a somewhat self-conscious charm but it has an outdoor terrace and good Croatian meat-based specialities. Holing up here on a snowy winter evening is one of the great Zagrebian pleasures.

Lower Town

Zinfandels (☎ 45 66 666; Mihanovićeva 1; meals 110-250KN; ☺ closed Sun) The new Belgian chef here in the Esplanade dining room grafts Mediterranean flavours onto Croatian dishes and polishes the result with a light Asian touch.

Purger (☎ 48 73 394; Petrinjska 33; meals from 75KN) This restaurant serves up a good assortment of meat and fish dishes at reasonable prices. It has an open-air terrace at the back. Recent graduates are inclined to blow their first pay cheque here.

Konoba Čiho (☎ 48 17 060; P Hatza 15; meals from 75KN; ☺ closed Sun) Tucked away downstairs, this cosy restaurant turns out a startling assortment of fish and seafood, grilled, fried and combined in delicious stews.

Mimiće (Jurišićeva 21; meals 20-40KN; ☺ closed Sun) It's a local favourite and deservedly so. The fish is sure to be fresh because turnover is high, especially at noontime when workers in the offices around Trg Jelačića turn out in droves for their lunch.

Gavrilović (Trg Jelačića; ☺ closed Sun) Pick up local cheese, smoked meat and cold cuts.

Vincek (☎ 45 50 834; Ilica 18) Slurp up dessert at Vincek, famous for its ice cream.

West of the Centre

Makronova (☎ 48 47 115; Ilica 72; meals 90KN; ☺ closed Sun) All very Zen, purely macrobiotic and more than welcome for those of the vegan persuasion. There's also shiatsu treatment, yoga classes and feng shui courses.

Frankopan (☎ 48 48 547; Frankopanska 8; meals 65-110KN) It's a gilt trip with chubby cherubs frolicking on the ceiling while you munch on relatively adventurous dishes. The prices are good because meals are prepared by a hostelry school.

There's also a **fruit and vegetable market** (Britanski trg; ☺ 7am-3pm).

DRINKING

The architecture may be sober but the nightlife definitely is not, especially as the weather warms up and Zagrebians take to the streets. Wander along **Tkalčićeva** in the Upper Town or around bar-lined Bogovićeva, just south of Trg Jelačića, which turns into prime meet-and-greet territory each evening. Tkalčićeva attracts a slightly funkier crowd. **Trg Petra Preradovića** is the most popular spot in the Lower Town, attracting street performers and occasional bands in mild weather. The places listed below open around noon for café society and turn into bars around dinner time.

Bulldog (☎ 48 17 393; Bogovićeva 6) Belgian beer loosens up a crowd of young execs, sales reps, minor politicos and expats.

Tolkien's House (☎ 48 51 776; Vranicanijeva 8) Decorated in the style of JRR Tolkien's books, it's very Frodo.

Indy's (☎ 48 52 053; Vranicanijeva 4) This friendly bar presents a dazzling assortment of juicy and fruity cocktails on an outdoor terrace.

Brazil (☎ 091 20 02 481; Veslačka bb) Parked on the Sava River, this bar on a boat refreshes a throng of thirsty revellers and offers occasional live music.

Kazališna Kavana (☎ 48 55 851; Trg Maršala Tita) Everyone seems to wind up at this café, known as Kav Kaz, at one time or another, even though it's beyond pretentious.

ENTERTAINMENT

Zagreb is definitely a happening city. Its theatres and concert halls present a great variety of programmes throughout the year. Many (but not all) are listed in the monthly brochure *Zagreb Events & Performances*, which is available from the tourist office. Otherwise, drop in at Art Net Club (p149) and peruse the many flyers which announce the latest breaking developments on the music scene.

Discos & Nightclubs

The dress code is relaxed in most Zagreb clubs but neatness counts. The cover charge usually runs to 40KN and the action doesn't heat up until near midnight.

Aquarius (☎ 36 40 231; Ljubeka bb) On Lake Jarun, this is the night temple of choice for Zagrebians of all ages and styles. The design cleverly includes an open-air terrace on the lake and the sound is usually house. Take tram 17 to the Jarun stop.

Purgeraj (☎ 48 14 734; Park Ribnjak) A funky, relaxed space to listen to live rock, blues, rock-blues, blues-rock, country rock. You get the idea.

Glob@l (☎ 48 76 146; P Hatza 14) Gays and lesbians are more than welcome to take in the friendly, tolerant vibes.

Sokol klub (☎ 48 28 510; Trg Maršala Tita 6) Across the street from the Ethnographic Museum, Sokol is fashionable without being snooty and the dance floor is always packed.

BP Club (☎ 48 14 444; Teslina 7; ☽ 5pm-1am) Famous for its high-quality musicians and occasional jam sessions, this is one of Zagreb's classic addresses.

Sport

Basketball is popular in Zagreb, and from October to April games take place in a variety of venues around town, usually at the weekend. The tourist office can provide you with the schedule.

Football (soccer) games are held every Sunday afternoon at the **Maksimir Stadium** (Maksimirska 128), on the eastern side of Zagreb; catch tram 4, 7, 11 or 12 to Bukovačka. If you arrive too early for the game, Zagreb's zoo is just across the street.

Theatre

It's worth making the rounds of the theatres in person to check their programmes. Tickets are usually available for performances, even for the best shows. A small office marked 'Kazalište Komedija' (look out for the posters) also sells theatre tickets; it's in the Oktogon, a passage connecting Trg Petra Preradovića to Ilica 3.

The neobaroque Croatian National Theatre (p197) was established in 1895. It stages opera and ballet performances.

Komedija Theatre (☎ 48 14 566; Kaptol 9) Near the cathedral, the Komedija Theatre stages operettas and musicals.

Vatroslav Lisinski Concert Hall (ticket office ☎ 61 21 166; Trg Stjepana Radica 4; ☽ 9am-8pm Mon-Fri, to 2pm Sat) Just south of the train station, this concert hall is a prestigious venue where symphony concerts are held regularly.

Academy of Music (☎ 48 30 822; Gundulićeva 6a) Concerts also take place at the Academy of Music, off Ilica.

Puppet Theatre (Baruna Trenka 3; performances 5pm Sat, noon Sun) Another entertainment option.

SHOPPING

Ilica is Zagreb's main shopping street.

Vartek's department store (Trg Jelačića) You can get in touch with true Croatian consumerism at this new store.

Kroata Cravata (Oktogon) Croatia is the birthplace of the necktie (cravat); Kroata Cravata has locally made silk neckties at prices that run from 200KN to 400KN.

Rokotvorine (Trg Jelačića 7) This place sells traditional Croatian handicrafts, such as red-and-white embroidered tablecloths, dolls and pottery.

Bornstein (☎ 48 12 361; Kaptol 19) If Croatia's wine and spirits have gone to your head, get your fix at Bornstein, which presents an astonishing collection of brandy, wine and gourmet products.

GETTING THERE & AWAY

Marko Polo (☎ 48 15 216; Masarykova 24) handles information and ticketing for Jadrolinija's coastal ferries.

Air

For information about the flights to and from Zagreb, see p225 and p225.

Bus

Zagreb's big, modern **bus station** (☎ 61 57 983; www.akz.hr in Croatian) has a large, enclosed waiting room and a number of shops, including eateries and grocery stores. You can buy most international tickets at windows 17 to 20.

Buses depart from Zagreb for most parts of Croatia, Slovenia and places beyond. Buy an advance ticket at the station if you're planning to travel far.

The following domestic buses depart from Zagreb:

CROATIA

Destination	Cost (KN)	Duration	Frequency
Dubrovnik	205-401	11hr	7 daily
Korčula	204	12hr	1 daily
Krk	148	4-5hr	4 daily
Ljubljana,			
Slovenia	203	2½hr	2 daily
Osijek	99-132	4hr	8 daily
Plitvice	48-70	2½hr	19 daily
Poreč	117-172	5hr	6 daily
Pula	120-174	4-6hr	17 daily
Rab	133-154	4½-5hr	2 daily
Rijeka	84-141	2½-3hr	21 daily
Rovinj	105-196	5-8hr	8 daily
Split	115-150	6-9hr	27 daily
Varaždin	53	1¾hr	20 daily
Zadar	102-165	4-5hr	20 daily

For international bus connections see p225.

Train
The following domestic trains depart from **Zagreb train station** (☎ 060 33 34 44):

Destination	Cost (KN)	Duration	Frequency
Osijek	102	4½hr	4 daily
Pula	14	5½hr	2 daily
Rijeka	91	5hr	5 daily
Split	152	6½-9hr	6 daily
Varaždin	55	3hr	13 daily
Zadar	148	8hr	4 daily

All daily trains to Zadar stop at Knin. Reservations are required on fast InterCity (IC) trains and there's a supplement of 5KN to 15KN for fast or express trains.

For international train connections see p225.

GETTING AROUND
Zagreb is a fairly easy city to navigate, whether by car or public transport. Traffic isn't bad, there's sufficient parking, and the efficient tram system should be a model for other polluted, traffic-clogged European capitals.

To/From the Airport
The Croatia Airlines bus to Zagreb airport, 17km southeast of the city, leaves from the bus station every half-hour or hour from about 5.30am to 7.30pm, depending on flights, and returns from the airport on about the same schedule (25KN). A taxi would cost about 250KN.

Car
Of the major car-hire companies, you could try **Budget Rent-a-Car** (☎ 45 54 936; Kneza Borne 2) in the Hotel Sheraton, **Avis Autotehna** (☎ 48 36 006; Kršnavoga 1) at the Hotel Westin and **Hertz** (☎ 48 46 777; Vukotinovićeva 4). Prices start at 300KN per day. Zagreb is relatively easy to navigate by car but remember that the streets around Trg Jelačića and up through Kaptol and Gradec are pedestrian only. Watch out for trams sneaking up on you.

The **Croatian Auto Club (HAK) Information Centre** (☎ 46 40 800; Derenčinova 20) helps motorists in need. It's just east of the centre.

Public Transport
Public transport is based on an efficient but overcrowded network of trams, though the city centre is compact enough to make them unnecessary. Trams 3 and 8 don't run at weekends. Buy tickets at newspaper kiosks for 6.50KN or from the driver for 8KN. Each ticket must be stamped when you board. You can use your ticket for transfers within 90 minutes but only in one direction.

A *dnevna karta* (day ticket), valid on all public transport until 4am the next morning, is 18KN at most Vjesnik or Tisak news outlets. (See p149 for details of the Zagreb Card.) Controls are frequent on the tram system with fines for not having the proper ticket starting at €30.

Taxi
Zagreb's taxis ring up 8KN per kilometre after a whopping flag fall of 25KN. On Sunday and from 10pm to 5am there's a 20% surcharge.

AROUND ZAGREB
Samobor
pop 14,000
It's almost too little-village-cute, but after a week of crowded trams in Zagreb, Samobor provides a perfect breather for stressed-out Zagrebians. A shallow stream stocked with trout curves through a town centre that is composed of trim pastel houses and several old churches. The town has conserved its culture as well as its architecture. The small family businesses involved in handicrafts, restaurants and the production of mustard and spirits have survived well, seemingly untouched by the political fads sweeping through the rest of the country.

The town's literary and musical traditions, which produced the poet Stanko Vraz and the composer Ferdo Livadić, are reflected in a number of annual festivals, most famously the Fašnik (Samobor Carnival) on the eve of Lent, which attracts some 300,000 visitors.

ORIENTATION & INFORMATION

The bus stop (no left-luggage office) is on Šmidheva, about 100m uphill from the town, which centres around Trg Kralja Tomislava.

In the town centre, the **tourist office** (☎ 33 60 044; www.samobor.hr in Croatian; Trg Kralja Tomislava 5; �} 8am-7pm Mon-Fri, 9am-7pm Sat, 10am-7pm Sun) has limited documentation but you can get hiking maps.

SIGHTS & ACTIVITIES

The **Town Museum** (Gradski Muzej; ☎ 33 61 014; Livadićeva 7; adult/student 8/5KN; �} 9am-3pm Tue-Sat, to 1pm Sun) has moderately interesting exhibits on regional culture. It's housed in Livadićev Dvor Villa, which once belonged to composer Ferdinand Livadić and was an important centre for the 19th-century nationalist cause.

Samobor is a good jumping-off point for **hikes** into the Samoborsko Gorje, a mountain system (part of the Žumberak Range) which links the high peaks of the alps with the karstic caves and abysses of the Dinaric Range. Carpeted with meadows and forests, the range is the most popular hiking destination in the region. Most of the hikes are easy and there are several mountain huts that make pleasant rest stops. Many are open weekends only except in the high season.

The range has three groups: the Oštrc group in the centre, the Japetić group to the west, and the Plešica group to the east. Both the Oštrc and the Japetić groups are accessible from Šoićeva Kuća, a mountain hut 10km west of Samobor only reachable by foot. From there, it's an easy 30-minute climb to the hill fort of Lipovac and an hour's climb to the peak of Oštrc (753m). Another popular hike is the 1½-hour climb from Šoićeva Kuća to Japetić (780m). You can also follow a path from Oštrc to Japetić which will take about two hours. If you want to explore the Plešica group, head east to the hunting cabin Srndać on Poljanice

(12km) from where it's a 40-minute climb to Plešivica peak (780m). The tourist office in town has maps and information on hikes in the region.

SLEEPING & EATING

Most people come to Samobor on a day trip from Zagreb but you can also stay here and commute into Zagreb. The one hotel in town offers better value for money than any of the Zagreb hotels.

Hotel Livadić (☎ 33 65 850; www.hotel-livadic.hr; Trg Kralja Tomislava 1; s/d 410/465KN) This atmospheric place is decorated in 19th-century style and provides spacious, comfortable rooms with TV and phone. Since cuisine is a major draw for Samobor, you can count on the quality of the restaurant and café. Prices stay the same year-round.

Meals tend to be more expensive than in Zagreb but are well worth it.

Pri Staroj Vuri (☎ 33 60 548; Giznik 2; 2-course meal 90-110KN) Sitting about 50m uphill from Trg Kralja Tomislava, this restaurant serves traditional dishes in a homy cottage, and sometimes hosts poetry readings. The specialities of the house are *hrvatska pisanica* (beef steak in a spicy mushroom, onion, tomato and red-wine sauce) and *struklova juha* (soup with *štrukli*).

U Prolazu (☎ 33 66 420; Trg Kralja Tomislava 5) This eatery, on the main square, serves the best *kremšnite* (custard slice) in town.

GETTING THERE & AWAY

Samobor is easy to reach by public transport. Local buses leave from the bus station in Zagreb every 30 minutes for the price of a local ride but it's quicker to take an express from the bus station (20KN, 30 minutes).

Varaždin

☎ 042 / pop 43,000

Varaždin, 81km north of Zagreb, is often ill-used as a mere transit point on the way to or from Hungary, but in fact it's well worth a visit in its own right. The town centre is a marvel of baroque architecture, scrupulously restored and well tended. It was once Croatia's capital and most prosperous city, which explains the extraordinary refinement of the architecture. In many ways, it's a mini-Prague without the crowds or the prices. Topping off the baroque symphony is the gleaming white and turreted

CROATIA

Stari Grad (Old City), which now contains a museum.

ORIENTATION

The bus and train stations are at opposite ends of town, about 2km apart, and are not linked by public transportation. The town centre lies between them and to the north. The main commercial street is Gundulića; it leads to the main square, Trg Kralja Tomislava, surrounded by Varaždin's famous baroque buildings.

INFORMATION

Atlas Travel Agency (☎ 313 618; B Radić 20) Represents American Express.

Garderoba bus station (per day 10KN; ☒ 6am-10pm); train station (per day 10KN; ☒ 24hr) Left luggage.

Post office (Trg Slobode 9)

T-Tours Agency (☎ 210 989; t-tours@vz.t-com.hr; Gundulićeva 2) Finds private accommodation and is a good source of information on town events.

Turistička Zajednica (☎ /fax 210 987; www.varazdin .hr; Padovčeva 3; ☒ 8am-6pm Mon-Fri, 9am-1pm Sat Apr-Oct, 8am-4pm Mon-Fri Nov-Mar) The tourist office has plenty of colourful brochures and is a wealth of information.

Varaždinska Banka (Kapucinski trg 5) This branch is opposite the bus station, but all branches have ATMs.

SIGHTS

In addition to several excellent museums, Varaždin offers a fine ensemble of baroque buildings in its centre, a number of which have been turned into museums. Many of the aristocratic mansions and elegant churches are being restored as part of the town's bid to be included in Unesco's list of World Heritage sites. Conveniently, most buildings have plaques out the front with architectural and historical explanations in English.

The **Town Museum** (Gradski Muzej; ☎ 210 339; Strossmayera 7; adult/student 15/12KN; ☒ 10am-5pm Tue-Fri, to 1pm Sat & Sun Jun-Aug, 10am-5pm Tue-Fri, to 1pm Sat & Sun Sep-May) is part of the **Stari Grad** (Old City), which is a beautifully preserved example of medieval defensive architecture. Construction of this fortress began in the 14th century, but it was the Earl of Celje who turned it into a strong fortress in the 15th century, adding the rounded towers that typify Gothic architecture in northern Croatia. By the early 16th century, it was the chief regional fortification against the encroaching Ottoman Turks, but the

two large courtyards and massive corridors made it look more like a castle. It remained in private hands until 1925 when it was turned into a museum. Today it houses furniture, paintings, decorative objects and weapons amassed during the course of Varaždin's history. The exhibits are divided into eight different rooms, each one reflecting a different historic period. The architecture alone is worth paying the admission; the exhibits are interesting enough.

Varaždin's other major museum is the fascinating **Entomological Collection** (Entomološka Zbirka; ☎ 210 474; Franjevački trg 6; adult/student 15/12KN; ☒ 10am-3pm Tue-Fri, to 1pm Sat & Sun). Housed in the baroque **Herczer Palace**, the collection comprises nearly 4500 exhibits of the bug world, including 1000 different insect species. The examples of insect nests, habitats and reproductive habits are informative and displayed with flair. The collection was amassed and mounted by a local entomologist, Franjo Košćec, who also created the tools to mount the tiny creatures.

FESTIVALS & EVENTS

Varaždin is famous for its baroque music festival, **Varaždin Baroque Evenings**, which takes place over three to four weeks each September. Local and international orchestras play baroque music in churches and theatres around the city for prices ranging from 30KN to 100KN, depending on the programme. Tickets are available about two hours before the beginning of the concert at travel agencies, the **Varaždin Concert Bureau** (☎ /fax 212 907) at the Croatian National Theatre, or at the cathedral. In July and August there's also a **Summer Cultural Festival** of music, dance and theatre; it's often held in the city's squares and parks.

SLEEPING

Accommodation is less expensive than in Zagreb and offers better value. Most hotels in Varaždin are clean, well maintained and offer good value for money. Their clientele is mostly visiting businesspeople from Zagreb and neighbouring countries; this means they are likely to be full on Monday to Friday and empty on weekends.

T-Tours Agency has single/double private rooms from about 95/180KN. There is generally no supplement for a single night's stay and prices stay the same year-round.

There aren't many rooms available, but then there aren't many people asking for them either.

Pansion Maltar (☎ 311 100; www.maltar.hr; F Preš-erna 1; s/d 250/380KN) This cheerful little *pension*, not far from the bus station, is the cheapest place in town but has only 10 rooms. Booking in advance is advised. Rooms are in excellent condition and have satellite TV but no phones.

Garestin Hotel (☎ /fax 214 314; Zagrebačka 34; s/d 310/445KN) This establishment has a glossy, modern décor that usually indicates high prices. Yet rooms with phone, TV and mini-bar are reasonably priced. The hotel is only a short walk from the bus station.

EATING & DRINKING

Pivnica Raj (☎ 213 146; Gundulića 11; meals from 65KN) The brew flows freely in this enormously popular local beer hall where the food is old-fashioned and hearty but with a nod to vegetarians. On weekends there's traditional *tamburitza* music but it's a good time here any time, whether on the terrace or in the cosy interior.

Zlatna Guska (☎ 213 393; Habdelića 4; mains around 70KN) The interior is designed to resemble a knights' dining hall with plenty of armour and equipment, and dishes called 'the last meal of a victim of an execution' among other evocative names. It's fun and the dishes are cooked to perfection. The portions would make a knight burst his tin suit.

There is a daily **market** (Trg Bana Jelačića; ⏲ 6am-2pm), and there are many bakeries that sell Varaždin's special finger-shaped bread, *klipići*.

GETTING THERE & AWAY

Varaždin is a major transportation hub in northern Croatia, with bus and train lines running in all directions. For information on long-haul buses to Germany and northern Europe, see the Land section in the Transport chapter (p402). Remember that northbound buses originate in Zagreb, stop at Varaždin and cost the same whether you buy the ticket in Zagreb or Varaždin.

All buses to the coast go through Zagreb. There are buses to Zagreb every 30 minutes to an hour (53KN, two hours).

There's a daily train to Rijeka (134KN, seven hours) and Zadar (189KN, 11 hours)

in the summer. There's one direct train a day to Budapest (195KN, five hours) and three unreserved trains to Nagykanizsa, Hungary (42KN, 1½ hours).

ISTRIA

Istria (Istra to Croatians) is the heart-shaped 3600-sq-km peninsula just south of Trieste, Italy, that retains a pronounced Italian influence. Sometimes called the 'new Tuscany', the Istrian interior is a peaceful landscape of green rolling hills, drowned valleys and fertile plains. The rugged and indented coastline is enormously popular with Italian tourists, comfortable with the excellent pasta and seafood on the menus and the fact that Italian is a second language for most Istrians.

Perhaps they dream of the days when the string of Istrian resorts was a part of Italy. Italy seized Istria from Austria-Hungary in 1918, was allowed to keep it in 1920, then had to give it to Yugoslavia in 1947. Tito wanted Trieste (Trst) as part of Yugoslavia too, but in 1954 the Anglo-American occupiers returned the city to Italy so that it wouldn't fall into the hands of the 'communists'. Today the Koper to Piran strip belongs to Slovenia while the rest is held by Croatia. Visit Piran quickly, and then make stops in Poreč and Rovinj on your way to Pula.

POREČ
☎ 052 / pop 10,450
Poreč (Parenzo in Italian) sits on a low, narrow peninsula halfway down the western coast of Istria. The town is the centre of a region dotted with sprawling tourist resorts, but vestiges of earlier times and a quiet, small-town atmosphere (at least in the low season) make it well worth a stop. There are the magnificent mosaics in the Euphrasian Basilica, and places to swim off the rocks north of the Old Town.

History
The Romans called the town Parentium and made it an important administrative base, leaving their mark on the rectangular street plan, which still is evident. After the fall of Rome, Poreč came under the rule of the Byzantines who constructed the famous

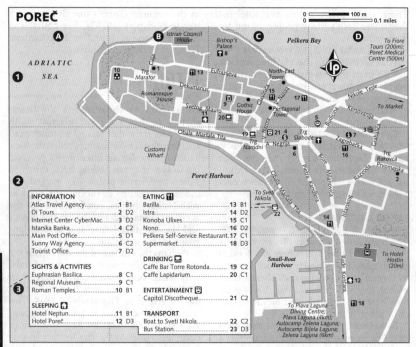

POREČ

INFORMATION
Atlas Travel Agency	1 B1
Di Tours	2 D2
Internet Center CyberMac	3 D2
Istarska Banka	4 C2
Main Post Office	5 D1
Sunny Way Agency	6 C2
Tourist Office	7 D2

SIGHTS & ACTIVITIES
Euphrasian Basilica	8 C1
Regional Museum	9 C1
Roman Temples	10 B1

SLEEPING
Hotel Neptun	11 B1
Hotel Poreč	12 D3

EATING
Barilla	13 B1
Istra	14 D2
Konoba Ulixes	15 C1
Nono	16 D2
Peškera Self-Service Restaurant	17 C1
Supermarket	18 D3

DRINKING
Caffe Bar Torre Rotonda	19 C2
Caffe Lapidarium	20 C1

ENTERTAINMENT
Capitol Discotheque	21 C2

TRANSPORT
Boat to Sveti Nikola	22 C2
Bus Station	23 D3

Euphrasian Basilica, now a World Heritage site. It was later ruled by Venice, then Austria.

Orientation

The compact Old Town is squeezed into the peninsula and packed with thousands of shops. The ancient Roman Dekumanus (a Roman longitudinal road) with its polished stones is still the main street. Hotels, travel agencies and excursion boats are on the quay, Obala Maršala Tita, which runs from the small-boat harbour to the tip of the peninsula. The bus station is directly opposite the small-boat harbour just outside the Old Town.

Information

INTERNET ACCESS
Internet Centre CyberMac (☎ 427 075; Grahalića 1; per hr 42KN) A full-service Internet and computer centre.

LEFT LUGGAGE
Garderoba (⏰ 6am-8pm Mon-Sat, 6am-5pm Sun) In the bus station.

MEDICAL SERVICES
Porec Medical Centre (☎ 451 611; Dr Mauro Gioseffi 2) Emergency services open 24 hours.

MONEY
You can change money at any of the town's travel agencies.
Istarska Banka (A Negrija 6) Has an ATM.

POST
Main post office (Trg Slobode 14) Has a telephone centre.

TOURIST INFORMATION
Tourist office (☎ 451 293; www.istra.com/porec; Zagrebačka 11; ⏰ 8am-10pm Mon-Sat year-round, 9am-1pm & 6-10pm Sun Jul & Aug)

TRAVEL AGENCIES
Atlas travel agency (☎ 434 933; Eufrazijeva 63) Represents Amex.
Di Tours (☎ 432 100, 452 018; www.di-tours.hr; Prvomajska 2) Finds private accommodation.
Fiore Tours (☎ /fax 431 397; www.fiore.hr.hr; Mate Vašića 6) Also handles private accommodation. It's northeast of the centre.

Sunny Way agency (☎ 452 021; A Negrija 1) Has information about boat connections to Italy.

Sights

The main reason to visit Poreč is to visit the 6th-century **Euphrasian Basilica** (☎ 431 635; admission free; ☼ 7.30am-8pm, to 7pm Oct-Mar), which features some wonderfully preserved Byzantine gold mosaics. The sculpture and architecture of the basilica are remarkable survivors of that distant period. For 10KN you may visit the 4th-century mosaic floor of the adjacent early Christian basilica or visit the baptistry and climb the bell tower for a spectacular view of the region.

The numerous historic sites in the Old Town include the ruins of two **Roman temples**, between Trg Marafor and the western end of the peninsula. Archaeology and history are featured in the **Regional Museum** (☎ 431 585; Dekumanus 9; adult/concession 10/5KN; ☼ 10am-1pm & 6-9pm Jul-Aug, 10am-1pm rest of year) in an old baroque palace. The captions are in German and Italian but there's an explanatory leaflet in English.

From May to mid-October there are passenger boats (20KN return) every half-hour to **Sveti Nikola**, the small island opposite Poreč Harbour, for some wonderful swimming. The boats depart from the wharf on Obala Maršala Tita.

Activities

Nearly every activity you might want to enjoy is outside the town in either Plava Laguna or Zelena Laguna. Most of the sports centres in Plava Laguna are affiliated with hotels and have tennis courts with basketball and volleyball, windsurfing, rowing, bungee jumping, water-skiing, parasailing, boat hire and canoeing. **Hotel Galijot** (☎ 415 800; www.plavalaguna.hr) in Plava Laguna has the largest and best equipped diving centre in the region. At nearby **Plava Laguna Diving Center** (☎ 451 549; www.plava-laguna-diving.hr) boat dives start at 107KN (more for caves or wrecks).

Sleeping

All of the travel agencies listed on opposite find private accommodation. Expect to pay from €25/32 for a room with shared/private bathroom in the high season, plus a 30% surcharge for stays less than three nights. There are a limited number of rooms available in the Old Town and it's wise to reserve far in advance for the July to August period.

BUDGET

Camping grounds are large, well-organised little cities with plenty of activities. Take the Zelena Laguna resort 'tourist train' (20KN), which runs half-hourly or hourly from the town centre between April and October, or the boat shuttle. Prices in high season run about €6.70 per person and €9.60 for a site.

Autocamp Zelena Laguna (☎ 410 541) Well-equipped for sports, this autocamp can house up to 2700 people.

Autocamp Bijela Uvala (☎ 410 551) Housing up to 6000 people, the camping ground can be crowded.

MIDRANGE

Most hotels are managed by **Riviera** (☎ 408 000; www.riviera.hr) or **Plava Laguna** (☎ 410 101; www.plavalaguna.hr). All hotels are open from April to October but there is only one hotel in town open in winter and it changes every year.

Hotel Hostin (☎ 432 112; www.hostin.hr; Rade Končara 4; s/d €85/122; P ☒ ☒ ☐ ☒) One of the newer entries on the hotel scene, this sparkling place is in verdant parkland just behind the bus station. An indoor swimming pool, fitness room and sauna are nice little extras plus the hotel is only 70m from a pebble beach.

Hotel Neptun (☎ 400 800; fax 431 531; Obala Maršala Tita 15; s/d from €55/110; P ☒) This is the best hotel in the town centre, which is an advantage if you want to be in the centre of the action, but it also means being in the centre of a traffic snarl in peak season. The front rooms with a harbour view are unbeatable.

Hotel Poreč (☎ 451 811; R Končara 1; www.hotel porec.com; s/d €59/90; ☒) Near the bus station and an easy walk from the Old Town, you'll find freshly renovated and comfortable rooms in this hotel.

Eating

Istra (☎ 434 636; Milanovića 30; meals from 80KN) This is where locals go for a special meal. In addition to the usual offerings of grilled fish, spaghetti and calamari there are delicious local specialities such as a mixed seafood starter and *mučkalica*, stewed chicken and vegetables in

CROATIA

a spicy sauce. There's a cosy interior and a covered terrace with wooden booths.

Nono (☎ 435 088; Zagrebačka 4; pizzas 28-35KN) You can tell that Nono serves the best pizzas in town because it's always crowded. With their soft, puffy crust and fresh toppings, these pizzas are actually memorable.

Barilla (☎ 452 742; Eufrazijana 26; meals 70-100KN) This authentic Italian restaurant serves delicious pasta and pizza as well as more sophisticated Italian dishes on two outdoor terraces.

Konoba Ulixes (☎ 451 132; Dekumanus 2; meals 70-100KN) Truffles are one of Istria's most precious products and you can taste them here in pasta, with beef or fresh tuna. The other fish and shellfish are also excellent, and be sure to look for the special asparagus dishes when in season.

Peškera Self-Service Restaurant (☎ 432 890; Nikole Tesle bb; meals 40KN; ⊗ 9am-10pm) Situated just outside the northeastern corner of the old city wall, this is one of the best of its kind in Croatia. You can get a cheap but good main course such as fried chicken, grilled calamari or rump steak and eat it on a terrace facing the sea.

A large supermarket and department store are situated next to Hotel Poreč, near the bus station.

Drinking

Caffe Lapidarium (Svetog Mauro 10) The sound of Croatian crooners sails forth from the sound system while you relax in a large courtyard or antique-filled inner rooms. Wednesday night is jazz night in the summer when all sorts of groups turn up to play.

Caffe Bar Torre Rotonda (Narodni trg 3a) In the historic Round Tower, this upstairs café is a good spot to watch the action on the quays in a soft, jazzy atmosphere.

Entertainment

Most nightlife is out of town at Zelena Laguna, where the big hotels host discos and various party nights, but the Old Town has its attractions as well.

Capitol Discotheque (V Nazora 9) This is the oldest disco in town, playing a mix of commercial music.

Getting There & Away

From the **bus station** (☎ 432 153; Karla Hugesa 2), buses depart for Rovinj (29KN, one hour,

seven daily), Zagreb (117KN to 167KN, five hours, six daily) and Rijeka (56KN to 67KN, 5½ hours, eight daily), and Pula (39KN to 51KN, 1¼ hours, 12 daily). Between Poreč and Rovinj the bus runs along the Lim Channel, a drowned valley. To see it clearly, sit on the right-hand side if you're southbound, or the left if you're northbound.

The nearest train station is at Pazin, 30km east (25KN, 12 daily).

For information about bus connections to Slovenia, see p225 and for information about boat connections to Italy, see p403.

ROVINJ

☎ 052 / pop 14,200

Yes, it is touristy and residents are developing a sharp eye for maximising their profits but Rovinj (Rovigno in Italian) is one of the last of the true Mediterranean fishing ports. Fishermen haul their catch into the harbour in the early morning, followed by a horde of squawking gulls, and mend their nets before lunch. Prayers for a good catch are sent forth at the massive Cathedral of St Euphemia, whose 60m tower punctuates the peninsula. Wooded hills and low-rise luxury hotels surround a town webbed by steep, cobbled streets. The 13 green, offshore islands of the Rovinj archipelago make for pleasant, varied views and you can swim from the rocks in the sparkling water below Hotel Rovinj.

Orientation & Information

The bus station is in the southeastern corner of the Old Town and there's an ATM next to the entrance, as well as the Autotrans Travel Agency, which will change money.

INTERNET ACCESS

Planet tourist agency (☎ 840 494; Sv Križ 1; per hr 30KN) The most convenient Internet access in Rovinj has a couple of computers.

LAUNDRY

Galax (☎ 814 059; M Benussi; per 5kg 50KN) It may be pricey but at least you can get your clothes washed.

LEFT LUGGAGE

Garderoba (⊗ 8am-9pm daily Jun-Sep, 8am-3pm Mon-Fri, to 2pm Sat Oct-May) At the bus station.

MEDICAL SERVICES

Ambulanta Rovinj (☎ 813 004; Istarska ul bb)

POST

Main post office (M Benussi 4) Situated across from the bus station; you can make phone calls here.

TOURIST INFORMATION

Tourist office (☎ 811 566; fax 816 007; www.tzgrovinj .hr; Obala Pina Budicina 12; ☷ 8am-9pm Mon-Sat, 9am-1pm Sun Jun-Sep, 8am-3pm Mon-Fri, to noon Sat Oct-May) Just off Trg Maršala Tita, this office is less than a fountain of information, more of a trickle.

TRAVEL AGENCIES

Futura Travel (☎ 817 281; futura-travel@pu.t-com.hr; M Benussi 2)

Marco Polo (☎ 816 616; www.marcopolo.hr; Istarska 2)

Planet tourist agency (☎ 840 494; www.planetrovinj .com; Sv Križ 1)

Sights

The **Cathedral of St Euphemia** (☷ 10am-noon & 2-5pm), which completely dominates the town from its hill-top location, was built in 1736 and is the largest baroque building in Istria. It reflects the period during the 18th century when Rovinj was the most populous town in Istria, an important fishing centre and the bulwark of the Venetian fleet.

Inside the cathedral, don't miss the tomb of St Euphemia (martyred in AD 304) behind the right-hand altar. The saint's remains were brought from Constantinople in 800. On the anniversary of her martyrdom (16 September) devotees congregate here. A copper statue of her tops the cathedral's mighty tower.

Take a wander along the winding narrow backstreets below the cathedral, such as **ul Grisia**, where local artists sell their work. Each year in August Rovinj's painters stage a big open-air art show in town.

The Rovinj **Regional Museum** (☎ 816 720; Trg Maršala Tita; adult/concession 10/8KN; ☷ 9am-noon & 7-10pm Tue-Sun mid-Jun–mid-Sep, 9am-1pm Tue-Sat rest of year) contains an interesting collection of Italian painters from the 15th to 19th centuries. Unfortunately the small size of the museum means that only a small percentage of its collection is on display at any given time. In the off season, a collection of works by contemporary Rovinj artists is mounted. There are also some Etruscan artefacts in the archaeology collection.

When you've seen enough of the town, follow the waterfront south past Hotel Park to **Punta Corrente Forest Park**, which was es-

tablished in 1890 by Baron Hütterodt, an Austrian admiral who kept a villa on Crveni otok (Red Island). Here you can swim off the rocks, climb a cliff or just sit and admire the offshore islands.

Activities

Most people hop aboard a boat for serious swimming, snorkelling and sunbathing. A trip to Crveni otok or Sveti Katarina (Katarina Island) is easily arranged (see below). **Divers Sport Center** (☎ 816 648; www.diver.hr; Villas Rubin) is 3km south of Rovinj and specialises in wreck diving, especially the wreck of the *Baron Gautsch*, an Austrian passengersteamer sunk in 1914 by an Austrian mine, causing 177 fatalities. The wreck lies in up to 40m of water and offers plenty of marine life.

Tours

Delfin Agency (☎ 813 383), near the ferry dock for Crveni otok, runs half-day scenic cruises to the Lim Channel for 130KN per person, or you can go with one of the independent operators at the end of Alzo Rismondo that run half-day and full-day boat trips around the region. There's an hourly ferry to the lovely and wooded Crveni otok (20KN return) and a frequent ferry to nearby Sveti Katarina (10KN return) from the same landing. Get tickets on the boat or at the nearby kiosk. These boats operate only from May to mid-October.

Festivals & Events

The city's annual events include the following. The tourist office has full details.

Rovinj-Pesaro Regatta Early May

Rovinj Summer Concert series in July and August.

Grisia Art Market On the 2nd Sunday of August.

Sleeping

Private rooms with two beds cost €30 to €50 in high season with a small discount for single occupancy. The surcharge for a stay of less than three nights is 50% and guests who stay only one night are punished with a 100% surcharge, but you should be able to bargain the surcharge away outside of July and August. You can book directly from www.inforovinj.com or consult one of the travel agencies listed on left. There are almost no rooms at all available in the Old Town, however.

Hotel Villa Angelo D'Oro (☎ 840 502; www.rovinj .at; Via Svalba 38-42; s/d €113/200; 🔀) This new luxury hotel in a renovated Venetian building has plush, lavishly decorated rooms with satellite TV and minibar, and a free sauna and Jacuzzi room.

Aparthotel Villa Valdibora (☎ 845 040; www .valdibora.com; Chiurca Silvana 8; s/d 180/200; P 🔀 🖵) This is a boutique hotel of the highest calibre. The restored 17th-century building has been lavishly done up with mementos recalling Rovinj's history and the rooms are exceptionally comfortable.

Vila Lili (☎ 840 940; www.cel.hr/vilalili; Mohorovicica 16; s/d from €60/100; 🔀) The comfort level at this small hotel is excellent, and includes satellite TV, a sauna and bright, modern rooms. It's just a short walk out of town past the marina.

Hotel Monte Mulin (☎ 811 512; www.adriaresorts .hr; s/d from €35/60; P) On the wooded hillside overlooking the bay just beyond Hotel Park, this hotel is about a 15-minute walk south of the bus station. Rooms are bland but perfectly serviceable.

Porton Biondi (☎ 813 557; per person/camp site €6.28/6) Less than a kilometre from the town (on the Monsena bus route).

Eating & Drinking

Most of the fish and spaghetti places along the harbour cater to the upmarket crowd.

Amfora (☎ 815 525; Rismondo 23; meals from 70KN) One of the best restaurants in town, it's expensive and packed in high season but you will eat well.

Giannino (☎ 813 402; A Ferri 38; meals from 90KN) If you like Italian food, it doesn't get much better than this. Everything from the olive oil to the grilled seafood is first rate.

Cantinon (☎ 811 970; Alzo Rismondo 18; fish meals from 65KN) This welcoming restaurant is becoming touristy but locals still come here for the variety of well-prepared fresh fish.

Veli Jože (☎ 816 337; Sv Križ 1; meals 65-140KN) In an interior crammed with knick-knacks or at tables outside, you can feast on a wide assortment of Istrian delicacies.

Zanzibar (☎ 813 206; P Budicina bb) Indonesian wood, palms, subdued lighting and various imaginative decorative touches create a vaguely tropical and definitely upscale ambience in this cocktail bar.

Monvi Centre (☎ 545 117; Adamovića bb) Next to the Hotel Eden, this entertainment complex harbours a bar, cabaret, disco and a variety of fast-food joints.

Picnickers can buy supplies at the supermarket only about 25m downhill from the bus station or in one of the kiosks selling *burek* near the vegetable market.

Getting There & Away

Eurostar Travel (☎ 813 144; Obala Pina Budicina 1) has schedules and tickets for boats to Italy.

From the **bus station** (⌚ 811 453; Trg na Lokvi 6), there are frequent buses to Pula (27KN, 45 minutes), which sometimes continue on to Poreč (29KN to 40KN, one hour), eight buses daily to Rijeka (86KN, three hours), nine daily to Zagreb (105KN to 196KN, five to eight hours), one daily each to Koper (80KN, 2¾ hours) and Split (319KN, 11¼ hours), and one daily to Dubrovnik (455KN, 16 hours) and Ljubljana (155KN, 5½ hours, July and August). Prices and durations vary between different companies and routes.

The closest train station is Kanfanar, 19km away on the Pula–Divača line.

PULA

☎ 052 / pop 62,400

Pula (the ancient Polensium) is a large regional centre with a wealth of Roman ruins to explore. Its star attraction is a remarkably well-preserved amphitheatre that dominates the town centre and is often the scene of concerts and shows. Despite its busy commercial life, Pula retains an easy-going small-town appeal. Nearby are some rocky wooded peninsulas overlooking the clear Adriatic waters, which explain the many resort hotels and camping grounds circling the city. Most residents head out to Verudela Peninsula for the nightlife and swimming coves.

Orientation

The bus station is 500m northeast of the town centre. The centre of town is Giardini, while the harbour is west of the bus station. The train station is near the water, about 500m north of town.

Information

You can exchange money in travel agencies or at either of the post offices where there is an ATM.

Atlas travel agency (☎ 393 040; atlas.pula@atlas.hr; Starih Statuta 1) Finds private accommodation and organises tours.

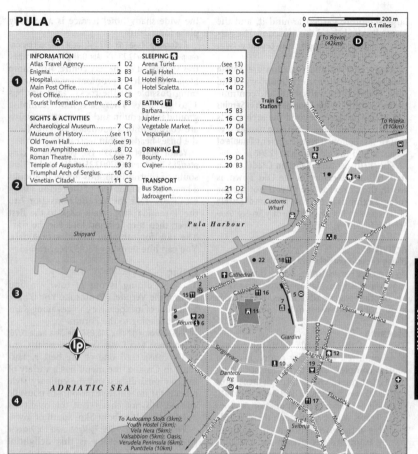

PULA

0 ——————— 200 m
0 ——————— 0.1 miles

INFORMATION
Atlas Travel Agency.................1 D2
Enigma.....................................2 B3
Hospital...................................3 D4
Main Post Office.....................4 C4
Post Office..............................5 C3
Tourist Information Centre......6 B3

SIGHTS & ACTIVITIES
Archaeological Museum...........7 C3
Museum of History..............(see 11)
Old Town Hall......................(see 9)
Roman Amphitheatre..............8 D2
Roman Theatre.....................(see 7)
Temple of Augustus................9 B3
Triumphal Arch of Sergius.....10 C4
Venetian Citadel....................11 C3

SLEEPING
Arena Turist........................(see 13)
Galija Hotel..........................12 D4
Hotel Riviera........................13 D2
Hotel Scaletta......................14 D2

EATING
Barbara................................15 B3
Jupiter.................................16 C3
Vegetable Market.................17 C3
Vespazijan...........................18 C3

DRINKING
Bounty.................................19 D4
Cvajner................................20 B3

TRANSPORT
Bus Station..........................21 D2
Jadroagent...........................22 C3

Pula Harbour

ADRIATIC SEA

To Rovinj
(42km)

To Rijeka
(110km)

To Autocamp Stoia (3km);
Youth Hostel (3km);
Vela Nera (5km);
Valsabbion (5km); Oasis;
Verudela Peninsula (6km);
Puntižela (10km)

CROATIA

Enigma (☎ 381 615; Kandlerova 19; per hr 20KN)
Internet access.
Hospital (☎ 214 433; Zagrebačka 34) Emergency
services are available 24 hours.
Main post office (Danteov trg 4; ☼ 7am-8pm) You can
make long distance calls. There's a branch post office to the
northeast of the Archaeological Museum.
Tourist Information Centre (☎ 219 197; www
.pulainfo.hr; Forum 2; ☼ 9am-8pm Mon-Sat, 10am-6pm
Sun) With knowledgeable and friendly staff, this centre
provides maps, brochures and schedules of upcoming
events in Pula and around Istria.

Sights
Pula's most imposing sight is the 1st-century
Roman amphitheatre (☎ 219 028; Flavijevska; adult/
concession 16/8KN; ☼ 8am-9pm Jun-Sep, 8.30am-4.30pm

Oct-May) overlooking the harbour and northeast of the Old Town.

Built entirely from local limestone, the
amphitheatre was designed to host gladi-
atorial contests and could accommodate up
to 20,000 spectators. The 30m-high outer
wall is almost intact and contains two rows
of 72 arches. Around the end of July a
Croatian film festival is held in the amphitheatre, and there are pop, jazz and classical
events, often with major international stars,
throughout summer.

The **Archaeological Museum** (☎ 218 603; Cara-
rina 3; adult/concession 12/6KN; ☼ 9am-7pm Mon-Sat,
10am-3pm Sun Jun-Sep, 9am-3pm Mon-Fri Oct-May) is
uphill from the town centre. Even if you
don't visit the museum be sure to visit the

large sculpture garden around it, and the **Roman theatre** behind the museum. The garden is entered through 2nd-century twin gates.

Along Istarska and Catarina are **Roman walls** that mark the eastern boundary of old Pula. Follow these walls south and continue down Giardini to the **Triumphal Arch of Sergius** (27 BC). The street beyond the arch winds right around old Pula, changing names several times. Follow it to the ancient **Temple of Augustus** and the **old town hall** (1296).

The 17th-century **Venetian Citadel**, on a high hill in the centre of the Old Town, is worth the climb for the view if not for the meagre exhibits in the tiny **Museum of History** (Kaštel; admission 7KN; ☯ 8am-7pm daily Jun-Sep, 9am-5pm Mon-Fri Oct-May) inside.

Activities

Diving Center Puntižela (☎ 517 517; www.wreckdiving-croatia.com; Puntižela) offers wreck diving, diving around Brijuni National Park and a variety of other watery adventures. Puntižela is about 10km southwest of the centre.

Sleeping

The tip of the Verudela Peninsula, about 6km southwest of the city centre, is a vast tourist complex with plenty of sprawling hotels that you can book through **Arena Turist** (☎ 529 483; www.arenaturist.hr; Hotel Riviera, Splitska 1a). It also finds private accommodation, as does Atlas Travel Agency, although there is little available in the town centre itself. Count on paying from €18 per person for a double room and up to €62 for an apartment.

Hotel Scaletta (☎ 541 599; www.hotel-scaletta.com; Flavijeska 26; s/d €70/101; P ☯) This hotel offers beautifully decorated and thoughtfully arranged rooms with every comfort accounted for. The hotel restaurant is also first-rate.

Galija Hotel (☎ 383 802; www.hotel-galija-pula .com; Epulonova 2; s/d from €80/120; ☯ ☯) This small family-owned hotel is another good bet if you want to stay in town. It feels more like staying in a private residence than a commercial establishment.

Hotel Riviera (☎ /fax 211 166; Splitska 1; s/d €54/92) Neither the service nor the comfort quite justifies the price (which eases in the low season) in this one-star hotel, but there is an undeniably appealing old-world elegance and the rooms are spacious. The front rooms have a view of the water and

the wide shady hotel terrace is a relaxing place for a drink.

Autocamp Stoja (☎ 387 144; fax 387 748; per person/ camp site & car €6/12.20; ☯ Apr-Oct) Three kilometres southwest of the city centre, Autocamp Stoja is on a shady promontory, with swimming possible off the rocks. Take city bus 1 to get here. There are more camping grounds at Medulin and Premantura, which are coastal resorts southeast of Pula (take the buses heading southeast from town).

Youth Hostel (☎ 391 133; pula@hfhs.hr; camp sites/B&B/half board €8.70/13.35/17.35) Only 3km south of central Pula, this hostel overlooks a beach and is near one of the region's largest discos. Take the Verudela bus 2 or 7 to the 'Piramida' stop, walk back to the first street, then turn left and look for the sign. The rate for camping includes breakfast. You can hire tents for €1.85, year round.

Eating

The best dining is out of town on and around the Verudela Peninsula. You'll have a number of inexpensive choices along Kandlerova leading to the Forum.

Valsabbion (☎ /fax 218 033; Pješčana uvala IX/26; 2-course meals from 120KN; ☯ noon-midnight) Generally considered one of the best restaurants in Croatia, the menu has a variety of international dishes and the culinary style reflects the imaginative flavours of nouvelle cuisine. It's not cheap, but the quality is outstanding. It's about 5km south of town.

Vela Nera (☎ 219 209; Pješčana uvala bb; 2-course meals from 100KN) Nearby is this delightful place, a rival of Valsabbion for renowned dining, with a terrace overlooking the sea and excellent seafood specialities.

Jupiter (☎ 214 333; Castropola 38; meals from 25KN) This popular place serves up the best pizza in town and the pasta is good, too.

Barbara (☎ 219 317; Kandlerova 5; meals from 25KN) It's your basic calamari and *ćevapčići* but well done and in a great people-watching location.

Vespazijan (☎ 210 016; Amfiteatarska 11; meals from 30KN) This unpretentious spot conjures up yummy risottos and a variety of seafood dishes.

Self-caterers can pick up vegetables, cold cuts and local cheese at the morning **vegetable market** (Smareglije Masovog Polja).

(Continued on page 177)

RAFAEL ESTEFANIA

Seaside restaurant terrace on the road from Vlora
to Himara, Ionian Coast (p69) Albania

Independence Monument (p68),
Vlora, Albania

PAUL DAVID HELLANDER

PAUL DAVID HELLANDER

Baptistry (p73) at the ruins of Butrinti, Albania

The castle (p63) at Kruja, Albania

RAFAEL ESTEFANIA

RAFAEL ESTEFANIA

Resurrected Saviour (p119) by Andrej Ajdič, Međugorje, Bosnia and Hercegovina

Gazi-Husrevbey Mosque (p98), Sarajevo, Bosnia and Hercegovina

RAFAEL ESTEFANIA

RAFAEL ESTEFANIA

Baščaršija (p98), Sarajevo, Bosnia and Hercegovina

Old Bridge (Stari Most; p111) and the cobbled Kujundžiluk (p114), Mostar, Bosnia and Hercegovina

RAFAEL ESTE

Museum Mimara (p154), Zagreb, Croatia

Cavtat (p215), near Dubrovnik, Croatia

Rovinj (p164), Istria, Croatia

Euphrasian Basilica (p163), Poreč, Croatia

Vegetable market, Rovinj (p164), Croatia

WAYNE WALTON

Diocletian's Palace (p195), Split, Croatia

WAYNE WA

RAFAEL ESTEFANIA

Treskavec Monastery (p255), near Prilep, Macedonia

RAFAEL ESTEFANIA

Daud Paša Baths (p238), Skopje, Macedonia

Man playing the *gadja* (traditional bagpipes; p235), Macedonia

RAFAEL ESTEFANIA

IZZET KERIBAR

Šarena Djamija mosque (p244), Tetovo, Macedonia

Bookshop, Knez Mihailova street (p275), Belgrade, Serbia

Sinan Pasha Mosque (p308), Prizren, Kosovo

Hotel Moscow (p284), Belgrade, Serbia

Trg Slobode in Novi Sad (p291), Serbia

PATRICK HORTON

Sveti Stefan (p313), Montenegro

PATRICK HORTON

Monastery of Ostrog (p319), near Nikšic, Montenegro

Quaint house on a street in Cetinje (p310), Montenegro

RAFAEL ESTEFANIA

Mountain hut, Bohinj (p356), Slovenia

Façade of decorated windows, Ljubljana (p339), Slovenia

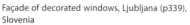

Piran (p366), Primorska, Slovenia

Bled Castle (p351), Bled, Slovenia

(Continued from page 168)

Drinking

The streets of Flanatička, Kandlerova and Sergijevaca are lively people-watching spots, and the Forum has several outdoor cafés that fill up in the early evening.

Cvajner (Forum) The trendiest café/gallery in town, with a stunning art-filled interior.

Bounty (☎ 218 088; Veronska 8) Irish beer and cheer are served up in liberal doses here.

Entertainment

Posters around Pula advertise live performances at the amphitheatre or details of rave parties at two venues in Verudela: Oasis and Fort Bourguignon.

Getting There & Away

BOAT

Jadroagent (☎ 210 431; jadroagent-pula@pu.t-com.hr; Riva 14) has schedules and tickets for boats connecting Istria with Italy and the islands. For more information about ferries to Italy, see p403.

BUS

The buses that travel to Rijeka (6KN, 2½ hours, 20 daily) are sometimes crowded, especially the eight that continue to Zagreb, so be sure to reserve a seat in advance. Going from Pula to Rijeka, be sure to sit on the right-hand side of the bus for a stunning view of the Gulf of Kvarner.

Other destinations you can reach from the **bus station** (☎ 502 997; Istarske Brigade bb) include: Rovinj (27KN, 40 minutes, 18 daily); Poreč (39KN to 51KN, one hour, 12 daily); Zagreb (88KN to 174KN, five hours, 11 daily); Zadar (194KN, seven hours, four daily); Split (300KN, 10 hours, two daily); and Dubrovnik (432KN, 15 hours, one daily).

TRAIN

There are two daily trains to Ljubljana (125KN, four hours) and two to Zagreb (134KN, 6½ hours), but you must board a bus for part of the trip.

Getting Around

The only city buses of use to visitors are buses 2 and 7 to Verudela, which pass the youth hostel. Frequency varies from every 15 minutes to every 30 minutes, with service from 5am to 11.30pm daily. Tickets are sold at newsstands for 10KN and are good for two trips.

Around Pula

BRIJUNI ISLANDS NATIONAL PARK

The Brijuni (Brioni in Italian) consists of two main pine-covered islands and 12 islets just northwest of Pula. Notable as the summer residence of Maršal Tito, the Brijuni Islands are now a highly groomed and scrupulously maintained national park. Some 680 species of plants grow here, including many exotic subtropical species which were planted at Tito's request. Tito's former private hunting grounds are now a safari park where elephants, zebras and antelope roam.

You may only visit Brijuni National Park with a group. Instead of booking an excursion with one of the travel agencies in Pula, Rovinj or Poreč, which costs €48 (400KN), you could take a public bus from Pula to Fažana (8km), then sign up for a tour (140KN) at the **Brijuni Tourist Service** (☎ 525 883) office near the wharf. You must book at least one day in advance.

PAZIN

☎ 052 / pop 5200

No fashionable foreigners are crowding Pazin's streets and that's part of its appeal. This workaday town in central Istria deserves a stop, not only for its famous chasm that so inspired Jules Verne or the stolid medieval castle that dominates the western portion of town, but also for its neighbourly small-town feel. The rolling Istrian countryside creeps right up to the town's outskirts while most of the centre is given over to pedestrian-only areas. Not only is Pazin the geographic heart of Istria, it's the county's administrative seat as well. As transport connections by road or rail put you within an hour's reach of virtually every other destination in Istria, Pazin makes an excellent, relaxed, inexpensive base to explore the region.

Orientation

From east to west, the town is relatively compact, stretching little more than a kilometre from the train station on the eastern end to the castle on the western end, which is at the edge of the Pazin Chasm. The bus station is 200m west of the train station and the old part of town comprises the 200m leading up to the castle.

CROATIA

Information

Futura Travel (☎ 621 045; Prolaz Ernesta Jelusica 2) Changes money, books excursions and provides regional information.

Hospital (☎ 624 021; Jurja Dobrile 1) Emergency services are available 24 hours. **Post office** (MB Rašana 7a)

Tourist office (☎ /fax 622 460; www.tzpazin.hr; Franine i Jurine 14; ☑ 8.30am-6pm daily Jul-Aug, 8am-3pm Mon-Fri Sep-Jun) Finds private accommodation.

Sights

Pazin's most renowned site is undoubtedly the **Pazin Chasm**, an abyss of about 100m through which the Pazinčica River sinks into subterranean passages forming three underground lakes. Its shadowy depths inspired the imagination of Jules Verne as well as numerous Croatian writers. There's a viewing point just outside the castle and a footbridge that spans the abyss about 30m further on.

Pazin's **Castle** (Kaštel; ☎ 625 040; Istarskog Razvoda 1; adult/concession 15/8KN; ☑ 10am-6pm Tue-Sun mid-Apr–mid-Oct, 10am-3pm Tue-Thu, noon-5pm Fri, 11am-5pm Sat & Sun mid-Oct–mid-Apr) is the largest and best-preserved medieval structure in Istria. Overlooking the Pazin Chasm, it was first mentioned in 983 but the current structure dates from about 1537. Within the castle, there's an **Ethnographic Museum** with a collection of medieval Istrian church bells as well as Istrian implements, garments and musical instruments.

Near the tourist office is the **Church of St Nickolas** (Svetog Nikola; Muntriljska; ☑ Mass only), notable for its late-Gothic polygonal presbytery and 15th-century frescoes of the Creation in the vault.

Festivals & Events

Town Fair Day First Tuesday of the month; features products from all over Istria.

Days of Jules Verne In the third week of June; Pazin's way of honouring the writer that put Pazin on the cultural map. There are races, reenactments from his novel, and journeys retracing the footsteps of Verne's hero Mathias Sandorf.

Sleeping & Eating

The tourist office helps arrange private accommodation, which is generally reasonably priced. Count on spending about 125KN per person for a room.

Hotel Lovac (☎ 624 384; tisadoo@inet.hr; Kurelića bb; d €45; Ⓟ) The only hotel in town is a not-especially-characterful place on the western edge of town.

Poli Luce (☎ 687 081; www.konoba-marino-gracisce .hr; Grašišće; per person €18; Ⓟ) If you don't mind being out of town, try these beautifully restored rooms in an old farmhouse. It's at Grašišće, a sleepy, rustic village about 7km south of Pazin.

Konoba Marino (☎ 687 081; meals from 60KN; ☑ closed Wed) The same owners of Poli Luce run Konoba, which is a good place to sample homemade Istrian sausage and other home-smoked meat in copious portions.

Getting There & Away

From the **bus station** (☎ 624 437; Šetalište Pazinske Gimnazije) there are services to Poreč (25KN, 40 minutes, 10 daily), Pula (18KN to 30KN, 50 minutes, nine daily), Rijeka (41KN, one hour, five daily) and Rovinj (29KN, one hour, five daily). Service is reduced on weekends. Pazin **train station** (☎ 622 710; Stareh Kostanje 1) has services to Ljubljana (83KN, four hours, one daily), Pula (29KN, one hour, eight daily) and Zagreb (99KN, eight hours, seven daily). There is reduced service on weekends.

MOTOVUN

☎ 052 / pop 590

Motovun is a captivating little town perched on a hill in Mirna River Valley, about 20km northeast of Poreč. It was the Venetians who decided to fortify the town in the 14th century, building two sets of thick walls. A Venetian lion scowls down from the outer gate and a cheerier lion adorns the inner gate. Venetian coats of arms on many buildings recall the noble families that once lived here. Once crumbling into ruin, the town is attracting artists who have set up studios in the tumble of Romanesque and Gothic houses, while newer houses have sprung up on the slopes leading up to the Old Town.

Orientation & Information

If you come in a car, leave it at the foot of the village. There's a 10KN charge in season which includes a little 'tourist train' to take you up the steep hill through the city gates. It also makes a nice walk.

The **tourist office** (☎ 681758; opcina-motovun@pu .t-com.hr; Zadrugarska 20b) has a limited amount of information. There's an ATM just after the entrance on the right.

Sights & Activities

The highlight of the town is the Renaissance church of **St Stephen** (Sveti Stjepan; Trg Andrea Antico; 10am-1pm & 4-8pm Apr-Oct), designed by Venetian artist Andrea Palladio. Venetian Francesco Bonazzo contributed the marble altar statues of St Stephen and St Laurence and an unknown 17th-century Venetian produced the painting of the Last Supper behind the altar.

Festivals & Events

Motovun's **International Film Festival** (www.motovunfilmfestival.com) takes place in the last week in July and presents independent and avant-garde films from the USA and Europe.

Sleeping & Eating

Hotel Kaštel (681 607; www.hotel-kastel-motovun.hr; Trg Andrea Antico 7; s/d €50/70; P) The town's only hotel is in a restored stone building with 28 simply furnished rooms. It has a good restaurant offering truffles and the local *teran* wine.

Restaurant Zigante (664 302; Livade 7, Livade; meals from 142KN) Just outside Motovun in Livade, this restaurant dominates the town centre. In fact, it *is* the town centre. The all-inclusive menu for 142KN is a truffle-taster's treat and the wine list is superb. There's no better place to sample the best of Istrian wine and cuisine in a refined, low-key atmosphere.

Getting There & Away

There are weekday bus connections from Pazin (19KN, 35 minutes, three daily).

GROŽNJAN

052 / pop 193

Until the mid-1960s, Grožnjan, 26km northeast of Poreč, was slipping towards oblivion. For the 14th-century Venetians, this strategic hill-top town was an important fortress in their Istrian defensive system. They created a system of ramparts and gates, built a loggia, a granary and several fine churches. With the collapse of the Venetian empire in the 18th century, Grožnjan suffered a decline in its importance and population.

In 1965 sculptor Aleksandar Rukavina and a small group of other sculptors and painters 'discovered' the crumbling medieval appeal of Grožnjan and began setting up studios in the abandoned buildings. As the town crawled back to life, it attracted the attention of the International Cultural Centre of Jeunesses Musicales Croatia, an international training programme for young musicians. In July, August and the start of September, concerts and musical events are held almost daily, and you can often overhear the musicians practising while you browse the many crafts shops and galleries.

Orientation & Information

The tiny town is a jumble of crooked lanes and leafy squares. Near the centre is the **Tourist Office** (Turistička Zajednica; /fax 776 131; www.groznjan-grisignana.hr; Gorjan 3; 9am-noon & 5-8pm Mon-Sat May-Sep). Its staff can help find private accommodation in and around town and provide a small map with a list of galleries.

Sights & Activities

There are nearly 20 galleries and studios scattered around town and most are open daily from May to September. The Renaissance **loggia** is immediately to the right of the town gate and on top of the loggia is the **granary**. Keep going and on your right you'll see the baroque **Spinotti Morteani Palace** and then the **Castle** (Kaštel) where many concerts are held. The town is dominated by the bell tower of the **Church of St Vitus, St Modest & St Crecsentius**, which was built in the late 18th century and contains striking baroque choir stalls.

Summer music concerts are organised by the **International Cultural Centre of Jeunesses Musicales Croatia** (ICCJMC; 01-611 600; www.hgm.hr in Croatian; Trg Stjepana Radića 4, Zagreb). The concerts are free and no reservations are necessary. They are usually held in the church, main square, loggia or the castle at 9pm (8pm in September).

Sleeping & Eating

The tourist office can put you in touch with private rooms. Count on about €15 per person.

Getting There & Away

If you don't have your own wheels, you can take the morning bus that runs from Pula to Poreč and Trieste (24KN, 1½ hours), and get off at the town of Krasica, before Buje. It's a 3.5km-walk to Grožnjan, but the road winds along a scenic ridge with great views.

GULF OF KVARNER

The Gulf of Kvarner (Quarnero in Italian) covers 3300 sq km between Rijeka and Pag Island in the south. Protected by the Velebit Range in the northeast, the Gorski Kotar in the north and the Učka massif in the east, the climate is gentle and the range of vegetation wide.

The largest city is the busy commercial port of Rijeka, only a few kilometres from the aristocratic Opatija riviera. The islands of Krk, Cres, Lošinj and Rab also have their share of admirers, who come for the luxuriant slopes dipping down to the sea.

RIJEKA

☎ 051 / pop 144,000

As Croatia's largest port, Rijeka (Fiume in Italian) is full of boats, cargo, fumes, cranes and the bustling sense of purpose that characterises most port cities. All of the buses, trains and ferries that form the network connecting Istria and Dalmatia with Zagreb and points beyond seem to pass through Rijeka, making the town almost impossible to avoid. Since Rijeka is hardly one of the 'must-see' destinations, the café-lined boulevard Korzo is refreshingly tourist-free, and few visitors make the trek up to Trsat Castle for the views over the gulf. With stately 19th-century buildings, a tree-lined promenade along the harbour and a smattering of museums and restaurants, you won't regret spending a day here.

Orientation

The **bus station** (☎ 060 333 444; Trg Žabica) is south of the Capuchin Church in the centre of town. The **train station** (ul Krešimirova) is a seven-minute walk west of the bus station.

The Jadrolinija ferry wharf (there's no left-luggage section) is just a few minutes east of the bus station. Korzo runs in an easterly direction through the city centre towards the fast-moving Rječina River.

Information

INTERNET ACCESS

Erste Club (☎ 320 072; Korzo 22; per hr 25KN; ☺ 8am-10pm Mon-Sat, 9am-4pm Sun)

RIJEKA

0 ———— 200 m
0 ———— 0.1 miles

INFORMATION	
Erste Club	(see 1)
Hostelling International	1 B2
Main Post Office	2 B2
Telephone Centre	(see 2)
Tourist Information Centre	3 B2

SIGHTS & ACTIVITIES	
Capuchin Church	4 A1
Church of St Jerome	5 B2
Church of St Vito	6 C2
City Tower	7 C2
Modern Art Gallery	8 B2
Natural History Museum	9 C1
Naval & Historical Museum	10 C1

SLEEPING	
Hotel Bonavia	11 B2

EATING	
Feral	12 C3
Grocery Stores	(see 15)
Zlatna Školja	13 B2

DRINKING	
Club Palach	14 B2

TRANSPORT	
Bus Station	15 A2
ITR Rent a Car	16 A2
Jadroagent	17 C2
Jadrolinija	18 A2

LAUNDRY

Blitz (☎ 215 219; Krešimirova 3a; ☺ 7am-8pm Mon-Fri, 7am-1pm Sat) Situated between the bus and train stations, Blitz will do a small load of laundry for 60KN.

LEFT LUGGAGE

Garderoba (per day 15KN) bus station (☺ 5.30am-10.30pm); train station (☺ 24hr)

MEDICAL SERVICES

Hospital (☎ 333 333; Krešimirova 52) Emergency services are available 24 hours. It's past the train station.

MONEY

There's an ATM at the train station, and the exchange offices adjacent to the train and bus stations keep long hours. There are a number of ATMs dotted along Korzo, as well as an exchange counter in the main post office.

POST

Main post office (Korzo) Opposite the old City Tower, the post office also houses a telephone centre.

TOURIST INFORMATION

Hostelling International (☎ 264 176; Korzo 22) Sells HI cards and is a good source of information about Croatian hostels, but it doesn't direct to hostels in Rijeka.
Tourist Information Centre (☎ 335 882; www.tz-rijeka.hr; Korzo 33) Distributes *Rijeka Tourist Route*, a walking-tour guide that is so well produced it makes you actually want to stay and look around.

Sights

Rijeka's main orientation point is the **City Tower** (Korzo), which was originally one of the main gates to the city, and is one of the few monuments to have survived the earthquake of 1750.

The **Modern Art Gallery** (Galerija Moderna; ☎ 334 280; Dolac 1; adult/concession 10/5KN; ☺ 10am-1pm & 5-8pm) is in the upstairs scientific library opposite Hotel Bonavia. The **Naval & Historical Museum** (Pomorski I Povijesni Muzej; ☎ 213 578; Muzejski trg 1; adult/student 10/1KN; ☺ 9am-1pm Tue-Sat) traces the development of sailing, with models and paintings of ships and portraits of the captains. The **Natural History Museum** (Pirodoslovni Muzej; ☎ 334 988; Lorenzov prolaz 1; adult/student 10/5KN; ☺ 9am-7pm Mon-Sat, to 3pm Sun) is devoted to regional geology and botany.

Also worth a visit is the 13th-century **Trsat Castle** (Trsatska Gradina; admission 15KN; ☺ 9am-11pm Tue-Sun Apr-Nov, to 3pm Tue-Sun Dec-Mar), which is on a high ridge overlooking Rijeka and

the canyon of the Rječina River. If you have some more time to kill, stroll into some of Rijeka's churches, such as **Church of St Vito** (Crkva Sv. Vida; Trg Grivica 11), **Church of St Jerome** (Crkva Sv. Jeronima; Trg Riječke Rezolucije) or the ornate **Capuchin Church** (Crkva Gospe Lurdska; Trg Žabica), all open for Mass only.

Festivals & Events

The **Rijeka Carnival** (www.ri-karnival.com) in February is the largest and most elaborate in Croatia with seven days of partying. Balls are by invitation only, but there are plenty of parades and street dances that are open to everyone.

Sleeping

The tourist office can direct you to the few options for private accommodation, most of which are a few kilometres out of town on the road to Opatija. It's just as easy to go on to Opatija, where there are more and better choices for hotels and private accommodation (for details on getting to/from Opatija, see p183).

Hotel Bonavia (☎ 333 744; www.bonavia.hr; Dolac 4; s/d from €125/150; P ✗ ✗ ☐ ☐) The four-star Bonavia is the only hotel in the centre of town and it has all of the niceties that businesspeople on generous expense accounts find indispensable.

Hotel Continental (☎ 372 008; www.jadran-hoteli.hr; Andrije Kašića Miočica; s/d €47/55; P ☐) This old building, northeast of the town centre, has spacious rooms that could use an overhaul. At least there's Internet access.

PJ Boarding House (☎ 551 246; Prvog Maja 34; per person with/without bathroom 225/135KN) The rooms are spartan but tidy and the boarding house is reachable by buses 4 and 5. Prices do not include breakfast.

Eating

If you're hungry on Sunday, head to one of the hotel restaurants, since nearly every restaurant in town will be closed.

Feral (☎ 212 274; Matije Gupca 5b; meals from 60KN) The marine theme runs strong here with slightly cheaper seafood than Zlatna Školja, but it's still beautifully prepared.

Zlatna Školja (☎ 213 782; Kružna 12; meals 100KN) The fetching maritime décor puts you in the mood to savour the astonishingly creative seafood dishes here. The wine list is also notable.

There are several 24-hour grocery stores in and around the bus station.

Drinking

Croatia's recent zero-tolerance approach to drink-driving has been good for Rijeka's nightlife. Everyone used to go to Opatija to drink, but now no-one wants to take the chance of getting stopped on the route back. Bar-hoppers cruise along Riva or Korzo for the liveliest bars and cafés.

Club Palach (☎ 215 063; Kružna 6) In the back alley, accessible through a small passageway off Jadranski trg, Club Palach caters to students who find it a good low-key place to drink and dance.

Getting There & Away

BOAT

Croatia's national boat carrier, **Jadrolinija** (☎ 211 444; www.jadrolinija.hr; Riva 16), has tickets for the large coastal ferries that run all year between Rijeka and Dubrovnik. For fares, see p226. For information on all boats to Croatia contact **Jadroagent** (☎ 211 276; Trg Ivana Koblera 2).

BUS

There are 13 buses daily between Rijeka and Krk (41KN, 1½ hours) via the huge Krk Bridge. Buses to Krk are overcrowded and a ticket in no way guarantees a seat. Don't worry – the bus from Rijeka to Krk empties fast so you won't be standing for long. There's also a daily bus transfer to the Zagreb airport at 5am and at 3.30pm from the bus station. The cost is 135KN. Call ☎ 51-330 207 to reserve.

Other buses departing from Rijeka are headed for:

Destination	Cost (KN)	Duration	Frequency
Baška (Krk Island)	53	2hr	1 daily
Dubrovnik	300-372	13hr	2 daily
Poreč	60	4½hr	5 daily
Pula	68	2½hr	17 daily
Rab	99	3½hr	2 daily
Rovinj	86	3½hr	10 daily
Split	185-248	8½hr	11 daily
Trieste	48	2-3hr	3 daily
Zadar	138	5hr	12 daily
Zagreb	81-116	2½-3hr	21 daily

For international connections see p225.

CAR

Close to the bus station, **ITR Rent a Car** (☎ 337 544; Riva 20) has hire cars for about 300KN per day.

TRAIN

Four trains run daily to Zagreb (120KN, five hours). There's also a daily direct train to Osijek (182KN, eight hours) and a daily train to Split that changes at Ogulin where you wait for two hours (154KN, 10 hours). Several of the seven daily services to Ljubljana (86KN, three hours) require a change of trains at the Slovenian border and again at Bifka or Bistrica in Slovenia, but there are also two direct trains. Reservations are compulsory on some *poslovni* (express) trains.

OPATIJA

☎ 051 / pop 12,719

Opatija, just a few kilometres due west of Rijeka, was where fashionable 19th-century aristocrats came to 'take the waters'. The Lungomare, a shady waterfront promenade that stretches for 12km along the Gulf of Kvarner, offers genteel exercise and a calming view of the mountainous coast. And to rest your weary head, there's a wide choice of hotels with baroque exteriors and high-ceilinged plush interiors that offer good value for money.

Information

There's no left-luggage facility at **Opatija bus station** (Trg Vladimira Gortana), which is in the town centre, but Autotrans Agency at the station will usually watch luggage.

Atlas travel agency (☎ 271 032; Maršala Tita 116) Accommodation and excursions.

Da Riva (☎ 272 482; www.da-riva.hr; Maršala Tita 162) Finds private accommodation and organises group transfers to regional airports.

Main post office (Eugena Kumičića 2; ⏲ 8am-7pm Mon-Sat) Behind the market.

Tourist office (☎ 271 310; www.opatija-tourism.hr; Maršala Tita 101; ⏲ 8am-7pm Mon-Sat & 2-6pm Sun Jun-Sep, 9am-noon & 2-4.30pm Mon-Sat Oct-May) Has some information on local events.

Activities

Opatija is not a museum/gallery kind of place. Come for the swimming in the coves along the Lungomare or just stroll the great seaside promenade. There's also hiking up

Mt Učka. Head to the tourist office for details.

Sleeping & Eating

Private rooms are abundant and reasonably priced. Along with the travel agencies listed earlier, **GIT travel agency** (☎ /fax 271 967; gi-trade@ri.t-com.hr; Maršala Tita 65) has rooms running from €22 to €45, depending on the amenities.

The hotel scene is competitive and offers good value for money, especially outside of July and August. Most hotels are handled by **Liburnia Hotels** (☎ 710 300; www.liburnia.hr).

Hotel Kvarner (☎ 271 233; www.liburnia.hr; P Tomašića 1-4; s/d from €75/120; P ☒) This genteel 19th-century establishment has indoor and outdoor swimming pools as well as easy access to the sea. The charming hotel oozes old-world elegance. More expensive rooms have a sea view and a balcony and there are cheaper rooms in the annexe, Vila Amalia.

Hotel Millennium (☎ 202 000; www.ugohoteli.hr; Maršala Tita 9; s/d €89/132; P ☒ ☒) This five-star wonder has plush air-con rooms with minibars, and all sorts of luxuries in its glistening bathrooms.

Hotel Residenz (☎ 271 399; www.liburnia.hr; Maršala Tita 133; s/d from €55/80KN) This place has stodgy but decent rooms in a classic building. You can use the swimming pool at the neighbouring Hotel Kristol and the Residenz is right on the sea. More expensive rooms with a balcony are available.

Camping Opatija (☎ 704 387; fax 704 112; Liburnjska 46, Ičići; per person/camp site €4.20/6.80; ⊙ May-Sep) Right on the sea and only 5km south of town.

Maršala Tita is lined with a number of decent restaurants offering pizza, grilled meat and fish.

Bevanda (☎ 712 769; Zert 8; meals from 90KN) For a special meal, the best choice is this place, located on the port, which has the freshest fish and a good wine list.

Entertainment

Open air-cinema (Park Angiolina) Screens films and presents occasional concerts nightly at 9.30pm from May to September.

There's a bar scene centred around the harbour, where you'll find the ever-popular Caffé Harbour or Hemingways, two of Opatija's liveliest cafe-bars.

Getting There & Away

Bus 32 stops in front of the train station in Rijeka (11KN, 30 minutes) and runs right along the Opatija Riviera, west of Rijeka, every 20 minutes until late in the evening. If you're looking for accommodation, it's easiest to get off at the first stop and walk downhill, passing hotels and other agencies on the way to the bus station.

KRK ISLAND

☎ 051 / pop 18,000

The comparatively barren and rocky Krk (Veglia in Italian) is Croatia's largest island, connected to the mainland in 1980 by the enormous Krk Bridge. The northern part of the island is the site of Rijeka airport, which was a boon to the island economy at the cost of rapid overdevelopment. Real estate was quickly snapped up leaving few areas untouched. Still, the main town (also called Krk) is rather picturesque, and the popular resort of Baška at the island's southern end has a 2km-long pebbly beach set below a high ridge.

GETTING THERE & AWAY

About 14 buses a day travel between Rijeka and Krk town (41KN, 1½ hours), of which six continue on to Baška (12KN, up to one hour). One of the Rijeka buses is to/from Zagreb (144KN, four hours). To go from Krk to Zadar, take one of the many buses to Kraljevica and then change to a southbound bus.

Krk Town

Tiny Krk town has a compact medieval centre on a scenic spot. From the 12th to 15th centuries, Krk town and the surrounding region remained semi-independent under the Frankopan Dukes of Krk, an indigenous Croatian dynasty, at a time when much of the Adriatic was controlled by Venice. This history explains the various medieval sights in Krk town, the ducal seat.

The bus from Baška and Rijeka stops by the harbour, a few minutes' walk from the Old Town of Krk. There's no left-luggage facility at Krk bus station. The **Turistička Zajednica** (☎ /fax 221 414; www.tz-krk.hr in Croatian; Velika Placa 1; ⊙ 8am-3pm Mon-Fri) is in the city wall's Guard Tower. You can change money at any travel agency and there's an ATM in the shopping centre near the bus station.

The **hospital** (☎ 221 224) is at Vinogradska bb (emergency services are available 24 hours).

The lovely 14th-century **Frankopan Castle** and 12th-century Romanesque **cathedral** are in the lower town near the harbour. In the upper part of Krk town are three old **monastic churches**. The narrow streets of Krk are worth exploring.

SLEEPING

There is a range of accommodation in and around Krk, but many places only open during summertime. Private rooms can be organised through **Autotrans** (☎ 222 661; www.autotrans.hr) at the bus station. You can expect to pay about €22 to €45 for a double room.

Hotel Marina (☎ 221 128; www.hotelikrk.hr; Obala Hrvatske Mornarice 6; s/d €36/72) It's really nothing special, but this is the only hotel right in the town centre.

Autocamp Ježevac (☎ 221 081; jezevac@zlatni-otok.hr; per person/camp site €4.80/6KN; ☼ mid-Mar–Oct) On the coast, a 10-minute walk southwest of Krk town, is this camping ground with easy sea access and merciful shade.

Veli Jože (☎ /fax 220 212; www.hostel-krk.hr; Vitezića 32; dm €17.50) This hostel is located in a spruced-up older building and is open year-round. Rooms have three, four or six beds, and rates include breakfast.

EATING & DRINKING

There are a number of restaurants around the harbour.

Konobo Nono (Krčkih iseljenika 8; meals from 90KN) For something different, try this place, which offers *šurlice* (homemade noodles topped with goulash), as well as grilled fish and meat dishes.

Jungle (☎ 221 503) To relax over cocktails, the best local hang-out is this place, right in the centre of town.

Baška

At the southern end of Krk Island, Baška is popular for its 2km-long pebbly beach set below a dramatic, barren range of mountains. Although crowded in summer, the Old Town and harbour make a pleasant stroll and there's always that splendid beach. The bus from Krk stops at the top of a hill on the edge of the Old Town, between the beach and the harbour.

The main street of Baška is Zvonimirova, which overlooks the harbour, while the beach begins at the western end of the harbour, continuing southwards past a big sprawling hotel complex. The town's **tourist office** (☎ 856 544; www.tz-baska.hr; Zvonimirova 114; ☼ 8am-8pm daily mid-Jun–Sep, 8am-3pm Mon-Fri Oct–mid-Jun) is just down the street from the bus stop. To arrange hotels or camping, contact **Hoteli Baška** (☎ 656 801; www.hotelibaska.hr). For private accommodation, there's **Guliver** (☎ 856 004; www.pdm-guliver.hr; Zvonimirova 98).

RAB ISLAND

Rab (Arbe in Italian), near the centre of the Kvarner island group, is the most enticing island in the northern Adriatic. The more densely populated southwest is green with pine forests and dotted with sandy beaches and coves. High mountains protect Rab's interior from cold northeasterly winds, allowing olives, grapes and vegetables to be cultivated. The Lopar Peninsula in the northeastern corner is a fertile oasis offering the island's best beaches along its two wide bays. The northwestern peninsula, which emerges from Supetarska Draga, is fringed with coves and lagoons that continue on to the Kalifront Peninsula and the Suha Punta resort.

The cultural and historical centre of the island is Rab town, characterised by four elegant bell towers rising from the ancient stone streets. The island has a strong tourist business, but outside of July and August you'll find it lively without being overrun.

Rab Town

☎ 051 / pop 592

Medieval Rab town has a unique and instantly recognisable look. Crowded onto a narrow peninsula, four bell towers rise like exclamation points over the red-roofed stone buildings. The steep streets that climb up from the harbour cross a series of richly endowed churches to reach lovely lookout points. Wandering the narrow old roads interspersed with shady parks is a pure joy and the churches often host concerts and art exhibitions. When you get 'churched out', there are excursion boats to whisk you off to beaches and coves around the island.

ORIENTATION

The Old Town lies directly across the bay from the marina. Narrow side streets climb up from the main north-south streets: Donja, Srednja and Gornja ul, literally, lower, middle and upper roads.

A five-minute walk north of the Old Town is the new commercial centre. Despite a sign at the bus station advertising a left-luggage office, it's not operational because the station is only open limited hours. The northwestern portion of the peninsula is given over to the 100-year-old Komrčar Park, bordered by the town's beaches. There are also beaches around the Hotel and Autocamp Padova, but you'll find better swimming further from town.

INFORMATION
Internet Access
Digital X (☎ 777 010; Donja ul bb; per hr 20KN; ☺ 10am-2pm & 6pm-1am Mon-Fri, 6pm-1am Sat)

Medical Services
Hospital (☎ 724 109; Banjol 20) Emergency services are available 24 hours.

Money
Riječka Banka (Commercial Centre) Changes money and has an ATM.

Post
You can get cash advances on your Master-Card or Diners Club card at the Commercial Centre and Trg Municipium Arba branches of the post office.

Tourist Information
Turistička Zajednica (☎ 771 111; www.tzg-rab.hr; Palit bb; ☺ 8am-noon & 7-9pm Oct-May, 8am-10pm Jun-Sep) It's the head office of the tourist association and there's an annexe around the corner from the bus station, opposite Merkur department store.

Travel Agencies
Atlas travel agency (☎ 724 585; www.atlas-rab.com; Biskupa Draga 2; ☺ 8am-1pm Mon-Sat Oct-Apr, to 10pm Jun-Sep)

Kristofor (☎ 725 543; www.kristofor.hr; Palit bb) Next to the bus station, this friendly and efficient agency finds private accommodation, changes money, hires boats and scooters and is a good source of information.

Turist Biro Mila (☎ 725 499; www.mila.hr; Palit 68) At the southeastern corner of the bus station, this is a helpful agency.

SIGHTS
Most of Rab's famous churches and towers are along Gornja ul, the upper road that continues on as Ivana Rablianina in the Kaldanac section. Unless otherwise indicated the churches are open only for Mass but, even when churches are closed, most have metal grates over the front door, through which you can glimpse the interior.

Start your walk from Trg Svetog Kristofora near the harbour. In the centre of the square is a **fountain** with sculptures of the two legendary figures Kalifront and Draga. According to the story, the passionate Kalifront attempted to seduce the shepherdess Draga, who had taken a vow of chastity. The goddess to whom Draga had pledged chastity turned her into stone to save her from the seducer.

Go up Bobotine and pause at the corner of Srednja ul to admire the **Dominis Palace** on the left. Built at the end of the 15th century for a prominent patrician family, the building's façade has decorated Renaissance windows and a striking portal decorated with the family coat of arms. Continue to the top and the **St Christopher Church** (Crkva Sveti Kristofor; ☺ 7.30-9pm Jun & Sep, 9am-noon & 7.30-10pm Jul & Aug) was part of the highest tower of the ramparts. Next to it is a **lapidarium** (admission 5KN; ☺ 9am-1pm & 6-8pm). From the tower a passage leads to Komrčar Park.

Continuing south along Gornja ul, you'll come to the ruins of the **Church of St John** (Sveti Ivan), which probably dates to the beginning of the 7th century. Little survives but the 13th-century bell tower next to it, which can be climbed. The church was part of a monastery that was occupied by Benedictine nuns in the 11th century, Franciscans from 1298 to 1783, and was later converted into a bishop's residence. Next to the bell tower is the 16th-century **Holy Cross Church** (Sveti Kriša; ☺ 7.30-9pm Jun & Sep, 9am-noon & 7.30-10pm Jul & Aug), which was briefly called the Church of the Weeping Cross after a legend circulated that Christ wept on the church's cross because of the immorality of the town's residents.

Further along Gornja ul is **St Justine Church** (Sveti Justina; ☺ 7.30-9pm Jun & Sep, 9am-noon & 7.30-10pm Jul & Aug) with a bell tower dating from 1572. Today the church hosts a collection of religious artefacts, including a portable altar donated to the town by King Koloman, fragments of the evangelistary-passages from the Gospel from the 11th century and the silver-plated reliquary for the head of St Christopher. There's also a polyptych by Paolo Veneziano and a Renaissance terracotta of the Madonna from the 15th century.

Pass Trg Slobode bearing right and on your right you'll see the Romanesque **bell tower** of the **Church of St Andrew** (Sveti Andrije), which dates from 1181. The biggest tower is coming up on the right. The **Cathedral of St Mary the Great** (Sveta Marija Velika; ☎ 724 195; ⌚ 10am-1pm & 7.30-10pm) and its bell tower were built in the 12th century. The 25m-tall tower stands on the remains of Roman buildings and is divided into four floors, terminating in an octagonal pyramid surrounded by a Romanesque balustrade. The pyramid is topped by a cross with five small globes, and reliquaries of several saints were placed in the highest globe. The symmetrical arrangement of windows and arches creates a wonderful sense of lightness and harmony that makes the tower one of the most beautiful on the Croatian coast. You can climb it for a small fee.

The extreme end of the cape accommodates a monastery of Franciscan nuns and the baroque **Church of St Anthony** (Sveti Antun; Gornja ul), built in 1675. The altar is decorated with 17th-century inlaid marble and a painting of St Anthony.

ACTIVITIES

From behind the Hotel Istra (the most visible landmark along the port), there's a marked hiking trail that leads northeast to the top of Sveti Ilija (100m). It only takes about 30 minutes and the view is great.

Kristofor travel agency hires motorboats, starting at about €51 a day depending on size. You can hire bicycles at the Hotel and Autocamp Padova or arrange to scuba dive for about €36 per dive from the **Mirko Diving information office** (☎ 721 154; www.mirkodiving center.com; Šetalište Markatuma). There's an office in town but the company's boats leave from its **main office** (☎ /fax 721 154; Barbat).

TOURS

Atlas and other travel agencies offer day tours of the island by boat, which include plenty of swim stops around the island and at nearby Sveti Grgur Island. In summer, tourist agencies offer day excursions to Lošinj or Pag Island once or twice a week.

SLEEPING

Everything from camping to expensive hotels can be found in and around Rab town. Many of the older hotels and all camping grounds are managed by **Imperial** (www.impe rial.hr). Travel agencies find private accommodation at prices that range from €9 to €12 per person in a double room with a €5 single supplement.

Hotel Ros Maris (☎ 778 896; www.rosmaris.com; Obala Krešimira IV; d €214; P ⊠ ♋ ☐) This brand-new address offers a spa, swimming pool, Internet access and fresh, bright rooms, some of which overlook the sea.

Hotel Imperial (☎ 724 522; imperial@imperial.hr; Palit bb; s/d €43/75; P) Set back from the town in a wooded park, the lush green surroundings do a lot to mitigate the white, charmless exterior.

Hotel & Autocamp Pavoda (☎ 724 355; Banjol; per person/camp site €4.80/5.60; ⌚ Apr-Oct) To sleep cheap, carry your tent around the bay and walk south along the waterfront for about 25 minutes (about 2km) to this camping ground.

EATING

Pizzeria Mare (☎ 771 315; Srednja Ul 8; meals from 33KN) It's reputed to be the best pizza place in town, which would explain why it's often crowded.

Restoran Rio (☎ 725 645; Palit 57; meals from 65KN) There is a fish theme in the décor and the menu, but the meat is good and there's a pleasant terrace.

Santa Maria (☎ 724 196; Dinka Dakulo 6; meals from 70KN) The unusual interior of Santa Maria is decked out with wooden tables and benches and there's an upstairs terrace with a sea view. The speciality here is meat although there are also some fish dishes.

There's a good supermarket for picnic supplies in the basement of the Merkur department store, and a fruit and vegetable market in the Commercial Centre on Trg Municipium Arba.

ENTERTAINMENT

Disco San Antonio (☎ 724 145; Trg Municipium Arba) Situated behind Trg Municipium Arba, this is the most popular disco in town.

AROUND RAB TOWN

The **Franciscan Monastery of St Euphemia** (Sa-mostan svete Fumije; ☎ 724 951; Kampor; admission 5KN;

(⊗ 9am-noon & 3-5pm Jun & Sep, 10am-noon & 4-6pm Jul & Aug) is about 3km southwest of town in Kampor. It's a peaceful spot, usually deserted, but worth the walk for the Gothic church of St Bernardin. The painted ceiling is ethereal, a stark contrast to the agony depicted on the late-Gothic wooden crucifix. Note also the 15th-century polyptych by the Vivarini brothers.

Lopar

The ferry from Baška lands at Lopar, but the ferry stop is the least attractive part of the peninsula, which is marked by beautiful coves, bays and hamlets. There are 22 sandy beaches bordered by pine groves around Lopar, and the shallow sea makes them perfect for small children. Lopar Bay is on one side of the peninsula and Crnika Bay is on the other. The northeastern part of the peninsula is steep and barren, with many naturist beaches.

ORIENTATION & INFORMATION

The 1500m-long **Paradise Beach** (Rajska Plaša) lies 3km south of the ferry landing on Crnika Bay. The road between the ferry landing and the San Marino Hotel and autocamp on Crnika Bay passes a small commercial centre and several restaurants.

In the commercial centre there is a **tourist office** (Turistička Zajednica; ☎ 775 508; www.lopar.com; Commercial Centre; ⊗ 8am-8pm Mon-Sat, to 1pm Sun Jul & Aug, 8am-5pm Mon-Fri Sep-Jun).

GETTING THERE & AWAY

The ferry between Baška on Krk Island and Lopar (31KN, one hour) operates between June and September from two to five times daily, but between October and May there's no service. Novalja on Pag Island, and a daily car ferry from Jablanac on the coast to Mišnjak on Rab (10KN, 20 minutes).

The most reliable way to come and go is on one of the two daily buses between Rab and Rijeka (99KN, three hours). In the high season there are two direct buses from Zagreb to Rab (154KN, five hours). These services can fill up, so book ahead if possible. There's no direct bus from Rab to Zadar, but there are two daily buses that connect at Senj with Rijeka buses travelling to Zadar (114KN, five hours). In order to avoid backtracking from Senj to Jablanac, and also to save some kuna, you can take the bus to the highway at Jablanac, wait for about 1½ hours and catch the Rijeka bus as it heads to Zadar (89KN, one hour). Another possibility is to take the daily catamaran to Novalja on Pag Island and then catch a bus to Zadar.

GETTING AROUND

From Lopar to Rab town (12km) there are nine buses daily in either direction (15KN, 20 minutes); some are timed to meet the Baška–Lopar ferry. There are eight daily buses from Rab town to Kampor (11KN, 15 minutes), eight to Barbat (11KN, 20 minutes) and five to Suha Punta (11KN, 25 minutes).

DALMATIA

Roman ruins, spectacular beaches, old fishing ports, medieval architecture and unspoilt offshore islands make a trip to Dalmatia (Dalmacija) unforgettable. Occupying the central 375km of Croatia's Adriatic coast, Dalmatia offers a matchless combination of hedonism and historical discovery. The jagged coast is speckled with lush offshore islands and dotted with historic cities.

Split is the largest city in the region and a hub for bus and boat connections along the Adriatic, as well as home to the late-Roman Diocletian's Palace. Nearby are the early Roman ruins in Solin. Zadar has yet more Roman ruins and a wealth of churches. The architecture of Hvar and Korčula recalls the days when these places were outposts of the Venetian empire. None can rival majestic Dubrovnik, a cultural and aesthetic jewel.

The dramatic coastal scenery is due to the rugged Dinaric Alps, which form a 1500m-long barrier that separates Dalmatia from Bosnia and Hercegovina. After the last ice age, part of the coastal mountains was flooded, creating the sort of long, high islands seen in the Gulf of Kvarner. The deep, protected passages between these islands are a paradise for sailors and cruisers.

ZADAR

☎ 023 / pop 72,700

The main city of northern Dalmatia, Zadar (ancient Zara) is one of Croatia's more underrated destinations. The marble, traffic-free streets of the Old Town are replete with Roman ruins, medieval churches and

CROATIA

several fascinating museums. Massive 16th-century fortifications still shield the city on the landward side, with high walls running along the harbour. The tree-lined promenade along Obala kralja Petra Krešimira IV is perfect for a lazy stroll or a picnic, and there are several small beaches east of the Old Town. More beaches lie to the northwest at Borik as well as on the islands of Ugljan and Dugi Otok, both within easy reach of the town.

History

In the past 2000 years Zadar has escaped few wars. Its strategic position on the Adriatic coast made it a target for the Romans, the Byzantine, Venetian and Austro-Hungarian empires and Italy. Although it was damaged by Allied bombing raids in 1943–44 and Yugoslav rockets in 1991, this resilient city has been rebuilt and restored, retaining much of its old flavour. Don't forget to sample Zadar's famous maraschino cherry liqueur.

Orientation

The train station and the **bus station** (☎ 211 035) are adjacent and are 1km southeast of the harbour and Old Town. From the stations, Zrinsko-Frankopanska ul leads northwest to the town and harbour. Buses marked 'Poluotok' run from the bus station to the harbour. Narodni trg is the heart of Zadar.

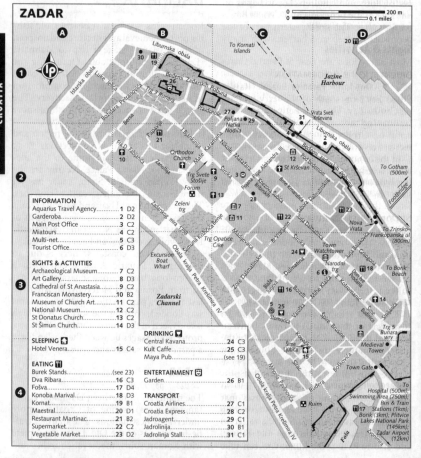

ZADAR

0 ——————— 200 m
0 ——————— 0.1 miles

To Kornati Islands

Jazine Harbour

Liburnska obala

To Gotham (500m)

To Zrinsko-Frankopanska ul (800m)

To Borik Beach

Zadarski Channel

Footbridge

To Hospital (500m); Swimming Area (750m); Bus & Train Stations (1km); Borik (3km); Plitvice Lakes National Park (145km); Zadar Airport (12km)

INFORMATION
Aquarius Travel Agency............1 D2
Garderoba............................2 D2
Main Post Office....................3 C2
Miatours.............................4 C2
Multi-net............................5 C3
Tourist Office.......................6 D3

SIGHTS & ACTIVITIES
Archaeological Museum............7 C2
Art Gallery..........................8 D3
Cathedral of St Anastasia..........9 C2
Franciscan Monastery...............10 B2
Museum of Church Art.............11 C2
National Museum.....................12 C2
St Donatus Church..................13 C2
St Šimun Church....................14 D3

SLEEPING
Hotel Venera........................15 C4

EATING
Burek Stands.....................(see 23)
Dva Ribara..........................16 C3
Fošva...............................17 D4
Konoba Marival.....................18 D3
Kornat..............................19 B1
Maestral............................20 D1
Restaurant Martinac................21 B2
Supermarket.........................22 C2
Vegetable Market...................23 D2

DRINKING
Central Kavana.....................24 C3
Kult Caffe..........................25 C3
Maya Pub........................(see 19)

ENTERTAINMENT
Garden..............................26 B1

TRANSPORT
Croatia Airlines....................27 C1
Croatia Express.....................28 C2
Jadroagent.........................29 C1
Jadrolinija.........................30 B1
Jadrolinija Stall....................31 C1

Information

Aquarius Travel Agency (☎ /fax 212 919; www.jur
eskoaquarius.hr; Nova Vrata bb) Books accommodation
and excursions.

Garderoba (per day 15KN) bus station (⊙ 7am-9pm
Mon-Fri); Jadrolinija dock (⊙ 7am-8pm Mon-Fri, to 3pm
Sat); train station (⊙ 24hr)

Hospital (☎ 315 677; Bože Peričića 5) Emergency
services are available 24 hours.

Main post office (Poljana Pape Aleksandra III) You can
make phone calls here.

Miatours (☎ /fax 212 788; www.miatours.hr; Vrata
Sveti Krševana) Books accommodation and excursions.
Vrata Sveti Krševana is an extremely tiny passage through
the walls that contains little more than the travel agency.

Multi-net (☎ 302 207; Stomorica 8; per hr 30KN)
Internet.

Tourist office (☎ 316 166; tzg-zadar@zd.t-com.hr;
Mihe Klaića 5; ⊙ 8am-8pm Mon-Sat, to 1pm Sun Jun-
Sep, 8am-6pm Mon-Sat Oct-May)

Sights & Activities

Most attractions are near **St Donatus Church**
(Sveti Donat; ☎ 250 516; Šimuna Kožičića Benje; admission
6KN; ⊙ 9.30am-1pm & 4-6pm Mar-Oct), a circular
9th-century Byzantine structure built over
the Roman forum. Slabs for the ancient
forum are visible in the church and there is
a pillar from the Roman era on the northwestern side. In summer ask about the musical evenings here (featuring Renaissance
and early baroque music). The outstand-
ing **Museum of Church Art** (Trg Opatice Čike bb; adult/
student 20/10KN; ⊙ 10am-12.30pm daily, 6-8pm Mon-
Sat), in the Benedictine monastery opposite
St Donatus, offers three floors of elaborate
gold and silver reliquaries, religious paintings, icons and local lacework.

The 13th-century Romanesque **Cathedral
of St Anastasia** (Katedrala Svete Stošije; Trg Svete Stošije;
⊙ Mass only) has some fine Venetian carvings
in the 15th-century choir stalls. The **Franciscan Monastery** (Samostan Svetog Frane; Zadarscog mira
1358; admission free; ⊙ 7.30am-noon & 4.30-6pm) is
the oldest Gothic church in Dalmatia (consecrated in 1280), with lovely interior Renaissance features and a large Romanesque
cross in the treasury, behind the sacristy.

The most interesting museum is the
Archaeological Museum (Arheološki Muzej; Trg Opatice
Čike 1; adult/student 10/5KN; ⊙ 9am-1pm & 6-9pm Mon-
Fri, 9am-1pm Sat), across from St Donatus, with
an extensive collection of artefacts, from
the Neolithic period through the Roman
occupation to the development of Croatian

culture under the Byzantines. Some captions
are in English and you are handed a leaflet in
English when you buy your ticket.

Less interesting is the **National Museum**
(Narodni Muzej; Poljana Pape Aleksandra III; admission
5KN; ⊙ 9am-1pm & 5-7pm Mon-Fri), just inside the
sea gate, featuring photos of Zadar from
different periods, and old paintings and
engravings of many coastal cities. The same
admission ticket will get you into the **Art Gallery** (Galerija; Smiljanića; ⊙ 9am-noon & 5-8pm Mon-Fri,
9am-1pm Sat). One church worth a visit is **St
Šimun Church** (Crkva Sveti Šime; Šime Budinica; ⊙ 8am-
1pm & 6-8pm Jun-Sep), which has a 14th-century
gold chest.

There's a swimming area with diving
boards, a small park and a café on the coastal
promenade off Zvonimira. Bordered by pine
trees and parks, the promenade takes you
to a beach in front of Hotel Kolovare and
then winds on for about a kilometre up the
coast.

Tours

Any of the many travel agencies around
town can supply information on tourist
cruises to the beautiful **Kornati Islands** (Kornati Islands National Park is an archipelago
of 147 mostly uninhabited islands), river-
rafting and half-day excursions to the Krka
waterfalls.

Festivals & Events

Major annual events include:

Town fair July and August.

Dalmatian Song Festival July and August.

Musical evenings In St Donatus Church in August.

Choral Festival October.

Sleeping

Most visitors head out to the 'tourist settlement' at Borik, 3km northwest of Zadar, on
the Puntamika bus (6KN, every 20 minutes
from the bus station). Here there are hotels,
a hostel, a camping ground, big swimming
pools, sporting opportunities and numerous *sobe* (rooms) signs; you can arrange
a private room through a travel agency in
town. Expect to pay from €22 to €50 for a
room, depending on the facilities.

Hotel Venera (☎ 214 098, 098 330 958; Šime
Ljubića 4a; d 300KN) If you want to stay in town,
the only choice is this 12-room guesthouse in the heart of town, with small but
adequate rooms with bathroom. The price

does not include breakfast but there are plenty of cafés around where you can have your morning meal. If you can't reach the owner, the rooms can be reserved through Aquarius travel agency.

Hotel President (☎ 333 464; www.hotel-president .hr; Vladana Desnice 16; s/d €105/160; P ✖ ▣) Near the beach at Borik, this place will give you the full first-class treatment.

Borik Youth Hostel (☎ 331 145; zadar@hfhs.hr; Obala Kneza Trpimira 76; B&B/half board €12.60/16.65) Friendly and well-kept, this hostel is also near the beach at Borik.

Autocamp Borik (☎ 332 074; per person/camp site €4.20/5.60) This large camping ground is just steps away from Borik beach.

Eating

Dva Ribara (Blaža Jurjeva 1; meals from 40KN) With a wide range of food and an outdoor terrace, Dva Ribara is justifiably popular with the local crowd.

Konoba Marival (☎ 213 239; Don Ive Prodana 3; meals from 65KN) If your mama married a fisherman, she'd probably dream up the kinds of dishes that are served here. The ambience is also homy and intimate.

Restaurant Martinac (Papavije 7; meals from 75KN) The secluded backyard terrace behind this restaurant provides a relaxed atmosphere in which to sample delicious risotto and fish.

Foša (☎ 314 421; Kralja Dmitra Zvonimira 2; meals from 60KN) If the funky '70s décor gets to you, concentrate on the view over the marina. An oldish crowd of regulars keeps coming back for the attentively prepared fish.

Maestral (☎ 430 455; Ivana Mažuranića 2; meals from 70KN) On the 1st floor of a waterfront building, Maestral's meat is tender, its variety of fish excellent and its panoramic view of the harbour most relaxing. There's no better place to view the sunset while you dine.

Kornat (☎ 254 501; Liburnska Obala 6; meals from 75KN) This place has an imaginative chef who's bringing a whiff of exoticism to traditional Croatian staples.

Local people usually head out to Borik to find something to eat. **Restaurant Albin** (☎ 331 137; meals 40-100KN), on the road to Borik, is one of the most popular establishments because its fish is extremely well prepared and it has a spacious outdoor terrace.

There's a **supermarket** (cnr Široka & Sabora) that is open longer than usual hours, and you'll also find a number of *burek* stands around the vegetable market, on the landward side of town.

Drinking

In summer the many cafés along Varoška and Klaića place their tables on the street; it's great for people-watching.

Central Kavana (Široka) A spacious café and hang-out that often has live music at the weekend.

Kult Caffe (Stomorica) Draws a young crowd who listens to rap music indoors or relax on the large shady terrace outside.

Maya Pub (☎ 251 716; Liburnska Obala 6) The Buddha Bar becomes the Shiva Bar in Zadar. The smooth electro sounds swirl around an imposing sculpture of Shiva and there are occasional live concerts. It's the latest place to go.

Bounty (Mate Gupca 2, Borik; ✖ closed Sun & Mon) Staying in Borik doesn't mean being out of the action. This new spot with a pirate theme is where Borikians hang out.

Entertainment

Garden (☎ 450 907; Bedemi Zadarskih Pobuna) The newest and hottest nightlife in Zadar enlivens this traditional walled garden. A top-of-the-line sound system and celebrated DJs have made this the primary spot to see and be seen.

Gotham (☎ 200 289; Marka Oreškovića 1; ✖ closed Mon) Go-go dancers, tropical fantasy nights and '70s nights liven up this club north of the Old Town.

Getting There & Away

AIR

Zadar's airport, 12km east of the city, receives charter flights and **Croatia Airlines** (☎ 250 101; Poljana Natka Nodila 7) flights from Zagreb daily (170KN to 350KIN, 40 minutes). A Croatia Airlines bus meets all flights and costs 15KN; a taxi into town costs around 175KN.

BOAT

The Jadrolinija coastal ferry from Rijeka to Dubrovnik calls at Zadar twice weekly (126/151KN low/high season, six hours). It arrives around midnight. The **Jadrolinija** (☎ 254 800; Liburnska obala 7) office is on the harbour and has tickets for all local ferries, or you can buy ferry tickets from the Jadrolinija stall on Liburnska obala.

Jadroagent (☎ 251 052; jadroagent-zadar@zd.t-com.hr; Poljana Natka Nodila 4) is just inside the city walls and has tickets and information for all boats.

For information on boat connections to Italy see p403.

BUS & TRAIN

Zadar is on the coastal route that goes from Rijeka down to Split and Dubrovnik. See the Getting There & Away sections of those towns for further details. There are four daily trains to Zagreb (134KN, 6½ hours) that change at Knin, but the bus to Zagreb is quicker and stops at the Plitvice Lakes National Park (32KN, three hours).

Croatia Express (☎ 211 660; croatiae@zd.t-com.hr; Široka) sells bus tickets to many German cities. See Land p402 for more information about bus connections to Germany.

Around Zadar

PLITVICE LAKES NATIONAL PARK

☎ 053

Plitvice Lakes National Park (admission Oct-May/Jun-Sep 75/95KN, students 45/55KN) lies midway between Zagreb and Zadar. The 19.5 hectares of wooded hills enclose 16 turquoise lakes, which are linked by a series of waterfalls and cascades. Wooden footbridges follow the lakes and streams over, under and across the rumbling water for an exhilaratingly damp 18km. In 1979 Unesco proclaimed the Plitvice Lakes a World Heritage site, and the lakes and forests are carefully regulated to ensure their continuing preservation.

The extraordinary natural beauty of the site merits at least a three-day visit but you can experience a lot simply on a day trip from Zadar or Zagreb. There's no bad time to visit: in the spring the falls are flush with water, in summer the surrounding hills are greener and in autumn there are fewer visitors and you'll be treated to the changing colours of leaves.

The lake system is divided into the upper and lower lakes. The upper lakes, lying in a dolomite valley, are the most impressive, surrounded by dense forests and interlinked by several gushing waterfalls. The lower lakes are smaller and shallower, surrounded only by sparse underbrush. Most of the water comes from the White and Black Rivers (Bijela and Crna Rijeka), which join south of Prošćansko Lake, but the lakes are also fed by underground springs. In turn, water disappears into the porous limestone at some points only to reemerge in other places. All the water empties into the Korana River near Sastavci.

The upper lakes are separated by dolomite barriers, which expand with the mosses and algae that absorb calcium carbonate as river water rushes through the karst. The encrusted plants grow on top of each other, forming travertine barriers and creating waterfalls. The lower lakes were formed by cavities created by the water of the upper lakes. They undergo a similar process, as travertine is constantly forming and reforming itself into new combinations so that the landscape is ever changing. This unique interaction of water, rock and plant life has continued more or less undisturbed since the last ice age.

The colours of the lakes also change constantly. From azure to bright green, deep blue or grey, the colours depend upon the quantity of minerals or organisms in the water, whether rain has deposited mud, and the angle of sunlight.

The luxuriant vegetation of the national park is another delight. The northeastern section of the park is covered with beech forests while the rest of it is covered with beech, fir spruce and white pine dotted with patches of whitebeam, hornbeam and flowering ash, which change colour in autumn.

Wildlife

Animal life flourishes in the unspoiled conditions. The stars of the park are bears and wolves but there are also deer, boar, rabbits, foxes and badgers. There are over 120 different species of bird such as hawks, owls, cuckoos, thrushes, starlings, kingfishers, wild ducks and herons. You might occasionally see black storks and ospreys, and flocks of butterflies flutter throughout the park.

Orientation & Information

At the main entrance to the park, the **tourist office** (☎ 751 015; www.np-plitvicka-jezera.hr; 🕐 7am-8pm) has its main entrance on Plitvička jezera and a secondary entrance at Velika Poljana, near the hotels. At the main entrance you can pick up brochures and a map to walk you around the lakes.

CROATIA

There are well-marked trails throughout the park and a system of wooden walkways that allow you to appreciate the beauty of the landscape without disturbing the environment. The admission ticket includes the boats and buses you need to see the lakes.

The post office is near the hotels and there's an ATM near the Hotel Bellevue. Luggage can be left at the tourist office or at one of the hotels.

Sights
The lower lakes string out from the main entrance and are rich in forests, grottoes and steep cliffs. **Novakovića Falls** is nearest the entrance and is followed by **Kaluđerovac Lake**, near two caves: the Blue Cave and Šupljara. Next is **Gavanovac Lake**, with towering waterfalls, and last is **Milanovac Lake**, notable for colours that are variously sky blue, azure or emerald green.

Kozjak is the largest lake and forms a boundary between the upper and lower lakes. Three kilometres long, the lake is surrounded by steep, forested slopes and contains a small oval island, composed of travertine. Past the hotels, you'll see **Gradinsko Lake**, bordered by reeds that often harbour nesting wild ducks. A series of cascades links Gradinsko to **Galovac Lake**, considered the most beautiful lake of all. An abundance of water has formed a series of ponds and falls. A set of concrete stairs over the falls, constructed long ago, have eventually been covered by travertine, forming even more falls in a spectacular panorama. Several smaller lakes are topped by the larger **Okrugljak Lake**, supplied by two powerful waterfalls. Continuing upward you'll come to **Ciginovac Lake** and finally **Prošćansko Lake**, surrounded by thick forests.

Sleeping
The Zagreb buses drop you off just outside the camping ground while the hotels are clustered on Velika Poljana overlooking Kozjak Lake. There are many *sobe* signs along the road from Korana village to the national park. The tourist office in the park or its branch in Zagreb (see p149) can refer you to rooms in the neighbouring villages, the closest of which is about 400m from the entrance. Expect to pay about 225KN for a double room. Hotels can be booked through the tourist office website.

Hotel Jezero (☎ 751 400; jezero@np-plitvicka-jezera .hr; Velika Poljana; s/d €81/114; (P) (🛋)) This is by far the most comfortable and best-appointed hotel in the park. There's even a sauna and swimming pool.

Hotel Plitvice (☎ 751 100; fax 751 165; Velika Poljana; s/d from €70/98KN; (P)) Completely renovated into a comfortable modern hotel, you'll find spacious, well-equipped rooms, each with TV, phone and minibar. There are more expensive rooms which are larger and have a view.

Korana (☎ 751 015; per person/camp site 35/50KN; (🌙) May-Oct) This is a large, well-equipped autocamp about 6km north of the main entrance on the main road to Zagreb.

Hotel Bellevue (☎ 751 700; Velika Poljana; s/d €52/72) It's the cheapest hotel around but the rooms and atmosphere are dreary.

Eating
There's an inexpensive self-service cafeteria next to the tourist office, at the second entrance, as well as a café, which sells sandwiches, pastries and roast chicken, and a minimarket for picnic supplies.

Lička Kuća (☎ 751 024; meals from 70KN) Just across from the main entrance, this sprawling place is usually crowded with tourists who come for the local sausages and roasted-meat dishes. Vegetarians will appreciate the *djuveč*, a stew of rice, carrots, tomatoes, peppers and onions, as well as the fine local cheese.

Getting There & Away
All the Zagreb–Zadar buses stop at Plitvice; it takes three hours from Zadar (75KN) and 2½ hours from Zagreb (62KN). It's possible to visit here for the day on the way to or from the coast, but be aware that bus drivers will not pick up passengers if their buses are full. On summer weekends you could spend a good part of the day stuck in traffic since the road to Plitvice is the main artery to the coast for holidaying city folk.

SPLIT
☎ 021 / pop 188,700
Split (Spalato in Italian), the largest Croatian city on the Adriatic coast, is a major industrial city ringed with apartment-block housing of stupefying ugliness, but the remarkable Diocletian's Palace (which

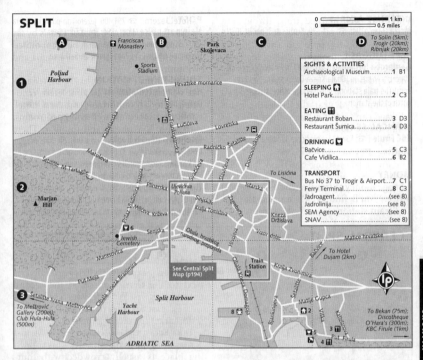

SPLIT

0	1 km
0	0.5 miles

To Solin (5km);
Trogir (20km);
Ribnjak (20km)

SIGHTS & ACTIVITIES
Archaeological Museum............1 B1

SLEEPING
Hotel Park.................................2 C3

EATING
Restaurant Boban....................3 D3
Restaurant Šumica...................4 D3

DRINKING
Bačvice....................................5 C3
Cafe Vidilica............................6 B2

TRANSPORT
Bus No 37 to Trogir & Airport....7 C1
Ferry Terminal.........................8 C3
Jadroagent...........................(see 8)
Jadrolinija............................(see 8)
SEM Agency..........................(see 8)
SNAV...................................(see 8)

CROATIA

is now a World Heritage site) makes a visit to the city worthwhile – and a visit is indispensable if you'll be visiting one of the many islands within reach of Split. In the centre of town, within the ancient walls of Diocletian's Palace, rises the majestic cathedral surrounded by a tangle of marble streets containing shops and businesses. The entire western end of town is a vast, wooded mountain park with beaches below and pathways above. A refurbished harbourside promenade lined with cafés makes for a pleasant stroll, and the high coastal mountains set against the blue Adriatic provide a striking frame, best appreciated as your ferry heads into or out of the port.

History

Split achieved fame when Roman emperor Diocletian (AD 245–313), who was noted for his persecution of the early Christians, had his retirement palace built here from 295 to 305. After his death the great stone palace continued to be used as a retreat by Roman rulers. When the neighbouring colony of Salona was abandoned in the 7th century, many of the Romanised inhabitants fled to Split and barricaded themselves behind the high palace walls, where their descendants continue to live to this day.

The town was hard-hit economically (although not militarily) when the former Yugoslavia split up, and is still struggling to regain its footing. It's clearly less prosperous than Zagreb or Dubrovnik, which helps explain why so many residents flock to the bus station and port to hawk their extra rooms to disembarking tourists.

Orientation

The bus, train and ferry terminals are adjacent on the eastern side of the harbour, a short walk from the Old Town. Obala hrvatskog narodnog preporoda, the waterfront promenade, is your best central reference point in Split.

Information
BOOKSHOPS

Algoritam (Map p194; Bajamontijeva 2) A good English-language bookshop.

INTERNET ACCESS

Mriža (Map p194; ☎ 321 320; Kružićeva 3; per hr 20KN)

LEFT LUGGAGE

Garderoba (per hr/day 2.20/20KN) bus station (🕒 6am-10pm); train station (Obala Kneza Domagoja 6; 🕒 7am-9pm) The train station's left-luggage office is about 50m north of the station.

MEDICAL SERVICES

KBC Firule (☎ 556 111; Spinčićeva 1) Split's hospital. Emergency services are available 24 hours.

MONEY

Change money at travel agencies or the post office. You'll find ATMs around the bus and train stations.

POST

Main post office (Map p194; Kralja Tomislava 9; 🕒 7.30am-7pm Mon-Fri, 8am-noon Sat) There's also a telephone centre (🕒 7am-9pm Mon-Sat) here.

TOURIST INFORMATION

Hostelling International (Map p194; ☎ 395 972; Domilijina 8) Sells HI cards and is a good source of information about Croatian hostels (however, there's no hostel in Split).

Internet Games & Books (Map p194; ☎ 338 548; Obala Kneza Domagoja 3) Luggage storage, information for backpackers, accommodation referrals, used books and an Internet connection for 30KN per hour.

Turist Biro (Map p194; ☎ /fax 342 142; turist-biro-split@st.t-com.hr; Obala hrvatskog narodnog preporoda 12) This office arranges private accommodation and sells

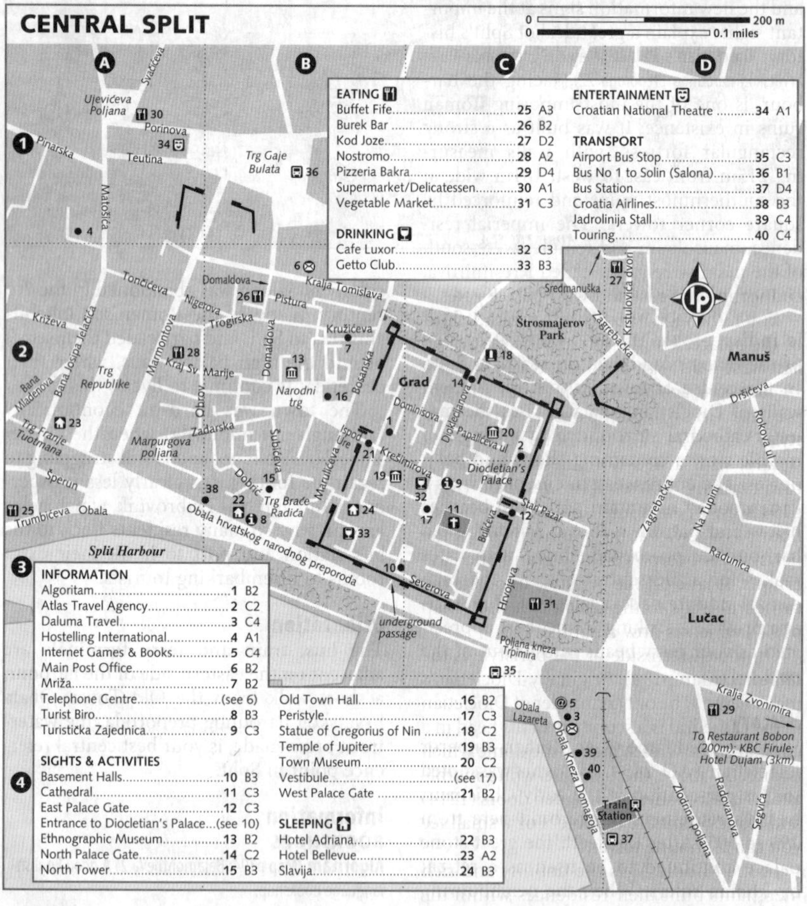
CENTRAL SPLIT
0 200 m
0 0.1 miles
EATING
Buffet Fife 25 A3
Burek Bar 26 B2
Kod Joze 27 D2
Nostromo 28 A2
Pizzeria Bakra 29 D4
Supermarket/Delicatessen 30 A1
Vegetable Market 31 C3
DRINKING
Cafe Luxor 32 C3
Getto Club 33 B3
ENTERTAINMENT
Croatian National Theatre 34 A1
TRANSPORT
Airport Bus Stop 35 C3
Bus No 1 to Solin (Salona) 36 B1
Bus Station 37 D4
Croatia Airlines 38 B3
Jadrolinija Stall 39 C4
Touring 40 C4
INFORMATION
Algoritam 1 B2
Atlas Travel Agency 2 C2
Daluma Travel 3 C4
Hostelling International 4 A1
Internet Games & Books 5 C4
Main Post Office 6 B2
Mriža 7 B2
Telephone Centre (see 6)
Turist Biro 8 B3
Turistička Zajednica 9 C3
SIGHTS & ACTIVITIES
Basement Halls 10 B3
Cathedral 11 C3
East Palace Gate 12 C3
Entrance to Diocletian's Palace (see 10)
Ethnographic Museum 13 B2
North Palace Gate 14 C2
North Tower 15 B3
Old Town Hall 16 B2
Peristyle 17 C3
Statue of Gregorius of Nin 18 C2
Temple of Jupiter 19 B3
Town Museum 20 C2
Vestibule (see 17)
West Palace Gate 21 B2
SLEEPING
Hotel Adriana 22 B3
Hotel Bellevue 23 A2
Slavija 24 B3
Split Harbour
Grad
Štrosmajerov Park
Diocletian's Palace
Manuš
Lučac
Trg Republike
Narodni trg
Trg Gaje Bulata
Marpurgova poljana
Trg Braće Radića
Trg Franje Tuđmana
Ujevićeva Poljana
Poljana kneza Trpimira
underground passage
Train Station
To Restaurant Bobon (200m); KBC Firule; Hotel Dujam (3km)
Kralja Tomislava
Obala hrvatskog narodnog preporoda
Obala Kneza Domagoja
Obala Lazareta
Kralja Zvonimira
Zagrebačka
Severova
Marulićeva
Bosanska
Dioklecijanova
Hrvojeva
Pinarska
Teutina
Porinova
Tončićeva
Križeva
Trumbićeva Obala
Šperun

guidebooks and the Split Card (€5, offers free and discounted admission to Split attractions).

Turistička Zajednica (Map p194; ☎ /fax 342 606; www.visitsplit.com; Peristyle; ☺ 9am-8.30pm Mon-Sat, 8am-1pm Sun) Has information on Split; sells the Split Card.

TRAVEL AGENCIES

Atlas travel agency (Map p194; ☎ 343 055; Nepotova 4) The town's Amex representative.

Daluma Travel (Map p194; ☎ /fax 338 484; www .daluma.hr; Obala Kneza Domagoja 1) Finds private accommodation and has information on boat schedules.

Sights

DIOCLETIAN'S PALACE

The Old Town is a vast open-air museum and the new information signs at the important sights explain a great deal of Split's history. **Diocletian's Palace** (Map p194; entrance: Obala hrvatskog narodnog preporoda 22), facing the harbour, is one of the most imposing Roman ruins in existence. It was built as a strong rectangular fortress, with walls measuring 215m from east to west, 181m wide at the southernmost point and reinforced by square corner towers. The imperial residence, mausoleum and temples were south of the main street, now called Krešimirova, connecting the east and west palace gates.

Enter through the central ground floor of the palace. On the left are the excavated **basement halls** (Map p194; adult/concession 6/3KN; ☺ 10am-6pm), which are empty but still impressive. Go through the passage to the **peristyle** (Map p194), a picturesque colonnaded square, with a neo-Romanesque cathedral tower rising above. The **vestibule** (Map p194), an open dome above the ground-floor passageway at the southern end of the peristyle, is overpoweringly grand and cavernous. A lane off the peristyle opposite the cathedral leads to the **Temple of Jupiter** (Map p194), which is now a baptistry.

On the eastern side of the peristyle is the **cathedral** (Map p194), originally Diocletian's mausoleum. The only reminder of Diocletian in the cathedral is a sculpture of his head in a circular stone wreath, below the dome which is directly above the baroque white-marble altar. The Romanesque wooden doors (1214) and stone pulpit are notable. For a small fee you can climb the tower.

In the Middle Ages the nobility and rich merchants built their residences within the old palace walls; the Papalic Palace is now the **town museum** (Gradski Muzej; Map p194; ☎ 341 240; Papalićeva ul 5; adult/concession 10/5KN; ☺ 9am-noon & 5-8pm Tue-Fri, 10am-noon Sat & Sun Jun-Sep, 10am-5pm Tue-Fri, 10am-noon Sat & Sun Oct-May). It has a tidy collection of artefacts, paintings, furniture and clothes from Split; captions are in Croatian.

OUTSIDE THE PALACE WALLS

The **east palace gate** (Map p194) leads to the market area. The **west palace gate** (Map p194) opens onto medieval Narodni trg, dominated by the 15th-century Venetian Gothic **old town hall** (Map p194). The **Ethnographic Museum** (Ethnografski Muzej; Map p194; ☎ 344 164; Narodni trg; adult/student 10/5KN; ☺ 10am-1pm Tue-Fri Jun-Sep, 10am-4pm Tue-Fri, 10am-1pm Sat & Sun Oct-May) has a mildly interesting collection of photos of old Split, traditional costumes and memorabilia of important citizens; captions are in Croatian.

Trg Braće Radića, between Narodni trg and the harbour, contains the surviving **north tower** (Map p194) of the 15th-century Venetian garrison castle, which once extended to the water's edge.

Go through the **north palace gate** (Map p194) to see Ivan Meštrović's powerful 1929 **statue of Gregorius of Nin** (Map p194), a 10th-century Slavic religious leader who fought for the right to perform Mass in Croatian. Notice that his big toe has been polished to a shine; it's said that touching it brings good luck.

OUTSIDE CENTRAL SPLIT

The **Archaeological Museum** (Arheološki Muzej; Map p193; ☎ 318 720; Zrinsko-Frankopanska 25; adult/student 10/5KN; ☺ 9am-2pm Tue-Fri, 9am-1pm Sat & Sun), north of town, is a fascinating supplement to your walk around Diocletian's Palace, and to the site of ancient Salona. The history of Split is traced from Illyrian times to the Middle Ages, in chronological order, with explanations in English.

The finest art museum in Split is **Meštrović Gallery** (Galerija Meštrović; ☎ 358 450; Šetalište Ivana Meštrovića 46; adult/student 15/10KN; ☺ 9am-9pm Tue-Sun Jun-Sep, 9am-4pm Tue-Sat, 10am-3pm Sun Oct-May). You'll see a comprehensive, well-arranged collection of works by Ivan Meštrović, Croatia's premier modern sculptor, who built the gallery as his home in 1931–39. Although Meštrović intended to retire here,

CROATIA

he emigrated to the USA soon after WWII. Bus 12 runs to the gallery from Trg Republike every 40 minutes.

From the Meštrović Gallery it's possible to hike straight up **Marjan Hill** (Map p193). Go up ul Tonća Petrasova Marovića on the western side of the gallery and continue straight up the stairway to Put Meja ul. Turn left and walk west to Put Meja 76. The trail begins on the western side of this building. Marjan Hill offers trails through the forest to lookouts and old chapels.

Tours

Atlas travel agency runs excursions to Krka waterfalls (€37) as well as other excursions.

Festivals & Events

February Carnival This traditional carnival is presented in the Old Town.
Feast of St Dujo 7 May.
Flower show May.
Festival of Popular Music End of June.
Split Summer Festival Mid-July to mid-August. Features open-air opera, ballet, drama and musical concerts.

Sleeping

Private accommodation is the best bet for budget travellers, as hotels in Split are geared towards business travellers with deep pockets. You will usually find packs of women at the bus, train and ferry terminals ready to propose rooms to travellers. Find out exactly where the room is and the exact price before heading out or you could get stuck. Prices rarely exceed 110KN for a room but you'll be sharing the bathroom with the proprietor. The travel agencies listed earlier are a surer bet for private rooms. Expect to pay 180/255KN for a single/double room with a shared bathroom and 200/295 with private facilities.

DIOCLETIAN'S PALACE

Slavija (Map p194; ☎ 323 840; www.hotelslavija.com; Buvinova 3; €70/90) Has a great location in the Old Town and freshly renovated but somewhat noisy rooms.

OUTSIDE THE PALACE WALLS

Hotel Adriana (Map p194; ☎ 340 000; www.hotel-adriana.com; Obala hrvatskog narodnog preporoda 9; s/d €77/105; ⊠) Rooms are beautifully decorated, soundproofed and graced with spacious bathrooms. They lie over the classiest café/

bar/restaurant on the waterfront. Prices stay the same all year.

Hotel Bellevue (Map p194; ☎ 345 644; www.hotel-bellevue-split.hr; bana Josipa Jelačića 2; s/d €69/96) The Bellevue is an old classic that has seen better days. Rooms on the street side can be noisy but the location is good and the rooms, though faded, are well tended. If you take a taxi from the port get ready for a long, meandering ride as the driver navigates the many one-way streets.

OUTSIDE CENTRAL SPLIT

Hotel Park (Map p193; ☎ 406 400; www.hotelpark-split.hr; Hatzeov perivoj 3; s/d €127/154; ⓟ ⊠ 🖳) Close to the centre, this hotel nonetheless provides a resort experience with a large shady terrace and an easy walk to the beach. Rooms are nicely decorated and comfortable, although not large.

Hotel Dujam (☎ 538 025; www.hoteldujam.com; Velebitska 27; s/d €55//74; dm €14) Although not particularly well-located, this combination hotel/hostel offers two floors of modern, fresh rooms. The hostel rooms are especially good value on the expensive Split accommodation scene. Rooms have two beds and the communal showers are well maintained. The hotel rooms are about the same except for they have an en-suite bathroom and satellite TV. To get here, take bus 9 from the port.

Eating

OUTSIDE THE PALACE WALLS

Kod Joze (Map p194; ☎ 347 397; Sredmanuška 4; meals from 60KN) A die-hard faction of locals keeps this informal *konoba* (a small family-owned bistro) alive and kicking. It's Dalmatian all the way – ham, cheese and green tagliatelle with seafood.

Nostromo (Map p194; ☎ 091 40 56 666; Kraj Sv Marije 10; meals from 75KN) Marine creatures of all persuasions form a delightful menu in this sweetly decorated spot next to the fish market.

Buffet Fife (Map p194; ☎ 345 223; Obala Ante Trumbića 11; meals from 45KN) Dragomir presides over a motley crew of sailors and misfits who drop in for the simple, savoury home cooking and his own brand of hospitality.

Pizzeria Bakra (Map p194; ☎ 488 488; Radovanova 2; pizzas from 35KN) Friendly and relaxed, this place offers the best pizza in town.

Burek Bar (Map p194; Domaldova 13) This spiffy place is near the main post office.

Supermarket/delicatessen (Map p194; Svačićeva 1) This vast place has a wide selection of meat and cheese for sandwiches.

The **vegetable market** (Map p194; ☽ 6am-2pm), outside the east palace gate, has a wide array of fresh local produce.

OUTSIDE CENTRAL SPLIT

Restaurant Šumica (Map p193; ☎ 389 897; Put Firula 6; meals from 65KN) For a splurge, you couldn't do better than this place. The pasta is home-made and is combined with salmon or other fish in imaginative sauces. The grilled scampi is perfection, but you pay a steep 340KN per kilogram. Before your meal you'll be served a dish of homemade fish pâté with bread to whet your appetite. Meals are served on an open-air terrace under pine trees with a view of the sea.

Restaurant Boban (Map p193; ☎ 543 300; Hektorovićeva 49; meals from 60KN) The décor may be sober and traditional but this family-owned restaurant devotes considerable effort to keeping its menu up to date. The risotto is perfection and the angler wrapped in bacon, mouth watering.

Bekan (☎ 389 400; Ivana Zajca 1; meals from 80KN) Bekan serves an array of fish prepared Dalmatian style. It's not cheap (unless you order the spaghetti with seafood for 55KN) but you can sample a savoury shrimp *buzara* (a sauce of tomatoes, white wine, onions and breadcrumbs) on an airy terrace overlooking the sea.

Drinking

Getto Club (Map p194; ☎ 346 879; Dosud) This serene and secluded café is tucked into a tranquil little courtyard inside Diocletian's Palace. Relax in an overstuffed chair amid flower beds and a trickling fountain, sampling various exotic coffees – or join the party indoors.

Cafe Vidilica (Map p193; ☎ 394 480; Nazorov prilaz 1) Any time of the day, you can come here to sip a coffee or cocktail and admire the view of Split from an outdoor terrace in front of the Jewish cemetery. There's no vehicle access but it's a nice walk.

Cafe Luxor (Map p194; Kralja Sv Ivana 11) In the heart of the peristyle, this is everyone's favourite café, maybe because of the Hollywood references and posters or perhaps it's the magic of the sphinx, casting her spell over the terrace.

Entertainment

In summer everyone starts the evening at one of the cafés along Obala hrvatskog narodnog preporoda and then heads towards the Bačvice (Map p193) complex on the beach. These former public baths offer restaurants, cafés, discos and venues for live rock and salsa.

Discotheque O'Hara's (☎ 519 492; Uvala Zenta 3; ☽ Jun-Sep) This open-air disco takes over summer nightlife and presents live concerts on Friday. If you're planning on staying late your best bet is to drive or walk as buses don't run after 11.30pm

Club Hula-Hula (☎ 398 589; Uvala Zvončać; ☽ Jun-Sep) There's a never-ending string of events here, including live music on weekends with local groups. Again, you're best to drive or walk.

Croatian National Theatre (Map p194; Trg Gaje Bulata; best seats about 60KN) During winter, opera and ballet are presented here. Tickets for the same night's performance are usually available. Erected in 1891, the theatre was fully restored in 1979 in its original style; it's worth attending a performance for the architecture alone.

Getting There & Away

AIR

The country's national air carrier, **Croatia Airlines** (Map p194; ☎ 062-777 777; Obala hrvatskog narodnog preporoda 8), operates flights between Zagreb and Split (170KN to 350KN, 45 minutes) up to four times every day. Rates are lower if you book in advance.

BOAT

You can buy tickets for passenger ferries at the **Jadrolinija stall** (Map p194; Obala Kneza Domagoja). There are also several agents in the large ferry terminal (Map p193) opposite the bus station that can assist with boat trips from Split: **Jadroagent** (Map p193; ☎ 338 335) represents Adriatica Navigazione for its connections between Split and Ancona; **Jadrolinija** (Map p193; ☎ 338 333) handles all car-ferry services that depart from the docks around the ferry terminal; **SEM agency** (Map p193; ☎ 060 325 523) handles tickets between Ancona, Split and Hvar. SEM also runs the daily fast boat from Split to Hvar (22KN, one to 1½ hours) and Korčula (55KN, one to 1½ hours). **SNAV** (Map p193; ☎ 322 252) has a four-hour connection to Ancona and Pescara.

CROATIA

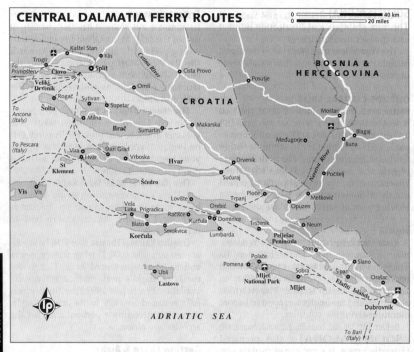

CENTRAL DALMATIA FERRY ROUTES

For more details on connections to/from Italy see p403.

BUS
Advance bus tickets with seat reservations are recommended. There are buses from the main **bus station** (Map p194; ☎ 060 327 327; www .ak-split.hr in Croatian) beside the harbour to:

Destination	Cost (KN)	Duration	Frequency
Dubrovnik	123	4½hr	12 daily
Međugorje, Bosnia & Hercegovina	64-98	3hr	4 daily
Mostar, Bosnia & Hercegovina	64-72	2-4hr	4 daily
Pula	300	10hr	2 daily
Rijeka	233	8hr	14 daily
Sarajevo, Bosnia & Hercegovina	93-128	7hr	11 daily
Zadar	66-89	3hr	26 daily
Zagreb	255	6-9hr	27 daily

Touring (Map p194; ☎ 338 503; Obala Kneza Domagojeva 10), near the bus station, represents Deutsche Touring and sells tickets to German cities.

Bus 37 to Solin, Split airport and Trogir leaves from a local bus station on Domovinskog, 1km northeast of the city centre (see Map p193).

TRAIN
From the train station there are three fast trains (138KN, six hours) and three overnight trains (138KN, 8½ hours) between Split and Zagreb. From Monday to Saturday there are six trains a day between Šibenik and Split (33KN, two hours) and four trains on Sunday.

Getting Around
There's an airport bus stop on Obala Lazareta 3 (see Map p194). The bus (30KN, 30 minutes) leaves about 90 minutes before flight times, or you can take bus 37 from the bus station on Domovinskog (11KN for a two-zone ticket).

Buses run about every 15 minutes from 5.30am to 11.30pm. A one-zone ticket costs 9KN for one trip in central Split. You can buy tickets on the bus and the driver can make change.

SOLIN (SALONA)

The ruins of the ancient city of Solin (known as Salona by the Romans), among the vineyards at the foot of mountains 5km northeast of Split, are the most interesting archaeological site in Croatia. Today surrounded by noisy highways and industry, Salona was the capital of the Roman province of Dalmatia from the time Julius Caesar elevated it to the status of colony. Salona held out against the barbarians and was only evacuated in AD 614 when the inhabitants fled to Split and neighbouring islands in the face of Avar and Slav attacks. With such a long, violent history, it's surprising that Solin is the site of a summer **Ethnoambient** (www.ethno ambient.net) music festival each August.

Sights

A good place to begin your visit is at the main entrance, near Caffe Bar Salona. There's a small **museum and information centre** (admission 10KN; 🕙 9am-6pm Mon-Sat Jun-Sep, 9am-1pm Mon-Sat Oct-May) at the entrance, which also provides a helpful map and some literature about the complex.

Manastirine, the fenced area behind the car park, was a burial place for early Christian martyrs before the legalisation of Christianity. Excavated remains of the cemetery and the 5th-century basilica are highlights, although this area was outside the ancient city itself. Overlooking Manastirine is **Tusculum**, with interesting sculptures embedded in the walls and in the garden.

The Manastirine-Tusculum complex is part of an archaeological reserve which can be freely entered. A path bordered by cypress trees runs south towards the northern **city wall** of Salona. Note the **covered aqueduct** along the inside base of the wall. The ruins in front of you as you stand on the wall were the early Christian cult centre, which include the three-aisled, 5th-century **cathedral** and a small **baptistry** with inner columns. **Public baths** adjoin the cathedral on the eastern side.

Southwest of the cathedral is the 1st-century east city gate, **Porta Caesarea**, later engulfed by the growth of Salona in all directions. Grooves in the stone road left by ancient chariots can be seen at this gate.

CROATIA

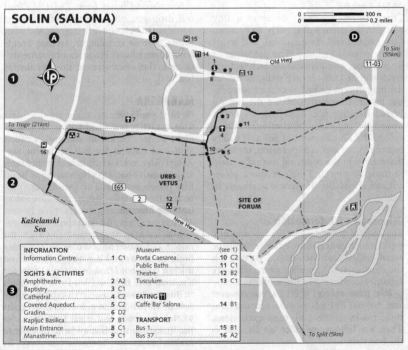

Walk west along the city wall for about 500m to **Kapljuč Basilica** on the right, another martyrs' burial place. At the western end of Salona you'll find the huge 2nd-century **amphitheatre**, which was destroyed in the 17th century by the Venetians to prevent it from being used as a refuge by Turkish raiders.

Getting There & Away

The ruins are easily accessible on Split city bus 1 direct to Solin every half-hour from the city bus stop at Trg Gaje Bulata.

From the amphitheatre at Solin it's easy to continue to Trogir by catching a west-bound bus 37 from the nearby stop on the adjacent new highway. If, on the other hand, you want to return to Split, use the underpass to cross the highway and catch an eastbound bus 37 (buy a four-zone ticket in Split if you plan to do this).

Alternatively, you can catch most Sinj-bound buses (7KN, 10 daily) from Split's main bus station to take you to Solin.

TROGIR

☎ 021 / pop 600

Trogir (formerly Trau) occupies a tiny island in the narrow channel lying between Čiovo Island and the mainland, and is just off the coastal highway. The profusion of Romanesque and Renaissance architectural styles within 15th-century walls, as well as the magnificent cathedral at the town centre, inspired Unesco to name the town a World Heritage site. A day trip to Trogir from Split can easily be combined with a visit to the Roman ruins of Solin. If you're coming by car and in high season, try to get there early in the morning to find a place to park. Staying in Trogir is also a pleasant and affordable alternative to staying in Split.

Orientation & Information

The heart of the Old Town is a few minutes' walk from the bus station. After crossing the small bridge near the station, go through the north gate. Trogir's finest sights are around Narodni trg to the southeast.

Atlas travel agency (☎ 881 374; www.atlas-trogir .com; Zvonimira 10) finds private accommodation, books hotels and runs excursions. There's a **left-luggage office** (per day 13KN) in the bus station.

Sights

The glory of the three-nave Venetian **Cathedral of St Lovro** (Trg Ivana Pavla II; ☺ 9.30am-noon year-round & 4.30-7pm daily summer) is the Romanesque portal of *Adam and Eve* (1240) by Master Radovan, the earliest example of the nude in Dalmatian sculpture. Enter the building via an obscure back door to see the perfect Renaissance Chapel of St Ivan and the choir stalls, pulpit, ciborium (vessel used to hold consecrated wafers) and treasury. You can even climb the cathedral tower, if it's open, for a great view. Also located on the square is the renovated **Church of St John the Baptist** with a magnificent carved portal and an interior showcasing a *Pietá* by Nicola Firentinac.

Getting There & Away

In Split, city bus 37 leaves from the bus station on Domovinskog. It runs between Trogir and Split every 20 minutes (19KN, one hour) throughout the day, with a short stop at Split airport en route. There's also a ferry (35KN, 2½ hours) once a week from Split to Trogir.

Southbound buses from Zadar (130km) will drop you off in Trogir, as will most northbound buses from Split going to Zadar, Rijeka, Šibenik and Zagreb. Getting north-bound buses from Trogir can be more difficult, as they often arrive from Split already full.

MAKARSKA

☎ 021 / pop 15,000

This attractive town and port is the centre-piece of the 'Makarska Riviera', a 50km stretch of coast at the foot of the Biokovo Range. The series of cliffs and ridges form an impressive backdrop to a string of beautiful pebble beaches. The foothills are protected from harsh winds and covered in lush Mediterranean greenery: pine forests, olive groves, figs and fruit trees.

Makarska is the largest town in the region and makes a good base for exploring both the coast and Mt Biokovo. Located on a large cove bordered by Cape Osejava in the southeast and the Sveti Petar Peninsula in the northwest, the landscape is dominated by Mt Biokovo looming over the town. The roads and trails that crisscross the limestone massif may be irresistible to hikers, but the less energetic can simply lie

CROATIA

on the beach and watch the day-long play of light and shadow on the mountain's cracks and crevices.

Orientation

The bus station on Ante Starčevića is about 300m uphill from the centre of the Old Town, which opens like an amphitheatre onto the sea. Take Kralja Zvonimira from the bus station downhill to Obala Kralja Tomislava and you'll be on the main promenade of the Old Town with travel agencies, shops and restaurants.

There's a long pebble beach that stretches from the Sveti Petar park at the beginning of Obala Kralja Tomislava northwest along the bay, which is where you'll find most of the large hotels. The southeastern side of town is rockier, but you can still find plenty of places to stretch out on the rocks and to take a swim.

Information

INTERNET ACCESS

Master (☎ 612 466; Jadranska 1; per hr 24KN; ⊗ 8am-midnight Mon-Sat, to 4pm Sun) Behind Hotel Biokovo.

LEFT LUGGAGE

Garderoba (per day 15KN; ⊗ 6am-10pm) At the bus station.

MEDICAL SERVICES

Hospital (☎ 612 033; Stjepana Ivičevića 2) Emergency services are available 24 hours.

MONEY

There are many banks and ATMs along Obala Kralja Tomislava and you can change money at the travel agencies on the same street.

Zagrebačka Banka (Irg Tina Ujevića 1) Has an ATM.

POST

Post office (Trg 4 Svibnja 533) You can change money, make phone calls or withdraw cash on MasterCard here.

TOURIST INFORMATION

Biokovo Active Holidays (☎ 098 225 852; www .biokovo.net; Obala Kralja Tomislava 2) A font of information on Mt Biokovo; it also organises hiking trips.

Turistička Zajednica (☎ /fax 612 002; www.makarska .com; Obala Kralja Tomislava 16; ⊗ 7am-9pm daily Jun-Sep, 7am-2pm Mon-Fri Oct-May) It distributes the useful *Official City Guide*, which you can pick up here or at any travel agency.

TRAVEL AGENCIES

Atlas travel agency (☎ 617 038; fax 616 343; Kačićev trg 8) It is at the far end of town and finds private accommodation.

Mariva Turist (☎ 616 010; www.marivaturist.hr; Obala Kralja Tomislava 15) In addition to money exchange and excursions, it books private accommodation along the whole Makarska coast, including Brela.

Turist Biro (☎ 611 688; www.turistbiro-makarska.com; Obala Kralja Tomislava 2) Finds private accommodation and books excursions.

Sights

Makarska is more renowned for its natural beauty than its cultural highlights, but on a rainy day you could check out the **Town Museum** (Gradski Muzej; ☎ 612 302; Obala Kralja Tomislava 17; adult/concession 5/3KN; ⊗ 7am-3pm Mon-Fri, 9am-noon Sat), which traces the town's history in a less-than-gripping collection of photos and old stones.

More interesting is the **Franciscan monastery** (Franjevački Samostan; Franjevački Put 1; ⊗ Mass only), built in 1400 and restored in 1540 and 1614. The monastery's single-nave church is worth visiting for the **shell collection** (☎ 611 256; admission 10KN; ⊗ 11am-noon) in the cloister and a painting of the Assumption by the Flemish artist Pieter de Coster (1760). The 18th-century **St Mark's Church** (Crkva Svetog Marka; ☎ 611 365; Kačićev trg; ⊗ Mass only) features a baroque silver altar from 1818 and a marble altar from 18th-century Venice.

Activities

Mt Biokovo, rising behind the city, offers wonderful **hiking** opportunities. The Vošac peak (142m) is the nearest target for hikers, only 2.5km from the city. From St Mark's Church in Kačićev trg, you can walk or drive up Put Makra, following signs to the village of Makar, where a trail leads to Vošac (one to two hours). From Vošac a good marked trail leads to Sveti Jure, the highest peak at 1762m (two hours). Take plenty of water.

Another popular destination is the Botanical Garden (near the village of Kotišina), which can be reached by a marked trail from Makar that passes under a series of towering peaks. Although once a major regional highlight, the garden has fallen into decay since the recent death of its caretaker.

Biokovo Active Holidays is an excellent source of hiking and other information about Mt Biokovo. For scuba diving, try:

CROATIA

More Sub (☎ 611 727, 098 265 241; Hotel Dalmacija, Kralja Krešimira bb).

Tours

Biokovo Active Holidays offers guided walks and drives on Mt Biokovo for all levels of physical exertion. You can go part way up the mountain by minibus and then take a short hike to Sveti Jure peak, take a 5½-hour hike through black pine forests and fields of chamois and sheep, or enjoy an early drive to watch the sun rise over Makarska.

Sleeping

All of the travel agencies listed earlier can find private rooms. Count on spending from €14 for a simple double with shared bathroom to €25 for better digs with private facilities. There are plenty available in the centre of town as well as the outskirts.

Hotel Porin (☎ 613 744; www.hotel-porin.hr; Marineta 2; s/d €53/84; 🍴 **P**) This new entry on the hotel scene is a solid choice if you're looking for maximum comfort in the town centre. The soundproofed rooms are shiny new with such welcome touches as hair dryers and satellite TV.

Hotel Makarska (☎ /fax 616 622; www.makarska -hotel.com; Potok 17; s/d €39/64; **P** 🍴) This small family-owned hotel in town is about 200m from the beach. The rooms are comfortable enough, with satellite TV and minibars, plus the service is attentive.

Hotel Biokovo (☎ 615 244; www.hotelbiokovo.hr; Obala Kralja Tomislava bb; s/d from €55/108; **P** 🍴) An attractive 50-room hotel right on the promenade, this place has double-glazed windows to keep out noise. There are a lot of business travellers, attracted by the well-outfitted rooms. Rooms facing the sea are slightly more expensive.

Meteor (☎ 602 600; www.hoteli-makarska.hr; Šatalište Donja Luka 1; s/d from €69/130; **P** 🍴 🏊) This three-star hotel 400m west of the town centre on a pebble beach is the most luxurious. Each of the 280 rooms is air-conditioned and has a balcony with a sea view. There are indoor and outdoor swimming pools, shops and tennis courts. Don't expect much of a discount in room rates outside the high season.

Baško Polje (☎ 612 329; per person/camp site €3.50/3.80; ☼ May-Oct) Four kilometres south of Brela, this is the closest autocamp to town and is on the beach.

Eating

Riva (☎ 616 829; Obala Kralja Tomislava 6; meals around 80KN) On one of their rare nights dining out, local people usually head here for good quality at low prices. The menu is the usual range of dishes such as scampi, beef cutlet and squid, and you can sit under the trees on an outdoor terrace.

Ivo (☎ 611 257; Starčevića 41; meals around 70KN) Because it's not near the beach, few tourists know about this place. Fish and meat dishes are cooked to perfection and expertly seasoned.

Susvid (☎ 612 732; Kačićev trg; meals from 40KN) It claims to be a 'health food' restaurant, which may simply mean that pleasure is good for your health. There are excellent vegetarian and fish dishes.

Picnickers can pick up supplies at the fruit and vegetable market next to St Mark's Church or at the **supermarket** (Obala Kralja Tomislava 14).

Entertainment

Art Cafe (☎ 615 808; Don M Pavlinovića 1) A former disco, Art Cafe now holds a changing series of concerts, exhibits and events. It's one of the best hang-outs on the coast.

Twister is a casual beach bar at the eastern end of town. It's popular for cocktails with names like 'Sex on the beach'.

Opera (☎ 616 838; Šetalište Fra Jure Radića) There's also this place, which, despite the name, is the town disco.

Getting There & Away

In summer there are three to five ferries a day between Makarska and Sumartin on Brač (23KN, 30 minutes), reduced to two a day in winter.

There are 10 buses daily from the **bus station** (☎ 612 333; Ante Starčevića 30) to Dubrovnik (99KN, three hours), 11 buses daily to Split (38KN, 1¼ hours), two buses daily to Rijeka (278KN, nine hours) and two buses daily to Zagreb (127KN to 150KN, six hours). The **Jadrolinija stall** (☎ 338 333; Obala Kralja Tomislava) is near the Hotel Biokovo.

There's also a daily bus to Sarajevo (127KN, six hours).

Around Makarska
BRELA

The town of Brela, 14km northwest of Makarska, is surrounded by the longest and loveliest coastline in Dalmatia, perhaps in all of Europe. Six kilometres of pebble beaches curve around gentle coves thickly forested with pine trees. A shady paved promenade winds around the coves, the sea is crystal clear and there are convenient outdoor showers on some beaches. Although there are far too many hotels and residences along the shore near town, the pine trees take over if you walk a few kilometres.

Orientation & Information
The bus stop (no left-luggage office) is behind Hotel Soline. From here it's a short walk downhill to Obala Kneza Domagoja, the harbour street and town centre.

Turistička Zajednica (☎ 618 455, 618 337; www .brela.hr; Obala Kneza Domagoja bb; ☺ 8am-9pm mid-Jun–mid-Sep, 8am-2pm Mon-Fri mid-Sep–mid-Jun). It provides a town map and a cycling map for the region, and **Bonavia travel agency** (☎ 619 019; www.bonavia-agency.hr; Obala Kneza Domagoja 18) finds private accommodation, changes money and books excursions.

Sights
Beaches and coves are on both sides of the town but the longest stretch is the 4km coast west of the town centre. The best beach is **Punta Rata**, a stunning pebble beach about 300m southwest of the town centre where there are showers and changing rooms.

Sleeping
The closest camping is available at Baško Polje (see opposite). For private accommodation you'll pay from €13 to €16 per person per day.

There are no cheap hotels in Brela but much of the private accommodation on offer from the tourist office or travel agencies are really small *pensions*. The four large hotels are managed by **Brela Hotels** (☎ 603 190; www.brelahotels.com).

Hotel Marina (☎ 603 608; marina@hoteli-brela .t-com.hr; s/d €66/100; **P** ✖) The Marina is the least expensive hotel in town and the newest. A wall of pine trees separates this rather standard-issue hotel from a luxuriant beach.

Hotel Soline (☎ 603 207; soline@hoteli-brela .t-com.hr; Trg Gospe od Karmela 1 s/d €72/119; **P** ✖ ✖) This well-turned-out establishment is the closest to town, on a beach, and sports an indoor swimming pool.

Hotel Berulia (☎ 603 599; berulia@hoteli-brela .t-com.hr; Frankopanska bb; s/d from €71/122; **P** ✖ ✖) About 300m east of the town centre, this hotel is a little more secluded than the others but also offers a full range of comforts.

Eating & Drinking
Konoba Feral (☎ 618 909; Obala Domagoja; meals from 70KN) This friendly place has wooden tables outside and a homy interior to enjoy superb grilled fish. Try the line-caught squid and finish with the sinful *palačinke Feral*, an amazing concoction of crepes, ice cream and chocolate.

Guliver (☎ 618 735; Obala Domagoja) This cocktail bar with live music manages to be both fun and romantic.

Getting There & Away
All buses between Makarska and Split stop at Brela, making it an easy day trip (1½ hours, 40KN) from either town.

HVAR ISLAND
☎ 021 / pop 12,600
Rapidly becoming the island of choice for a swanky international crowd, Hvar admittedly deserves the honour, for it is the sunniest and greenest of the Croatian islands. Called the 'Croatian Madeira', Hvar receives 2724 hours of sunshine each year. The stunning interior is a panorama of lavender fields, peaceful villages and pine-covered slopes.

Hvar Town
Within the 13th-century walls of medieval Hvar lie beautifully ornamented Gothic palaces and traffic-free marble streets. A long seaside promenade, dotted with small rocky beaches, stretches from each end of the harbour. A few tasteful bars and cafés along the harbour are relaxing spots for people-watching. For more activity, hop on a launch to the Pakleni Islands, famous for nude sunbathing.

ORIENTATION
Car ferries from Split deposit you in Stari Grad but local buses meet most ferries in summer for the trip to Hvar town. The town centre is Trg Sv Stjepana, 100m west of the bus station. Passenger ferries tie up on Riva, the eastern quay, across from Hotel Slavija.

INFORMATION

Atlas travel agency (☎ 741 670) On the western side of the harbour.

Clinic (☎ 741 300; Sv Katarina) About 200m from the town centre, it's past the Hotel Pharos. Emergency services are available 24 hours.

Garderoba (per day 15KN; ⏰ 7am-midnight) The left-luggage office is in the bathroom next to the bus station.

Internet Leon (☎ 741 824; Riva; per hr 30KN; ⏰ 8am-9pm Mon-Fri, to 10pm Sat, to 6pm Sun) Internet access next to the Hotel Palace.

Pelegrini Travel (☎ /fax 742 250; pelegrini@inet.hr) Also finds private accommodation.

Post office (Riva) You can make phone calls here.

Tourist office (☎ /fax 742 977; www.tzhvar.hr; ⏰ 8am-1pm & 5-9pm Mon-Sat, 9am-noon Sun Jun-Sep, 8am-2pm Mon-Sat Oct-May) In the arsenal building on the corner of Trg Sv Stjepana.

SIGHTS & ACTIVITIES

The full flavour of medieval Hvar is best savoured on the backstreets of the Old Town. At each end of Hvar is a monastery with a prominent tower. The Dominican **Church of St Marko** at the head of the bay was largely destroyed by Turks in the 16th century but you can visit the local **archaeological museum** (admission 10KN; ⏰ 10am-noon Jun-Sep) in the ruins. If it is closed you'll still get a good view of the ruins from the road just above, which leads up to a stone cross on a hill top offering a picture-postcard view of Hvar.

At the southeastern end of Hvar you'll find the 15th-century Renaissance **Franciscan Monastery** (⏰ 10am-noon & 5-7pm Jun-Sep & Christmas week & Holy Week), with a wonderful collection of Venetian paintings in the church and adjacent **museum** (admission 15KN; ⏰ 10am-noon & 5-7pm Mon-Sat Jun-Sep), including *The Last Supper* by Matteo Ingoli.

Smack in the middle of Hvar is the imposing Gothic **arsenal**, its great arch visible from afar. The local commune's war galley was once kept here. Upstairs off the arsenal terrace is Hvar's prize, the first **municipal theatre** (admission 15KN; ⏰ 10am-noon & 5-7pm) in Europe (1612), rebuilt in the 19th century. Hours can vary and you enter through the adjoining **Gallery of Contemporary Croatian Art** (arsenal; admission for gallery & theatre 15KN; ⏰ 10am-noon & 7-11pm Jun-Sep & Christmas week & Holy Week, 10am-noon rest of year).

On the hill high above Hvar town is a **Venetian fortress** (1551), and it's worth the climb up to appreciate the lovely, sweeping panoramic views. The fort was built to defend Hvar from the Turks, who sacked the town in 1539 and 1571.

There is a small town beach next to the Franciscan Monastery, but the best beach is in front of the Hotel Amphora, around the western corner of the cove. Most people take a launch to the offshore islands that include the naturist Pakleni Islands of Jerolim and Stipanska and lovely Palmižana.

In front of the Hotel Amphora, **Diving Centar Viking** (☎ 742 529; www.viking-diving.com) is a large operation in Podstine that offers a certification course, dives (€30) and hotel packages.

SLEEPING

Accommodation in Hvar is extremely tight in July and August: a reservation is highly recommended. For private accommodation, try Pelegrini Travel (see Information). Expect to pay from 160/280KN per single/double with bathroom in the town centre.

Jagoda & Ante Bracanović Guesthouse (☎ 741 416, 091 520 37 96; virgilye@yahoo.com; Poviše Škole; s 100-120KN, d 190-220KN) This friendly place is close to the town centre and offers six spacious rooms, each with a bathroom, balcony, small refrigerator and kitchen access.

Aparthotel Pharia (☎ 778 080; www.orvas-hotels .com; Majerovica bb; s/d/apt from €55/78/116; 🖭) This small 10-room hotel provides a more personal level of service than the giants crowding the town outskirts. Rooms are snug but well-appointed and the apartments are a great deal.

Hotel Slavija (☎ 741 820; fax 741 147; Riva; s/d from €66/94) The great thing here is that you step off the passenger boat from Split and into hotel reception. The location on the harbour is the main selling point and the rooms are more than acceptable. Reservations for this and the other large hotels in and around the Old Town are handled by **Sunčani Hvar** (☎ 741 026; www.suncanihvar.hr).

Mala Milna (☎ 745 027; per person/camp site 40/30KN) This restful camping ground is the closest, only 2km southeast of town.

EATING

The pizzerias along the harbour offer predictable but inexpensive eating.

Macondo (☎ 741 851; meals from 75KN) Head upstairs from the northern side of Trg Sv Stjepana for mouth-watering seafood.

Konoba Menego (☎ 742 036; meals 60KN) On the stairway over the Benedictine convent, this eatery is an excellent choice. The menu offers the best of the Hvar specialities, and vegetarians will appreciate the marinated vegetables.

Bounty (☎ 742 565; meals from 50KN) This place on the quay is a long-time favourite among the locals for its tasty fish, pasta and meat dishes at reasonable prices. There's a special soup, main course and salad deal for 50KN.

Paradise Garden (☎ 741 310; meals 65-85KN) This eatery, up some stairs on the northern side of the cathedral, serves up a memorable spaghetti with seafood, as well as the usual excellent assortment of grilled or fried fish. You will dine outdoors on an enclosed patio.

The **grocery store** (Trg Sv Stjepana) is a viable restaurant alternative, and there's a morning market next to the bus station.

DRINKING
Hvar has some of the best nightlife on the Adriatic coast, mostly centred around the harbour.

Carpe Diem (☎ 742 369; Riva) From a groggy breakfast to late-night cocktails, there is no time of day when this swanky place is dull. The music is smooth, the drinks fruity and expensive, and the sofas more than welcoming.

Nautika (Fabrika) Offering tall, juicy cocktails and nonstop dance music, from techno to hip-hop, this place is ground zero for Hvar's explosive nightlife. Just up the street is Kiva Bar, where you can chill out and talk between dance numbers.

GETTING THERE & AWAY
The Jadrolinija ferries between Rijeka and Dubrovnik stop in Stari Grad before continuing to Korčula. The **Jadrolinija agency** (☎ 741 132; Riva) sells boat tickets.

Car ferries from Split call at Stari Grad (32KN, one hour) three times daily (five daily in July and August) and there's an afternoon passenger boat from Split to Hvar town (22KN, 50 minutes) that goes on to Vela Luka on Korčula Island (22KN, one hour). Even more convenient are the daily passenger boats from Hvar to Split (33KN, 1¼ hours) or Korčula (33KN, 1½ hours). See p403 for information on international connections. Buses meet most ferries that

dock at Stari Grad in July and August, but if you come in the off season it's best to check at the tourist office or at Pelegrini to make sure the bus is running. A taxi costs from 150KN to 200KN. **Radio Taxi Tihi** (☎ 098 338 824) is cheaper if there are a number of passengers to fill up the minivan. It's easy to recognise with the photo of Hvar painted on the side.

It's possible to visit Hvar on a (hectic) day trip from Split by catching the morning Jadrolinija ferry to Stari Grad, a bus to Hvar town, then the last ferry from Stari Grad directly back to Split.

KORČULA ISLAND
☎ 020 / pop 16,200
Rich in vineyards and olive trees, the island of Korčula was named Korkyra Melaina (Black Korčula) by the original Greek settlers because of its dense woods and plant life. As the largest island in an archipelago of 48, it provides plenty of opportunities for scenic drives, particularly along the southern coast.

Swimming opportunities abound in the many quiet coves and secluded beaches, while the interior produces some of Croatia's finest wine, especially dessert wines made from the *grk* grape cultivated around Lumbarda. Local olive oil is another product worth seeking out.

Korčula Town
On a hilly peninsula jutting into the Adriatic sits Korčula Town, a striking walled town of round defensive towers and red-roofed houses. Resembling a miniature Dubrovnik, the gated, walled Old Town is crisscrossed by narrow stone streets designed to protect its inhabitants from the winds swirling around the peninsula. Korčula Island was controlled by Venice from the 14th to the 18th centuries, as is evident from the Venetian coats of arms adorning the official buildings. If you don't stop in Korčula, one look at this unique town from the Jadrolinija ferry will make you regret it.

ORIENTATION
The big Jadrolinija car ferry drops you off either in the west harbour next to the Hotel Korčula or the east harbour next to Marko Polo Tours. The Old Town lies between the two harbours. The large hotels and main

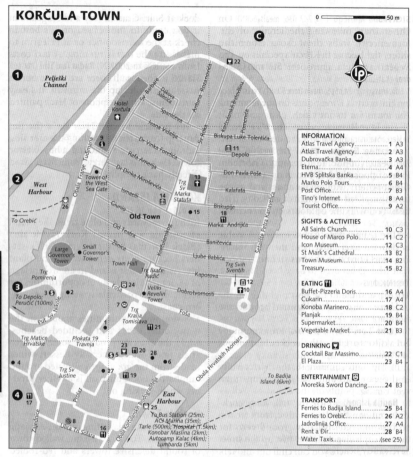

KORČULA TOWN

INFORMATION	
Atlas Travel Agency................1	A3
Atlas Travel Agency................2	A3
Dubrovačka Banka.................3	A3
Eterna..............................4	A4
HVB Splitska Banka................5	B4
Marko Polo Tours..................6	B4
Post Office..........................7	B3
Tino's Internet......................8	A4
Tourist Office.......................9	A2

SIGHTS & ACTIVITIES	
All Saints Church...................10	C3
House of Marco Polo...............11	C2
Icon Museum........................12	C3
St Mark's Cathedral................13	B2
Town Museum.......................14	B2
Treasury.............................15	B2

EATING	
Buffet-Pizzeria Doris...............16	A4
Cukarin..............................17	A4
Konoba Marinero...................18	C2
Planjak..............................19	B4
Supermarket........................20	B4
Vegetable Market..................21	B3

DRINKING	
Cocktail Bar Massimo...............22	C1
El Plaza.............................23	B4

ENTERTAINMENT	
Moreška Sword Dancing...........24	B3

TRANSPORT	
Ferries to Badija Island............25	B4
Ferries to Orebić...................26	A2
Jadrolinija Office...................27	A4
Rent a Đir..........................28	B4
Water Taxis.....................(see 25)	

beach lie south of the east harbour, and the residential neighbourhood Sveti Nikola (with a smaller beach) is southwest of the west harbour. The town bus station is 100m south of the Old Town centre.

INFORMATION

There are ATMs in the town centre at HVB Splitska Banka and Dubrovačka Banka. You can change money there, at the post office, or at any of the travel agencies. The post office is hidden next to the stairway up to the Old Town. The post office also has telephones.

Atlas travel agency (☎ 711 231; Trg Kralja Tomislava) Represents Amex, runs excursions and finds private accommodation. There's another office nearby.

Marko Polo Tours (☎ 715 400; marko-polo-tours@du .t-com.hr; Biline 5) Finds private accommodation and organises excursions.

Eterna (☎ 716 538; eterno.doo@du.t-com.hr; Put Sv. Nikola bb) Finds private accommodation and offers Internet access (per hr 25KN).

Hospital (☎ 711 137; Ul 59, Kalac) It's south of the Old Town, about 1km past the Hotel Marko Polo. Emergency services are available 24 hours.

Tino's Internet (☎ 091 50 91 182; ul Tri Sulara; per hr 25KN) Tino's other outlet is at the ACI Marina; both are open long hours.

Tourist office (☎ 715 701; tzg-korcule@du.t-com.hr; Obala Franje Tudjmana bb; ⏰ 8am-3pm & 5-9pm Mon-Sat, 8am-3pm Sun Jun-Sep, 8am-1pm & 5-9pm Mon-Sat Oct-May) An excellent source of information, located on the west harbour.

SIGHTS

Other than following the circuit of the former city walls or walking along the shore, sightseeing in Korčula centres on Trg Sv Marka Statuta. The Gothic **St Mark's Cathedral** (Katedrala Svetog Marka; 10am-noon, 5-7pm Jul & Aug, Mass only rest of year) features two paintings by Tintoretto (*Three Saints* on the altar and *Annunciation* to one side).

The **Town Museum** (Gradski Muzej; ☎ 711 420; Trg Sv Marka Statuta; admission 10KN; 10am-1pm Nov-Mar, 10am-2pm Apr-May, 10am-2pm & 7-9pm Jun & Oct, 10am-9pm Jul-Aug) in the 15th-century Gabriellis Palace opposite the cathedral has exhibits of Greek pottery, Roman ceramics and home furnishings, all with English captions. The **treasury** (☎ 711 049; Trg Sv Marka Statuta; admission 15KN; 9am-2pm & 5-8pm May-Oct), in the 14th-century Abbey Palace next to the cathedral is also worth a look. It's said that Marco Polo was born in Korčula in 1254; you can visit what is believed to have been his **house** (Depolo; admission 10KN; 10am-1pm & 5-7pm Mon-Sat Jul & Aug) and climb the tower.

There's also an **Icon Museum** (Trg Svih Svetih; admission 7.50KN; 9am-2pm & 5-8pm May-Oct) in the Old Town. It isn't much of a museum, but visitors are let into the beautiful old **All Saints Church**.

In the high summer season, water taxis at the east harbour collect passengers to visit various points on the island, as well as to **Badija Island**, which features an historic 15th-century Franciscan Monastery in the process of reconstruction, plus **Orebić** and the nearby village of **Lumbarda**, which both have sandy beaches.

TOURS

Both Atlas travel agency and Marko Polo Tours offer a variety of boat tours and island excursions.

SLEEPING

The big hotels in Korčula are overpriced, but there are a wealth of guesthouses that offer clean, attractive rooms and friendly service. Atlas and Marko Polo Tours arrange private rooms, charging from 200KN to 220KN for a room with a bathroom, and starting at about 400KN for an apartment. Or you could try one of the following options.

Depolo (☎ /fax 711 621; tereza.depolo@du.t-com.hr; d with/without sea view €35/32; 🐾) In the residential neighbourhood close to the Old Town

of Sveti Nikola and 100m west of the bus station, this guesthouse has spiffy and modern rooms equipped with satellite TV.

Tarle (☎ 711 712; fax 711 243; Stalište Frana Kršinića; d with/without kitchen €37/29) Next to the Hotel Marko Polo, about 500m southeast of the bus station, this place has a pretty enclosed garden and attractive rooms, each with a balcony.

Other guesthouses nearby for about the same price include **Peručić** (☎ /fax 711 458), with great balconies, and the homy **Ojdanić** (☎ /fax 711 708; roko-taxi@du.t-com.hr). Local Ratko Ojdanić has a water taxi and a lot of experience with fishing trips around the island. He's also available for private boat transfers and excursions.

Autocamp Kalac (☎ 711 182; fax 711 146; per person/camp site €5.40/8.20) This attractive camping ground is behind Hotel Bon Repos, about 4km from the west harbour, in a dense pine grove near the beach.

EATING & DRINKING

Planjak (☎ 711 015; Plokata 19 Travnja; meals from 50KN) This restaurant-grill, between the supermarket and the Jadrolinija office in town, is popular with a local crowd who appreciates the fresh Dalmatian dishes as much as the low prices.

Konoba Maslina (☎ 711 720; Lumbarajska cesta bb; meals from 70KN) It's well worth the walk out here for the authentic Korčulan home cooking. The multibean soup is a standout but all is scrumptious. It's about a kilometre past the Hotel Marko Polo on the road to Lumbarda but you can often arrange to be picked up or dropped off in town.

Konoba Marinero (☎ 711 170; Marka Andrijića 13; meals from 65KN) Friendly and efficient, this place serves up outstanding fish prepared in true Dalmatian style.

Buffet-Pizzeria Doris (☎ 711 596; ul Tri Solara; meals from 35KN) Simple but tasty dishes are served up indoors or outdoors on a shaded terrace. The grilled vegetable platter is a welcome vegetarian treat.

Cukarin (☎ 711 055; Zajednice) The Cukarin serves up scrumptious local pastries such as *cukarini*, which is a sweet biscuit, *klajun*, a pastry stuffed with walnuts, and *amareta*, a round, rich cake with almonds.

Cocktail Bar Massimo (Šetalište Petra Kanevelića) It's original, you have to grant them that. Lodged in a turret and accessible only by ladder, the drinks are brought up by pulley. You also get lovely views.

El Plaza (Plokata 19 Travnja) It's a large, smoky hang-out for locals who watch sports on the TV and check their email on one of the computers.

Pick up fresh fruit and veggies at the **vegetable market** (Trg Kralja Tomislava) or grab other supplies at the **supermarket** (Plokata 19 Travnja).

ENTERTAINMENT

Between June and October there's **moreška sword dancing** (tickets 80KN; ☣ show 9pm Thu) by the Old Town gate; performances are more frequent during July and August. The clash of swords and the graceful movements of the dancers/fighters make an exciting show. Atlas, the tourist office and Marko Polo Tours sell tickets.

GETTING THERE & AROUND

Transport connections to Korčula are good. There's one bus every day to Dubrovnik (77KN, three hours), one to Zagreb (195KN, 12 hours), and one a week to Sarajevo (152KN, eight hours).

There's a **Jadrolinija office** (☎ 715 410) about 25m up from the west harbour.

There's a regular afternoon car ferry between Split and Vela Luka (35KN, three hours), on the island's western end, that stops at Hvar most days. Six daily buses link Korčula town to Vela Luka (28KN, one hour), but services from Vela Luka are reduced at the weekend.

The daily fast boat running from Split to Hvar and Korcula is great for locals working in Split but not so great for tourists who find themselves leaving Korčula at 6am. Nevertheless, you can go quickly from Korčula to Hvar (33KN, 1½ hours) and to Split (55KN, 2¾ hours). Get tickets at Marko Polo.

From Orebić, look for the passenger launch (15KN, 15 minutes, at least five times daily on weekdays), which will drop you off near Hotel Korčula below the Old Town's towers. There's also a car ferry to Dominče (10KN, 15 minutes) which stops near the Hotel Bon Repos, where you can pick up the bus from Lumbarda (10KN) a few times a day or a water taxi to Korčula town. For international connections see p403.

Next to Marko Polo, **Rent a Đir** (☎ 711 908; www.korcula-rent.com) hires autos, scooters and small boats.

MLJET ISLAND

☎ 020 / pop 1111

Of all the Adriatic islands, Mljet (Meleda in Italian) may be the most seductive. Over 72% of the island is covered by forests and the rest is dotted by fields, vineyards and small villages. Created in 1960, **Mljet National Park** occupies the western third of the island and surrounds two saltwater lakes, Malo Jezero and Veliko Jezero. Most people visit the island on excursions from Korčula or Dubrovnik, but it is now possible to take a passenger boat from Dubrovnik or come on the regular ferry from Dubrovnik and stay a few days for hiking, cycling and boating.

Orientation & Information

Tour boats arrive at Pomena wharf at Mljet's western end. Jadrolinija ferries arrive at Sobra on the eastern end and they are met by a local bus for the 1½-hour ride to Pomena and little town of Polače, about 5km from Pomena. The *Nona Ana* passenger boat from Dubrovnik docks at Sobra and then Polače. You can enter the national park from either Pomena or Polače. The **tourist office** (☎ 744 125; np-mljet@np-mljet.hr; ☣ 8am-1pm & 5-8pm Mon-Fri Oct-May, 8am-8pm Mon-Sat, to 1pm Sun Jun-Sep) is in Polače, and the only ATM on the island is at the Odisej hotel in Pomena. The admission price for the national park is 90/30KN adult/concession which includes a bus and boat transfer to the Benedictine Monastery; there is no park admission price if you stay overnight on the island.

Sights & Activities

From Pomena it's a 15-minute walk to a jetty on **Veliko Jezero**, the larger of the two lakes. Here you can board a boat to a small lake islet and have lunch at a 12th-century **Benedictine Monastery**, which now houses a restaurant.

Those who don't want to spend the rest of the afternoon swimming and sunbathing on the monastery island can catch an early boat back to the main island and spend a couple of hours walking along the lakeshore before taking the late-afternoon excursion boat back to Korčula or Dubrovnik. There's a small landing on the main island opposite the monastery where the boat operator drops off passengers upon request. It's not possible to walk right around Veliko Jezero because there's no bridge over the channel that connects the lakes to the sea.

Mljet is good for cycling; several restaurants along the dock in Polače and the Odisej hotel in Pomena hire bicycles (90KN per half day). If you plan to cycle between Pomena and Polače be aware that the two towns are separated by a steep mountain. The bike path along Veliko Jezero is an easier pedal but it doesn't link the two towns.

Tours

See p206 and p211 in Korčula and Dubrovnik respectively for agencies offering excursions to Mljet. The tour lasts from 8.30am to 6pm and includes the park entry fee. The boat trip from Korčula to Pomena takes at least two hours, less by hydrofoil; from Dubrovnik it takes longer. Lunch isn't included in the tour price and the opportunities for self-catering are limited.

Sleeping & Eating

The Polače tourist office arranges private accommodation at 200KN per double room in summer but it is essential to make arrangements before arrival in peak season. There are more *sobe* signs around Pomena than Polače, but practically none at all in Sobra.

Odisej (☎ 744 022; Pomena; s/d from €62/88; 🍴) Rooms are pleasant enough here, plus you are right on the port, and you can hire bicycles, snorkelling equipment etc.

There's no camping permitted inside the national park but there are two grounds outside it.

Camping Mungos (☎ 745 060; fax 745 125; Babino Poje; per person/camp site €8/7.50; 🗓 May-Sep) Not very shady, but well located, this camping ground is not far from the beach and the lovely grotto of Odysseus.

Marina (☎ 745 071; fax 745 224; per person/camp site €4/4; 🗓 Jun-Sep) This is a small camping ground in Ropa, about 1km from the park.

Nine (☎ 744 037; Pomena; meals from 100KN) The Nine, opposite Odisej hotel, is by the sea and, though touristy in high season, turns out succulent seafood.

Getting There & Away

It's possible to make a quick visit to Mljet by a regular morning ferry (26KN to 32KN, 2½ hours) from Dubrovnik in July and August.

The rest of the year the ferry leaves from Dubrovnik in the mid-afternoon Monday to Saturday, or Sunday evening. The ferry docks in Sobra where it is met by a bus. The big Jadrolinija coastal ferries also stop at Mljet twice a week in summer and once a week during the rest of the year.

The *Nona Ana* is a small boat that makes a 2¾-hour run between Dubrovnik and Polače three times a week, leaving in the morning and returning in the late afternoon (45KN).

Tickets are sold in the **Turistička Zajednica** (Map pp210-11; ☎ 417 983; Obala Papa Ivana Pavla II) in Gruž, at **Atlantagent** (Map pp210-11; ☎ 419 044; obala Stjepana Radića 26; 🕑 10am-4pm) in Dubrovnik, or on board, but it's wise to buy in advance as the boat fills up quickly.

DUBROVNIK

☎ 020 / pop 43,770

Whether you call it 'paradise on earth' (George Bernard Shaw) or merely 'the pearl of the Adriatic' (Lord Byron), Dubrovnik is clearly special. Enclosed in a curtain of stone walls, the town centre is radiant with the light reflected from its white marble paving stones. The main pedestrian thoroughfare, Placa, is a melange of cafés and shops with outstanding monuments at either end. Churches, monasteries and museums ornamented with finely carved stone recall an eventful history, and the vibrant artistic tradition is continued with regular concerts and plays. Beyond the walls stretch the crystal blue waters of the southern Adriatic, sprinkled with tiny islands for the hedonistically inclined.

History

Founded 1300 years ago by refugees from Epidaurus in Greece, medieval Dubrovnik (Ragusa until 1918) shook off Venetian control in the 14th century, becoming an independent republic and one of Venice's more important maritime rivals, trading with Egypt, Syria, Sicily, Spain, France and later Turkey. The double blow of an earthquake in 1667 and the opening of new trade routes to the east sent Ragusa into a slow decline, ending with Napoleon's conquest of the town in 1806.

The deliberate and militarily pointless shelling of Dubrovnik by the Yugoslav army in 1991 sent shockwaves through the

DUBROVNIK

INFORMATION	
Atlantagent	1 D1
Atlas Travel Agency	2 C1
Dubrovnik Internet Centar	(see 7)
Garderoba	(see 24)
Gulliver	3 D1
Hospital	4 C2
Lapad Post Office	5 C2
Turistička Zajednica	6 C1
Turistička Zajednica	7 E3

SIGHTS & ACTIVITIES	
Lazareti	8 F3
Ploče Beach	9 F3

SLEEPING 🏠	
Apartments Silva Kusjanović	10 B1

Begović Boarding House	11 B1
Hotel Lapad	12 C1
Hotel Petka	13 D1
Hotel Sumratin	14 B2
Solitudo	15 B1
YHA Hostel	16 D2

international community but, when the smoke cleared in 1992, traumatised residents cleared the rubble and set about repairing the damage. With substantial international aid, the famous monuments were rebuilt and resculpted, the streets sealed and the clay roofs retiled. Reconstruction has been extraordinarily skilful but you will notice different shades of rose-tiled roofs as you walk around the city walls.

After a steep postwar decline in tourism, visitors are once again flocking to Dubrovnik. It has become a main port of call for Mediterranean cruise ships, whose passengers are sometimes elbow-to-elbow in peak season. Come in June or September if you can but, whatever the time of year, the interlay of light and stone is enchanting. Don't miss it.

Orientation

The Jadrolinija ferry terminal and the bus station are next to each other at Gruž, several kilometres northwest of the Old Town, which is closed to cars. The main street in the Old Town is Placa (also called Stradun).

Most accommodation is on the leafy Lapad Peninsula, west of the bus station.

Information
BOOKSHOPS
Algoritam (Map p212; Placa) Has a good selection of English-language books, including guidebooks.

INTERNET ACCESS
Dubrovnik Internet Centar (Map pp210-11; ☎ 311 017; Dubrovačkih branitelja 7; ☺ 9am-9pm; per hr 20KN)

LEFT LUGGAGE
Garderoba (Map pp210-11; ☺ 5.30am-9pm) At the bus station.

MEDICAL SERVICES
Hospital (Map pp210-11; ☎ 431 777; Dr. Roka Mišetića bb) Emergency services are available 24 hours.

MONEY
You can change money at any travel agency or post office. There are numerous ATMs in town, near the bus station and near the ferry terminal.

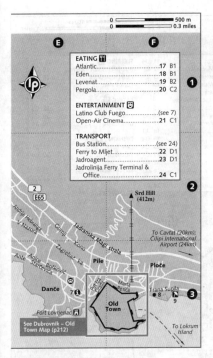

EATING 🍴
Atlantic.................................**17** B1
Eden....................................**18** B1
Levenat...............................**19** B2
Pergola...............................**20** C2

ENTERTAINMENT 🎭
Latino Club Fuego................(see 7)
Open-Air Cinema..................**21** C1

TRANSPORT
Bus Station...........................(see 24)
Ferry to Mljet.......................**22** D1
Jadroagent...........................**23** D1
Jadrolinija Ferry Terminal &
Office...................................**24** C1

POST
Main post office (Map p212; cnr Široka & Od Puča)
Lapad post office (Map pp210-11; Šetalište Kralja Zvonimira 21)

TOURIST INFORMATION
Tourist Information Centar (Map p212; ☎ 323 350; tic-stradun@du.t-com.hr; Placa 1) Across from the Franciscan monastery in the Old Town, this private agency finds accommodation, changes money and books excursions.
Turistička Zajednica (www.tzdubrovnik.hr; ☑ 8am-8pm daily Jun-Sep, 9am-7pm Mon-Fri, to 1pm Sat Oct-May) Dubrovačkih branitelja (Map pp210-11; ☎ 427 591; Dubrovačkih branitelja 7); Obala Papa Ivana Pavla II (Map pp210-11; ☎ 417 983; Obala Papa Ivana Pavla II 44a); Placa (Map p212; ☎ 321 561; Placa bb) Offers maps and the indispensable *Dubrovnik Riviera* guide. The Dubrovačkih branitelja branch is outside Pile Gate, the Placa branch is in the Old Town. The harbour branch at Obala Papa Ivana Pavla II has limited information.

TRAVEL AGENCIES
Atlas travel agency Obala Papa Ivana Pavla II (Map pp210-11; ☎ 418 001; Obala Papa Ivana Pavla II 1); Sv Đurđa (Map p212; ☎ 442 574; Sv Đurđa 1) In convenient locations (the Sv Đurđa branch is outside Pile Gate and the Obala

Papa Ivana Pavla II branch is at the harbour), this agency is extremely helpful for general information as well as finding private accommodation. All excursions are run by Atlas.
Gulliver (Map pp210-11; ☎ 313 300; www.gulliver .hr; Obala Stjepana Radića 32) Near the Jadrolinija dock, Gulliver finds private accommodation, changes money and hires cars and scooters.

Sights
OLD TOWN
You will probably begin your visit of Dubrovnik's World Heritage-listed Old Town at the city bus stop outside **Pile Gate** (Map p212). As you enter the city Dubrovnik's wonderful pedestrian promenade, Placa, extends before you all the way to the **clock tower** (Map p212) at the other end of town.

Just inside Pile Gate is the huge 1438 **Onofrio Fountain** (Map p212) and **Franciscan Monastery** (Muzej Franjevačkog Samostana; Map p212; ☎ 426 345; ☑ 9am-5pm) with a splendid cloister and the third-oldest functioning **pharmacy** (Map p212; ☑ 9am-5pm) in Europe; it's been operating since 1391. The **church** (Map p212; ☑ 7am-7pm) has recently undergone a long and expensive restoration to startling effect. The **monastery museum** (Map p212; adult/concession 15/7.50KN; ☑ 9am-5pm) has a collection of liturgical objects, paintings and pharmacy equipment.

In front of the clock tower at the eastern end of Placa (on the square called Luža) is the 1419 **Orlando Column** (Map p212) – a favourite meeting place. On opposite sides of the column are the 16th-century **Sponza Palace** (Map p212) – originally a customs house, later a bank, and which now houses the **State Archives** (Državni Arhiv u Dubrovniku; Map p212; ☎ 321 032; admission free; ☑ 8am-3pm Mon-Fri, 8am-1pm Sat) – and **St Blaise's Church** (Map p212), a lovely Italian baroque building built in 1715 to replace an earlier church destroyed in the 1667 earthquake. At the end of Pred Dvorom, the wide street beside St Blaise, is the baroque **Cathedral of the Assumption of the Virgin** (Map p212). Located between the two churches, the 1441 Gothic **Rector's Palace** (Map p212; Knežev Dvor; ☎ 426 469; adult/concession 20/7KN; ☑ 9am-2pm Mon-Sat Oct-May, 9am-6pm daily Jun-Sep) houses a museum with furnished rooms, baroque paintings and historical exhibits. The elected rector was not permitted to leave the building during his one-month term without the permission of the senate. The narrow street

CROATIA

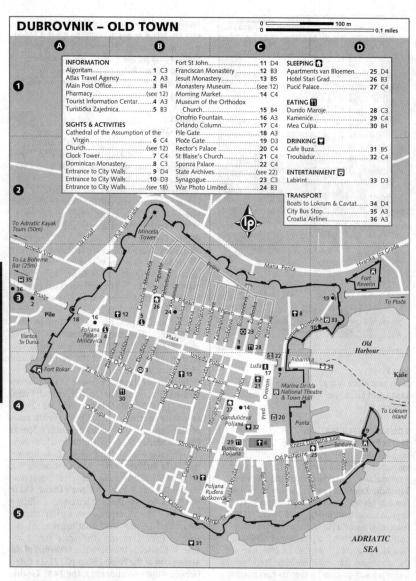

DUBROVNIK – OLD TOWN

0 _____ 100 m
0 _____ 0.1 miles

INFORMATION		
Algoritam	1	C3
Atlas Travel Agency	2	A3
Main Post Office	3	B4
Pharmacy	(see 12)	
Tourist Information Centar	4	A3
Turistička Zajednica	5	B3

SIGHTS & ACTIVITIES		
Cathedral of the Assumption of the Virgin	6	C4
Church	(see 12)	
Clock Tower	7	C4
Dominican Monastery	8	C3
Entrance to City Walls	9	D4
Entrance to City Walls	10	D3
Entrance to City Walls	(see 18)	

Fort St John	11	D4
Franciscan Monastery	12	B3
Jesuit Monastery	13	B5
Monastery Museum	(see 12)	
Morning Market	14	C4
Museum of the Orthodox Church	15	B4
Onofrio Fountain	16	A3
Orlando Column	17	C4
Pile Gate	18	A3
Ploče Gate	19	D3
Rector's Palace	20	C4
St Blaise's Church	21	C4
Sponza Palace	22	C4
State Archives	(see 22)	
Synagogue	23	C3
War Photo Limited	24	B3

SLEEPING		
Apartments van Bloemen	25	D4
Hotel Stari Grad	26	B3
Pucić Palace	27	C4

EATING		
Dundo Maroje	28	C3
Kamenice	29	C4
Mea Culpa	30	B4

DRINKING		
Cafe Buza	31	B5
Troubadur	32	C4

ENTERTAINMENT		
Labirint	33	D3

TRANSPORT		
Boats to Lokrum & Cavtat	34	D4
City Bus Stop	35	A3
Croatia Airlines	36	A3

CROATIA

opposite opens onto Gundulićeva Poljana, a bustling **morning market** (Map p212). Up the stairs south of the square is the 1725 **Jesuit Monastery** (Map p212; Poljana Ruđera Bošovića).

As you proceed up Placa, make a detour to the **Museum of the Orthodox Church** (Muzej Pravoslavne Crkva; Map p212; ☎ 426 260; Nikole Bozidaverica; adult/concession 10/5KN; ☺ 9am-1pm Mon-Fri) for a

look at a fascinating collection of 15th- to 19th-century icons.

By now you'll be ready for a leisurely walk around the **city walls** (Map p212; adult/concession 30/10KN; ☺ 9am-7pm), which has entrances just inside Pile Gate, across from the Dominican monastery and near Fort St John. Built between the 13th and 16th centuries, these powerful walls are the finest in the world and Dubrovnik's main claim to fame. They enclose the entire city in a protective veil over 2km long and up to 25m high, with two round and 14 square towers, two corner fortifications and a large fortress. The views over the town and sea are great – this walk could be the high point of your visit.

Whichever way you go, you'll notice the 14th-century **Dominican Monastery** (Muzej Dominikanskog Samostana; Map p212; ☎ 426 472; adult/concession 10/5KN; ☑ 9am-6pm) in the northeastern corner of the city, whose forbidding fortress-like exterior shelters a rich trove of paintings from Dubrovnik's finest 15th- and 16th-century artists.

Dubrovnik has many other sights, such as the unmarked **synagogue** (Sinagoga; Map p212; ☎ 412 219; ul Žudioska 5; admission free; ☑ 10am-1pm Mon-Fri) near the clock tower, which is the second oldest synagogue in Europe. The uppermost streets of the Old Town below the north and south walls are pleasant to wander along.

For a change from the ancient and the artsy, try the excellent **War Photo Limited** (Map p212; ☎ 326 166; Antuninska 6; admission 25KN; ☑ 9am-9pm May-Sep, 10am-4pm Tue-Sat, 10am-2pm Sun Oct, Mar & Apr), managed by former photojournalist Wade Goddard. The award-winning photos on display here concentrate on the subtleties of human violence rather than on its carnage. The permanent exhibition focuses on the Balkan wars but temporary exhibits will include other wars.

BEACHES

Ploče (Map pp210–11), the closest beach to the old city, is just beyond the 17th-century **Lazareti** (Map pp210–11; a former quarantine station) outside **Ploče Gate** (Map p212). There are also hotel beaches along the **Lapad Peninsula** (Map pp210–11), which you are able to use without a problem. The largest is outside the Hotel Kompas.

An even better option is to take the ferry that shuttles half-hourly in summer to lush **Lokrum Island** (return 35KN), a national park with a rocky nudist beach (marked FKK), a botanical garden and the ruins of a medieval Benedictine monastery.

Activities

Adriatic Kayak Tours (☎ 312 770; www.kayakcroatia.com; Frankopanska 6) offers a great series of kayak tours for experienced and beginning kayakers. Guided tours to and around Lokrum and other islands start at €47.

Tours

Atlas travel agency offers full-day tours to Mostar (€43), Međugorje (€37.50), the Elafiti Islands (€40) and Mljet (€53.50), among other destinations. Its tour to Montenegro (€45.50) is a good alternative to taking the morning bus to Montenegro, since the bus schedules make a day trip there impractical.

Festivals & Events

Feast of St Blaise 3 February.
Carnival February.
Dubrovnik Summer Festival Mid-July to mid-August. A major cultural event, with over 100 performances at different venues in the Old Town.

Sleeping

Private accommodation is generally the best option in Dubrovnik, but beware of the scramble of private owners at the bus station or Jadrolinija wharf. Some offer what they say they offer, others are rip-off artists. Be aware that most accommodation in the Old Town involves sharing the flat with the owner's family. The owners listed below meet you at the station if you call in advance. Otherwise head to any of the travel agencies or the Turistička Zajednica. Expect to pay about €28 to €50 a room in high season.

OLD TOWN
Midrange

Apartments van Bloemen (Map p212; ☎ 323 433, 091 33 24 106; www.karmendu.tk; Bandureva 1; apt €75-110; 🔀) This is Dubrovnik's most personal and original accommodation, with a great location in the Old Town. All four apartments are beautifully decorated with original art; three of them sleep three people comfortably.

Hotel Stari Grad (Map p212; ☎ 322 244; www.hotelstarigrad.com; Palmoticeva; s/d €91/130; 🔀) Staying in the heart of the Old Town in a lovingly restored stone building is an unmatchable experience. There are only eight rooms, each one furnished with taste and a sense of comfort. From the rooftop terrace, you have a marvellous view over the town. Prices stay the same all year.

Top End

Pucić Palace (Map p212; ☎ 324 111; www.thepucicpal ace.com; Od Puća 1; s/d €370/584; **P** 🞨) Right in the heart of the Old Town, these palatial digs have been designed and decorated to the cutting edge of fashion. Warm and cosy it's not but the countesses and moguls that stay here probably don't care.

OUTSIDE THE OLD TOWN

Budget

Begović Boarding House (Map pp210-11; ☎ 435 191; bega@beg-board.com; Primorska 17; per person 110KN) A long-time favourite with our readers, this friendly place in Lapad has three rooms with shared bathroom and three apartments. There's a terrace out the back with a good view. Breakfast is an additional 30KN.

Apartments Silva Kusjanović (Map pp210-11; ☎ 435 071, 098 244 639; silva_dubrovnik@yahoo.com; Kardinala Stepinća 62; per person 100KN) Sweet Silva has four large apartments that can hold four to eight beds. All have terraces with gorgeous views and barbecues.

Solitudo (Map pp210-11; ☎ 448 200; Iva Dulčića 39; per person/camp site €5.40/10.20) This pretty and renovated camping ground is within walking distance of the beach.

YHA hostel (Map pp210-11; ☎ 423 241; dubrovnik@ hfhs.hr; Vinka Sagrestana 3; B&B/half board €14.65/18.65) It's not exactly restful here, but there are plenty of bars and cafés in the vicinity.

Midrange

Hotel Lapad (Map pp210-11; ☎ 432 922; www.hotel -lapad.hr; Lapadska Obala 37; s/d €87/112; 🞨 🞨) This hotel is a solid, old limestone structure with simple but cheerful rooms and an outdoor swimming pool.

Hotel Sumratin (Map pp210-11; ☎ 436 333; hot-sum ratin@du.t-com.hr; Šetalište Kralja Zvonimira 31; s/d €64/ 111; **P**) About 200m from the water, this calm hotel offers good value for money.

Hotel Petka (Map pp210-11; ☎ 410 500; www.hotel petka.com; Obala Stjepana Radića 38; s/d from €80/114; **P** 🞨) Situated opposite the Jadrolinija ferry landing, Hotel Petka won't bowl you over with charm but the location is great for getting back and forth to the ferry.

Eating

OLD TOWN

There are dozens of places to chow down in the Old Town but there's not a great deal of variety. Pizza, pasta, pasta, pizza. Yawn.

Dundo Maroje (Map p212; ☎ 321 445; Kovačka; meals from 75KN) Nothing adventurous here, but everything is cooked exactly as it should be. The menu is wide ranging with an accent on seafood.

Kamenice (Map p212; ☎ 421 499; Gundulićeva poljana 8; meals from 50KN) Portions are huge at this convivial hang-out known for its mussels. Plus, its outdoor terrace is on one of Dubrovnik's more scenic squares.

Mea Culpa (Map p212; ☎ 323 430; Za Rokom 3; pizzas from 30KN) Everyone agrees that the best pizza in town is served here beneath the Tiffany lights. The crowd is young and relaxed.

LAPAD

The better dining is in Lapad.

Atlantic (Map pp210-11; ☎ 098 435 89 11; Kardinala Stepinca 42; meals from 60KN) The homemade pasta and vegetarian lasagne are outstanding here, even if the ambience is not terribly atmospheric.

Levenat (Map pp210-11; ☎ 435 352; Šetalište Nika i Meda Pucića 15; meals 65-180KN) The interior of this eatery is classic and the outdoor terrace has a smashing view. The food is superb and there's even a vegetarian plate.

Pergola (Map pp210-11; ☎ 436 848; Kralja Tomislava 1; meals from 60KN) This is another consistently satisfying place with an outdoor terrace and good seafood.

Eden (Map pp210-11; ☎ 435 133; Kardinala Stepinca 54; meals 75-110KN) The leafy terrace upstairs is an agreeable spot to enjoy meat, pasta or fish dishes.

Drinking

Bars sprang up like mushrooms on Bana Josipa Jelačića near the YHA hostel but these days thirsty young singles fill the cafés and terraces on Bunićeva in the Old Town.

The ineffably romantic Cafe Buza (Map p212) offers nothing but drinks served on outdoor tables overlooking the sea. It's just outside the city walls and you can find it by looking for the 'Cold Drinks' sign and going through a hole in the walls. Get there for the sunset.

Troubadur (Map p212; ☎ 412 154; Gundulićeva Poljana) It's a long-time favourite for jazz; the ambience is joyous, especially when the owner, Marko, plays.

La Boheme (☎ 312 688; Dubrovačkih branitelja 29) Located in the midst of gardens, this trendy cocktail bar is a relaxing spot to while away the evening hours.

Entertainment

The summer months are chock-full of concerts and folk dancing. The tourist office has the full schedule.

Open-air folklore shows are conducted in front of St Blaise's Church (p211) at 11am on Sunday through May, June and September.

Latino Club Fuego (Map pp210–11; Dubrovačkih branitelja 2) Despite the name, at this disco you'll find a gamut of dance music that includes techno and pop.

Open-air cinema (Map pp210–11; Kumičića) In Lapad, this spot allows you to watch movies, in their original language, by starlight.

Labirint (Map p212; ☎ 322 222; Svetog Dominika 2) A vast restaurant, nightclub, disco and cabaret complex that caters to high rollers. It can chew through your wallet pretty quickly unless you just come for a romantic cocktail on the roof terrace.

Getting There & Away

AIR

Daily flights to/from Zagreb are operated by **Croatia Airlines** (Map p212; ☎ 413 777; Brsalje 9). The fare runs about 400KN one way, higher in peak season; the trip takes about an hour.

There are also nonstop flights to Rome, London and Manchester between April and October.

BOAT

In addition to the **Jadrolinija** (Map pp210–11; ☎ 418 000; Gruž) coastal ferry north to Hvar, Split and Rijeka (Rijeka–Split 12½ hours, Split–Hvar 1¾ hours, Hvar–Korcula 3¾ hours, Korcula–Dubrovnik 3¼ hours; deck passage from Rijeka to Dubrovnik low/high season is €26/31 – these prices can change by season and there are many different prices according to the comfort level), there's a local ferry that leaves from Dubrovnik for Sobra on Mljet Island (26KN to 32KN, 2½ hours) throughout the year. In summer there are two ferries a day. There are several ferries a day year-round to the outlying islands of Šipanska, Sugjuraj, Lopud and Koločep. See also the Central Dalmatia Ferry Routes Map (p198).

Jadroagent (Map pp210–11; ☎ 419 009; fax 419 029; Radića 32) handles ticketing for most international boats from Croatia.

For information on international connections see p403.

BUS

Buses from Dubrovnik include:

Destination	Cost (KN)	Duration	Frequency
Korčula	77	3hr	1 daily
Mostar	77	3hr	2 daily
Orebić	77	2½hr	1 daily
Rijeka	372	12hr	4 daily
Sarajevo	160	5hr	1 daily
Split	82-111	4½hr	14 daily
Zadar	168-210	8hr	7 daily
Zagreb	205-401	11hr	7 daily

There's a daily 11am bus to the Montenegrin border, from where a Montenegro bus takes you to Herceg Novi (60KN, two hours) and on to Kotor (100KN, 2½ hours) and Bar (130KN, three hours). In a busy summer season and at weekends buses out of Dubrovnik can be crowded, so book a ticket well before the scheduled departure time.

Getting Around

Čilipi international airport is 24km southeast of Dubrovnik. The Croatia Airlines airport buses (25KN, 45 minutes) leave from the main **bus station** (Map pp210–11; ☎ 357 088) 1½ hours before flight times. Buses meet Croatia Airlines flights but not all others. A taxi costs around 200KN.

Dubrovnik's buses run frequently and generally on time. The fare is 10KN if you buy from the driver but only 8KN if you buy a ticket at a kiosk.

Around Dubrovnik

Cavtat is a small town that curves around an attractive harbour bordered by nice beaches. Although it does not have as many interesting sights as Dubrovnik, Cavtat does make a good alternative place to stay if Dubrovnik is fully booked out or the summer crowds become overwhelming. Don't miss the memorial chapel to the Račić family designed by Ivan Meštrović.

A day trip can be made from Dubrovnik to this resort town, just to the southeast. Bus 10 to Cavtat runs often from Dubrovnik's bus station and there are three daily boats (see Map p212) during the summer (40KN).

CROATIA

SLAVONIA

For a visitor, Slavonia provides a landscape nearly untouched by tourism yet with some unique wonders. The region's largest town is Osijek, well worth a visit for its remarkable fortress and secession architecture. Throughout the region are peaceful farming villages and an extraordinarily tasty cuisine.

Slavonia is Croatia's breadbasket, a fertile region that yields wheat, corn, sugar beets, sunflowers, alfalfa and clover, in addition to some of Croatia's finest wines. In contrast to the rugged Croatian coastline, the terrain is pancake-flat; as locals say, 'the highest mountain is a cabbage'. Stretching from the Ilova River in the west, over the Sava and Drava basins to the Hungarian border in the north, to the border of Bosnia and Hercegovina in the south and the Serbia and Montenegro border in the east, it's a region of cultural, if not geographic, diversity.

There is a small Hungarian minority in Slavonia, recalling the days when its powerful neighbour to the north ruled the region. Other traces of Hungarian influence include a scattering of baroque architecture in the cities. Few Serbs remain after the bitter war of the early 1990s, but their presence is a powerful and tragic reminder of the ethnic diversity that once characterised Slavonia.

Dangers & Annoyances

Osijek and the surrounding region was heavily laid with land mines during the 1990s war. Although the city and its outskirts along the main road have been de-mined and are completely safe, it would be unwise to wander through the swampland north of the Drava River which leads to Kopački Rit Nature Park.

In summer, the mosquitoes are bloodthirsty little devils, chewing through every bit of flesh they can find. Wear long sleeves and trousers or slather on a lot of insect repellent after dark.

OSIJEK

☎ 031 / pop 114,600

Photographs of Osijek before the 1990s reveal a relaxed river city of wide avenues, leafy parks and stately 19th-century Viennese architecture. The avenues and parks are still there, but the fine old mansions were badly scarred by the shells that fell on the town as part of the 1991 Yugoslav offensive.

Although many major buildings along the avenues were patched up and restored to their former lustre, the pits and pockmarks on other buildings are grim reminders of the war that ravaged eastern Slavonia in the early 1990s.

Nevertheless, through the general aura of decay you can still perceive the resilient spirit of the city. A shortage of decent accommodation makes a visit here problematic and expensive, but if you're willing to put up with the hassle there's a pleasant waterfront promenade and an imposing 18th-century fortress on the hill, and you can swim in the Drava River.

Orientation

Stretching along the southern bank of the Drava River, Osijek is composed of three settlements: the Gornji Grad (Upper Town) the Donji Grad (Lower Town) and the 18th-century fortress, Tvrđa. The bus station and train station are adjacent in the southern part of the Gornji Grad, and you'll find most of the sights, hotels, cafés and shopping between the river and the train and bus stations.

The main shopping street is Kapucinska, which becomes Europska Avenija in the east, bordered by three parks planted with chestnut and linden trees. A promenade stretches along the riverbanks until the city's outskirts.

Information

INTERNET ACCESS

Internet Caffe (☎ 204 250; Sunčana 18; per hr 20KN; ⏰ 7am-7pm)

LEFT LUGGAGE

Garderoba (bus station; ⏰ 7am-8pm Mon-Sat, to 4pm Sun)

MONEY

Croatia Express (train station) Changes money.

Privredna Banka (Kapucinska 25) Has an ATM.

Zagrebačka Banka (Strossmayera 1) In town; you can change money here.

POST

Main post office (Kardinala Alojzja Stepinca 17) Here you can change money, make phone calls and get cash advances on MasterCard.

TOURIST INFORMATION

Tourist office (☎ /fax 203 755; www.tzosijek.hr; Županijska 2) Has brochures and maps. Ask for the helpful *Gradski Vodić*, which lists each month's events and has dozens of useful phone numbers.

TRAVEL AGENCIES

Generalturist (☎ 211 500; Kapucinska 39) Sells air tickets and package tours to European destinations.

OK Tours (☎ 212 815; www.ok-tours.hr; Slobode trg 8) Good local information and some private accommodation.

Panturist (☎ 214 388; www.panturist.hr; Kapucinska 19) The largest travel agency in Slavonia; runs buses to the coast as well as Germany, Switzerland and Bosnia and Hercegovina. It sells bus and air tickets and arranges accommodation along the Adriatic coast.

Sights

TVRĐA

Built under Habsburg rule as a defence against Turkish attacks, the 18th-century fortress was relatively undamaged during the recent war, leaving its baroque architecture intact. Because most of it was designed solely by the Austrian architect Maximilian de Gosseau between 1712 and 1721, the buildings present a remarkable architectural unity.

The main square, Trg Svetog Trojstva, is marked by the elaborate **Holy Trinity Monument**, erected in 1729 to commemorate the victims of the 15th-century plague that swept through the city.

The **Museum of Slavonia** (Muzej Slavonije Osijek; ☎ 208 501; Trg Svetog Trojstva 6; adult/student 12/6KN; ☾ 10am-1pm), on the eastern side of the square, is housed in the former 1702 Magistrate Building. It traces Slavonia's long history, beginning with implements from the Bronze Age and displays of coins, pottery, sculpture and utensils from the Roman occupation.

GORNJI GRAD

The towering **Church of St Peter & St Paul** (☎ 369 626; ☾ 7am-noon & 3-8pm) looms over Trg Ante Starčevića. The 90m-high tower is the second highest in Croatia, surpassed only by the cathedral in Zagreb. Although often referred to as the 'Cathedral' because of its size and majesty, in fact this brick neo-Gothic structure is a parish church which was built at the end of the 19th century. The style is Viennese, from the overall design to the 40 stained-glass windows inside, as well as the stonework from the Viennese

sculptor Eduard Hauser. The wall paintings have long been attributed to Croatian painter Mirko Rački, but recent scholarship indicates that they were in fact executed by one of his disciples.

The **Gallery of Fine Arts** (☎ 213 587; Europska Avenija 9; adult/student 10/5KN; ☾ 9am-1pm & 5-8pm Tue-Fri) is housed in an elegant 19th-century mansion and contains a collection of paintings by Slavonian artists and some contemporary Croatian works.

Sleeping

There are no camping grounds or hostels and only limited private accommodation in Osijek. Ask at OK Tours.

Hotel Central (☎ 283 399; www.hotel-central-os.hr; Trg Ante Starčevića 6; s/d €47.50/73) This has the most character of any of the hotels, with its stunning Art Deco lobby and café. Rooms are comfortable but could use a face-lift.

Waldinger (☎ 250 450; www.waldinger.hr; Županijska 8; s/d €100/126) Osijek's most elegant tea-room-art gallery (where the pastries are outstanding) has recently expanded into a smart little guesthouse. The rooms don't quite equal the lavishness of the tearoom (or the assertive prices) but they'll do nicely.

Hotel Osijek (☎ 201 333; Šamačka 4; s/d from 400/500KN) This hotel could use a makeover but at least some rooms overlook the Drava. Other than that, there's nothing that special here.

Hotel Ritam (☎ 310 310; www.hotel-ritam.hr; Kozjačka 76; s/d €48/62) This new place offers large, bright rooms with modern furnishings and satellite TV. Some rooms have a balcony.

Eating

Food is the strong point of Osijek and it offers much better value for money than the accommodation available here. The cuisine is spicy and strongly influenced by neighbouring Hungary, although Slavonia does produce its own brand of hot paprika. As elsewhere in Croatia, there is a strong emphasis on meat but you can also find freshwater fish, which is often served in a delicious stew called *riblji paprikaš*, with noodles.

Confucius (☎ 210 104; Kapucinska 34; meals from 65KN) The people of Osijek are probably the only Croats with enough of a taste for spicy food to support a Szechuan Chinese restaurant. The décor is Chinese-red and the dishes are authentic.

CROATIA

Bijelo Plavi (☎ 571 000; Divaltova 8; meals from 90KN) Visiting businesspeople come here for a meaty meal in a slightly formal atmosphere. It's about 2km southeast of the train station.

Slavonska Kuća (☎ 208 277; Kamila Firingera 26, Tvrđa; meals from 90KN) One of the best places to try *riblji paprikaš* as well as other regional specialities, it is in an appealingly rustic old house with wooden booths and lace curtains. Wash your meal down with Krauthaker, a fruity white *graševina* wine.

Restaurant Muller (☎ 204 270; Trg Križanića 9; meals from 70KN) The culinary concept is 'international', with good old standards like roast turkey plus a smattering of local specialities.

There's a daily **vegetable market** (Trg LJ Gaja) open until mid-afternoon.

Getting There & Away

Osijek is a major transport centre, with buses and trains arriving and departing in all directions.

BUS

Following are some of the international buses that depart from Osijek. Many more buses leave for Germany than can be listed here. To get to Sarajevo, take the bus to Tuzla and get a connecting bus (€7, 3½ hours); from Vukovar you can catch another bus to Belgrade.

Destination	Cost (KN)	Duration	Frequency
Belgrade	92	3¾hr	daily
Mostar	220	10hr	daily
Tuzla	85	3½hr	daily
Vienna	418	10hr	twice weekly
Zürich	665	19½hr	Sat & Sun

The following domestic buses depart from Osijek.

Destination	Cost (KN)	Duration	Frequency
Bizovačke Toplice	21	25min	19 daily
Đakovo	27	40min	17 daily
Požega	52	2hr	5 daily
Rijeka	175	8¾hr	1 daily
Slavonski Brod	50	1¾hr	20 daily
Split	295	11hr	1 daily
Vukovar	26	40min	14 daily
Zagreb	99-132	4hr	8 daily

TRAIN

There are two trains per day in either direction between Pećs (Hungary) and Osijek (454KN, three hours). The trains from Osijek connect to Budapest (162KN, 7½ hours).

The following domestic trains depart from Osijek.

Destination	Cost (KN)	Duration	Frequency
Bizovačke Toplice	11	15min	13 daily
Đakovo	19	40min	6 daily
Požega	44	2½hr	3 daily
Rijeka	162	8hr	2 daily
Šibenik	199	12hr	1 daily
Slavonski Brod	53	1½hr	15 daily
Zagreb	117	4hr	5 daily

Getting Around

Osijek has a tram line that dates from 1884 and makes transportation within the city easy. The fare is 7KN each way if you buy from the driver, or you can buy a *karnet* of 10 tickets for 55KN at a Tisak news outlet.

For visitors, the most useful tram lines are the No 2, which connects the train and bus station with Trg Ante Starčevića in the town centre and the No 1, which connects the town centre with Tvrđa.

CROATIA DIRECTORY

ACCOMMODATION

Accommodation listings in this guide have been arranged in order of preference. Many hotels, rooms and camping grounds issue their prices in euros but some places to stay have stuck with the kuna. Although you can usually pay with either currency, we have listed the primary currency the establishment uses in setting its prices.

Along the Croatian coast accommodation is priced according to three seasons, which tend to vary from place to place. Generally October to May are the cheapest months, June and September are midpriced, but count on paying top price for the peak season, which runs for a six-week period in July and August. Prices quoted in this chapter are for the peak period and do not include 'residence tax', which runs from about 4KN to 7.50KN depending on the location and season. Deduct about 25% if

---

PRACTICALITIES

■ Electrical supply is 220V to 240V/50Hz to 60Hz. Croatia uses the standard European round-pronged plugs.

■ Widely read newspapers include *Vecernji List, Vjesnik, Jutarnji list, Slobodna Dalmacija* and the *Feral Tribune*. The most popular weeklies are *Nacional* and *Globus*.

■ The radio station HR2 broadcasts traffic reports in English every hour on the hour from July to mid-September; Croatian Radio broadcasts news in English on 88.9, 91.3 and 99.3FM.

■ Croatia uses the metric system.

■ Mobile phones are GSM 900/1800, which is compatible with the rest of Europe and Australia, but not with the North American GSM 1900.

■ The video system is PAL.

---

you come in June, the beginning of July and September, about 35% for May and October and about 50% for all other times. Note that prices for rooms in Zagreb are pretty much constant all year and that many hotels on the coast close in winter. Some places offer half board, which is bed and two meals a day, usually breakfast and one other meal. It can be good value if you're not too fussy about what you eat.

Accommodation takes the largest chunk of a travel budget, and costs vary widely depending on the season. If you travel in March you'll quite easily find a private room for 100KN per person, but prices climb upward to double that in July and August.

Camping

Nearly 100 camping grounds are scattered along the Croatian coast. Opening times of camping grounds generally run from mid-April to September, give or take a few weeks. The exact times change from year to year, so it's wise to call in advance if you're arriving at either end of the season.

Many camping grounds, especially in Istria, are gigantic 'autocamps' with restaurants, shops and row upon row of caravans. Expect to pay up to 100KN for a camp site

at some of the larger establishments but half that at most other camping grounds, in addition to 38KN to 48KN per person.

Nudist camping grounds (marked FKK) are among the best because their secluded locations ensure peace and quiet. However, bear in mind that freelance camping is officially prohibited. A good site for camping information is www.camping.hr.

Hostels

The **Croatian YHA** (☎ 01-48 47 472; www.hfhs.hr; Dežmanova 9, Zagreb) operates youth hostels in Dubrovnik, Zadar, Zagreb and Pula. Non-members pay an additional 10KN per person daily for a stamp on a welcome card; six stamps entitles you to a membership. Prices in this chapter are for high season during July and August; prices fall the rest of the year. The Croatian YHA can also provide information about private youth hostels in Krk, Zadar, Dubrovnik and Zagreb.

Hotels

Hotels are ranked from one to five stars with the most in the two- and three-star range. Features, such as satellite TV, direct-dial phones, high-tech bathrooms, minibars and air-con, are standard in four- and five-star hotels, and one-star hotels have at least a bathroom in the room. Many two- and three-star hotels offer satellite TV but you'll find better décor in the higher categories. Unfortunately the country is saddled with too many 1970s concrete-block hotels, built to warehouse package tourists, but there are more and more options for those looking for smaller and more personal establishments. Prices for hotels in this chapter are for the pricey six-week period that begins in mid-July and lasts until the end of August. During this period some hotels may demand a surcharge for stays of less than four nights but this surcharge is usually waived during the rest of the year, when prices drop steeply. In Zagreb prices are the same all year.

Breakfast is included in the prices quoted for hotels in this chapter, unless stated otherwise.

Private Rooms

Private rooms or apartments are the best accommodation in Croatia. Service is excellent and the rooms are usually extremely well kept. You may very well be greeted by offers of *sobe* as you step off your bus and boat but rooms are most often arranged by travel agencies or the local tourist office. Booking through an agency is somewhat more expensive but at least you'll know who to complain to if things go wrong.

The most expensive rooms are three star and have private bathrooms, in establishments resembling small guesthouses. Some of the better ones are listed in this chapter. It's best to call in advance as the owners will often meet you at the bus station or ferry dock. In a two-star room, the bathroom is shared with one other room; in a one-star room, the bathroom is shared with two other rooms or with the owner who is usually an elderly widow. Breakfast is usually not included but can sometimes be arranged for an additional 30KN; be sure to clarify whether the price agreed upon is per person or per room. If you're travelling in a small group it may be worthwhile to get a small apartment with cooking facilities, which are widely available along the coast.

It makes little sense to price-shop from agency to agency since prices are fixed by the local tourist association. Whether you deal with the owner directly or book through an agency, you'll pay a 30% surcharge for stays of less than four nights and sometimes 50% or even 100% more for a one-night stay, although you may be able to get them to waive the surcharge if you arrive in the low season. Prices for private rooms in this chapter are for a four-night stay in peak season.

ACTIVITIES
Diving
The clear waters and varied underwater life of the Adriatic have led to a flourishing dive industry along the coast. Cave diving is the real speciality in Croatia; night diving and wreck diving are also offered and there are coral reefs in some places, but they are in rather deep water. You must get a permit for a boat dive: go to the harbour captain in any port with your passport, certification card and 100KN. Permission is valid for a year. If you dive with a dive centre, they will take care of the paperwork. Most of the coastal resorts mentioned in this chapter have dive shops. See **Diving Croatia** (www.diving-hrs.hr) for contact information.

Hiking
Risnjak National Park at Crni Lug, 12km west of Delnice between Zagreb and Rijeka, is a good hiking area in summer. Hiking is advisable only from late spring to early autumn. The steep gorges and beech forests of Paklenica National Park, 40km northeast of Zadar, also offer excellent hiking.

Kayaking
There are countless possibilities for anyone carrying a folding sea kayak, especially among the Elafiti and Kornati Islands. Lopud makes a good launch point from which to explore the Elafiti Islands; there's a daily ferry from Dubrovnik. Sali on Dugi Otok is close to the Kornati Islands and is connected by daily ferry to Zadar.

Rock Climbing
The karstic stone of Croatia's coast provides excellent climbing opportunities. Paklenica National Park has the widest range of routes – nearly 400 – for all levels of experience. Spring, summer and autumn are good seasons to climb, but in winter you'll be fighting the fierce *bura* (cold northeasterly wind). Other popular climbing spots include the rocks surrounding Baška on Krk Island, which can be climbed year-round (although if you come in summer, you can combine climbing with a beach holiday). Brela on the Makarska Riviera also allows climbing and beach-bumming, but in winter there's a strong *bura*. Also on the Makarska Riviera is the wall from Baška Voda to Makarska on Mt Biokovo, with 200m to 400m routes. For more information, contact the **Croatian Mountaineering Association** (☎ /fax 01-48 24 142; http://hps.inet.hr; Kozaričeva 22, 10000 Zagreb).

Yachting
There's no better way to appreciate the Croatian Adriatic than by boat. The long, rugged islands off Croatia's mountainous coast all the way from Istria to Dubrovnik make this a yachting paradise. Fine, deep channels with abundant anchorage and steady winds attract yachties from around the world. Throughout the region there are quaint little ports where you can get provisions, and yachts can tie up right in the middle of everything.

There are 40 marinas along the coast, some with more facilities than others. Every coastal town mentioned in this chapter has a marina, from little Sali on Dugi Otok to the large marinas in Opatija, Zadar, Split and Dubrovnik. Most marinas are open throughout the year but it's best to check first. A good source of information is **Udruženje Nautičkog Tourism** (Association of Nautical Tourism; ☎ 051-209 147; fax 051-216 033; Bulevar Oslobođenja 23, 51000 Rijeka). You could also try the **Adriatic Croatia International** (ACI; ☎ 051-271 288; www.aci-club.hr; M Tita 51, Opatija), which represents about half the marinas.

Although you can row, motor or sail any vessel up to 3m long without authorisation, for larger boats you'll need to get authorisation from the harbour master at your port of entry, which will be at any harbour open to international traffic. Come equipped with a boat certificate, documents proving your sailing qualifications, insurance documents and money.

Yachting enthusiasts may wish to charter their own boat. Experienced sailors can charter a yacht on a 'bareboat' basis or you can pay for the services of a local captain for a 'skippered' boat. **Sunsail** (☎ 0870 777 0313 in UK, ☎ 888 350 3568 in USA; www.sunsail.com) is an international operator with offices in the UK and the USA. It offers bareboat and skippered charters from Pula and Rogoznica near Trogir. In the UK, you could also try **Cosmos Yachting** (☎ 0800 376 9070; www.cosmos yachting.com), which offers charters out of Dubrovnik, Pula, Rovinj, Split, Trogir and Zadar, or **Nautilus Yachting** (☎ 01732-867 445; www.nautilus-yachting.com), which offers rentals from Pula and Split. The price depends upon the size of the boat, the number of berths and the season.

An interesting option for sailing enthusiasts is **Katarina Line** (☎ 051-272 110; www.katarina -line.hr; Tita 75, Opatija), which offers week-long cruises from Opatija to Krk, Rab, Dugi Otok, Lošinj and Cres, or cruises from Split to Dubrovnik that pass the Kornati Islands. Prices run from €370 to €490 a week per person depending on the season and cabin class and include half board. For specific tours in individual regions, see Tours in the destination sections.

BOOKS

Lonely Planet's *Croatia* is a comprehensive guide to the country. There's also Zoë Brân's *After Yugoslavia*, part of the Lonely Planet Journeys series, which recounts the author's return to a troubled region.

As Croatia emerges from the shadow of the former Yugoslavia, several writers of Croatian origin have taken the opportunity to rediscover their roots. *Plum Brandy: Croatian Journeys* by Josip Novakovich is a sensitive exploration of his family's Croatian background. *Croatia: Travels in Undiscovered Country* by Tony Fabijancic recounts the life of rural folks in a new Croatia. *Café Europa* is a series of essays by a Croatian journalist, Slavenka Drakulić, which provides an inside look at life in the country since independence. Marcus Tanner's *Croatia: A Nation Forged in War* provides an excellent overview of Croatia's history.

BUSINESS HOURS

Banking and post office hours are 7.30am to 7pm on weekdays and 8am to noon on Saturday. Many shops are open 8am to 7pm on weekdays and until 2pm on Saturday. Along the coast life is more relaxed; shops and offices frequently close around noon for an afternoon break and reopen around 4pm. Restaurants are open long hours, often noon to midnight, with Sunday closings outside of peak season. Cafés are generally open from 10am to midnight, bars from 9pm to 2am. Internet cafés are also open long hours, usually seven days a week.

CUSTOMS

Travellers can bring their personal effects into the country, along with 1L of liquor, 1L of wine, 500g of coffee, 200 cigarettes and 50mL of perfume. The import or export of kuna is limited to 15,000KN per person.

DISABLED TRAVELLERS

Because of the number of wounded war veterans, more attention is being paid to the needs of disabled travellers. Public toilets at bus stations, train stations, airports and large public venues are usually wheelchair accessible. Large hotels are wheelchair accessible but very little private accommodation is. The bus and train stations in Zagreb, Zadar, Rijeka, Split and Dubrovnik are wheelchair accessible but the local Jadrolinija ferries are not. For further information, get in touch with **Savez Organizacija Invalida Hrvatske** (☎ /fax 01-48 29 394; Savska cesta 3; 10000 Zagreb).

CROATIA

EMBASSIES & CONSULATES
Croatian Embassies & Consulates

Croatian embassies and consulates abroad include:

Australia Canberra (☎ 02-6286 6988; 14 Jindalee Cres, O'Malley, ACT 2601)

Canada Ottawa (☎ 613-562 7820; 229 Chapel St, Ottawa, Ontario K1N 7Y6)

France Paris (☎ 01 5370 0287; 2 rue de Lubeck, Paris)

Germany Berlin (☎ 030-219 15 514; Ahornstrasse 4, Berlin 10787); Bonn (☎ 022-895 29 20; Rolandstrasse 52, Bonn 53179)

Ireland Dublin (☎ 1 4767 181; Adelaide Chambers, Peter St, Dublin)

Netherlands The Hague (☎ 70 362 36 38; Amaliastraat 16; The Hague)

New Zealand Auckland (☎ 09-836 5581; 131 Lincoln Rd, Henderson, Box 83200, Edmonton, Auckland)

South Africa Pretoria (☎ 012-342 1206; 1160 Church St, 0083 Colbyn, Pretoria)

UK London (☎ 020-7387 2022; 21 Conway St, London W1P 5HL)

USA Washington DC (☎ 202-588 5899; www.croatiaemb.org; 2343 Massachusetts Ave NW, Washington, DC 20008)

Embassies & Consulates in Croatia

The following addresses are in Zagreb (area code ☎ 01):

Albania (Map pp150-1; ☎ 48 10 679; Jurišićeva 2a)

Australia (☎ 48 91 200; www.auembassy.hr; Kaptol Centar, Nova Ves 11) North of the centre.

Bosnia & Hercegovina (☎ 46 83 761; Torbarova 9) Northwest of the centre.

Bulgaria (☎ 48 23 336; Novi Goljak 25) Northwest of the centre.

Canada (Map pp150-1; ☎ 48 81 200; zagreb@dfait-maeci.gc.ca; Prilaz Gjure Deželića 4)

Czech Republic (Map pp150-1; ☎ 61 77 239; Savska 41)

France (Map pp150-1; 48 93 680; consulat@ambafrance.hr; Hebrangova 2)

Germany (☎ 61 58 105; www.deutschebotschaft-zagreb.hr in German; ul grada Vukovara 64) South of the centre.

Hungary (☎ 48 22 051; Pantovčak 128/I) Northwest of the centre.

Ireland (Map pp150-1 ☎ 66 74 455; Turinina 3)

Netherlands (Map pp150-1; ☎ 46 84 880; nlgovzag@zg.t-com.hr; Medveščak 56)

New Zealand (☎ 61 51 382; Trg Stjepana Radića 3) Southwest of the centre.

Poland (Map pp150-1; ☎ 48 99 444; Krležin Gvozd 3)

Romania (☎ 45 77 550; roamb@zg.t-com.hr; Mlinarska ul 43) North of the centre.

Serbia & Montenegro (☎ 45 79 067; Pantovčak 245) Northwest of the centre.

Slovakia (Map pp150-1; ☎ 48 48 941; Prilaz Gjure Deželića 10)

Slovenia (Map pp150-1; ☎ 63 11 000; Savska 41)

UK (☎ 60 09 100; I Lučića 4) East of the centre.

USA (☎ 66 12 200; www.usembassy.hr; Ul Thomasa Jeffersona 2) South of the centre.

FESTIVALS & EVENTS

In July and August there are summer festivals in Dubrovnik, Split, Pula and Zagreb. Dubrovnik's summer music festival emphasises classical music with concerts in churches around town, while Pula hosts a variety of pop and classical stars in the Roman amphitheatre and also hosts a film festival. Mardi Gras celebrations have recently been revived in many towns with attendant parades and festivities, but nowhere is it celebrated with more verve than in Rijeka.

GAY & LESBIAN TRAVELLERS

Homosexuality has been legal in Croatia since 1977 and is tolerated, but not welcomed with open arms. Public displays of affection between members of the same sex may be met with hostility, especially outside major cities. Exclusively gay clubs are a rarity outside Zagreb, but many of the large discos attract a mixed crowd. Raves are also a good way for gays to meet.

On the coast, gays gravitate to Rovinj, Hvar, Split and Dubrovnik and tend to frequent naturist beaches. In Zagreb, the last Saturday in June is Gay Pride Zagreb day, an excellent opportunity to connect with the local gay scene.

Most Croatian websites devoted to the gay scene are in Croatian only, but a good starting point is the English-language www.touristinfo.gay.hr which has articles on the gay scene and links to other relevant websites.

HOLIDAYS

New Year's Day 1 January
Epiphany 6 January
Easter Monday March/April
Labour Day 1 May
Corpus Christi 10 June
Day of Antifascist Resistance 22 June; marks the outbreak of resistance in 1941
Statehood Day 25 June
Victory Day and National Thanksgiving Day 5 August
Feast of the Assumption 15 August

Independence Day 8 October
All Saints' Day 1 November
Christmas 25 & 26 December

INTERNET ACCESS

Internet cafés are springing up everywhere. The going rate is about 25KN per hour, and connections are usually good. They can be busy, especially with kids playing online games.

INTERNET RESOURCES

Croatia Homepage (www.hr.hr) Hundreds of links to everything you want to know about Croatia.

Croatia Traveller (www.croatiatraveller.com) All ferry schedules, flights, forums, accommodation, sightseeing and travel planning.

Dalmatia Travel Guide (www.dalmacija.net) All about Dalmatia, including reservations for private accommodation.

Find Croatia (www.findcroatia.com) More Croatia links, with an emphasis on tourism and outdoor activities.

MONEY
Credit Cards

Amex, MasterCard, Visa and Diners Club cards are widely accepted in large hotels, stores and many restaurants, but don't count on cards to pay for private accommodation or meals in small restaurants. ATMs accepting MasterCard, Maestro, Cirrus, Plus and Visa are available in most bus and train stations, airports, all major cities and most small towns. Many branches of Privredna Banka have ATMs that allow cash withdrawals on an Amex card.

Currency

The currency is the kuna. Banknotes are in denominations of 500, 200, 100, 50, 20, 10 and 5. Each kuna is divided into 100 lipa in coins of 50, 20 and 10. Many places exchange money, all with similar rates.

Moneychangers

Exchange offices may deduct a commission of 1% to change cash or travellers cheques, but some banks do not. Hungarian currency is difficult to change in Croatia and Croatian currency can be difficult to exchange in some neighbouring countries.

Tax

A 22% VAT is usually imposed upon most purchases and services, and is included in the price. If your purchases exceed 500KN

in one shop you can claim a refund upon leaving the country. Ask the merchant for the paperwork, but don't be surprised if they don't have it.

Tipping

If you're served well at a restaurant, you should round up the bill, but a service charge is always included. (Don't leave money on the table.) Bar bills and taxi fares can also be rounded up. Tour guides on day excursions expect to be tipped.

POST

Mail sent to Poste Restante, 10000 Zagreb, Croatia, is held at the **main post office** (Branimirova 4; ☉ 24hr Mon-Sat, 1pm-midnight Sun) next to the Zagreb train station. A good coastal address to use is c/o Poste Restante, Main Post Office, 21000 Split, Croatia. If you have an Amex card, most Atlas travel agencies will hold your mail.

TELEPHONE
Mobile Phones

Croatia uses GSM 900/1800 and the two mobile networks are T-Mobile and VIP. If your mobile is compatible, SIM cards are widely available and cost about 400KN.

Phone Codes

To call Croatia from abroad, dial your international access code, ☎ 385 (Croatia's country code), the area code (without the initial zero) and the local number. When calling from one region to another within Croatia, use the initial zero. Phone numbers with the prefix 060 are free and numbers that begin with 09 are mobile numbers which are billed at a much higher rate – figure on about 6KN a minute. When in Croatia, dial ☎ 00 to speak to the international operator.

Phonecards

To make a phone call from Croatia, go to the town's main post office. You'll need a

EMERGENCY NUMBERS
▪ Ambulance ☎ 94
▪ Fire Service ☎ 93
▪ Police ☎ 92
▪ Roadside Assistance ☎ 987

phonecard to use public telephones, but calls using a phonecard are about 50% more expensive. Phonecards are sold according to *impulsa* (units), and you can buy cards of 25 (15KN), 50 (30KN), 100 (50KN) and 200 (100KN) units. These can be purchased at any post office and most tobacco shops and newspaper kiosks.

TOURIST INFORMATION

The **Croatian National Tourist Board** (☎ 45 56 455; www.htz.hr; Iblerov trg 10, Importanne Gallerija, 10000 Zagreb) is a good source of information with an excellent website. There are regional tourist offices that supervise tourist development, and municipal tourist offices which have free brochures and good information on local events. Some arrange private accommodation.

Tourist information is also dispensed by commercial travel agencies such as **Atlas** (www.atlas-croatia.com), Croatia Express, Generalturist and Kompas, which also arrange private rooms, sightseeing tours and so on. Ask for the schedule for coastal ferries.

Croatian tourist offices abroad include:
UK (☎ 020-8563 7979; info@cnto.freeserve.co.uk; Croatian National Tourist Office, 2 Lanchesters, 162-64 Fulham Palace Rd, London W6 9ER)
USA (☎ 212-279 8672; cntony@earthlink.net; Croatian National Tourist Office, Suite 4003, 350 Fifth Ave, New York, NY 10118)

VISAS

Visitors from Australia, Canada, New Zealand, the EU and the USA do not require a visa for stays of less than 90 days. For other nationalities, visas are issued free of charge at Croatian consulates. Croatian authorities require all foreigners to register with the local police when they first arrive in a new area of the country, but this is a routine matter that is normally handled by your hotel, hostel or camping ground, or the agency that organises your private accommodation.

TRANSPORT IN CROATIA

GETTING THERE & AWAY

Connections into Croatia are in a constant state of flux with new air and boat routes opening every season. Following is an overview of the major connections into Croatia

but you should refer to the Transport in Western Balkans chapter (p399) for more detail.

Air

The major airports in the country are as follows:
Dubrovnik (code DBV; ☎ 020-773 377; www.airport-dubrovnik.hr)
Pula (code PUY; ☎ 052-530 105; www.airport-pula.com)
Rijeka (code RJK; ☎ 051-842 132)
Split (code SPU; ☎ 021-203 506; www.split-airport.hr)
Zadar (code ZAD; ☎ 023-313 311; www.zadar-airport.hr)
Zagreb (Code ZAG; ☎ 01-62 65 222; www.zagreb-airport.hr)

In addition to domestic connections to Zagreb, Pula has direct flights to London (Gatwick) and Manchester while Split has direct flights to Amsterdam, Frankfurt, Manchester, London (Gatwick and Heathrow), Lyon, Munich, Paris, Prague, Rome (Fiumicino) and Vienna.

Dubrovnik has direct flights to Manchester, London (Gatwick), Glasgow, Nottingham, Paris, Frankfurt, Rome, Tel Aviv and Vienna, as well as flights to Zagreb and Split. Many of the international connections to the coast are available only from April or May to September or October.

Zagreb is connected domestically to Dubrovnik, Split, Pula, Rijeka and Zadar and internationally to all European capitals plus Milan, Munich, Frankfurt, Istanbul and Sarajevo.

Zadar receives domestic flights from Zagreb only.

The following are the major airlines flying into the country:
Adria Airways (code JD; www.adria-airways.com; ☎ 01-48 10 011) Hub Ljubljana.
Aeroflot (code SU; www.aeroflot.ru; ☎ 01-48 72 055) Hub Moscow.
Air Canada (code AC; www.aircanada.ca; ☎ 01-48 22 033) Hub Toronto.
Air France (code AF; www.airfrance.com; ☎ 01-48 37 100) Hub Paris.
Alitalia (code AZ; www.alitalia.it; ☎ 01-48 10 413) Hub Milan.
Austrian Airlines (code OS; www.aua.com; ☎ 062 65 900) Hub Vienna.
British Airways (code BA; www.british-airways.com) Hub London.
Croatia Airlines (code OU; ☎ 01-48 19 633; www.croatiaairlines.hr; Zrinjevac 17, Zagreb) Hub Zagreb.

Croatia's national carrier has recently stepped up its service to serve many more routes.

ČSA (code OK; www.csa.cz; ☎ 01-48 73 301) Hub Prague.

Delta Airlines (code DL; www.delta.com; ☎ 01-48 78 760) Hub Atlanta.

KLM-Northwest (code KL; www.klm.com; ☎ 01-48 78 601) Hub Amsterdam.

LOT Polish Airlines (code LO; www.lot.com; ☎ 01 48 37 500) Hub Warsaw.

Lufthansa (code LH; www.lufthansa.com; ☎ 01-48 73 121) Hub Frankfurt.

Malév Hungarian Airlines (code MA; www.malev.hu; ☎ 01-48 36 935) Hub Budapest.

Turkish Airlines (code TK; www.turkishairlines.com; ☎ 01-49 21 854) Hub Istanbul.

Land

BUS

Bosnia & Hercegovina

There are daily connections from Sarajevo (160KN, five hours, daily) and Mostar (105KN, three hours) to Dubrovnik; from Sarajevo to Split (110KN, seven hours, five daily), which stop at Mostar; and from Sarajevo to Zagreb (199KN, eight hours) and Rijeka (255KN, 10 hours).

Serbia & Montenegro

There's one bus each morning from Zagreb to Belgrade (151KN, six hours). At Bajakovo on the border, a Serbian bus takes you on to Belgrade. The border between Serbia and Montenegro and Croatia is open to visitors, allowing Americans, Australians, Canadians and Brits to enter visa-free. There's a daily bus from Kotor to Dubrovnik (105KN, 2½ hours, daily) that starts at Bar and stops at Herceg Novi.

Slovenia

Slovenia is also well connected with the Istrian coast. There is one weekday bus between Rovinj and Koper (80KN, three hours) and Poreč and Portorož (38KN, 1½ hours), as well as a daily bus in summer from Rovinj to Ljubljana (84KN, 5½ hours) and Piran (73.50KN, 2½ hours).

There are also buses from Ljubljana to Zagreb (112KN, three hours, two daily), Rijeka (83KN, 2½ hours, one daily) and Split (299KN, 10½ hours, one daily).

CAR & MOTORCYCLE

The main highway entry/exit points between Croatia and Hungary are Goričan

(between Nagykanisza and Varaždin), Gola (23km east of Koprivnica), Terezino Polje (opposite Barcs) and Donji Miholjac (7km south of Harkány). There are dozens of crossing points to/from Slovenia, too many to list here. There are 23 border crossings into Bosnia and Hercegovina and 10 into Serbia and Montenegro, including the main Zagreb to Belgrade highway. Major destinations in Bosnia and Hercegovina, such as Sarajevo, Mostar and Međugorje, are accessible from Zagreb, Split and Dubrovnik.

Motorists require vehicle registration papers and the green insurance card to enter Croatia. Bear in mind that if you hire a car in Italy, many insurance companies will not insure you for a trip into Croatia. Border officials know this and may refuse you entry unless permission to drive into Croatia is clearly marked on the insurance documents. Most car-hire companies in Trieste and Venice are familiar with this requirement and will furnish you with the stamp. Otherwise, you must make specific inquiries.

See p227 for road rules and further information.

TRAIN

Serbia & Montenegro

There are five daily trains which connect Zagreb with Belgrade (€17.50, six hours).

Slovenia

There are up to 11 trains daily between Zagreb and Ljubljana (€12.50, 2¼ hours) and four between Rijeka and Ljubljana (€12, three hours). A new service runs daily from Ljubljana to Pula from late June to August (€19, four hours).

Sea

Regular boats from several companies connect Croatia with Italy and Slovenia. See p403 for information about ferries back and forth to Italy. All of the boat-company offices in Split are located inside the ferry terminal.

Lošinska Plovidba (☎ 051-352 200 in Rijeka; www.losinjska-plovidba.hr) runs boats connecting Koper, Slovenia, with Pula (€9, 4½ hours) and Zadar (€23, 13½ hours).

GETTING AROUND
Air

Croatia Airlines is the one and only carrier for flights within Croatia. The price of flights depends on the season and you get better deals if you book ahead. Seniors and people aged under 26 get discounts. There are daily flights between Zagreb and Dubrovnik (256KN, one hour), Pula (185KN, 45 minutes), Split (170KN to 350KN, 45 minutes) and Zadar (170KN to 350KIN, 40 minutes).

Bicycle

Cycling is a great way to see the islands and bikes are fairly easy to hire in most tourist spots. Many tourist offices have helpful maps of cycling routes. Bike lanes are nearly unknown in Croatia, however; you'll need to exercise extreme caution on the many narrow two-lane roads.

Boat

Year-round Jadrolinija car ferries operate along the Bari–Rijeka–Dubrovnik coastal route, stopping at Zadar, Split and the islands of Hvar, Korčula and Mljet. Services are less frequent in winter. The most scenic section is Split to Dubrovnik, which all Jadrolinija ferries cover during the day. Ferries are a lot more comfortable than buses, though somewhat more expensive. From Rijeka to Dubrovnik the deck fare is €26/31 low/high season with high season running from about the end of June to the end of August; there's a 20% reduction on the return portion of a return ticket. With a through ticket, deck passengers can stop at any port for up to a week, provided they notify the purser beforehand and have their ticket validated. This is much cheaper than buying individual sector tickets but is only good for one stopover. Cabins should be booked a week ahead, but deck space is usually available on all sailings.

Deck passage on Jadrolinija is just that: *poltrone* (reclining seats) are about €6 extra and four-berth cabins (if available) begin at €48.50/58 low/high season from (Rijeka to Dubrovnik). You must buy tickets in advance at an agency or the Jadrolinija office as they are not sold on board. Cabins can be arranged at the reservation counter aboard the ship, but advance bookings are recommended if you want to be sure of a place. Bringing a car means checking in at least two hours in advance, more in the summer.

Local ferries connect the bigger offshore islands with each other and the mainland. Some of the ferries operate only a couple of times a day and, once the vehicular capacity is reached, the remaining motorists must wait for the next available service. During summer the lines of waiting cars can be long, so it's important to arrive early.

Foot passengers and cyclists should have no problem getting on but you must buy your tickets at an agency before boarding since they are not sold on board. You should bear in mind that taking a bicycle on these services will incur an extra charge, which depends on the distance.

Bus

Bus services are excellent and relatively inexpensive. There are often a number of different companies handling each route so prices can vary substantially, but the prices in this book should give you an idea of costs (and unless otherwise noted, all bus prices are for one-way fares). Generally, the cheaper fares are on overnight buses. Following are some prices for the most popular routes:

Destination	Cost (KN)	Duration	Frequency
Dubrovnik-Rijeka	372	12hr	4 daily
Dubrovnik-Split	82-111	4½hr	14 daily
Dubrovnik-Zadar	168-210	8hr	7 daily
Zagreb-Dubrovnik	205-401	11hr	7 daily
Zagreb-Korčula	204	12hr	1 daily
Zagreb-Pula	120-174	4-6hr	17 daily
Zagreb-Split	115-150	6-9hr	27 daily

It's generally best to call or visit the bus station to get the complete schedule but the following companies are among the largest:

Autotrans (☎ 051-660 360; www.autotrans.hr) Based in Rijeka with connections to Istria, Zagreb, Varaždin and Kvarner.

Brioni Pula (☎ 052-502 997; www.brioni.hr in Croatian) Based in Pula with connections to Istria, Trieste, Padua, Split and Zagreb.

Contus (☎ 023-315 315; www.contus.hr) Based in Zadar with connections to Split and Zagreb.

At large stations bus tickets must be purchased at the office; book ahead to be sure of a seat. Tickets for buses that arrive from somewhere else are usually purchased from the conductor. Buy a one-way ticket only or you'll be locked into one company's schedule for the return. Most intercity buses are air-conditioned and make rest stops every two hours or so. Some of the more expensive companies charge extra for a video system that allows you to watch Croatian soap operas during your trip. If you plan to catch a nap, bring earplugs since there's bound to be music playing. Luggage stowed in the baggage compartment under the bus costs extra (10KN a piece, including insurance).

On schedules, *vozi svaki dan* means 'every day' and *ne vozi nedjeljom ni praznikom* means 'not Sunday and public holidays'. Check www.akz.hr (in Croatian) for information on schedules and fares to and from Zagreb.

Car & Motorcycle

You have to pay tolls on the motorways around Zagreb, to use the Učka tunnel between Rijeka and Istria, the bridge to Krk Island, as well as the road from Rijeka to Delnice and from Zagreb to Split. Tolls can be paid in foreign currencies. The long-awaited motorway connecting Zagreb and Split opened in 2005 cutting travel time to the coast to around four hours. Tolls add up to about 160KN. Over the next few years, look for completion of the final leg running from Split to Dubrovnik. For general news on Croatia's motorways and tolls, see www.hac.hr.

DRIVING LICENCE

Any valid driving licence is sufficient to legally drive and hire a car; an international driving licence is not necessary. **Hrvatski Autoklub** (HAK; Croatian Auto Club; www.hak.hr) offers help and advice, plus there's the nationwide **HAK road assistance** (vučna služba; ☎ 987).

FUEL

Petrol stations are generally open 7am to 7pm and often until 10pm in summer. Petrol is Eurosuper 95, Super 98, normal or diesel. See www.ina.hr for up-to-date fuel prices.

HIRE

The large car-hire chains represented in Croatia are Avis, Budget, Europcar and Hertz. Throughout Croatia, Avis is allied with the Autotehna company, while Hertz is often represented by Kompas.

Independent local companies are often much cheaper than the international chains, but Avis, Budget, Europcar and Hertz have the big advantage of offering one-way rentals that allow you to drop the car off at any one of their many stations in Croatia free of charge.

Prices at local companies begin at around €40 a day with unlimited kilometres. Shop around as deals vary widely and 'special' discounts and weekend rates are often available. Third-party public liability insurance is included by law, but make sure your quoted price includes full collision insurance, called collision damage waiver (CDW). Otherwise your responsibility for damage done to the vehicle is usually determined as a percentage of the car's value. Full CDW begins at 50KN a day extra (compulsory for those aged under 25), theft insurance is 15KN a day and personal accident insurance another 40KN a day.

Sometimes you can get a lower car-hire rate by booking the car from abroad. Tour companies in Western Europe often have fly-drive packages that include a flight to Croatia and a car (two-person minimum).

ROAD RULES

Unless otherwise posted, the speed limits for cars and motorcycles are 50km/h in the urban zones, 90km outside urban zones, 110km/h on main highways and 130km/h on motorways. On any of Croatia's winding two-lane highways, it's illegal to pass long military convoys or a line of cars caught behind a slow-moving truck. The maximum permitted amount of alcohol in the blood is – none at all! It is also forbidden to use a mobile phone while driving. Drive defensively, as some local drivers lack discipline, to put it mildly.

Hitching

Hitching is never entirely safe, and we don't recommend it. Hitchhiking in Croatia is unreliable. You'll have better luck on the islands, but in the interior cars are small and usually full.

Local Transport

Zagreb and Osijek have well-developed tram system as well as local buses, but in the rest of the country you'll only find buses. In major cities such as Rijeka, Split, Zadar and Dubrovnik buses run about every 20 minutes, and less often on Sunday. Small medieval towns along the coast are generally closed to traffic and have infrequent links to outlying suburbs.

Taxis are available in all cities and towns, but they must be called or boarded at a taxi stand. Prices are rather high (meters start at 25KN).

Train

Train travel is about 15% cheaper than bus travel and often more comfortable, although slower. The main lines run from Zagreb to Rijeka, Zadar and Split and east to Osijek. There are no trains along the coast. Local trains usually have only unreserved 2nd-class seats. Reservations may be required on express trains. 'Executive' trains have only 1st-class seats and are 40% more expensive than local trains.

On posted timetables in Croatia, the word for arrivals is *dolazak* and for departures it's *odlazak* or *polazak*. For train information check out **Croatian Railway** (www.hznet.hr).

Macedonia

RAFAEL ESTEFANIA

Macedonia

The southernmost Slavic nation, Macedonia is rich in vineyards, forests, old villages and a wealth of Orthodox churches and monasteries. The gorgeous town of Ohrid on the lake of the same name is one of the crucibles of the Orthodox faith and Slavic culture, and Macedonia's tourism trump card. Centuries of Ottoman rule have also bestowed on it some wonderful mosques and shrines.

This small country is mostly made up of farming towns in the middle of broad fertile valleys, separated by forested ranges. The frescoes in dozens of monasteries and old churches illuminate this pastoral culture – the images of saints and angels follow strict Byzantine formulas, but the vines, goats and sheep in the margins are painted with detail and flair.

For people from the rest of old Yugoslavia, Macedonia reminds them a lot of the old days. Yugo hatchbacks buzz like motorised roller skates around streets with socialist titles such as Leninova and Maksim Gorki. Modern Macedonia is not without its problems – the local economy is still in the doldrums and there is a lingering ethnic divide between the Slavic, Orthodox Macedonians and the mostly Muslim ethnic Albanian minority. That said, visitors are greeted warmly in every part of the country and plied with hearty food and luscious drinks. Outside of Skopje, the cost of travel is low, and while public transport is a bit worn it stretches to nearly every corner of the country.

FAST FACTS

- **Area** 25,713 sq km
- **Capital** Skopje
- **Currency** Macedonian Denar (MKD); €1 = 60.8MKD; US$1=50.8MKD; UK£1 = 88.6MKD; A$1 = 38.1MKD; ¥100 = 42.5MKD; NZ$1 = 32.5MKD
- **Famous for** Lake Ohrid, old monasteries, name dispute with Greece
- **Key phrases** *Zdravo* (hello), *blagodaram/fala* (thanks), *molam* (please), *prijatno* (goodbye)
- **Official languages** Macedonian, Albanian
- **Population** 2 million
- **Telephone codes** country code ☎ 389; international access code ☎ 99
- **Visas** not needed for EU passport holders; some others do require one, see p261

MACEDONIA

HIGHLIGHTS

- The ancient holy town of **Ohrid** (p247) is rich in cultural treasures and is artfully positioned on a beautiful highland lake.
- The dinky little capital **Skopje** (p236) is an interesting mix of old bazaars, cool cafés and chunky communist influences.
- The highland wilderness of **Mavrovo National Park** (p245) is home to skiing, the splendid Sveti Jovan Bigorski Monastery and the wedding-festival village of Galičnik.
- Busy little **Bitola** (p252) is a great base for exploring the Roman ruins of Heraclea Lyncestis and the Treskavec Monastery at Prilep.
- **Pelister National Park** (p252) offers highland treks and the fine old Vlach village of Malovište.

HOW MUCH?

- **Dorm bed in Skopje** 936MKD
- **Loaf of bread** 15MKD
- **Souvenir icon** 1800MKD
- **Kebapci (kebabs)** 150MKD
- **Short taxi ride** 50MKD

LONELY PLANET INDEX

- **Litre of petrol** 55MKD
- **Litre of bottled water** 30MKD
- **Skopsko beer** 100MKD
- **Souvenir T-shirt** 450MKD
- **Street snack (burger)** 50MKD

ITINERARIES

- **One week** Spend two days in Skopje in the old-town bazaar and visit the enchanting Turkish baths-cum-art galleries, mosques and churches. Take a day trip to Tetovo and visit a Sufi monastery, the Painted Mosque and maybe the World's Smallest Museum at Džepčište. Then head to Ohrid and spend two days simply exploring. Next, aim for cosy little Bitola and make an excursion to the rare old village of Malovište.
- **Two weeks** Take an extra day in Skopje to visit Lake Matka. Hire a car and stay in a ski hotel in Mavrovo National Park. Visit the Sveti Jovan Bigorski Monastery on a stunning mountain ride to Ohrid. Go forth to the Sveti Naum Monastery and the village of Vevčani for an extra couple of days at Ohrid. Head down to Brajčino above Lake Prespa and explore one of Macedonia's prettiest villages. Stay in Bitola and visit both Pelister National Park and Prilep's Treskavec Monastery. Then take an excursion out to highland Berovo or to the Sveti Joachim Osogovski Monastery.

CLIMATE & WHEN TO GO

Macedonia's summers are hot and dry. Warm winds drift up from the Aegean into the Vardar Valley. The temperatures vary widely: summer temperatures can reach 40°C, while in winter it can drop as low as -30°C. The average annual temperatures are above 10°C almost everywhere. Snow falls on all the mountainous areas from November to April, but in the higher mountains the snow can stay until the end of May, which makes it great for skiing.

The best time to enjoy Macedonia is between May and September. The busiest season is from mid-July to mid-August, when Macedonians take their holidays.

See Climate Charts p388.

HISTORY

Historical Macedonia is divided between the Republic of Macedonia, the Greek province of Macedonia and a corner of Bulgaria geographers call Pirin Macedonia. The largest portion of the historic Macedonia region is now Greek territory, a point that Greeks are always quick to make when disputing Macedonia's use of the name, as they invariably do. In any case, the region was the homeland of Alexander the Great, who sallied forth to conquer the ancient world in the 4th century BC. Rarely independent, the territory of the Republic of Macedonia has often been a staging post point for invaders. Roman rule was entrenched after the conquest of Macedonia in 168 BC, and over the next 500 years the ancestors of the Vlach people developed a Latin dialect. Today's Vlach community speak a language called Aromanian, which, as the names suggest, is related to Romanian and the Romans.

Many Vlach villages lie along the route of the Roman Via Egnatia, a vital military

MACEDONIA

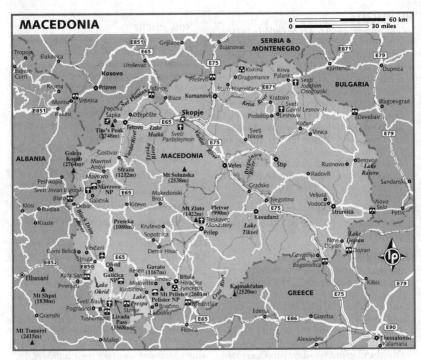

road and trade route which stretched from Durrësi in Albania to Bitola in Macedonia, and then down to Thessaloniki. When the Roman Empire was divided in the 4th century AD, this region came under the Eastern Roman Empire ruled from Constantinople. Slavs started settling in the area in the 7th century AD, and not long after adopted the Christian faith of earlier residents.

In the 9th century the region was conquered by Car Simeon (r 893–927) and later, under Car Samoil (r 980–1014), Macedonia was the centre of a powerful Bulgarian state. Samoil's defeat by Byzantium in 1014 ushered in a long period when Macedonia passed back and forth between Byzantium, Bulgaria and Serbia. Around this time, the first Roma (Gypsy) people arrived in the area after a long migration from northern India. After several defeats of Serbia by the Ottomans in the 14th and 15th centuries, the Balkans and therefore Macedonia became a part of the Ottoman Empire. Turkish administrators and small communities of Turkish peasants settled in the region, and over the centuries many of the local Albanians converted to Islam. The Slavic Macedonians largely remained faithful to the Orthodox Church. As Ottoman power waned in the 18th century, the Greek Orthodox Church began to take over local Christian life, and many monasteries and churches changed their liturgy to Greek. The Macedonians resented this almost as much as Turkish rule.

In 1878 Russia defeated Turkey, and the Treaty of San Stefano ceded Macedonia to Bulgaria. The Western powers, fearing the creation of a powerful Russian satellite in the heart of the Balkans, forced Bulgaria to return Macedonia to Ottoman rule. Macedonia was left as a predominantly Christian, Muslim-ruled region surrounded by Christian states competing to expand. The 'Macedonian Question' introduced a period of 40 years of rebellions, invasions and bloody reprisals.

In 1893, Macedonian nationalists formed the Vnatresno-Makedonska Revolucionerna Organizacija (VMRO), which in English means Internal Macedonian Revolutionary Organisation, to fight for independence from Turkey. The struggle culminated in the Ilinden (St Elijah's Day) uprising of August 1903, which was brutally suppressed in October of the same year. Although the nationalist leader Goce Delčev died before the revolt, he has become the symbol of Macedonian nationalism.

The First Balkan War of 1912 saw Greece, Serbia, Bulgaria and Montenegro fighting together against Turkey, and Macedonia was unlucky enough to become a major battlefield – repeatedly. During the Second Balkan War, in 1913, Greece and Serbia ousted the Bulgarians and shared Macedonia. Montenegro was part of the anti-Turkish alliance, but it didn't occupy any part of Macedonia. These wars were pioneers of the worst of 20th-century warfare. The use of heavy artillery and trench warfare coincided with numerous massacres of civilians. After WWI, the region was granted to the Kingdom of Serbs, Croats and Slovenes and renamed Yugoslavia in 1929.

Frustrated by this, VMRO continued the struggle against the new rulers, and, in response, the interwar government in Belgrade banned the Macedonian language and the name Macedonia. Although some VMRO elements supported Bulgarian occupation during WWII, many more joined Josip Broz Tito's partisans, and in 1943 it was agreed that postwar Macedonia would have full republican status within the future Yugoslavia. Tito led the communist resistance to German occupation in WWII and later became prime minister, then president, of Yugoslavia.

The end of WWII brought Macedonians hope of unifying their peoples. This was encouraged by the Greek Communist Party and Bulgaria's recognition of its Macedonian minorities. However the Stalin-Tito split of 1948 and the end of the Greek civil war in 1949 put an end to such hopes. Nonetheless, the first Macedonian grammar was published in 1952 and an independent Macedonian Orthodox Church was formed. After Kosovo, Macedonia was the most economically backward region of Yugoslavia, and depended on financial support from the wealthier republics.

On 8 September 1991, Macedonians went to a referendum on independence. Seventy-four per cent voted in favour, and in January 1992 the country declared its full independence from the former Yugoslavia. Macedonian leader Kiro Gligorov artfully negotiated the only peaceful withdrawal of the Yugoslav army from any of the republics, and relations with Serbia's leadership remained friendly.

Meanwhile, Greece withheld diplomatic recognition of Macedonia and demanded that the country find another name. The Greeks say that the term Macedonia implies territorial claims on northern Greece, but what really fuels their ire is the idea that 'others' are claiming the legacy of illustrious ancient Macedonia for themselves. At Greek insistence, Macedonia was forced to use the 'provisional' title the Former Yugoslav Republic of Macedonia (FYROM) in order to be admitted to the UN in April 1993. When the USA (following six EU countries) recognised FYROM in February 1994, Greece declared an economic embargo against Macedonia and closed the port of Thessaloniki to trade. The embargo was lifted in November 1995 after Macedonia changed its flag and agreed to discuss its name with Greece. The discussions on the name issue went nowhere, and gradually more and more countries are dropping FYROM and recognising Republic of Macedonia as the title. Just after crossing the Greek border on the highway to Thessaloniki there's a billboard which says 'Welcome to the Real Macedonia'. The Greek disapproval of Macedonia's name is driven by a proud sense that historical Macedonia is Greek and can only ever be Greek, which makes the issue almost impossible to resolve. The Greek government still makes it difficult for Macedonians to get visas, though things are looking up on the trade front.

In the meantime, the country's ethnic Albanian minority was seeking better representation on political and cultural fronts, and tried to set up an Albanian-speaking university in Tetovo in 1995. Since Macedonian was the only official language according to the country's constitution, the authorities declared the university illegal and tried to close it down. Soon after, President Kiro Gligorov lost an eye in an assassination attempt and tensions increased.

At the end of the 1990s, an Albanian rebel group called the Ushtria Člirimtare Kombetare (UČK; National Liberation Army) claimed responsibility for a number of bombings. This escalated in February 2001 into armed conflict in western Macedonia between security forces and the UČK. Hostilities did not last long, however. With the signing of the Ohrid Framework Agreement in August 2001, the Macedonian government agreed to greater political participation for the Albanian minority, official recognition of the Albanian language, as well as an increase in the number of ethnic Albanian police officers throughout the country.

After the unfortunate death of Macedonian president Boris Trajkovski in a plane accident in Bosnia and Hercegovina in February 2004, the presidency was taken by former prime minister, Branko Crvenkovski, in elections in April the same year. Macedonia is keen to enter the EU, but the EU doesn't seem too anxious about it.

PEOPLE

According to 2004 estimates, the republic's 2,071,210 population is divided as follows: Macedonians of Slav ethnicity (66.6%); Albanians (22.7%); Turks (4%); Roma (2.2%); Serbs (2.1%); and others (2.4%). Relations between Macedonians and Albanians are problematic, in Skopje in particular. There are high schools in Skopje where relations between students from the two communities are so bad that the authorities came up with the following solution.

Every day, the school is divided into two. For example, if Macedonian students attend in the morning, the Albanians attend in the afternoon, with a one-hour period during the changeover, so that the students won't clash. Not only do the students change, but the entire teaching staff as well. In addition, the school itself changes name – a Macedonian name in the morning, and an Albanian name in the afternoon.

A big factor behind all this is the different growth rates behind the Macedonian and Albanian communities. Basically, the average Albanian family currently has twice as many kids as Macedonian ones. If this trend continues, the two communities will be roughly the same size in about 30 years. In the meantime Macedonians are moving out of majority Albanian towns, and vice versa. The other communities more or less try to stay out of all of this. The Turkish people generally live in big towns, descendants of the Ottoman administrators and traders. They seem to be aligned, at least in Macedonian eyes, with their Albanian Muslim coreligionists. The Roma, who are mostly Muslim, get lumped in with the Albanians as well, but they seem to invariably live in the part of town with the fewest public services and don't have much of a say in anything.

Despite all of this, it is absolutely the case that every community is generous and hospitable. If the topic of community relations comes up, most people will say they get along just fine with everyone and it's the politicians who stir up trouble for their own benefit. Just be aware that it is a sensitive topic. Preaching to the wrong people on the idea of Greater Albania or a pure Macedonia for Macedonians wouldn't win you any friends.

RELIGION

Most Macedonians belong to the Macedonian Orthodox Church, and most Albanians to Islam. There is also a smallish Catholic community – nearly all ethnic Albanian. Mother Theresa of Calcutta grew up as Agnes Bojaxhiu in a pious Albanian Catholic family in Skopje. Even if people aren't regular church or mosque attendees, they still generally identify with one or other religion. After an interminable tug-of-war between the Greek, Serbian and Bulgarian Orthodox churches, the Macedonian Orthodox Church declared itself autocephalous (literally 'self-headed' or self-governing) in 1967. As often happens in Orthodox church politics, the other churches have resisted recognising the independence of the Macedonian church. Monastic life in the Macedonian Orthodox Church has been reviving since the end of communism, and roughly 70 monasteries and convents have been reoccupied.

ARTS
Cinema

The most significant Macedonian film is *Before the Rain* (1995) directed by Milčo Mančevski. Visually stunning, the film is a manifold take on the tensions between Macedonians and ethnic Albanians. Filmed partly in London and partly in Macedonia, you will be able to spot the Sveti Jovan at Kaneo church in Ohrid, and the Treskavec Monastery. Mančevski released *Dust* in 2001, an interesting account of 20th-century Ottoman Macedonia.

Dance

The most famous Macedonian folk dance is probably *Teškoto oro* (difficult dance). Music for this beautiful male dance is provided by the *tapan* (two-sided drum) and *zurla* (double-reed horn). Performed in traditional Macedonian costume, it is often included in festivals or concerts. Other dances include *Komitsko oro,* symbolising the struggle of Macedonian freedom fighters against the Turks, and *Tresenica,* a women's dance from the Mavrovo region.

The *oro* is similar to the *kolo,* a circle dance, danced throughout the Balkans.

The Ministry of Culture website at www .culture.in.mk has a comprehensive list of dates and venues for performances of modern and traditional dance.

Music

The oldest form of Macedonian folk music involves the *gajda* (bagpipes). This instrument is played solo or is accompanied by the *tapan,* each side of which is played with a different stick to obtain a different tone. These are often augmented by the *kaval* (flute) and/or *tambura* (small lute with two pairs of strings). In addition, Macedonia has inherited (from a long period of Turkish influence) the *zurla,* also accompanied by the *tapan,* and the *Čalgija* music form, involving clarinet, violin, *darabuk* (hourglass-shaped drum) and *doumbuš* (banjolike instrument).

Bands playing these instruments may be heard and enjoyed at festivals such as the Balkan Festival of Folk Dances & Songs in Ohrid in mid-July (p249) or the Ilinden festival in Bitola in early August. Nearly all Macedonian traditional music is accompanied by dancing.

ENVIRONMENT
The Land

Most of Macedonia's 25,713 sq km consists of a plateau between 600m and 900m above sea level. The Vardar River crosses the middle of the country, passing Skopje on its way to the Aegean Sea near Thessaloniki. Ohrid and Prespa lakes, in the southwest, drain into the Adriatic Sea via Albania. At a depth of 294m, Lake Ohrid is the deepest lake on the Balkan Peninsula. In the northwest, the Šar Planina marks the border with Kosovo. Mt Korab (Golem Korab; 2864m)

on the border with Albania is the country's highest peak.

Wildlife

Macedonia belongs to the eastern Mediterranean and Euro-Siberian vegetation region and is home to a large number of plant species in a relatively small geographical area. The high mountains are dominated by pines, while on the lower mountains beech and oak predominate.

Macedonia is a boundary area between two different zoological zones – the high mountain region and the low Mediterranean valley region. The fauna of the forests is abundant and includes bear, wild boar, wolf, fox, squirrel, chamois and deer. The lynx is found, although very rarely, in the mountains of western Macedonia, particularly on Šar Planina, while deer inhabit the region of Demir Kapija. Forest birds include the blackcap, grouse, black grouse, imperial eagle and forest owl.

The shepherd dog, *šar planinec,* from the Šar Planina, stands some 60cm tall and is a brave, fierce fighter in guarding and defending flocks from bears or wolf packs.

Lakes Ohrid, Prespa and Dojran are separate fauna zones, a result of territorial and temporal isolation. Lake Ohrid's fauna is a relic of an earlier era. The lake is known for letnica trout, lake whitefish, gudgeon and roach, as well as certain species of snails of a genus older than 30 million years. It is also home to the mysterious European eel, which comes to Lake Ohrid from the distant Sargasso Sea to live for up to 10 years. It makes the trip back to the Sargasso Sea to breed, then dies; its offspring start the cycle anew.

National Parks

Macedonia's three national parks all protect mountain wilderness. They are: Pelister (near Bitola, p252), Galičica (between Lakes Ohrid and Prespa) and Mavrovo (between Ohrid and Tetovo, p245). Pelister and Galičica are both part of a broader nature protection zone around Lake Prespa, shared with adjacent areas in Albania and Greece. Being mountains, the three national parks are only really open for hiking during the warmer months, from April to October, though Mavrovo has a great little ski resort. All three are accessible by road (though not really by public transport), and none require any tickets or permits from park officers. With this in mind, the onus is really on visitors to keep the parks as tidy and pristine as possible.

Environmental Issues

Soil erosion is a problem in areas where there has been clear felling on steep slopes, but UN reports suggest that the strain on farming land has eased with the fall in the rural population (down about 30 per cent since 1945).

FOOD & DRINK

If one word sums up Macedonian cuisine, it's *skara* (barbecue). Whether it's pork, chicken or lamb, there's a lot of *skara* served in the country. Balkan *burek* (cheese, spinach, potato or meat in filo pastry) and yogurt make for a cheap and delicious breakfast. Try it in a *burekdžinica* (*burek* shop). Taste the Macedonian *tavče gravče* (beans cooked in a skillet).

Other dishes to try are *pastrmajilija*, a bit like a pizza or a Turkish pide with meat and sometimes egg, *kebapci* (kebabs), *mešana salata* (mixed salad) and the *šopska salata* (mixed salad with grated white cheese). *Ajvar* is a sauce named from sweet red peppers available everywhere. Typical cheeses include the white *sirenje* and the yellow *kaskaval*. Italian food (eg pizza) is available just about everywhere.

Skopsko Pivo is the most popular local beer. It's strong and quite cheap. Big-brand European beers are also available. The national firewater is *rakija*, a strong distilled spirit made from grapes. *Mastika*, an ouzo-like spirit, is also popular. See the boxed text In Vino Veritas (p254) for details on Macedonia's impressive array of wines.

SKOPJE СКОПЈЕ

☎ 02 / pop 640,000

While not anyone's idea of an architectural gem, Skopje has enough urban buzz to fill a few days. What strikes you most about the city is the weighty communist paw in its design. Most of the city was rebuilt after an earthquake in 1960s' communist concrete style. In about 50 years or so pundits

SKOPJE IN TWO DAYS

Catch the morning sun crossing the 15th-century **Kamen Most** (p238) to the heart of Skopje's old town. Step into the old Turkish baths, **Daud Paša Baths** (p238) and **Čifte Amam** (p238), now art galleries. Wander around the old town, **Čaršija**, (p238) and lunch alfresco. Spend the afternoon visiting the **Sveti Spas** (p238) and **Skopje's mosques** (p239). Take in the street scene at **Dal Met Fu** (p241) or sample traditional fare at **Pivnica An** (p241).

On day two, head for **Lake Matka** (p243), outside Skopje, for hiking, climbing, or just plain relaxing by the smooth mirror of the lake. Have dinner in the restaurant at the **Sveti Pantelejmon Monastery** (p239) on the slopes of Mount Vodno overlooking the city.

may well be raving about this superb period ensemble of concrete apartment towers, vast avenues suitable for tank parades and weird space-age public buildings. To the current eye, though, it might seem a tad ugly. The locals do have a sense of humour about it all. One described the bunker-like National Theatre as just like the Sydney Opera House, only square.

During the day you can take in the view from the Tvrdina Kale (the city fort) and wander around the old bazaar. Check out the small shops, and step into the beautiful old Turkish baths, now the city's art galleries. Skopje has a number of beautiful old mosques and churches you can spend a quiet moment in.

The city is divided into the mostly Albanian and Turkish north and the mostly Macedonian south by the Vardar River. The 15th-century Kamen Most (Stone Bridge) connects the two city centres.

ORIENTATION

Skopje's central zone is mostly a pedestrian area where you can stroll along the river and cross the Kamen Most which divides the old and new towns. South of the river is the Ploštad Makedonija (the city's main square) and north is Čaršija (the city's ancient Turkish bazaar). The Gradski Trvgovki Centar is a complex of shops, clubs, bars and cafés along the southern side of the

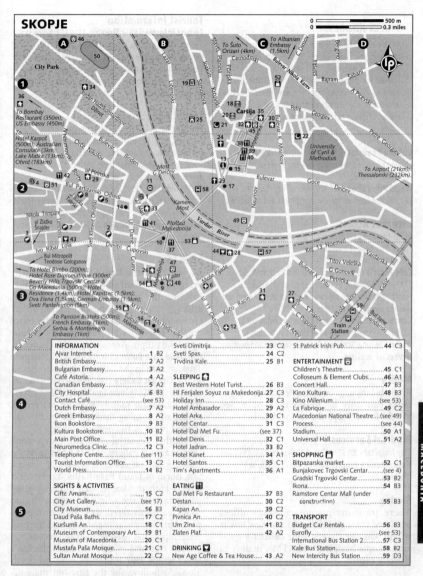

SKOPJE

0 — 500 m
0 — 0.3 miles

INFORMATION	
Ajvar Internet	1 B2
British Embassy	2 A2
Bulgarian Embassy	3 A2
Café Astoria	4 A2
Canadian Embassy	5 A2
City Hospital	6 B3
Contact Café	(see 53)
Dutch Embassy	7 A2
Greek Embassy	8 A2
Ikon Bookstore	9 B3
Kultura Bookstore	10 B2
Main Post Office	11 B2
Neuromedica Clinic	12 C3
Telephone Centre	(see 11)
Tourist Information Office	13 C2
World Press	14 B2

SIGHTS & ACTIVITIES	
Cifte Amam	15 C2
City Art Gallery	(see 17)
City Museum	16 B3
Daud Paša Baths	17 C2
Kuršumli An	18 C1
Museum of Contemporary Art	19 B1
Museum of Macedonia	20 C1
Mustafa Paša Mosque	21 C1
Sultan Murat Mosque	22 C2

Sveti Dimitrija	23 C2
Sveti Spas	24 C2
Trvdina Kale	25 B1

SLEEPING	
Best Western Hotel Turist	26 B3
Hl Ferijalen Soyuz na Makedonija	27 C3
Holiday Inn	28 C3
Hotel Ambasador	29 A2
Hotel Arka	30 C1
Hotel Centar	31 C3
Hotel Dal Met Fu	(see 37)
Hotel Denis	32 C1
Hotel Jadran	33 B2
Hotel Kanet	34 A1
Hotel Santos	35 C1
Tim's Apartments	36 A1

EATING	
Dal Met Fu Restaurant	37 B3
Destan	30 C2
Kapan An	39 C2
Pivnica An	40 C2
Um Zina	41 B2
Zlaten Plat	42 A2

DRINKING	
New Age Coffee & Tea House	43 A2

St Patrick Irish Pub	44 C3

ENTERTAINMENT	
Children's Theatre	45 C1
Colloseum & Element Clubs	46 A1
Concert Hall	47 B3
Kino Kultura	48 B3
Kino Milenium	(see 53)
La Fabrique	49 C2
Macedonian National Theatre	(see 49)
Process	(see 44)
Stadium	50 A1
Universal Hall	51 A2

SHOPPING	
Bitpazarska market	52 C1
Bunjakovec Trgovski Centar	(see 4)
Gradski Trgovski Centar	53 B2
Ikona	54 B3
Ramstore Centar Mall (under construction)	55 B3

TRANSPORT	
Budget Car Rentals	56 B3
Eurofly	(see 53)
International Bus Station 2	57 C3
Kale Bus Station	58 B2
New Intercity Bus Station	59 D3

MACEDONIA

Vardar. The train station and main bus stations are a 15-minute walk southeast of the stone bridge, and the domestic bus station is just north of the bridge.

Maps

Good maps published by Trimaks can be found at the **Kultura Bookstore** (Ploštad Make-donija bb). The *New Skopje City Map* costs 200MKD.

INFORMATION
Bookshops

Ikon Bookstore (☎ 3065 312, ul Luj Paster) This nifty little bookstore a few doors from the Kultura Kino off Maršal Tito has a good range of English-language novels.

> **STREET ADDRESSES**
>
> At the end of a number of addresses in this chapter, you'll notice the letters 'bb' instead of a street number. This shorthand, which stands for *bez broja* (without a number) is used by businesses or other non-residential institutions, indicating that it's an official place without a street number.

Kultura Bookstore (☎ 3235 862l Ploštad Makedonija bb) Good for maps and colour souvenir books on Macedonian culture and sights.

World Press Shop (☎ 3298 082; ul Vasil Glavinov 3) Best place in town for foreign newspapers and magazines.

Internet Access

Ajvar Internet (27th Mart bb; per hr 40MKD; ☺ 9am-10pm) Bare bones basement Internet café with handy central location.

Café Astoria (Bunjakovec Centar; Bul Partizanski Odredi 27A; per hr 100MKD; ☺ 9am-11pm) An atmospheric French-style café with old computers. Scanning, faxing and printing services are available.

Contact Café (2nd fl, Gradski Trgovski Centar; per hr 120MKD; ☺ 9am-10pm) More expensive but it is a smoke-free zone. Scanning, faxing, telephone and printing services are available.

Media

English-language newspapers and magazines can only be found in Skopje. See World Press Shop, above, for details.

Medical Services

City hospital (☎ 3130 111; ul 11 Oktomvri 53; ☺ 24hr)
Neuromedica private clinic (☎ 3133 313; ul 11 Oktomvri 25; ☺ 24hr)

Money

There are many private exchange offices scattered throughout the old and new towns where you can change your cash at a good rate. Skopje has plenty of ATMs, mainly in the city centre.

Post & Telephone

Main post office (☎ 3141 141; ul Orce Nikolov 1; ☺ 7am-7.30pm Mon-Sat, 7.30am-2.30pm Sun) Located 75m northwest of Ploštad Makedonija, along the river.
Telephone centre (ul Orce Nikolov 1; ☺ 24hr) Inside the main post office. You can also phone from kiosks (newsagents) with private telephones. The price of your call is displayed digitally as you speak.

Tourist Information

Tourist information office (☎ 3116 854; Kruševska; ☺ officially 8am-6pm Mon-Fri, 9am-5pm Sat) This neglected little office was open exactly once in the 20 or so times we walked past over two months. If open, they sell maps and can arrange rooms in private homes starting at around 1500MKD.

Travel Agencies

Eurofly (☎ 3136 619; fax 3136 320; 1st fl, Gradski Trgovski Centar) Of Skopje's abundance of travel agencies, the best and most practical for airline tickets is this modern travel agency, where ticket prices are listed boldly at the door in both euros and US dollars.
Go Macedonia (☎ 3232 273, www.gomacedonia.com .mk; Trgovski Centar Beverly Hills lok 32, ul Naroden Front 19) Lively 'alternative' travel agency offering hikes, bicycle tours, caving and other adventure sports, homestays and wine tours.

SIGHTS

As you cross the **Kamen Most**, its arch will bring you right into the old town or **Čaršija**. Just over the bridge on the left is **Sveti Dimitrija** (☺ 9am-6pm), a handsome, three-aisled Orthodox church built in 1886. The most notable feature is a lovely spiral staircase up to the pulpit. Across from the church is the **Daud Paša Baths** (1466), once the largest Turkish bath in the Balkans, and now home to the **City Art Gallery** (☎ 3133 102; Kruševska 1A; admission 100MKD; ☺ 9am-3pm Tue-Sun). The seven rooms housing mainly modern art are lit by the sun coming through the small star-shaped holes in the domed ceiling.

Another beautiful old bath, now a contemporary art gallery, is **Čifte Amam** (admission 50MKD; ☺ 9am-4.45pm Mon-Fri, 9am-3pm Sat, 9am-1pm Sun), north of Daud Paša Baths. The second largest bath in Skopje, this building gives you a taste of the original baths with one room left unplastered, its walls showing exposed brickwork, stone arches and the clay waterpipes that used to heat the rooms.

Step out and wander around Čaršija's small shops and teahouses, and go north along Samoilova for the tiny but magnificent **Sveti Spas** (admission to church & tomb 100MKD; ☺ 8am-3pm Tue-Sun). The church was built below ground, since during Ottoman times it was illegal for a church to be taller than a mosque. It boasts an iconostasis 10m wide and 6m high, beautifully carved in the early 19th century by the master-craftsmen Makarije Frčkovski and the Filipovski brothers.

MACEDONIA

The church courtyard leads to a room with the **Tomb and Museum of Goce Delčev**, leader of VMRO and the national hero, killed by the Turks in 1903. The latter is a somewhat less-splendid experience than the church; however, the ticket gives you access to both.

The 1492 **Mustafa Paša Mosque** (Samoilova bb), beyond the church, has an earthquake-cracked dome and a shady garden with a fountain. Climb up to the ruins of **Tvrdina Kale** (city fort), across the street, for panoramic views of Skopje from the 11th-century Cyclopean wall. If you want more art, the **Museum of Contemporary Art** (☎ 3117 735; Samoilova bb; admission 100MKD; ⊙ 9am-3pm Tue-Sun) is higher up the hill.

Back in Čaršija, beyond the mosque, is the white **Museum of Macedonia** (☎ 3116 044; Ćurčiska 86; admission 50MKD; ⊙ 9am-3pm Tue-Sun), which traces the region's civilisations over the centuries. One wing holds a permanent ethnographical exhibition (buy tickets here) with costumes and models of traditional houses, while the second wing covers the historical angle, from Neolithic times through the Greek, Roman, Byzantine and Turkish eras, ending with a rather comprehensive section on communist achievements. The highlight is the collection of icons and carved wooden iconostases. Some of the archaeological collection is gathering dust in the **Kuršumli An** (1550), an impressive old caravanserai or inn, where traders would stop off and rest during Ottoman times.

On the other side of the city, in the new town, the sights are less obvious, but pay attention to the bizarre architecture of the **main post office building** (ul Orce Nikolov 1; ⊙ 7am-7.30pm Mon-Sat, 7.30am-2.30pm Sun) near Kamen Most. It's a futuristic, insect-like structure, apparently an abstract take on church architecture. Further down there's the slightly dull **City Museum** (☎ 3114 742; Mito Hadživasilev bb; admission free; ⊙ 9am-3pm Tue-Sun), housed inside the old train station. Its **clock** is frozen at 5.17 on the morning of the great Skopje earthquake of 27 July 1963, which killed 1066 people and almost demolished the entire city.

For something completely different, there's **Šuto Orizari**, Europe's biggest Roma settlement, on the northern edge of the city (artfully situated between a cemetery and a prison). Commonly called Šutka, this suburb of 40,000 is one of the few places in Europe where the Roma run their own local government. The local architecture is quite interesting, especially some of the more nouveau riche designs. The settlement sprang up here after the 1963 earthquake when the old Roma neighbourhood closer to the centre was destroyed. A taxi to Šutka from central Skopje costs about 100MKD. Non-Roma locals will think you're a bit weird to want to visit, but while poor it's quite safe. It's reminiscent of many towns in India – a bit scruffy, but vibrant and colourful. The bazaar in Šutka is renowned as the cheapest place in Skopje to buy clothes and simple household items.

Up on Mount Vodno the sweet, little, 12th-century **Sveti Pantelejmon Monastery** has a beautiful fresco of the Lamentation of Christ. The church is about a 20-minute taxi ride from the centre of Skopje. The **restaurant** (☎ 3081255; meals 400MKD; ⊙ 9am-11pm) outside the church serves traditional food – very good *burek* and brandy.

SLEEPING

Prices are relatively high in Skopje's inflated accommodation scene – partly because many of the overseas visitors are working to resolve the Kosovo Question, and have the benefit of expense accounts. The cheapest budget hotels are in the Čaršija district on the north side of the river.

Budget

Hotel Kapištec (☎ 3081 424; www.hotel-kapistec.com; ul Mile Pop Jordanov 3; s €25-35, d €32-50) A rambling, little B&B with a range of rooms – some of the cheaper ones are small and a bit frayed, but the double rooms are quite nice. The friendly owners live on site and are very helpful. Good breakfast too.

Hotel Bimbo (☎ 321 4517, 070 827 511; fax 321 7663; ul 29 Noemvri 63; s/d incl breakfast €35/50) What a fantastic hotel! This is a cheerful little family-run hotel with basic but spotless rooms, a nice lounge area on the 1st floor and a cosy breakfast room. It's in a handy part of town too – close to the centre but in a quiet residential area. Ul 29 Noemvri runs along the side of Skopje's 1960s-style Catholic church.

Pansion Brateks (☎ 3176 606, 070 243 232; ul Aco Karamanov 3; s/d 1920/3200MKD) Another good B&B with tidy, airy rooms. It's often full, despite being a 20-minute walk from the centre. It's positioned in an upscale neighbourhood at the foot of Mt Vodno.

Hotel Ambasador (☎ 3215 510; fax 3121 383; ul Pirinska 36; s/d 2800/4340MKD) Next to the Russian Embassy, it has pleasant, simple rooms with breakfast. On the top of the building, a 'Statue of Liberty' wields its torch.

HI Ferijalen Soyuz na Makedonija (Ferijalen Dom; ☎ 3114 849; www.myfa.org.mk; ul Prolet 25; members s/d 935/1280MKD, nonmembers s/d 1280/1590MKD; ☺ 24hr Apr-mid-Oct) The rooms are clean and fairly comfortable, but otherwise this is a rather sterile version of a youth hostel. No communal areas, for example. Still, it's well positioned between the city centre and the bus and train stations, and all the taxi drivers know where it is. All prices include breakfast.

Hotel Kanet (☎ 3238 353; ul Jordan Hadžikonstantinov Džinot 20; s/d 2500/3700MKD) A bit like a hunting lodge in the heart of the city, this curious little wooden building sits on the edge of a park. It offer comfy rooms with TV and a buffet breakfast.

Hotel Santos (☎ 3226 963; ul Bitpazarska 69; s/d €20/25) This is the nicest of the cheap hotels in the Čaršija – newly refurbished rooms with TV and clean bathrooms. The managers don't speak English but budgeters can get by with sign language and an approximation of Macedonian and Albanian. It's set back from the corner of ul Bitpazarska and ul Evliya Čelebi. The hotel is very close to the luxury Hotel Arka, and a short walk from the Bitpazarska market. If you get a taxi to the Arka, walk into the Čaršija and you'll find yourself on ul Bitpazarska. The little alley leading to the Hotel Santos is next to a money exchange and telephone business on the corner of Bitpazarska and a street leading uphill called ul Evliya Čelebi.

Hotel Denis (☎ 3116 792; ul Evliya Čelebi 7; s/d €15/20) This little lodge has small, simple rooms, but it has the basics like cleanliness and hot water. It's uphill about 100m from the Hotel Santos – you pass the Children's Theatre and it's one block up on the left.

Midrange

Hotel Dal Met Fu (☎ 323 9584; www.dalmetfu.com .mk; Ploštad Makedonija; s €59-69, d €69-79, apt s €85-145, apt d €100-170; ☒) A bright and cheerful mini hotel (three rooms and three apartments) above the restaurant of the same name –

head up the marble stairs to reception. It has very nicely designed rooms with a fashionable edge, friendly staff, room service from the restaurant, and a location that is unbeatably central. For real sybarites, the biggest suite has a Jacuzzi.

Hotel Rose Diplomatique (☎ 3135 469; rosediplomatique.tripod.com; ul Roza Luksemburg 13; s €65-85, d €85-105) Boutique B&B has eight charming rooms, caring staff and a cute little garden. The décor has a gentle feminine touch (lots of frills and ornaments) plus necessities like hair dryers.

Hotel Residence (☎ 3081 528; fax 3084 816; ul Vasil Gjorgjov 32; s/d €55/70) This charming little boutique B&B has eight rooms of varying dimensions – rooms 205 and 203 are the pick of the bunch. It has a quiet location at the base of Mount Vodno. There's a very pleasant downstairs lounge cum bar cum breakfast room.

Hotel Centar (☎ 312 0430; pcentar@mt.net.mk; ul Kočo Racin bb; s/d €63/73; ☒) Tucked into the side of an indoor swimming pool complex, the peculiar setting belies a central location, tasteful lounge areas and handsomely appointed rooms. The rooms on the ground floor have kitchenettes. The exterior surroundings are distinctly bleak, but at least there's plenty of parking.

Tim's Apartments (☎ 323 7650; www.tims.com .mk; ul Orce Nikolov 120; r €69-98, ste €89-110) This handsome apartment-hotel has a range of rooms, one-bedroom apartments and two-bedroom 'residences' on a quiet street in an inner suburb. It's a good option for people staying long term or who have just moved to Skopje and are looking to rent a house or apartment. Several guests have remarked on the friendly service.

Hotel Jadran (☎ 3118 427; fax 3118 334; ul 27 Mart bb; s/d €40/75) This venerable Ottoman-style hotel has a great location in the centre of town, but more charm than comfort. There are some lovely wooden carvings, but the bathrooms are rather ancient.

Top End

Best Western Hotel Turist (☎ 3289 111; bestwestern@ hotelturist.com.mk; ul Gjuro Strugar 11; s/d €120/150) Fab position in the city centre, right on Maršal Tito (the main entrance on a side street). The old Hotel Turist has been nicely renovated up to Best Western standards, plus we've had good reports on the service here. Some of the rooms have balconies. The ground floor café is a nice place for a bite and a drink.

Holiday Inn (☎ 3292 929; www.holiday-inn.com/skopje; ul Vasil Adžilarski 2; r €120-250) Another conveniently located, business-class establishment, next to the Gradski Trgovski Centar on the south side of the Vardar. Free car parking, last renovated in 2000.

Hotel Karpoš (☎ 3088 388; www.hotelkarpos.com.mk; cnr ul Šekspirova & Partizanski Odredi; r €110-150, ste €170-200) This bright new business hotel a little out of the city centre offers spacious rooms and well-appointed bathrooms. Some of the rooms are studios with kitchenettes, and there are a couple of rooms with wheelchair access. The staff are switched on and attentive.

Hotel Arka (☎ 3230 603; www.hotel-arka.com.mk; ul Bitpazarska 90/2; s €88-107, d €118-138, ste €127-158) New upmarket hotel in an interesting location next to the Čaršija. There are great views from the 7th floor, which has a swimming pool and café-bar. The spacious rooms have all the mod cons you'd expect for the price.

EATING

The Čaršija has lots of cheap and quick *kebapčićis* (shops selling kebabs), cafés and *burek* eateries where you can grab a fast, filling meal for not very much.

Dal Met Fu Restaurant (☎ 3112 482; Ploštad Makedonija; mains 280MKD; ☽ 7.30am-midnight) A popular, glass-fronted restaurant with tables outside facing the main square, it serves good thin base pizza and al dente pasta.

Kapan An (Čaršija, behind Čifte Amam; meals 200MKD) This shady cobblestone courtyard contains a number of restaurants. Buy delicious *kebupci* with mouth-watering warm bread and enjoy al fresco dining.

Bombay Restaurant (☎ 3067 373; blvd Illindenska 94; meals 500-700MKD; ☽ noon-midnight Mon-Sat) This delightful Indian restaurant is good enough to attract regular diners from Kosovo. The menu is mostly north Indian with a few south Indian classics. A vegetarian *thali* (platter) costs 350MKD, suitably chilli-packed vindaloo 355MKD, plus raita, pickles, naan bread and basmati rice. The perfect antidote to pork *skara*! It's next to the city zoo, in a laneway off Illindenska.

Dva Elena (☎ 3082 383; ul Zagrebska 31; mains 300MKD; ☽ 10am-midnight) This is a traditional

Macedonian steakhouse with excellent, hearty grills, a big open fire on cold nights and a decent wine list. It's at the foot of Mount Vodno about a five-minute taxi ride from the city centre.

Um Zina (☎ 3128 345; ul 27 Mart 5; meals 400MKD; ☽ 9.30am-midnight Mon-Sat) The restaurant serves delicious Lebanese food in either a warm, cosy basement with lots of cushions and flowers or a cheerful outdoor area. It has belly dancers every Friday night. A huge shish kebab costs 250MKD, and there are several vegetarian options such as tabouleh (100MKD) and hummus (80MKD).

Pivnica An (☎ 3212 111; Čaršija; mains 270-300MKD; ☽ 9am-midnight) Excellent traditional eating plus beer, located in a restored Ottoman building in the old town, serving a wide range of Macedonian dishes in a relaxing atmosphere.

Destan (☎ 3127 324; Čaršija; kebabs 75-230MKD; ☽ 7am-11pm) A typical *kebapčići* which serves kebabs with delicious spongy Turkish bread, tomato and cucumber.

Zlaten Plat (☎ 3228 100; cnr Leninova & Partizanska Odredi; meals around 600MKD; ☽ 11am-midnight) Not the best Chinese restaurant in the world, but it's reasonably good. Boiled dumplings cost 120MKD and sautéed chicken with peanuts 280MKD.

DRINKING

There are hundreds of bars and cafés to choose from. The riverside promenade of Key 13 Noemvri in front of the Gradski Trgovski Centar has about 20 cafés in a row, all trying to outdo each other with the funkiest sounds and décor. Skopje's bars used to stay open phenomenally late, but in 2003 the government closed all girlie bars and enforced a 1am closing time for the rest – after which the only option is a nightclub.

New Age Coffee and Tea House (☎ 3117 559; ul Kosta Šahov 9; ☽ 9am-midnight) Plush floor cushions indoors, chaise longues and peacocks in the garden, teas, beers or cocktails, the choice is yours in this bohemian hangout. A bit tricky to find, it's on a side-street off Ivo Robar Lola.

St Patrick Irish Pub (☎ 3220 431; Kej 13 Noemvri; mains 280MKD; ☽ 7.30am-midnight) As the place favoured by the expat community, this resembles Irish pubs around the world. Sip your Guinness while you munch on Irish breakfasts from 7.30am onwards and meals such as beef in Guinness or Gaelic steak.

ENTERTAINMENT

Universal Hall (☎ 3224 158; ul Partizanski Odredi bb; tickets 100-200MKD) Classical and other music performances, as well as Skopje's jazz festival, take place here in October every year, plus classical and jazz concerts two or three times per week.

Macedonian National Theatre (☎ 3114 060; Key Dimitar Vlahov bb; tickets 100-400MKD) This stunningly chunky concrete behemoth on the north side of the Vardar is Macedonia's home of opera and ballet and also holds classical music recitals.

Children's Theatre (☎ 3222 619; ul Evliya Čelebi 4; tickets 100MKD) This cute little theatre in the Čaršija puts on excellent musicals, puppet shows and more for the little 'uns.

Colosseum (City Park; www.colosseumsummerclub .com) and **Element** (City Park; www.element.com.mk) in the city park are *the* places for summer outdoor clubbers and international DJs. Colosseum has cheap drinks and rooms for 3000 movers and shakers. Tickets to special events cost around 250MKD to 400MKD.

La Fabrique (☎ 3220 767; Kej Dimitar Vlahov) Downstairs, below the Macedonian National Theatre, the crowd in this place gets grooving to disco music after 10pm.

Kino Kultura (☎ 3236 578; ul Luj Paster 2; tickets 60-120MKD) Be entertained by some recent English-language movies. Tickets prices vary depending on the viewing time.

Kino Milenium (☎ 3111 111; Gradski Trgovski Centar; tickets 60-120MKD) A smaller cinema in the city's main shopping centre.

Process (Kej 13 Noemvri, www.process.com.mk) Often hosts touring DJs. It mainly plays house music but has hip hop and R&B nights as well. It's next to the St Patrick Irish Pub.

For up-to-date info on clubs and special events, check out www.skopjeclubbing .com.mk.

SHOPPING

The Čaršija teems with little shops selling souvenirs such as copper coffee pots, rugs, or animal skins. The two shopping centres, **Gradski Trgovski Centar** (ul 11 Oktomvri; ⏰ 9am-7pm) and **Trgovski Centar Bunjakovec** (Bulevar Partizanski; ⏰ 9am-7pm), stock anything your heart may desire: from clothes, to music (warning:

not entirely legal CDs are being sold in the basement level of the Gradski Trgovski Centar) to books. The **Trgovski Centar Beverly Hills** (⏰ 9am-7pm) is a more upmarket shopping centre with lots of clothing boutiques, trendy cafés and jewellery stores. The new **Ramstore Centar**, next to the City Museum, wasn't open at the time of research but will apparently be an upscale mall. Some shops within the centres close for lunch, anywhere between 1pm and 3pm.

One excellent souvenir store is **Ikona** (☎ 3215 330; ul Luj Paster 19; ⏰ 9am-9pm Mon-Fri, 9am-4pm Sat) which sells beautiful reproductions of Macedonian icons painted by artists schooled in the old techniques. They start from around 1250MKD up to 7500MKD or even 50,000MKD for more unusual pieces. Ikona also sells dolls, pottery, painted boxes and other souvenir items in traditional styles.

GETTING THERE & AWAY

Air

A host of airlines serve Skopje's **Petrovec Airport** (information ☎ 02-3148 333, www.airports.com .mk), 21km east of the city.

It may be cheaper to fly into Thessaloniki in northern Greece; try to coordinate the flight times with the two daily trains that connect Thessaloniki with Skopje.

Bus

Skopje's **New Intercity Bus Station** (Nova Avtobuska Stanica; ☎ 3166 254) is underneath the train station on bulevar Jane Sandanski. There is a comprehensive network to all Macedonian towns, and there are a dozen or so offices selling tickets to Serbia, Bulgaria, Croatia and Turkey as well. Most buses to Tetovo leave from the **Kale Bus Station**, just over the Kamen Most under the walls of the castle. You have to go to Tetovo to catch a direct bus to Tirana in Albania. There are no buses to Greece, as Macedonians find it very difficult to get Greek visas. There are two bus routes from Skopje to Ohrid: the 167km route through Tetovo takes about three hours, while the 261km route that goes via Veles and Bitola takes four hours. Book a seat to Ohrid the day before if you're travelling in high season (May to August). International buses usually leave from the main Intercity Bus Station or from the car park in front of the Holiday Inn.

The following buses depart daily from the New Intercity Bus Station:

Destination	Cost	Duration	Frequency
Berovo	350MKD	3hr	8 daily
Bitola	350MKD	2½hr	10 daily
Kriva Palanka	200MKD	2hr	12 daily
Kumanovo	100MKD	40min	28 daily
Mavrovo	170MKD	1½hr	6 daily
Ohrid	380MKD	3-4hr	15 daily
Prilep	270MKD	2hr	13 daily
Strumica	300MKD	2½	16 daily
Tetovo	100MKD	40min	21 daily

Train

Frequent trains shoot out of Skopje's ageing 'Zheleznicka Stanica'. For details on international trains, see p262). Domestic rail destinations include Bitola and Kičevo (in the west of the country), Veles (south of Skopje), Tabanovce (on the border with Serbia and Montenegro), and Gevgelija (on the Greek border north of Thessaloniki).

You will have to understand the Cyrillic alphabet to make any sense of timetables. The staff at the Information desk will be of limited use so come prepared with your phrasebook.

GETTING AROUND
To/From the Airport

There is no public transport to and from the airport. If you are flying to Skopje, try to arrange pick up through your hotel or hostel before you arrive, as you will otherwise be at the mercy of the airport taxi drivers who can charge anything between 1290MKD to 2200MKD. Getting to the airport from Skopje is a much more pleasant affair and will cost you around 660MKD. Avoid taxis that don't have the official 'taxi' sign.

Bus

Inner-suburban city buses in Skopje cost 15MKD to 30MKD per trip, depending on what kind of bus it is and whether you buy your ticket on board or in advance.

Car

Skopje is awash with car hire agencies, from the large ones (Hertz and Avis) to the smaller local companies. Prices generally start at around 2000MKD per day. Try Budget Car Rental (☎ 3290 222; Mito Hadzivasilev

Jasmin bb; 🕙 9am-5pm). The tourist office has a complete listing of car agencies in town.

Taxi

Skopje's **taxi system** is excellent, once you get beyond the taxis at the airport. All taxis have meters and drivers turn them on without prompting. The first few kilometres are 50MKD, and then 15MKD per kilometre.

LAKE MATKA ЕЗЕРО МАТКА

Only half an hour's drive away from busy Skopje, Lake Matka is a place of calm nature, where the steep Treška limestone canyon reflects in the green mirror of the lake. Matka means 'womb' in Macedonian, suggesting a link with the Virgin Mary. There is plenty to do for those who want action, with opportunities for hiking and rock climbing, or take a €10 boat ride and a peek at the caves and their dark life.

The lake is artificial, created by the damming of the River Treška, and there are restaurants along the dam, serving excellent fish and traditional Macedonian dishes. A cluster of interesting churches lies around the lake: Sveti Bogorodica below the wall, from where a steep path leads up to the churches of Sveti Spas, Sveti Trojica and Sveti Nedela – the latter about a 90-minute walk. There are caves along the path (which is very slippery after rain – wear hiking boots), where hermits once meditated and early Macedonian revolutionaries took refuge from the Turkish authorities. The church of Sveti Nikola is located just after the dam, across the bridge, and the church of Sveti Andrej lies further on. Sveti Andrej dates from 1389 and has important frescoes. Next door is the mountaineering hut **Matka** (☎ 3052 655; per bed 500MKD) where you can sleep and hire guides and basic rock climbing gear.

To get to Lake Matka take bus 60 (40 minutes, 50MKD), which leaves on the hour from bus stands along Skopje's Bulevar Partizanski Odredi.

WESTERN MACEDONIA

TETOVO ТЕТОВО
☎ 044 / pop 53,000

Tetovo is the unofficial capital of the majority Albanian region of the country. In Albanian the city is called Tetova. Despite its lovely setting on the slopes between the bulk of the Šar mountains and the verdant plains of the upper Vardar, it's a fairly workaday place without any great architectural merit, bar two stunning exceptions. These can be visited in an unhurried day trip from Skopje, which is only 30 to 40 minutes away by motorway. There is only one hotel on the main street, and at the time of research it was being renovated. Being overwhelmingly ethnic Albanian, it helps if you talk in Shqip (Albanian) or English first, rather than launching straight into Macedonian.

The city layout is fairly simple. Buses from Skopje turn off the motorway and head up the main drag, bulevar Maršal Tito. They come to a major intersection where they either turn left to go on towards Gostivar, or else they turn right, cruise past a Vero supermarket and then take another right to the bus station on ul Vasil Kidrič. Either way, if you want to head straight into town, get off here at this intersection and walk or catch a taxi uphill along bulevar Maršal Tito, which leads to the main square (about 800m away).

About halfway along on the left is Tetovo's interesting and substantial **market**, brimming with fresh groceries and merchandise. Once you get to the main square and marvel at the concrete blockiness of it all, turn right onto bulevar Ilindenska and after about 500m you cross the little Pena

River and the Šarena Djamija is unmissable on the right.

The **Šarena Djamija** (painted or coloured mosque) is one of the most beautiful Islamic buildings in the Balkans. Modest in scale, it was built in 1459 with money from two women, Mensure and Hurshida, who are buried in the mosque's grounds. The feminine touch is immediately apparent in the panels of delicately painted geometric murals on the outside.

About 2km from the city centre is Tetovo's other outstanding monument, the **Baba Arabati tekke**. A *tekke* is a monastery for dervishes belonging to an Islamic sect, the Bektashi, and this is the finest remaining *tekke* in Europe. Founded in 1538, most of the buildings date from the 18th century. The compound is surrounded by a handsome rough stone wall at the foot of the Šar Planina mountains, on the town's outskirts. A large Muslim cemetery lies in front of it. The complex has spacious gardens and is dotted with prayer halls, dining halls, traditional lodgings and a very handsome marble fountain inside a decorated wooden pavilion. The *tekke* has had a difficult recent history. In 1992 a group of Bektashi dervishes reoccupied the *tekke*, but in August 2002 armed members of a militant Sunni Muslim group invaded the compound and converted one of the buildings into a Sunni mosque. Some of the buildings were damaged in 2002, and are

---

THE BEKTASHI ORDER

Bektashi Islam is quite different from mainstream Sunni Islam. It allows the consumption of alcohol, for example. It takes a more mystical approach, with emphasis on a spiritual relationship with Allah built through prayer and the contemplation of mystical poetry.

The word 'bektashi' means secret or mysterious. The order's founder, Haji Bektash Veli, was born in Iran in the 13th century. He wrote the cornerstone of the order's beliefs, the *Makalaat*, which lays out a four-stage path to enlightenment. In the first stage, dervishes learn the difference between right and wrong; in the second, they pray constantly; in the third, they come to understand God's love; and in the fourth, they arrive at an understanding of reality through self-effacement and the constant awareness of God. Haji Bektash died in central Turkey, where he is buried at the great *tekke* in the little town named after him, Hacībektaş. The order grew quite powerful in the 18th century. The Janissaries, the Christian boys taken in the Turkish army and made to convert to Islam, were followers and patrons of the Bektashi order. The order was suppressed in many countries during the 20th century. In its main base, in Turkey, the republican government under Ataturk harshly suppressed the order in the 1920s. In 1925 the headquarters shifted to Albania, where, in turn, the movement was crushed by the communists after WWII. It has undergone something of a revival in Albania since the early 1990s, but, as the tensions in Tetovo show, the order is facing a difficult comeback.

slowly being repaired. Baba Tahir Emini, the head of the *tekke*, lives in corner of the compound near a fine old tower. Next to his quarters is a shrine containing the tombs of Bektashi holy men.

The easiest way to get there is by taxi. It takes about 15 minutes to walk back to the centre of town.

About 5km north of Tetovo in the village of Džepčište is the **Smallest Ethnological Museum in the World** (Najmal Etno Muzej na Svetot; ☎ 070 555 165; entry free but 50MKD donation appreciated; ☒ 10am-5pm). The museum is just 7.2 sq metres – enough for one visitor at a time – but packs in 1150 items, including a metre wide copper *sofra* (a large tray for serving food). The museum is located in one room of the home of the museum's founder, Simeon Zlatev-Mone, who has been building his collection for 30 years. His house is in the middle of Džepčište – the villagers assume anyone coming here is headed for the museum and will direct you to it. A taxi from Tetovo costs about 200MKD.

Getting There & Away
BUS

There are 21 buses per day between Tetovo and Skopje (100MKD, 40 minutes), starting at 6am and finishing at 7pm. In Skopje, the buses that go direct to the Tetovo bus station leave from the old bus station at the foot of the Kale, just over the Kamen Most. These services are run by the **Polet bus company** (☎ 337 221; ul Ilindenska 266, Tetovo). The buses from the main bus station stop at Tetovo on the way to Gostivar, Debar, Ohrid and other points south. These stop briefly on Maršal Tito and then turn off towards Gostivar. So if you're coming here from Skopje to catch the bus to Albania, go to the old bus station under the Kale and save yourself a short taxi ride or a five-minute walk when you reach Tetovo. There are three daily buses to Ohrid (310MKD, 2½ hours), or you can take a bus to Struga (310MKD, five buses per day, last one at 6.20pm) and take a short bus ride to Ohrid from there. For Mavrovo National Park (140MKD, 1½ hours) or Sveti Jovan Bigorski Monastery (200MKD, 2½ hours) jump on a bus heading for Debar (7.20am, 8.50am, 10.50am, 3.05pm, 5.50pm).

The Polet bus company runs two buses per day from Tetovo via Struga to Tirana,

Albania (one way/return €15/25, seven to eight hours). The buses leave at 9am and 9pm, and drop passengers by Tirana's train station at 5pm and 5am respectively. Polet's head office is on ul Ilindenska, but you can also buy a ticket from its office at the **bus station** (☎ 334 194). In July and August there are additional services to Albania from Tetovo, catering to locals taking beach holidays there. Most of these go to Durrës.

POPOVA ŠAPKA ПОПОВА ШАПКА

Some 1800m up in the Šar Planina mountains and 18km by road from Tetovo, Popova Šapka could be Macedonia's secret weapon in the struggle for Europe's best undiscovered ski resort. Unfortunately, the resort has become a victim of regional conflicts, and the facilities are in poor shape. It is rather close to the frontier with Kosovo, and it also lies within the majority Albanian region of Western Macedonia. Ethnic Macedonians prefer to ski at Mavrovo. There used to be a cable car from Tetovo hoisting visitors 1km up to Popova Šapka, but it now closed and shows no immediate signs of reopening. Although the area around the resort was cleared of landmines after the end of the Kosovo War, there are still understandable fears of stray mines. This is a real shame, because the region would be ideal for hiking in summer. The top of Tito's Peak (Titov Vrv), at 2748m the highest mountain entirely within Macedonia, can be seen from the resort.

MAVROVO NATIONAL PARK
МАВРОВО

Macedonia's biggest and oldest national park is also home to its biggest ski resort. Roughly halfway between Skopje and Ohrid, the park is quite difficult to get around on public transport but a cinch with your own wheels. Besides the 73,088 hectares of birch and pine forest, gorges, karst fields, waterfalls and alpine plain, the park contains Sveti Jovan Bigorski, Macedonia's most scenic monastery, and quite a few mountain villages including Galičnik with its famous July wedding festival.

Accommodation is mostly in the ski resort village of Mavrovo, on the southern side of Lake Mavrovo. Alas, public transport only goes directly to the village of Mavrovi Anovi on the *other* side of the lake. The lake itself is artificial, and curiously enough has two overflows – the old one going west into the Radika River and down to the Adriatic Sea via the Black Drim, and the new one going north into the Vardar River and eventually to the Aegean Sea.

Sights

The **Zare Lazarevski ski centre** (www.zarelaz.com) based at Mavrovo village is Macedonia's biggest and most modern ski resort, and by all accounts the skiing is very good. As a brochure says 'The average snow cover is 70cm, which makes skiing possible, as well as other snow foolish games'. Which is a pretty good description for the snowboarding scene. There are a couple of cafés up on the ski fields, which lie between 1860m and 1255m above sea level. Ski hire costs 600MKD per day, a ski pass for the three chairlifts and eleven ski lifts costs 700MKD per day (or 3500MKD per week) and there's a ski school. The whole operation is run from the Hotel Bistra (see right).

Sveti Jovan Bigorski is a fully working monastery and is one of the most popular with visitors in Macedonia. It was first established in 1020 on the spot where the icon of Sveti Jovan Bigorski (St John the Forerunner, ie St John the Baptist) appeared, and has been rebuilt many times over the centuries. The miraculous icon kept reappearing and the monastery kept being 'resurrected'. The present-day structures date from the 18th and 19th centuries, and inside the church you can see what is supposedly the fore-arm of Sveti Jovan himself. The church also holds one of the three iconostases and chairs carved by Makarije Frčkovski and the Filipovski brothers, who also carved the iconostasis of Sveti Spas in Skopje. The monastery has **dormitories** (☎ 042 478 675; per person €4) where you can stay overnight, with self-catering facilities.

To get to the monastery, take either the Skopje-Ohrid bus going via Debar, or catch a bus to Tetovo and change to a Debar bus. Either way, ask to be let off at the turning point for the Sveti Jovan Bigorski Monastery (*manastir*).

The old Vlach village of **Galičnik** lies deep within the park, about 17km from Mavrovo. The road to Galičnik from Mavrovo is often snowed in as late at May and closes as early as November. The village hosts a very popular

wedding festival in the middle of July – couples go into a lottery for a chance to be married here. The bridal costumes weigh up to 30kg! The festival is rich in traditions, with lots of dances, folk music…and a few tears.

Sleeping & Eating

Hotel Bistra (☎ 042-489 002; www.bistra.com; 15 Mar-15 Nov s €45 d €60-70, 16 Nov-14 Mar s €65, d €90-110; Mavrovo) This sprawling resort hotel has comfortable rooms with satellite TV, a large restaurant, a bar (of course), plus swimming pool, fitness centre and sauna. The more expensive rooms have Jacuzzis. The Bistra also runs the Hotel Ski Škola and Hotel Mavrovski during the ski season, which have single rooms from €20 to €40 and doubles from €40 to €70. The rooms are a bit simpler but new and comfortable. These lodges are just down the hill from the Bistra, near the bottom of the chairlift. Staying at either gives you access to the Bistra's pool and other facilities free of charge. There's a nightclub at the Mavrovski.

Hotel Srna (☎ 042-388 083; www.hotelsrna.cjb.net; std s/d €20/40, apt s/d €30/60; Mavrovo) This friendly little hotel is about 400m away from the chairlifts. The light, airy, standard rooms are spotless and the apartments (most with three beds) have balconies. Half board costs an extra €5 per person. The Srna has a cheerful bar and a restaurant with lots of antlers and pelts.

Hotel Makpetrol (☎ 042-489 022; hotelmavrovo@makpetrol.com.mk; s/d €36/60, ste €130; Mavrovo) Run by – guess what – a petrol company, this hotel's staff might benefit from some tickling but the facilities are quite good. The restaurant is cavernous and the rooms, though a tad socialist in character, are comfortable.

Getting There & Away

Buses don't go directly to Mavrovo but pass through the town of Mavrovo Anovi on the other side of the lake. The best thing to do to get from Mavrovo Anovi to Mavrovo would be to ring one of the hotels to send a car to come and pick you up, or if you feel brave you could get off at the dam wall where the Mavrovo road branches off and try to flag down a lift for the final couple of kilometres to Mavrovo. There are seven buses per day to Debar (120MKD), five per day to Tetovo (140MKD), and three to Skopje (180MKD).

SOUTHERN MACEDONIA

OHRID ОХРИД
☎ 046 / pop 50,000

Ohrid is Macedonia's jewel, and the most popular town with visitors. Resting by the still waters of Lake Ohrid, the town has stunning Byzantine churches, small cobbled streets, art galleries, good budget accommodation and picturesque pebbly beaches to relax on. During the summer the town is packed with people and there are numerous festivals to entertain you. For quieter moments, Galičica National Park is nearby, on the way to the marvellous monastery of Sveti Naum 20km south, towards the Albanian border.

Lake Ohrid, a natural tectonic lake shared with Albania, is one of the oldest in the world and, at 294m, the deepest in the Balkans. It might remind you of the sea with its vastness and sometimes stormy behaviour.

Under Byzantium, Ohrid became the episcopal centre of Macedonia. The first Slavic university was founded here in 893 by Bishop (Saint) Kliment of Ohrid, a disciple of the inventors of the first Slavic script, St Cyril and St Methodius. The revival of the archbishopric of Ohrid in 1958 and its independence from the Serbian Orthodox

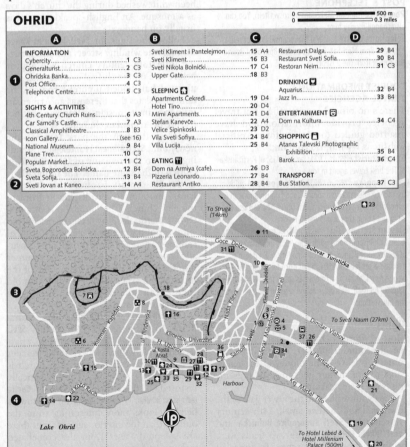

OHRID

INFORMATION		
Cybercity	1	C3
Generalturist	2	C3
Ohridska Banka	3	C3
Post Office	4	C3
Telephone Centre	5	C3

SIGHTS & ACTIVITIES		
4th Century Church Ruins	6	A3
Car Samoil's Castle	7	A3
Classical Amphitheatre	8	B3
Icon Gallery	(see 16)	
National Museum	9	B4
Plane Tree	10	C3
Popular Market	11	C2
Sveta Bogorodica Bolnička	12	B4
Sveta Sofija	13	B4
Sveti Jovan at Kaneo	14	A4
Sveti Kliment i Pantelejmon	15	A4
Sveti Kliment	16	B3
Sveti Nikola Bolnički	17	C4
Upper Gate	18	B3

SLEEPING		
Apartments Čekređi	19	D4
Hotel Tino	20	D4
Mimi Apartments	21	D4
Stefan Kanevče	22	A4
Velice Sipinkoski	23	D2
Vila Sveti Sofija	24	B4
Villa Lucija	25	B4

EATING		
Dom na Armiya (cafe)	26	D3
Pizzeria Leonardo	27	B4
Restaurant Antiko	28	B4

Restaurant Dalga	29	B4
Restaurant Sveti Sofia	30	B4
Restoran Neim	31	C3

DRINKING		
Aquarius	32	B4
Jazz In	33	B4

ENTERTAINMENT		
Dom na Kultura	34	C4

SHOPPING		
Atanas Talevski Photographic Exhibition	35	B4
Barok	36	C4

TRANSPORT		
Bus Station	37	C3

To Struga (14km)

Goce Delčev

7 Noemvri

Bulevar Turistička

To Sveti Naum (27km)

Dimitar Vlahov

Kliment Ohridski Prosvetitel

Naum Fileva

Klimentov Univerzitet

ul Uzunov

ul Kosta Abraš

ul Ilindenska

Koroman Kapidan

ul Kočo Racin

Kej Maršal Tito

ul Partizanska

ul Ičafim Klanoski

Jane Sandanski

Bulevar Makedonski Prosvetiteli

Car Samoil

Harbour

Lake Ohrid

To Hotel Lebed & Hotel Millenium Palace (500m)

MACEDONIA

Church in 1967 were important steps on the road to Macedonia's modern nationhood.

Orientation

The Old Town of Ohrid is easy to get around on foot. The lake is to the south, and the picturesque Old Town rises from Sveti Kliment Ohridski street, the main pedestrian mall.

Information

INTERNET ACCESS

Cybercity (☎ 231 620; www.cybercity.com.mk; 3rd fl, ul Sveti Kliment Ohridski; per hr 60MKD) Cheap overseas calls at 15MKD per minute can also be made from here.

POST & TELEPHONE

Post office (Bulevar Makedonski Prosvetiteli). You can also change money here.

Telephone centre (Bulevar Makedonski Prosvetiteli; ⊗ 7am-8pm Mon-Sat, 9am-noon & 6-8pm Sun) Round the corner from the post office.

TOURIST INFORMATION & TRAVEL AGENCIES

There's no official tourist office, but travel agencies provide information and have assorted guided tours. The town's official website is www.ohrid.com.mk.

Generalturist (☎ 261 071; fax 260 415; ul Partizanska 6) The best travel agent in town.

Jana Poposka (☎ 263 875) To hire a personal guide, try the voluble Jana who speaks good English and knows everything there is to know about Ohrid. She can usually be found at the church of Sveti Kliment.

Slavian Stefanovski (http://gradinar.freeservers.com) A local philosopher and guide who leads informative tours of the town and arranges accommodation. He doesn't demand a set fee but €10 is a fair price for a tour. His 'vegan hotel' at his apartment has space for two sleeping bags for €5 each. He's often found waiting for travellers at the bus station.

Sights

Most of Ohrid's churches charge an entry fee of around 100MKD; if not, it is customary to leave some money at the icons. Most of this money goes towards preserving these historical sites.

Start your walk from the lower gate of the town wall and the two small, 14th-century churches, of **Sveti Bogorodica Bolnička** and **Sveti Nikola Bolnički**. These two gems were originally hospital churches. In times of

plague people wanting to enter Ohrid were quarantined here for up to 40 days before being allowed into the town. The churches boast delicate frescoes. A great example of 19th-century Macedonian architecture is the 1827 **National Museum** (☎ 267 173; Car Samoil 62; adult/student 100/50MKD; ⊗ 10am-3pm Tue-Sun). The museum collection is divided into the Robev Residence, which houses an archaeological display, and the Urania Residence with an ethnographic display. Both rooms make for an interesting hour of exploring Macedonia's history.

Further up Car Samoil is the grandiose 11th-century church of **Sveta Sofija**, originally built as a cathedral. The frescoes are extremely well preserved thanks to having been whitewashed during the church's days as a mosque. An English-speaking guide is usually on hand.

Follow the signs for **Sveti Jovan at Kaneo** through the winding streets and this amazing little 13th-century church will appear before you on the cliffs above the lake. The unusual half-folded umbrella roof of the dome indicates that there was an Armenian influence in its design – this is a distinct feature of Armenian churches.

Go up through the park towards the newly built **Sveti Kliment i Pantelejmon**, standing next to the remains of Ohrid's oldest church of the same name. The foundations of the 5th-century basilica with their intricate mosaics are on display in front of the new church. The foundations of a **4th-century church** close by have been covered with a roof on pylons to show the original roofline. There are more mosaics here, usually covered with sand outside the summer months to help preserve them. One of the mosaics shows a swastika symbol – an old Indo-Aryan sun symbol long before the Nazis appropriated it.

Continue towards the **Upper Gate** (Gorna Porta) to the gorgeous, 13th-century **Sveti Kliment** (admission 100MKD; ⊗ 9am-5pm), patterned inside with vividly restored frescoes of biblical scenes. Opposite this church is an **icon gallery** (⊗ 9am-3pm). The emphatically restored, 10th-century **Car Samoil's Castle** (admission 30MKD; ⊗ 9am-6.30pm), on the town's heights, looks more interesting from the outside than the interior suggests, but there are splendid views from the crenellated walls and towers.

Ohrid's **Classical Amphitheatre** was first built around the time of the birth of Christ, and wasn't fully uncovered until 1984. The amphitheatre was originally built for plays and oratory, but in the late Roman era the first 10 rows were pulled out and replaced with a wall, so the theatre could be used as an arena for bloodspots. Its original purpose has been restored and the amphitheatre is used for Summer Festival performances.

A gnarled, 900-year-old **plane tree**, which apparently used to house a café and a barber shop at different points of its long life, stands at the town's northern end. The medieval town wall isolates the Old Town from the surrounding valley.

Festivals & Events

The five-day **Balkan Festival of Folk Dances & Songs**, held at Ohrid in early July, draws folkloric groups from around the Balkans. The **Ohrid Summer Festival**, held from mid-July to mid-August, features classical concerts in the Church of Sveta Sofija, open-air theatre, and many other events. An international **poetry festival**, replete with food and drink in the streets, is held annually in nearby Struga on 25 and 26 August.

Ohrid hosts a **swimming marathon** each August, when swimmers race the 30km across Lake Ohrid from Sveti Naum to Ohrid.

Sleeping

BUDGET

Villa Lucija (☎ 265 608; luciya@mt.net.mk; ul Kosta Abraš 29; s/d €15/25, apt €40) A fantastic place in the centre of the Old Town and near all the bars, its rooms are white, clean and spacious, balconies overlook the lake, and the patio is right on the water for a swim. Book early though, this place is popular.

Private rooms or apartments (per person €5-10) Your best bet in Ohrid, private rooms or apartments can be organised in advance either through Generalturist (opposite) or other local agencies, or chances are someone will approach you at the bus station and offer you a room. Rooms in the Old Town are more expensive.

Stefan Kanevče Rooms (☎ 070-212 352, 234 813; apostolanet@yahoo.co.uk; ul Kočo Racin 47, Kaneo; per person €10) This spot is lakeside in Kaneo, the small settlement you can see west from the Church of Sveti Jovan. The rooms are in a 19th-century house with carved wooden ceilings, generous hospitality and Macedonian home cooking. Be warned that it is a bit of a hike from the Old Town. Stefan also arranges rooms in other houses around Ohrid.

Mimi Apartments (☎ 250 103; mimioh@mail.com.mk; ul Strašo Pinđur 2; r incl breakfast 800MKD) Friendly Mimi Apostolov lets eight comfortable, heated rooms, each of which has a fridge and satellite TV.

Veliče Šipinkoski (☎ 070 854 651, 252 345; ul 7 Noemvri 120; s/d €7.50/15) There are five simple rooms at this house in a quiet neighbourhood about 250m from the market. Breakfast costs €3. Veliče is a friendly chap – you may well meet him at the bus station.

MIDRANGE & TOP END

Apartments Čekređi (☎ 261 733, 070 570 717; Kej Maršal Tito 27; d/tr 1500/2700MKD) These roomy, immaculate and spacious quarters close to the lake are good for a stay of a few days, as you can self-cater.

Hotel Lebed (☎ 250 004; www.hotellebed.com.mk; Kej Maršal Tito bb; incl breakfasts €32-37, d €52-57) This friendly little eight-room hotel is about 1km from the town centre (a 50MKD taxi ride). The more expensive rooms have lake views. The rooms have relaxing wooden décor, phones, satellite TV, central heating and air-conditioning. Visa and MasterCard are accepted.

Hotel Tino (☎ 261 665; www.hoteltino.com.mk; Kej Maršal Tito 55; s/d €39/49) This mid-sized hotel by the lakeshore in the new part of town has a ground-floor restaurant serving Italian and Macedonian cuisines and quite nice rooms – the lakeside ones have little balconies. The rooms have satellite TV, phone and

---

THE AUTHOR'S CHOICE

Vila Sveti Sofiya (☎ 254 370, www.vilasofiya.com; ul Kosta Abraš 64; s €35, d €60, suite €80-120) Tucked into the lower part of the old city just 50m from the Sveti Sofiya church, this bijou establishment hotel combines opulent traditional furnishings and old-world charm with the latest in bathroom design. The luxury suite is impossibly romantic, and the entire building is a wonderful example of an Ohrid mansion. For my money this is the best boutique hotel in Macedonia.

MACEDONIA

air-conditioning. Visa and Mastercard aren't accepted here – cash only.

Hotel Millenium Palace (☎ 263 361; www.millen iumpalace.com.mk; Kej Maršal Tito bb; s/d €49/66, ste €99) The exterior may not win prizes for classic beauty but the facilities within are very good – all mod cons such as satellite TV, minibar and very comfy beds. Plus, for exercise fanatics it has a small gym, sauna and an indoor swimming pool with a cocktail bar! The suites have terraces overlooking the lake. Accepts Visa, MasterCard and Diners cards.

Eating & Drinking

Restaurants, quick eats, cafés and bars are dotted all around Ohrid.

Restaurant Sveti Sofia (☎ 267 403; ul Car Samoil 88; meals around 500MKD; ☽ 10am-midnight) Classy bistro just uphill from the Sveti Sofia church, with a wide range of modern and traditional Macedonian dishes. The view from the terrace onto the ancient church is the very soul of Ohrid.

Restoran Neim (☎ 254 504; ul Goce Delčev 71; ☽ 9am-midnight) Check out the local characters at this working man's hangout about 100m west of the old plane tree, and try some delicious moussaka or *polneti piperki* (stuffed peppers).

Restaurant Antiko (☎ 265 523; ul Car Samoil 30; mains from 350MKD; ☽ 9am-midnight) This traditional place, located in an old Ohrid house, is one of the most popular restaurants in town, although it's rather pricey. Special warning: if you want to eat Macedonian specialities, you have to order them three hours in advance.

Pizzeria Leonardo (☎ 260 359; ul Car Samoil 31; ☽ 9am-midnight) For a pizza and half a litre of draught wine at around 250MKD, this cosy little spot is the place to be.

Restaurant Dalga (☎ 31 948; ul Kosta Abraš bb) Here you can enjoy glorious lake views along with some Californian trout at 800MKD per kilo.

Dom na Armiya (☎ secret; ul Partizanka bb; ☽ 7am-6pm) For something different, the Army House is a classic communist café, remaining unchanged since Tito took his holidays at Ohrid, and serving coffee for only 10MKD. The waiters in ageing tuxedos refused to divulge the telephone number to this foreign spy, but subterfuge helped me get the opening hours.

Jazz Inn (ul Kosta Abraš 27; admission free; ☽ 10.30pm-2am) A vibrant, jazzy atmosphere, with live music on Thursdays and weekends, this must be the most popular place in town. Opens late and stays open until much later.

Aquarius (ul Kosta Abraš bb; ☽ 10am-midnight) A local radio station broadcasts from this groovy lakeside bar in summer. The lakeside terrace was the first of its kind, an idea picked up by adjacent bars. The bar features a big sound system and lots of cocktails.

Entertainment

Dom na Kultura (ul Grigor Prličev; admission 50-100MKD) Ohrid's movie theatre, Dom na Kultura, faces the lakeside park. Cultural events are also held here.

Shopping

Pick up some interesting woodcarvings at **Barok** (☎ 263 151; barokohrid@yahoo.com; ul Car Samoil 24; ☽ 10am-2pm & 5-8pm), or some fine prints of photographs of rural Macedonia by photographer **Atanas Talevski** (☎ 254 059; Kosta Abraš bb; ☽ 9am-9pm). Small prints cost 200MKD and large ones 900MKD.

Getting There & Away

AIR

Four airlines serve **Ohrid Airport** (information ☎ 252 820, www.airports.com.mk), which is 10km north of Ohrid. JAT flies to Belgrade via Skopje on Mondays and Fridays. A taxi to the airport costs 250MKD.

BUS

About 10 buses per day run between Ohrid and Skopje (380MKD, three hours, 167km), via Kičevo. Another four or five go via Bitola. The first route is shorter, faster, more scenic and cheaper, so try to take it. The last bus to Skopje leaves around 6.30pm. During the summer rush, it pays to book a seat the day before.

There are 10 buses per day travelling to Bitola (70MKD, 1¼ hours). Buses to Struga (70MKD, 14km) leave about every 15 minutes (5.30am to 8.30pm) from stand 1 at the **bus station** (☎ 262 490; ul Dimitar Vlahov). Enter through the back doors and pay the conductor (30MKD).

There are three buses per day to Belgrade (1500MKD, about 12 hours).

To go to Albania, catch a bus or boat to Sveti Naum Monastery, which is very near the border crossing. In summer, there are six buses every day from Ohrid to Sveti Naum (120MKD, 29km), in winter, three daily. The bus continues on to the border post. From Albanian customs it's 6km to Pogradeci; taxis are waiting and should charge only €5 for the ride. A taxi from Ohrid to Sveti Naum costs €10/15 one way/return.

Around Ohrid

SVETI NAUM СВЕТИ НАУМ

The magnificent grounds of the Sveti Naum Monastery, close to the Albanian border 29km south of Ohrid, are a real treat. Standing just over the lake, the grounds are guarded by peacocks and hide the source of Lake Ohrid's water. The beautiful 17th-century **Church of Sveti Naum** rises on a hill above the lake, surrounded by the buildings of the Hotel Sveti Naum which has taken over the old monastery complex.

The original church of the Holy Archangels was built here in 900 by St Naum, and St Naum himself was buried here in 910. They say that you can still hear his heart beat if you put your ear on his tomb inside the chapel. The charming frescoes of the archangels inside the church are mostly 19th century, though fragments of 16th- and 17th-century work remain. You can probably find an English speaker on hand to act as a guide. There's no need to pay the guide, but do leave some money by the icons. The monastery grounds also offer a view of the Albanian town of Pogradeci across the lake. In the summer months you can take a half-hour boat trip from the monastery to bubbling springs that feed Lake Ohrid (100MKD per person).

Sleeping & Eating

Hotel Sveti Naum (☎ 046 283 244; www.hotel-stnaum .com.mk; r €35-60, ste €80) Standing at the heart of the monastery, this hotel has magical views, and excellent rooms with satellite TV, central heating and traditional styling. Book in advance during the popular summer months; prices drop at other times of the year. The hotel restaurant serves meals for about 600MKD per person.

Getting There & Away

Six buses per day run from Ohrid to Sveti Naum; it's 80MKD one way, payable on the bus. Buses generally return 40 minutes after they set out – the last one leaves Sveti Naum at 7pm. The bus makes a stop at the Albanian border before turning back.

In summer, you can also come by boat but it only leaves when a group of about five to eight people is present; ask about times at the wharf or at the travel agencies in town. The fare is about 150/200MKD one way/return.

VEVČANI ВЕВЧАНИ

Vevčani is a Christian village surrounded by Muslim villages 14km northwest of Struga. In the early 1990s, its residents saw how the new post-Yugoslav nationalisms were destroying the region and came up with their own solution – they declared independence. In 1991, 99 per cent of the villagers voted for an independent Republic of Vevčani, which now has its own flag, passports and currency. The push for independence began in 1987, when the government planned to tap Vevčani's springs and pipe water to Struga. The villagers built barricades to block the construction work, and after several weeks of violent protests the government backed off. After the independence vote in 1991 the villagers let it be known they had stockpiled weapons and again warned the government to leave them alone. The Macedonian government has studiously ignored the unilateral declaration of independence, but the tactic seems to have worked – the villagers of Vevčani have the respect of their Muslim neighbours and local relations are in good shape.

Vevčani is one of the region's prettiest villages, with some fine old houses and a splendid 19th-century church, Sveti Nikola. Many of the local men are builders and masons by trade. There's a good traditional restaurant called **Domakinska Kukja** (☎ 046-790 505; meals around 500MKD; ☺ noon-10pm Wed-Sun) near Sveti Nikola at the top of the village. The restaurant sells Vevčanian passports and currency.

The town also has a famous annual **festival** on January 13 and 14 – the Orthodox New Year's Eve. The festival culminates in a satirical carnival, where villagers dress up as politicians, policemen and other dubious characters and send up the lot.

From Vevčani it is possible to walk up to the old mountain village of **Gorno Belica** –

MACEDONIA

population, two. The village lies above the treeline on the high slopes of Jablanica mountain. The walking trails are marked.

A taxi from Ohrid and back with a two-hour wait costs about 1800MKD. There are minibuses to the village from Struga.

PELISTER NATIONAL PARK & LAKE PRESPA

Macedonia's oldest national park (it was proclaimed in 1948) covers 12,500 hectares of pine forest and the great granite dome of Mt Pelister (2601m). The park protects some 88 species of trees, included the rare five-leafed Molika pine (Pinus peuce).

There is a very small **ski resort** (with one ski run) on the northern side of the mountain near Bitola. The chairlift is next to the Hotel Molika. Besides the chairlift there is also one ski lift operating on weekends from December until the end of March – a day pass costs 300MKD. The resort used to be bigger in Yugoslav times, and it looks like more lifts and lodges will reopen here over the next few years.

The main cultural attraction inside the park is the rugged old Vlach village of **Malovište**. The village has been slowly losing its population for decades, but its collection of two-storey, stone houses are one of the finest ensembles of traditional architecture in Macedonia. The little Shemnica River burbles through the village, crossed by many quaint little bridges. The village lanes are made of rough cobble stones – sturdy footwear helps to save your ankles. The massive church of **Sveti Petka** at the top of the village (built in 1856) shows how wealthy the community had grown through cattle breeding. The interior is full of frescoes and over one hundred icons. About 2km from the village, in the middle of a dense beech forest, is the little church of **Sveti Ana**. It takes about 30 minutes to hike there – it's 400m higher in altitude. Hotels in Bitola can arrange transport to and from Malovište with one hour at the village for about 500MKD. Malovište is 4km off Highway E65 between Bitola and Resen – turn off at Kazani, take the first left and then another left through a tunnel under the highway.

Hotel Molika (☎ 047-229 406; www.hotelmolika .com.mk; s/d €28/44) is 12km from Bitola, high up in the Molika pine forests at an altitude of 1420m. This very pleasant resort hotel

has simple but comfortable rooms, a cheerful wood-panelled restaurant (meals around 700MKD), fresh highland air and tremendous views down the mountain to Bitola. A taxi from Bitola costs about 400MKD.

The eastern shore of **Lake Prespa** is a very pretty area of orchards and villages, between the Pelister mountain and the reedy shores of the lake. This used to be a popular holiday spot in the past, and the communist-era lakeside resorts are looking rather tired, the views over the lake are as magical as ever.

The village of **Kurbinovo** is as typical a Macedonian village as you could find, but the little church of **Sveti Gjorgi** about 1km uphill from the village is one of the country's cultural treasures. The church was thought to have been an 18th century construction for many years, until art historians took another look and realised its frescoes date back to 1191. The images on the 50 denar note come from the church's frescoes. You'll have to ask in the village for the custodian with the key to the church.

Just before the Greek border a road leads to the utterly captivating villages of **Ljubojno** and **Brajčino**. The villages share a lovely setting between wooded slopes and a wealth of old stone houses. Brajčino has six churches, while Ljubojno sits below the domes of **Sveti Petar i Pavle**. The area used to prosper from growing apples for the Greek market, but since the Greeks closed the border here trading has languished. Brajčino is the start of a 17km trek into Pelister National Park. The hike takes about six hours, with two natural springs on the way, up to a **mountain hut** (☎ 070 497 751) with 25 beds near Stone Lake (Golemo Ezero). There are buses to Brajčino from Resen at 6am, 9am, 11.30am, 2.30pm and 3.30pm, and about 10 buses in either direction every day between Ohrid and Bitola which stop in Resen.

BITOLA БИТОЛА
☎ 097 / pop 77,000

Bitola, sits on a 660m-high plateau between mountains 16km north of the Greek border. It was an important commercial centre in the late Ottoman era (when it was called Manastir), and it still has a substantial Turkish population. Its past prosperity has graced it with a fine collection of 19th-century buildings, interspersed with some

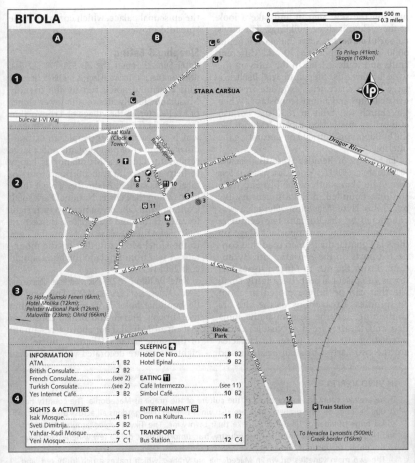

BITOLA

STARA ČARŠIJA

Saat Kula
(Clock
Tower)

Dragor River

bulevar I-VI Maj

To Prilep (41km);
Skopje (169km)

To Hotel Šumski Feneri (6km);
Hotel Molika (12km);
Pelister National Park (12km);
Malovište (23km); Ohrid (66km)

Bitola
Park

To Heraclea Lyncestis (500m);
Greek border (16km)

Train Station

INFORMATION	
ATM	1 B2
British Consulate	2 B2
French Consulate	(see 2)
Turkish Consulate	(see 2)
Yes Internet Café	3 B2

SIGHTS & ACTIVITIES	
Isak Mosque	4 B1
Sveti Dimitrija	5 B2
Yahdar-Kadi Mosque	6 C1
Yeni Mosque	7 C1

SLEEPING	
Hotel De Niro	8 B2
Hotel Epinal	9 B2

EATING	
Café Intermezzo	(see 11)
Simbol Café	10 B2

ENTERTAINMENT	
Dom na Kultura	11 B2

TRANSPORT	
Bus Station	12 C4

wildly inappropriate communist monoliths. The town has a vibrant arts scene and some decent hotels. It makes a good base for visiting Pelister National Park and Prilep.

One of the town's curiosities is its three consulates – Turkish, British and French. They are the last of 15 or so European consulates based here in the late 19th century. The Turkish consulate is still here because of the local Turkish minority; the British consulate is still here because they don't want to leave before the French do; and the French won't leave until the British pack up. All three share the same premises on ul Maršal Tito.

The **Ilinden festival**, the most important event of the year, takes place on 2 August, when the Macedonians celebrate their uprising against the Ottomans with traditional food, music and general joy.

Information

There is no tourist office in town, but a good source of information online is www .bitola.de, in English, German and Macedonian – 'only in Bitola life can be discovered' it says. The **Yes Internet Café** (ul Boris Kidrič; per hr 40MKD; 7am-3am) in the centre of town is cheap, quick and serves drinks.

Sights

As you enter, you will notice the magnificent minarets of the 16th-century **Yeni Mosque**, **Isak Mosque** and **Yahdar-Kadi Mosque**

MACEDONIA

piercing the sky. Step in and take a look at these elegant stone buildings. The city's colourful **old bazaar**, Stara Čaršija, has about 6000 shops supporting 70-odd different crafts and trades. Relax in the cafés on the wide boulevards. Step into **Sveti Dimitri**, a large lavish space with exquisite frescoes, ornate lamps and a huge iconostasis. When the church was built in 1830 the Turkish authorities insisted on a plain exterior, so the builders concentrated on decorating the interior.

The ruins of **Heraclea Lyncestis** (admission 100MKD, photos 500MKD; ☺ 9am-3pm winter, to 5pm summer) lie 1km south of the bus and train stations. Founded in the 4th century BC by Philip II of Macedon, Heraclea was conquered by the Romans two centuries later and became an important stage on the Via Egnatia, the Roman road that connected ports on the Adriatic with Byzantium. From the 4th to 6th centuries AD it was an episcopal seat. It's a fairly small site that can be fully explored in about 30 minutes. Excavations of the site are continuing, but the Roman baths, portico and theatre are now visible. Other interesting attractions to see in Heraclea are the two early Christian basilicas and the episcopal palace, which contains some splendid mosaics.

Sleeping & Eating

Hotel Šumski Feneri (☎ 293 030, 070 682 244; sfeneri@mt.net.mk; Trnovo village; s/d €30/45, apt €60) This charming hotel, run by the friendly Musulanov family, lies on the lower slopes of Mt Pelister, in the village of Trnovo 4km from Bitola. The hotel has four apartments which can each fit four people, an extraordinary number of potted plants and a large restaurant. Ljubmila Musulanov is happy to help guests with transport and tours of local sights such as Malovište. To get there head out on the Pelister National Park road. Coming from Ohrid you need to turn right towards Bitola and then take a quick turn right again up to the park – follow the signs to the Hotel Molika further up the mountain. A taxi from Bitola to the hotel should cost 200MKD.

Hotel De Niro (☎ 229 656; www.hotel-deniro.com; ul Kiril i Metodij 5; s/d €35/50, ste €80) This new little boutique hotel is in the street behind the Turkish, French and British consulates just off ul Maršal Tito, above a restaurant of the same name (Italian of course). All eight rooms are decorated with individual

---

IN VINO VERITAS

There are few countries as drenched in the culture of the grape as Macedonia. The country has 20,000 hectares of wine grapes. There are also vines trailing over gardens all across the country, and a huge number of households make their own wine. The Tikveš region around Kavadarci and Negotino is the heart of the wine industry, but, unfortunately, only a few wineries are open to the public for tastings and sales.

The two main varieties grown in Macedonia are Vranec, which makes a rich fruity red, and Smederevka, a light white with citrus notes. These varieties used to account for 80 per cent of all wine made, but recently there's been a switch towards French varieties including Merlot, Chardonnay, Pinot Noir and Cabernet Sauvignon. The giant of the industry is Tikveš, based in Kavadarci, which alone makes up about 60 per cent of the local wine market. Tikveš wines, such as its popular T'ga za Jug, are practically national icons – and quite moderately priced at around 400MKD per bottle. Skovin is a mid-sized winery close to Skopje, and its wines are popular in the capital. Fonko Wines is one of Macedonia's biggest premium wineries, producing Chardonnay, Smederevka, Merlot, Pinot Noir, Vranec and Cabernet Sauvignon. Its Alexander the Great range is quite expensive – around 1000MKD per bottle – but well worth the splurge. The following are a couple of premium wineries which can be visited:

Bovin Winery (☎ 043-365 322; Industriska zone 1440, Negotino) Macedonia's first private winery, established in 1998. Bovin has since won a clutch of awards and medals for its Pinot Noir and Vranec. It also makes a very good Merlot.

Čekorovi Winery (☎ 043-400 317; bulevar Edvard Kardelj 11/10, Kavadarci) Boutique wines made by veteran winemaker Kiril Čekorov. Čekorov produces just two wines – a white Riesling and a red Vranec – in limited quantities from grapes grown in the heart of the Tikveš wine region.

flair – some in traditional Bitolan style, others with leather sofas and Jacuzzis. All have air-conditioning, cable TV and Internet connections.

Hotel Epinal (☎ 224 777; www.hotelepinal.com; ul Maršal Tito bb; s/d €65/100), in the centre of Bitola is a marginally revamped communist-era tower block. The casino, spa and restaurant are all fine but the rooms are small and poor value. The open-air café under a wrought-iron roof at the front of the hotel, on the other hand, is an excellent spot for a bite to eat, with pizzas and pasta dishes from 200MKD and steaks for around 600MKD.

Ul Maršal Tito is lined with cafés, restaurants and bars – one popular spot is the **Café Intermezzo** (☎ 225 115; Kej Domot na Kulturata; ☺ 9am-midnight), a wood-lined pub/café/restaurant on the ground level of the Dom na Kultura (House of Culture), opposite the Hotel Epinal. Another stylish place is the **Simbol Café** (☎ 203 750; ul Maršal Tito 65; ☺ 8am-midnight), with a modern twist on 19th-century design and up-to-date tunes.

Getting There & Away

The **bus station** (☎ 391 391; ul Nikola Tesla) and the **train station** (☎ 392 904; ul Nikola Tesla) are adjacent to each other, about 1km south of the town centre. There are 10 buses per day to Skopje between 5am and 5.25pm (2½ hours, 350MKD) via Prilep, and six trains daily. There are between 12 and 18 buses per day to Ohrid – the higher number being in summer (1¼ hours, 70MKD). To get to the Greek border, you must take a taxi from the bus station (350MKD to 450MKD), then look for a taxi on the Greek side to the nearest town, Florina.

TRESKAVEC MONASTERY
МАНАСТИР ТРЕСКАВЕЦ

This is the most magnificent – and perhaps the most remote – place in the country. Planted on the top of Mt Zlato 10km above the town of Prilep, you couldn't get a more breathtaking and dramatic setting. You will most certainly feel deliriously light-headed upon reaching the monastery when, after the two-hour climb, you breathe the fresh air at the top. The valley stretches out on all sides beneath you. The mountain itself is bare and the rock formations are like dinosaurs turned to stone mid-step, with a solitary tree grazed by the sweeping winds.

Prepare to be amazed by some of the most colourful and intricate frescoes to be found in Macedonia at the 14th-century **Sveti Bogorodica**, the monastery's spiritual heart. The incisions on the bare walls reveal yet more frescoes to be uncovered, like small windows into history. The church was built on the foundations of the original 6th-century basilica, and inside you can see some more Roman remains.

Inside the monastery you will be welcomed by the lovely Naumovski couple who will cook you dinner and let you sleep in the rooms for free; beds and blankets are provided. Leave a donation of 200MKD at the icons.

To get to the monastery, you must first get to Prilep. There are frequent buses from Ohrid, Bitola and Skopje, and four trains from Skopje go every day (300MKD, three hours). From Prilep, there are two ways of getting to the monastery: one is by 4WD up a muddy mountain track. Ask for directions to the new town cemetery where you will have to watch out for a small sign for *Manastir Sveti Bogorodica, Treskavec*. Head straight up. The second option is on foot, and is far more rewarding, because you get to see the fantastic scenery around you and experience the priceless sight of the monastery appearing above you. Take a taxi to Dabnica village outside Prilep to the north and head for the cobbled track leading you up Mt Zlato. If you cannot see the cobbled track straight away, ask the driver to point you in the right direction. Go up the road, and after you reach the water fountain, continue on the straight path.

At the end of your mountain excursion, check out **Markovi Kuli** (Marko's Towers) on the hill above Prilep. Archaeological findings show that the site dates back to the 3rd and 4th centuries BC, but most of the remains you will be able to see are from medieval times. This is another place from which to enjoy spectacular views.

EASTERN MACEDONIA

The eastern half of the country is not high on most visitors' priorities. The mountains are lower, the land is drier and the region is strongly agricultural with scattered places of interest. Public transport out here is OK if you just want to go to and from Skopje, but trips between regional cities tend to test your patience. The easiest and least frustrating way to explore the region is by car. If you don't mind putting in a few hours behind the wheel dodging tractors and farm trucks, Eastern Macedonia has some wonderful monasteries and churches, some of the best preserved traditional villages and a couple of real oddities like a 4000-year-old astronomical observatory.

NORTHEASTERN MACEDONIA

If Orthodox churches and monasteries really ring your bell, then there are a couple of worthwhile detours off the main highway to Sofia in Bulgaria. **Kumanovo** is Macedonia's third biggest city, but it is a rather dull, dusty regional commercial centre. Like most of eastern Macedonia's towns, its historic quarter was thoroughly damaged by the wars of the early 20th century. Some maps show a monastery about 20km west of Kumanovo, near the village of **Matejče** on the eastern slopes of the Skopska Crna Gora mountains. The villages in the vicinity are ethnic Albanian, and the monastery of **Sveti Spas** (built in the 14th century by the Serbian Emperor Dusan the Mighty) was heavily vandalised by UČK militants in 2001. The monastery has been partially repaired, but visiting here was a salutary lesson in stumbling into the embers of ethnic conflict. Asking for directions to the monastery in Matejče led me being directed to the local mosque instead, which had been sprayed with gunfire and had its minaret blown in half. On the way back to Kumanovo I was stopped and questioned by bullying policemen for 30 minutes – not a particularly pleasant experience.

Northeast of Kumanovo is the village of Staro Nagoričane. It lies 4km north of the E871 Kumanovo-Sofia highway – turn off at the sign for Prohor Pčinski, take a left at the T-intersection and then the first right. The village lies on a broad rolling plain, and is fairly undistinguished except for the handsome church of **Sveti Gjorgi**, a 14th-century construction on top of an earlier shrine. The rich frescoes date from 1318. Ask at the police station next to the church and they'll help track down the custodian who

has the key. The church is in the centre of Staro Nagoričane, about 1km off the main road (look for a sharp left turn to get on the road into the village – it's easy to miss). To reach the **Kokino megalithic observatory** on the peak of Taticev Kamen, get back onto the main road, head north for 5km and take a right to the village of Dragomance. This minor road heads northeast for 15km past the hamlet of Stepanče. Just after Stepanče, look for a small sign on the left at the crest of a hill. This leads uphill for a couple of hundred metres, and then it's a stiff climb up to the observatory on top of the volcanic ridge.

The site was confirmed as an observatory in 2002. It is believed to have been built around 1815 BC to measure the movements of the sun and moon. To the uninformed eye there isn't much to see, but the marks and niches in the rocks were finely calibrated to mark the winter and summer solstice, the vernal and autumnal equinox and the four main positions of the moon over a year. Some of the markings indicate the optimal time for harvesting different crops.

Back on the E871 the road continues through rolling pasture lands, past low volcanic outcroppings and down into fertile valleys. The roads starts to climb as you approach Kriva Palanka. The town straggles along the Kriva River for several kilometres. Evidently the local economy is in a slump, and while the townsfolk are friendly there is very little in the way of places to stay or eat. At the far (upriver) end of town a sign points south to the monastery of **Sveti Joakim Osogovski**, one of the largest in Macedonia. The monastery is tucked away in a wooded valley high above the town. There's a semi-derelict hotel at the turn-off. It's a twisty, five-minute drive or a 30-minute walk from the turn-off. It is possible to stay at the monastery in either the old monk's quarters (300MKD for a simple double) or in a new pilgrims' lodge (600MKD). Make a booking by calling during the day on ☎ 031-375 063. If you don't speak Macedonian, it is worth getting someone to call for you.

The complex has two churches and several impressive monastic buildings. Parts of the smaller Sveti Bodorodica church date from the monastery's founding in the

12th century. The larger, multidomed Sveti Joakim Osogovski church dates from the mid-19th century. The 12 cupolae on the roof represent the Twelve Apostles. The frescoes around the main door and on the inside of the cupolae mostly date from the 1850s. The monastery's main festival is on Sveti Joakim Osogovski's feast day, 29 August. Other buildings in the complex include a bell tower with a charnel house in its base, a three-storey dormitory and a guardhouse.

The ancient mining town of **Kratovo** lies in an old volcanic crater 18km south of the E871 highway. The town has been a source of iron ore for millennia. Kratovo is known for its stone towers, built as the town's defence system. The turn-off to Kratovo is just after the Stracin Pass. After you cross the Kriva River a rough road (4WD recommended) leads off on the right to the bizarre rock formations called the **kukla** (stone dolls), pinnacles of rocks set in a deeply eroded ravine.

Further south of Kratovo near the village of Lesnovo is another fine monastery, **Sveti Gavril Lesnovski**. It is the third monastery in Macedonia to sport an iconostasis carved by the Filipovski brothers and Makarije Frckovski, who also created the masterpieces at Sveti Spas in Skopje and Sveti Jovan Bigorski in Mavrovo National Park. The 14th-century church also has some fine frescoes.

BEROVO БЕРОВО

☎ 033 / pop 7,000

This quiet farming town is tucked into the rolling, pine-forested highlands by the Bulgarian border. In communist times this little mountain town (altitude 850m) was a minor, all-seasons holiday resort. It has no epic attractions, but it's an easy-going retreat from Skopje's summer heat and there are some superb examples of traditional architecture in the town and in nearby hamlets and villages. The town itself is very pleasant – residential districts on either side of the little Bregalnica River overlook pastures, fields and public buildings in the middle.

SIGHTS

The **Sveti Arhangel Mihail** convent isn't the biggest complex in Macedonia, but it is one of the prettiest. It's at the far end of town from Skopje, next to the Hotel Manastir. The most obvious feature is its charming octagonal belltower, set on a square stone base. The convent was built in the 19th century and was at the forefront of education in Macedonia in that era. At its height in the early 20th century, 60 nuns lived here. Enter through the fine wooden gate and the peaceful atmosphere strike you immediately. The wooden and stone convent quarters surround an inner garden and a small but elegant main chapel with a large wooden portico. At the time of research there were five nuns in residence; they have a sideline in painting icons according to the old techniques.

Otherwise the main attractions are either a tour of nearby villages such as Rusinovo, a centre for traditional weaving, or a short drive (or longish walk) 4km up the valley to the artificial Lake Ratevo, surrounded by pine and beech forests.

SLEEPING & EATING

Hotel Manastir (☎ 472 28; fax 472 283; ul Kiril i Metodij; s €20, d €30-40, ste €60) This lovely, traditional-style hotel has modern comfy rooms with minibars, couches and snazzy bathrooms. Some face onto the little monastery, others overlook the town. The restaurant on the ground floor is very more-ish (mains around 250MKD to 300MKD and the best chips in Macedonia) and has outdoor seating. The local *belo cirenje* (white cheese) is particularly good.

Loven Dom (☎ 470 454; r €25, full board €32) The name means 'hunting lodge' but thankfully taxidermy is not in evidence. The lodge has four rooms (two apartments and two standard rooms, all the same price) above a large dining hall. The rooms are quite decent, fairly simple but comfortable. The main attraction is the spacious grounds, backing onto a forest. The lodge has an outdoor restaurant in summer.

About 4km out of town at Lake Ratevo is the **Maleševo Recreation Centre** (☎ 471 212; www.malesevo.com.mk; cabin 1240MKD). The main building is looking rundown, but the cabins down by the lakeshore are pretty good, if simple. Next to the cabins is a popular local restaurant with grills from around 350MKD, outdoor seating and lots of inexpensive wines and beers.

MACEDONIA

GETTING THERE AND AWAY

Skopje is 161km away. The bus station is in the centre of town – there are eight buses per day to Skopje, from 4.30am to 6pm (four hours, 350MKD). If you have a car, there's a very pretty 47km drive to Strumica through highland forests and down a dramatic escarpment.

SOUTHEASTERN MACEDONIA

The town of Strumica is about as interesting as my hometown of Seymour in central Victoria, Australia – in short, not very interesting at all, unless perhaps you're shopping for tractors. There are, however, two lovely little churches in nearby villages. The hamlet of Vodoča, 5km west of Strumica is home to the monastery of **Sveti Leonthius**, which has been demolished and rebuilt several times in its 1000-year history. There are some restored pilgrims' quarters next to the church. Three kilometres further on, the village of Veljusa is home to the monastery of **Sveti Bogorodica-Eleusa**, which dates back to 1080. The floor of the church shows some of the mosaic from the original construction.

South of Strumica is the third and least interesting of Macedonia's big lakes, **Lake Dojran**, which straddles the Greek border. The lake is in poor shape ecologically because too much water has been diverted for irrigation, and the water level has dropped several metres in the last 20 years. The main attraction here is a casino built to extract money from Greek gamblers. There is a small border crossing into Greece.

MACEDONIA DIRECTORY

ACCOMMODATION

The listings of accommodation are given in order of preference. Skopje's hotels are relatively expensive but there are some alternatives, such as private-room agencies. Skopje's convenient HI hostel is open throughout the year. Beds are also available at student dormitories in Skopje in summer. Prices in more expensive hotels are usually quoted in euros. The accommodation in Ohrid is generally good and affordable, with plenty of budget and midrange

---

PRACTICALITIES

- The press is varied with *Nova Makedonija, Vest,* and *Dnevnik* among the most popular of half-a-dozen daily Macedonian-language newspapers. Most newspapers are closely aligned to major political parties. *Forum* is an influential bi-weekly news magazine, also in Macedonian. The two main Albanian-language newspapers are *Fakti* and *Flaka*. There are also newspapers in Roma and Turkish.

- There are six Macedonian-language TV stations, A1 being the most credible for news reporting. There are also two Albanian-language TV channels. There are dozens of local radio stations, two of the more popular being City Radio and Radio Uno.

- Macedonia uses standard European electricity (220V to 240V/50Hz to 60Hz).

- The system used for measurements and weights is metric.

- Macedonia uses the PAL video system.

---

options. Booking early is recommended for visits during the summer high season, Orthodox Christmas (7 January) and Orthodox Easter.

ACTIVITIES

The Mavrovo ski resort in the national park of the same name is Macedonia's premier resort, with a lot of new ski runs and lifts constructed in recent years. There is also skiing at Popova Šapka (1845m), on the southern slopes of Šar Planina west of Tetovo. However, because Popova Šapka is in the 'Albanian' part of the country and it is close to the Kosovo border, the resort has languished during the last 15 years and the facilities are distinctly dated. There is also a very small ski centre (one chairlift) in Pelister National Park.

Hiking is spectacular in any of the three national parks (Galičica and Pelister in the south, and Mavrovo) or at Lake Matka near Skopje, which offers climbing and sailing. For a dose of pure Balkan machismo, hunting is also quite popular.

One excellent resource for mountain climbing and alpine trekking is the website of the **Korab Mountain Club** (www.korab .org.mk/indexen.html), Macedonia's most active mountaineering club. The website contains details on tackling 14 mountain routes in Macedonia and other useful info (including, gulp, rescue-service numbers).

BOOKS

Lonely Planet's *Eastern Europe phrasebook* will help you with the language.

A decent background book is *Who Are the Macedonians?*, a political and cultural history by Hugh Poulton. Rebecca West's *Black Lamb & Grey Falcon*, a between-the-wars Balkan travelogue, makes a brief mention of Macedonia. A recent study is *The New Macedonian Question* edited by James Pettifer – a collection of academic essays discussing this complex issue.

BUSINESS HOURS

Businesses tend to stay open late in Macedonia. Travellers will generally find them open from 8am to 8pm weekdays and 8am to 2pm on Saturday. Post offices open from 6.30am to 4pm and banks from 7am to 5pm, Monday to Friday.

CUSTOMS

Customs checks are generally cursory, though travellers with private cars may attract more attention at land borders. You may bring one litre of alcohol and 200 cigarettes in with you, and the maximum amount of currency that can be brought into the country without having to declare it is €10,000. You can take MKD freely back over the border with you, but there is not much point in doing so because it cannot be exchanged into any currency outside of Macedonia.

DANGERS & ANNOYANCES

Macedonia is a safe and easygoing country in general. The usual cautions apply – pickpockets and other dodgy types tend to hang out at train and bus stations, and some taxi drivers will try to charge exorbitant fees if you're just arrived by bus, train or plane.

Tread carefully if you go to villages which saw fighting during the ethnic disturbances of recent years. These lie in a belt along the frontier with Kosovo, from Tetovo to Kumanovo.

DISABLED TRAVELLERS

Few public buildings or streets have facilities for wheelchairs, but some newer buildings and some of the most expensive hotels provide wheelchair ramps. There is no disabled access on public transport.

EMBASSIES & CONSULATES
Macedonian Embassies & Consulates

A full list of Macedonian embassies abroad and embassies and consulates in Macedonia can be found on the Ministry of Foreign Affairs website at www.mfr.gov.mk. Macedonian embassies include the following:

Albania (☎ 04-233 036; makambas@albnet.net; rruga Lek Dukagjini, Vila 2, Tirana)

Australia (☎ 02-6249 8000; macedonian .embassy@netspeed.com.au; Perpetual Bldg, Suite 2:05, 10 Rudd St, Canberra ACT 2601)

Bulgaria (☎ 02-870 1560; todmak@bgnet.bg; ul Frederic Joliot-Curie 17, Block 2, 1st Flr, Suite 1, Sofia 1113)

Canada (☎ 613-234 3882; www3.sympatico.ca/emb .macedonia.ottawa; 130 Albert St, Suite 1006, Ottawa ON, K1P 5G4)

France (☎ 331-45 77 10 50; ambassade@fr.oleane.com; 5 Rue de la Faisanderie, 75116 Paris)

Germany (☎ 030-890 6950; jpopovski@t-online.de; Koenigsallee 2, 14193 Berlin)

Greece Athens (☎ 1-674 9585, lormak@teledomenet.gr; Marathonoudromou 13, Psychico, 154 52 Athens) Thessaloniki (☎ 31-027 7347, dkpsolun@mfa.gov.mk; Tsimiski 42, Thessaloniki)

Netherlands (☎ 070-427 44 64; repmak@wanadoo.nl; Laan van Meerdevoort 50-C, 2517AM The Hague)

Serbia and Montenegro (☎ 011-328 49 24; macemb@eunet.yu; Gospodar Jevremova 34, 11000 Belgrade)

UK (☎ 020-7976 0535; www.macedonian embassy.org.uk; Suites 2.1-2.2, Buckingham Court, Buckingham Gate 75/83, London, SW1E 6PE)

USA (☎ 202-337 3063; www.macedonianembassy .org; 1101 30th St NW, Suite 302, Washington DC, 20007)

Embassies & Consulates in Macedonia
SKOPJE

Albania (☎ 02-614 636; ambshqip@mt.net.mk; ul HT Karpoš 94a)

Australia (☎ 02-3061 114; austcon@mt.net.mk; ul Londonska 11b)

Bulgaria (☎ 02-3229 444; bgemb@unet.com.mk; ul Ivo Ribar Lola 40)

MACEDONIA

Canada (☎ 02-3225 630; honcon@unet.com.mk;
bul Partizanska Odredi 17a)
France (☎ 02-3118 749; www.ambafrance-mk.org;
ul Salvador Aljende 73)
Germany (☎ 02-3093 900; dt.boskop@mol.com.mk;
ul Lerinska 59)
Greece (☎ 02-3219 260; grfyrom@unet.com.mk;
ul Borka Taleski 6)
Netherlands (☎ 02-3129 319; www.nlembassy.org.mk;
ul Leninova 69-71)
Serbia and Montenegro (☎ 02-3129 298;
yuamb@unet.com.mk; ul Pitu Guli 8)
UK (☎ 02-3299 299; beskopje@mt.net.mkl;
ul Dimitrie Čupovski 26)
USA (☎ 02-3116 180; skopje.usembassy.gov;
bul Ilinden bb)

BITOLA
France (☎ 047-223 192; fax 047-223 594;
ul Maršal Tito 42)
UK (☎ /fax 047-228 765; ul Maršal Tito 42)

FESTIVALS & EVENTS

There are a good few festivals in Macedonia,
especially in the summer time. July brings
open-air evening concerts, opera and theatre to both Ohrid and Skopje. There is also a
fun Balkan Festival of Folk Dances & Songs
in Ohrid in early July (see p249).

One festival that all Macedonians rave
about is the Galičnik village's wedding
festival (p246). Skopje's autumn days are
brightened up with the flickering screens of
the international film festival and the warm
sounds of Skopje Jazz Festival in October.

HOLIDAYS

New Year 1 and 2 January
Orthodox Christmas 7 January
International Women's Day 8 March
Orthodox Easter Week March/April
Labour Day 1 May
Sts Cyril and Methodius Day 24 May
Ilinden or Day of the 1903 Rebellion 2 August
Republic Day 8 September
1941 Partisan Day 11 October

INTERNET RESOURCES

www.exploringmacedonia.com The official tourism portal. This well-organised site has a good depth of
information on things to do, see, eat and drink in
Macedonia.
faq.macedonia.org A comprehensive portal with information on everything from travel to embassy addresses to
sports and cuisine.

www.skopjeonline.com.mk Nifty, up-to-date site
with lots of info on cultural happenings in the capital,
plus nightclub listings, city bus schedules and lots
more.
www.culture.in.mk A useful resource on the cultural
life of Macedonia, including information on music, film
and performing arts festivals.

LANGUAGE

Macedonia's two official languages are
Macedonian and Albanian. Macedonian,
a South Slavic language, is spoken by the
majority of the population. It is divided into
two large groups, the western and eastern
Macedonian dialects. The Macedonian literary language is based on the central dialects of Veles, Prilep and Bitola. Its script
is Cyrillic, but you will see advertisements
or place names in Latin script. There are
certain grammatical similarities between
Macedonian and Bulgarian, such as the
omittance of cases, and speakers of Bulgarian, Serbian or Croatian should easily
understand Macedonian. Russian speakers
should also be able to get by without too
much difficulty. For others, we recommend
a good phrasebook, such as Lonely Planet's
Eastern Europe phrasebook.

The first alphabet for Slavic languages
was the Glagolitic script developed by
two Thessaloniki brothers, St Cyril and
St Methodius, in the 9th century. One of
their disciples modified this alphabet with
the Greek alphabet, and gradually the
medieval Cyrillic alphabet emerged from
this fusion.

Despite the use of Latin script on road
signs and some shop names, the Cyrillic
alphabet is still predominant and street
names are printed in Cyrillic script only,
so it is a good idea to learn the Cyrillic
alphabet before you travel to the country.

For a quick introduction to some useful Macedonian words and phrases, see the
Language chapter, p417.

MONEY

Macedonian denar (MKD) notes come in
denominations of 10, 50, 100, 500, 1000
and 5000, and there are coins of one, two
and five denar. The denar is nonconvertible
outside Macedonia. Restaurants, hotels and
some shops will accept payment in euros
(usually) and US dollars (sometimes);
prices are often quoted in these currencies.

Where prices are quoted in denars, we've given denars, but hotels that quote rates in euros are therefore given in euros.

Small, private exchange offices throughout central Skopje and Ohrid exchange cash for a rate that is only slightly better than that which you can get at the banks. ATMs can be found in all of the major towns and tourist centres (Skopje, Ohrid, Bitola, Tetovo, etc) but not in out-of-the-way places like Mavrovo and Berovo. Travellers cheques are a real hassle to change and we advise against relying on them, except as a form of emergency back-up money.

POST

Mail services to and from Macedonia are efficient and reasonably fast, although sending money or valuables through normal post is not recommended. Letters to the USA cost 38MKD, to Australia 40MKD and to Europe 35MKD. There are poste restante services available at major post offices.

RESPONSIBLE TRAVEL

Ohrid Lake trout is almost extinct and in 2004 the government issued a seven-year ban on catching it. Despite this, many restaurants still offer it, thereby encouraging illegal trout fishing. Do try to resist ordering one and opt for Californian trout instead, which is just as tasty.

TELEPHONE & FAX

A long distance call costs less at main post offices than in hotels. Drop the initial zero in the city codes when calling Macedonia from abroad. Buy phonecards in units of 100 (200MKD), 200 (300MKD), 500 (650MKD) or 1000 (1250MKD) from post offices. Some of the larger kiosks also sell the 100-unit cards. You can make cheap international phone call at Internet cafés for around 15MKD per minute for all countries.

Macedonia has a digital mobile phone network (Mobimak); mobile numbers are

---

EMERGENCY NUMBERS

- Ambulance ☎ 94
- Police ☎ 92
- Highway & roadside assistance ☎ 987

---

preceded by ☎ 070. Your provider may have a global-roaming agreement with Macedonia's domestic network. Check before you leave home.

Fax services are available at the main post offices in Skopje and Ohrid.

TOURIST INFORMATION

Macedonia's tourist information office is in Skopje but it may not be very useful.

VISAS

Citizens of EU countries, Iceland, New Zealand, Norway, Switzerland and the USA don't need visas for Macedonia and are allowed to stay for up to three months. Visas are required for most others. Australians can buy a visa on arrival at Petrovets airport (800MKD), but not at any land border – so if you're travelling overland you need to get one from a Macedonian embassy. Canadians and South Africans should get a visa in advance. Visa fees vary for different countries, but are mostly around US$30 for a single-entry visa and US$60 for a multiple-entry visa. The regulations have changed quite a bit in the past few years – check www.mfr.gov.mk for the latest alterations. Note that if you need a visa to enter Macedonia and you intend to visit Kosovo and then return to Macedonia, you will need a Macedonian multiple-entry visa. There is no Macedonian embassy, consulate or visa-issuing office in Kosovo.

TRANSPORT IN MACEDONIA

GETTING THERE & AWAY

This section covers travel options to and from the other countries in this book. For information on getting to Macedonia from, say, Greece or Bulgaria, see the Transport chapter at the end of this book (p399).

Air

Macedonia has two international airports. **Petrovec** (pronounced 'petrovets'; ☎ 02-3148 651), 21km from Skopje is the main one, while the little **Ohrid** (☎ 046-252 820) airport is between Ohrid and Struga. The website www.airports.com.mk has comprehensive information on both, from arrival and departure times to weather conditions. There is no departure tax. There are currency exchange offices and desks to book hotels and car hire at Petrovec.

AIRLINES FLYING TO/FROM MACEDONIA WITHIN WESTERN BALKANS

Adria Airways (airline code JP; ☎ 02-117 009; www.adria.si; hub Ljubljana)

Croatia Airlines (airline code OU; ☎ 02-3115 858; www.croatiaairlines.hr; hub Zagreb)

JAT (airline code JU; ☎ 02-3116 532; www.jat.com; hub Belgrade)

Macedonian Airlines (MAT; airline code IN; ☎ 02-3292 333; www.mat.com.mk; hub Skopje)

Land

Macedonia shares land borders with Greece, Albania, Bulgaria, and Serbia and Montenegro and one UN-monitored territory – Kosovo. This section covers getting to and from the other countries in this region. Access to/from all neighbouring states is trouble free and unrestricted.

BORDER CROSSINGS

Albania

There are four border crossings with Albania – the two main ones are on either side of Lake Ohrid (Kafa San/Qafa e Thanës, 12km southwest of Struga, and Sveti Naum/Tushëmishti, 29km south of Ohrid). There are two smaller ones at Blato, 5km northwest of Debar, and at Stenje on the western shore of Lake Prespa. None of the crossings present any problems, though Kafa San/Qafa e Thanës tends to be the busiest and therefore the slowest. There are no buses from Skopje to Albania, but there are buses from Tetovo which also pick up passengers in Struga. See the Tetovo section (p243) for details.

Serbia & Montenegro

Visas are not necessary for travel to Kosovo (though this may change if/when Kosovo becomes independent) and it is quite easy to get there; the main border crossing at Blace is just a 20-minute trip north from Skopje. There is another crossing point close by at Jazince, used by vehicles coming from Tetovo.

The main crossing point into Serbia is Tabanovce, either on the motorway or by train. There's a much smaller crossing point

at Pelince about 25km northeast of Tabanovce. There are several buses every day to Prizren and Prishtina and Belgrade from both Tetovo and Skopje.

BUS

Most international buses leave from Skopje's Intercity Bus Station, though a few leave from in front of the Holiday Inn on Kej 13 Noemvri. Buses travel to Belgrade (1350MKD, six hours, four daily) and Zagreb (1900MKD, 15 hours, daily).

Buses between Skopje and Prishtina, the capital of Kosovo, are fairly frequent. To/from Albania you can travel from Tetovo to Tirana by bus (900MKD, six to seven hours, two daily).

CAR & MOTORCYCLE

There are several major highway border crossings into Macedonia from neighbouring countries. You will need a Green Card endorsed for Macedonia to bring a car into the country.

TRAIN

There are four trains daily between Skopje and Belgrade via Niš (1209MKD, nine hours). Sleepers are available. One daily Belgrade train continues on to Zagreb (2050MKD, 17 hours) and Ljubljana (2690MKD, 20 hours). You can find timetables for international routes on the Macedonian Railways (Makedonski Zheleznici) website (www.mz .com.mk/patnichki/timetable.htm), and on the Euro Railways website (www.eurorail ways.com).

GETTING AROUND
Bicycle

Cycling around Macedonia is becoming more popular. The country offers generally good road conditions and relatively light traffic – though beginners should be warned it is a fairly mountainous country.

Bus

The bus network is well developed in Macedonia, with frequent services from Skopje to all major centres. The domestic bus fleet is a motley collection of ageing rattlers and slightly newer coaches – generally speaking it's fairly dilapidated and can be quite uncomfortable in the hotter months. It is a good idea to book in advance when travelling to Ohrid in the busy summer season. Some bus companies levy a fee of about 10MKD to store bags in the luggage compartments.

Car & Motorcycle

AUTOMOBILE ASSOCIATIONS
AMSM (Avto Moto Soyuz na Makedonija) (☎ 02-318 1181; www.art.com.mk; ul Ivo Ribar Lola 51, Skopje) offers road assistance, towing services and information to members (in German and English as well as Macedonian), and has offices all over the country.

DRIVING LICENCE
Usually your national driving licence will suffice, but it is a good idea to have an International Driving Permit as well.

FUEL & SPARE PARTS
Petrol stations are easily found on the tollways and in major towns, but apart from on the tollways they often aren't open after dark. Unleaded and regular petrol are widely available, and cost about 60MKD per litre, while diesel costs around 44MKD per litre. Spare parts are mostly only available in Skopje and to a lesser extent in Bitola, Tetovo and Kumanovo.

HIRE
Skopje is full of car hire agencies, from the large ones (Hertz, Avis, Sixt) to dozens of local companies, though the choices in Ohrid and Bitola are limited. Tourist brochures give comprehensive lists. A smallish sedan like a Ford Focus costs about €40 a day, including insurance. The rates in Skopje are such good value that quite a few people holidaying in Greece make a detour here to hire a car. As a result, car hire agencies tend to be pleasantly surprised if you tell them you're going to be touring Macedonia instead. You need to present your passport, driving licence and a credit card. You normally need to have held a full driving licence for one year.

INSURANCE
Car hire agencies provide insurance for around €15 to €25 a day, depending on the type of car, with a nonwaivable excess of €1000 to €2500. Green Card insurance is accepted, and third party insurance is compulsory.

ROAD CONDITIONS
Major roads and highways are generally safe and in good condition. Local driving habits are fairly civilised, except for the usual minority of hot-blooded idiots. Secondary rural roads are often in poor condition and used by livestock, tractors and horse-drawn carts. Minor mountain roads require particular care, as they can be very narrow and poorly marked and can become very tricky in bad weather. Seek local advice before tackling the drive to a mountain road to an isolated village such as Galičnik. Signage in rural areas is wildly variable – sometimes it's very good, other times you have no idea where one village begins and another ends.

ROAD RULES
Driving is on the right side of the road. Speed limits for cars and motorcycles are 120km/h on motorways, 80km/h on the open road and 50km/h to 60km/h in towns. Speeding fines start from around 1500MKD. It is compulsory to wear a seat belt and to have the headlights on (dipped) at all times for both cars and motorcycles. It is also compulsory to carry a replacement set of bulbs, two warning triangles and a first-aid kit. Between 15 November and 15 March, cars must carry snow chains. Motorcyclists and the passenger must wear helmets. Macedonia has a relatively high death toll from accidents and the busy traffic police are vigilant on speeding, drink driving and headlights in particular. Fines are issued on the spot. The legal blood-alcohol limit is 0.05 per cent.

Taxi
Taxis are a snappy way of getting to out-of-the-way monasteries and other sights if buses aren't convenient. Macedonian taxis are very cheap by European standards – Skopje has some of the cheapest capital city taxis anywhere. A half-hour trip, from Skopje to Lake Matka for example, should cost around 350MKD.

Train
Macedonia has a small but interesting network of domestic destinations, but the trains are in a similar condition to public buses – not so good. There's a timetable (at the time of writing in Macedonian only,

though an English section is under construction) on the Macedonian Railways (Makedonski Zheleznici) website at www .mz.com.mk/patnichki/timetable.htm. The most useful one for travellers is the scenic, four-hour, four-times-daily service from Skopje to Bitola via Prilep. Other destina-

tions from Skopje are: via Tetovo to Kičevo (two hours) in western Macedonia; to Veles, in the centre of the country; via Kumanovo to Tabanovce on the Serbian border; and to Gevgelija on the Greek border. The most you'll pay for a domestic ticket is 370MKD for a return to Bitola.

Serbia & Montenegro

RAFAEL ESTEFANIA

Serbia & Montenegro

Although the two countries may soon no longer be one, Serbia and Montenegro together currently make an interesting and diverse whole.

Landlocked Serbia has Belgrade as its beating heart, with everything you'd expect from a gritty, kicking capital: arts and culture, food and wine, and great nightlife To the north, flat Vojvodina is where the Balkan and Hungarian cultures mix. The plains of Fruška Gora hide numerous monasteries amid peaceful vineyards. Serbia's sleepy south is filled with stories of former rebellion, with the forts of Topola and Niš keeping the memories alive. Nestling under the heights of Kopaonik is the Sandžak region, with the small kasbah-like town of Novi Pazar. This is a good base for forays into Kosovo, a UN-NATO protectorate since 1999, and still a part of Serbia.

To the southwest, amid harsh mountains, river canyons and by the beautiful coast of the Adriatic lies Montenegro. Its coast, bordering with Croatia in the north, is just as stunning as its better-known neighbour. The Bay of Kotor is dotted with gems: the walled town of Kotor is like Dubrovnik's smaller sister; the tiny town of Perast is a perfect slice of the Mediterranean. Further down is Budva with its fortified old town, and seductive seaside towns such as Petrovac or the curious holiday island of Sveti Stefan. Inland is Cetinje, the old capital that crowns the country at 800m above sea-level. There is skiing and trekking in the heights of the mighty Durmitor range and rafting on the foamy whirls of the Tara River Canyon.

FAST FACTS

- **Area** 102,350 sq km
- **Capital** union and Serbian capital – Belgrade; Montenegro – Podgorica
- **Currency** Serbia – dinar (DIN): €1 = 85.2DIN; US$1 = 71.1DIN; UK£1 = 124DIN; A$1 = 53.4DIN; ¥100 = 63DIN; NZ$1 = 48DIN; Kosovo and Montenegro – euro (€): US$1 = €0.82; UK£1 = €1.5; A$1 = €0.63; ¥100 = €0.75; NZ$1 = €0.58
- **Famous for** Monica Seles, basketball players
- **Key phrases** Serbian *zdravo* (hello), *doviđenja* (goodbye), *hvala* (thanks); Kosovar Albanian *allo* (hello), *lamturmirë* (goodbye), *ju falem nderit* (thanks)
- **Official language** Serbia and Montenegro – Serbian; Kosovo – Albanian
- **Population** 7.5 million excluding Kosovo (estimate 1.9 million)
- **Telephone codes** country code ☎ 381; international access code ☎ 99
- **Visas** not required by most European, Australian, New Zealand, American and Canadian citizens; see p324 for details

SERBIA & MONTENEGRO

HIGHLIGHTS

- Belgrade is notorious for partying, its mighty **Kalemegdan Citadel** (p277) that dominates the landscape, and plentiful culinary offerings in the city's many restaurants
- The quiet town of **Novi Sad** (p291), with smart café-lined streets and the baroque Petrovaradin Citadel that goes wild every year in July when it hosts the Exit music festival
- The walled, dramatically beautiful labyrinthine old city of **Kotor** (p316), proudly sitting at the helm of southern Europe's biggest fjord
- Sharp mountains – veined by the Tara River Canyon, over one kilometre deep – shelter pretty lakes in **Durmitor National Park** (p320); tons of winter and summer activities
- The former medieval capital of 'Old Serbia', **Prizren** (p307), dominated by the old castle, Turkish-influenced architecture, riverside bars and cafés

ITINERARIES

- **One week** Two days of partying and culture in Belgrade, a day trip to Novi Sad, then head south for sightseeing in Cetinje, and down to Budva's beaches and gorgeous Kotor.
- **Two to three weeks** The above plus Subotica and Novi Pazar, relax in the natural beauty of Žabljak, find peace in the tiny village of Rijeka Crnojevića, and walk the long beach at Ulcinj before spending a day or two by the sea in Perast or Petrovac.

CLIMATE & WHEN TO GO

The north has a continental climate with cold winters and hot, humid summers. The coastal region has hot, dry summers and relatively cold winters with heavy snowfall inland.

The Montenegrin coast is at its best in May, June and September, but avoid July and August, when accommodation becomes quite scarce and expensive. The ski season is generally December to March, with January and February providing the best sport.

HISTORY

Celts supplanted the original inhabitants of the region, the Illyrians, from the 4th century BC; the Romans arrived in the 3rd century BC. In AD 395 Theodosius I

HOW MUCH?

- **Short taxi ride** 200DIN/€3
- **Internet access** per hour 80DIN to 150DIN/€1.50
- **Cup of coffee** 100DIN/€1
- **Bottle of plum brandy** 500DIN/€7
- **Postcard** 30DIN/€0.50

LONELY PLANET INDEX

- **Litre of petrol** Serbia 66DIN, Kosovo €0.80, Montenegro €0.88
- **Litre of water** 70DIN/€1
- **Half-litre of beer** 60DIN/€1
- **Souvenir T-shirt** Serbia 600DIN
- **Street snack (burek)** 30DIN/€0.50

---

divided the empire, with Serbia passing to the Byzantine Empire.

During the 6th century, Slavic tribes crossed the Danube and occupied much of the Balkan Peninsula. In 879 Saints Cyril and Methodius converted the Serbs to Christianity.

Serbian independence briefly flowered from 1217 with a 'Golden Age' during Stefan Dušan's reign (1346–55). After Stefan's death Serbia declined. At the pivotal Battle of Kosovo in 1389 the Turks defeated Serbia, ushering in 500 years of Islamic rule. A revolt in 1815 led to de facto Serbian independence and complete independence in 1878.

On 28 June 1914 Austria-Hungary used the assassination of Archduke Ferdinand by a Bosnian Serb as a pretext to invade Serbia, sparking WWI. After the war, Croatia, Slovenia, Bosnia and Hercegovina, Vojvodina, Serbia and its Kosovo province, Montenegro and Macedonia formed the Kingdom of Serbs, Croats and Slovenes under King Alexander of Serbia. In 1929 the country was renamed Yugoslavia.

In March 1941 Yugoslavia joined the fascist Tripartite Alliance. This sparked a military coup and an abrupt withdrawal from the Alliance. Germany replied by bombing Belgrade.

The Communist Party, under Josip Broz Tito, assisted in the liberation of the country and gained power in 1945. It abolished

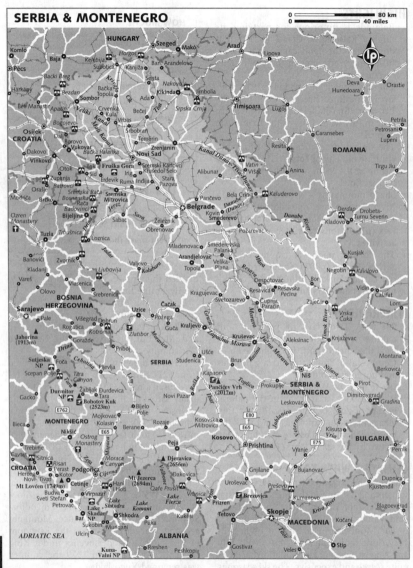

the monarchy and declared a federal republic. Serbia's size was reduced; Bosnia and Hercegovina, Montenegro and Macedonia were granted republic status but Kosovo and Vojvodina were denied it and became autonomous provinces.

Tito broke with Stalin in 1948 and Yugoslavia became a nonaligned nation

(ie belonging to neither of the post-WWII power blocks led by the USA and the USSR), albeit bolstered by Western aid. Growing regional inequalities pushed demands by Slovenia, Croatia and Kosovo for greater autonomy to counter Serbian dominance.

By 1986 Serbian nationalists were espousing the idea of a Greater Serbia, a doctrine adopted by Slobodan Milošević, the Serbian Communist Party leader. This horrified the other republics, which managed to gain independence by 1992.

While the violent collapse of Yugoslavia resulted in wars in the neighbouring Croatia and Bosnia and Hercegovina, the remaining parties of Serbia and Montenegro formed the 'third' Yugoslav federation in April 1992. The new constitution made no mention of 'autonomous provinces', infuriating Albanians in Kosovo, who had been stripped of their autonomous status by Milošević and had long been brutally repressed by Serbia. Violence in Kosovo erupted in January 1998, largely provoked by the federal army and police.

This incited a storm of protest from the international community, plus an arms embargo. In March 1999 peace talks in Paris failed when Serbia rejected a US-brokered peace plan. In reply to resistance in Kosovo, Serbian forces moved to ethnically cleanse the country of its Albanian population. Hundreds of thousands fled into Macedonia and Albania galvanising NATO into a 78-day bombing campaign. On 12 June 1999 Serbian forces withdrew from Kosovo.

In the September 2000 federal presidential elections the opposition, led by Vojislav Koštunica, declared victory, a claim denied by Milošević. Opposition supporters took over the streets, called a general strike and occupied parliament. When Russia recognised Koštunica's presidency, Milošević's last support evaporated.

Koštunica restored ties with Europe, acknowledged Yugoslav atrocities in Kosovo and rejoined the UN. In April 2001 Milošević was arrested for misappropriating state funds and extradited to the International War Crimes Tribunal in The Hague.

In April 2002 Yugoslavia was replaced by a loose union of Serbia and Montenegro. The EU-brokered deal was intended to stabilise the region by settling Montenegrin demands for independence and preventing further changes to Balkan borders. The union will be tested in a referendum in 2006.

In March 2003 Serbia's first democratically elected prime minister since WWII, Zoran Đinđić, was assassinated. He had been instrumental in handing over Milošević to

---

> **MONEY MATTERS**
>
> During the 1990s economic sanctions and gross mishandling of the economy led to severe hyperinflation, the highest in European history. It became cheaper to use banknotes to paper walls than to buy the wallpaper. At one point a 500 billion dinar banknote was issued, making every Serb an instant multimillionaire.
>
> Many state industries were unable to pay their employees; they were paid in kind or issued worthless shares in the company. When a multinational bought up the local brewery in the small town of Apatin, the locals found their shares to be worth a fortune. Apatin is now one of the richest municipalities, per capita, in Serbia.

---

the International War Crimes Tribunal and had been trying to purge politics and business of crime and corruption. His alleged killers were crime bosses and Milošević-era paramilitary commanders.

At the end of his term in January 2003, the Serbian president Milan Milutinović surrendered to The Hague tribunal to plead not guilty to charges of crimes against humanity. Between 2003 and 2004 three attempts to elect a new president failed, due to low voter turnout. Parliamentary elections in December 2003 were inconclusive but saw the resurgence of nationalism, worrying the rest of Europe. A series of power-sharing deals installed Koštunica as head of a centre-right coalition that now relies on the support of Milošević's Socialist Party. Finally, in June 2004, Serbia and Montenegro gained a new president in the pro-European Boris Tadić.

PEOPLE

The last full census was taken in 1991. Only Serbia took a census in 2002, revealing a population of estimated an 7.5 million. Estimates for Montenegro are 651,000 and Kosovo 1.9 million.

These figures split into Serbs 62%, Albanians 17%, Montenegrins 5%, Hungarians 3% and other groups 13%.

Vojvodina is more multicultural, with perhaps 28 ethnic groups and sizable populations of Hungarians (25%), Ukrainians and Romanians.

Central Serbia is predominantly Serb Orthodox and the southern region of Sandzak is mainly Muslim.

There are large Slavic Muslim and Albanian minorities in Montenegro and southern Serbia; Belgrade has about 10,000 Muslims.

Serbs and Montenegrins have always seen eye to eye but in Kosovo things have never been easy, particularly so since the late '90s conflict. Minority Serbs live in Kosovo Force (KFOR) protected ghettoes. Relations between Albanians and Serbs remain extremely tense.

RELIGION

Religion and ethnicity broadly go together. About 65% of the population is Orthodox; Roman Catholics, who are Vojvodinan Hungarians, comprise 4%; and Albanian Kosovars and Slavic Muslims make up 19%. The remaining 12% are 'other', including Romanians, Croatians, Bulgarians, Roma and Vlachs.

ARTS

Literature

The oral tradition of epic poetry was the most important way of recording historical events and figures in both Serbia and Montenegro (and other parts of former Yugoslavia) for centuries. None of it was written down and the singers composed the poems as they performed them, having to confine themselves to the rigid form of 10 or eight syllables per line. Accompanying it was the sound of the gusle, a one-stringed instrument held upright like a cello. Poems most often depicted battles and brave kings, or tragic love stories.

With the arrival of the 19th-century writer and linguist Vuk Karadžić epic poetry was first written down. Karadžić not only collected and wrote down the epic poems, but he went on to reform the language and formalise the rules of Serbian grammar. The epics were translated into English, French and German by the likes of Goethe and Walter Scott. A good read on the subject of oral verse is *The Singer of Tales* by Albert B Lord (Harvard University Press).

On the Montenegrin side, Petar II Petrović Njegoš (1813–51), a poet and a prince, produced one of the country's most impor-

tant works of literature *Gorski vijenac* (The Mountain Wreath), a verse play depicting the Montenegrin struggle to maintain Orthodox Christianity under Ottoman rule. Njegoš was and still is one of the most popular and revered figures in Montenegrin history.

Another significant figure in late 19th-century Serbian literature was Jovan Jovanović Zmaj (1833–1904), who wrote a large volume of works of poetry, fiction and essays. Contemporary writers include the poet Vasko Popa, whose work has been translated into English and many other languages. Other interesting reads are *In the Hold* by Vladimir Arsenijević, *Words Are Something Else* by David Albahari, *Petrija's Wreath* by Dragoslav Mihailović and *Fear and its Servant* by Mirjana Novaković.

Bosnian-born, but a past Belgrade resident, Ivo Andrić was awarded the Nobel prize for his *Bridge over the Drina*. The excellent works of Danilo Kiš are available in English. *A Tomb for Boris Davidovich* is recommended.

The perennial *Black Lamb and Grey Falcon* by Rebecca West is always a good read for those wishing to get a taste of pre-WWII travels around the Balkans.

A relatively new and popular portrait of the life of a Serb in Yugoslavia, and later the UK, is Vesna Goldsworthy's memoir *Chernobyl Strawberries* (Atlantic, 2005).

Cinema

Cinema is a thriving industry in Serbia, but not many of the films made in the country ever get past the borders of the former Yugoslavia. If you are really keen on seeing some of these, you can find DVDs or videos of the Serbian cinema classics with English subtitles in Serbia. Titles to look out for are *Ko to tamo peva?* (Who's That Singing Over There?), *Petrija's Wreath* and *Balkan Express*.

The award-winning film *Underground,* by Sarajevo-born director Emir Kusturica, is worth seeing, as are his other films. *Underground* is told in a chaotic, colourful style, reminiscent of Fellini's movies. Bosnian director Danis Tanović's *No Man's Land* superbly deals with an encounter between a Bosnian soldier and a Serb soldier stuck in a trench on their own during the Bosnian war.

SERBIA & MONTENEGRO

Music

Serbia's vibrant dances are led by musicians playing bagpipes, flutes and fiddles. Kosovar music bears the deep imprint of five centuries of Turkish rule, with high-whine flutes carrying the tune above the beat of a goat-skin drum.

Blehmuzika (brass music influenced by Turkish and Austrian military music) is the national music of Serbia, with an annual festival at Guča in August. This type of music is most commonly played by Roma, and traditionally at weddings or funerals. One of the most popular recordings of this music is the soundtrack to the film *Underground* and albums by the trumpet player Boban Marković.

Modern music covers anything from wild Romani music to house, techno, blues, jazz, drum'n'bass. Two of Serbia's favourite modern bands are Darkwood Dub and Eyesburn.

Ethnic folk updated and crossed with techno is the rather painful 'turbofolk' that the visitor will doubtlessly come across in Serbia and Montenegro. The queen of turbofolk is Svetlana Ražnatović 'Ceca', the heavy-bosomed wife of the late war criminal Arkan. She attracts sell-out numbers not only across Serbia and Montenegro, but even in the supposedly more 'civilised' Slovenia. Wars may rage, but in the Balkans some things never change.

Serbia and Montenegro entered the Eurovision hall of fame by coming second in 2004 with a haunting love ballad that effectively blended Serbian and Turkish influences. Its 2005 entry with the Montenegrin No Name boy band didn't fare as well.

Architecture

Serbia and Montenegro displays the architecture of those who once ruled the country. Towns in the south bear a Turkish imprint whereas the north has a dominance of 19th-century imperial Austro-Hungarian style. In Vojvodina, especially in Subotica, there are some magnificent buildings of the Hungarian Secessionist period. Montenegro is all Socialist blocks in Podgorica, and gleaming-white Mediterranean marble houses along the coast. Cetinje's architecture is an interesting collection of mansions and palaces remaining from its days as a royal capital.

Overlaying all are the post-WWII buildings bearing the modernist imprint of concrete and central planning.

Visual Arts

Artists in Serbia and Montenegro have been happy to follow European trends in art, although there is a significant interest in icon painting. Galleries throughout the country present an eclectic range from landscapes and figurative art to abstract work.

The works of the Croatian sculptor Ivan Meštrović (1883–1962) are ubiquitous and you will notice them in several places around Belgrade, most notably the *France* and *Messenger of Victory* statues in the Kalemegdan Citadel and the war memorial in Avala. The Munich-educated impressionist painter Nadežda Petrović (1873–1915) produced some wonderfully energetic portraits. Her earthy 'Serbian period' (1903–10) paintings show a change in perception from the earlier, more impassioned 'Munich period' (1898–1903). Her final and perhaps most accomplished paintings come from the 'Parisian period' (1910–12) shortly before she died of typhoid, which she contracted in a Serbian WWI hospital where she worked as a voluntary nurse. Her paintings are displayed in Belgrade's National Museum (p279) as well as in Cetinje's National Museum (p310).

ENVIRONMENT

Vojvodina is pancake-flat agricultural land. South of the Danube the landscape rises through rolling green hills, which crest at the point where the eastern outpost of the Dinaric Alps slices southeastwards across the country. In among these mountains lie the vales of Kosovo.

The Land

Đeravica (2656m) in western Kosovo is the highest mountain; Bobotov Kuk (2525m) in the Durmitor Range is Montenegro's. Zlatibor and Kopaonik in Serbia, and Durmitor in Montenegro provide the winter snow playgrounds.

Montenegro's mountains are mainly limestone and carry the features of arid karst scenery, craggy grey-white outcrops, sparse vegetation and, beneath, caves. To the east the vast Lake Skadar, an important European bird sanctuary and pelican habitat, spans Montenegro and Albania.

Wildlife

Around two hundred species of birds live in the woods of Fruška Gora in Serbia, including a rare species of imperial eagle *(Aquila heliaca)*. Wild boar, wildcat, lynx and mouflon are among the mammals. The golden eagle and crossbill are the rare birds, and the uncommon species of the viviparous lizard crawls around the Kopaonik mountain. Birds such as the griffon vulture *(Gyps fulvius)* fly above Tara National Park, and hopefully you will not encounter the brown bear, wildcat and chamois, who all live in its woods.

Among the mammals that live in Montenegro's mountains are chamois, fox and hare. Bears and wolves are a very rare sight. Grey mountain eagles, white-headed vultures and falcons can be spotted in the skies above the peaks.

National Parks

The major national parks of Serbia include: Vojvodina's Fruška Gora, which stretches over 10,000 hectares of orchards and vineyards on the plains and takes in maple, oak and linden forests in the hills.

Kopaonik, in southern Serbia, is a mountainous area slashed with canyons of the Ibar, Jošanica, Toplica and Brzeća Rivers. The famous ski slopes are part of the national park, and outside of the resorts are some of the most important centres of biodiversity in the Balkans. Kopaonik houseleek, Kopaonik violet and Pančić cuckoo flower are among the endemic species of flora.

The Tara National Park in western Serbia spreads over 20,000 hectares in width, and varies between 250m and 1500m in altitude. Mountain peaks and deep river gorges make for spectacular and dramatic scenery in this park. Most impressive is the gorge of the Drina River, the park's main waterway. Among the endemic species of the Tara and Zvijezda mountain ranges are the Pančić spruce and Pančić locust.

Other parks in Serbia are Šar National Park in Kosovo and the Đerdap National Park in eastern Serbia.

Montenegro's most interesting and popular national park is Durmitor, a truly magnificent place for nature-lovers. Spread over 39,000 hectares, the mountain peaks reach over 2200m. The Tara and Piva Canyons take

your breath away, glacial lakes mirror your soul, and springs of clear mountain water quench your thirst. Tara, the longest river in Montenegro, is raftable and is hidden in the deepest canyon in Europe (1300m at times). Durmitor is under Unesco protection as is the Tara River. There is plenty of choice for cave-lovers, with Ice Cave (Ledena Pećina) being the most notable. At 2100m at Obla Glava on the north face of Bobotov Kuk, the cave is reachable from a mountain path.

Lake Skadar National Park has one of the largest lakes in Europe, taking up 391 sq km of the 40,000-hectare parkland. Surrounded by mountains from three sides, the lake borders on Albania (where it is called Lake Shkodra), has 40 different kinds of fish, and counts as one of the largest bird reserves in Europe, with rarities such as the Dalmatian pelican residing on its shores.

Environmental Issues

Sewage pollution of coastal waters, air pollution around Belgrade and rubbish dumping out in the countryside are the environmental issues the country has to face. Some of the remains of the NATO bombing campaign in 2000 are ecological hazards, such as the destruction of the petrol factory in Novi Sad. Destroyed bridges over the Danube have also caused heavy river pollution.

FOOD & DRINK
Staples & Specialities

The cheapest and ubiquitous Western Balkan snack is *burek*, a filo-pastry pie made with *sir* (cheese), *meso* (meat), *krompir* (potato) or occasionally *pečurke* (mushrooms), most commonly consumed with yogurt. It's a great breakfast filler, especially if not greasy and made *ispod saća* (baked on hot coals, in a covered tray). A fingerlicking midday meal might consist of soup or *ćevapčići*.

Serbia is famous for its grilled meats, such as *ćevapčići*, *pljeskavica* (spicy hamburger), *ražnjići* (pork or veal kebabs). Another speciality is Karađorđe's schnitzel, a long tubular roll of veal meat, stuffed with *kajmak* (curdled, salted milk). *Đuveč* is grilled pork cutlets with spiced stewed peppers, courgettes and tomatoes on rice.

For dishes that have more than just meat, although they still contain meat, try *musaka* (layers of aubergine, potato and minced meat), *sarma* (minced meat and rice rolled in sour-cabbage leaves), *kapama* (stewed lamb, onions and spinach with yogurt) and *punjene tikvice* (courgettes stuffed with minced meat and rice).

Regional cuisines range from spicy Hungarian goulash in Vojvodina to Turkish kebab in Kosovo.

Pivo (beer) is universally available. Nikšićko *pivo* (both light and dark), brewed at Nikšić in Montenegro, is terribly good. Many people distil their own *rakija* (brandy), made of grapes or out of plums (*šljivovica*). There are other varieties such as *orahovača* (walnut), *kruškovača* or *viljamovka* (pear) or *jabukovača* (apple). If you ask for *domaća rakija* in a restaurant, you will be offered homemade *rakija* made of a choice of fruit.

Montenegrin red wine is a rich drop. Vranac is the most popular wine and is widely available.

A bittersweet aperitif, *pelinkovac*, a herbal liquor that tastes just like medicine with a kick, is currently popular in Belgrade. A more upmarket and less bitter version of this is the German variety, Jagermaister, also available in bars.

Coffee is usually served Turkish-style, 'black as hell, strong as death and sweet as love'. Superb espresso and cappuccino can be found but mostly in the north. If you want anything other than herbal teas (camomile or hibiscus), then ask for Indian tea.

Where to Eat & Drink

The country abounds with eating options, so you won't go hungry. You might well go hungry though, if you want to eat anything that does not have meat as the main ingredient. Meat in pastry, meat with potatoes, meat on its own, and meat stuffed with meat is ever-present. Some love this, others do not.

Many locals eat on the go so there are plenty of hole-in-the-wall counters, kiosks and bakeries that offer *burek*, pizza, *ćevapčići* or sandwiches. Plenty of small restaurants offer cheap, satisfying but limited menus. Many can be found around the bus and train stations.

Hotel restaurants also figure in providing fine food. Resort areas have fewer restaurants, as the hotels capture their clients with half- and full-board accommodation.

The distinction between café and bar is blurred. Cafés usually sell alcohol except in Muslim areas; the more upmarket ones add cocktails to their range.

Vegetarians & Vegans

Priroda (p286) is the country's only vegetarian restaurant, but top-end restaurants will have some vegetarian dishes. In general, eating in Serbia and Montenegro can be a trial for vegetarians and almost impossible for vegans. There's always the ubiquitous vegetarian pizza. Satisfying salads are *Srpska salata* (Serbian salad) of raw peppers, onions and tomatoes, seasoned with oil, vinegar and maybe chilli, and *šopska salata*, consisting of chopped tomatoes, cucumber and onion, topped with grated soft white cheese. Also ask for *gibanica* (cheese pie), *zeljanica* (cheese pie with spinach) or *pasulj prebranac* (a dish of cooked and spiced beans). If you're happy with fish, then there are plenty of fish restaurants.

Habits & Customs

People tend to skimp on breakfast and catch something on the way to work. Work hours are usually 7.30am to a 3.30pm finish that then becomes the time for lunch; this slides dinner back to 8, 9 or 10pm if eating out.

SERBIA СРБИЈА

The most exciting spot in Serbia (Srbija) is undoubtedly its capital, Belgrade. Vojvodina's flat plains and the tranquil Fruška Gora monasteries provide an effective antidote to urban chaos, and the northern cities of Novi Sad and Subotica are an interesting combination of Hungarian and Balkan life.

Serbia's central and southern towns are quiet and good for those interested in the country's history. Snow fun can be had at the country's ski resorts of Zlatibor and Kopaonik.

The Unesco-protected Sopoćani Monastery sits on the hills outside the lovely little town of Novi Pazar, where minarets scrape the sky, in the predominantly Muslim southern region of Sandžak that mixes mosques with monasteries.

All the way south is Kosovo: administered as a UN-NATO protectorate, but still part of Serbia. This is a disputed land torn by different interpretations of history. For Serbs it is the cradle of their nationhood, for Kosovo Albanians it is their independent land.

BELGRADE БЕОГРАД

☎ 011 / pop 1.58 million

It's been described as 'hip', 'hot', 'urban', 'underground', 'gritty', 'pulsating'. Aptly so. For Belgrade is a ragged party capital that is quickly gaining a reputation as the Bad Boy of the Balkans. And if Serbia's tourist attractions have been largely unsuccessful as tourist magnets, Belgrade's culture and nightlife are drawing in night owls from across the globe.

Picturesque it is not. Belgrade's architecture is a mishmash of grandiose old build-ings that speak of a better past, and weary Soviet-style concrete blocks that look like they might collapse into a cloud of dust before your very eyes.

Still, the city holds some real gems. Perched over two rivers, the Danube and the Sava, Belgrade's central crowd puller is the ancient Kalemegdan Citadel. Knez Mihailova street is dotted with fascinating historical buildings. Dozens of museums and galleries will quench the thirst of the culturally parched.

But Belgrade's ultimate appeal is its nightlife. It's easy never to go to sleep in this city for there's always another place to go to: underground clubs, apartment-block bars, river-barge dance floors. Needing no

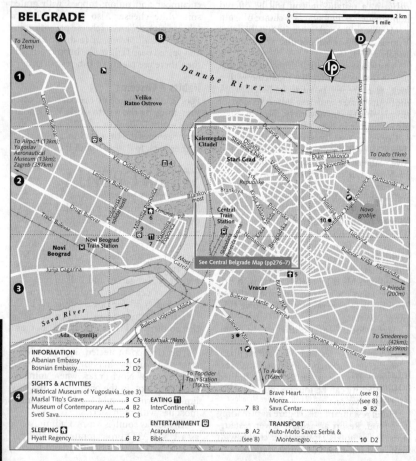

BELGRADE

0 ——— 2 km
0 ——— 1 mile

To Zemun (1km)

Danube River

1

Veliko
Ratno Ostrovo

To Airport (13km);
Yugoslav
Aeronautical
Museum (13km);
Zagreb (387km)

Kej Oslobođenja

Kalemegdan
Citadel

Dušana
Stražilića Bana

Dunavska

Vasina

Đure Đakovića
29 Novembra

To Dačo (1km)

Pančevački most

2

Lenjinov Bulevar

Stari Grad

Trg
Republike

Brankova

Kneza Miloša

Resavska

Partizanski Put

Novo
groblje

Dimitrija Tucovića Milje Kovačevića

Bulevar Kralja Aleksandra

Brankov most

Central
Train
Station

Nemanjina

Beogradska

10

Tucovića

Drugi Bulevar

Jadranska Popovića

Zemunski put

Vojislava Ilića

Karađorđeva

Pop Lukina

Balkanska

See Central Belgrade Map (pp276-7)

Novi Beograd

Treći Bulevar

Proleterske solidarnosti

Novi Beograd
Train Station

Most
Gazela

Bulevar JNA

5

Vracar

Jurija Gagarina

Bulevar Franše D'Epered

To Priroda
(200m)

3

Sava River

Bulevar voivode Mišića

Bulevar
Mira

Stevana Provençanoga

To Smederevo
(42km);
Niš (239km)

Ada Ciganlija

To Košutnjak (8km)

3

1

To Avala
(16km)

To Topčider
Train Station
(100m)

4

INFORMATION
Albanian Embassy.................................1 C4
Bosnian Embassy..................................2 D2

SIGHTS & ACTIVITIES
Historical Museum of Yugoslavia..(see 3)
Maršal Tito's Grave..............................3 C3
Museum of Contemporary Art........4 B2
Sveti Sava...5 C3

SLEEPING ☐
Hyatt Regency.....................................6 B2

EATING ☐
InterContinental...................................7 B3

ENTERTAINMENT ☐
Acapulco..8 A2
Bibis...(see 8)

Brave Heart.......................................(see 8)
Monza..(see 8)
Sava Centar...9 B2

TRANSPORT
Auto-Moto Savez Serbia &
Montenegro....................................10 D2

excuse to throw a good party, Belgraders are happy to dance all night and go straight to work the next day.

When it all gets too much, there are places to escape to and relax. Ada Ciganlija swarms with swimmers during hot summer days. The nearby Košutnjak park has forests to walk in. Alternatively, you can dive into one of the city's galleries or excellent museums and learn about Belgrade's contemporary art or ancient history.

History

The lumpy hill flanked by the Sava and Danube Rivers was ideal for a fortified settlement. The trouble was that it attracted enemies – Belgrade has been destroyed and rebuilt 40 times in its 2300-year history. Those fortifications – the massive Kalemegdan Citadel, changed by succeeding conquerors and defenders – are now no more than fortified parkland. At first it was the Celts who decided to settle on the hill overlooking the confluence of the two rivers. The Romans came in 1st century AD and remained for around 400 years. Then there were Goths and Huns wreaking havoc in the area, before the Serbs came to settle here and make it their capital in 1403. In 1521 the Turks conquered the Balkans, and with it Belgrade. In the 19th century Belgrade was capital of the union of Serbs, Croats and Slovenes, and then capital of Socialist Yugoslavia between 1945 and 1990. Air attacks by the Germans in 1941 left Belgrade in ruins and much of the pick'n'mix architecture seen today is the result of postwar rebuilding.

Orientation

The central train station and two adjacent bus stations are on the southern side of the city centre. A couple of blocks northeast lies Terazije, the heart of modern Belgrade. Knez Mihailova, Belgrade's lively pedestrian boulevard, runs northwest through the old town from Terazije to the Kalemegdan Citadel.

Information

BOOKSHOPS

Mamut (Map pp276-7; ☎ 639 060; cnr Knez Mihailova & Sremska; ☺ 9am-10pm Mon-Sat, noon-10pm Sun) Big browse-around shop with many floors; it sells books, magazines and newspapers in English as well as CDs, DVDs and gifts.

> **BELGRADE IN TWO DAYS**
>
> Grab breakfast on the go and catch tram 2 anywhere on its circular route. Get off and roam **Kalemegdan Citadel** (p277), stroll through Knez Mihailova and have a coffee in the **Russian Tsar** (p287) or somewhere on **Trg Republike** (p285). Check out the **National Museum** (p279) and the **Ethnographical Museum** (p279), dine out to Roma violins in **Skadarska** (p280), and catch some cocktails in **Ben Akiba** (p288) or a gig in **Akademija** (p289).
>
> Have a peek at the mighty Sveti Sava and Sveti Marko churches in **central Belgrade** (p281), catch a bus to **Zemun** (p290) for a late lunch, have an afternoon drink on one of the **Danube River barges** (p289) and head back to the city to go clubbing at **Andergraund** (p288), **Oh! Cinema!** (p289) or **Plastic** (p289).

Plato Bookshop (Map pp276-7; ☎ 625 834; 48 Knez Mihailova; ☺ 9am-midnight Mon-Sat, noon-midnight Sun) University bookshop with a small Internet café. Stocks English literature, maps, books on Serbia and stationery.

INTERNET ACCESS

IPS (Map pp276-7; ☎ 323 3344; off Makedonska 4; per hr 90DIN; ☺ 24hr)

Plato Cyber Club (Map pp276-7; ☎ 635 363; Vase Čarapića 19; per hr 65DIN; ☺ 24hr)

INTERNET RESOURCES

Belgrade City site (www.beograd.org.yu)

Tourist Organisation of Belgrade (www.belgrade tourism.org.yu)

LEFT LUGGAGE

Central train station (Map pp276-7; Savski Trg 2; per piece per day 60DIN)

MEDICAL SERVICES

Boris Kidrič Hospital Diplomatic Section (Map pp276-7; ☎ 643 839; Miloša Porcerca Pasterova 1; ☺ 7am-7pm Mon-Fri)

Klinički Centar (Map pp276-7; ☎ 361 8444; Miloša Porcerca Pasterova 2; ☺ 24hr) Medical clinic.

Prima 1 (Map pp276-7; ☎ 361 0999; Nemanjina 2; ☺ 24hr) Pharmacy.

MONEY

You won't be stuck for cash on the streets of Belgrade; there is an ATM on every corner.

CENTRAL BELGRADE

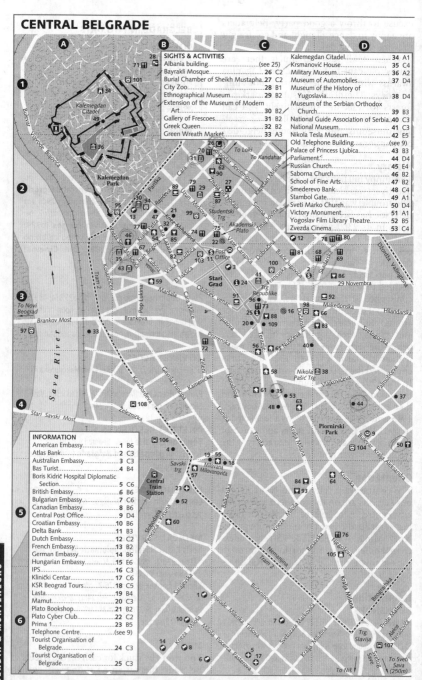

SIGHTS & ACTIVITIES
Albania building	(see 25)
Bayrakli Mosque	26 C2
Burial Chamber of Sheikh Mustapha	27 C2
City Zoo	28 B1
Ethnographical Museum	29 B2
Extension of the Museum of Modern Art	30 B2
Gallery of Frescoes	31 B2
Greek Queen	32 B2
Green Wreath Market	33 A3
Kalemegdan Citadel	34 A1
Krsmanović House	35 C4
Military Museum	36 A2
Museum of Automobiles	37 D4
Museum of the History of Yugoslavia	38 D4
Museum of the Serbian Orthodox Church	39 B3
National Guide Association of Serbia	40 C3
National Museum	41 C3
Nikola Tesla Museum	42 E5
Old Telephone Building	(see 9)
Palace of Princess Ljubica	43 B3
Parliament	44 D4
Russian Church	45 E4
Saborna Church	46 B2
School of Fine Arts	47 B2
Smederevo Bank	48 C3
Stambol Gate	49 A1
Sveti Marko Church	50 D4
Victory Monument	51 A1
Yogoslav Film Library Theatre	52 B5
Zvezda Cinema	53 C4

INFORMATION
American Embassy	1 B6
Atlas Bank	2 C3
Australian Embassy	3 C3
Bas Turist	4 B4
Boris Kidrič Hospital Diplomatic Section	5 C6
British Embassy	6 B6
Bulgarian Embassy	7 C6
Canadian Embassy	8 B6
Central Post Office	9 D4
Croatian Embassy	10 B6
Delta Bank	11 B3
Dutch Embassy	12 C2
French Embassy	13 B2
German Embassy	14 B6
Hungarian Embassy	15 E6
IPS	16 C3
Klinički Centar	17 C6
KSR Beograd Tours	18 C5
Lasta	19 B4
Mamut	20 C3
Plato Bookshop	21 B2
Plato Cyber Club	22 C2
Prima 1	23 B5
Telephone Centre	(see 9)
Tourist Organisation of Belgrade	24 C3
Tourist Organisation of Belgrade	25 C3

Kalemegdan Citadel

Kalemegdan Park

To Loki
To Kandahar

Studentski Trg

Akademski Plato

Post Office

Stari Grad

Trg Republike

Makedonska

Hilandarska

Svetogorska

To Novi Beograd

Brankov Most

Sava River

Stari Savski Most

Nikola Pašić Trg

Vlajkovićeva

Piornirski Park

Central Train Station

Savski trg

Milovana Milovanovića

Trg Slavija

To Sveti Sava (250m)

To Niš

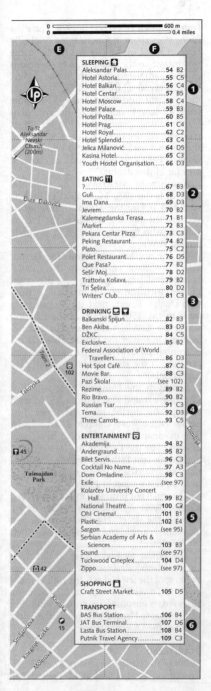

Exchange offices, recognisable by a large blue diamond sign, are also widespread.

Atlas Bank (Map pp276-7; ☎ 302 4000; Emilijana Joksimovića 4; ⏰ 8am-5pm Mon-Fri, 8am-1pm Sat) Cashes travellers cheques.

Delta Banka (Map pp276-7; ☎ 302 2624; Knez Mihailova 30; ⏰ 6.30am-10pm) ATM and cashes travellers cheques.

POST

Central post office (Map pp276-7; ☎ 633 492; Takovska 2; ⏰ 8am-7pm Mon-Sat)

TELEPHONE & FAX

Telephone centre (Map pp276-7; ☎ 323 4484; Takovska 2; ⏰ 7am-midnight Mon-Fri, 7am-10pm Sat & Sun) In the central post office building.

TOURIST INFORMATION

Tourist Organisation of Belgrade (Map pp276-7; www.belgradetourism.org.yu) Knez Mihailova (☎ 629 992; Knez Mihailova 18; ⏰ 9am-8pm Mon-Fri, 9am-6pm Sat, 11am-5pm Sun); Terazije Underpass (☎ 635 622; fax 635 343; ⏰ 9am-8pm Mon-Fri, 9am-4pm Sat) Cheery and friendly with useful brochures, city maps and a *Yellow Cab* events mag.

TRAVEL AGENCIES

Bas Turist (Map pp276-7; ☎ 638 555; fax 784 859; BAS bus station) International bus tickets.

KSR Beograd Tours (Map pp276-7; ☎ 641 258; fax 687 447; Milovana Milovanovića 5; ⏰ 6.30am-8pm) Train tickets at station prices without the crowds.

Lasta (Map pp276-7; ☎ 641 251; www.lasta.co.yu; Milovana Milovanovića 1; ⏰ 7am-9pm) International bus tickets.

Sights

KALEMEGDAN CITADEL

When approaching Kalemegdan (Map pp276-7) from Knez Mihailova street it looks like a fortified park full of youngsters and the older generation, with souvenir sellers displaying their goods on the benches. Seeing it from the river gives it a more imposing look, the large fortification is perched on the hill (and above the city zoo) and behind it sprawls central Belgrade. This is the most important of Belgrade's sights.

Kalemegdan Citadel looks out onto the confluence of the Danube and Sava Rivers, Belgrade's two main arteries. Fortifications were started in Celtic times and extended down onto the flood plain during the Roman settlement of Singidunum,

SERBIA & MONTENEGRO

Belgrade's Roman name. Over the centuries the fortifications were attacked, destroyed and rebuilt as one conqueror removed another. The statistics for this piece of real estate, the key to power in the region, are staggering. Some 115 battles were fought over it and parts of it and the outer city were razed no fewer than 40 times.

Much of what can be seen today dates from the 18th century when the Austro-Hungarians and the Turks reconstructed the citadel three times.

Entering the fortifications from Knez Mihailova street on the southern side, you will start with the essence of the fortification: the Upper Citadel. The main entrance is **Stambol Gate** (Map pp276–7) built by the Turks around 1750.

Passing through Stambol Gate you will find yourself surrounded by cannons and tanks. Fear not, it's only the **Military Museum** (Map pp276–7; ☎ 334 4408; admission 20DIN; ☺ 10am-5pm Tue-Sun), a large complex presenting a complete military history of the former Yugoslavia. Captured Kosovo Liberation Army (KLA) weapons and bits of a downed American stealth fighter are on display as successful 'catches'. Outside are a number of bombs and missiles contributed from the air by NATO in 1999 and a line-up of old guns and tanks, some quite rare. There are basketball grounds nearby, which turn into an ice rink in the winter months and gliding is free.

Crossing through Clock-Tower Gate just by the museum, you will see the Clock Tower above, built during the Austrian occupation in the 18th century. Further on is the mausoleum of Damad Ali-Pasha, where the Turkish dignitary was buried. If you peek through the window you will notice what looks like a coffin covered in a green rug, with an elegant Turkish water jug on the table next to it. No-one knows who it's for.

The large Ottoman-style house behind is the Belgrade Landmarks Preservation office, housed in what used to be a military building. Nearby is the Great Well, 62m deep, at the foot of a double stairway that descends 30m underground, built by the Austrians from 1721 to 1731 to provide a safe water supply to the fortress. The well's depth makes it 10m deeper than the Sava River.

Look up from the well, and you will see the **Victory monument** (Map pp276–7), sculpted by Ivan Meštrović (see p271) in 1928. There is a funny story about this monument: originally built to stand in the city centre, the statue was moved to the citadel due to numerous prudish complaints about its frontal nudity. Now its reveal-all front is facing away from the city and into the distance. The statue holds a falcon in one hand – the symbol of Slav freedom – and a sword in the other, representing the defence of peace. Beyond the statue is the Sava River and Veliko Ratno Ostrvo (The Great War Island), an excellent area for bird-watching.

Another of Meštrović's monumental legacies is the 1930 Monument to France, seen just before the Military Museum. It was erected out of gratitude to the French soldiers who fought and died in Belgrade during WWI.

On the northeastern side is the Despot Gate, the main entrance to the Citadel in medieval times and the best preserved of the fortifications from that period. The Dizdar Tower, next to the gate, was built in the 15th century at the location where the Citadel was entered by a drawbridge. On top of the Dizdar Tower is the Astronomical Observatory, from where you can gaze at the stars (Friday and Saturday nights only).

Nearby is the Dungeon Gate with two impressive round towers on each side, used as a prison during medieval times. Just below is the Rose Church of Our Lady. The original church is said to have been destroyed by the Turks in the 16th century, and the present 18th-century one was originally an arsenal and then a military chapel, until its restoration in 1925.

The small but pleasant **City Zoo** (Map pp276–7; admission 300DIN; ☺ 8am-8pm) is further down, towards the street. How do those hippos, elephants, camels and tigers survive a Belgrade winter?

The Lower Citadel, closer to the river, suffered heavy destruction. The most impressive of the few sights is the 15th-century Nebojša Tower built to protect the harbour. It served its purpose bravely for a while, but was conquered by fire after which the Turks invaded the Lower Citadel.

STARI GRAD

South of the citadel and along Knez Mihailova street is **Stari Grad** (Old Town; Map pp276–7). The mishmash of architecture covers the last two centuries, starting from when Belgrade was snatched from the dying Ottoman Empire and given a boost by the Habsburgs. Pedestrian **Knez Mihailova street** (Map pp276–7) is central to this area and to the city as a whole. It was the first street in Belgrade with an official name. This is where the cafés spill onto the pavements in the summer and where people stroll in their multitudes. Many of the restaurants and some of the hotels reviewed in this chapter are located on Knez Mihailova.

Knez Mihailova itself has some fine buildings, such as the elegant pink and white, neo-Renaissance **School of Fine Arts** (Map pp276–7) sitting on the corner with Rajićeva street. The **Greek queen** (Grčka kraljica; Map pp276–7) hotel and restaurant was built in the mid-19th century and is one of Belgrade's oldest buildings outside the fortified citadel. A little further down is the Serbian Academy of Arts & Sciences (pp276–7), an early-20th-century Art Nouveau-style building, with the goddess Nike at its helm crowning Industry and Trade with two wreaths. A young, arty crowd hangs out here wearing dark shades and cigarettes suspended from their lower lip, so if you feel like belonging, just assume the pose and look cool.

At the other end of Knez Mihailova is Trg Republike (Republic Sq) with the lovely **National Museum** (Map pp276–7; ☎ 624 322; Trg Republike; admission 200DIN, free Sun; ☿ 10am-5pm Tue, Wed & Fri, noon-8pm Thu, 10am-2pm Sat & Sun). The lower two floors of prehistory and early Serbian art and culture were closed for restoration at the time of research. You can see the modern-art gallery on the 3rd floor, which displays a fraction of a large collection of national and European art, including work by Picasso and Monet. If you are interested in seeing some local art, Nadežda Petrović (1873–1915), one of Serbia's first female artists, is well represented. A few blocks away is the **Ethnographical Museum** (Map pp276–7; ☎ 328 1888; Studentski Trg 13; admission 60DIN; ☿ 10am-5pm Tue-Sat, 9am-2pm Sun), with traditional costumes, living spaces and working utensils on display. Pay attention to the elaborate 19th-century bridal costume with a 'Smiljevac' hat (on the ground floor). The woman's hat is made out of coins and mimosas with peacock feathers at the front – it may have been the fash-

ion two centuries ago, but it wouldn't look out of place at Rio Carnival. Montenegrin men's costumes are also fascinating, with guns in shawls wrapped around their waists like belts, revealing their warrior past.

The 2nd floor displays historical living conditions and 19th-century mountain village interiors. It is interesting to compare this with the almost 'real' thing in the museum village of Sirogojno (p300) where museum houses are displayed on a mountainside as a real village would have been 200 years ago. All displays are marked in English.

The 1831 **Palace of Princess Ljubica** (Map pp276–7; ☎ 638 264; Kneza Sime Markovića 8; admission 50DIN; ☿ 10am-5pm Tue-Fri, 10am-4pm Sat & Sun) is a Balkan-style palace built for the wife of Prince Miloš. The spacious rooms are filled with period furniture, but you don't get much of a feeling of how the princess might have lived here. Perhaps the only thing that brings the idea closer to life is the little *hammam* (Turkish bath) where Ljubica would have had steams and massages, and, were she the woman of today, the odd yoga or Pilates class.

To the right of the Palace is the 19th-century **Saborna church** (Orthodox Cathedral; Map pp276–7), a mixture of late baroque and neoclassical styles. The church itself is not as impressive as some others you will encounter in the city, but it is nevertheless important because it holds the tombs of Prince Miloš Obrenović and his two sons. Vuk Karadžić, the man responsible for phoneticising the Serbian language, is buried in the church's graveyard. Opposite is the Patriarchate (Patrijaršija) building with the **Museum of the Serbian Orthodox Church** (Map pp276–7; ☎ 328 2593; Kralja Petra 5; admission 50DIN; ☿ 8am-3pm Mon-Fri), housing valuable items such as the robes of King Milutin (12th and 14th century), Ivan The Terrible's cup and various icons, prints and engravings.

Just up on Kralja Petra, by the church, is the '?' restaurant (see p285), apparently the oldest restaurant in the city. Laid out in the traditional style, this place has acquired its peculiar name because of a long-ago dispute with the church authorities. Built in 1823 and known as Ećim Toma's Café-Restaurant for a while, it eventually changed its name to Cathedral Café because of its location. This rubbed the ecclesiastical authorities up the wrong way and they protested and protested, claiming the café 'desecrated the name of God's temple'. The owner, baffled by all the fuss, put a simple question mark above the front door.

For some quality art exhibitions in the centre, pop into the **Extension of the Museum of Modern Art** (Salon Muzeja Savremene Umetnosti; Map pp276-7; ☎ 630 940; Pariška 14; admission free; 🕙 11am-5pm). The two large rooms house temporary art exhibitions by high-profile international artists. Abbas Kiarostami's photography exhibition 'Roads' was here before it went to London.

DORĆOL

Dorćol gets its name from the Turkish *dört yol*, meaning 'four roads'. The area initially encompassed only the crossing of Dubrovačka and Dušanova streets, but now includes the northern area from Studentski Trg (Student Sq) to the Danube, and from Skadarska to Kalemegdan in the east. Dorćol was once the most cosmopolitan area of Belgrade. A mixture of Turkish, Greek, Jewish, German, Armenian and Vlach merchant communities filled the streets, and Christmas, Passover and Ramadan were celebrated side by side. Unfortunately, no tzatziki can be bought on these streets any more, nor can you sink your teeth into a *kugel* (yeasted sweet bread) in the Dorćol restaurants. But you can still enjoy a stroll and get a feel of the old Dorćol in Jevrem restaurant (see p285).

The area has had a few nips and tucks over the years, depending on who ruled the city: the Turks gave it a distinct oriental look, with small houses and cobbled winding streets; during the brief Austrian command between 1717 and 1739, the streets were 'straightened'; when Belgrade was returned to Turkish power in 1739, the streets got their curves back. Now the area has a pleasant residential feel, but none of the oriental architecture remains, apart from the 18th-century **Burial Chamber of Sheik Mustafa** (Map pp276-7; cnr Braće Jugovića & Višnjićeva), a dervish sheik from Baghdad.

Dorćol's last remaining mosque, and indeed the last mosque in Belgrade, is the **Bayrakli Mosque** (Map pp276-7; cnr Kralja Petra & Gospodar Jevremova). It dates back to the 17th century and is being reconstructed after it

was damaged in the March 2004 riots, a backlash against the anti-Serb pogroms in Kosovo at the time.

One of Belgrade's first synagogues was built in this area, but sadly it no longer stands. The **St Aleksandar Nevski church** (Cara Dušana) is the first Christian place of worship to have been built in the area and is still here. For a bit of free music, catch the Roma bands playing outside the church when the wedding crowds come out on Saturday afternoons.

The **Gallery of Frescoes** (Map pp276-7; ☎ 621 491; Cara Uroša 20; admission 50DIN; 🕙 10am-5pm Mon, Tue & Thu-Sat, 10am-2pm Sun) gives you a good idea of Serbian church art with its full-size replicas (and some originals) of paintings from churches and monasteries. The replicas are exact down to the last detail, even reproducing scratches and wear. Some fascinating Roman floor mosaics are being reconstructed and can be seen under their protective sheets.

SKADARSKA

East of Trg Republike, Skadarska (Map pp276-7) or 'Skadarlija' is what some like to call 'Belgrade's Montmartre'. Although a perhaps slightly ambitious comparison, Skadarska earned this name for being the place where bohemians hung out at the turn of the 20th century, discussing their latest poems or art in thick clouds of cigarette smoke. It's a small street and still has its old-fashioned charm. Although the sight of men in bowler hats, or – even better – berets, writing poetry or discussing philosophy is now a thing of the past, they still would not look out of place on this cobbled street. For a true Serbian experience, dine in one of the traditional restaurants that hide in the small houses, while the compulsory Roma fiddle plays into your ear. It's especially good if you're doing a bit of wooing: Skadarska is definitely a street for romantics.

In the 1830s this area was a collection of abandoned trenches outside of Belgrade's defensive walls and was populated by the city's Roma community. The Roma shantytown was removed and houses were built for craftsmen and poorer civil servants. The street got its name in honour of the Albanian city of Skadar (Shkodra). By the early 20th century, Skadarska had become the stomping ground of Belgrade's artists, actors, writers and musicians and even today you may dine next to a Belgrade film star in one of the restaurants.

Further up, off Skadarska, is the Association of Serbian Writers with a famous restaurant (the Writers' Club, p286), where Belgrade's men and women of the pen met and ate during socialist times. Now, anyone is welcome and the restaurant still retains its old-time atmosphere.

Skadarska is at its best in the summer months when musical, theatrical and cabaret performances enliven outdoor eating. The food is mainly traditional and the restaurants rejoice in unusual names: Three Hats (Tri Šešira; once a hatmaking shop), There Are Days (Ima Dana), Two Deer (Dva Jelena) and Two White Doves (Dva Bela Goluba).

There is a market at the end of the street, called Bajlonova pijaca, and a copy of the Sarajevo Sebilj fountain given to Belgrade by Sarajevo in 1989.

CENTRAL BELGRADE

From Skadarska, across Trg Republike is **Terazije** street, the core of Belgrade's hustle and bustle. The grandiose Hotel Moscow with its water fountain in the front dominates the square. The wide Terazije street is traffic-laden, advertisement lights flicker from the buildings, and shops line the street. Terazije street has some lovely architecture that gets somewhat lost among all the lights and noise.

Look up at the charming Art Nouveau **Smederevo Bank** (Map pp276-7; Terazije 39), a slim white construction built in 1912 for a local merchant. Opposite is another Art Nouveau building, now the **Zvezda cinema** (Map pp276-7; Terazije 40), but originally a photography studio of Milan Jovanović, a locally known portrait photographer. If you look at the wall of the building on the left-hand side, you will see a reproduction of one of Jovanović's elegant photographs called 'A Girl with a Parasol'.

A fine example of a neobaroque-style house on Terazije is the **Krsmanović House** (Map pp276-7; Terazije 34), where the Kingdom of Serbs, Croats and Slovenes was first pronounced in 1918, a unification that would some years later lead to the federation of Yugoslavia.

The Hotel Moscow (see the boxed text, p284), apart from being a luxurious structure, is a legendary meeting place. It was built between 1906 and 1907 as a hotel and office building for an insurance company from St Petersburg. The hotel restaurant and bar are never empty and you may want to sip a coffee here too and watch Belgrade go by.

The tall modernist tower-block building **Albania** (Map pp276-7) marks the point where Terazije meets Knez Mihailova street. The building's underground passage hides shops and tourist information offices.

From Terazije, across Trg Nikola Pašić, is the grandiose 1938 **Post Office Building** (Map pp276-7), for mailing in style. Constructed to accompany the 1908 **Old Telephone Building** (Map pp276-7), it is a good example of Serbian-Byzantine style buildings, standing a few streets away from the post office.

Behind the post office is the **Sveti Marko church** (Map pp276-7; ☎ 323 1940; Bulevar Kralja Aleksandra 17), based on the design of the Gračanica Monastery in Kosovo. It is five-domed, with a bell tower above the main entrance. The church contains the grave of the Emperor Dušan (1308–55). Behind it is the tiny white **Russian church** (Map pp276-7) with blue domes, erected by Russian refugees who fled the October Revolution.

Surrounding these two churches is **Tašmajdan park** (Map pp276-7), a former quarry, and the ground where the Belgrade cemetery stood. After the post office building was constructed, the park was laid out behind it, and for a while in the 20th century, Tašmajdan park became an extension of the Belgrade racetrack.

Opposite the post office is the **Parliament** (Map pp276-7). This building gained fame in October 2000 when anti-Milošević rallies took place here. TV screens around the world were filled with crowds of people storming this very building.

Trg Nikola Pašića is adjacent, with the **Museum of the History of Yugoslavia** (Trg Nikole Pašića 11; admission free; ☽ Tue-Sun noon-7pm) sitting on the corner. Temporary exhibitions show work by artists from all over former Yugoslavia and are definitely worth a look.

If vehicles are your thing, the **Museum of Automobiles** (Map pp276-7; ☎ 334 2625; Majke Jevrosime 30; admission 50DIN; ☽ 11am-7pm) is a compelling collection of cars and motorcycles.

Choice for our garage would be the '57 Cadillac convertible: only 25,000km and one careful owner – President Tito.

For film buffs, the **Yugoslav Film Library Theatre** (Map pp276-7; ☎ 324 8250; www.kinoteka .org.yu; Kosovska 11) has more than 82,000 films, stills, books and film magazines, all illustrating the technical development of film throughout the years. It also shows classic films, and prints a monthly programme of upcoming screenings.

Back on Terazije and down towards the river behind Hotel Moscow is the **Green Wreath market** (Zeleni Venac; Map pp276-7), a covered market that has been a place of trade since the 19th century. The construction of the place is interesting, with unusual, almost Chinese-style roofs on the chequerboard towers. The rest of the market area is covered with a patchwork of tin, wood and textile, to keep out the sun. Unfortunately, it seems to also have the effect of keeping the smell in. If your airline loses your luggage, fret not: you can stock up on anything here, from cheap clothes to washing products, dodgy DVDs and, of course, food. This is also a starting and ending

point for many of the city buses, including Zemun and Ada Ciganlija.

One of Belgrade's best museums is the **Nikola Tesla Museum** (Map pp276-7; ☎ 433 886; Krunska 51; www.tesla-museum.org; admission 50DIN; ⏲ 10am-noon & 4-8pm Tue-Fri, 10am-1pm Sat & Sun). For more about Nikola Tesla, see the boxed text below. Apart from seeing demonstrations of Tesla's fascinating inventions, you will get to play a part in a *Star Wars*–like episode where a crazy machine produces noisy sparks, and lights the cableless neon lamp in your hand – excellent for a sword fight. A truly interactive museum experience, even for those who have no comprehension of science.

OUTER BELGRADE

Head down across Trg Slavija, where the tall 'Belgrade' building stands. Behind it is the massive Orthodox church of **Sveti Sava** (Map p274; Svetog Save). Billed as the biggest Orthodox church in the world, which is not hard to believe, it is a work in progress. Started in 1935, and interrupted by Hitler, communism and lack of cash, it's at the lock-up stage. Still, if the door's open for the builders, have a peek inside and feel

---

NIKOLA TESLA: AN ELECTRIC LIFE

If you happened to see Jim Jarmusch's film *Coffee and Cigarettes* (2003) and wondered who on earth that guy Nikola Tesla was that everyone in the film was banging on about, now's your chance to find out.

Nikola Tesla was the embodiment of the idea of a crazy scientist, minus the wild hair sported by Einstein. In fact, the moustachioed Serb who spent most of his working life in America was about as influential in the world of physics and electronic engineering as Einstein himself. He was the inventor of the rotating magnetic field and the complete production and distribution of electrical energy based on alternate currents. For you and me that means he invented motors and generators, and without him, you'd still be using a wind-up mechanism to start your car.

Born in northern Serbia in 1856, Tesla studied at Graz and Prague universities before moving to Paris in 1882 to work for Edison's Continental Company, where he made the prototype of the induction motor. Two years later he moved to New York and after resigning from Edison's company for not getting paid, Tesla started playing around with X-rays and wireless power transmission. He invented the first neon light tube and forever changed the look of America's streets. He was also responsible for coming up with a way to transmit electricity over long distances, those large power stations and towers, attached to miles of cables across many a country's landscape, are all thanks to Tesla. He played around with remote controls and electric motor ignition, both of which are integral to the modern world, and was an early starter at radio astronomy. But his more idiosyncratic inventions like the 'electric laxative' somehow didn't become household items.

Unfortunately, Tesla didn't have a business head and did not patent many of his inventions, leaving himself frequently out of pocket. He was also often tricked out of money by more shrewd businessmen, and ended up dying half-forgotten in the New Yorker hotel in Manhattan in 1943. A book entitled *The Man Who Invented the Twentieth Century: Nikola Tesla* by Robert Lomas (Headline) is a detailed account of this fascinating man's life.

puny under its massive dome. The church is built on the site where the Turks apparently burnt the relics of St Sava, the youngest son of a 12th-century ruler, and founder of the independent Serbian Orthodox church. In front of it is a statue of Serbia's former ruler, the legendary Karađorđe, which in turn is surrounded by Karađorđe park where people lounge about in the sun.

Further south, don't miss **Maršal Tito's grave** (Kuća Cveća or House of Flowers; Map p274; ☎ 367 1485; Bulevar Mira; admission free; 🕓 9am-5pm Tue-Sun Jun-Sep, to 3pm rest of year) with an interesting museum of gifts (embroidery, dubious-purpose smoking pipes, saddles and weapons) given by toadying comrades and fellow travellers. Check if the adjacent **Historical Museum of Yugoslavia** (Map p274; ☎ 367 1485; exhibitions 🕓 9am-2pm Tue-Sun) is open for one of its occasional exhibitions. Take trolleybus 40 or 41.

At the airport, the exceptional **Yugoslav Aeronautical Museum** (☎ 670 992; Suračin; admission 300DIN; 🕓 9am-2pm Tue-Sun Nov-Apr, 9am-7pm Tue-Sun May-Oct) is engrossing if you're an aircraft buff. There are some rare planes here, including a Hurricane, Spitfire and Messerschmitt from WWII, and bits of that infamous American stealth fighter that air defences downed in 1999.

The **Museum of Contemporary Art** (Muzej Savremene Umetnosti; Map pp276-7; ☎ 311 5713; admission 80DIN; 🕓 10am-5pm Mon, Wed, Fri & Sat, noon-8pm Thu, 10am-2pm Sun) is in New Belgrade (Novi Beograd) on the banks of the Danube River. The permanent collection covers three periods: impressionist (1900–18); expressionist, constructivist and surrealist (1918–41); neosurrealist, modern and contemporary (1945 to present day). A collection of sculptures scans the period between 1900 and the 1970s, and the temporary exhibitions gallery has retrospectives of Serbian and foreign artists. Note that this is probably the only museum in the country (and possibly in Eastern Europe) that is open on Mondays. It's closed on Tuesdays though. Get there by buses 15, 84, 704E or 706 from the Green Wreath market (Zeleni Venac).

Ada Ciganlija (Map p274), an island park on the Sava River, is Belgrade's summer retreat. Gentle choices are swimming in a lake (get your kit off with the naturists 1km upstream), hiring a bicycle or just strolling among the trees. Adrenaline junkies might fancy the bungee jumping or trying the water-ski tow. Plenty of places overlooking the lake sell restorative cold beers. To get to Ada take bus 53 or 56 from the Green Wreath market.

Avala is a mountain 16km south of Belgrade and is another popular summer outing place. There are water springs and walking opportunities here, as well as WWI and WWII monuments, the most famous being ubiquitous Ivan Meštrović's **Monument to the Unknown Hero**, essentially a tomb for a Serbian soldier, with eight tall granite female figures symbolising the Yugoslav peoples.

Košutnjak is a park on Belgrade's southwestern outskirts where many come to walk on the 'health path' marked with suggestions of exercise. These are the remains of the country's socialist past, when the government made sport one of the axes for a happy existence, adopting the slogan from ancient Greece: 'A healthy spirit is in a healthy body' to get the masses jogging. Get bus 53 from the Green Wreath market or jog the 9km.

Tours

The Tourist Organisation of Belgrade (p277) runs bus, boat and guided walking tours. **National Guide Association of Serbia** (Map pp276-7; ☎ 323 5910; www.utvs.org.yu; 5th fl, Dučanska 8; 🕓 9.30am-3pm Mon-Fri) Independent and licensed guides for city or country tours.
Romantika Steam-hauled train to Austro-Hungarian Sremski Karlovci. Contact KSR Beograd Tours (p277).

Festivals & Events

FEST film festival (www.fest.org.yu) International and local films are screened from February to March every year, with talks by various directors.
Beer festival (www.belgradebeerfest.com) August.
BEMUS Music Festival (www.bemus.co.yu) A classical music festival with a good choice of local and international artists.
BITEF international theatre festival (www.bitef .co.yu) A September festival originating in the avant-garde of the '60s and '70s, it now stages Serbia's best thespian talent and international theatre companies.
Classical music festival October.

Sleeping

Belgrade's hotel scene is really rather under-developed, apart from a couple of big boys like Hyatt Regency and Aleksandar Palas, which go slightly overboard both in price and in comfort. The lower end of the market leaves a lot to be desired. The midrange options are mostly decent, and provide guests with all the basics in slightly more polished surroundings. The real shame though is the lack of imaginative and different places to stay.

CITY CENTRE
Budget

The **Youth Hostel organisation** (Ferijalni Savez Beograd; Map pp276-7; ☎ 324 8550; www.hostels.org .yu; 2nd fl, Makedonska 22; ☯ 9am-5pm) does deals with local hotels for discounts. You need HI membership (300DIN to join) or an international student card. It also books the **Jelica Milanović** (Map pp276-7; ☎ 323 1268; Krunska 8; per person from €7.50; ☯ Jul & Aug), which offers college accommodation during holiday time. No food is available.

Hotel Royal (Map pp276-7; ☎ 634 222; www.hotel royal.co.yu; Kralja Petra 56; s/d 1888/2628DIN; ☐) Possibly the best value for money: it's central (Dorćol area), cheap and clean. The rooms are simply decorated, pleasant and tidy, the staff are friendly, and the reception buzzes with action around a bizarre glass-mosaic staircase in the centre. There is live music in the basement restaurant, if you're up for the folk experience.

Hotel Splendid (Map pp276-7; ☎ 323 5444; www .splendid.co.yu; D Jovanovića 5; s/d 1974/3168DIN) More splendid in name than in appearance, this place is slightly run-down, but in a good location (off Terazije) and has a friendly home-away-from-home feeling.

Hotel Astoria (Map pp276-7; ☎ 264 5422; www.as toria.co.yu; Milovana Milovanovića 1a; s/d 2684/2868DIN, d with shared bathroom 2208DIN) If there is no room in any of the other similarly priced hotels, you could stay a night here – but mind the scraggly gauze curtains and the dingy rooms. Oh, and its business card doubles as a small sewing kit, should you need one in a hurry.

Hotel Pošta (Map pp276-7; ☎ 361 4260; Slobodana Penezića 3; s/d 1590/2400DIN) A conspiratorial feeling stirs as you enter the hotel's reception area: a gambling-machine room flickers on one side; passengers killing time until their next train fix their gazes upon you through thick clouds of cigarette smoke. In front is a reception with former Yugoslav memorabilia all around. The rooms are run-down but clean, with funny bar stools for sitting at the window-sills-come-tables. No credit cards are accepted.

Midrange

Hotel Balkan (Map pp276-7; ☎ 268 7466; fax 268 7581; Prizrenska 2; r €50-70) Opposite Hotel Moscow, but a little less grandiose, Balkan is great value for money. Rooms are spacious with lovely views of Terazije street, and the bathrooms are tiled in a seductive dark brown. There is a busy café on the ground floor and a terrace on the square in the summer.

Kasina Hotel (Map pp276-7; ☎ 323 5574; www .kasina.stari-grad.co.yu; Terazije 25; s/d from 2904/5808DIN) In the Balkan-Moscow triangle on Terazije street, this place has decent and comfortable rooms. Depending on whether you go for the 'comfort' or 'standard' option you get air-conditioning and a minibar, or neither of those and slightly darker rooms. In the latter case try compensating by getting a room with a view of the square. A good location in any case.

Hotel Palace (Map pp276-7; ☎ 185 585; www.pal acehotel.co.yu; Topličin Venac 23; s/d €60/82; ☐) Slightly better than other state hotels, it may still be a little overpriced for what it has to offer. The lobby is dolled up with a water feature and some leather armchairs. The rooms are equipped with a phone, TV and a massive bathroom. There is a good view of the city from the upstairs Panorama restaurant.

> ### THE AUTHOR'S CHOICE
> **Hotel Moscow** (Map pp276-7; Hotel Moskva; ☎ 268 6255; hotelmoskva@absolutok.net; Balkanska; s €33-56, d from €102; ☒) This is the most famous hotel in Belgrade and a lovely building it is too – an Art Nouveau structure dating from 1906 with a large terrace out front. Rooms range from cheaper singles, which are small but comfortable, to more spacious doubles and luxurious apartments with writing desks that'll make you feel like Lord Byron. If you can't remember what day it is, pop into the lift and check the carpet, changed each day with the weekday written on them. The bar downstairs is a gathering place for locals to have a drink, eat a cake and relax as Belgrade rushes by.

Hotel Prag (Map pp276-7; ☎ 361 0422; www.hotel prag.co.yu; Narodnog Fronta 27; s/d €34/63; 🌐) This small hotel, hidden in what looks like someone's house, shows what a lick of paint can do to freshen up a room. The doubles are spacious and light, but the singles are a little cramped. The bathrooms have a scary blue light that does no favours to anyone's complexion in the morning.

Top End

Aleksandar Palas (Map pp276-7; ☎ 330 5300; Kralja Petra 13-15; apt €260; www.aleksandarpalas.com; 🌐 💻) An ultraposh place where you can have a pad to yourself. In fact, there are no rooms as such, only classy apartments, each with a living room, bedroom and bathroom. Then there are DVD players and home cinema systems with six speakers, Turkish baths, Finnish saunas, need we go on? So if your pockets are deep and you want to feel like the king of the hill for the night, look no further.

OUTER BELGRADE

Hyatt Regency (Map p274; ☎ 301 1234; www.belgrade .regency.hyatt.com; Milentija Popovića 5; s/d from €245/265; 🌐 💻) A little less central than the Aleksandar Palas, this stately marble monument in New Belgrade has all the usual mod cons and luxury shops this kind of a place has to offer, and is close to the Museum of Contemporary Art.

Eating

Meat's the word on the modern (and traditional) Belgrader's tongue. And the Serbs are into their food. Big piles of it. Whether you choose to go for a traditional restaurant or a more modern affair, the atmosphere in Belgrade's restaurants is boisterous and the food affordable. Pick a place along Knez Mihailova, 29 Novembra or Makedonska, or one of the famous Skadarska street restaurants. If you don't mind floating while you eat, restaurants on the Danube are also a good option.

Many eat on the go, so the quality of quick bites is ensured, too. Kralja Petra street has some notable fast-food kiosks, green in colour and at the bottom of the street. Those around Trg Republike are open 24 hours, as are most of the ones by the train and bus stations. You can fill up for under 100DIN.

RESTAURANTS

¿Que Pasa? (Map pp276-7; ☎ 330 5377; Kralja Petra 13-15; www.que-pasa.co.yu; meals 600-700DIN; ☽ 8am-midnight) Is it a busy restaurant with a great bar, or a funky bar that does food? The menu is a curious mishmash of Mexican and Serbian, but the music is definitely Latin. Spacious, luminous and chic, this bar/restaurant has a happening buzz.

Jevrem (Map pp276-7; ☎ 328 4746; Gospodar Jevremova 36; meals 300-500DIN; ☽ 10am-2am Mon-Sat, 2-10pm Sun) Set in a lovingly restored old Dorćol house and entered through a heavy walnut door, Jevrem is decorated to look like a place out of the 1920s. It has separate drinking and dining areas furnished with plush armchairs. Photographs of Belgrade from the '20s adorn the walls. This place breathes comfort. The food is traditional and simple. We recommend the Serbian beans at 280DIN, accompanied by one of the wines from the excellent selection. There's some live music, too.

Šešir Moj (My Hat; Map pp276-7; ☎ 322 8750; Skadarska 21; meals 300-500DIN; ☽ 8am-late) An intimate little restaurant with alcove rooms and walls obscured with an art gallery of oils and pastels. A place for romantics, especially when members of a Roma band swirl in playing their hauntingly passionate music. Go for the *punjena bela vešalica*, which is a pork fillet stuffed with *kajmak*. Finish with Serbian coffee and a piece of *orašnica* (walnut cake) if you've any room left.

Guli (Map pp276-7; ☎ 323 7204; Skadarska 13; meals 400-600DIN; ☽ 11am-1am) And now for

---

THE AUTHOR'S CHOICE

? (Map pp276-7; ☎ 635 421; Kralja Petra 6; meals 200-350DIN) There's no question about this being one of the best places in town for traditional food and décor. You'll be beckoned in by one of the smiling moustachioed old men standing outside. Tender lamb or veal *ispod saća* (baked in a special earthen pot under hot coals) is mouth-watering and plenty, with roast potatoes accompanied by shiny pickled peppers. The wooden interior is of an old-style Serbian tavern, with low tables and half-moon stools, and the service is jolly. The name is a result of a dispute between a previous owner and the Orthodox cathedral opposite.

something completely different. A Skadarska restaurant that is as spankingly modern and different from its neighbours as can be. Not only that, but Belgraders consider this a place of pilgrimage for the pizza and pasta on the menu. If you're not hungry, you can have some cocktails and snuggle up to what might be a Belgrade film star next to you. Great wine selection from Italy, Australia, Chile and Argentina.

Writers' Club (Klub Književnika; Map pp276-7; Francuska 7; meals 400-600DIN; ☻6pm-1am) This is a legendary institution that has been popular since the Tito era and was once frequented by the state-approved literati of the time. Despite not having the same cult status nowadays, it remains a Belgrade favourite. Many reminisce about the stuffed courgettes and roast lamb with potatoes, both of which have kept their cult status. Enter through the gate on the street and go into the grand stucco mansion, to the restaurant downstairs.

Dačo (☎ 278 1009; Patrisa Lumumbe 49; meals 250-500DIN; ☻10.30am-midnight) Dačo is a legend on the Belgrade dining scene. This all-Serbian restaurant has waiters in national dress, traditional music and fluttering trumpets attracting a crowd from across the city. It's a haul from the centre, so allow yourself half a day here. The boisterous atmosphere is great fun; try resisting the jocular musicians as they lure you into belting out traditional songs (or at least being an accompanying vocal). For authenticity the menu's in Cyrillic but English-speaking waiters will help you out. The entrées – kajmak, cheeses, pršuta (prosciutto) and other cold meats and salad items – served on wooden platters are the restaurant's speciality. Check out the Serbian mementos at the small shop. You will have to catch a taxi to get here from the city centre.

Priroda (☎ 411 890; Batutova 11; meals 25-400DIN; ☻9am-9.30pm, food from 12.30pm) Give the owner a medal for battling against adversity: here is a superb vegetarian restaurant in a land of human carnivores. Rediscover the delicate flavours of vegetables and pulses that don't normally appear in traditional Serbian cuisine. The macrobiotic cake is a mouth stunner. Priroda is about 6km east of the central train station.

Trattoria Košava (Map pp276-7; ☎ 627 344; Kralja Petra 6; meals 400-600DIN; ☻9am-1am Mon-Fri, noon-

1am Sat & Sun) A small eatery in which the kitchen is decidedly Italian. There's not much space at all in this cross between a family kitchen and a café/restaurant. If you like it cosy, this is your perfect lunch spot. The menu has pastas and pizzas for a proper lunch, or you can snack on a yummy cherry strudel and a coffee in the downstairs café.

Peking Restaurant (Map pp276-7; ☎ 181 931; Vuka Karadžića 2; meals 600-700DIN; ☻11am-midnight Mon-Sat, 2pm-midnight Sun) Boldly striking across national borders is this two-floor Chinese restaurant draped in red lanterns and Chinese décor, with tinkling music fortifying the oriental feeling (or compensating for the fact that none of the staff is Chinese). The meals are varied (40 different options), with inviting recipes like duck with walnuts and maybe a not-so-inviting deep-fried ice cream.

Kalemegdanska Terasa (Map pp276-7; ☎ 328 2727; Kalemegdan bb; meals 400-900DIN; ☻noon-1am) This slick peach-coloured restaurant in the grounds of Kalemegdan Citadel steals the city's views. Lovely terraces for summer dining alfresco beat the faux ancient interior. The menu consists of grilled meat and cutlets and diners seem to be charged for the location as well as the tasty food. For dessert, sample a Serbian walnut pie at 150DIN.

Plato (Map pp276-7; ☎ 658 863; Akademski Plato 1; meals 250-400DIN; ☻9am-2am Mon-Thu, 9am-3am Fri, 10am-3am Sat, noon-2am Sun) Plato (plar-to) is an eclectic mix of restaurant, café, bar and live-music venue. It provides enjoyable food, mostly Italian, in a relaxed atmosphere where you can eat, drink or just listen to jazz or Cuban rhythms.

Polet Restaurant (Map pp276-7; ☎ 323 2454; Kralja Milana 31; meals 200-500DIN; ☻11am-11pm) With fat, shiny brass railings surrounding the upper mezzanine floor, and blue-and-white décor, you feel as if you're out at sea. Eat low or eat high here: a tasty fish soup at 90DIN or scampi à la Parisienne at 1150DIN. The succulent calamari (390DIN) is char-grilled to perfection.

Intercontinental (Map p274; ☎ 311 333; Vladimira Popovića, Novi Beograd; buffet breakfast 650DIN; ☻7am-10pm) Massive breakfasts. In fact, all-you-can-eat breakfasts, if your body is in need of a multitude of nutrients.

Also recommended in Skadarska street are **Ima Dana** (There Are Days; Map pp276-7; ☎ 323

4422; Skadarska 38; meals 250-350DIN; ◉ 11am-5pm & 7pm-1am) and **Tri Šešira** (Three Hats; Map pp276-7; ☎ 324 7501; Skadarska 29; meals 300-460DIN; ◉ lunch & dinner), both offering similar menus and entertainment.

QUICK EATS
Loki (Kralja Petra; 100-200DIN; ◉ 24hr) Dorćol's Loki is the most renowned of the fast-food kiosks. Its exquisite *pljeskavica* (a Serbian burger) is responsible for the long line of people at 1am. Recommended.

Pekara Centar Pizza (Map pp276-7; Kolarčeva 10; pizza 40DIN; ◉ 24hr) With its bright and cheery interior and French breads and pretzels hanging above the counter, its the freshly baked pizzas and pastry here that passers-by pop in for.

Belgrade's main fruit and veg **market** (Map pp276-7; cnr Brankova Prizrenska & Narodnog Fronta; ◉ 6am-1pm) is a scrounging ground for DIY food; there are also many supermarkets around Belgrade.

Drinking
Sometimes it's hard to distinguish between a café and a bar in Belgrade: both serve coffee and booze and some serve food. Many are quiet coffee places during the day and noisy, busy and smoky at night. All are open daily from early morning to at least midnight with a later start on Sunday. All around Belgrade, but particularly in the centre, café and bar terraces spread onto pavements in the spring and summer months.

Apart from serving excellent pizza, Belgraders flock to Guli (p285) for the cocktails. The exposed-brick walls, low-hanging subdued lights and long wooden tables are ideal for whispering sweet nothings into your sweetheart's ear.

CAFÉS
Hot Spot Café (Map pp276-7; ☎ 263 905; Studentski Trg 2; ◉ 8am-midnight) Glass-fronted and elegantly decorated with small sculptures and soft seats, this is a great (hot) spot for breakfast/brunch as well as night-time drinking. There is freshly squeezed orange juice, toasted sandwiches and delicious coffee. During the day, young and old come here to drink coffee and chat. In the evening the music is good and there's plenty to drink.

Russian Tsar (Ruski Car; Map pp276-7; ☎ 633 628; Obilićev venac 28; ◉ 8am-midnight) A grandiose,

---

SILICON VALLEY
You may think that this has something to do with the high-tech boom in California, and if you do, you're most certainly mistaken. The only boom occurring on the trendy Strahinjića Bana street (aka 'Silicon Valley') in Dorćol is the silicone attributes of trophy girlfriends coming here to accompany their gangsta boyfriends. Strahinjića Bana is a quiet daytime street with a string of fashionable bars. Approaching the pumpkin hour, there's nowhere to park, and hardly anywhere to walk. The only thing to do is to stand back and enjoy the show.

---

faded café with heavy chandeliers that feels like a Moscow salon that found itself in the middle of Knez Mihailova by surprise. This classic hang-out has comforted thirsty Belgraders for the last hundred years. Teas, coffees and alcoholic drinks are served and there is a leafy garden outside in summer as well as a fast-food takeaway hole-in-the-wall.

Rezime (Map pp276-7; ☎ 328 4276; Kralja Petra 41) Classy Rezime with its leather armchairs and sleek glass'n'gold tables is on the ground floor of a magnificently ornate Art Nouveau building. The waiters wear bow ties and local businessmen sip their coffees while flicking through the fashion magazines displayed on each table. A great selection of hot chocolate.

Balkanski Špijun (Map pp276-7; ☎ 639 903; Vuka Karadžića 7a; ◉ 8am-midnight) Named after a cult Yugoslav film called *The Balkan Spy*, this small bar has spy memorabilia hanging on the walls: Lomo cameras, small notebooks and multipurpose can't-work-out-what-they-are-unless-you're-a-spy tools. The atmosphere is relaxed and the coffee good.

Tema (Map pp276-7; ☎ 337 3859; Makedonska 11-13; ◉ 8am-midnight) Subtly lit modern bar that both young and old are welcome to linger in. It does a pleasant line in coffees with a spirit kick.

BARS
Kandahar (☎ 064 334 3970; Strahinjića Bana 48; ◉ 8am-late) On the 'Silicon Valley' beat (see above), this place brings home the true meaning of a 'lounge' bar. The décor is Arabic with gentle drapes hanging overhead, and the reclining

position is obligatory on the soft cushions scattered on the floor and benches. This is a popular hang-out and apart from cocktails (200DIN to 300DIN), exotic types of tea are served, such as desert tea (which curiously includes mango) or tea for lovers. Or you could try Kandahar coffee, served with Turkish delight.

Ben Akiba (Map pp276-7; ☎ 323 7775; Nušićeva 8; ❧ 9am-late) Unless you're a part of Belgrade's 'in' crowd, you're not supposed to know about this place. Hidden away in a 'secret' location (a converted flat), it started out as a haven for liberals to sip cocktails and discuss freedom during the Milošević years. Now it's Belgrade's chic who frequent this place renowned for its cocktail range. You can even choose a painting by a local artist from a selection displayed on the walls.

Movie Bar (Map pp276-7; ☎ 262 3818; Kolarčeva 6; ❧ 9am-1am) A long, long white room with a longish bar and many, many drinks. Under the Albania building, and next to the cinema (hence the name), this is a cool oasis during the summer heat and a cool jazz joint at night. Italian-style *aperitivo* (snacks and wine) is served in the afternoons between 5pm and 8pm.

Pazi Škola! (Map pp276-7; ☎ 328 5437; cnr Dalmatinska & Takovska; ❧ 7pm-1am Mon-Thu, 7pm-late Fri, Sat & Sun) This is a great bar. Adjacent to the nightclub Plastic, Pazi Škola! is a blue room with a few sofas, tables and chairs, as well as a bit of standing room, so everyone can fit in. Classed best as a DJ bar, it's subdued during weeknights, with a few barflies enjoying a quiet drink, and then kicking on the weekends, with most of Belgrade's 'alternative' club crowd dancing until all hours.

DžKC – Džepni Kulturni Centar (Pocket Culture Centre; Map pp276-7; Kralja Milana 18; ❧ 9am-late) Don't be afraid when you enter the courtyard that looks like a nuclear wasteland (that someone actually lives in – note the clothes drying among the rubble), boldly approach the old house. Run and frequented by those not interested in fashion or sleek places, DžKC is what has been described as a neopunk gathering ground and drinking den that hosts cultural evenings and workshops. It's a lively place with colourful walls, local art, and a fabulous panoramic photo of Belgrade stretching across one of its walls.

Federal Association of World Travellers (Map pp276-7; ☎ 324 2303; 29 Novembra 7; ❧ 1pm-midnight Mon-Fri, 3pm-late Sat & Sun) Open the big black gate, follow the lights that suddenly come on and enter a place that looks like an eccentric granny's house. Cats roam around the three rooms all decorated with ornaments from the four corners of the globe. Tables are anything from a piano to an old sewing machine, lamps are crooked on table edges and facing you are photos of relatives you never knew. The Association hosts hedonistic house parties on weekends. Try a cocktail of the day at 250DIN.

Exclusive (Map pp276-7; ☎ 328 2288; Knez Mihailova 41-45; ❧ 9am-2am Mon-Sat, noon-1am Sun) This basement beer joint is Belgrade's answer to a Munich beer hall. There's plenty of knees-up music for this lads' bar, with big snacks – sausage, bread and chips (70DIN) – as a sound bedrock for serious drinking.

Rio Bravo (Map pp276-7; ☎ 328 5050; Kralja Petra 54; ❧ 11am-2am Mon-Sat, 5pm-2am Sun) Hitch yer horse outside, mosey in and shoot down some hard liquor in this bar kitted out with redundant Western film sets.

Three Carrots (Map pp276-7; ☎ 683 748; Kneza Milosa 16; ❧ 9am-1am) Allegedly Belgrade's first Irish pub, although it only vaguely resembles a pub at all. It does have a wooden interior. Importantly it has Guinness, serves snacks and, 'authentically', plays a lot of U2.

Entertainment

Welcome to club central. Belgrade's nightlife is well and truly awake and in this city you can have a lot of fun. Belgraders are party animals, and clubs are everywhere: in the city centre, off centre, on the river barges. The music stretches from well-known European and local DJs playing house, R&B, hip-hop or drum'n'bass to the beats of turbofolk pounding into the night.

If you'd rather take it easy, cinemas screen films in English (with Serbian subtitles) and concerts are held at Sava Centar.

CLUBS
City Clubs
Anderground (Underground; Map pp276-7; ☎ 625 681; www.anderground.com; Pariška 1a; ❧ noon-midnight Sun-Thu, to 2am Fri & Sat) The city's most famous nightspot parties hard. Big names in the DJ world spin records on Saturdays. Dancers shake it all on two elevated platforms. There's whooping, whistling, sweating and

jigging. Drenched waiters collect glasses and dodge flying limbs with unbelievable skill. The club, set in an old cavern, has a large dancing area and a smaller area for when you can dance no more. About the only nightclub with wheelchair access.

Šargon (Map pp276-7; ☎ 063 667 722; Pariška 1a; ◷ noon-midnight Sun-Thu, to 2am Fri & Sat) Next door to Andergraund but with a markedly different atmosphere. It's all disco, disco, disco here with '80s and '90s music and a more subdued crowd. Nevertheless, it's packed on weekends.

Akademija (Map pp276-7; ☎ 627 846; www.aka demija.net in Serbian; Rajićeva 10; ◷ 6pm-late) This dark, graffitied underground club is where it was at in the Belgrade '80s. The big names of Belgrade's pop and rock scene played and drank within the dark walls. After suffering a decline in the '90s, Akademija is on the up again with a young crowd, a buzzing atmosphere and a minifootball table. Bands like Darkwood Dub or the up-and-coming Sila play here alongside good DJs.

Oh! Cinema! (Map pp276-7; ☎ 328 4000; Kalemeg-dan Citadel; ◷ 9pm-5am) A rock-till-dawn café/bar on the eastern bulwarks of the citadel, overlooking the Danube and zoo. Open only in summer months so the tigers get to have some sleep during winter.

Plastic (Map pp276-7; cnr Dalmatinska & Takovska; ◷ 11pm-late Fri & Sat only) This is where the alternative crowd lets loose. A more intimate venue than Anderground, Plastic has great DJs spinning anything from house to trance and techno, and an electric atmosphere, with Pazi Škola! (see opposite) in the back to chill your danced-out bones.

Danube River Barges

Adjacent to Hotel Jugoslavija in Novi Belgrade is a kilometre-long strip of some 20 barges. Buses 15, 68, 603 and 701 from Trg Republike go to the Hotel Jugoslavija. Most barges are closed in winter.

Brave Heart (Hrabro Srce; Map p274; ☎ 851 1480; ◷ 10pm-4am) The 'Hagar cartoon strip'-style chunky wood-slab furniture would make Mel Gibson proud. A place to chill out, with DJ music to midnight and then live music.

Bibis (Map p274; ☎ 319 2150; ◷ 10am-2am) A subdued place, good for a chat and a drink before hitting its larger and louder neighbouring barges for an all-nighter. Popular in winter when other barges close.

Acapulco (Map p274; ☎ 784 760; ◷ noon-3am) Where young men who work out come to flaunt their money and female attachments. Mockingly referred to as sponsorship girls, they work on the basis of 'you look after me (plenty of gifts), and I'll look gorgeous beside you'. Music is fast and furious turbofolk.

Monza (Map p274; ☎ 319 0712; ◷ 10am-2am) More of an afternoon place where you can sunbathe on the large outdoor terrace and listen to the sounds of R&B.

Sava River Barges

On the western bank of the Sava River is a 1.5km strip of floating bars, restaurants and discos. Here you'll find Cocktail No Name playing pop and '80s music, Zippo for Serbian folk music, Exile pounding out techno and nearby Sound playing house and disco. Get there by walking over the Brankov Most or by tram 7, 9 or 11. Most of these are only open in summer.

CONCERTS & THEATRE

Bilet Servis (Map pp276-7; ☎ 628 342; Trg Republike 5; ◷ 9am-8pm Mon-Fri, 9am-3pm Sat) A ticketing agency that sells tickets for concerts and theatre.

National Theatre (Map pp276-7; ☎ 620 946; Trg Republike; box office ◷ 10am-2pm Tue-Sun) In winter there's opera at this elegant theatre.

Kolarčev University Concert Hall (Map pp276-7; ☎ 630 550; Studentski Trg 5; box office ◷ 10am-noon & 6-8pm) The Belgrade Philharmonia often performs at this concert hall.

Serbian Academy of Arts & Sciences (Map pp276-7; ☎ 334 2400; Knez Mihailova 35; concerts 6pm Mon & Thu) Hosts a number of free concerts and exhibitions; check its window for details.

Dom Omladine (Map pp276-7; ☎ 324 8202; Make-donska 22) Has nonclassical music concerts, film festivals and multimedia events.

Sava Centar (Map p274; ☎ 213 9840; www.sava centar.com; Milentija Popovića 9, Novi Beograd) Hosts major concerts.

For some free entertainment on a Sunday, wander along to the outer part of the Kalemegdan Citadel, where folk come to dance hand in hand the traditional way to pipe, accordion and drum.

CINEMAS

Tuckwood Cineplex (Map pp276-7; ☎ 323 6517; Kneza Miloša 7; tickets 150-280DIN) For the latest in

Hollywood blockbusters, this cineplex shows films in English or with English subtitles.

Shopping

Belgrade's main street, Knez Mihailova, is decked out with all the usual shops that are best at showing what globalisation is really about: fashion. Mango, Zara, Benetton and the likes are always crowded.

If you're after a souvenir, you'll be happy to know that there isn't a tacky Belgrade fridge magnet to be found. Instead you can get something a bit lacy to perk up your table, or hand-knitted woollens from the sellers in Kalemgdan Park.

Snoop around the **craft street market** (Map pp276-7; cnr Kralja Milana & Njegoševa; 8am-5pm Mon-Sat) for handcrafted jewellery items and original oil paintings.

Street sellers may offer you a set of 1990s currency, a period when unimaginable hyperinflation ruined Serbia (see the boxed text, p269). A 500 billion dinar note should be included; its only value now is the chance to boast multibillionaire status.

Getting There & Away
BUS

The country is well served by buses: Belgrade has two adjacent bus stations: **BAS** (Map pp276-7; ☎ 636 299; Železnička 4) serves regional Serbia and some destinations in Montenegro, while **Lasta** (Map pp276-7; ☎ 625 740; Železnička bb) deals with destinations around Belgrade.

Sample services are Subotica (440DIN, three hours), Niš (460DIN, three hours), Podgorica (940DIN, nine hours), Budva (1160DIN, 12 hours) and Novi Pazar (580DIN, three hours) for Kosovo.

International services to Western Europe are good with daily buses to destinations there; see p325.

TRAIN

The **central train station** (Map pp276-7; ☎ 629 400; Savski Trg 2) has a very helpful **information office** (☎ 361 8487; platform 1; 7am-7pm). There's also a **tourist office** (☎ 361 2732; 7am-9.30pm Mon-Sat, 10am-6pm Sun) for basic city information, an **exchange bureau** (6am-10pm) and **sales counter** (☎/fax 265 8868; 9am-4pm Mon-Sat) for Eurail passes at the track end of the station.

You can buy your tickets (bus or train) in the city centre at **Putnik Travel Agency** (Map pp276-7; ☎ 334 5619; Trg Nikole Pašića 1; 8am-8pm Mon-Fri, 9am-3pm Sat) for no extra charge.

Overnight trains run from Belgrade to Bar (1000DIN plus three-/six-berth couchette 1000/564DIN, 11½ hours). Frequent trains go to Novi Sad (199DIN, 1½ hours) and Subotica (420DIN, three hours).

For international trains, see p326.

Getting Around
TO/FROM THE AIRPORT

Surcin airport is 18km west of Belgrade. The **JAT bus** (☎ 675 583) connects the airport with the JAT bus terminal at Trg Slavija (120DIN, 5am to 9pm hourly airport–town, 7am to 8pm hourly town–airport) and the central train station. Ignore the taxi sharks prowling in the airport; go outside and catch a cab to town for 450DIN to 600DIN.

CAR & MOTORCYCLE

Belgraders park on the pavements. It's even regulated, with three parking zones requiring tickets bought from a street kiosk.

PUBLIC TRANSPORT

Belgrade has trams and trolleybuses with limited routes, while buses ply all over the city, New Belgrade and the suburbs.

Tickets cost 20DIN from a street kiosk or 30DIN from the driver; make sure you validate the ticket in the machine on board.

Tram No 2 is useful for connecting the Kalemegdan Citadel with Trg Slavija, bus stations and the central train station.

TAXI

Belgrade's taxis are plentiful and most use meters. Flag fall is 35DIN to 45DIN (depending on the company) and a 5km trip should cost around 200DIN. If the meter's not running, then point it out to the driver.

Taxi sharks, usually in flash cars, prey around the airport, train and bus stations looking for a rich fare. Airport to city should be about 500DIN; at the stations move away from the entrance and pick up a cruising cab.

Have your hotel call you a taxi or phone **Maxis** (☎ 581 111) or **Plavi** (☎ 555 999).

Around Belgrade
ZEMUN ЗЕМУН

Once a separate little town on Belgrade's outskirts, Zemun is now part of the big city. But despite its integration, Zemun retained its 'a town within a city' feel, with a slow pace, and elegant Austro-Hungarian houses lining the little streets. Who would have thought that one of the most notorious mafia groups in the country (the 'Zemun clan', credited for, among other things, the smooth arrest of Slobodan Milosević and the murder of Zoran Đinđić) comes from a quiet little place like this? But don't be alarmed, it's all firmly underground.

Zemun sits on the southern bank of the Danube, some 8km northwest of Central Belgrade. This was the most southerly point of the Austro-Hungarian empire when its opponents, the Turks, were in control of Belgrade. Visitors come for the fish restaurants, boating or just ambling along the Danube.

Catch bus 83 from outside Belgrade's central train station and get off in the main street, Glavna, where the pedestrian-only Lenyinova street leads through a market down to the Danube. You can also walk there (takes around 45 minutes), across the Branko Bridge (Brankov most) and over the green meadows alongside the river.

Above the market area and up the narrow cobbled street of Grobnjačka, remnants of the old village lead uphill towards the **Gardoš**, a fortress with origins going back to the 9th century. Fifteenth-century walls remain and, more importantly, the **Tower of Sibinjanin Janko**. Built in 1896 to celebrate the millennial anniversary of the Hungarian state and to keep an eye on the Turks, the tower guards the city like a misplaced lighthouse.

Down the stairs that descend from the tower is **Nikolajevska church** (Njegoševa 43), an Orthodox church dating back to 1731. Inside this high-vaulted building, gleaming out of the gloom, is an astoundingly beautiful iconostasis carved in the baroque style, gold plated on black and with rows of saints painted on golden backgrounds.

Zemun Museum (☎ 617 766; Glavna 9; admission 100DIN; ☺ 9am-4pm Tue-Fri, 9am-3pm Sat & Sun) has a huge collection demonstrating the development of Serbian applied arts.

A great way to spend the afternoon, after you've had a look around town, is to go down to the river and choose one of the fish restaurants for a dinner accompanied with music and wine or hard liquor like the notorious *šljivovica* (plum brandy) before hitting the barges for night-time fun.

A suggestion for a good fish lunch is **Aleksandar** (☎ 199 462; Kej Oslobođenja 49; meals 500DIN; ☺ 9am-midnight), with an expansive fish menu drawn from both sea and river. Try its fiery-red *riblja čorba* (a peppery fish soup) and a huge chunk of bread to mop up the remains.

SMEDEREVO СМЕДЕРЕВО

If you like fortresses, head to Smederevo. Forty-six kilometres southwest of Belgrade, this small, otherwise unremarkable town boasts an imposing fortress that guards the southern bank of the Danube. A frequent bus service (130DIN, 1½ hours) from Belgrade's Lasta bus station makes this a pleasant day trip.

Smederevo Fortress (admission 10DIN; ☺ daylight hr) is a triangular fort with 25 towers and a water moat. An inner citadel overlooks the river. Built by despot Đurađ Brankovic, it served as his capital from 1428 to 1430. The fortifications were never really tested in battle, the only damage being wrought by time and the massive explosion of an ammunition train in WWII.

Smederevo Museum (admission 10DIN; ☺ 10am-5pm Mon-Fri, 10am-3pm Sat & Sun) is a 'history of the town' museum with artefacts dating from Roman times and some interesting frescoes.

VOJVODINA ВОЈВОДИНА

North of the Danube, this flat fertile plain provides much of the food that fills the nation's larders. Vojvodina is a rich mix of Hungarian and Balkan cultures and traditions, and comprises a mixed population of Serbs, Hungarians, Croats, Romanians, Germans, Slovaks and Roma. The region divides into the three smaller geographical parts of Bačka, Banat and Srem. Towns like the region's capital Novi Sad or the more Hungarian Subotica have wide streets and charming buildings. The hilly Fruška Gora National Park is an 80km-long upland of rolling landscape, vineyards and some 14 monasteries as well as the charming little town of Sremski Karlovci, once the home of the Serbian Orthodox Patriarchate.

Novi Sad Нови Сад

☎ 021 / pop 299,000

Novi Sad, once an anonymous name to a Western ear, is fast gaining notoriety as the host of Serbia's biggest music festival, Exit.

SERBIA & MONTENEGRO

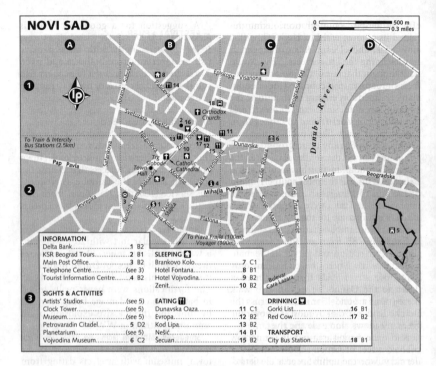

NOVI SAD

INFORMATION	
Delta Bank	1 B2
KSR Beograd Tours	2 B1
Main Post Office	3 B2
Telephone Centre	(see 3)
Tourist Information Centre	4 B2

SIGHTS & ACTIVITIES	
Artists' Studios	(see 5)
Clock Tower	(see 5)
Museum	(see 5)
Petrovaradin Citadel	5 D2
Planetarium	(see 5)
Vojvodina Museum	6 C2

SLEEPING	
Brankovo Kolo	7 C1
Hotel Fontana	8 B1
Hotel Vojvodina	9 B2
Zenit	10 B2

EATING	
Dunavska Oaza	11 C1
Evropa	12 B2
Kod Lipa	13 B2
Nešić	14 B1
Šecuan	15 B2

DRINKING	
Gorki List	16 B1
Red Cow	17 B2

TRANSPORT	
City Bus Station	18 B1

A quiet town with wide streets, interesting cafés, bars, museums and the mighty Petrovaradin Citadel that dominates the town from the volcanic rock upon which it sits, Novi Sad becomes a young (and old) clubbers' mecca in July when the festival takes over the citadel. A jazz festival is held at various venues in town in November.

The town is definitely worth a day visit and makes a great base for exploring the Fruška Gora monasteries over a weekend, and Exit is highly recommended.

ORIENTATION
The adjacent train and intercity bus stations lie at the northern end of Bulevar Oslobođenja. It's a 2.5km walk to the city centre or a bus ride (11A) to the city bus station. One block south of the city bus station is Zmaj Jovina, leading into Trg Slobode, the heart of Novi Sad and dominated by the Catholic cathedral with its chequered roof tiles. Leading off Zmaj Jovina is the small cobbled street of Dunavska, the cultural hub of Novi Sad with a mix of brand-name clothing shops, cafés, restaurants and antique shops.

Two road bridges lead over the Danube to the eastern bank and the old town. Stairs beside the large church lead up to Petrovaradin Citadel.

INFORMATION
Delta Bank (☎ 487 0000; Mihajla Pupina 4; ☸ 8am-6pm Mon-Fri, 8am-1pm Sat) Cashes travellers cheques and has an all-cards ATM.
KSR Beograd Tours (☎ 27 455; fax 27 423; Svetozara Miletića 4; ☸ 7am-7pm Mon-Fri, 7am-1pm Sat) Train tickets at train station prices.
Main post office (☎ 614 708; Narodnih Heroja 2; ☸ 7am-7pm Mon-Sat, 8am-3pm Sun) The telephone centre is also located here.
Tourist information centre (☎ 421 811; www .novisadtourism.org.yu; Mihajla Pupina 9; ☸ 9am-8pm Mon-Fri, 9am-2pm Sat) On-the-button office with plenty of info.
Voyager (16 Stražilovska; per hr 60DIN; ☸ 24hr) Internet just southwest of the centre.

SIGHTS
Petrovaradin Citadel
The most impressive sight in Novi Sad is the Petrovaradin Citadel. A massive piece

of work perched on a hill overlooking the river, it is often referred to as the 'Gibraltar of the Danube'. Designed by the French architect Vauban, it was built by slaves, murderers and thieves who were 'earning their purgatory' in the process dubbed by many as hell. It is estimated that 70 to 80 men died per day in the 88 years it took to build the citadel (from 1692 to 1780). Petrovaradin was built to protect the town from Turkish invasions and was mainly populated by Austro-Hungarian army soldiers, although historical characters like Karađorđe and Tito were held prisoners within its walls, albeit not at the same time. The village below was where the good life was, according to some. The town's 'ladies of the night' entertained the soldiers and the best Hungarian Roma came to play.

Within the citadel's walls is a **museum** (☎ 433 155; admission 70DIN; ☽ 9am-5pm) and a **planetarium** (☎ 433 308; admission 40DIN; ☽ shows 7pm Thu, 5pm Sat & Sun). The most fun part of the citadel is walking around it, exploring the many alcoves and enjoying the fantastic view of the river glistening in the sun.

The citadel's **clock tower** was erected by the Germans, who then introduced a 'clock tax' for each house that could see the clock – practically the entire town. The old clockwork has not been changed since (perhaps because the tax is no more) so the clock is a little slow in the winter, when the cold temperatures make the metal contract, and fast in the summer, when the mechanism relaxes. The hour hand is the longer one, so that everyone can tell what the hour is from a distance.

The charming **artists' studios** (☽ 9am-5pm Mon-Sat) are in the inner citadel, and visitors are welcome to explore. The artists are relaxed and friendly, chatting or snoozing when not busy working. Maybe over a coffee you'll find just that piece for back home.

Muzej Vojvodine

The main museum in Novi Sad is **Vojvodina Museum** (Muzej Vojvodine; ☎ 420 566; Dunavska 35-37; admission 70DIN; ☽ 9am-7pm Tue-Fri, 9am-2pm Sat & Sun), housed in two buildings. No 35 covers the history of Vojvodina from Palaeolithic times to the late 19th century; No 37 takes the story to 1945 with an emphasis on WWI

and WWII. The collection is impressive in its thoroughness, with the main explanatory panels in English.

SLEEPING

Zenit (☎ 621 444; www.hotelzenit.co.yu; Zmaj Jovina 8; s/d 3900/5400DIN; Ⓟ 🖳 🖾) A glass-fronted hotel with comfortable, cosy rooms and chocolates balanced on the folded fresh linen. Zenit is very popular with foreign visitors and it is clear why: the place feels luxurious, comfortable and personal. The restaurant is for breakfast use only, and there is an Internet room in the hotel at a pricey 250DIN for a half-hour.

Hotel Vojvodina (☎ 622 122; vojvodina@visit novisad.com, Trg Slobode 7; s/d from 2100/3000DIN) An atmospheric old hotel looking over the central square of Novi Sad with large but slightly run-down rooms.

Hotel Fontana (☎ 621 779; fax 621 779; Pašićeva 27; s/d 1500/2000DIN; Ⓟ) The Fontana is a good find in a town stretched for cheap accommodation, plus it's close to the local bus station and there's a restaurant below. The rooms are simply decorated but clean and a geyser powers the hot water.

Brankovo Kolo (☎ /fax 528 263; www.hostelns.com; Episkopa Visariona 3; d/tr/q per person €8/7/6; ☽ 1 Jul-25 Aug) Novi Sad's cheapie is student accommodation only available in summer.

EATING & DRINKING

Kod Lipa (☎ 615 259; Svetozara Miletića 7; meals from 290DIN; ☺ 10am-11pm) A great atmosphere that beams you into a different age and good traditional Vojvodinian cooking are a seductive combination, making this the place to eat in Novi Sad. Opened in the late 19th century, the yellowed photographs on the wall show the place looking exactly the same then and now. Descend into the converted cellars and smell mellow wine in the vast barrels; there is seating among them within secluded alcoves.

Šecuan (☎ 529 693; Dunavska 16; meals 300-400DIN; ☺ 9am-11pm Mon-Fri, 9am-1am Sat & Sun) It's unlikely that you will eat a better Chinese meal in Serbia. Opened especially for 1981 when Novi Sad hosted the world table tennis championship, it wowed the Chinese team back in the 1980s and still excels today.

Plava Frajle (☎ 613 675; Sutjeska 2; meals 300-400DIN; ☺ 9am-midnight) A popular knees-up restaurant just southwest of the centre. On Thursdays and weekends traditional music bands play their hearts out, the clientele join in with gusto and the party rips on until dawn. A good taster of local food is the *paprika u pavlaci* (an appetiser of yellow peppers in crème fraîche). We never understood why there were chairs fixed to the ceiling.

Dunavska Oaza (☎ 528 020; Dunavska 25; meals 400-600DIN; ☺ 9am-11pm) A fish restaurant that looks as if it were designed by a nostalgic sailor, with dangling fish nets and blue-and-white life buoys on the walls. Try some of the fresh Danube fish at 1000DIN per kilo.

Evropa (Dunavska 6; cakes 50-100DIN; ☺ 8am-midnight) A place every calorie-fearing woman should run a mile from because the cakes and ice creams are so beguiling. You can sit down or takeaway. Try *žito*, the traditional dessert made of crushed wheat and walnuts.

Nešić (Pašića 23; cakes 10-60DIN; ☺ 8am-9pm, closed Sun) Worth a visit as much to buy a squidgy cake as to appreciate the interior of this 1950s cake shop that's still spick-and-span with red leatherette bench seats.

Gorki List (☎ 622 029; Zmaj Jovina 11; ☺ 8am-midnight) Zebra-print armchairs and comfy cushions are ideal for lounging over a morning coffee, afternoon tea or evening drink. Slap bang in the centre.

Red Cow (cnr Dunavska & Zmaj Jovina; ☺ 8am-1am) Is this the long-lost partner of Red Bull?

A young crowd spends its evenings in this busy Irish publike bar with a wooden interior and tons of seating in the bar area and the upstairs attic room. A relaxed atmosphere and 16 different kinds of bottled beer, as well as draught Guinness and Nikšičko. Go into the courtyard opposite the city library on Zmaj Jovina, and climb to the 1st floor.

GETTING THERE & AWAY

There are frequent trains linking the **train station** (☎ 443 200; Bulevar Jaše Tomića 4) with Belgrade (199DIN, two hours) and Subotica (179DIN, 1½ hours).

Buses leave from the **bus station** (☎ 442 021; Bulevar Jaše Tomića 6) frequently for Belgrade (250DIN, 1½ hours).

AROUND NOVI SAD

Fruška Gora Фрушка Гора

A small area of land with rolling hills rising from the Vojvodina plain, Fruška Gora is given over to farming, vineyards and orchards. Thirty-five monasteries were built between the 15th and 18th centuries to protect Serbian culture and religion from the Turks to the south. Fifteen of those monasteries are preserved today.

In all of the monasteries you will hear the murmur of people chatting inside, see dirty wellies, clothes pegs, smoke out of the chimneys, and smell food being prepared; these monasteries are where important parts of life take place and many villagers come here on weekends for christenings and weddings. Krušedol and Novo Hopovo are perhaps the best known and the most easily accessible. All of the following are within 10km of each other and are well signposted.

Krušedol Monastery, near Krušedol Selo, was built by the Serbian ruler Đorđe Branković in the early 1500s. Like many monasteries in this area the church was severely damaged during one of the Turkish invasions and later rebuilt. The four central pillars are 16th-century originals and are very well preserved. Vivid frescoes, some original, leap out from the walls as a storyboard for biblical events.

Novo Hopovo, near Irig, is one of the oldest of the region's monasteries (1576), and in one of the loveliest settings for walks. It influenced the design of later churches but suffered severe damage during WWII. Restoration of the frescoes revealed earlier work painted under the influence of Cretan masters who also worked at the Mt Athos Monastery in Greece. Many of the frescoes are incomplete but nevertheless they present powerful images.

Grgeteg is different from most other Orthodox monasteries – the church has no frescoes, but is adorned with paintings of flowers and has ochre walls and a light interior. Its centrepiece is the icon of the Holy Mother Trojeručica (meaning 'of three hands'), a copy of the famous icon from Hilander Monastery at Mt Athos, in front of which prayers are sung.

The 16th-century **Velika Remeta** was built entirely out of bricks rather than stone like others. It has the highest bell tower (built between 1733 and 1735) in the region, at nearly 40m. There are only new frescoes inside the church.

Other monasteries in the area are **Mala Remeta**, **Vrdnik** (or Ravanica) and **Jazak**.

Sremski Karlovci Сремски Карловци

Sremski Karlovci takes you by surprise. It's hidden away in the midst of Fruška Gora, but it has some of the most beautiful buildings in the country, all concentrated on the main town square. It's strange that such a historic little town never expanded to become a bigger, more important place in later years.

There is a **tourist office** (☎ 882 127; Branka Radičevića 7; ☒ 8am-6pm) on the main square.

Sremski Karlovci was the centre of the Serbian Orthodox Church in the 19th century and has a magnificent baroque **Orthodox cathedral** (1758–62) with an impressive iconostasis and 18th-century icons. Also on the square are the neoclassical **town hall** (1806–11) and the **high school building**, a cross between Art Nouveau and traditional Serbian style.

Off the square, down Mitropolita Stratimirovića street, is the small white **Lower church** with a ghostly white plane tree.

The round **Peace Chapel** sits on the southern side of town, and is highly significant for it commemorates the signing of the Peace Treaty between the Turks and Austrians in 1699. The chapel (1817) was designed to resemble a Turkish military tent with four entrances enabling everyone

to enter at the same time and thus be equal to each other.

If you decide to stay the night in Sremski Karlovci, **Hotel Boem** (☎ 881 038; Branka Radičevića 5; per person 800DIN) has clean and tidy rooms. The **Četri Jelena** (Branka Radičevića 1; meals 200-400DIN) is a small and cosy restaurant with the usual traditional meat and good-value set menus.

Subotica Суботица

☎ 024 / pop 148,400

This is as close as you will get to being in Hungary, without actually crossing the border. Serbian and Hungarian languages mix in the streets, the smell of fresh goulash fills the nostrils, and the lovely Art Nouveau buildings (1908–12) add sparkle to this relaxed provincial town. The lakeside resort of Palić, 10km from the Hungarian border, is a crowd puller in the summer months. Subotica makes for a lovely day trip from Belgrade, or a stopover on your way to Hungary.

ORIENTATION

Walk out of the train station and through the park to Đure Đakovića. Left (southeast) leads to the bus station and on to Palić. On the right is the amazing Art Nouveau Modern Art Gallery. Also to the left, about 100m from the park, is a pedestrian street (Korzo) that leads down to the old heart of Subotica, Trg Republike and the town hall.

INFORMATION

Delta Bank (☎ 554 011; Cara Dušana; ☒ 8am-3pm Mon-Fri, to noon Sat) All-cards ATM, cashes travellers cheques.

Exchange office (Train station; ☒ 7am-7pm Mon-Sat, 7am-noon & 3-7pm Sun)

IPS (☎ 551 004; Korzo 8; ☒ 9am-9pm Mon-Fri, to 3pm Sat) Some English titles plus books on Subotica.

Left-luggage office (Train station; per item 60DIN; ☒ 24hr)

Tourist information office (☎ 554 809; ticsu@ yunord.net; Korzo 15; ☒ 8am-8pm Mon-Sat, to noon Sun) Very helpful folk with maps, pamphlets and advice on what to see.

SIGHTS

Subotica's main attraction is the Art Nouveau architecture, especially if you are coming from inland Serbia, where the Serbian-Ottoman architecture prevails. The majority of the sights are along the main street, Korzo, and on the main square, Trg Republike.

The **town hall** (Trg Republike), built in 1910, is a curious mixture of Art Nouveau and something Gaudí may have had a playful dab at. It houses an engaging **historical museum** (admission 50DIN; ☺ 9am-2pm Tue-Sat) displaying regional life and the skull of a mammoth. If the exquisitely decorated council chambers are open, don't miss seeing them. It seems that even the proprietors of McDonald's know beauty when they see it, for the fast-food giant has a branch in this fabulous town hall building.

An even more beautiful piece of Art Nouveau architecture is the gracefully decorated **Modern Art Gallery** (☎ 553 725; Trg Lenjina 5; ☺ 7am-1pm Mon, Wed & Fri, 7am-6pm Tue & Thu, 9am-noon Sat). Adorned with mosaics, floral patterns, ceramic tiles and stained-glass windows, this is one of the most stunning buildings in the country.

The 1854 **National Theatre building** on the main square is a Romanesque terracotta structure resting on six heavy pillars which houses Serbia's oldest theatre.

Along Korzo, the **Continental Bank building** is another Art Nouveau gem. A little further away is the first Art Nouveau building to have sprung up in Subotica, the **synagogue**. This grandiose building is now out of use, since most of Subotica's Jewish population was either killed in WWII or emigrated in the postwar years.

SLEEPING & EATING

Hotel Patria (☎ 554 500; www.patria-su.com in Serbian; Đure Đakovića; s/d 1950/3050DIN) An overpriced hotel with dorm-like retro rooms and tiger-print shower curtains. Unfortunately, there isn't much choice in the area. The reception is super-equipped, however, with currency exchange and rent-a-car offices, a souvenir shop, a casino, and a men's and women's hairdresser. You can have a lot of fun!

Student Centar (☎ 546 637; M V Tošinice 7; ☺ 15 Jun-30 August; per person 600DIN) This is a student hall that rents rooms over the summer. The rooms are doubles and triples with a kitchenette and a shared bathroom, generally in a good state. It's worth calling in advance, since this is a new venture, or checking with the Youth Hostels website (www.hostels.org .yu) or the tourist information office first.

Népkör (☎ 555 480; Žarka Zrenjanina 11; meals 250-400DIN; ☺ 8am-midnight Mon-Sat, to 4pm Sun) A large, airy restaurant where you can sample quality Hungarian cuisine. Have a steaming, spicy goulash for 300DIN or *gombásztál* (mushroom and cheese dish) for 280DIN. On Sundays gorge yourself on a buffet lunch for 400DIN.

Ravel (☎ 554 670; Nušićeva 2; cakes 50-100DIN; ☺ 9am-10pm Mon-Sat, 11am-10pm Sun) This is one of the loveliest cafés you are likely to set foot in. The beautiful Art Nouveau interior is as if untouched for a century, with pastel green walls, stained-glass partitions and golden lamps and tables. You can soak up the sun by the large windows and enjoy delicious cakes and coffee.

Vento Pizza (Korzo; ☺ 8am-midnight) A pizza slice from a hole in the wall at 85DIN.

GETTING THERE & AWAY

From the **train station** (☎ 555 606) there are two local trains to Szeged, Hungary (155DIN, 1¾ hours) and one international train. Trains to Belgrade (155DIN, 3½ hours) also call at Novi Sad.

For day trips to Subotica there's a handy train leaving from Belgrade at 8.20am, arriving in Subotica at 11.28am; the return is at 5.14pm arriving back in Belgrade at 8.15pm.

The **bus station** (☎ 555 566; Marksov Put) has regular buses to Szeged (135DIN, 1½ hours) and hourly buses to Novi Sad (300DIN, two hours) and Belgrade (400DIN, 3½ hours).

Palić Палић

Eight kilometres west of Subotica is the park resort of Palić. Crowds flock here in the summer to escape the heat by the 5.5-sq-km lake, where you can go boating, swimming, fishing and sailing. Outside the park on the Subotica road is a string of shops, pizza joints and a supermarket. In mid-July Palić hosts an international film festival.

Bus 6 from outside the Hotel Patria in Subotica goes to Palić (20 minutes, 35DIN); alternatively a taxi will cost 150DIN to 200DIN.

SOUTHERN SERBIA

Despotovac Деспотовац
☎ 035 / 25,500
The rural idyll of Southern Serbia is complete with peasants working the land, ruffled

haystacks along the roadside, dogs barking aimlessly, and people going about their day-to-day business in the small towns and villages. Among them is the tiny town of Despotovac, a quiet place on an eastern off-shoot of the Belgrade–Niš corridor. It would be of no interest to the visitor were it not for the fascinating Resava Cave and the placid Manasija Monastery outside of the town.

SIGHTS

Manasija Monastery

The magnitude of this fortresslike mon-astery may be surprising to those who expect monasteries to be small and intimate places. But the 11 towers encircling the for-tified walls were built for a reason. And the reason is (you guessed it) the Turks.

During the first half of the 15th century, Manasija was a refuge for artists and writers fleeing the Turkish invasion of Kosovo. The church was built during this time and the remaining frescoes date back to the early 1400s, the heyday of the Morava school of painting. The artists belonging to this school were either trained in Salonica or heavily influenced by Greek masters.

Despite their efforts to defend them-selves and the monastery, the Serbs were conquered and Manasija taken over by the Turks on several occasions. This is why the remaining frescoes are only patchy. Many consider the Manasija frescoes to be the predecessors of the Serbian equivalent to Renaissance art (which might have hap-pened had the artists not been so rudely interrupted).

The monastery is about 2km north of Despotovac.

Resava Cave

Up in the hills 20km beyond Despotovac **Resavska Pećina** (Resava Cave; ☎ 611 110; respec@ milnet.co.yu; adult/child 150/80DIN; ◷ 9am-5pm 1 Apr-1 Nov) was not discovered until 1962. Some 4km have been explored, but only 80m are open to the public. The guided tour takes around 40 minutes and goes through several halls where lonely stalagmites and stalactites drip, with only some moss or a bat for company. It's suspected that the cave explorers were often hungry during their expedition for they named many of the 45 million-year-old formations things like 'Turkey Thigh' or 'Chicken Drum'. The

temperature inside the cave is a constant 7°C, so bring a jacket in the summer.

There's no public transport to the cave from Despotovac, so it'll cost about 1500DIN by taxi.

SLEEPING & EATING

The **Kruna Motel** (☎ 611 659; Rudnička bb; s/d 1050/ 1900DIN; P) is good value if you wish to stay the night. The bedroom slippers make you feel at home. The hotel staff will organise transport to the cave and monastery for 1500DIN.

Aside from the usual fast-food kiosks with grilled meat, you can try **Grand Restaurant** (☎ 611 552; bus station; meals 200-300DIN; 6am-midnight Mon-Sat, 3pm-midnight Sun), a bus-station café with some good food such as grilled trout.

GETTING THERE & AWAY

Belgrade buses leave four times a day (350DIN, three hours).

Topola Топола

☎ 034 / 25,000

There's not much in Topola, but many Serbs regard this small rural town some 40km south of Belgrade as sacred since it was from here that Karađorđe Petrović pitched the Serbian insurrection against the Turks in 1804.

ORIENTATION & INFORMATION

The bus station is 10 minutes' walk north of the centre on the Belgrade road. From the Tourist Organisation office it's a five-minute walk south to the museum and 15 to the Church of St George. There are no ATMs in town.

The **Tourist Organisation** (☎ 811 172; Kneginje Zorke 13; ◷ 8am-4pm Nov-Mar, 8am-7pm Apr-Oct) has some pieces in English on Karađorđe plus a town map.

SIGHTS

The **museum** (Kralijice Marije; admission 100DIN; ◷ 9am-5pm) is one of the remnants of the fortified town built by Karađorđe and from where he led his rebellion. It houses artefacts of that period plus personal effects. Within the entrance stands Karađorđe's personal canon with one handle missing. This was removed by his grandson, King Petar I, to be made into his crown when he ascended to the Serbian throne in 1904.

The admission ticket also gets you in to the Church of St George and Petar House. Set in wooded parkland atop a hill, the **Church of St George** (Avenija Kralja Petra I; ☒ 8am-7pm Apr-Oct, 8am-4pm Nov-Mar) is a white marble, five-domed church built between 1904 and 1912 by King Petar I as a memorial to his grandfather, Karađorđe. The interior is decorated with copies of the best Serbian medieval frescoes executed in millions of mosaic pieces. Similar mosaics depict the medieval kings of Serbia holding the monasteries they founded. The southern tomb is Karađorđe's while the other is King Petar's.

Just downhill from the Church of St George is a small house, **Petar House** (Avenija Kralja Petra I; ☒ 8am-7pm Apr-Oct, 8am-4pm Nov-Mar), used by workmen building the church. King Petar also stayed here on occasions when he came to inspect progress on the church. Today it houses temporary historical and art exhibitions.

SLEEPING & EATING
Hotel Oplenac (☎ 811 430; Avenija Kralja Petra I; s/d 1280/1760DIN) This is the only hotel in town, and sits at the foot of the church park. Built in 1934 by King Aleksandar, the hotel has an old and a new part. Although you can see a smudge of its former sparkle, the Oplenac is now a run-down state hotel.

Breza (☎ 812 463; Krajiskih Brigada 25; meals 120-250DIN; ☒ 8am-late) Five minutes' walk downhill from the town centre, this local favourite is a restaurant built into someone's house. The food is traditional, hearty and cheap.

Alternatively, there are a number of food kiosks on the main street serving grilled meat.

GETTING THERE & AWAY
Frequent buses travel to Belgrade (400DIN, three hours).

Niš Ниш
☎ 018 / pop 250,000

A city that most will stop in on their way to somewhere else (like, say, Sofia, Skopje or Thessaloniki), Niš feels a little forgotten. Although there is not much to lure the visitor, plenty of life fills the streets, with horse-drawn carriages racing alongside cars, and casino lights that hope to seduce the idle youngster. The Ottoman Tower of Skulls (Ćele Kula) is an infamous tourist attraction you may want to see.

HISTORY
Niš was first settled in pre-Roman times and flourished during the time of local-boy-made-good Emperor Constantine (AD 280–337), whose extensive palace ruins lie 4km east of town.

Turkish rule lasted from 1386 until 1877 despite several Serb revolts; the Ćele Kula, a Turkish victory tower of Serbian skulls, is a grim reminder of their failure. The massive Tvrđava Citadel is another remnant of Turkish domination.

Niš had a tough time in the last century. The Nazis built one of the more notorious concentration camps in the country here, ironically named 'the Red Cross', where many perished.

During the '90s conflict, Niš was an infamous gathering place for Serb nationalists, and this kind of 'redneck' attitude is still evident with pictures of characters like Karadžić and Mladić on sale on the main street.

ORIENTATION
North of the Nišava River is the mighty Tvrđava Citadel, which shelters the adjacent market and the bus station. The train station is to the west on Dimitrija Tucovića; south of the river is the CBD.

The citadel hosts a blues, rock and pop festival in July and a jazz festival in October.

INFORMATION
Komercijalna Bank (Nikole Pašića 45) All-cards ATM.
KSR Beograd (☎ /fax 523 808; Trg Oslobođenja 9; ☒ 8am-4pm Mon-Fri, 9am-2pm Sat) Sells train tickets.
Post office (Voždova Karađorđa 13a; ☒ 8am-8pm) There's also Internet access for 50DIN per hour.
Tourist Organisation of Niš (☎ 542 588; torg@bankerinter.net; Voždova Karađorđa 7; ☒ 7.30am-7pm Mon-Fri, 9am-1pm Sat) Basic tourist literature; books domestic buses.

SIGHTS
The **Tvrđava Citadel** (Jadranska; ☒ 24hr) was built in the 18th century to consolidate the Turks' hold on the region. Enter through the Stambol Gate into the spacious courtyard filled with souvenir shops, restaurants and cafés that attract the local crowd.

The macabre **Tower of Skulls** (Ćele Kula; ☎ 322 228; Braće Tankosić bb; adult/child 40/30DIN; ☒ 8am-

8pm May-Oct, 9am-4pm Mon-Sat, 10am-2pm Sun Nov-Apr) was erected by the Turks in 1809 as a ghoulish warning to would-be Serbian rebels. During 1809 a force under the duke of Resava trying to liberate Niš attacked a larger Turkish force. The Serbs suffered heavily and the duke desperately rushed the Turkish defences firing his pistol into their powder magazine. The resulting explosion reportedly wiped out 4,000 Serbs and 10,000 Turks but not enough to deny the Turks victory. The dead Serbs were beheaded, scalped and their skulls embedded in this squat tower. Only 58 skulls remain; the rest have disappeared over time.

Mediana (☎ 550 433; Bulevar Cara Konstantina bb; admission museum adult/child 40/30DIN; site free; ☺ 9am-4pm Tue-Sat, 10am-2pm Sun), on the eastern outskirts of Niš, is what remains of a 4th-century Roman palace complex, that of Constantine. Archaeological digging has revealed a palace, forum and an expansive grain-storage area with some sizable, almost intact, pottery vessels.

SLEEPING & EATING

Hotel Ambassador (☎ /fax 541 800; Trg Oslobođenja bb; s/d 2800/4100DIN) Right in the middle of the city centre, the tall glass building of Hotel Ambassador is the city's skyscraper pride and joy. The rooms are a little overpriced since you don't even get a TV, but the views are great. It's clean and bright, with laundry service. The retro reception is a hub of middle-aged activity.

Hamam (☎ 513 444; Tvrđava; meals 200-400DIN; ☺ 9am-midnight) A restaurant in a converted Turkish bath sounds like a great idea, but this feels like the space was slightly wasted on the owner. Considering the wonderful interior, surely an Eastern or more daring style would have been better. Nevertheless, the separate alcoves are pleasant, with warm lighting and a man tinkling on a keyboard. The food is a choice of Italian meals and national fare like *dimljena vešalica* (a roll of smoked pork stuffed with cream cheese and almonds).

Mama Pizza (☎ 45 044; Dušanova 43; meals about 350DIN; ☺ 9am-midnight) A restaurant decorated in Tuscan yellow, burnt umber and sienna, the colours of Italy all to accompany the pasta and pizza. It's very popular with the thirty-something crowd who come to munch, drink wine and listen to the smooth live music.

Sharing the same turn-of-the-19th-century building, adorned with winsome cherubs, are two interesting café/bars.

Tramvaj (Tramway; ☎ 547 909; Pobede 20; ☺ 8am-midnight) Get on the tram, sit down in your very own compartment and, instead of a ticket, order a coffee or ice-cream.

Broz (☎ 064 979 9909; Pobede 20; ☺ 10am-late) A shiny bar dedicated in its entirety to the late Josip Broz (Tito) that, given his sense of style, the man himself would surely have approved of. A large photomontage of Broz and Castro chuckling in the Havana heat covers a wall, and a bust of the Marshal guards the ladies' toilet. A fine range of single-malt whiskies is available for hours of sampling.

GETTING THERE & AWAY

The **bus station** (Kneginje Ljubice) has frequent services to Belgrade (440DIN, three hours), Brus for Kopaonik (230DIN, 1½ hours), four daily to Novi Pazar (345DIN, four hours) and three to Užice for Zlatibor (455DIN, five hours).

Eight trains go to Belgrade (500DIN, 4½ hours) and two to Bar (1060DIN plus three-/six-berth couchette 680/317DIN, 11½ hours).

Kopaonik Копаоник

Kopaonik, Serbia's prime ski resort and a national park, is great for those looking for snow fun without the glamour or prices to match and a rather long season. It is based around the Pančićev Peak (Pančićev Vrh, 2017m), overlooking Kosovo. Ski runs totalling 44km range from nursery slopes to difficult, served by 22 lifts also linked to 20km of cross-country runs. Depending on the weather, the ski season here runs from the end of November to the end of March, or even early April.

ORIENTATION & INFORMATION

Commercial and Delta banks cash travellers cheques and have ATMs dotted around the resort. The website www.kopaonik.net has some basic information and an area map.

There are several ski schools, equipment-rental places, and daily and weekly lift passes are available.

ACTIVITIES

There's all the usual winter activities you'd expect: skiing and snowboarding plus snowmobiles. In summer there's hiking, horse riding and mountain biking.

SLEEPING & EATING

There are several large-scale hotels with restaurants, gym facilities, pizzerias, discos and shops. Expect to pay from 1300DIN to 3000DIN for a single and 2250DIN to 4000DIN per double depending on the time of year and whether you take bed and breakfast or full board.

Possible accommodation options are the two-star **Hotel Jugobank** (☎ 036-71 040; Kopaonik) and **Hotel Junior** (☎ 037-825 051; fax 823 033; Brzeće), which is part of the Youth Hostel organisation. Inquiries can be made through the Youth Hostel organisation in Belgrade (see p284).

Balkan Holidays (www.balkanholidays.co.uk) A British outfit that books ski holidays in Kopaonik. Its website has a topographical map showing the ski runs.

GETTING THERE & AWAY

In summer and winter seasons there are three daily buses from Belgrade and one from Niš.

Zlatibor Златибор

☎ 031 / pop 156,000

Another ski resort, but the season is from December to February – shorter than Kopaonik's due to the lower altitude. Its stunning mountain scenery and walks along marked routes draw crowds during the summer months.

ORIENTATION & INFORMATION

Zlatibor is a patchwork of small settlements centred on Tržni centar, a village of shops, eating and drinking places, a market and a bus stop.

Anitours (☎/fax 841 855; www.anitours.co.yu; Tržni centar; 8am-6pm) Books accommodation and half-/one-day tours for €10/20.

Gr@nd CyberCenter (Naselje Sloboda; per hr 100DIN; 10am-2am) In the shopping complex near the Olimp hotel.

Komercijalna Bank (☎ 845 182; Tržni centar; 8am-8pm Mon-Fri, 9am-3pm Sat Jan, Feb, Jul & Aug, 8am-4pm Mon-Fri 8am-3pm Sat rest of year) Cashes travellers cheques and has an all-cards ATM.

M Tours (☎ 841 911; office@m-tours.co.yu; Tržni centar; 8am-6pm) Books accommodation and organises tours.

Tourist Organisation (☎ 845 103; 8am-6pm Mar-Jun, 8am-10pm Jul-Feb) At the bus stop; provides tourist information, arranges private accommodation and sells bus tickets.

SIGHTS & ACTIVITIES

Zlatibor is a great skiing place for kids or faint-hearted adults. But don't dismiss it just yet; harder runs are being prepared and a couple are already in use. Ski schools and equipment-rental places are in Tržni centar.

Spend a day in the wonderful museum village of **Sirogojno** (☎ 802 291; admission 70DIN; 9am-4pm Oct-Apr, 9am-7pm rest of year). Set on a picturesque mountainside, Sirogojno is a meticulous reconstruction of a 19th-century Serbian village. The high-roofed wooden houses are furnished, and under the cooking utensils warm ashes smell as if someone had just heated a pot of stew. If you visited Belgrade's Ethnographic Museum, you'll have noticed many of the same items, but here in Sirogojno, they are in their 'natural habitat'. After a walk among the pines your appetite will be roaring for a homemade lunch in the wooden-hut restaurant (meals 100DIN to 300DIN) and a hot *rakija*.

Other activities include visits to the Stopića cave at Rožanstvo, the Uvac Monastery at Stublo and old wooden churches at Dobroselica, Jablanica and Kucani. It's also possible to visit the Mileševa Monastery, which houses the famous white angel fresco. Summer activities include paragliding, walking, horse riding and mountain biking.

A day trip from Zlatibor can also incorporate the **Šargan 8 narrow gauge steam railway** (Morca Gora to Sargan Vitas; 2½hr trip 400DIN; Apr-Sep), famous for its figure of eight ascension of the mountains towards Bosnia and Hercegovina.

SLEEPING & EATING

Most visitors choose to stay in private rooms and apartments. There are two peak seasons: winter (January and February) and summer (June to August). Apartments in season typically cost €30 to €80 for two to six people and €7 to €13 less out of season; full board costs an extra €18. Cheaper rooms with shared bathrooms are available for €8 to €15 in season and €7 out of season.

The following hotels are open all year.

Olimp (☎ 842 555; fax 841 953; Naselje Sloboda bb; s/d/tr B&B from 2200/3600/4500DIN, s/d/tr half board

3000/4800/7500DIN; ⓟ ⓧ) Smashing works of art decorate this modern hotel. You can have your morning coffee on the balcony and breathe in the fresh mountain air. Prices remain the same all year but reduce after three days' stay. The penthouse apartment at 2500DIN per person is suitable for six and massive with three double bedrooms.

Hotel Jugopetrol (☎ 841 467; s/d/tr B&B from 2100/3600/4800DIN, s/d/tr half board 2400/4200/5400DIN) You could expect anything from a hotel with the word 'petrol' in its name. But this is a large and welcoming place with spacious, comfortable rooms with TV, phone, small balconies and sweets on the pillows. Off the lobby is a glass conservatory selling naughty cakes. This hotel is about 200m southwest of Tržni centar.

There are more pizza and ćevapčići joints, cafés and bars than you could visit in a month.

Zlatni Bor (☎ 841 638; meals from 250DIN; ☽ 7am-midnight) A hunger-stopping place for breakfast with a view over the lake. About 50m northeast of Tržni centar.

Zlatiborska Koliba (☎ 841 638; meals 250-600DIN; ☽ 8am-midnight) Wooden ceilings, a big brick-arched bar, an open fireplace and good Serbian food chased by slugs of rakija make this a suitable place to recover from the exhaustion of skiing or hiking. In season there's live traditional music. The house speciality is teleća prsa (a stew of veal, potatoes, kajmak and vegetables in an earthenware pot cooked over an open fire). It's at the foot of the ski slopes.

SHOPPING
Apart from fruit and veg, the market sells all manner of interesting things. For the nippy weather there's a range of brightly coloured chunky pullovers and gloves; for presents you could buy intricate lacework, a pair of opanci (traditional Serbian leather shoes) with the curly toes or ćutura (wooden bottles) for holding your rakija stash.

On the food and drink front there's plenty of domestic rakija, honey, pickles, several varieties of kajmak, pršuta (smoked meats) and dried herbs for tea.

GETTING THERE & AROUND
Three daily express buses leave the **bus stand** (☎ 841 587) for Belgrade (400DIN, four hours), one bus daily heads to Niš (425DIN,

four hours) and hourly ones go to Užice (65DIN, 45 minutes), the nearest railhead.

Minibuses ply the villages in season.

Novi Pazar Нови Пазар
☎ 020 / pop 86,000

Novi Pazar is an explosion of bizarre architectural diversity in a small space: an Ottoman kasbah centre on one side of the Raška River, arched by a bridge attached to the UFO-like Hotel Vrbak, and backed by elaborate buildings and apartment blocks that whiff of socialism. All of this is speared with minarets reaching for the sky.

The Turks were not ousted from here until 1912. Novi Pazar is a gateway town for Kosovo, and there are some interesting churches to visit as well as the Unesco-protected Sopoćani Monastery.

ORIENTATION & INFORMATION
The Raška River runs through the town, placing the old Turkish fortress, Turkish quarter and the mosque of Altun Alem on the southern side. The peculiar Hotel Vrbak spans the river. The street of 28 Novembar, on the other side of the river, has numerous cafés, bars and restaurants.

SIGHTS
Checking out the old town's little shops, each individually dedicated to selling meat, coffee or nuts, and having a Turkish coffee in one of the old cafés, is good fun for a half-day. Perhaps you can find a copper souvenir too.

Sopoćani Monastery
Nestling in one of the most beautiful settings in Serbia, the Sopoćani Monastery is Unesco protected and a real treat. Built by King Uroš in mid-13th century, not only did the frescoes inside miraculously survive three centuries of exposure to the elements, they also remained very well preserved. Destroyed by the Turks at the end of the 17th century, the monastery was abandoned until it was restored in the 1920s. It displays the definite influence of Romanesque art, giving the frescoes a rhythm and vibrancy that makes the painted figures actors in their own stories. Some of the monks speak English and will be more than happy to give you the historical lowdown and a drink in their lush garden.

Church of St Peter

On a bluff on the Kraljevo road at the edge of town is the small stone Church of St Peter (Petrova Crkva). It's the oldest in Serbia with parts dating from the 8th century. Surrounding it is an ancient cemetery; if locked ask at the nearest house for the keeper of the huge iron key.

Inside the rough masonry, a step-down baptismal well and feet-polished flagstones provide a tangible sense of the ancient. The 13th-century frescoes are incomplete due to damage.

Columns of St George Monastery

Rising out of a copse 3km uphill from the Church of St Peter is the still-damaged Columns of St George (Đurđevi Stupovi) Monastery, the oldest monastery in Serbia, dating from 1170. The story goes that Stefan Nemanja, ruler of much of what is now southern Serbia, was captured by the Turks in 1172 and promised God that if he gained his freedom he would endow a monastery to St George. He was eventually released, and later in life he abdicated in favour of his son and became the monk and saint Simeon. St Simeon did indeed endow this monastery as promised, and was eventually buried here. The church was extensively damaged by the Turks in the same fit of destruction that befell Sopoćani. Repairs were done in the 1900s but undone in WWII when German troops removed stonework for their defences. Consequently only the western and northern sides of the church remain today.

SLEEPING & EATING

Hotel Vrbak (☎ 315 300; Maršala Tita bb; s/d from 1800/2500DIN) Once considered an architectural masterpiece and the most impressive hotel in the former Yugoslavia, the Vrbak is mind-boggling. As you approach its extraterrestrial grounds, you might be swept along by a Roma band accompanying a wedding crowd into the hotel's buzzing restaurant. A cross between a beehive and a spaceship, with elements of the Orient, this is a place you shouldn't miss the chance to stay the night. The rooms are a little run-down due to lack of funds, but the low Ottoman tables and leather puffs on the floor make them quite comfortable. The round reception area has a marble fountain in the centre and a glass onion-dome roof letting the sunshine in.

Hotel Kan (Cannes; ☎ /fax 315 300; Rifata Burdžovića 10; s/d 2050/3040DIN) This small hotel, built in an oriental style, has rather cramped rooms but compensates with the fact that you don't have to get up to reach the minibar while you're watching the telly. Or is that just being too lazy? It's clean and no-frills, with staff who are mountain-trekking enthusiasts (and they have pictures to prove it).

Ukus (1 Maj 59; meals 150-200; 🕙 8am-11pm) A down-to-earth joint on the main street of the old town. There's freshly cooked food every day. Delicious stews, stuffed peppers and fresh salads all taste amazing – just get there in time before it all gets munched away.

Kafana Centar (☎ 27 799; 28 Novembar 21; meals 150-170DIN; 🕙 7am-midnight) In a street of open cafés this traditional *kafana* (café), hiding behind lace curtains, is a favourite hang-out of the older generation of the town. The smiling matron welcomes foreigners and can dish up a mighty helping of *ćevapčići* and salad to be washed down with a local beer.

Hotel Tadž (☎ 311 904; Rifata Burdževića 79; meals 150-350DIN; 🕙 7am-late; P) The poshest place in town, in the new hotel, this restaurant is a little soulless, but the *pastrmka* (trout) with a luscious garlic sauce makes the heart race.

GETTING THERE & AWAY

Frequent buses go to Belgrade (432DIN, four hours), an overnight bus goes to Sarajevo (€13, seven hours) and four daily buses head to Prishtina in Kosovo (330DIN, three hours).

AROUND NOVI PAZAR

Studenica Monastery

Built around 1190 and set amid beautiful mountains and forests, and alongside Studenica River, Studenica Monastery holds a sacred place in Serbian psyche and history. The working monastery was established by monarch Stefan Nemanja (who is entombed here) and later further built by his sons Vukan and Stefan (also entombed here), and its monastic life was nurtured by Rastko, a monk whose piety has given him an almost saintly status in Serbian Orthodoxy. There are three churches within an oval complex. The central and most important is **Bogorodičina crkva** (The Church of Our Lady), built in 1191, which is unique in Serbia's medieval architecture for its polished marble exterior and elaborately decorated windows and doorways. Inside, the frescoes, originally dating back to the early 13th century, were repainted in 1569, with wonderful, vivid rich colours. A pilgrimage gathers at Bogorodičina crkva annually on 24 May to celebrate the feast day of Stefan Nemanja.

Kraljeva crkva (King's church) is next door and occupies a much smaller space. It was built in 1314 by King Milutin, and houses some of the best preserved and most interesting frescoes in the country. The very realistic *Birth of the Virgin* illustrates the uniqueness of style and technique taken by Serbian fresco artists at the time. **Crkva Svetog Nikole/Nikoljača** (St Nicholas' church) is the smallest and the simplest structure. The church revealed medieval tombs and fresco remains upon removal of soil in which it was half-buried for centuries.

KOSOVO

Kosovo, or Kosova as it's called in Albanian, seems like a hidden vale surrounded by the mountains of Serbia, Montenegro and Albania. Often, while winter still blankets those countries in snow, Kosovo will be enjoying the first touches of spring.

Your government's travel advisory may have warned against travel to Kosovo. They are of necessity cautious and if you do decide to ignore their advice, then it is safer to avoid areas of potential Serb/Kosovo Albanian tension such as Mitrovica and the boundary area with Serbia. Fortunately for visitors the sites of interest are outside these zones.

The ebb and flow of Islam and Orthodox Christianity has left Kosovo a legacy of several artistically beautiful buildings, such as Gračanica Monastery near Prishtina, Decani Monastery near Peja and the Sinan Pasha Mosque in Prizren. These all escaped the violence of 1999 and 2004.

The countryside is pictorially attractive: wide-open plains in some places, rolling hills patchworked with fields in others. Rearing up to the south, behind Peja in the southwest, are a set of tall mountains, often snow-clad, that include Đeravica (2656m), the tallest mountain in pre-1999 Serbia. Further east, nearer Macedonia, the mountains provide the ski slopes of Brezovica, closed as a result of the 2004 riots but expected to open again for the next season.

Serb influence in the province has ended to be replaced by an Albanian one and new buildings are no longer in the Yugoslav socialist style of concrete blocks. In Prishtina new monuments celebrate Albanian heroes while the displays in the museums of Prishtina and Prizren are exploring the province's Illyrian and Albanian past.

As Kosovo is a small province with an extensive bus network, it's perfectly reasonable to use Prishtina as a base and visit Peja and Prizren as day trips.

HISTORY

Following their defeat in 1389 by the Turks, the Serbs abandoned the region to the Albanians, descendants of the Illyrians, the original inhabitants.

Serbia regained control when the Turks departed in 1913. In the ensuing years some 500,000 Albanians emigrated and Serbs were brought in to settle the vacated land. In WWII the territory was incorporated into Italian-controlled Albania and then liberated in October 1944 by Albanian partisans.

Tito wanted Albania united with Kosovo in the new Yugoslavia. It never happened. Three decades of pernicious neglect ensued until an autonomous province was created in 1974 and economic aid increased. However, little changed and the standard of living in Kosovo remained a quarter of the Yugoslav average. In 1981 demonstrations calling for full republic status were put down by the Serbian military; 300 died and 700 were imprisoned.

Trouble began anew in November 1988 with demonstrations against the sacking of local officials and Kosovo's President Azem Vllasi. Further unrest and strikes in February 1989 led to the suspension of Kosovo's autonomy and a state of emergency.

Serious rioting followed with 24 Albanian Kosovars shot dead. In July 1990 Kosovo's autonomy was cancelled, broadcasts in Albanian ceased and the only Albanian-language newspaper was banned. Some 115,000 Albanians had their jobs taken by loyalist Serbs. Against Serbian opposition, a referendum with a 90% turnout produced a 98% vote for independence.

The Kosovo Liberation Army (KLA) was formed in 1996 out of frustrated attempts to negotiate autonomy. Using guerrilla tactics they began to fight the Serbs.

In March 1999, a US-backed plan to return Kosovo's autonomy was rejected by Serbia. Stepping up attacks on the KLA, Serbia moved to empty the province of its non-Serbian population. Nearly 850,000 Kosovo Albanians fled to Albania and Macedonia. Serbia ignored demands to desist and NATO unleashed a bombing campaign on 24 March 1999. On 2 June Milošević acquiesced to a UN settlement, Serbian forces withdrew and the Kosovo Force (KFOR) took over. Since June 1999 Kosovo has been administered as a UN-NATO protectorate.

Peace has not been easy. KFOR had to persuade the KLA to demilitarise and Serbian refugees to return home. Potential and real revenge attacks on the remaining Serbs made them isolated communities protected by KFOR.

The elections in November 2001 led to a coalition government with Ibrahim Rugova as the president of Kosovo. There was a gradual process to normalise relations with post-Milošević Serbia.

Kosovo slipped from the world's eye until March 2004, when three Kosovo Albanian children were allegedly chased into a river by Kosovo Serbs, and two drowned. This sparked a simmering discontent, mostly among youths, who attacked Serbian people, homes and churches. Nineteen people were killed, 600 homes burnt out and 29 monasteries and churches, many medieval, were destroyed. KFOR, which could have controlled much of the outrage, was disastrously slow to act.

In March 2005 Kosovo's then Prime Minister Ramuš Haradinaj surrendered to the International Tribunal in The Hague after he was indicted for war crimes. This sparked some temporary unrest in the area, but no serious trouble ensued.

DANGERS & ANNOYANCES

Various government travel advisories warn against visiting Kosovo. The events of March 2004 have shown that civil insurrection is but an incident away in which a foreign visitor may unwittingly get caught.

The country is thought to have been cleared of landmines but there is still unexploded ordnance about, so if you are off the beaten track you will need KFOR and local advice (try the police).

GETTING THERE & AWAY

> **VISITING KOSOVO FIRST**
>
> Visitors coming into Kosovo first can then only legally enter Serbia via Macedonia, as there are no immigration facilities at the crossings between Kosovo and Serbia or Montenegro.

Air

For air services see p325. Passengers with more than €10,000 have to complete a currency declaration form on arrival.

Bus

International bus services serve much of Europe; some sample fares from Prishtina are Skopje, Macedonia (€5.50, 1½ hours), Tirana, Albania (€20, 10 hours), Istanbul, Turkey (€30, 20 hours), and Sarajevo, Bosnia and Hercegovina (€30, 10 hours).

From Peja there's an overnight bus to Podgorica (€16, seven hours) in Montenegro. Alternatively minibuses (€5) and taxis (€20) go to the Montenegrin town of Rožaje from outside the Peja bus station.

Four daily buses connect Prishtina and Novi Pazar in Serbia (€5.50, three hours) with onward connections to Belgrade.

Getting Around

There is an excellent bus service linking all the main towns and villages. Buses operate very frequently between Prishtina, Prizren and Peja (€3 to €4, about two hours). There was a stab at resurrecting the railway but it ended after a short trial.

Prishtina

☎ 038 / pop 160,000

Prishtina is a bustling capital engorged with the activity and personnel of foreign

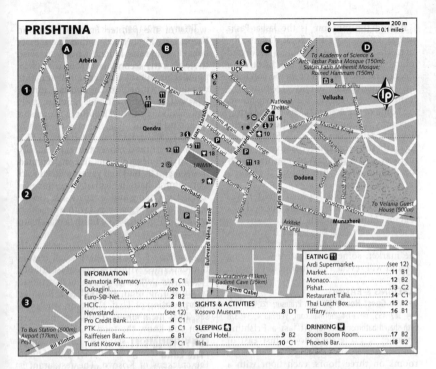

PRISHTINA

INFORMATION	
Barnatorja Pharmacy	1 C1
Dukagjini	(see 1)
Euro-S@-Net	2 B2
HCIC	3 B1
Newsstand	(see 12)
Pro Credit Bank	4 C1
PTK	5 C1
Raiffeisen Bank	6 B1
Turist Kosova	7 C1

SIGHTS & ACTIVITIES	
Kosovo Museum	8 D1

SLEEPING	
Grand Hotel	9 B2
Iliria	10 C1

EATING	
Ardi Supermarket	(see 12)
Market	11 B1
Monaco	12 B2
Pishat	13 C2
Restaurant Talia	14 C1
Thai Lunch Box	15 B2
Tiffany	16 B1

DRINKING	
Boom Boom Room	17 B2
Phoenix Bar	18 B2

agencies. Some postwar reconstruction has taken place but a lot has still to happen. Apart from the city and its activities there's not a lot to see and it's really a jumping-off point to Peja and Prizren.

ORIENTATION
Bulevardi Nëna Terezë and Agim Ramadani run from the south and converge near the National Theatre in central Prishtina. The UN Interim Administration Mission in Kosovo (Unmik) headquarters are off Nëna Terezë and west of this is the Sports Complex shopping mall. Bil Klinton (yes, him) runs southwest from Bulevardi Nëna Terezë passing the bus station, the airport (17km) and onto Peja.

INFORMATION
Barnatorja Pharmacy (☎ 224 245; Bulevardi Nëna Terezë; 7.30am-8pm Mon-Sat, 7.30am-8pm every 3rd Sun) Notice on window for Sunday opening times of other pharmacies.

Dukagjini (☎ 248 143; Bulevardi Nëna Terezë 20; 8am-8pm Mon-Sat) Sells novels and art books in English, and city maps.

Euro-s@-net (☎ 227 225; Luan Haradinaj; per hr €1; 9am-11pm Mon-Sat) Also phone calls worldwide for €0.30 per minute.

Humanitarian Community Information Centre (HCIC; ☎ 549 169; Luan Haradinaj 8; 8.30am-5pm Mon-Fri) Information on Kosovo as well as maps and books.

Newsstand (Luan Haradinaj; 9am-late) Foreign newspapers and magazines; latest papers arrive at 6pm. It's outside Monaco restaurant.

Post Telephone Kosova (PTK; ☎ 245 339; Bulevardi Nëna Terezë; 8am-9pm) Post and telephone.

Pro Credit Bank (☎ 240 248; Skënderbeu; 9am-4pm Mon-Fri) Cashes travellers cheques and has a MasterCard ATM.

Raiffeisen Bank (☎ 226 400; Migjeni 1; 8.30am-4.30pm Mon-Fri, 9am-noon Sat) Cashes travellers cheques and has a Visa card ATM.

Turist Kosova (☎ 223 815; Bulevardi Nëna Terezë 36; 8am-6pm Mon-Sat, 8am-noon Sun) Travel information, flights and international bus booking.

SIGHTS
Kosovo Museum (☎ 249 964; Marte e Driele; citizen/foreigner €1.50/5; 10.30am-7pm Tue-Sun) has a thoughtful and well-captioned exhibition on premedieval Kosovo.

Behind the museum is the **Jashar Pasha mosque**. Of note are the floral designs, the huge chandelier and the finely decorated mihrab (the niche showing the direction of Mecca, and the position of the person leading the congregation in prayer). Around the corner is a well-restored Balkan-style house, the home of the **Academy of Science and Arts**.

Nearby, a second mosque, the **Sultan Fatih Mehemit**, dates from the mid-15th century. Again there's exquisite decorative work and interestingly some carved marble stones from some earlier use among the courtyard flagstones.

Much of the old Turkish quarter was destroyed by WWII bombing but odd bits remain. Almost opposite Jashar Pasha is a **ruined hammam** (Vasil Andori) and if you walk down this street to Xhemajl Prishtina and the market, some investigative wandering around will reveal a number of old houses.

SLEEPING & EATING

Velania Guest House (Pansion Profesor; ☎ 531 742, 044 167 455; besa-h4@hotmail.com; Velania 4, 34; s/d with shared bathroom €13/18) At last a Prishtina cheapie! A professor's house just east of the centre welcoming budget travellers; 10 rooms on three floors, each floor with a small kitchen. There's free tea/coffee ingredients and laundry.

Iliria (☎ 224 275; fax 548 117; Bulevardi Nëna Terezë; s/d €30/60; P) A large former Serbian state hotel that's right in the thick of things, and a central safe haven for the party animal. Comes with very helpful staff.

Grand Hotel (☎ 220 210; reception@grandhotel -pr.com; Bulevardi Nëna Terezë; s/d/tr €60/90/105; P) Prishtina's top-notch hotel with all the facilities you'd expect for the price but rated five stars, two too many in our opinion; it's a bit shabby round the edges. Booking is advisable as it's the hotel for the big shots when they come to town.

Cafés abound in the centre selling *burek* and hamburgers for €1 to €2; pasta and pizza cafés charge up to €2.50.

Restaurant Talia (☎ 244715; meals €3.50-5; 9am-midnight) Good pizza offered with Tabasco sauce to add heat if you feel like something spicy. It's behind the National Theatre.

Monaco (☎ 227 490; Luan Haradinaj; pizzas €3-6; 8am-late) Buy your newspaper from the vendor outside, sit down with a drink and mull over day-old news.

Tiffany (☎ 244 040; meals from €6; 8am-11pm Mon-Sat, 6-11pm Sun) A crisp-white-linen, best-behaviour establishment where it's wise to come early to secure a table. This very popular restaurant is off Fehmi Agani, hidden down by the side of the Sports Stadium; a lack of signage doesn't help. Soups, grills and salads are on offer but for some reason there's no menu.

Pishat (☎ 245 333; Qamil Hoxha; meals €2.50-5; 8am-11pm) Brand-new restaurant, centrally located off Bulevardi Nëna Terezë, decorated in strong earth, blue and yellow colours with a brightness that's like a blast of sunshine on a dull day. Feeling midday snack-ish? Go for *tavë e kuge*, a veggie hotpot with a large flap of newly baked bread. To finish, a macchiato coffee, the best in town.

Thai Lunch Box (☎ 044 140 791; meals €7-11; 11am-3pm & 6-11pm Mon-Sat) A small restaurant decorated with Kosovar cubist art, but just as the paintings are an interpretation of cubism so then the food is a Kosovar interpretation of Thai. However, when you see Thai members of Unmik eating here then you know the food's OK. It's a welcome relief from standard Eastern European fare although heavily dependent upon the chickens of Kosovo. The restaurant is between Unmik & Luan Haradinaj.

Ardi Supermarket (Luan Haradinaj; 8am-8pm Mon-Sat) and the fruit and veg section of the **market** (8am-2pm Mon-Fri), off Fehmi Agani, can provide your DIY supplies.

DRINKING

Phoenix Bar (7am-midnight) A favourite with the expats and decorated with football team strips as tribal identities rather than flags. Cholesterol-damage breakfasts, coffee and snacks (€2.50 to €4) all day plus booze are on offer. There's live music some weekends. It's opposite Unmik.

Boom Boom Room (Kosta Novakoviq; 10am-late) Behind and west of Unmik, this is a grungy big barn of a drinking joint with a considerable range of drinks, and it's popular with the locals. There's live music on Wednesday nights when the room does go boom boom.

GETTING THERE & AWAY

Air

For airlines operating from Prishtina **airport** (☎ 548 430) see p325. Unless included in your ticket, departure tax is €15.

Bus
International and domestic services leave from the **bus station** (☎ 550 011; Mitrovicë-Prishtinë). For details see p326.

GETTING AROUND
Numbered minibuses roam the streets. Numbers 1 and 2 go down Bil Klinton, from where it's a short walk back up Mitrovicë-Prishtinë to the bus station. The fare is €0.50.

The easiest way between town and the airport is by taxi. Try **Radio Taxi Victory** (☎ 550 889) or **Radio RGB** (☎ 515 515); the fare should be about €20.

AROUND PRISHTINA
Gračanica
Some 13km southeast of Prishtina is the superbly decorated Gračanica Monastery, built by the Serbian King Milutin in the early 14th century. It's in the shape of a five-dome building on a cross-in-a-square plan typical of the best Byzantine architecture of the period. Most of the frescoes date from then and cover all the walls.

Entry is no problem once you've identified yourself to KFOR at the entrance. Catch one of the frequent buses to Gjilan which pass outside.

Marble Cave
Some 35km south of Prishtina, **Marble Cave** (Gadimë Cave; adult/child €2.50/0.50; ☻ 9am-6pm), the only show cave in Kosovo, is definitely worth a plunge underground. It's renowned for its helictites, thin stalactites growing at strange angles. There are several buses to Gadimë Cave from Prishtina or a taxi, wait and return, would cost €30.

Outer Kosovo
PEJA (PEĆ)
☎ 039
The nearness of Peja and Prizren to Prishtina means that you can avail yourself of the better sleeping and eating options in Prishtina and do day trips. While there are a number of eating places in Peja and Prizren, hotels are very few and overexpensive. Peja's attractions stand outside town, and the medieval Patrijaršija Monastery and the Decani Monastery. Much work remains to be done restoring the old buildings in the market area but there's a superb picture-postcard backdrop of 2000m-plus mountains shearing straight up.

Orientation & Information
After the Serbian departure in 1999 all Serbian names were removed. Peja, unlike Prishtina and Prizren, still hasn't renamed its streets so they remain nameless or are numbered. The Prishtina road runs into the northern part of town. Striking south, and into town, is the main road. The bus station is at the intersection of these two routes.

Sights
Many of Peja's mosques and old buildings remain severely damaged but the colourful **bazaar** is the place to engage with the oriental atmosphere.

Two kilometres west of Peja is **Patrijaršija Monastery**, seat of the Serbian Orthodox Peč patriarchy. Although the monastery is open to visitors, KFOR at the gate may decide otherwise; if not you'll be rewarded with three mid-13th-century churches with glorious medieval frescoes.

Decani Monastery (1335) is 15km south and accessible by frequent local buses and a 2km walk. The monastery was the endowment of King, later Saint, Stefan, whose body is buried within the church. According to the monks it is still uncorrupted (not yet decayed), which is the hallmark of a saint.

Getting There & Away
The **bus station** (☎ 31 152; Geromin de Rada) is on the Peja road, about 2km northwest from the centre.

PRIZREN
☎ 029
Although Prizren was the medieval capital of 'Old Serbia', the architectural influence is Turkish. It seems like a party town as people throng the many bars and cafés along the river and in the plaza Shadrvan. The delight is wandering through cobbled streets soaking up the history and atmosphere.

Unfortunately the Albanian Kosovar vandalism of March 2004 has added to the Serbian vandalism of 1999 and left an ugly scar of burnt-out houses up the hillside.

Orientation & Information
The town revolves around the river and Shadrvan, a small cobblestone plaza with a

fountain in the middle. The **bus station** (☎ 31 152; Geromin de Rada) is on the Peja road about 2km from the centre. Crossing the river just west of the main bridge is a 'new' medieval bridge built to replace the old one destroyed by floods in 1979.

A documentary film and photographic exhibition, Dokufest, happens in the first week of September.

Sights

A slow plod up from behind the Shadrvan brings you to the castle that's passed through Roman, Turkish, Serbian and KFOR army hands. The views are quite stupendous and if you're there when the imams call for prayers you'll hear a wave of chants sweep across the town.

The Orthodox churches were mostly destroyed in the March 2004 violence with little left except collapsed and burnt-out interiors.

The 1561 **Sinan Pasha Mosque** on the riverside dominates the centre and can be visited for its fine, decorated high-domed ceiling.

Near the Theranda Hotel, the newly restored **Gazi Mehmed Pasha Baths** (1563) have become an occasional exhibition space. The internal upper floor was destroyed during WWII; maybe it couldn't cope with being an Italian bordello.

Opposite the post office is a solitary **minaretlike tower** with the Star of David; it's believed to be the remnants of a synagogue.

Some 200m upriver from the Theranda Hotel is a small **museum complex** (☎ 44 487; adult/child €1/0.20; ☯ 10am-10pm Sun-Tue) celebrating the Albanian League of Prizren. This was an independence movement in Turkish times and the museum illustrates the League and historical Prizren.

BREZOVICA

This ski resort, 60km south of Prishtina, was seen as a bright spot in Kosovo's tourism future: Albanians working together with Serbs in a Serbian enclave to make a success of the resort. However, with the violence of March 2004 it was closed; it was also the end of the ski season. Hopefully it's a temporary closure.

Nine ski runs, served by seven chairlifts, lead down from 2500m; ski equipment and snowboards could be hired and lessons were available. Even if you're not a skier

a trip up the ski lift was worth it to see the stunning snow scenery.

The **Molika Hotel** (☎ 290-70 452), with a restaurant, bars and cafés, was the only hotel.

MONTENEGRO
ЦРНА ГОРА

The tiny republic of Montenegro has got it all: dramatic mountains with sharp, rugged peaks reaching into steely blue skies, slashed with giddy, capricious canyons and scented with tufts of pine forests; the sapphire Adriatic Sea with its perfect Mediterranean towns; Kotor Bay, the biggest fjord in southern Europe, hemmed in by majestic limestone mountains. And all of that packed into 13,812 sq km.

Montenegrin culture is a curious cocktail. The key components are Montenegrin, Serb, Albanian and Croatian, with a relaxed Mediterranean air, and you'll see Orthodox and Catholic churches alongside mosques. Montenegro and Crna Gora both mean 'black mountain'. Crna Gora is a Slavic name, but the name Montenegro might come from the old Dalmatian language, a relative of Italian which died out in the 19th century.

Fantastic walled towns like Budva, Kotor or Herceg Novi are wonderful for exploring, and small, pretty seaside village-towns like Petrovac or Perast are perfect for resting and having a real summer holiday by the beach. Mountains such as Durmitor are great for skiing in winter, and many trek its fells in the summer. Fishing and bird-watching are favourites on the shores of Lake Skadar.

A small drawback is that Montenegro is a very popular local holiday spot, with crowds from the cities cascading onto the beaches in July and August, and things can get quite crowded. So the best times to go are May, June and September. Visitors with time or transport can choose their accommodation from a range of 'sobe', 'Zimmer' or 'private room' signs all along the coast.

The railway connects Belgrade to Bar, where ferries sail to Italy. Frequent bus services (fares €2 to €4) link the coastal towns with Podgorica and Cetinje.

History

Only tiny Montenegro was able to keep its head above the Turkish tide that engulfed the Balkans for over four centuries from the 14th century onwards. From 1482 Montenegro was ruled from Cetinje by *vladike* (prince-bishops). With the defeat of the Turks in 1878, Montenegrin independence was assured and later recognised by the Congress of Berlin. Nikola I Petrović, Montenegro's ruler, declared himself king in 1910 but was evicted by the Austrians in 1916. After the end of WWI Montenegro was incorporated into Serbia.

During WWII Montenegrins fought valiantly in Tito's partisan army and afterwards the region was rewarded with republic status within Yugoslavia.

The republic has been a stalwart of all Yugoslav federations and is now in a union with Serbia that may last no longer than the 2006 referendum.

PODGORICA ПОДГОРИЦА

☎ 081 / pop 170,000

Unfortunately, Montenegro's capital, Podgorica, is its most unattractive spot. With no sights and only expensive hotels, it is really a place to go to for only a half-day, if you need to do your errands. It also becomes cauldron-hot in the summer, so don't say you weren't warned. It is a much wiser choice to go south and stay on the coast.

Orientation

The commercial hub of the town centres around Slobode, and intersecting with it is Hercegovačka, the shopping/café heart of the town.

Information

Atlas Bank (☎ 407 211; Stanka Dragojevića 4; ☻ 8am-6pm Mon-Fri, 8am-12.30pm Sat) Cashes travellers cheques.

Crnogorska Komercijalna Bank (cnr Slobode & Novaka) MasterCard ATM.

Gorbis (☎ 230 624; Slobode 47; ☻ 8am-5pm) Tourist information, organises tours and books flights and ferries.

Internet cg (☎ 248 844; Vučedolska 13; per hr €1.50; ☻ 8am-8pm Mon-Fri, 9am-2pm Sat)

Meridian (☎ 234 944, 069 316 666; Cetinjski put; ☻ 8am-2pm & 6-8pm Mon-Fri, 8am-2pm Sat) Rents cars from €30 a day.

Sleeping & Eating

There are some cheap eating places around and in the bus station, and some pleasant cafés in Hercegovačka.

Europa (☎ 623 444; shole@cg.yu; Orahovačka 16; s/d €45/70) In a city of overexpensive hotels, this modern and well-equipped hotel near the train station is a weary traveller's best option if a night in Podgorica is necessary.

Mimi Pekara (bakery snacks €0.50-1.25; ☻ 6am-3am) There's always the *burek* option available for those in need of a quick snack, and here they make 'em good.

Buda Bar (☎ 344 944; Stanka Dragojevića 26; sandwiches €2.50; ☻ 8am-2am) This is the coolest place in town, popular as a daytime coffee-drinking spot and an evening meeting place. The interior is swish and smooth, with little Buddha statues adorning the room, and outside is a spacious garden with a bamboo bar.

Getting There & Away

The **train station** (☎ 633 663) and **bus station** (☎ 620 430) are adjacent in the eastern part of the town. There are eight buses daily to Belgrade (€14, nine hours), one each at 9am and 3.30pm to Žabljak (€7.50, four hours), many to Rožaje, for Kosovo (€7, four hours), and four buses to Sarajevo (€12, nine hours).

You can fly to Belgrade for €43, or take the scenic train route to Bar (€15 plus €15/8 for a three-/six-berth sleeper on overnight trains, eight hours).

Montenegro Airlines (☎ 664 411; www.montenegro-airlines.cg.yu; Slobode 23; ☻ 8.30am-7pm Mon-Fri, to 2pm Sat) flies to Frankfurt, Zürich and Budapest. There is a €15 departure tax charge at Podgorica airport.

Around Podgorica

LAKE SKADAR & VIRPAZAR

СКАДАРСКО ЈЕЗЕРО & ВИРПАЗАР

A causeway carries the road and railway from Podgorica to Bar over the western edge of the 44km-long Lake Skadar, part of Lake Skadar National Park. The biggest lake in the Balkans, it's one of the largest bird sanctuaries and remaining pelican habitats in Europe. Jutting westward from the causeway is the 400-year-old Turkish castle of Lesendro. Check with **Gorbis** (☎ 230 624; Slobode 47; ☻ 8am-5pm) in Podgorica about trips on the lake and water activities.

Alternatively, nose around Virpazar, where in summer there'll be sightseeing boats. You'll also find one of Montenegro's more interesting restaurants, the **Pelican** (☎ 081-711 011; Virpazar; d with shared bathroom €30, meals €6-8; ☺ 8am-midnight), exotically decorated with dried plants and herbs, old photographs and nautical ephemera. The service is top-notch and dessert is on the house. For starters try *dalmatinsko varvo* (a potato, onion and spinach pie) and follow that with a fish salad of perch, eel or trout – all fresh from the lake. Weekend evenings, May to September, there's live music. The Pelican also has accommodation.

CETINJE ЦЕТИЊЕ

☎ 086 / pop 20,000

The former capital of Montenegro sits in the country's crowning position amid Montenegro's tallest mountains. The green vale is like a nest, and the sharp-edged grey mountains surround it protectively. The residual air of Cetinje's former importance is still visible in many a palace dating from its royal past and the mansions that used to house various embassies; for Montenegrins this small place still occupies a special place in their hearts.

Many of the grandiose buildings have been turned into schools for music and the arts and some into museums. Cetinje Monastery, renowned throughout the country and with a good museum, is still the place in which many seek spiritual solace.

The area around Cetinje has some of the most stunning scenery: the panoramic view of Lake Skadar from Pavlova Strana; the old bridge at the tranquil village of Rijeka Crnojevića; or the plummeting road down to Kotor.

Cetinje's accommodation choice is highly limited and the town is best visited as a day trip from the coast or Podgorica. The transport to the town is very good. On a hot summer's day, Cetinje is always cooler thanks to the altitude.

Orientation & Information

A short walk from the bus stand leads to Balšića Pazar, the main square, with a big wall map to help you get your bearings.

There are no banks here for exchanging your money, so be prepared and arrange cash before you arrive.

Sights

Strolling around the town gives you some idea of what kind of a place this used to be. Cetinje's 500 years of capital glory are still reflected in the elegant little houses painted in greens and reds, juxtaposed against palaces and mansions that used to hold embassies from all over the world. Try working out which building used to represent which nation and you'll soon realise that most carry something of an 'architectural denomination' in them. The former Russian embassy, now a hip art academy, is as if plucked straight out of St Petersburg and planted on the Montenegrin soil; the former Italian embassy is all classic lines and Mediterranean freshness; and the former French embassy has Moorish elements with tiles and mosaics. Some say this building was supposed to have been built somewhere in North Africa, but the building plans got confused, so Cetinje got this building and the real embassy building is now God-knows-where.

There have been reports that if Montenegrins vote for independence from Serbia in 2006, the old embassies might be reinstated. So watch this space.

MUSEUMS

The most important building, the former parliament, is now the **National Museum of Montenegro** (☎ 231 477; Novice Cerovića bb; admission €5; ☺ 9am-5pm). The ticket also covers entry to the Art Gallery, the Billiard Hall and the State Museum (all in the same place as the museum). The neobaroque structure was built at the beginning of the 20th century, and was once the number one institution in Cetinje. The museum shows periods from pre-Slavic Montenegro all the way to the Yugoslav times, together with exhibits of a large variety of weapons and the coat (three bullet holes in the back) of Duke Danilo, the last *vladika*, who was killed in Kotor in 1860. The prime exhibit is the precious 5th-century icon of the Madonna's face, *Our Lady of Philermos*.

The **Art Gallery** celebrates 19th- and 20th-century Montenegrin and regional art. If you have any interest in art from the former Yugoslav period, this is a good place to see paintings and sculptures by artists such as Đuro Jakšić, Nadežda Petrović, Ivan Meštrović and Tomo Rosandić, among others. Milo Milunović's paintings, which have their own separate space, are a real treat with touches of Picasso or Cézanne.

Opposite the National Museum, the **Billiard Hall** (Biljarda; ☎ 231 050; ☺ 9am-5pm Apr-Oct, 9am-3pm Mon-Fri Nov-Mar), built and financed by the Russians in 1838, was the residence of *vladika* and Montenegro's most celebrated poet Petar II Petrović Njegoš; it is now a museum dedicated to him. The hall housed the nation's first billiard table, hence the name. There is a special area for displays of original manuscripts and early editions of his lyrical work *The Mountain Wreath* (see p270), his most important epic poem and the piece that made him famous around the entirety of the former Yugoslavia. Also, there is a fascinating scale relief map of Montenegro created by the Austrians in 1917.

The **State Museum** (☎ 230 555; Trg Kralja Nikole; ☺ 9am-5pm Apr-Oct, 9am-5pm Mon-Fri Nov-Mar) was the former residence (built 1871) of Nikola Petrović I, last king of Montenegro. Although looted during WWII, sufficient furnishings, many stern portraits and period weapons remain to give a picture of the times.

CETINJE MONASTERY
Founded in 1484, and rebuilt in 1785, **Cetinje Monastery** (☎ 231 021; ☺ 8am-7pm May-Oct) has for the curious, or devout, a portion of the true Cross and some of the mummified right hand of St John the Baptist (although this seems to be the *pièce de résistance* of almost every monastery). To underline its significance as the hand that baptised Christ, it's set in a bejewelled casket with a little glass window.

The monastery **museum** is only open to groups. But if you are persuasive enough, you may be able to get in. The museum holds a copy of the 1494 *Oktoih* (Book of the Eight Voices), one of the oldest collections of liturgical songs in a Slavic language. There's also a collection of portraits, vestments, ancient handwritten texts and gifts from Russian churches.

Around Cetinje
Around 7km along the road to Podgorica a turning leads another 7km to **Rijeka Crnojevića** village. At the end of Lake Skadar, this little village is a magical place. When you approach it, having come down the winding mountain road, you'll be engulfed by silence and tranquillity. A little marble stone promenade is a platform for junior and senior fishermen, and the highlight of the village is the four-arched stone bridge that descends into a path alongside the river. Its mirror-smooth stillness is only occasionally disturbed by ripples from boats.

Carry on another 5km from Rijeka Crnojevića and you'll arrive at **Pavlova Strana**. This place has stunning views of the river flowing into the lake, around a rock island shaped like a giant tortoise. In the distance, a double hunchbacked mountain shelters the town of Virpazar. The view stretches for miles and creates a visual harmony of rock and water.

Twenty kilometres from Cetinje is **Mt Lovćen** (1749m), the 'Black Mountain' that is said to have given Montenegro its name (*crna* – black; *gora* – mountain) for it's covered with dark pines. On the mountain's summit is the mausoleum of Njegoš. If you don't have your own transport, take a taxi and then climb the 461 steps to the mausoleum where the views are of a sea of mountains, the Adriatic and, on a (very) clear day, the Italian coast.

COASTAL MONTENEGRO
The coastal area, although rather small, is diverse in its choice of beaches and swimming areas, and places to see and stay. Perhaps the most sensible way to divide it is in two: the stretch of towns and beaches south of Budva, via Petrovac and Bar, all the way to the Albanian border at Ulcinj; and the area of Kotor Bay (Boka Kotorska), curling south from the Croatian border with towns such as Kotor, Perast and Herceg Novi.

Budva Будва
☎ 086 / pop 11,700
Budva is the most popular holiday spot on the entire coast. This is hardly surprising: its old town is like a miniature Dubrovnik, with smooth narrow streets and old limestone houses. Dozens of bars and restaurants bulge with people in the hot summer days and nights, and the beaches are fine and plentiful.

In June the town hosts a national music festival and a summer festival in July and August.

ORIENTATION & INFORMATION

The **bus station** (☎ 456 000; Ivana Milutinovića bb) is about 1km from the Stari Grad (Old Town). The road called Mediteranska leads into Budva, ending at the harbour and Stari Grad.

Crnogorska Komercijalna Bank (☎ 451 075; Mediteranska 7; ⏰ 8am-7.30pm Mon-Sat Jul & Aug, 8am-1pm Mon-Fri Sep-Jun) Has a MasterCard ATM, cashes travellers cheques.

Euromarket Bank (☎ 455 106; Mediteranska 4; ⏰ 8.30am-2.30pm Mon-Fri, 8.30am-12.30pm Sat) Has a Visa ATM, cashes travellers cheques.

JAT (☎ 451 641; Mediteranska 2; ⏰ 8am-4pm Mon-Fri, 8am-1pm Sat) Airline office.

SIGHTS

Budva's best feature and star attraction is the walled Stari Grad. Narrow marble streets and old Mediterranean houses, as well as galleries, museums, shops, bars and restaurants, make this small old part the focus of all the summer fun. Much of the old town was ruined in two earthquakes in 1979, but it has since been completely rebuilt and is a tourist attraction, rather than a place where people live.

The recently renovated **Budva Museum** (☎ 457 994; Petra I Petrovića, Stari Grad; adult/child €1.50/0.50; ⏰ 9am-7pm Mon-Fri, 11am-5pm Sat & Sun), is neat and interesting, with three floors of artefacts showing pre-Roman and Roman findings from the area, as well as many artefacts from the time of the Ottoman rule. The seafarers' wooden chests painted and embroidered with images of land and home are captivating. There is a sample of an original Budva street displayed on the ground floor.

The tiny island of **St Nikola**, locally known as Hawaii, is an uninhabited green spot where Montenegrins go to eat fish in the restaurant (there's only one). A nautical mile away off the coast, boats ply to and from the island from almost any area in the city during the summer. You can also go snorkelling or simply sunbathing.

Budva's main beach is pebbly and average. **Mogren beach** is better: follow the coastal path southwards for 500m from the Grand Hotel Avala.

Bečiči beach is south of Budva. It's a long crescent of sand and the sea is calm, so if you have children, this is a good place to go, especially since there are many beach games at hand.

SLEEPING & EATING

Villa Balkan (☎ 454 401; Vuka Karadžića 2; 3-person apt Sep-Jun €70, Jul & Aug €110; ☒) On the north-western side of the old town walls, this place is a great deal if you are sharing the costs between three or two. The five apartments are spacious, with a kitchenette and great views of the bay, and the building is an elegant old Budva house that feels a lot more intimate than a big hotel.

Hotel Mogren (☎ 451 780; fax 452 041; Mediteranska 1; s/d Sep-Jun €30/60, Jul & Aug €42/84, half board €6) The 'cheapest' hotel option, but you may very well wonder if it's worth it. The hotel is large and formerly state owned, with rooms painted in aquatic blue and white. The furniture is a little old and decrepit. The more acceptable rooms are those with small balconies looking on to the sea.

Two options for camping are **Autocamp Avala** (☎ 451 205; ⏰ Jun-Sep) at Boreti, 2km on the road to Bar, and **Budva Autocamp** (tent & 2 people €4). **JAMB travel** (☎ 452 992; www.jamb-travel .com; Mediteranska 23; r €5.90-13.50, 2-/5-person apt €16/80, half/full board €10/15; ⏰ 8am-8pm Jun-Oct, 8am-3pm Mon-Fri Nov-May) books accommodation and organises day tours around Montenegro.

Join the crowds eating and drinking in Budva's Stari Grad or along the harbourside.

Restaurant Jadran (☎ 451 028; Slovenska Obala 10; meals €5-10; ⏰ 8am-late) With three terraces ranging from an elegant sea-view restaurant, to a canteenlike eatery with views of the street, you can find your own space in Jadran. Equally, you can eat high with lobster at €60 per kilogram or eat low with a substantial soup or ćevapčiči for €2. If you decide to go for something in the middle, mussels Jadran are good: the fresh molluscs are served in a delicious sauce of olive oil, lemon and garlic and go very well with a chilled Montenegrin white wine.

Lazo i Milan (☎ 451 468; 13 Jul bb; meals €4-8; ⏰ 9am-11pm) Pasta dishes just like mama makes them except this mama is a burly Montenegrin chef who can cook up a storm of gastronomic delight with his sauces.

Konoba Stari Grad (☎ 454 443; Njegoševa 14; meals €5-8; ⏰ 8am-late) Bang in the middle of the old town, this small place looks like an Italian mama's kitchen, with a cosy atmosphere, chequered tablecloths and good-smelling food. A real advantage is the menu of the day (available only in the summer months) where for €12 to €15 you get starters, *primi* *piati* (first course), *secondi piati* (second course) and dessert.

Donna kod Nikole (☎ 451 531; Budva Marina; meals €5-8; ☺ 8am-late) A recommended harbourside restaurant with maritime décor (surprise, surprise). Its fish soup is excellent, and individual seafood/fish meals are good, but beware the seafood platters – a little overpriced.

Bus station café (Ivana Milutinovića; meals €2-3; ☺ 7am-9pm) The best cheap eats in town in a choose-and-point cafeteria.

MB Ice Club (☎ 452 552; Starogradski Trg; treats €3-6; ☺ 9am-2am) This place has a huge terrace, and cocktails go down easily with the silky Cuban rhythms.

AROUND BUDVA
Sveti Stefan
About 5km south of Budva is the former fishing island of Sveti Stefan. Until 50 years ago it was a simple little fishing community, but since the people on the island grew increasingly poor, families kept moving away in search of bigger and better things. Then someone had the idea to buy the entire island, a wondrous-looking thing in itself, and turn it into a luxury hotel. It became a big hit with the glamorous layer of socialist Yugoslavia, and the likes of Sofia Loren and Doris Day strutted their stuff around here. But, like so many other things in the former Yugoslavia, it lost its appeal during the '90s.

The island is like a slice of Mediterranean heaven, with oleanders, pines and olives scenting the air and the little houses looking straight onto the expansive Adriatic. There is a charge of €5 to enter the resort, and it's worth the wander around. A small 15th-century church remains in the centre of the island, and there is a sense of nostalgia when you think how the villagers' life must have been in this beautiful isolated spot. At the time of research Sveti Stefan awaited its future, and it's possible that the resort will once again charge astronomical prices and attract an exclusive crowd.

Petrovac
Seventeen kilometres away from Budva, on the road to Bar, this used to be the place where rich Romans had their summer villas. Petrovac is a beautiful small town with a red sandy beach, a pretty promenade and lush Mediterranean plants perfuming the air. A 16th-century **Venetian fortress** guards the harbour, and many dance the nights away in the club inside it.

The restaurants are mainly by the fortress, with places like Lazaret and Caffe Cuba, where you can have a breakfast of fried eggs for €3.50 and pizzas for €5. Sleeping can be arranged through any of the tourist agencies in Budva or Bar, but if you don't mind splashing out, the local **Hotel Rivijera** (☎ 422 100; www.riviera-petrovac.com; per person €50; ✗ ⬚ ⬚) is a luxurious hotel with plasma-screen TVs in the gleaming rooms and luxurious brand-new bathrooms. There is a small swimming pool, plus a bit of the beach belongs to the hotel.

Petrovac gets crowded in the months of July and August, so you won't be able to find an inch of space on the beach.

Bar Бар
☎ 085 / pop 37,000
This might be your first stop in coastal Montenegro if you decide to ferry it across from Italy. Bar is a modern city, a port with all that entails: tower blocks, a run-down feeling and a hint of oil threading the air. But Stari Bar (Old Bar), a thousand-year-old town in ruins up on the mountainside, is an enchanting site worth visiting.

ORIENTATION & INFORMATION
The ferry terminal in Bar is 300m from the town centre; the **bus station** (☎ 314 499) and adjacent **train station** (☎ 312 210) are about 2km southeast of the centre.

There are several ATMs around town.

Komercijalna Bank (☎ 311 827; Obala Kralja Nikole bb; ☺ 8am-4pm Mon-Fri, 8am-noon Sat) Cashes travellers cheques.

Montenegro Express (☎ /fax 312 589; Obala 13 Jula bb; ☺ 8am-8pm Mon-Sat Jul & Aug, 8am-2pm Mon Sat Sep-Jun) Books accommodation along the coast and organises tours.

Tourist Information Centar (☎ 311 633; Obala 13 Jula bb; ☺ 7am-8pm Jul & Aug, 7am-2pm Mon-Fri Sep-Jun) Limited tourist information.

SIGHTS
The beautiful remains of **Stari Bar** (admission €1; ☺ 9am-5pm Apr-Oct) lie 5km east of the modern town, off the Ulcinj road. Stari Bar sits on top of Lundža hill and its setting is amazing. Steep cliffs surround the old town and render it inaccessible but from one side.

Findings of pottery and metal have dated occupancy as far back as 800 BC. During the 3rd century, the occupying Romans destroyed the old settlement and abandoned it for a location nearer to the sea. Three centuries later, the Byzantine Emperor Justinian built a fortified tower on the same hill, and Stari Bar started to develop into an active centre on the Adriatic coast. In the 10th century, Stari Bar was referred to as 'the Antinbaris, as in, opposite to the Italian city, Bari'. Hence its current name. In the 11th century, it was part of Duklja or Zeta, the first Slavonic littoral state, and soon after became one of the most important political, economic and cultural places on the coast. Nearly all the 240 buildings lie in ruin, a result of Montenegrin shelling when they captured the town back from the Turks in 1878.

Climbing the steep cobbled street will take you to the entrance of the old town, where the buzzing of insects and a serene atmosphere will make you feel you've entered a huge garden. Wandering around you'll notice the **upper fortress** in the northern corner. Built in the 11th century, the fortress was used as a prison in WWII, and looking out from its 'balcony', the view shows Stari Bar's isolated and beautiful setting, amid mountains and olive groves. Also in the north are the foundations of the **Church of St George**, the patron saint of Bar. Originally a Romanesque church, the Turks rebuilt it into a mosque in the 17th century, but the unlucky spot was yet again in ruins after an accidental explosion of gunpowder. Nearby are two preserved churches, **St Veneranda** and **St Catherine**, both from the 14th century. Around the corner is a **Turkish bath** from the 17th or 18th century, a solid, charming building. In the western part of the town are the remains of the **Church of St Nicolas** with glimpses of Serbo-Byzantine frescoes.

It's as if the murmur of people and the scurrying of everyday life are embedded in the air of the many living spaces you might be able to imagine among the ruins. They show the sophistication and the complexity of ancient life in Stari Bar.

SLEEPING & EATING

Putnik Gold (☎ 311 588; putnikgold@cg.yu; Obala 13 Jula bb; ☒ 8am-3pm Mon-Sat) Books accommodation along the coast. Private rooms without breakfast start at €9, B&B apartments from €12, half-board apartments from €17 and hotels from €30 to €100.

Montenegro Express (☎ /fax 312 589; Obala 13 Jula bb; private rooms €7-20, hotels €30-100; ☒ 8am-8pm Mon-Sat Jul & Aug, 8am-2pm Mon-Sat Sep-Jun) Another agency with similar deals.

Places to eat are limited with drinks-only cafés and bars outnumbering restaurants.

Pizeria Bell (Vladimira Rolovića bb; pizzas €3, pastas €4-5; ☒ 7am-11pm) A small cosy pizza/pasta joint that's open year-round, with juicy portions and efficient service.

Primorka Supermarket (☎ 312 619; Vladimira Rolovića bb; ☒ 8am-8pm) Sells all you need for a feed-yourself holiday.

GETTING THERE & AWAY

Four daily trains link Bar and Belgrade (€15 plus €15/8 for a three-/six-berth sleeper, nine hours).

Boats to Italy

Barska Plovidba (☎ 312 336; mlinesagency@cg.yu; Obala 13 Jula bb; ☒ 8am-10pm) is the agent for Montenegro Lines, which sails several times a week to Bari (Italy). For times and prices check www.montenegrolines.net.

Mercur (☎ 313 617; www.mercuradriatica.com in Serbian; Obala 13 Jula bb; ☒ 8am-8pm Mon-Fri, 9am-2pm Sat) books Adriatica ferries to Ancona (Italy). A Thursday service leaves at 5.30pm and arrives at 9.30am, and costs from €51/61/82 for passage only/deck seat/cabin bed.

Ulcinj Улцињ
☎ 085 / 24,000

The closest seaside town to the Albanian border is a rich bustle of Albanian and Montenegrin cultures. Although the new part of town is not as beautiful as, say, Kotor, Ulcinj still has a great coast. As well as Mala Plaža (Small Beach) in the town itself (a fine grin of a cove), Ulcinj has the longest sandy beach in the whole of Montenegro, aptly called Velika Plaža (Big Beach). Stretching east, towards the Albanian border, it is 12km long and provides a great escape from the crowded Ulcinj town beaches. Some of it is nudist, too.

The Stari Grad (Old Town) is a mire of stone houses and fortified walls that are present so often in Montenegrin seaside towns due to historical events that called for defence. But Ulcinj has a bit of a

---

PIRATES OF THE MEDITERRANEAN

The Venetians handed control of Ulcinj to the Turks in 1571, and over the next 300 years the town gained notoriety as a pirate base. Initially, the pirates comprised mainly a few hundred North Africans and Maltese, but soon others joined in – Serbs, Albanians and Turks also took their eye patches out and got a hold of a hook or two.

They are said to have made great fortunes from their innumerable robberies, swapping small galleys for galleons in a relatively short time (a bit like progressing from a Yugo 55 to a Ferrari in a few weeks). Legendary leaders became 'celebrities' across the eastern Mediterranean with stories of the Karamindžoja brothers, Lika Ceni, Ali Hodža and the like fuelling the imaginations of avid listeners. It is said that the gangs changed their flags frequently while at sea, thus causing confusion and chaos, and, their day's work done, partied on Ulcinj's Mala Plaža and boiled halvah in massive cauldrons. Always faithful only to the sea, they stirred the piping halvah with an oar.

One tale tells of Cervantes being captured by some of these pirates in 1575, after the battle of Lepanto, and held prisoner in the vaults by the main square. There were rumours also that Don Quixote's Dulcinea was an Ulcinj girl, although one may question the verity of this.

There was a less romanticised side to this time too. Ulcinj was the centre of a thriving slave trade, and the slaves – some of them small children of only two or three, and mainly North African – were sold on the town's main square.

---

different history, and a fascinating one at that (see the boxed text, above).

ORIENTATION & INFORMATION

The **bus station** (☎ 413 225) is on the edge of town. Travel into town by turning right onto 26 Novembar at the first major junction. Mala Plaža and Stari Grad are 3km down at the end of 26 Novembar. Just up from Mala Plaža is a small market area.

Velika Plaža begins about 5km southeast of the town (take the Ada bus or a minibus in season).

Euromarket Bank (☎ 422 370; 26 Novembar bb; ⏳ 8.30am-3pm Mon-Fri, 8.30am-12.30pm Sat) Cashes travellers cheques, has a Visa ATM.

Integral Caffe (☎ 401 144; 26 Novembar bb; per hr €2.50; ⏳ 9am-2pm) Internet, up an alley opposite the mosque.

SIGHTS

The ancient Stari Grad walls overlook the sea and are lovely to wander around. The damaged buildings you will no doubt come across are result of an earthquake that shattered the town in 1979 – the repair works seem to be taking a rather long time. At the western entrance, the **Upper Gate**, is a **museum** (☎ 421 419; Stari Grad; admission €1; ⏳ 8am-2pm Mon-Fri) containing Montenegrin and Turkish artefacts such as cannon balls and old Muslim tombstones, as well as some Roman ruins.

Just outside the western entrance is the **Church of St Nicholas** with an ancient olive orchard. The olive trees are gnarled and beautiful on this part of the coast. The smiling **Mala Plaža** is Ulcinj's town beach.

On your way south towards **Velika Plaža**, whether you walk or go by transport, stop at the **Milena canal**, part of the Bojana River, where the local fishermen use traditional methods to catch their prey. Long willow rods are suspended above the river along with large nets catching unsuspecting fish as they swim by. The entire device is attached to a wooden house sitting on stilts above the water, and since there are many of these, they create an unusual sight that reminds you of Thailand or Vietnam. There are more of these on the banks of the **Bojana River**, beyond Velika Plaža. Along the river banks are fish restaurants with fresh catches lining your plate.

SLEEPING

The **Real Estate Tourist Agency** (☎ 421 612; 26 Novembar bb; ⏳ 8am-9pm) has accommodation available in private rooms (from €10, no meals), hotels (doubles from €16, half board) and two-/three-/four-person apartments (€27/36/43, half board). The agency also runs tours.

Dvori Balšića & Palata Venecija (☎ /fax 421 457; leart@cg.yu; Stari Grad; 2-/4-/6-person apt low season from €40/63/95, Jul & Aug €50/83/111) No better place than these adjacent places in Ulcinj: spacious two-room (and more) apartments with kitchenettes in an old stone house that looks like a small castle, and endless views of the sea. The restaurant downstairs has a spacious terrace where you can guzzle and swill. Breakfast/half board/full board is €3/8/10.

Albatros (☎ 423 266; s/d from €22.10/34; ☒) Among pine trees, this pleasant holiday hotel is 1km up the hill from Mala Plaža. Guests have access to a sauna, fitness room and swimming pool.

Tomi camping ground (☒ May-Sep) A camping ground under the trees, located east of Milena and adjacent to Velika Plaža.

HTP Velika Plaža (☎ 413 145; www.velikaplaza .cg.yu; Ada road) Further towards Ada, this holiday camp has a variety of accommodation from €19 to €23 per person or €35 to €100 for an apartment, full board.

EATING & DRINKING

On the seafront is a string of restaurants specialising in seafood.

Marinero (☎ 423 009; Mala Plaža; meals €5-9; ☒ 7am-late) The owner was once a ship's cook and ship's cooks don't last long unless they're good. Seafaring mates gather, speaking three or four languages, so for a coffee or *rakija* you'll get the history of the town and tales of the sea. Come for a slap-up seafood meal.

Bazar (☎ 421 639; 26 Novembar bb; meals €5-8; ☒ 8am-late) A great place if you want to have some seafood in a quiet spot during the summer bustle. *Lignje na žaru* (grilled calamari) is the restaurant's speciality and finger-licking good.

Gallo Nero (☎ 315 245; 26 Novembar bb; meals €5-12; ☒ 10am-late) Friendly service and a good Italian menu draw the crowds to this place. You can snack or feast, it's your choice.

Bella Vista (☎ 067 315 266; 26 Novembar bb; meals €4-8; ☒ 7am-late) If you don't have breakfast included in your accommodation, this is a good place to come and feed yourself. Equally, you can drink late here. Or just stay the night, since the owners also have accommodation (half board from €25).

Rock (26 Novembar bb; ☒ 8am-late) An attempt at an Irish pub with some of the atmosphere, and live music on the weekend. If that pint of Guinness ain't available, there are plenty of other beers to replace it.

GETTING THERE & AWAY

Many minibuses ply the road to Ada (and Velika Plaža) from the marketplace for €1.50 in season.

Bay of Kotor (Boka Kotorska)
Бока Которска
KOTOR КОТОР
☎ 082 / pop 22,500

Imagine a place at the head of southern Europe's deepest fjord, with a fortified old town nestled at the foot of a high cliff, labyrinthine streets where bars, pizza joints, churches, shops, hotels and restaurants surprise you on hidden piazzas, and you start getting the idea of Kotor. It's probably the most beautiful place on the Montenegrin coast, and its setting couldn't be more dramatic. Brooding mountains protect the bay and the sea is a moody indigo blue.

Kotor attracts a fair amount of visitors during July and August, so it's best to avoid it during these times, if you can. If not, remember that during these months partying is a priority, so if you can't beat 'em, join 'em.

Orientation

The western flank of the funnel-shaped Stari Grad (Old Town) lies against Kotor Fjord (Kotorski Zaliv). An 18th-century gateway off Jadranski Put, which runs along the waterside, leads into the city and Stari Grad, where Kotor's places of interest lie. The **bus station** (☎ 325 809) is 1km away on the Budva road.

Information

Euromarket Bank (☎ 323 946; Trg Octobarske Revolucije; ☒ 8am-8pm Mon-Fri, 8am-4pm Sat, until 8pm Sat Jun-Sep) Cashes travellers cheques, has a Visa ATM.

IDK Computers (☎ 301 046; Stari Grad; per hr €2; ☒ 2pm-midnight summer, 5pm-midnight rest of year)

Information booth (☎ 325 950; western gateway; ☒ 9am-1pm & 5-8pm Mon-Sat) Information on the town and private accommodation.

Opportunity Bank (Trg Octobarske Revolucije) Has a MasterCard ATM.

Sights

The best thing to do in Kotor is just let yourself get lost and found again in the mazy streets. You'll soon know every corner, since the town is quite small. But there's plenty to see and many coffees to be drunk in the shady squares. If you have the energy, climb the 1500 steps up to the old fortifications on the mountainside above Kotor. The views of the fjord are stunning and you get a good idea of the town below.

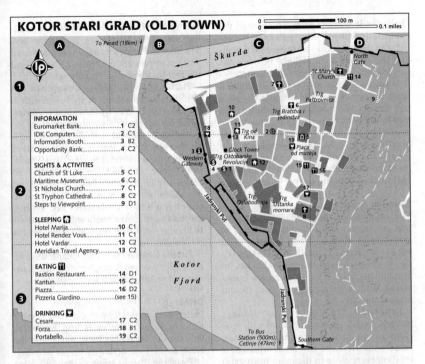

KOTOR STARI GRAD (OLD TOWN)

INFORMATION
Euromarket Bank.....................1 C2
IDK Computers.........................2 C1
Information Booth....................3 B2
Opportunity Bank....................4 C2

SIGHTS & ACTIVITIES
Church of St Luke....................5 C1
Maritime Museum....................6 C2
St Nicholas Church..................7 C1
St Tryphon Cathedral...............8 C2
Steps to Viewpoint..................9 D1

SLEEPING
Hotel Marija...........................10 C1
Hotel Rendez Vous.................11 C1
Hotel Vardar..........................12 C2
Meridian Travel Agency.........13 C2

EATING
Bastion Restaurant.................14 D1
Kantun...................................15 C2
Piazza....................................16 D2
Pizzeria Giardino.................(see 15)

DRINKING
Cesare....................................17 C2
Forza......................................18 B1
Portabello..............................19 C2

Within the town itself, the **Maritime Museum** (☎ 325 646; Stari Grad; admission €1; ☼ 9am-5pm Mon-Fri, to noon Sat) shows Kotor's formerly high position as a Mediterranean naval power and how important the sea is to the town. The displays show a proud history and tell that in the 18th century, the Bay of Kotor sent out over 400 ships to sail the world's seas. Note the brightly painted bottles reading 'For My True Love' and 'Think of Me', probably given to the sailors by their sweethearts upon departure. A leaflet in English is available.

The **St Tryphon Cathedral** (Trg Ustanka mornara), originally built in the 11th century, has been reconstructed several times since due to damage by a number of severe earthquakes. The entire western front was destroyed in 1667 and the replacement stone bell towers add a baroque aspect to the building. The interior is a masterpiece of Romanesque-Gothic architecture with slender columns thrusting upwards to support a series of vaulted roofs. The gilded silver-relief altar screen, in the form of an iconostasis, is held to be the most valuable exhibit in Kotor. There are 14th-century frescoes

which were discovered in the last few years, but the experts can't decide whether their painters were Greek or Serbian. Some of the remains of St Tryphon, Kotor's patron saint, are held at the reliquary chapel as well as parts of the Holy Cross.

The **Church of St Luke** (Trg bratstva i jedinstva) is a 12th-century Romanesque building with original frescoes remaining. The church became a place of worship for Orthodox Christianity in the 17th century, and a hundred years later a chapel to St Spiridon was built alongside it with a baroque façade. The church was restored to its original 12th-century form in 1979 after the strong earthquake that shattered so many of Montenegro's coastal towns. One of the most interesting things about this church is that it has two altars: a Catholic one and an Orthodox one, showing the historic closeness of these two faiths and the religious tolerance of the Kotor area. Confusion was avoided by the simple practice of holding Mass at separate times.

Breathe in the smell of incense and beeswax in the plain and unadorned 1909

Orthodox **St Nicholas Church**. The silence, the iconostasis with its silver panels in bas relief, the dark wood against bare grey walls and the filtered rays of light through the upper dome create an eerie atmosphere.

If you have your own transport, embark upon a journey that has become almost a cult among the inhabitants of Kotor: the **road to Cetinje**. The serpentine bends curve over the mountains and the views are breathtaking. Take the compulsory trip around the Bay of Kotor seeing all the little stone harbours protecting small boats against the chopping waves.

Sleeping & Eating

The information booth has some information on private accommodation. The ever-helpful **Meridian Travel Agency** (☎ 322 968; travel@cg.yu; r €8-15, apt €30-55, s €25-44, d €41-63; ☺ 9am-2pm & 6-7pm Mon-Fri, 9am-2pm Sat), in a small lane behind the clock tower, books private and hotel accommodation in and around the city.

Hotel Vardar (☎ 325 084; Trg Oktobarske Revolucije; s/d from €25/41) A great-value hotel with spacious rooms in dark browns and whites, some with views of the main square. Its location (very close to the main town gate) makes it the most hassle-free place for lugging your luggage across the no-traffic marble paving stones of the old town.

Hotel Marija (☎ 325 062; fax 325 073; Stari Grad; s/d €45/65; ❉) A boutique hotel with a wood-panelled interior boasts of each room being different from the other. Tucked in a small side street, this cosy little place can become a little noisy at weekends with pumping music coming from the street below, so ask for a quiet(er) room.

Hotel Rendez Vous (☎ 322 447; Pjaca od mljeka; s/d/apt €15/25/45) Possibly the cheapest hotel in town, with a TV and a fridge even, and a noisy old men's drinking den downstairs. The rooms are small and a little frumpy, but clean. The Pjaca od mljeka (Milk Piazza) is quiet and the hotel building is a lovely old stone structure.

There are tons of small eateries on the streets of Kotor, from bakeries to takeaway pizza joints. For the sweet-toothed, cherry-filled strudel is a speciality of the region.

Kantun (☎ 325 757; Pjaca od muzeja; meals €3-6; ☺ 9am-midnight) This wood-beam hut serving fabulous food is a place you could imagine

seafarers having their last feast before treading the ship's boards for months at sea. Traditional Montenegrin food abounds and good examples are the Njegoša cheeses and the *roštiljska kobasica* (grilled sausages).

Piazza (☎ 069 205 720; Pjaca od muzeja; pizza slices €2; ☺ 8am-late) Best pizza in town with a thin base and perfectly measured toppings. Great for snacks or a sit-down meal.

Bastion Restaurant (☎ 322 116; meals €6-9; ☺ 10am-late) By St Mary's church, Bastion Restaurant is more favoured as a lunch-time venue, in which case it's best to go early. Any slight indecision in ordering and the waiter will wheel in a platter of fish to tempt you and if those don't say 'eat me' there's an expansive menu with veg options to choose from. The seafood salad starter is recommended.

Pizzeria Giardino (☎ 323 324; Pjaca od muzeja; pizzas €4-5; ☺ 9am-late) A neighbour to the Kantun and recommended for the pizza.

Drinking

In terms of nightlife, you can have a great time in Kotor. The cafés and bars play various, but invariably loud, music and the Kotorians (?) are definitely up for partying.

Portabello (Pjaca od muzeja; ☺ 9am-1am) Next door to the Piazza pizza joint, the bar itself is tiny, but the DJ lets his music roar outside, where people jig to the beats.

Cesare (☎ 325 913; Stari Grad 327; ☺ 7am-1am) An elongated café/bar popular with the fashionable crowd, Cesare is a place to come to drink and dance, to see and be seen. Take a trip to the toilets and feel like you've stepped onto an MTV music video set, with aluminium capsule cubicles padded in white leather behind shiny sliding doors.

Forza (☎ 304 352; Stari Grad bb; ☺ 8am-late) An Internet café, a bookshop, a cake shop and a sleek café with leather armchairs and soft lighting, popular with a cigar-smoking, distinguished older crowd. If you want to read in silence or just sit and relax, this is your place.

Getting There & Away

Buses go to Budva (€2), Cetinje (€3), Bar (€3) and Podgorica (€5) every 15 to 20 minutes.

If you are driving, the shortest way to Herceg Novi is by ferry from Tivat (€3.50 per car, every 10 minutes, half-hour after midnight). Otherwise, it's a leisurely 43km drive around the bay, compared with 27km by ferry.

Around Kotor

Perast is a small waterside town about 18km from Kotor on the road around the bay. It's a beautiful old place, with fantastically preserved original Mediterranean charm. The entire town is made up of old houses, and none of the wonders of modern architecture have touched its grounds.

Quiet Perast boasts a parish **Church of St Nikola** on the waterfront, with the tallest bell tower in the bay (35m). Also on the waterfront is the **Perast Museum** (☎ 373 519; Obala Marka Martinovića bb; ☼ 8am-2pm Mon-Fri, 9am-2pm Sat & Sun; admission €1.50), exhibiting documents about the history of the town and seafaring artefacts.

As soon as you hit this part of the bay, you'll notice two peculiarly small islands in the fjord, opposite Perast. These are the **Gospa od Škrpjela** (Lady of the Rock Island) and the **island of St George** (Ostrvo Svetog Đurđa). The remarkable Lady of the Rock Island was artificially created by the locals over a period of 550 years. Every 22 July they took stones over to the island site and dropped them in the water, on top of an underwater rock. A later sinking of 87 captured ships loaded with rocks made creating the island a little easier. The St George is balanced on a natural reef and houses the Benedictine Monastery of St George shaded by cypress trees.

Between mid-May and mid-October boats regularly ply between the island and Perast for €1 return; just ask on the waterfront. An hourly minibus service connects with Kotor for €1.

The small village of **Risan**, a little further from Perast on the road to Kotor, has **3rd-century mosaics**. There are signposts on the road, leading you to the site. Discovered in the 19th century, the dig was carried out in 1930. The mosaics are part of the remains of the foundations of a Roman villa rustica, where they covered the floors of five rooms. The loveliest is the mosaic of the Greek god of sleep, Hypnos, reclining in the centre of what must have been the bedroom.

HERCEG NOVI ХЕРЦЕГ НОВИ
☎ 088 / pop 30,000

Herceg Novi is the first place you will come upon if you cross into Montenegro from Croatia. It's a lovely place, with sunny squares and a lively atmosphere. Herceg Novi has some great gardens and parks with rare trees and plants, and the beaches here and in the neighbouring Topla and Igalo are good for swimming.

A good general Herceg Novi information website is www.hercegnovi.cc/adresar/index.php.

There are plenty of ATMs in the city.

Crnogorska Komercijalna Bank (☎ 322 666; Trg Nikole Đurkovića; ☼ 7am-8pm Mon-Sat) Cashes travellers cheques and has a MasterCard ATM.

Euromarket Bank (☎ 323 523; by Njegoševa 12; ☼ 8.30am-3pm Mon-Fri, 8.30am-12.30pm Sat) Cashes travellers cheques and has a Visa ATM.

Gorbis (☎ 326 085; Njegoševa 64; r €5-8, s/d €25/36; ☼ 8am-7pm) A travel agency that books accommodation, transfers to Dubrovnik and flight and ferry tickets.

Sights

The old city centre is surrounded by walls, and the **Španjola tower**, started by the Spanish and finished by the Turks, is well preserved. The Venetians built towers overlooking the sea, and called them, imaginatively, Fortemare. In the city centre is the **clock tower**, marking the border between the old and new parts of town.

One of the loveliest places in town is **Trg Belvista**, a gleaming white piazza with the **Church of the Archangel Michael** (1900) in the centre, surrounded by palm trees. Many relax, drink and chat in the shade.

The seafront area is as active as the old town and is popular for restaurants and bars. One of the best places for breakfast, possibly in the entire country, is the **Sports Café** (☎ 322 018; Šetalište 5, Danica 34; breakfast €3-4; ☼ 8am-late) on a barge at the waterfront. Breakfasts are a variety of massive omelettes, fresh bread rolls and jam, or delicious wraps.

Getting There & Away

The **bus station** (☎ 321 225) is on the main highway. There are two buses to Dubrovnik, at 3.50pm and 8.10pm (€7). There are frequent buses to Kotor (€2.50, 1½ hours) and Budva (€3, 1¾ hours).

NORTHERN MONTENEGRO
Ostrog Острог

Some 20km south of Nikšić off the road from Podgorica is the **monastery of Ostrog**. Built in 1665 by St Vasilije Jovanović, who fled from the Turks, the monastery looks as if it has grown out of the rock of the cliff it rests on, 900m above the Zeta valley floor. Once you get on the winding road that snakes off the main Podgorica–Nikšić road, you will eventually make it to the Lower Monastery, a newer structure built in 1824. The Lower Monastery is, allegedly, the place where Montenegrin and Boka (Bay of Kotor) patriots met to agree that their country should join Tito's Yugoslavia in 1942.

The Upper Monastery (the impressive one) is dubbed St Vasilije's miracle, because no-one seems to understand how it was built. The Saint's bones are still inside and apparently heal all sorts of illnesses. There are original frescoes inside the monastery, as well as curious mosaics in rock. To get to the Upper Monastery, a 3km walk uphill, you can either join the pilgrims and get your cardiovascular system going, or if you'd rather drive and not be a sport, there's an upper car park.

Durmitor National Park Дурмитор
☎ 089 / pop 4900

A Unesco World Heritage site, Durmitor is the kind of mountain that sets off *Carmina Burana* in your head when you see its dramatic, imposing peaks. Slapped around by the elements, the sharp shapes of the rock stab the vast skies above. Relief comes in around 20 lakes that dot the Durmitor Range, dubbed 'Mountain Eyes' (Gorske oči).

In winter (December to March) Durmitor is Montenegro's ski resort; in summer (June to September) it's a popular place for hiking, rafting and many other activities. Be prepared though, as the weather is very changeable, even in summer.

ORIENTATION & INFORMATION
Žabljak town centre is where the Nikšić road meets the Đurđevića Tara bridge road. Here there's a **tourist information centre** (☎ 361 802; Stanka Dragojevića 26; ☉ 8am-8pm Dec-Mar, 8am-3pm Apr-Nov), with maps and fine picture books, a taxi stand and a bus stop.

Check out the informative Durmitor website www.durmitorcg.com.

SIGHTS & ACTIVITIES
Durmitor is fun, fun, fun. In winter there's skiing, snowboarding or having fun with a dog-drawn team. In summer there's rafting trips through the steeply forested Tara Gorge and over countless foaming rapids. There's also horse riding, hiking, cycling, mountaineering and paragliding.

Ski Centar Durmitor (☎ 61 144; www.durmitorcg .com/ski_centar.php; ☉ 8am-6pm Mon-Sat), in the Hotel Žabljak adjacent to the tourist information centre, arranges ski passes (€6.15/35.79 per day/week), ski lessons (€3.07/17.90 for one/seven lessons) and also equipment rental (€3.07/17.90 per day/week).

The largest lake in the area, **Black Lake** (Crno jezero), is a 3km walk from Žabljak. Dominating all is the rounded mass of 'Bear' (Međed, 2287m) rearing up behind the lake and flanked by other peaks, including Bobotov Kuk (2525m). **Škrčko Lake** is in the centre of a tectonic valley and the scenery is magnificent here. This lake is particularly popular with mountaineers, who walk the fells surrounding it and then go for a cool dip at the end of the day. **Modro Lake** is more accessible, even walkable (8km from Žabljak), and many drink its pure water.

The 1.3km-deep **Tara Canyon** that slits open the earth's crust for 80km is best seen from a rock promontory at Ćurevac, a €10 taxi ride away from Žabljak. It is popular for rafting. The entire length of the course is 85km, but you can choose to raft only 15km. Rafting is a group activity but individuals can join by prior arrangement. **Sveti Đorđije** (☎ /fax 61 367; tasaint@cg.yu; Njegoševa bb; ☉ 8am-8pm) is a fount of information (English spoken) and offers two-/three-day trips for €200/250 per person including transfers, accommodation and food. An inclusive day trip costs €80.

Sveti Đorđije also organises summer day tours, typically for six to eight people (individuals may join) at €30 each, to the **Piva Monastery**, near the Bosnian border, which has remarkable frescoes.

The **Durmitor National Park office** (☎ 61 474; fax 61 346; ☉ 7am-2pm Mon-Fri), by Hotel Durmitor, has park maps and runs rafting trips for €150 for a group of 10, horse-riding tours (half/whole day €25/50), led by an English-speaking guide, and walking tours.

SLEEPING & EATING
Sveti Đorđije (☎ /fax 361 367; tasaint@cg.yu; Njegoševa bb; s/d €10/16, 2-/3-/4-person apt €26/30/39, B&B/half-board €3/9; ☉ 8am-8pm) is an agency with its finger on private accommodation.

Hotel Jezera (☎ 361 103; fax 61 579; Njegoševa bb; s/d/tr B&B €25/36/45, half board €28/46/54; Ⓟ) If you feel like really joining the crowds, this large hotel has big groups of skiers and summer holidaymakers. The rooms are spacious and the hotel has a pleasant restaurant and apéritif bar.

Planinka (☎ 361 344; Njegoseva bb; s/d B&B €20/36, half board €25/46; Ⓟ) Offers much the same as the Jezera, plus a relief map of Durmitor in the reception, to feel all those sharp peaks under your fingertips.

Autocamp Ivan-do is just a fenced-off field, without facilities, uphill from the national park office.

All the hotels have restaurants open to nonresidents.

National Restaurant (☎ 361 337; Božidara Žugića 8; meals €3-8; ☺ 8am-late) A pearl of a place! Small, but not crowded, it's a happy restaurant offering the best food around: broths and hot appetisers with slugs of domestic brandy to defeat the winter chill, or grilled trout and salad in summer.

Restaurant Durmitor (☎ 637 316; Božidara Žugića bb; meals €4-8; ☺ 7am-11pm) Home cooking at its best in a small hut-restaurant proudly bearing the mountain's name. The small space guarantees a cosy winter atmosphere.

GETTING THERE & AWAY

The **bus station** (☎ 61 318), on the Nikšić road, is at the southern end of town. There's one bus daily to Belgrade (€18, 10 hours, departs 4.30pm), several to Nikšić (€3.50, two hours) and four to Podgorica (€6, 3½ hours).

SERBIA & MONTENEGRO DIRECTORY

ACCOMMODATION

The availability of hostel accommodation has declined but contact the Youth Hostel Organisation (p284) for current hotel deals. Belgrade hotels are rather expensive for what they have to offer, but there are a couple of good-value midrange hotels. Montenegrin hotels outside the coast and Žabljak are iniquitously expensive, while in Kosovo accommodation is scarce and pricey.

The cheapest option is private rooms (along the coast, seldom inland and not in

Belgrade) organised through travel agencies. The Montenegrin coast has some summer camping grounds. 'Wild' camping would be possible outside national parks, but not in Kosovo due to the odd chance of an undiscovered mine. An overnight bus or train will always save you a night's accommodation.

The quoted accommodation prices in Montenegro are for the high season. Unless otherwise mentioned the tariff includes breakfast, and rooms have a private bathroom. Places listed in our Sleeping sections are ordered by preference.

ACTIVITIES

Serbia's main ski resorts are Zlatibor (p300) and Kopaonik (p299), while Montenegro's is Durmitor (opposite). Kosovo's resort is at Brezovica (p308). The ski season is from December to March; the resorts are also popular for hiking in summer. For whitewater rafting, the Tara River in Montenegro's Durmitor National Park is the most important river in the country.

BOOKS

Rebecca West's 1941 *Black Lamb & Grey Falcon* is a classic piece of travel writing but now extremely dated. Consider *The Serbs: History, Myth and the Destruction of Yugoslavia* by Tim Judah and *Balkan Babel* by Sabrina Ramet, an engaging look at Yugoslavia from Tito to Milošević. Specifically for Kosovo read *Kosovo: A Short History* by Noel Malcolm. Ismail Kadare's *Three Elegies for Kosovo*, which centres around the myth of the 1389 Kosovo battle (the centre of the antagonism between the Serbs and the Albanians) is a recommended read.

SERBIA & MONTENEGRO

BUSINESS HOURS

Banks are open from 8am to 5pm Monday to Friday and 8am to 2pm Saturday, but are closed Sunday. On weekdays many shops open at 8am and close at 6pm. Most government offices close on Saturday; although shops stay open until 2pm, many other businesses close at 3pm. Restaurants are open from 8am to 11pm or midnight and bars from 9pm to 3am.

CUSTOMS

If you're bringing in more than €2000, then you have to complete a currency declaration form on arrival and show it on departure. In practice it's ignored but the reality is that if customs officials wanted to play by the rules they could confiscate your money. Play it safe and declare.

DANGERS & ANNOYANCES

Travel nearly everywhere is safe but your government travel advisories will warn against travel to Kosovo. Avoid southeastern Serbia, where Serb-Albanian tension remains. Kosovo is thought to have been cleared of landmines but there is still unexploded ordnance about, so if you are off the beaten track you will need KFOR (who are omnipresent) and local advice (try the police).

Many people are chain-smokers and give the same consideration to nonsmokers as lift farters do to their fellow passengers.

It's fine to discuss politics if you're also willing to listen.

Check with the police before photographing any official building they're guarding.

DISCOUNT CARDS

The EURO<26 discount card (www.euro26 .org.yu) can provide holders with discounts on rail travel, air travel with JAT and Montenegro Airlines, and some selected hotels.

EMBASSIES & CONSULATES
Serbian & Montenegrin Embassies & Consulates

Albania (☎ 042-232 042, 042-232 091; ambatira@icc-al .org; Skender Beg Bldg 8/3-II, Tirana)
Australia (☎ 02-6290 2630; yuembau@ozemail.com.au; 4 Bulwarra Close, O'Malley, ACT 2606)
Bosnia and Hercegovina (☎ 033-260 090; yugoamba@ bih.net.ba; Obala Marka Dizdara 3a, Sarajevo 71000)
Bulgaria (☎ 02-946 16 35, 02-946 10 59; ambasada-scg -sofija@infotel.bg; Veliko Târnovo 3, Sofia 1504)

Canada (☎ 613-233 6289; www.embscg.ca /consular.html; 17 Blackburn Ave, Ottawa, Ontario, K1A 8A2)
Croatia (☎ 01-457 90 6; ambasada@ambasada-srj.hr; Pantovcak 245, Zagreb)
France (☎ 01 40 72 24 24; ambasadapariz@wanadoo.fr; 54 rue Faisanderie, 75116 Paris)
Germany (☎ 030-895 77 00; info@botschaft-smg.de; Taubert Strasse 18, Berlin D-14193)
Hungary (☎ 1-322 9838; ambjubp@mail.datanet.hu; Dozsa Gyorgy ut 92/b, Budapest H-1068)
Netherlands (☎ 070-363 23 97; yuambanl@bart.nl; Groot Hertoginnelaan 30, The Hague 2517 EG)
Romania (☎ 021-211 98 71; ambiug@ines.ro; Calea Dorobantilor 34, Bucharest)
UK (☎ 0207-235 9049; www.yugoslavembassy.org.uk; 28 Belgrave Sq, London, SW1X 8QB)
USA (☎ 202-332 0333; www.yuembusa.org; 2134 Kalorama Rd NW, Washington, DC, 20008)

Embassies & Consulates in Serbia & Montenegro

The following countries have representation in Belgrade:
Albania (Map p274; ☎ 306 6642; Bulevar Mira 25A)
Australia (Map p276-7; ☎ 330 3400; Čika Ljubina 13)
Bosnia and Hercegovina (Map p274; ☎ 329 1277; Milana Tankosića 8)
Bulgaria (Map pp276-7; ☎ 361 3980; Birčaninova 26)
Canada (Map pp276-7; ☎ 306 3000; Kneza Miloša 75)
Croatia (Map pp276-7; ☎ 361 0535; Kneza Miloša 62)
France (Map pp276-7; ☎ 302 3500; Pariska 11)
Germany (Map pp276-7; ☎ 306 4300; Kneza Miloša 74-6)
Hungary (Map pp276-7; ☎ 244 0472; Krunska 72)
Netherlands (Map pp276-7; ☎ 328 2332; Simina 29)
UK (Map pp276-7; ☎ 264 5055; Resavska 46)
USA (Map pp276-7; ☎ 361 9344; Kneza Miloša 50)

FESTIVALS & EVENTS

There's plenty of variety for all tastes. Pop, techno and electronic aficionados from all over Europe flock to Novi Sad's **Exit festival** in July, while those who like beer with their rock will want to sink a few at Belgrade's August **Beer festival**. On a different note there's the famous festival of brass band music (www.guca.co.yu). This crazy festival where the musical energy beats anything from Kusturica's films takes place annually from 1-7 August in Guča near Čačak, a village in southern Serbia. For those who want to hear something different and tap directly into an exhibition of Serbian pride and culture, this is the festival to attend.

GAY & LESBIAN TRAVELLERS

Homosexuality has been legal in Yugoslavia since 1932 (the age of consent for male-male sex is 18 in Serbia but 14 in Montenegro, female-female sex is 14 in both), but significant homophobia has meant that gay and lesbian events and meeting places are very underground. For more information check www.gay-serbia.com.

HOLIDAYS

Public holidays in Serbia and Montenegro include:

New Year 1 January
Orthodox Christmas 7 January
Nation Day 27 April
International Labour Days 1 and 2 May
Victory Day 9 May
Republic Day 29 Nov

Additionally Montenegro has Uprising Day (13 July).

Orthodox churches celebrate Easter between one and five weeks later than other churches.

In Kosovo, 28 November is Flag Day and Easter Monday is a public holiday.

INTERNET RESOURCES

Fruška Gora (www.fruskagora-nat-park.co.yu)
Montenegro Tourist Organisation (www.visit-montenegro.cg.yu)
Serbian Government (www.srbija.sr.gov.yu)
Serbia in Your Hands (www.serbiainyourhands.com)This excellent tourism website offers an increasing amount of information on sights, restaurants and hotels throughout Serbia, plus the lowdown on wildlife, wine, spas and more.
Serbian Tourist Organisation (www.serbia-tourism.org)

LANGUAGE

Serbian is the common language in Serbia and Montenegro, although in Montenegro some also now refer to the language as Montenegrin. Only Albanian is spoken in Kosovo. Many people know some English and German.

Hungarians in Vojvodina use the Latin alphabet, Montenegrins and Serbs use both Latin and Cyrillic. See the language chapter (p414) for useful phrases and the Cyrillic alphabet.

MAPS

The Freytag & Berndt map *Yugoslavia, Slovenia, Croatia* covers the former republics of Yugoslavia. The *Savezna Republika Jugoslavija Autokarta* map shows the new borders and has some maps of towns too. *Plan Grada Beograd* is a detailed Belgrade city map. The latter two are available free from the Tourist Organisation of Belgrade (p277). M@gic M@p's *Crna Gora* is good for navigating around Montenegro and International Travel Maps' *Kosovo* is a decent topographical map.

MONEY

Montenegro and Kosovo use the euro; Serbia retains the dinar although some hotels may want payment in euros. Some international train journeys may require part payment in dinar and part in euros. **Western Union** (www.westernunion.com) transfers can be made at most banks and major post offices. ATMs accepting Visa, MasterCard and their variants are widespread in major towns. MasterCard, Visa and Diners Club are widely accepted by businesses too. The euro is the favoured hard currency. Many exchange offices in Serbia will readily change these and other hard currencies into dinars and back again when you leave. Look for their large blue diamond signs hanging outside. Some Belgrade banks are installing 24-hour machines for changing foreign notes. A large number of banks cash hard currency travellers cheques – the euro is preferable.

POST

Parcels should be taken unsealed to the main post office for inspection. Allow time to check the post office's repacking and complete the transaction.

You can receive mail, addressed poste restante, in all towns for a small charge.

TELEPHONE & FAX

Press the *i* button on public phones in Serbian and Montenegro for dialling commands in English.

Calls to Serbia to Europe/Australia/North America costs 42/76/76DIN a minute.

Montenegro to Europe/Australia/North America costs €0.90/1.64/1.64 per minute

Kosovo to Europe/Australia/North America costs €0.65/1.42/1.42 per minute.

Some premises do not have land-line telephones but can be contacted through mobile phones. These numbers usually start with 06 or 04.

SERBIA & MONTENEGRO

EMERGENCY NUMBERS

- Ambulance ☎ 94
- Fire service ☎ 93
- Motoring assistance in Belgrade ☎ 987
- Motoring assistance outside Belgrade ☎ 011 9800
- Police ☎ 92

Fax

Faxes can be sent from any large hotel or from post offices. In Serbia it costs 172/236/236DIN per page to Europe/Australia/North America; from Kosovo €2.10/3/3. Faxes can be sent from post offices but take a photocopy as they keep the original.

Phonecards

Phonecards don't give enough time for an international call, so use telephone centres at post offices.

TOURIST INFORMATION

Serbia is getting it together with its tourist offices and top marks go to Belgrade, Novi Sad and Subotica. They have plenty of maps and brochures and their English-speaking staff are a fountain of useful information. Montenegro's facilities, given the tourist potential, are woeful, with little literature and offices only open for short periods of time outside the tourist season. Better are the travel agencies listed in the Montenegro section. Kosovo has a tourist office in Prishtina but its non-English-speaking staff are of little assistance and have no literature. Again, try the travel agencies, but even their knowledge is limited.

TOURS

Ace Cycling & Mountaineering Center (☎ /fax 018-47 287; www.ace-adventurecentre.com; B. Krsmanovica 51/8 Niš) organises guided cycling and walking tours in Serbia.

VISAS

Tourist visas for less than 90 days are not required for citizens of many European countries, Australia, New Zealand, Canada and the USA. The website of the **Ministry of Foreign Affairs** (www.mfa.gov.yu) has details.

If you're not staying at a hotel or in a private home then you have to register with the police within 24 hours of arrival and subsequently on changing address.

WOMEN TRAVELLERS

Other than a cursory interest shown by men towards solo women travellers, travelling is hassle-free and easy. In Muslim areas a few women wear a headscarf but most young women adopt Western fashions.

Dress more conservatively in Muslim areas of Kosovo.

TRANSPORT IN SERBIA & MONTENEGRO

This section deals with travel into or out of Serbia and Montenegro, and includes getting around information. For details of travel within Western Balkans, see p399.

GETTING THERE & AWAY
Air

Serbia and Montenegro is well served by regional airlines that pick up at intercontinental hubs. Travellers from Australasia can fly to Dubai and pick up a JAT flight to Belgrade or with Lufthansa via Frankfurt or Austrian Air via Vienna. Travellers from North America would pick up regional connecting flights in London or Frankfurt. As of yet none of the European discount airlines flies to or near Belgrade.

Belgrade's **Surčin Airport** (☎ 011-601 424, 011-601 431; www.airport-belgrade.co.yu) handles the majority of international flights. The following office telephone numbers are in Belgrade (area code ☎ 011).

Aeroflot (airline code SU; ☎ 323 5814; www.aeroflot .com; hub Moscow Sheremetyevo)

Air France (airline code AF; ☎ 638 378; www.airfrance .com; hub Paris Charles de Gaulle)

Air India (airline code AI; ☎ 133 551; www.airindia .com; hub New Delhi, Mumbai)

Alitalia (airline code AZ; ☎ 324 5344; www.alitalia.com; hub Rome)

Austrian Airlines (airline ode OS; ☎ 324 8077; www .aua.com; hub Vienna)

British Airways (airline code BA; ☎ 328 1303; www .britishairways.com; hub London Heathrow)

ČSA (Czech Airlines; airline code OK; ☎ 361 4592; www .csa.cz; hub Prague)

Emirates (airline code EK; ☎ 624 435; www.ekgroup .com; hub Dubai)

DEPARTURE TAX

Departure tax for domestic/international flights is 500/1000DIN, although this may be covered in the price of your ticket. A €15 departure tax is charged at Podgorica airport.

JAT (airline code JU; ☎ 311 2123; www.jat.com; hub Belgrade)

KLM (airline code KL; ☎ 328 2747; www.klm.com; hub Amsterdam)

LOT Polish Airlines (airline code LOT; ☎ 324 8892; www.lot.com; hub Warsaw)

Lufthansa (airline code LH; ☎ 322 4975; www.lufthansa.com; hub Frnakfurt)

Macedonian Airlines (MAT; airline code IN; ☎ 187 123; www.mat.com.mk; hub Skopje)

Malév (Hungarian Airlines; airline code MA; ☎ 626 377; www.malev.hu; hub Budapest)

Montenegro Airlines (airline code YM; ☎ 262 1122; www.montenegro-airlines.com; hub Podgorica)

Olympic Airways (airline code OA; ☎ 322 6800; www.olympic-airways.gr; hub Athens)

Royal Jordanian (airline code RJ; ☎ 645 555; www.rja.com.jo; hub Amman)

Swiss International Air Lines (airline code LX; ☎ 3030 140; www.swiss.com; hub Zurich)

Turkish Airlines (airline code TK; ☎ 323 2561; www.turkishairlines.com; hub Istanbul)

AIRLINES SERVING PODGORICA & TIVAT IN MONTENEGRO

Charter and other airlines fly into **Podgorica** (☎ 081-242 912) and **Tivat** (☎ 082-671 894) airports in Montenegro. The following office telephone numbers are in Podgorica (area code ☎ 081).

Adria Airlines (airline code JP; ☎ 310 000; www.adria-alrways.com, hub Ljubljana) **JAT** (airline code JU; ☎ 230 027; www.jat.com; hub Belgrade)

Malév (Hungarian Airlines; airline code MA; ☎ 626 377; www.malev.hu; hub Budapest)

Montenegro Airlines (airline code YM; ☎ 664 411; www.montenegro-airlines.cg.yu; hub Podgorica)

AIRLINES SERVING PRISHTINA IN KOSOVO

Kosovo's airport is at **Prishtina** (☎ 038-548 430). The following office telephone numbers are in Prishtina (area code ☎ 038).

Adria Airlines (airline code JP; ☎ 548 437; www.adria-airways.com; hub Ljubljana)

Austrian Airlines (airline code OS; ☎ 548 661; www.aua.com; hub Vienna)

British Airways (airline code BA; ☎ 548 661; www.britishairways.com; hub London Heathrow)

Kosova Airlines (airline code KOS; ☎ 249 158; www.kosovaairlines.com; hub Prishtina)

Malév (Hungarian Airlines; airline code MA; ☎ 535 535; www.malev.hu; hub Budapest)

Turkish Airlines (airline code TK; ☎ 502 052; www.turkishairlines.com; hub Istanbul)

Land

You can easily enter Serbia and Montenegro by land from any of its neighbours. Make sure you are registered with the police (it is the duty of your hotel/host to do this) and have the registration paper(s) with you when leaving the country.

Decent maps of the region such as the Freytag & Berndt map (see p323) and the National Tourist Organisation of Serbia brochure *In Serbia by Car* show borders.

BICYCLE

There are no problems bringing a bicycle into the country, but remember it's hilly. There are not many cyclists here, so road-users are not cycle savvy.

BORDER CROSSINGS
Albania

From Kosovo you can cross at Qafe Prušit, Đakovica and Vrbnica. From Montenegro, cross at Božaj by Lake Skadar.

Bosnia & Hercegovina

Border crossings are at Kotroman, Sremska Rača, Badovinci, Trbušnica, and Zvornik.

Croatia

Crossing points are at Bijela, Batrovci, Bačka Palanka, Bogojevo, Apatin, Bezdan, and Šid.

Macedonia

There are crossings at Preševo and Đeneral Janković.

BUS

There's a well-developed bus service to Western Europe and Turkey. Contact any of the travel agencies mentioned in this chapter for information. Sample routes from Belgrade are Malmö in Sweden (€103, 34 hours, Friday), Munich (€55, 17 hours, daily), Paris (€97, 28 hours, Monday, Tuesday, Thursday and Friday) and Zurich (€87, 23 hours, Saturday).

CAR & MOTORCYCLE

Drivers need an International Driving Permit and vehicles need Green Card insurance, or insurance (from €80 a month) must be bought at the border. See also right.

TRAIN

All international rail connections out of Serbia originate in Belgrade with most calling at Novi Sad and Subotica heading north and west, and at Niš going east. Montenegro and Kosovo have no international connections. Curiously, tickets for international trains have to be paid for in euros, but sleeper supplements have to be paid for in DIN. Sample services from Belgrade are:

Dest	Frequency	Duration	Cost (€)	Sleeper (DIN)
Bucharest	daily	14hr	27	680
Budapest	daily	7hr	37	980
Istanbul	daily	26hr	44	360*
Ljubljana	daily	10hr	28	810
Moscow	daily	50hr	125	1520
Munich	daily	17hr	87	870
Sofia	daily	11hr	12	360
Thessaloniki	daily	16hr	30	680
Vienna	daily	11hr	65	980
Zagreb	daily	7hr	18	870

* to Thessaloniki only

Sea

A ferry service operates between Bar and Italy (see p314).

GETTING AROUND

Air

AIRLINES IN SERBIA & MONTENEGRO

JAT and Montenegro Airlines fly daily between Belgrade and Podgorica or Tivat. For Belgrade and Podgorica details see p324.

Bicycle

Cyclists are rare on the country's roads, even in the cities, and there are no special provisions. For cycling tours see p324.

Bus

The bus service is extensive and reliable and covers all of Serbia and Montenegro and Kosovo. Buses are rarely full and there's usually a row available for everyone; luggage carried below is charged at 50DIN/€0.50 per piece.

RESERVATIONS

Reservations are only worthwhile for international buses, at holiday times and where long-distance journeys are infrequent.

Car & Motorcycle

Independent travel by car or motorcycle is an ideal way to gad about and discover the country.

Traffic police are everywhere, so stick to speed limits: 120km/h on motorways, 100km/h on dual carriageways, 80km/h on main roads and 60km/h in urban areas. Carry an International Driving Permit, available from your home motoring organisation.

Serbia and Montenegro has right-hand drive, seat belts must be worn and the drink-driving limit is .05.

AUTOMOBILE ASSOCIATIONS

The **Auto-Moto Savez Serbia & Montenegro** (Serbia & Montenegro Automotive Association; Map p274; ☎ 011 9800; www.amsj.co.yu; Ruzveltova 18, Belgrade) web page has details on road conditions, tolls, insurance and petrol prices.

FUEL & SPARE PARTS

Filling up is no problem in any medium-sized town but don't leave it until the last drop as there are few late-night petrol stations. Spare parts for major brands (check with your dealer before you travel) will be no problem in the cities, and mechanics are available everywhere for simple repairs.

HIRE

There are plenty of hire companies; **VIP** (☎ 011-690 107), **Hertz** (☎ 011-600 634) and **Europcar** (☎ 011-601 555) all have offices at Belgrade airport. The typical cost of small-car hire in Serbia is €45 a day.

Car hire is cheaper in Montenegro with a small car costing from €30 a day from **Meridian Rent a Car** (☎ 081-234 944, 069 316 66) in Podgorica, Budva and Bar.

Train

Jugoslovenske Železnice (JŽ; www.yurail.co.yu in Serbian) provides adequate railway services from Belgrade serving Novi Sad, Subotica and the highly scenic line down to Bar; the website gives timetable details. Trains are slower than buses due to lack of infrastructure investment.

No trains run in Kosovo at present.

Slovenia

DAMIEN SIMONIS

Slovenia

Imagine alpine meadows crisscrossed with quiet country lanes. Imagine baroque steeples rising over stone villages. Picture soaring snow-tipped peaks presiding over virgin forests and turquoise lakes. Switzerland? No, Slovenia, the tiny republic of immense natural beauty squeezed between Croatia, Italy, Austria and Hungary.

With more than half its interior blanketed with forests, Slovenia is one of the world's greenest countries and the sporty Slovenes take full advantage of their bounty. For adrenaline junkies, the rugged interior offers canyoning, white-water rafting, rock climbing, skiing and anything else you can think of doing on mountains. Swing down to the coast and scuba dive to WWII wrecks. Or burrow into one of Slovenia's majestic caves at Postojna or Škocjan.

The urban landscape is equally varied. Slovenia's capital, Ljubljana, is young and dynamic with museums, galleries, a graceful baroque Old Town and the countercultural Metelkova centre. The country's architectural heritage includes Venetian fishing ports, Romanesque churches and a wealth of turreted castles that evoke the days of princes and peasants.

As you relax in a thermal spa or sample one of Slovenia's wines in a local café, strike up a conversation with a Slovene. Genial, multilingual and hardworking, Slovenes are sometimes called the Swiss of the Balkans but they have never considered themselves part of that volatile region. Even as war was engulfing its neighbours to the east, Slovenes worked to build their economy and solidify their links to Europe. With Slovenia's thoroughly European heart and soul, it was only natural for the political arrangements to follow. In 2004 Slovenia became the first country of the former Yugoslavia to attain membership in the EU.

FAST FACTS

- **Area** 20,256 sq km
- **Capital** Ljubljana
- **Currency** tolar (SIT); €1 = 239SIT;
  US$1 = 200SIT; UK£1 = 349SIT; A$1 = 150SIT;
  ¥100 = 176SIT; NZ$1 = 131SIT
- **Famous for** mountain sports, Lipizzaner horses, plonky Ljutomer riesling
- **Key phrases** dober dan (good day); pozdravljen (hi); nasvidenje (goodbye); hvala (thanks); oprostite (sorry)
- **Official language** Slovene; English, Italian and German are widely understood
- **Population** 2 million
- **Telephone codes** country code ☎ 386; international access code ☎ 00; ☎ toll free 080
- **Visas** not required for most; see p381 for details

HIGHLIGHTS

- The glory days of Venice echoing in the old streets of **Piran** (p366)
- The Julian Alps' glimmering lakes of **Bled** (p351) and **Bohinj** (p356)
- Gliding down the icy blue **Soča River** (p359) in a kayak or raft
- Ljubljana's stately Old Town and its wild side, **Metelkova** (p343).
- The **Škocjan Caves** (p363), recalling both *The Lord of the Rings* and the *Ring Cycle*

ITINERARIES

- **Three days** Enjoy the zesty street life and nightlife of Ljubljana then zip up to Bled to relax by the lake.
- **One week** From Ljubljana and Bled, fan out to the Soča Valley making stops in the Bohinj Valley. Descend to the coast for a look at Piran and the majestic Škocjan Caves.
- **Two weeks** As above, adding some extreme sports in Bovec or plenty of hiking around Bohinj.

CLIMATE & WHEN TO GO

The ski season lasts from December to March, though avalanche risks may keep the Vršič Pass closed until May. Lake Bled freezes over in winter, but the short coastline has a contrastingly mild, typically Mediterranean climate. April is often wet, but this means accommodation is cheaper and the vivid blossom-dappled forests are at their scenic best. May and June are warmer, but during these months hotel prices start to rise, peaking in August, when rooms can be hard to find at any price. Nonetheless, midsummer is the only time of year that cheap student hostels are open. Moving into autumn, warm September days are calm and ideal for hiking and climbing, while October can be damp.

See Climate Charts p388.

HISTORY
The Romans

In 181 BC the Romans established the colony of Aquileia (Oglej in Slovene) on the Gulf of Trieste and then went on to annex the rest of Slovenia and Istria. After subdividing the area into provinces and establishing military bases in each one, they built an extensive road system connecting their new settlements. From these bases

---

HOW MUCH?

- **Plain ajdovi žganci (buckwheat groats)** 450SIT
- **Bottle of cheap Teran wine** 900SIT to 1200SIT
- **Litre of wine from the winemaker's barrel** 330SIT to 380SIT
- **One day's bicycle hire** 3000SIT
- **One day ski pass** 4900SIT

LONELY PLANET INDEX

- **Litre of petrol** 193SIT to 196SIT
- **1.5-litre bottle of water** 95SIT to 130SIT
- **Half-litre of Laško beer** 165SIT (shop), 330SIT to 450SIT (bar)
- **Souvenir T-shirt** 2700SIT to 3200SIT
- **Street snack (burek)** 350SIT to 450SIT

---

developed the important towns of Emona (Ljubljana), Celeia (Celje) and Poetovio (Ptuj), where reminders of the Roman presence can still be seen.

The Roman Empire and its territories fell to a wave of invasions in the 5th century AD and a period of instability followed. The ancestors of today's Slovenes arrived from the Carpathian Basin in the 6th century and spread outward, settling the Sava, Drava and Mura River valleys, the eastern Alps, the Friulian plain and east as far as Lake Balaton in Hungary. At that time these people were called Sclavi or Sclaveni, as were most Slavs. As a social group they made no class distinctions, but chose a leader – a *župan* (now the word for 'mayor') or *vojvoda* (duke) – in times of great danger.

The Duchy of Carantania

When the Avars failed to take Byzantium in 626, the Alpine Slavs united under their leader Valuk and founded the Duchy of Carantania (Karantanija), the first Slavic state, with its seat at Krn Castle (now Karnburg in Austria).

By the early 8th century, a new class of ennobled commoners *(kosezi)* had emerged, and it was they who publicly elected and crowned the new *knez* (grand duke) on the 'duke's rock' *(knežni kamen)* in the courtyard

SLOVENIA

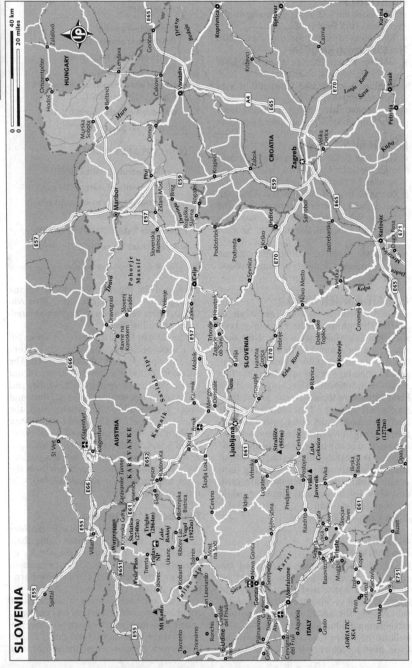

of Krn Castle. Such a democratic process was unique in the feudal Europe of the early Middle Ages.

The Carinthian Kingdom

In 748 the Frankish empire of the Carolingians incorporated Carantania as a vassal state called Carinthia and began converting the population to Christianity. When the Frankish state collapsed, a Carinthian prince named Kocelj established a short-lived independent Slovenian 'kingdom' (869–74) in Lower Pannonia. It was here that calls for a Slavic archdiocese were first heard.

In about 900, the Magyars subjugated the Slovenian regions of Lower Pannonia and along the Sava, cutting them off from Carinthia. It wasn't until 955 that they were stopped by forces under King Otto I at Augsburg who introduced German control of the region.

The Germans decided to reestablish Carinthia, dividing the area into half a dozen border counties (or marches). Control of the land was shared between the nobility and various church dioceses and German gentry were settled on it. The population remained essentially Slovenian, however, and it was largely due to intensive educational and pastoral work by the clergy that the Slovenian identity was preserved.

Early Habsburg Rule

In the early Middle Ages, the Habsburgs were just one of many German aristocratic families struggling for hegemony on Slovenian soil, but as dynasties intermarried or died out the Habsburgs consolidated their power. Between the late 13th and early 16th centuries, almost all of the lands inhabited by the Slovenes passed into Habsburg hands except for Istria and the Littoral, which were controlled by Venice, and parts of Prekmurje, which belonged to the Hungarian crown.

Attacks by the Ottomans on southeastern Europe began in 1408 and continued for more than two and a half centuries; by the start of the 16th century, thousands of Slovenes had been killed or taken prisoner. The assaults helped to radicalise landless peasants and labourers who were required to raise their own defences *and* continue to pay tribute and work for their feudal

lords. More than a hundred peasant uprisings and revolts occurred between the 14th and 19th centuries, but they reached their peak between 1478 and 1573. None of the revolts succeeded, however.

In the early 18th century, Habsburg economic decline brought on by a series of wars was reversed, and Empress Maria Theresa (1740–80) introduced a series of reforms that awarded limited self-government, greater religious freedom and the introduction of obligatory schooling. As a result, agricultural output improved, manufacturing intensified and shipping from Austria's main port at Trieste increased substantially. The reforms also produced a flowering of the arts and letters in Slovenia. The playwright and historian Anton Tomaž Linhart and the poet and journalist Valentin Vodnik produced their finest and most influential works at this time.

Napoleon & the Illyrian Provinces

The French Revolution of 1789 convinced the Austrian rulers that the reform movement should be nipped in the bud, and a period of reaction began that continued until the Revolution of 1848. Napoleon, after being defeated by the Austrians at Wagram in 1809, decided to cut the Habsburg empire off from the Adriatic. To do so he created six 'Illyrian Provinces' from Slovenian and Croatian regions and made Ljubljana the capital.

Although the Illyrian Provinces lasted only from 1809 to 1813, France instituted a number of reforms, including equality before the law and the use of Slovene in primary and lower secondary schools and in public offices. Most importantly, the progressive influence of the French Revolution brought the issue of national awakening to the Slovenian political arena for the first time.

Return to Austria

Austrian rule, restored in 1814, was now guided by the iron fist of Prince Clemens von Metternich. He immediately reinstituted the Austrian feudal system and attempted to suppress every national movement from the time of the Congress of Vienna (1815) to the Revolution of 1848. But the process of change had already started in Slovenia.

SLOVENIA

In 1848 Slovenian intellectuals drew up their first national political program under the banner of Zedinjena Slovenija (United Slovenia). In essence it called for the unification of all historic Slovenian regions within an autonomous unit of the Austrian monarchy, the use of Slovene in education and the establishment of a local university. The demands were rejected as they would have required the reorganisation of the empire along ethnic lines.

The only tangible results for Slovenes in the 1848 Austrian constitution were that laws would henceforth be published in Slovene and that the Carniolan (and thus Slovenian) flag should be three horizontal stripes of white, blue and red. Towards the end of the 19th century a new idea emerged. The distinguished Croatian bishop Josip Strossmayer argued that the southern Slavs should unite and demand greater autonomy within the Austro-Hungarian empire.

WWI & the Kingdom of Serbs, Croats & Slovenes

Although Slovenian political parties generally tended to remain faithful to Austria-Hungary, the heavy loss of life and the destruction of property during WWI lent support to demands for greater autonomy. Finally, in 1918, Slovenes, Croats and Serbs banded together and declared the independent Kingdom of Serbs, Croats and Slovenes, under Serbian King Peter I.

The kingdom was dominated by the notion of Yugoslav ('south Slav') unity, Serbian control and imperialistic pressure from Italy. Slovenia was reduced to little more than a province in this centralist kingdom, although it did enjoy cultural and linguistic autonomy.

In 1929 Peter I's son King Alexander seized absolute power, abolished the constitution and proclaimed the Kingdom of Yugoslavia. But the king was assassinated five years later during an official visit to France, and his cousin, Prince Paul, was named regent.

WWII & the Partisan Struggle

Prince Paul, under pressure from Berlin and Rome, signed a treaty with the Axis powers in March 1941. He was overthrown in a coup and the new king (the son of Alexander I) attempted neutrality, but German armies invaded and occupied Yugoslavia in April. Slovenia was split up among Germany, Italy and Hungary.

Slovenian communists and other left-wing groups quickly formed a Liberation Front (Osvobodilne Fronte; OF), and the people took up arms for the first time since the peasant uprisings. The OF, dedicated to the principles of a united Slovenia in a Yugoslav republic, joined the all-Yugoslav Partisan army of the KPJ (Communist Party of Slovenia) and its secretary-general Josip Broz 'Tito'. The Partisans received assistance from the Allies and were the most organised and successful of any resistance movement during WWII.

After Italy capitulated in 1943, the anti-OF Slovenian Domobranci (Home Guards) were active in Primorska and, in a bid to prevent the communists from gaining political control in liberated areas, began supporting the Germans. Despite this and other support the Germans were forced to evacuate Belgrade in 1944, losing control of the Kingdom of Croats, Serbs & Slovenes (later Yugoslavia).

Slovenia was liberated in May 1945, and as many as 12,000 Domobranci and anti-communist civilians were sent back to Slovenia from refugee camps in Austria. Most of them were executed by the communists over the next two months.

Postwar Division

Of immediate concern to Slovenia after the war was the status of liberated areas along the Adriatic, especially Trieste. A peace treaty signed in Paris in 1947 put Trieste and its surrounds under Anglo-American administration (Zone A) and the Koper and Buje (Istria) areas under Yugoslav control in Zone B.

In 1954 Zone A (with both its Italian and ethnic Slovenian populations) became the Italian province of Trieste. Koper and a 47km stretch of coast later went to Slovenia, and Istria to Croatia.

Tito & Socialist Yugoslavia

Tito moved quickly after the war to consolidate his power under the communist banner. It soon became obvious that Slovenia's rights to self-determination and autonomy would be very limited and that Serbian domination from Belgrade would continue as it did under the Kingdom of Yugoslavia.

Tito had distanced himself from the Soviet Union as early as 1948, but initially remained committed to creating a communist state. It didn't work. By the 1960s Tito was forced to introduce elements of a market economy. He also allowed greater freedom of movement over the objection of Communist Party officials.

A new constitution in 1974 gave the Yugoslav republics more independence (and autonomy to the ethnic Albanian province of Kosovo in Serbia); by the end of the decade Slovenia was the most advanced republic in the federation.

Crisis, Renewal & Change

The death of Tito and the economic decline in Yugoslavia in the early 1980s led to interethnic tensions, particularly when Serbia proposed scrapping elements of the 1974 constitution in favour of more uniformity of the state. This was anathema to Slovenes, who saw themselves under threat. Murmurings of independence appeared in influential magazines.

In June 1988 three Slovenian journalists working for the Mladina (Youth) weekly and a junior army officer who had given away 'military secrets' were tried by a military court and sentenced to prison. Mass demonstrations were held throughout the country in protest.

In the spring of 1989 the new opposition parties published the May Declaration demanding a sovereign state for Slovenes based on democracy and respect for human rights. In September the Slovenian parliament amended the constitution to legalise management of its own resources and peacetime command of the armed forces. In April 1990 Slovenia became the first Yugoslav republic to hold free elections. A coalition of seven opposition parties won 55% of the vote, and Kučan was elected 'president of the presidency'.

On 23 December 1990, 88.5% of the Slovenian electorate voted for an independent republic – effective within six months. The presidency of the Yugoslav Federation in Belgrade labelled the move secessionist and anticonstitutional. Serbia then proceeded to raid the Yugoslav monetary system and misappropriated almost the entire monetary issue planned for Yugoslavia in 1991 – US$2 billion. The Slovenian government began stockpiling weapons, and on 25 June 1991 Slovenia pulled out of the Yugoslav Federation altogether. 'This evening dreams are allowed,' President Kučan told the jubilant crowd in Ljubljana's Kongresni trg the following evening. 'Tomorrow is a new day.'

And so it was. On 27 June the Yugoslav army began marching on Slovenia but met great resistance from the Territorial Defence Forces, the police and the general population. Within several days, units of the federal army began disintegrating; Belgrade threatened aerial bombardment and total war. Belgrade apparently never expected Slovenia to resist, believing that a show of force would be sufficient. Since no territorial claims or minority issues were involved (unlike other republics in former Yugoslavia), the Yugoslav government agreed on 7 July to a truce brokered by leaders of the European Community (EC). The war had lasted just 10 days and taken the lives of 66 people.

The Road to Europe

To everyone's surprise, Belgrade announced that it would withdraw the federal army from Slovenian soil within three months, and did so on 25 October 1991, less than a month after Slovenia introduced its new currency, the tolar. In late December, Slovenia got a new constitution that provided for a parliamentary system of government. The head of state, the president, is elected directly for a maximum of two five-year terms. Milan Kučan, the nation's most popular politician, held that role from independence until October 2000, when Prime Minister Janez Drnovšek was elected. Executive power is vested in the prime minister – Janez Janša at the time of writing – and his 17-member cabinet.

The EC formally recognised Slovenia on 15 January 1992, and it was admitted to the UN four months later as the 176th member-state.

Slovenia began negotiations for entry into the EU in 1998 and, along with nine other countries, was invited to join the union four years later. In a referendum held in March 2003, an overwhelming 89.6% of the electorate voted in favour of Slovenia's joining the EU, and 66% approved its membership in NATO. Slovenia became a full member of the EU in May 2004.

PEOPLE

Slovenes are ethnically Slavic, typically multilingual, friendly without being pushy, and miraculously manage to combine a Germanic work ethic with an easy-going, Mediterranean *joie de vivre*.

Almost 90% of the population is ethnic Slovene, with the remainder being Croat, Serbian and Bosnian minorities and small, long-term enclaves of Italians and Hungarians. Although always a relatively homogeneous population, the new government of Slovenia took no chances after its independence, allegedly 'erasing' up to 130,000 nonethnic Slovenes from public records. The newly nonexistent found it impossible to get passports, health insurance and state benefits. Bowing to EU pressure, the government passed a law in 1999 allowing the victims of 'administrative cleansing'

to apply for citizenship. Only 14,000 applied. Some were unaware of the law; some couldn't get their documents together to meet the tough deadline; others had simply given up and left the country.

RELIGION

Constitutionally, Slovenes are left free to choose (and not obliged to publicly declare) their religion. A 2003 survey estimated that 67.9% consider themselves at least nominally Catholic, 26% atheist or agnostic, 2.3% Orthodox Christian and 1.2% Muslim. Although Sundays remain 'holy' (ie shops close), many locals prefer to use their uncluttered weekends to find spirituality through mountain sports rather than by churchbound worship.

ARTS
Architecture

Fine examples of Romanesque architecture can be found in many parts of Slovenia,

---

SLAVENAKIA

Let's get one thing straight. We are talking about Slovenia (formerly attached to ex-Yugoslavia) not Slovakia (formerly attached to the Czech Republic) and certainly not Slavonia (now attached to Croatia). First Slovenia declared independence, then Slavonia descended into war, then Slovakia separated from Czechoslovakia. Confusion has reigned ever since. We won't name names but a certain US presidential candidate in 2000 mixed up Slovenia and Slovakia, a certain Dutch diplomat visited Slavonia and lamented war-torn Slovenia, a certain major German weekly extolled Czech spas in Slovenia and a certain major US daily moved Slovakia into Slovenia's map position on the Adriatic. Reports are that no less than 600 tons of mail addressed to Slovakia ends up in Slovenia. Or maybe Slavonia. Since Slovenes are understandably sensitive about this issue, we would like to highlight the major differences.

	Slovenia	Slovakia	Slavonia
Capital	Ljubljana	Bratislava	Zagreb, Croatia
Official language	Slovene (Slavic roots)	Slovak (Slavic roots)	Croatian (Slavic roots)
Call them	Slovenes	Slovaks	Croatians
Borders	Austria & Italy	Austria & Hungary	on Croatia's eastern border with Hungary, Serbia & Bosnia & Hercegovina
Mountaineering	in the Julian Alps	in the High Tatra	no mountaineering, no mountains
Menus include	trout	trout & carp	carp
Independence	after tense 10-day standoff	after genteel divorce	part of independent Croatia after violent convulsion & ethnic cleansing
Part of EU	as of 2004	as of 2004	if & when Croatia is accepted

including the churches at Stična Abbey and at Podsreda Castle.

Much Gothic architecture in Slovenia is of the late period; the earthquake of 1511 took care of many buildings erected before then (although Koper's Venetian Gothic Loggia and Praetorian Palace date back a century earlier). Renaissance architecture is mostly limited to civil buildings (eg the town houses in Škofja Loka and Kranj).

Italian-influenced baroque of the 17th and 18th centuries abounds in Slovenia, particularly in Ljubljana (eg the Cathedral of St Nicholas). Classicism prevailed in architecture here in the first half of the 19th century; the Tempel pavilion in Rogaška Slatina is a good example.

The turn of the 20th century was when the secessionist (or Art Nouveau) architects Maks Fabiani and Ivan Vurnik began changing the face of Ljubljana after the devastating earthquake of 1895. But no architect has had a greater impact on his city or nation than Jože Plečnik (1872–1957), who cut his professional teeth working on Prague's Hradčany Castle. Many of Ljubljana's most characteristic features, including the Park Tivoli and Ljubljana's idiosyncratic recurring pyramid motifs, were his inspired design.

Literature

Far and away Slovenia's best-loved writer is romantic poet France Prešeren (1800–49), whose statue commands old Ljubljana's central square, Prešernov trg. Prešeren's patriotic yet humanistic verse was a driving force in raising Slovene national consciousness. Fittingly a stanza of his poem Zdravljica (The Toast) is now the national anthem. It calls for neighbourliness and an end to war, a very marked contrast to the enemy confounding sentiment of Britain's anthem. Visit www.preseren.net/ang for English translations of this and other works by Prešeren.

In the latter half of the 19th century, Fran Levstik (1831–87) brought the writing and interpretation of oral folk tales to new heights with his Martin Krpan, legends about the eponymous larger-than-life hero of the Bloke Plateau in Notranjska. But it was Josip Jurčič (1844–81) who published the first full-length novel in Slovene, Deseti Brat (The 10th Brother, 1866).

The period from the turn of the 20th century up to WWII is dominated by two men who single-handedly introduced modernism into Slovenian literature: the poet Oton Župančič (1878–1949) and the novelist and playwright Ivan Cankar (1876–1918). The latter has been called 'the outstanding master of Slovenian prose'. His works, notably Hiša Marije Pomočnice (The Ward of Our Lady of Mercy) and Hlapec Jernej in Njegova Pravica (The Bailiff Yerney and His Rights), influenced a generation of young writers.

Slovenian literature immediately before and after WWII was influenced by socialist realism and the Partisan struggle, as exemplified by the novels of Prežihov Voranc (1893–1950). Since then, Slovenia has tended to follow Western European trends: late expressionism, symbolism (poetry by Edvard Kocbek, 1904–81) and existentialism (novels by Vitomil Zupan, 1914–87, and the drama of Gregor Strniša, 1930–87). Contemporary writers and poets making use of avant-garde techniques include Drago Jančar (1948–), Tomaž Šalamun (1941–) and Kajetan Kovič (1931–).

Music

The conversion of the Slavs to Christianity from the 8th century brought the development of choral singing – the oldest Slovenian spiritual song dates from 1440 – in churches and monasteries. Baroque music had gone out of fashion by the time the Filharmonija was founded in Ljubljana in 1701, and classicist forms had become all the rage. Belin, the first Slovenian opera, was written by Jakob Francisek Zupan in 1780, and Janez Novak composed classicist music for a comedy written by Slovenia's first playwright, Anton Tomaž Linhart. The 19th-century romantics like Benjamin Ipavec, Fran Gerbič and Anton Foerster incorporated traditional Slovenian elements into their music as a way of expressing their nationalism. Perhaps Slovenia's best-known composer was Hugo Wolf (1860–1903), born in Slovenj Gradec.

Slovenian music between the wars is best represented by the expressionist Marij Kogoj and the modernist Slavko Osterc. Contemporary composers whose reputations go well beyond the borders of Slovenia include Primož Ramovš, Marjan Kozina, Lojze Lebič and the ultramodernist Vinko Globokar, who lives in Paris. Opera buffs won't want to miss out on the chance to hear Marjana Lipovšek, the country's foremost mezzo-soprano.

Popular music runs the gamut from Slovenian *chanson* (song) and folk to jazz and mainstream polka. However, it was punk music in the late 1970s and early 1980s that put Slovenia on the world stage. The most celebrated groups were Pankrti, Borghesia and Laibach, and they were imitated throughout Eastern Europe. (Laibach's leader, Tomaž Hostnik, died tragically in 1983 when he hanged himself from a *kozolec*, the traditional Slovenian hayrack.) The most popular rock band in Slovenia at present is Siddharta, which managed to fill Ljubljana's 30,000-seat Central Stadium – 1.5% of the national population! – in September 2003.

Folk music *(ljudska glasba)* in Slovenia has developed independently from other forms of music over the centuries. Traditional folk instruments include the *frajtonarica* (button accordion), *cymbalom* (a curious stringed instrument played with sticks), zither, *zvegla* (wooden cross flute), *okarina* (a clay flute), *šurle* (Istrian double flute), *trstenke* (reed pipes), Jew's harp, *lončeni bajs* (earthenware bass) and *brač* (eight-string guitar).

One of the best commercial folk groups in Slovenia is Katice. Another group definitely worth checking out is Katalena, who play traditional Slovene music with a modern twist. Brina & String.si combine the folk vocalist Brina Vogelnik-Saje with the world-music five-man String.si band. Šukar plays traditional Balkan Roma (Gypsy) music. Terra Folk is the quintessential world-music band.

Visual Arts

Examples of Romanesque fine art are rare in Slovenia, surviving only in illuminated manuscripts. Gothic painting and sculpture is another matter, however, with excellent works at Bohinj. Important painters of this time were Johannes de Laibaco (John of Ljubljana); Jernej of Loka, who worked mostly around Škofja Loka near Kranj; and Johannes Aquila of Radgona.

For baroque sculpture, look at the work of Francesco Robba in Ljubljana (Robba fountain in Mestni trg). Fortunat Bergant, who painted the Stations of the Cross in the church at Stična Abbey, was a master of baroque painting.

Classicism prevailed in Slovenian art in the first half of the 19th century in the works of the painter Franc Kavčič and the romantic portraits and landscapes of Josip Tominc and Matevž Langus. Realism arrived in the second half of the century in the work of artists like Ivana Kobilca, Jurij Šubic and Anton Ažbe. The most important painters of that time, however, were impressionists Rihard Jakopič, Matija Jama, Ivan Grohar and Matej Sternen, who exhibited together in Ljubljana in 1900.

In the 20th century, the expressionist school of Božidar Jakac and the brothers France and Tone Kralj gave way to the so-called Club of Independents (the painters Zoran Mušič, Maksim Sedej and France Mihelič) and later the sculptors Alojzij Gangl, Franc Berneker, Jakob Savinšek and Lojze Dolinar. The last two would later create 'masterpieces' of socialist realism under Tito without losing their credibility or (sometimes) their artistic sensibilities. Favourite artists of recent years include Janez Bernik, Rudi Španzel (who designed the tolar notes now in circulation) and Jože Tisnikar from Slovenj Gradec.

ENVIRONMENT
The Land

Slovenia has a surface area of only 20,273 sq km. It borders Austria to the north and Croatia to the south and southeast. Much shorter frontiers are shared with Italy to the west and Hungary to the northeast.

There are basically four topographical regions. The Alps, including the Julian Alps, the Kamnik-Savinja Alps, the Karavanke chain and the Pohorje Massif, are to the north and northeast. Spreading across their entire southern side are the pre-Alpine hills of Idrija, Cerkno, Škofja Loka and Posavje. The Dinaric karst lies below the hills and encompasses the 'true' or 'original' Karst plateau between Ljubljana and the Italian border. The Slovenian littoral follows 47km of coastline along the Adriatic Sea, and the essentially flat Pannonian plain spreads to the east and northeast.

Much of the interior of Slovenia is drained by the Sava (221km) and Drava (144km) Rivers, both of which flow southeastward and empty into the Danube. Other important rivers are the Soča to the west, which flows into the Adriatic; the Mura in the northeast; the Krka to the southeast; and the Kolpa, which forms part of the southeastern border with Croatia. There are several 'intermittent' rivers (eg the Unica, Pivka and Reka), which disappear into karst caves and potholes, only to resurface elsewhere under different names. Slovenia's largest natural lakes are Cerknica, which is dry for part of the year, and Bohinj.

MAIN REGIONS

Slovenia has eight traditional *krajine* (regions): Gorenjska, Primorska, Notranjska, Dolenjska, Bela Krajina, Štajerska, Koroška and Prekmurje.

Greater Ljubljana, by far the nation's largest city and its capital, is pinched between two groups of hills to the west and east and the non-arable Ljubljana Marsh to the south. Gorenjska, to the north and northwest of the capital, is Slovenia's most mountainous province and contains the country's highest peaks, including Triglav (2864m) and Škrlatica (2740m). Primorska, a very diverse region of hills, valleys, karst and a short coastline on the northern end of the Istrian peninsula, forms the country's western border, and the countryside feels Mediterranean. Notranjska, to the south and southeast of Ljubljana, is an underdeveloped area of forests and karst – Slovenia's 'last frontier'. Dolenjska lies south of the Sava River and has several distinct areas, including the Krka Valley, the hilly Kočevje and also the remote Posavje regions. Bela Krajina, a gentle land of rolling hills, birch groves and folk culture south of Dolenjska, is washed by the Kolpa River. Štajerska – Slovenia's largest region – stretches to the east and northeast and is a land of mountains, rivers, valleys, vineyards and ancient towns. Maribor and Celje are the centres and Slovenia's second- and third-largest cities respectively. Sitting north of Štajerska, little Koroška, with its centre at Slovenj Gradec, is all that is left of the once great historical province of Carinthia. Prekmurje, 'beyond the Mura River' in Slovenia's extreme northeast, is basically a flat plain, although there are hills to the north.

HABITATION

Slovenia is predominantly hilly or mountainous; about 90% of the surface is more than 300m above sea level. Forest, some of it virgin, and woodland cover more than half of the country, making Slovenia the greenest country in Europe outside

Finland and Sweden. Land under agricultural use (pastures, fields, orchards, vineyards) is rapidly diminishing as farms are abandoned' now accounts for less than 25%.

What has mushroomed in recent years is the number of organic farms – from just 41 in 1998 to 1150 in 2002 – raising and processing everything from cereals, dairy products and meat to fruits and vegetables, oils, nuts and wine. Only products inspected and certified by the Ministry of Agriculture, Forestry and Food may bear the government's *ekološki* label or the organic farmers' union logo 'Biodar'.

The population density of Slovenia is just over 98 people per square kilometre, with the urban-rural ratio being almost half and half. The five largest settlements in Slovenia are Ljubljana (269,800), Maribor (116,000), Celje (40,000), Kranj (37,000) and Velenje (26,750).

Wildlife

ANIMALS

Common European animals such as deer, boar, chamois, brown bear, wolves and lynx live in Slovenia in abundance, especially in the Alpine regions and the Kočevje region of Dolenjska. There are also some rare species such as the moor tortoise, cave hedgehog, scarab beetle and various types of dormice. Two species unique to Slovenia are the marbled Soča trout *(Salmo trutta marmoratus)* and *Proteus anguinus*, a blind salamander that lives in karst cave pools. Slovenia also abounds in important habitats for our feathered friends.

PLANTS

Slovenia is home to 3200 plant species, and about 70 of them – many in the Alps – are unique to Slovenia or were first classified here. Triglav National Park is especially rich in endemic flowering plants, including the Triglav 'rose' (actually a pink cinquefoil), the blue Clusi's gentian, yellow hawk's-beard, Julian poppy, Carniola lily and the purple Zois bellflower.

National Parks

About 8% of the countryside is protected under law. Further statutes have already been approved by parliament, and gradually almost a third of the territory will be conservation area of some kind.

At present, there is only one national park – the 83,807-hectare Triglav National Park, which encompasses almost all of the Julian Alps – although proposals have been made to set aside four more: in the Kamnik-Savinja Alps, the Pohorje Massif, the Karst and the Kočevje-Kolpa regions. There are two regional parks (in the Kozjansko region of southeast Štajerska and the area around the Škocjan Caves in Primorska) and 40 designated as country (or 'landscape') parks. These range in size from the 310-hectare park and nature reserve on the Strunjan Peninsula south of Izola in Primorska to the pristine Logarska Dolina (2438 hectares) in Štajerska. There are also about 50 protected nature reserves, including 200 hectares of primeval forest in the Kočevski Rog region of Dolenjska, and more than 600 natural heritage sites, such as tiny Wild Lake (Divje Jezero) near Idrija in Primorska.

Environmental Issues

Although Slovenia is a very 'green' country in both senses of the word, pollution is a problem here, and it is now being tackled by the National Environment Protection Program approved by parliament in 1999 and the Environmental Agency (Agencija za Okolje) set up two years later.

Over the past two decades the biggest concern has been air pollution. Nitrogen oxide emitted by cars, between Gorenjska and the coast in particular, were hurting the pine forests of Notranjska and damaging buildings and outdoor sculptures and other artwork in many historical cities. Sulphur dioxide levels were high in cities and towns like Šoštanj, Trbovlje and Ljubljana where coal was the main fuel. The nation's sole nuclear power plant (at Krško in Dolenjska) provides about 40% of electric power, but half of it is owned by Croatia, and Slovenia plans to stop using it by 2023.

Steps taken to clean up the mess – which include the construction of water-purifying plants, monitoring of those companies discharging waste, installation of filters on power plants and the introduction of gas heating – from 1985 to 2000 saw sulphur dioxide emissions fall by almost 40% and nitrogen oxide levels reduced by 20%.

The government has now shifted its priorities to halt the overuse and pollution of surface waters and the increasing problem of refuse disposal. The Sava, Mura and lower Savinja Rivers are especially vulnerable, rain has washed all sorts of filth dumped in the Karst region underground, and waste carried by the 'disappearing' Unica and Ljubljanica Rivers could threaten the Ljubljana Marsh. Slovenia produces 1.2 million tonnes of waste a year, almost half of it domestic, much of which still ends up in illegal tips.

FOOD & DRINK

It's relatively hard to find archetypal Slovene foods like *žlikrofi* (potato-filled ravioli) in *bakalca* (lamb sauce), *mlinci* (corn-pasta sheets in gravy) and *ajdovi žganci* (buckwheat groats). Inns (*gostilna* or *gostišče*) or restaurants (*restavracija*) more frequently serve pizzas, *rižota* (risotto), *klobasa* (sausage), *zrezek* (cutlet/steak), *golaž* (goulash) and *paprikaš* (stew). Fish (*riba*) meals are sometimes priced by the *dag* (0.1kg). Trout (*postrv*) generally costs half the price of other fish, though grilled squid (*lignji na žaru*) doused in garlic butter is a ubiquitous bargain at 1200SIT to 1500SIT per plate. For favourites popular throughout the region see p36.

Certain better restaurants ask 100SIT to 300SIT for bread/cover charge, and at some of the cheapest it is customary to share tables with other customers when things get busy. Some restaurants have bargain-value four-course *dnevno kosilo* (daily lunch) menus, including *juha* (soup) and *solata* (salad), for 1000SIT to 1600SIT. This can be less than the price of a cheap main course, and usually one option will be vegetarian.

Tap water is safe to drink. Distinctively Slovenian wines (*vino*) include hearty red Teran made from Refošk grapes and the light-red Cviček with a plummy sourness. Slovenes are justly proud of their top vintages. However, cheaper bar-standard 'openwines' (90SIT to 200SIT per glass) are often pure gut-rot. Some fascinating *suho* (dry) whites are made from sweet grapes like Tokaj and Muskat but *sladko* and *polsladko* (sweet/semisweet) wines can be very sugary indeed.

Beer (*piva*), whether *svetlo* (lager) or *temno* (dark), is best on draught (*točeno*).

There are dozens of hard-hitting *žganje* fruit liquors, including *češnovec* (from cherries), *sadjevec* (apples), *brinjevec* (juniper), *hruška* (pears) and *slivovka* (plums). *Na zdravje!* (Cheers!).

LJUBLJANA

☎ 01 / pop 269,800

Inspiring Ljubljana (pronounced 'Loob-li-yana') has a small but charming old core, a vibrant street-café culture, a buzzing student community, and an alternative-lifestyle centre at Metelkova. Viewed from Ljubljana Castle, the less exciting skirt of concrete suburbs is overshadowed by a magnificent alpine horizon, which seems to be almost leaping distance from the ramparts. Although the city may lack big-name attractions, the great galleries, atmospheric bars and varied, accessible nightlife make it tempting to while away weeks here.

HISTORY

If the city really was founded by the Golden Fleece-stealing Argonauts, they left no proof of their sojourn. All that survives of the later Roman city of Emona is a ragged wall on Mirje ul, which was wrecked by the Huns and rebuilt by Slavs. The city took its present form (as 'Laibach') under the Austrian Habsburgs, but it gained regional prominence in 1809, when it became the capital of Napoleon's short-lived Illyrian Provinces. Some fine Art Nouveau buildings filled up the holes left by an 1895 earthquake, and fortunately most later 20th-century development was relegated to the suburbs. The brutal, concrete Trg Republike is a marked exception.

LJUBLJANA IN TWO DAYS

Starting at **Ljubljana Castle** (p342), explore the Old Town surrounding **Prešernov trg** (p343). Museum-hop from the **National Gallery** (p343) to the **Modern Art Museum** (p343). Have a traditional Slovene dinner at **Sokol** (p346) and finish the day at lively **Metelkova** (p343).

Next day stroll through **Park Tivoli** (p344) to the **Museum of Contemporary History** (p344), check out some of the area's art galleries, including the **International Centre of Graphic Arts** (p344), and then return to dine in the Old Town. Alternatively, do the 2pm **Celica Hostel tour** (p345), then hop on the 4.15pm train for a four-hour sunset excursion to **Kamnik** (p370).

ORIENTATION

Prešernov trg is the heart of Ljubljana's delightful, if relatively small, old-town area, which follows the northern and western flanks of castle hill on both sides of the Ljubljanica River. Walk 10 minutes north up Miklošiceva c to the bus and train stations.

Despite being called 'Ljubljana Aerodrome', the airport is actually at Brnik near Kranj, some 23km north of Ljubljana.

Maps

Excellent free maps, some of which show the complete bus network, are available from the various tourist information offices. Even better are Kod-&-Kam maps, sold at bookshops and Tourist Information Centres (TICs).

INFORMATION
Bookshops

Geonavtik (www.geonavtik.com in Slovene; Kongresni trg 1; ☻ 8.30am-8.30pm Mon-Fri, to 3pm Sat) Stocks Lonely Planet guides.

Kod-&-Kam (Trg francoske revolucije 7; ☻ 9am-7pm Mon-Fri, 8am-1pm Sat) Map specialist.

Internet Access

Web connection is available at many hostels and hotels, plus the following:

Kotiček (Bus station; per 10min 100SIT; ☻ 7am-8.30pm)

Napotnica.com (Trg Ajdovščina 1; per 15min 200SIT; ☻ 8am-11pm) Small café in the city centre mini-mall above the Pelican Pub.

Xplorer (Petkovškovo nab 23; per 5min 110SIT, per hr 800SIT; ☻ 9am-11pm Mon-Fri, 1-11pm Sat & Sun) Good connection, plus discounts of 20% before noon, and 10% for students.

Laundry

Washing machines are available, even to nonguests, at the Celica Hostel (see the boxed text, p345) for 1200SIT per load, including powder.

Left Luggage

Bus station (320SIT; ☻ 5am-8.30pm)

Train station (400SIT or €2; ☻ 24hr) Coin lockers on platform No 1.

Medical Services

Klinični Center (☎ 232 30 60; Bohoričeva 9; ☻ 24hr) Emergency clinic.

Zdravstveni Dom Center (☎ 472 37 00; Metelkova 9; ☻ 7.30am-7pm) Non-emergency doctors.

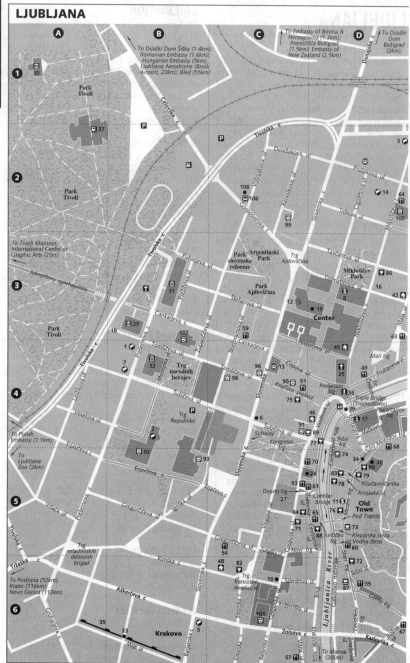

LJUBLJANA

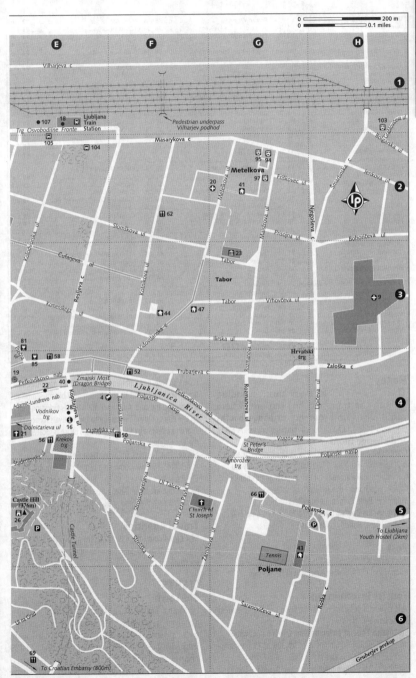

SLOVENIA

Money

There are ATMs at every turn, including in both the train and bus stations, where you'll also find **currency exchange booths** (🕑6am-10pm). Dozens of banks have ATMs and change money:

Gorenska Banka (Dalmatinova 4; 🕑9am-11.30am & 2-5pm Mon-Fri, 8am-11am Sat) Pseudo Art Nouveau furnishings make amends for the travesty of this bank's façade, which mars the architectural splendour of Miklošičev Park. Exchanges travellers cheques.

Ljubljanska Banka (Mestni trg 16; 🕑8am-noon & 2.30-4.30pm) Handily central ATM.

Post

Post office (Slovenska c 32; 🕑7am-8pm Mon-Fri, to 1pm Sat) Holds poste restante mail for 30 days.

Tourist Information

All three TICs have great free maps, themed brochures, tips and events listings.

Ljubljana Tourist Information Centre (TIC; www .ljubljana-tourism.si) Stritarjeva 2 (☎ 306 12 15; 🕑8am-9pm Jun-Sep, to 7pm Oct-May); train station (☎ 433 94 75; 🕑8am-10pm Jun-Sep, to 7pm Oct-May) This

centre's three-day Ljubljana Card (3000SIT) gives free city transport and various discounts, but only big museum fans will recoup the cost. A new service handles ticketing for all the city's cultural events, including festivals, concerts, sporting events and fairs. The branch office is located at the train station.

Slovenian Tourist Information Centre (STIC; ☎ 306 45 75; www.slovenia-tourism.si; Krekov trg 10; 🕑8am-9pm Jun-Sep, to 7pm Oct-May) Internet and bicycle hire available. Also, a free basic course in Slovenian is offered each Wednesday from 5pm to 6.30pm.

Travel Agencies

STA Ljubljana (☎ 439 16 90; Trg Ajdovščina Mall; 🕑10am-1pm & 2-5pm Mon-Fri) Offers discount airfares for students.

SIGHTS
Old Town

Ljubljana Castle (Ljubljanski Grad) crowns an abrupt, wooded hill that forms the city's focal point. It's an architectural mishmash, including early-16th-century walls, a 1489 chapel and a 1970s concrete café. Admission to the central courtyard and some north-facing ramparts is free. However, there are even better 360-degree views from the 19th-century **tower** (adult/student 790/490SIT; ☽ 10am-6pm Tue-Sun), and visits include an excellent 'virtual museum'. Don your 3-D spectacles and 'fly' around the Ljubljana of various historical epochs. Reaching the castle takes about 15 minutes, either on foot or by taking the hourly **tourist tram** (adult/child 550/350SIT; ☽ 9am-9pm) from Prešernov trg.

Prešernov trg is Ljubljana's central square, with the pink **Franciscan Church of the Annunciation** (1660) and a **statue** (1905) of national poet France Prešeren. Furtively observing Prešeren from a fake window on Wolfova is a bust of his unrequited love (and poetic inspiration), Julija Primic (Primicova).

Wander north of the square to admire the fine **Art Nouveau buildings** of Miklošičeva c, including the still-grand Grand Hotel Union Executive (p345). Built in 1905, the hotel was commandeered during WWI for use as the command centre for the Soča/Isonzo-front campaign. Today it retains many elements of Jugendtstil style, including the 'Blue' meeting room, the Unionska Klet cellar-restaurant, and a sweeping interior stone stairway with splendid original brass lantern stands.

South of Prešernov trg you cross the small but much celebrated **Triple Bridge** (Tromostovje). The original 1842 span had two side bridges added in 1931 by Ljubljana's superstar architect Jože Plečnik (who also plonked the curious **Pyramid Gateway** on top of the city's minimal **Roman Walls** at Mirje ul, southwest of the centre). A baroque **Robba Fountain** stands before the Gothic **Town Hall** (1718) in Mestni trg, which leads south into **Stari trg** and **Gornji trg**. These squares wind picturesquely around the castle bluff – delightfully sprinkled with cafés, they are arguably Ljubljana's greatest overall attraction.

East of the Triple Bridge, the 1708 **Cathedral of St Nicholas** (Stolnica; ☽ 8am-noon & 3-7pm) is filled with a riot of splendid frescoes (partly hidden during ongoing renovation at the time of research). To get inside, heave open what appear to be superheavy bronze sculptures, but which, on closer inspection, turn out to be the doors. Behind the cathedral is a lively **market** (☽ closed Sun) selling all kinds of stuff, a Plečnik **colonnade** and the 1901 **Dragon Bridge** (Zmajski Most), a bridge guarded by cute verdigris dragons which have become city mascots.

The grand if rather pompous main building of **Ljubljana University** (Kongresni trg 12) was formerly the regional parliament (1902). The more restrained **Filharmonija** (☎ 241 0800; Kongresni trg 10) dates from an 1898 reconstruction, despite the prominent 1701 plaque. It's home to the Slovenian Philharmonic Orchestra.

City Centre

Of the major galleries and museums west of Slovenska c, the best are the impressive **National Gallery** (☎ 241 54 34; www.ng-slo .si; Prešernova c 24; adult/student 800/600SIT, Sat afternoon free; ☽ 10am-6pm Tue-Sun), and the vibrant but outwardly drab 1940s **Modern Art Museum** (☎ 251 41 06; www.mg-lj.si; Cankarjeva c 15; adult/student 1000/700SIT; ☽ 10am-6pm Tue-Sat, to 1pm Sun).

The **National Museum** (☎ 241 44 04; www.nar muz-lj.si; Muzejska 1; adult/student 1100/800SIT; ☽ 10am-6pm Fri-Wed, 10am-8pm Thu) occupies an elegant 1888 building that was recently renovated. The archaeological collection ranges from prehistoric objects to Slavic jewellery, the 19th-century throne of Archduke Charles and mementos from WWI. Other galleries include a coin collection and an extensive collection of graphics.

Metelkova

An ex-army garrison taken over by squatters after independence, Metelkova is now a somewhat daunting, free-living commune – a miniature version of Copenhagen's Christiania. To really 'feel' Metelkova (which is around 500m east of the train station), visit the nightclubs after midnight (see p348). Even if you're staying there, a free 2pm tour of Metelkova's ultrahip Celica Hostel (p345) is intriguing, especially on Tuesday and Wednesday when you usually get to meet one of the architects. Sadly, as of the time of research, the authorities have announced plans to close some Metelkova structures. Naturally, there are petitions against it. See www.metelkova.org/indexe.htm for the latest developments and to register your protest, if you like.

The **Ethnographic Museum** (☎ 432 54 03; www .etno-muzej.si; Metelkova 2) has a very extensive collection, but was still undergoing renovation at the time of research. Meanwhile, there's a temporary exhibit devoted to ethnographic museums in Europe on the 1st floor and a look at contemporary and folk design on the 2nd floor.

Park Tivoli

You can reach Tivoli, the city's leafy playground laid out in 1813 and measuring 5 sq km, via an underpass from Cankarjeva c. Straight ahead, at the end of **Jakopičevo sprehajališče**, the monumental Jakopič Promenade designed by Plečnik in the 1920s and 30s, is the 17th-century **Tivoli Mansion** (Tivolski Grad), which now contains the **International Centre of Graphic Arts** (Mednarodni Grafični Likovni Center, MGLC; ☎ 241 38 18; www.mglc-lj.si; Pod turnom 3; adult/student 800/400SIT; ☻ 11am-6pm Wed-Sun), with new exhibitions every three months. The centre hosts the International Biennial of Graphic Arts in odd-numbered years (see opposite).

The **Museum of Contemporary History** (Muzej Novejše Zgodovine; ☎ 300 96 10; www.muzej-nz.si; Celovška c 23; adult/child 2-14, student & senior 500/300SIT, free Sun; ☻ 10am-6pm), housed in the 18th-century Cekin Mansion (Cekinov Grad) just northeast of the Tivoli Recreation Centre, traces the history of Slovenia in the 20th century through multimedia. The gloriously baroque **Ceremonial Hall** (Room F) is how the whole mansion once looked. Note the contrast between the sober earnestness of the communist-era Room G and the exuberant, logo-mad commercialism of the neighbouring industrial exhibit in Room H. A portrait of Stalin lies 'discarded' behind the door between the two.

The 45-hectare **Ljubljana Zoo** (Živalski Vrt Ljubljana; ☎ 244 21 88; www.zoo-ljubljana.si in Slovene; Večna pot 70; adult/child 2-14 1100/700SIT; ☻ 9am-7pm Tue-Sun Jun-Aug, 9am-4pm Tue-Sun Sep-May), on the southern slope of **Rožnik Hill** (394m), contains 500 animals representing 120 species. There's also a petting zoo for children.

ACTIVITIES
Hiking

The marked **Trail of Remembrance** (Pot Spominov), which runs for 34km around the city where German barbed wire once completely enclosed Ljubljana during WWII, is popular with walkers and joggers. The easiest places to reach the trail are from AMZS headquarters on Dunajska c 128 (catch bus 6, 8 or 21 to AMZS stop) or from Trg Komandanta Staneta just northwest of

the central office of the public transport authority LPP (Celovška c 160; bus 1 to Remiza stop). You can also join it from the northwestern side of Žale Cemetery (bus 19 to Nove Žale stop) – Ljubljana's own Père Lachaise or Highgate – or south of Trnovo (bus 19 to Veliki Štradon stop). These buses all leave from the bus station near the train station.

Swimming & Sauna

Tivoli Recreation Centre (☎ 431 51 55; Celovška c 25) in Park Tivoli has an indoor swimming pool (open September to May), a fitness centre, clay tennis courts and a roller-skating rink (which becomes an ice rink from mid-August to February). It also has a popular sauna called **Zlati Klub** (Gold Club; morning 2100SIT, afternoon 2400SIT; ☻ 10am-8pm Mon, Wed, Thu & Sun men only, 10am-10pm Tue women only, 10am-midnight Fri & Sat mixed) with saunas, steam room, splash pools and outside swimming pool surrounded by high walls so you can sunbathe *au naturel*. Towels are an extra 500SIT.

TOURS

Guided **city tours** (adult/student 1550/800SIT) start from in front of the Town Hall. At the time of writing, departures of English-language tours were 6pm (May to September) and 10am (October to April), but times vary year by year; check with the TIC.

A one-hour river-boat tour makes a pleasant summer outing. Boats leave at 6.30pm (weather permitting) from the Ribji trg pier, just southwest of the TIC.

FESTIVALS & EVENTS

The number-one event on Ljubljana's social calendar is the **Ljubljana Summer Festival** (www .festiva-lj.si), a summer celebration of music, opera, dance and street theatre held in venues throughout the city, but principally in the open-air theatre at the **Križanke** (☎ 252 65 44; Trg francoske revolucije) – originally a 13th-century monastic complex. The festival, now in its fifth decade, runs from early July to late August.

Druga Godba (Other Music; www.drugagodba.si) A festival of alternative and world music; takes place in the Križanke in early June.

Vino Ljubljana An international wine fair held in early June at the **Ljubljana Fairgrounds** (Ljubljanski Sejem; www.ljubljanski-sejem.si; Dunajska c 10) north of the train station.

International Biennial of Graphic Arts (www.mglc -lj.si) At the International Centre of Graphic Arts in Park Tivoli, the Modern Art Museum and several other venues; held from mid-June to September in odd-numbered years.

Ljubljana Jazz Festival (www.cd-cc.si) At the Križanke in late June; has been taking place for 45 years.

Summer in the Old Town Ljubljana is at its most vibrant in July and August during the so-called Summer in the Old Town season when there are four or five free cultural events a week in the city's historic squares, courtyards and bridges. Contact the tourist office for more information.

Trnfest (www.kud-fp.si) An international festival of alternative arts and culture organised by KUD France Prešeren; takes place in Trnovo in late July and August.

Young Lions (Mladi Levi; bunker@siol.net) A 10-day festival of theatre and dance held in late August.

City of Women (www.cityofwomen-a.si) Held in October in venues throughout Ljubljana; showcases all forms of artistic expression by women.

Ljubljana Marathon (www.slo-timing.com) Starts and ends in Kongresni trg; held on the last Saturday in October.

SLEEPING

Ljubljana is not overendowed with accommodation choices. The selection following includes all of the central budget and mid-range options. The TICs have comprehensive details of other hotels further out in the suburbs, of similarly inconvenient private rooms and of the four other central top-end hotels, all of which charge over €140 for a double.

Old Town

Hotel Emonec (☎ 200 15 20; www.hotel-emonec.com; Wolfova 12; s/d €49/59; [P] [🖳]) The décor is coldly modern but everything is gleamingly clean and you can't beat the central location. A

TV and Internet access in every room are unusual niceties for the price, making this hotel excellent value for money.

City Centre

Pri Mraku (☎ 433 40 49; www.daj-dam.si/ang/Mrak /mrakmain.htm; Rimska c 4; s/d from €58.80/71.80) Above a well-respected but misleadingly dowdy-looking restaurant of the same name, this hotel offers inviting rooms with all the creature comforts: great value for such an ideal location. Higher-priced rooms have air-con.

Grand Hotel Union Executive (☎ 308 12 70; www .gh-union.si; Miklošičeva c 1; s €136-165, d €145-177, ste €300; [🖳]) Although not the capital's most expensive hotel, the Union is nonetheless its star address, thanks to the great 1905 architecture and perfect position. For all the Art Nouveau flourishes, including brilliant brass lantern stands on sweeping stone stairways, be sure to choose the executive section. The slightly cheaper business section is a comfortable but entirely functional later addition.

Park Hotel (☎ 433 13 06; www.hotelpark.si; Tabor 9; s/d €53/70; [P]) In a handily central if rather uninviting area, this tower-block hotel is central Ljubljana's best-value midrange choice. Pleasant, well-renovated standard rooms are bright and unpretentiously well equipped. Cheaper rooms have ensuite toilet but share showers.

Cityhotel Turist (City Hotel, Hotel Turist; ☎ 432 91 30; www.hotelturist.si; Dalmatinova 15; s/d from €57/109; [🖳]) When they offer you a 'small' room here, they're not joking. This functionally businesslike property has recently had a much-needed modernisation, but the only compelling attraction remains its position. The nearby Park Hotel is less polished but better value.

Several fairly spartan student hostels with shared bathrooms only accept travellers during midsummer. Breakfast is not included. The most central are **Dijaški Dom Tabor** (☎ 234 88 40; ssljddta1s@guest.arnes.si; dm €17-20; [☾] Jul-Aug), entered from Kotnikova ul, and **Dijaški Dom Ivana Cankarja** (☎ 474 86 00; dd.lj-ic@guest.arnes.si; Poljanska c 26B; s/d/tr 3960/6520/8580SIT; [☾] Jul) with 10% student discounts. Ignore the misleading sign on the door of Poljanska c 26: the actual entrance is from the western side of block B. The correct doorway faces onto a tennis court.

THE AUTHOR'S CHOICE

Celica Hostel (☎ 230 97 00; www.souhostel .com; Metelkova 8; dm/s/d 3750/9500/10,500SIT; [☒] [🖳] [🐾]) Even if you're not in the habit of staying in hostels, Celica is the place to make an exception. Who would think of turning a military prison into a hostel and getting different architects to design each 'cell'? The result is a highly original survey of design styles, including everything from Finnish modern to traditional Slovenian. It's not The Ritz but the comfort level is more than adequate for the price and you can experience prison without imprisonment.

SLOVENIA

Outer Suburbs

Prenočišča Bežigrad (☎ 231 15 59; www.prenocisca-bezigrad.com; Podmilščakova 51; s/d/tr without breakfast 8000/11,000/14,000SIT) Bright, well-equipped new rooms off hospital-style corridors are good value, despite the road noise and semi-industrial location, 2km north of the centre (catch bus 14).

Ljubljana Youth Hostel (BIT Center Hotel; ☎ 548 00 55; www.bit-center.net; Litijska 57; dm/s/d €13/28.50/40, breakfast €3.50; ⓟ) Stylish new HI bunk-dorms and functionally modern ensuite rooms are attached to the large BIT sports centre 3km east of the centre. Take bus 9 from opposite the bus and train stations to the Emona bus stop, walk 250m further east, turn north onto Pesarska c, then immediately right through an expansive car park.

North of the centre are the less convenient **Dijaški Dom Bežigrad** (☎ 534 28 67; dd.lj-bezigrad@guest.arnes.si; Kardeljeva pl 28; dm from €12; ⓨ Jul-Aug), which you can reach on bus 6, and **Dijaški Dom Šiška** (☎ 500 78 04; www.ddsiska.com; Aljaževa 32; dm adult/student €11/9; ⓨ Jun-Aug) near pointy-towered Sv Frančišek Church (Verovškova ul). Take bus 1, 3, 15 or 16 west-bound to the Stara Cerkev stop, walk 500m due north on Aljaževa, and the hostel is on your right.

EATING

The Old Town has plenty of appealing restaurants, though the choice here isn't quite as overwhelming as that of cafés. For cheaper options you can try Poljanska c or the dull but functional snack bars around the stations.

Old Town

Pri Sv Florijanu (☎ 251 22 14; Gornji trg 20; meals from 1900SIT; ⓨ noon-11pm) This top-rate restaurant, housed in an old building with a stylishly modern interior, is famed for its creative nouveau-Slovene cuisine. Come before 4pm and you can choose three-course vegetarian, fish or meat menus for just 1900SIT. Or venture downstairs (open from 6pm), and you are atmospherically transported to North Africa for Moroccan food or a puff on a water pipe.

Gostilna Vodnikov Hram (☎ 234 52 60; Vodnikov trg 2; meals from 1700SIT; ⓨ 8am-8pm Mon-Sat, food to 4pm) Vegetarian and meaty lunch specials are a bargain at 780SIT to 1100SIT in this inviting vaulted pub.

Ajdovo Zrno (☎ 041 690 478; Trubarjeva c 7; meals from 1000SIT) Right in the centre of town, this cheery hangout serves no meat, fish or eggs and has a yummy salad bar.

Julija (☎ 425 64 63; Stari trg 9; meals from 1400SIT; ⓨ 8am-10pm, café to midnight) At Julija, rissotos and pastas are served outside or in a pseudo-Delft tiled back room behind a café decorated with 1920s prints.

Gostilna Pri Pavli (☎ 425 92 75; Stari trg 1; pizzas from 900SIT, meals from 1500SIT; ⓨ 6am-11pm) This attractive, country-style inn serves Slovene food that's unspectacular, but surprisingly affordable for such a perfect location. Service is homely, if slow, and the atmosphere calmly sedate.

Sokol (☎ 439 68 55; Ciril Metodov trg 18; meals from 2500SIT; ⓨ 6am-11pm) In this old vaulted house, traditional Slovene food is served on heavy tables by costumed waiters, who stop just short of Disneyesque self-parody. Pizzas and vegetarian options are available if sausage and groats don't appeal. Even if you think you'd hate blood pudding, the country feast platter may pleasantly surprise you.

Taverna Tatjana (☎ 421 00 87; Gornji trg 38; fish per kg 6000-20,000SIT, garnish extra 600SIT; ⓨ 5pm-midnight) Looking like an old-world wooden-beamed cottage pub, this is actually a rather exclusive fish restaurant with a tiny, brilliant two-seat bar for your apéritif. As you leave, the view from the doorway is one of Ljubljana's most picturesque.

Delikatesen Ljubljana Dvor (Gosposka ul; pizza slices 250-350SIT; ⓨ 9am-midnight Mon-Sat) Locals queue for huge, bargain pizza slices, salads and sold-by-weight braised vegetables to takeaway or stand and eat.

Paninoteka (Jurčičev trg 3; sandwiches 450-650SIT; ⓨ 8am-1am Mon-Sat, 9am-11pm Sun) Healthy sandwich creations on olive ciabatta are sold here to takeaway or to eat outside on a lovely little square with castle views.

A good pizzeria is the riverfront **Ljubljanski Dvor** (☎ 251 65 55; Dvorni trg 1; pizzas from 850SIT; ⓨ 10am-midnight Mon-Sat, 1-11pm Sun).

The minimarket **Živila** (Kongresni trg 9; ⓨ 7am-9pm) is open even on Sunday.

City Centre

Harambaša (☎ 041 675 155; Vrtna 8; meals from 1500SIT; ⓨ 10am-10pm Mon-Fri, noon-10pm Sat, noon-6pm Sun) Here you'll find Bosnian cuisine served at low tables in a charming modern cottage atmosphere with quiet Balkan music.

Alamut Orient House (☎ 031 545 595; Poljanska c 7; meals from 1500SIT; ⏰ 8am-10pm Mon-Sat) Persian rugs and Lurish swords decorate this cosy little Iranian restaurant, whose 1400SIT lunch menus are popular with intellectuals and vegetarians. Subtle herbs and yogurt are used to masterful effect in the 1200SIT *polnjen malancan* (stuffed aubergine).

Manna (☎ 283 52 94; Eippova 1a; meals from 3500SIT; ⏰ noon-midnight Mon-Sat) Plush red interiors with Klimt prints and a tempting Viennese bar area make this the most stylishly upmarket of several eateries and pubs along an attractive tree-shaded stretch of canal, a short walk south of the city centre. Try the rocket dumplings with scampi and saffron (1500SIT).

Joe Pena's (☎ 421 50 00; Cankarjeva c 6; meals from 2500SIT; ⏰ 10am-1am Mon-Sat, noon-midnight Sun) Lazily whirring ceiling fans, earth-tone walls and wooden floors create plenty of atmosphere at Joe Pena's, Ljubljana's best, mood-lit Mexican restaurant.

Cantina Mexicana (☎ 426 93 25; Knafljev prehod; ⏰ 11am-late) This luridly colourful Mexican place has a fabulous terrace equipped with sofas and lanterns; perfect for a preprandial margarita.

Nobel Burek (Miklošičeva c 30; burek 450SIT; ⏰ 24hr) This place serves up Slovenian-style fast food.

Hot Horse (Trubarjeva c 31; snacks 350-800SIT; burgers 400-700SIT; ⏰ 8am-midnight Mon-Sat, noon-midnight Sun) Fill up with giant 'horseburgers' and vegeburgers or pop next door for sandwiches.

Pinki (☎ 544 11 11; Poljanska c 22; meals 700-800SIT; ⏰ 6.30am-10pm Mon-Sat) Serving lasagnes, tortillas and pizzas, this cheap and cheerful student-oriented diner also does a 240SIT coffee-and-doughnut breakfast.

Pre-eminent pizzerias include the warmly vaulted **Foculus** (☎ 251 56 43; Gregorčičeva 3; ⏰ 10am-midnight Mon-Fri, noon-midnight Sat & Sun), good-value **Napoli** (☎ 231 29 49; Prečna 7) and trusty **Čerin** (☎ 232 09 90; Trubarjeva c 52; ⏰ 10am-11pm Mon-Fri, noon-11pm Sat & Sun), which has bargain 980SIT lunch menus before 3pm. Otherwise pizzas range from 1200SIT to 1800SIT almost anywhere.

The minimarket **Market Tabor** (Kotnikova 12; ⏰ 7.30am-10pm) is open on Sunday.

DRINKING

Few cities have central Ljubljana's concentration of fabulously inviting cafés and bars, many with outdoor seating. Unless noted, those listed below open daily till late and charge from 160SIT to 200SIT for an espresso, 300SIT to 350SIT for small beers, and 900SIT to 1000SIT for cocktails. Just choose the ambience that appeals.

Movia Vinoteka (☎ 425 54 48; Mestni trg 2; ⏰ noon-midnight Mon-Sat) If you've been disappointed by mediocre Slovenian vintages, this atmospheric 1820 wine bar beside the Town Hall is the place to taste the really good ones. Sip slowly, however, as the 0.07L measures barely wet the bottom of the giant globe glasses. And at 600SIT to 3500SIT a pop, you'll need a few before you're tipsy.

BiKoFe (Gosposka 7) This spot has a soft, jazzy, mellow vibe, attracting both a straight and gay clientele.

Pr'skelet (Ključavničarska 5; ⏰ 10am-1am) Here skeletons enjoy all-day two-for-one cocktails in an amusing *Rocky Horror*–style basement.

Makalonca (Hribarjevo nab) An unpretentious, cult bar on a glassed-in jetty, Makalonca is at the bottom of some easy-to-miss steps.

Salon (☎ 433 20 06; Trubarjeva c 23) This dazzling designer-kitsch cocktail bar features gold ceilings and leopard-skin couches.

Petit Café (Trg francoske revolucije 4) The wonderful Petit Café magically transports you to Montmartre.

Oriental Café (Metelkova 8) Many backpackers are so enchanted by the Celica Hostel's Oriental Café they forget to explore next-door Metelkova (p348).

Riverside classics:

Maček (☎ 425 37 91; Cankarjevo nab 19) Happy hour 4pm to 7pm.

Zlata Ladjica (☎ 241 06 95; Jurčičev trg) Has DJs at weekends.

CN7 Patisserie (Cankarjevo nab 7; coffee 200SIT; beers from 350SIT; ⏰ 8am-1pm) CN7's willow-whipped stools offer arguably the best-positioned riverbank perch.

For *Clockwork Orange* designer cool try **Fraga Gallery-Bar** (Mestni trg 15), audacious, white-on-white **Minimal** (Mestni trg 4; small beers 450SIT) or the less exclusive cake-café **Zvezda** (☎ 121 90 90; Wolfova 1).

If it had longer opening hours, Gostilna Vodnikov Hram (opposite) would knock the spots off Anglo-Irish pubs like **Patrick's** (Prečna 6), **Sir William's** (Tavčarjeva 8a; ⏰ closed Sun) or the ever-popular **Cutty Sark** (☎ 425 14 27; Knafljev prehod).

SLOVENIA

Quaint 'olde'-style places include **Café Antico** (☎ 426 56 28; Stari trg), wood-panelled **Roza** (Židovska 6) and patisserie cafés such as **Čajna Hisa** (Stari trg 3; ☺ 9am-11pm Mon-Sat) and **Slaščičarna Pri Vodnjaku** (Stari trg 30).

ENTERTAINMENT

Where to? In Ljubljana and **Ljubljana Calling** (www.ljubljana-calling.com) list cultural events, sports and nightlife options. Glossy **Ljubljana Life** (www.ljubljanalife.com) has some refreshingly frank reviews. All are free from TICs, hotels and some restaurants.

Nightclubs & Live Music

Global (☎ 426 90 20; www.global.si in Slovene; Tomšičeva 2; admission before midnight free, after midnight 1000SIT) After 11pm, Thursday to Saturday, this retro cocktail bar with Ljubljana's best city views becomes a popular dance venue. Take the bouncer-guarded elevator on Slovenska c to the top.

K4 (www.klubk4.org; Kersnikova 4; ☺ 10pm-4am) Two stark dance floors beneath the student organisation Roza Klub (p380) – enter from rear – feature rave-electronic music Friday and Saturday (1000SIT to 1500SIT), with other styles of music weeknights, and a popular gay-and-lesbian night on Sunday (500SIT after 11pm).

Bachus (☎ 241 82 44; www.bachus-center.com in Slovene; Kongresni trg; ☺ 8am-1am Mon-Wed, 8am-4am Thu-Sat, 6pm-4am holidays) This well-designed, smart and trendy bar-restaurant complex holds weekend discos.

As (☎ 425 88 22; www.gostilnaas.si in Slovene; Knafljev prehod; ☺ 9am-3am) Thursday to Saturday DJs transform this candle-lit basement bar, hidden beneath this incongruously upmarket restaurant, into a pumping, crowd-pulling nightclub.

Jazz Club Gajo (☎ 425 32 06; www.jazzclubgajo .com; Beethovnova 8; admission free; ☺ 11am-2am Mon-Fri, 7pm-midnight Sat & Sun, closed mid-Jul–mid-Aug) For Monday night student jams, midweek concerts or just a convivial drink, the Gajo is always inviting.

Orto Bar (☎ 232 16 74; Grablovičeva 1; ☺ 8pm-4am) Popular for late-night drinking and dancing with occasional live music, the Orto has red padded walls, whirring steel propeller fans and a taste for Joy Division. It's just five minutes' walk from Metelkova.

Metelkova (www.metelkova.org) In this two-courtyard block, half a dozen wonderfully idiosyncratic venues hide behind mostly unmarked doors, coming to life after midnight Thursday to Saturday. You might well feel uncomfortable amid the street-art, graffiti and shadow-lurking youth gangs, but this is all part of Metelkova's unique atmosphere. Entering from Masarykova c, to the right is **Gala Hala** (www.ljudmila.org/kapa/program in Slovene) with live bands and club nights. Easy to miss in the first building to the left are Club Tiffany (a gay café-club) and Monokel Club (for lesbians). Beyond the first courtyard, well-hidden Gromka (folk, improv, possibly anything) is beneath the bodyless heads. Cover charges and midweek openings are rare but erratic for all Metelkova venues.

Theatre & Classical Music

Cankarjev Dom (☎ 241 73 00; www.cd-cc.si; Trg Republike) is a complex of around a dozen venues offering a remarkable smorgasbord of performance arts. Its **ticket office** (☎ 241 71 00; ☺ 11am-1pm & 3-8pm Mon-Fri, 11am-1pm Sat, & 1hr before performances) lurks within the basement floor of Maximarket Mall.

Also check for classical concerts at the attractive Filharmonija (p343) and for ballet at the neo-Renaissance 1882 **Opera House** (☎ 425 48 40; Župančičeva ul).

Cinemas

Kinoteka (www.kinoteka.si in Slovene; Milošičeva c 28; admission 1400SIT) Offers the most imaginative programme, including rare, old and cult movies, in an Art Deco mansion. If the linguistic challenges of following a Slovene soundtrack are getting you down, slope off for a drink in the atmospheric, movie-themed Marilyn Caffe (big beers 380SIT).

GETTING THERE & AWAY

The shed-like **bus station** (Avtobusna postaja; ☎ 234 46 00; www.ap-ljubljana.si; Trg Osvobodilne Fronte; ☺ 5.30am-9pm) has bilingual info-phones, and its timetable is very useful once you get the hang of it – nominate your destination first. Hourly weekday buses serve Bohinj (1940SIT, two hours) via Bled (1400SIT, 1¼ hours). Most buses to Piran (2910SIT, 2½ to three hours, up to eight daily) go via Koper (2460SIT, 2½ hours, up to 10 daily) and Postojna (1340SIT, 1¼ hours, 20 daily). Most Maribor buses (2760SIT, three hours, seven daily) leave in the afternoon. All services are much less frequent at weekends.

Ljubljana **train station** (☎ 291 33 32; Trg Osvobodilne Fronte) has up to 19 daily services to Maribor (1710SIT to 2895SIT, 1¾ to 2¾ hours). There are five trains daily to Koper (2040SIT, 2½ hours). For international services see p382.

GETTING AROUND

The cheapest way to **Ljubljana Aerodrome** (Brnik Airport; www.lju-airport.si) is by city bus from bus station lane 28 (740SIT, 45 minutes). These run hourly, from 5.10am to 8.10pm Monday to Friday, but only seven times daily at weekends. Another seven Marun/Adria coaches (1000SIT, 30 minutes) run daily. Big hotels offer an airport shuttle for 2500SIT per person, or 8800SIT per shuttle if there are few passengers. A taxi to the city centre costs about 7000SIT.

The heavily pedestrianised city centre's one-way system makes driving confusing. Street parking is feasible, though not always easy in the museum area and near Metelkova. Once you've found a space it's generally most efficient to walk.

Ljubljana has excellent city buses, most lines operating every 10 to 20 minutes from 3.15am to midnight. However, the central area is perfectly walkable, so buses are really only necessary if you're staying out of town. Buy tokens in advance (190SIT) from newsstands, or pay 300SIT once aboard. Ljubljana Cards (3000SIT for 72 hours; see p342) give you free city-bus travel.

In summer you can hire bicycles at the train station, Petit Café (p347) and the STIC (p342) for 100SIT per hour, or at **Hotel Lev** (Vošnjakova 1; per day 3000SIT) and at a kiosk near Maček café (p347).

AROUND LJUBLJANA

Stična

☎ 01 / pop 715 / elev 325m

The abbey at Stična (Sittich in German) is the oldest monastery in Slovenia and one of the country's most important religious and cultural monuments. At only 35km from Ljubljana and within easy walking distance of the train station at Ivančna Gorica (population 1580), Stična can be visited on a day trip from the capital or en route to Novo Mesto, the valley of the lower Krka or Bela Krajina.

The monastery was established in 1136 by the Cistercians, a branch of the Bene-

dictines who worked as farmers, following a vow of silence. It became the most important religious, economic, educational and cultural centre in Dolenjska, but it was abandoned in 1784 when Emperor Joseph II dissolved all religious orders – many of them very powerful and corrupt – in the Habsburg Empire.

The Cistercians returned in 1898, and today almost the entire complex is again in use. There are seven priests (including the abbot) and six monks in residence.

ORIENTATION

The village of Stična is about 2.5km north of Ivančna Gorica, where you'll find the **train station** (Sokolska 1).

SIGHTS

The entrance to the walled **Stična Abbey** (Stiški Samostan; ☎ 787 71 00; www2.pms-lj.si/sticna in Slovene; Stična 17; adult/student & child 600/300SIT; ☻ 8am-noon & 2-5pm Tue-Sat, 2-5pm Sun, tours 8.30am, 10am, 2pm & 4pm Tue-Sat, 2pm & 4pm Sun), an incredible combination of Romanesque, Gothic, Renaissance and baroque architecture, is on the eastern side across a small stream. On the northern side of the central courtyard is the **Old Prelature**, a 17th-century Renaissance building that contains the **Slovenian Religious Museum** (Slovenski Verski Muzej) on two floors. Its permanent collection (History of Christianity in Slovenian) is on the 2nd floor. The museum is a hotchpotch of antique clocks, paintings, furniture and farm implements mixed with chalices, monstrances and icons. There are a few 16th-century missals and medical texts in Latin and German, but all the medieval documents are facsimiles of the originals carted off to libraries in Vienna and Ljubljana when the order was banned in the 18th century.

On the western side of the courtyard, the **Abbey Church** (1156) was built as a buttressed, three-nave Romanesque cathedral, but it was rebuilt in the baroque style in the 17th and 18th centuries. Inside, look for the Renaissance red-marble tombstone of Abbot Jakob Reinprecht in the north transept and the blue organ cupboard with eight angels (1747) in the choir loft. The greatest treasures here are the **Stations of the Cross** painted in 1766 by Fortunat Bergant, who spelled his surname with a 'W' on the last one.

South of the church is Stična's celebrated **vaulted cloister**, which mixes Romanesque and early Gothic styles. The cloister served as an ambulatory for monks in prayer and connected the church with the monastery's other wings. The arches and vaults are decorated with frescoes of the prophets and Old Testament stories as well as allegorical subjects such as the Virtues, the Four Winds and so on. Look for the carved stone faces on the western side that were meant to show human emotions and vices – upon which the clergy were expected to reflect.

On the southern side of the cloister is a typically baroque monastic **refectory** with an 18th-century pink ceiling and decorative swirls and loops made of white stucco. One floor above is the much impoverished **library**. **Neff's Abbey**, built in the mid-16th century by Abbot Volbenk Neff, runs to the west. The arches in the vestibule on the ground floor are painted with a dense network of leaves, blossoms, berries and birds.

The Cistercians sell their own products (honey, wine, herbal teas, liqueurs) in a small **shop** (8am-12.30pm & 1-3pm Mon-Fri, 8am-12.30pm Sat) at the abbey entrance.

SLEEPING & EATING
Grofija (County; /fax 787 81 41; Vir pri Stični 30; per person €20) This 19th-century farmhouse with four rooms for guests is 2km southeast of the abbey. Horses are available for hire. A major Hallstatt settlement dating from 800 BC once stood near the site of the tennis court here.

Krčma Deseti Brat (787 80 62; Stična 27; meals from 2200SIT; 8am-10pm Tue-Sun) Just uphill from the monastery, the '10th Brother Tavern' serves up dishes of game, Dolenjska sausage, wild mushrooms and *štruklji* (dumplings).

Pri Jurčku (At the Mushroom; 787 71 10; Ljubljanska c 38; pizzas 1100SIT; 10am-10pm) This cute little place in Ivančna Gorica, about 150m northeast of the train station and just off the road to the abbey, serves local favourites and quite decent pizza.

In Stična you'll also find a small supermarket called **Vele** (Stična 27a), just up from the abbey.

GETTING THERE & AWAY
Stična is served by up to 14 buses (one hour) a day from Ljubljana on weekdays, reducing to five on Saturday.

JULIAN ALPS

Dramatic rocky mountain spires straddle the Italian border. Within Slovenia these Julian Alps (named for Caesar) climax at tri-peaked Mt Triglav (2864m), the country's highest summit. Along with the neighbouring mountains, forests and breathtakingly beautiful valleys, the area forms the Triglav National Park. At weekends, half of Ljubljana's population decamps here to ski, cycle, fish, climb or hike. There are adventure sports to suit every level of insanity, many based in Bovec, and few places in Europe offer better rafting, paragliding or canyoning at such affordable prices.

KRANJ
04 / pop 37,000
Backed by a threatening battalion of mountains, Kranj's old core looks most picturesque when seen from across the Sava River, looking to the northeast. This is a view you'll enjoy briefly from the right-hand windows of buses headed from Ljubljana to Bled/Kranjska Gora, between gaps in the light-industrial foreground.

The frequent weekday buses between Kranj and 'Ljubljana Aerodrome' (in Brnik) make it possible to head straight from the plane to the Julian Alps without diverting to Ljubljana. While awaiting your Bled- or Kranjska Gora-bound bus, consider poking around the mildly appealing Kranj Old Town. It starts near the Art Nouveau **former post office** (Maistrov trg), a 500m walk south from the bus station. Most places of interest are along just three southbound pedestrianised streets – Prešernova, Britov and Tomišičeva ulicas – two of which bring you to the impressive **Sv Kancijan Church**, with its frescoes and ossuary. As far south again, the Old Town dead-ends near the **Serbian Orthodox church** with a 16th-century **defence tower**.

If you need a place to stay, there's the overpriced **Hotel Creina** (202 45 50; www.hotel-creina.si; Koroška c; s/d/tr 13,500/18,000/21,900SIT), south of the former post office.

Colourfully stylish, student-oriented **Cukrama** (Britov 73; beers 400SIT; 11am-late) is a great place for a drink, and boasts a gas-heated balcony overlooking an abyss.

From Kranj it's a relatively easy 10km excursion to **Škofja Loka**, which has one of Slovenia's most beautiful town squares (Mestni trg) and a fine **castle** (Loški Grad; 13 Grajski pot) containing a decent **ethnographical museum** (☎ 517 04 00; adult/child 600/400SIT; ☒ 10am-6pm Tue-Sun Apr-Oct). Buses run approximately hourly from Kranj (490SIT, 25 minutes).

BLED

☎ 04 / pop 5467

Genteel, millennium-old Bled is the gateway to the mountains. Its attraction is an absolutely idyllic setting on a 2km-long subalpine lake with a castle crag and romantic island placed exactly where you'd want them. It's a scene that seems designed for some god of tourism, not for the 13th-century bishops of Brixen. Bled town is not architecturally memorable, but it's small, convenient and a delightful base from which to simply stroll and gaze. Beware: in midsummer the beauty is diluted a little by the ever-expanding crowds and prices.

Information

Bled Health Centre (☎ 575 40 00; Mladinska c 1; ☒ 7am-7pm)

Kompas (☎ 572 75 00; Bled Shopping Centre; ☒ 9am-7pm) Sells maps, hires bicycles, offers tours and changes money.

SKB Banka (Bled Shopping Centre; ☒ 9-11.30am & 2-5pm Mon-Fri) One of several banks with an ATM.

TIC (☎ 574 11 22; www.bled.si; ☒ 9am-6pm Mon-Sat, noon-5pm Sun, later in summer) On the lakefront near the Park Hotel.

Union 99 (www.union-bled.com; Ljubljanska c 9; per 15min 300SIT; ☒ 8am-midnight) An appealing upstairs café-bar with an Internet connection.

Sights

On its own romantically tiny island (Blejski Otok), the baroque **Church of the Assumption** (☒ 8am-dusk, variable in winter) is Bled's photogenic trademark. Getting there by piloted *plenta* (gondola; €10 per person, 1½ hours return) is the archetypal tourist experience. Gondola prices are standard from any jetty, and you'll stay on the island long enough to ring the 'lucky' bell. Ordinary row-yourself boats cost 2000SIT per hour.

Topping a sheer 100m-cliff, **Bled Castle** (☎ 578 05 25; Blejski Grad; adult/student 1200/1100SIT; ☒ 8am-8pm May-Sep, 8am-5pm Oct-Apr) is the perfect backdrop to lake views, notably those

from Mlino, on the lake's southern bank. One of many access footpaths leads up from beside Bledec Hostel. Admission includes a historical **museum** section and the fabulous views.

Hidden away in its own lakeside park beyond Mlino is **Vila Bled** (☎ 579 15 00; www .vila-bled.com; C Svobode 26). This is now a Relais & Chateaux hotel, but it started life as Tito's summer retreat. Its basic design is somewhat forbiddingly 1950s, but there are some brilliant communist murals and a delightful outside terrace between arches of a colonnade. It's well worth the price of a drink to look around.

Activities

For perfect photos, stroll right around the lake. This 6km walk should take around two hours, including the short, steep climb to the brilliant **Osojnica viewpoints**.

Another popular, easy walk is to and through the 1.6km-long **Vintgar Gorge** (adult/child 900/600SIT; ☒ May-Oct). The highlight is an oft-renovated, century-old wooden walkway (no bicycles) which crisscrosses the fizzing Radovna River for the first 700m or so. Thereafter the scenery becomes tamer, passing a tall railway bridge, a spray-spouting weir, and ending at the anti-climactic **Sum Waterfall**. The gorge is officially but not physically closed in winter. Easiest access is via the appealing Gostilna Vintgar (an inn), three well-signed kilometres away on quiet, attractive roads from the Bledec Hostel. An alternative path back to Bled via Zasip is easy to lose track of before St Catherine's Church (Cerkev Sv Katarina).

For something tougher ask at the tourist office about multiday **hikes** and **mountain-bike** routes between semiabandoned, roadless hamlets in the mountains. The TIC can also help you arrange **gliding** (from €30) from nearby Lesce aerodrome. What a view!

Sleeping

Sobe (private rooms) are offered by dozens of homes. Agencies Kompas and **Globtour Bled** (☎ 574 18 21; www.globtour-bled.com; Hotel Krim, Ljubljanska c 7) have extensive lists, with prices for singles starting at €17. There is a 30% surcharge for stays under three nights.

Grand Hotel Toplice (☎ 579 10 00; www.hotel -toplice.com; C Svobode 12; s €100-170, d €130-200, ste €210-250; Ⓟ ☒ ☒) With a history that goes

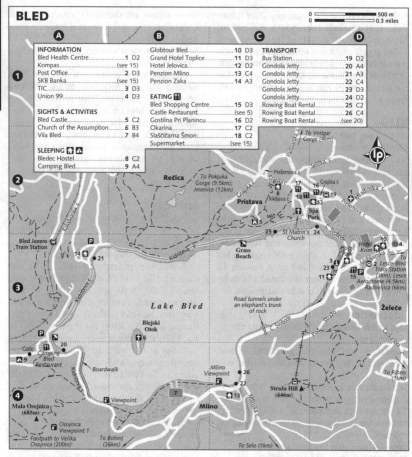

BLED

0 — 500 m
0 — 0.3 miles

INFORMATION
Bled Health Centre...............**1** D2
Kompas..............................(see 15)
Post Office..........................**2** D3
SKB Banka..........................(see 15)
TIC....................................**3** D3
Union 99............................**4** D3

SIGHTS & ACTIVITIES
Bled Castle..........................**5** C2
Church of the Assumption......**6** B3
Vila Bled............................**7** B4

SLEEPING
Bledec Hostel......................**8** C2
Camping Bled......................**9** A4

Globtour Bled......................**10** D3
Grand Hotel Toplice..............**11** D3
Hotel Jelovica.....................**12** D2
Penzion Mlino......................**13** C4
Penzion Zaka......................**14** A3

EATING
Bled Shopping Centre............**15** D3
Castle Restaurant.................(see 5)
Gostilna Pri Planincu.............**16** C2
Okarina..............................**17** C2
Slaščičarna Šmon..................**18** C2
Supermarket........................(see 15)

TRANSPORT
Bus Station.........................**19** D2
Gondola Jetty......................**20** A4
Gondola Jetty......................**21** A3
Gondola Jetty......................**22** C4
Gondola Jetty......................**23** D3
Gondola Jetty......................**24** D2
Rowing Boat Rental...............**25** C2
Rowing Boat Rental...............**26** C4
Rowing Boat Rental...............(see 20)

back to the mid-19th century, the 87-room Toplice is Bled's 'olde worlde' hotel, with attractive public areas, exquisitely outfitted rooms and superb views of the lake on its northern side. The hotel also has a couple of restaurants. The hotel's two extensions – the **Trst** (C Svobode 19; s €45-75, d €60-90), just opposite, and the more attractive **Jadran** (C Svobode 23; s €45-75, d €60-90), up on the hill – are half the price.

Penzion Mlino (☎ 574 14 04; www.mlino.si; C Svobode 45; s/d Nov-Apr €35/50, May-Oct €40/60) The lake-facing Mlino is on the Bohinj road, 900m southwest of town. The great views of the castle and lake counter the slightly cramped rooms and *Fawlty Towers*–style breakfast service.

Hotel Jelovica (☎ 579 60 00; www.hotel-jelovica.si; C Svobode 8; s/d July & August €50/76, rest of year €40/56) This handily central hotel is a decently renovated communist-era resort, and charges €5 extra for lake-glimpse rooms.

Penzion Zaka (☎ 574 17 09; www.bled-zaka.com; Župančičeva 9; s/d Sep-Jun €32/48, Jul & Aug €40/64) This *penzion* offers seven spacious if unsophisticated rooms with balconies and kitchenette above the good-value Regatni Center restaurant. Four of the rooms have lake views.

Bledec Hostel (☎ 574 52 50; www.mlino.si; Grajska c 17; dm low/high season €17/19, IYHA discount €2; ☐) Outwardly a typical *penzion*, this well-organised youth hostel has new four-bed dorms with attached bathrooms. It's quiet yet very central. Laundry (1500SIT per load) is available and Internet costs 500SIT per half-hour).

Camping Bled (☎ 575 20 00; www.camping.bled.si; adult/child €10/7; ☽ Apr–mid-Oct) This well-kept, popular site fills a rural valley behind a waterside restaurant at the western end of the lake. It hires mountain bikes (2500SIT per day) and can arrange ballooning, rafting, parachuting and more.

Eating

The venerable old Grand Hotel Toplice conjures up the best dining in town and there's a choice of restaurants. The most formal dining is at the toney (and aptly named) **Grand Restaurant** (meals from 5000SIT), where seafood and game done up in sauce rule the menu. Julijana is 'smart casual' and offers lighter more adventurous food with a Mediterranean accent for about the same price. The cheaper Panorama overlooks the lake and offers a wide range of well-prepared dishes. And there's no classier place to nibble a slice of cake or linger over cocktails than the hushed, hallowed lounge bar where princes, diplomats and celebrities have passed.

Okarina (☎ 574 14 58; Riklijeva c 9; meals €11-22; ☽ 6pm-midnight) Like its cuisine, Okarina's décor is an imaginative assortment of top-quality traditional Slovene and exotic Indian dishes. Relatively affordable vegetarian curries are available.

Gostilna Pri Planincu (☎ 574 16 13; Grajska c 8; meals from 1500SIT; ☽ noon-10pm) This 1903 village pub serves good-value food in its back rooms and pizza in the airy new bar upstairs.

Slaščičarna Šmon (Grajska 3; ☽ 7.30am-9pm) This renowned patisserie-café is the place to try *kremu snežna rozina*, Bled's scrumptiously light if anaemic-looking speciality, cream-and-custard pastry.

Castle Restaurant (Restavracija Blejski Grad; ☎ 574 16 07; meals from 3500SIT, beers 470SIT; ☽ 9am-10pm) Enjoy a meal or just a sunset beer on the superbly situated terrace of this restaurant.

Stock up on supplies at the supermarkets on Prešernova c or in **Bled shopping centre** (Ljubljanska c 4). The latter also has several decent café-bars.

Getting There & Around

Hourly buses to Bohinj (from 7.20am) and Ljubljana (1460SIT, 1½ hours) use the help-

fully central **bus station** (Gtajska c). Buses to Radovljica via Lesce-Bled station (370SIT, 15 minutes) run every 30 minutes. Bled has no central train station. Trains for Most na Soči and Nova Gorica use sweet little Bled Jezero station, which is 2km west of central Bled – handy for the camping ground and Pension Zaka but nothing else. Trains for Austria (up to eight daily) and Ljubljana (1050SIT, 55 minutes, frequent) use Lesce-Bled station, 4km to the east of town. However, if you're off to Ljubljana it's much nicer (if marginally less convenient) to wait for your train in attractive Radovljica.

In summer, pint-sized 'tourist-trains' (adult/child 550/350SIT) trundle around the lakeside every 40 minutes, passing *penzions* Mlino and Zaka.

RADOVLJICA

☎ 04 / pop 5950 / elev 488m

A charming town full of historic buildings, Radovljica enjoys an enviable position atop an outcrop 75m above a wide plain called the Dežela (Country). A short distance to the west, two branches of the Sava join to form Slovenia's longest and mightiest river.

Radovljica (Ratmansdorf in German) was settled by the early Slavs and grew into an important market town by the early 14th century. With increased trade on the river and the addition of iron forgeries at nearby Kropa and Kamna Gorica, Radovljica expanded. The town was built around a large rectangular square fortified with a wall and defence towers. Radovljica's affluence in the Middle Ages can be seen in the lovely buildings still lining Linhartov trg today.

Radovljica is an easy day trip from Bled, just 6km to the northwest.

Orientation

The centre of old Radovljica is Linhartov trg; the new town extends primarily northward along Gorenjska c towards Lesce. Radovljica's bus station is 500m northwest of Linhartov trg on Kranjska c. The train station is below the town on C Svobode.

Information

Gorenjska Banka (Gorenjska c 16; ☽ 8am-6pm Mon-Fri, 8am-noon Sat)

Post office (Kranjska c 1; ☽ 7am-7pm Mon-Fri, 7am-noon Sat)

SLOVENIA

SKB Banka (Gorenjska c 10; 8.30am-noon &
2-5pm Mon-Fri)
Tourist office (531 53 00; tdradovljica@s5.net;
Gorenjska c 1; 8am-6pm Mon-Fri, 8am-noon Sat)

Sights

BEEKEEPING MUSEUM

Although it might not sound like a crowd-
pleaser, this **museum** (Čebelarski Muzej; 532 05
20; www.muzeji-radovljica.si; Linhartov trg 1; adult/child
500/400SIT; 10am-1pm & 3-6pm Tue-Sun May-Oct,
10am-noon & 3-5pm Wed, Sat & Sun Mar, Apr, Nov & Dec) is
one of the most interesting in the country,
and there isn't a whole lot you won't know
about things apiarian after an hour inside.
The museum is housed in **Thurn Manor**,
which began life as Ortenburg Castle in
the early Middle Ages but was rebuilt with
a large hall on the ground floor after the
earthquake of 1511. The cream-and-white
structure has interesting reliefs and stucco
work on its façade.

The museum's exhibits take a close look at
the history of beekeeping in Slovenia (which
was at its most intense in the 18th and 19th
centuries), the country's unique contribution
to the industry with the development of the
Carniolan grey bee species (Apis mellifera
carnica) and the research of men like Anton
Janša (1734–73), who set up a research station in the Karavanke and is considered
around the world to be the father of modern beekeeping. And the museum doesn't
fail to pass on a few 'fun facts to know and
tell'. Did you realise that bees cannot see
the colour red but go gaga over yellow? The
museum's collection of illustrated beehive
panels (panjske končnice) from the 18th and
19th centuries, a folk art unique to Slovenia,
is the largest in the country.

LINHARTOV TRG

Radovljica's main square – named in honour of Slovenia's first dramatist and historian, Anton Tomaž Linhart (1756–95),
who was born here – is lined with houses
from the 16th century and is an absolute
delight to explore. It has been called 'the
most homogeneous Old Town core in Slovenia', with interesting details at every step.

Several lovely buildings are opposite the
Beekeeping Museum, including **Koman House**
(Linhartov trg 23), which has a baroque painting
on its front of St Florian, the patron saint
of fires (he douses, not sets, them) and **Mali**

House (Linhartov trg 24), which has a barely visible picture of St George slaying the dragon.
The 17th-century **Vidič House** (Linhartov trg 3)
has a corner projection and is colourfully
painted in red, yellow and blue.

The most important house here is 16th-
century **Šivec House** (Šivčeva Hiša; 532 05 20;
Linhartov trg 22; adult/child 400/300SIT; 10am-noon
& 6-8pm Tue-Sun Jul & Aug, 10am-noon & 5-7pm Tue-Sun
Jun & Sep, 10am-noon & 4-6pm Tue-Sun Jan-May, Oct-Dec),
which is an interesting hybrid: Renaissance
on the outside and Gothic on the inside.
On the ground floor there is a vaulted hall,
which now serves as a **gallery**, and on the 1st
floor there's a wood-panelled late-Gothic
drawing room with a beamed ceiling used
as a wedding hall. There is also a chim-
neyless 'black kitchen' and an interesting
collection of **children's book illustrations** by
celebrated Slovenian artists. The fresco on
the exterior shows the Good Samaritan performing his work of mercy.

East of the square is the Gothic **Parish
Church of St Peter** (Cerkev Sv Petra), a hall
church modelled after the one in Kranj.
The three portals are flamboyant Gothic,
and the sculptures inside were done by
Angelo Pozzo in 1713. The building with the
arcaded courtyard south of the church is
the **rectory** (župnišče).

Activities

There is a public **swimming pool** (531 57 70;
Kopališka c; 9am-9pm Jun-Aug) near the camping ground, with tennis courts nearby.

The **Sport Riding Centre** (532 52 00; per hr
400SIT; 7am-7pm) at Podvin Castle (Grad
Podvin; opposite), about 4km southeast of
Radovljica, has horses available for riding
individually or with an instructor.

Festivals & Events

The biggest event of the year is the two-
week long **Festival Radovljica** (http://festival-ra
dovljica.amis.net), one of the most important
festivals of ancient classical music in all
Europe, held in mid-August.

Sleeping

Camping Sobec (535 37 00; www.sobec.si; Šobčeva
c 25; camping per person €9.20-10.70, bungalows for 2
€73-87; May-Sep) The largest (15 hectares)
and arguably the best-equipped camping
ground in Slovenia is in Lesce, about 2.5km
northwest of Radovljica. Situated on a small

lake near a bend of the Sava Dolinka River, the camping ground can accommodate 1350 people, which this popular place often does in summer. In a small pine wood in the centre are bungalows for up to six people.

Hotel Grajski Dvor (☎ 531 55 85; www.hotel-grajski-dvor.si; Kranjska c 2; s/d 8700/12,600SIT; P) Radovljica's only hotel, the four-storey, 65-room 'Castle Courtyard' has recently been renovated although the décor remains rooted in the 1970s. At least check out the delightful Grajska Gostilnica restaurant.

Grad Podvin (☎ 532 52 00; www.robas.si/grad-podvin; s/d €54/67; P ☒ ☙) It's a rather boxy affair about 4km southeast of Radovljica in the village of Mošje but, hey, it's still a castle. Podvin Castle is surrounded by a lovely park and has tennis courts, an outdoor pool and a popular horse-riding centre.

Eating

Grajska Gostilnica (☎ 531 44 45; meals 1500-2400SIT; ☉ 11am-11pm Sun-Thu, 11am-midnight Fri & Sat) The flagship at the Hotel Grajski Dvor, this place has quickly become the town's best. It has a mixed cuisine of Italian and Slovenian, a great wine list and an atmospheric cellar below. All the metalwork was produced by UKO in Kropa (see p356).

Gostilna Lectar (☎ 537 48 00; Linhartov trg 2; meals from 2000SIT; ☉ noon-11pm Wed-Mon) The Lectar, in yet another historic Linhartov trg house, is highly recommended by locals.

Gostilna Augustin (☎ 531 41 63; Linhartov trg 14; lunch Mon-Fri 1100SIT; ☉ 8am-midnight) This welcoming bar-restaurant has a terrace out the back with stunning views towards Triglav.

Shopping

Vinoteka Sodček (☎ 531 50 71; Linhartov trg 8; ☉ 9am-7pm Mon-Fri, 8am-noon Sat) This shop has an excellent selection of Slovenian wines.

Getting There & Away

Buses leave from Radovljica almost every half-hour between 7am and 10pm for Bled and Ljubljana. They go hourly to Bohinjska Bistrica (via Bled), Kranj, Kranjska Gora and Kropa. Other destinations, and daily frequencies, include: Bovec via Kranjska Gora and the Vršič Pass (one bus daily in July and August), Brezje (one), Jesenice via Vrba (up to six), Novo Mesto (one at the weekend), Škofja Loka (one) and Tržič (up to four).

Radovljica is on the rail line linking Ljubljana (780SIT, 50 minutes) with Jesenice (340SIT, 20 minutes) via Škofja Loka, Kranj and Lesce-Bled. Up to 15 trains a day pass through the town in each direction. About eight of the northbound ones carry on to Villach in Austria.

KROPA

☎ 04 / pop 840 / elev 531m

While in Radovljica, don't miss the chance for an easy half-day trip to this delightful village. The inhabitants of Kropa (Cropp in German) have been 'workhorses' for centuries, mining iron ore and hammering out the nails and decorative wrought iron that can still be seen in many parts of Slovenia. Today Kropa has turned to screws – the Novi Plamen factory is based here – but artisans continue their work, clanging away in the workshop on the village's single street. The work of their forebears is evident in ornamental street lamps shaped like birds and dragons, weather vanes and shutters.

Sights

BLACKSMITH MUSEUM (KOVAŠKI MUZEJ)

The fascinating collection at the **museum** (☎ 533 67 17; Kropa 10; adult/child 400/300SIT, with film & forge display 500/400SIT; ☉ 10am-1pm & 3-6pm Tue-Sun May-Oct, 10am-noon & 3-5pm Wed, Sat & Sun Mar, Apr, Nov & Dec) traces the history of iron mining and forging in Kropa and nearby Kamna Gorica from the 14th to the early 20th centuries. Nail manufacturing was the town's main industry for most of that period: from giant ones that held the pylons below Venice together to little studs for snow boots, Kropa produced 130 varieties in huge quantities. You did not become a master blacksmith here until you could fit a horseshoe around an egg – without cracking the shell.

The museum has working models of forges, a couple of rooms showing how workers and their families lived in very cramped quarters (up to 45 people in one house) and a special exhibit devoted to the work of Joža Bertoncelj (1901–76), who turned out exquisite wrought-iron gratings, candlesticks, chandeliers and even masks. The museum shows a period-piece black-and-white film about the town and its work produced in the very socialist 1950s.

The house itself was owned by a 17th-century iron baron called Klinar, and it

SLOVENIA

contains some valuable furniture and paintings. Among the most interesting pieces is a 19th-century wind-up 'jukebox' from Bohemia.

OTHER SIGHTS

The **UKO forgers' workshop** (☎ 533 73 00; Kropa 7b; ☉ 7am-2pm Mon-Fri, 9am-noon Sat) across from the museum can be visited. The smiths sell their wares at the **shop** (Kropa No 7a) next door, which keeps the same hours.

An 18th-century furnace called **Purgatory Forge** (Vigenj Vice) lies a short distance north of the museum near the Kroparica, a fast-flowing stream that once turned the wheels that powered the furnaces for the forges. Close by is the birthplace of the Slovenian painter Janez Potočnik (1749–1834), whose work can be seen in the baroque **Church of St Leonard** (Cerkev Sv Lenarta), on the hill to the east, and in Kamnik. Kropa has many other lovely old houses, including several around **Trg Kropa**, the main square, which also has an interesting old wayside shrine.

Eating & Drinking

Gostilna Pri Kovač (☎ 533 63 20; Kropa 30; meals from 2500SIT; ☉ 10am-11pm Tue-Sun) Convivial 'At the Smith's' is in an interesting old house just north of the museum.

Pri Jarmu (☎ 533 67 50; Kropa 2; pizzas from 1000SIT; ☉ 10am-midnight Fri-Tue) This humble *gostilna* at the southern end of Kropa serves hearty pizzas but is more a place to drink than eat.

Getting There & Away

Public transport from Radovljica is minimal. You need your own car.

BOHINJ
☎ 04

Bohinj is not a town but a delightful valley of quaint meadowland villages culminating at magnificent Lake Bohinj. The mirrored waters are hemmed by high mountains that rise almost vertically from the walking trail along the lake's 3km-long northern shore.

The minuscule main tourist hub is **Ribčev Laz**, at the lake's eastern end. Its five-shop commercial centre contains a supermarket, pizzeria, post office (with ATM) and the obliging **tourist office** (☎ 572 32 70; www.bohinj.si; ☉ 8am-6pm Mon-Sat, 9am-3pm Sun mid-Sep–Jun, 7am-7pm Mon-Fri, 9am-4pm Sat & Sun Jul & Aug), which changes money, sells fishing licences and

can help with accommodation, including mountain-hikers' huts. **Alpinsport** (☎ 572 34 86; www.alpinsport.si; ☉ closed Apr) hires kayaks, canoes, bicycles and skis from a kiosk near the stone bridge.

For brochure-worthy photos of Lake Bohinj, climb 25 minutes up Peč Hill from Stara Fužina village, 1.5km further north. Stara Fužina also has an appealing little **Alpine Dairy Museum** (Planšarski Musej; ☎ 572 34 86; adult/child 400/300SIT; ☉ 10am-noon & 4-6pm Tue-Sun, 11am-7pm Tue-Sun Jul & Aug). Along with similarly attractive villages **Studor** and **Češnica**, it makes a delightful but easy bike ride from Ribčev Laz. The route is dotted with specially fine *kozolci* and *toplarji*, Slovenia's unique single and double hayracks.

Summer tourist boats (€6.50 return, 15 minutes, seven or eight per day) from Ribčev Laz terminate in Ukanc (aka Zlatorog) at the lake's far western end. Just 300m from the jetty a cable car (return €7, half hourly from 9am to 6pm, or 8am to 8pm July and August) whisks you up a vertical kilometre to 1540m; from here, ski lifts or hiking paths, according to season, continue up **Mt Vogel** for astonishing views.

Bohinjska Bistrica (population 3080), Bohinj's biggest village, is 6km east of Ribčev Laz and useful mainly for its train station.

Sleeping & Eating

Private rooms (€8.50 to €14.10 per person), mainly in outlying villages, are available through the tourist office. Nightly rates are cheaper for three-day stays.

Hotel Ski (☎ 572 16 91; d €36-40) With a stupendous position at the top of the Mt Vogel cable car, this is one of five hotels run by **Alpinum** (☎ 577 80 00; www.alpinum.net).

Penzion Rožic (☎ 572 33 93; www.penzion-rozic.com; per person without breakfast €19-27; ⌨) This unpretentious chalet-style guesthouse and restaurant is cheaper than most Ribčev Laz hotels. It's just 100m east of the tourist office, behind a bike-hire kiosk.

Hotel Jezero (☎ 572 91 00; hotel.jezero@cc-line.si; s/d from €51/62) This relatively comfortable place is the closest hotel to the lake, right by the stone bridge in Ribčev Laz. Rooms with a balcony cost slightly more.

Autokamp Zlatorog (☎ 572 34 82; camp sites per person 1700-2400SIT; ☉ May-Sep) A pine-shaded caravan site, with camping spots too, right beside the Ukanc jetty.

Getting There & Around

Buses run hourly (except Sunday) from Ukanc to Ljubljana via Ribčev Laz (470SIT), Bohinjska Bistrica and Bled, with six extra buses daily between Bohinjska Bistrica and Ukanc. Buses to Ukanc will be marked to 'Bohinj Zlatorog'. From Bohinjska Bistrica, passenger trains to Nova Gorica (1040SIT, 1½ hours, eight daily weekdays, less on weekends), plus six daily Avtovlak trains to Most na Soči (470SIT, 50 minutes), use a long tunnel that offers the only direct option for reaching the Soča Valley. Avtovlak trains carry cars for 2600SIT.

KRANJSKA GORA

☎ 04 / pop 2000

As ski resorts go, compact little Kranjska Gora is relatively cute and sits right beside the ski lifts to Slovenia's best-regarded pistes. There are world record-setting ski jumps 4km west at Planica.

Borovška c, 300m south of the bus station, is the old heart of the village, with an endearing **museum** (Borovška 61), an attractive **church** and a few wooden-roofed old houses. At its newer western end it passes the helpful **tourist office** (☎ 588 17 68; www .kranjska-gora.si; Tičarjeva 2; 8am-7pm Mon-Fri, to 8pm Sat, 9am-1pm Sun Jul-Aug, 8am-3pm Mon-Fri, 9am-6pm Sat, 9am-1pm Sun Sep-Jun), a bank with ATM and money exchange, a couple of supermarkets and the post office.

Several places, including **Skipass Travel** (☎ 582 1000; Boroškova 5; www.skipasstravel.si), hire skis, poles and boots and sell lift passes.

The in-your-face mountain valleys also beckon summer climbers, hikers and anglers alike. For cyclists and motorists there's the awesome drama of the Vršič Pass.

Sleeping & Eating

Accommodation pricing is very complex, peaking December to February, at Mardi Gras and in midsummer. April is the cheapest season, though many hotels close for repairs at this time. Private rooms (single/double from €18/26) and mountain huts can be arranged with help from the tourist office.

Hotel Kotnik (☎ 588 15 64; kotnik@siol.net; Borovška 75; d €56-64) In the old centre, this appealing, very well-appointed hotel has 'turrets', red-tiled roofs, and flowers in the window boxes. It's painted in unmissable bright yellow.

There's a cosy little lounge, a well-reputed restaurant and a good pizzeria attached.

Gostilna Pri Martinu (☎ 582 03 00; Borovška 61; d €46-52, meals around 1700SIT; 10am-10pm, bar 10am-11pm) This atmospheric tavern-restaurant serves up giant portions and offers four vegetarian options. It's *ajdova kaša* (buckwheat with fresh mushrooms in garlic-cream sauce) is superb. It also has rooms.

Youth Hostel Nika (Penzion Portentov Dom; ☎ 588 14 36; Čičare 2; dm €13; 8am-11pm) Somewhat institutional dorm-rooms are available in this large black-and-lilac house 800m northeast of the centre, some 200m beyond the Šanghai Chinese restaurant.

Getting There & Away

Buses run hourly to Ljubljana via Jesenice (change for Bled or Villach), and direct to Bled at 9.15am and 1.10pm, weekdays only. In July and August there's a service to Bovec (1530SIT, 1¾ hours, one daily) via the spectacular Vršič Pass.

TRIGLAV NATIONAL PARK

pop 2705 / elev to 2864m

Although there are 40 country (or 'landscape') parks and two regional ones in Slovenia, this is the country's only gazetted national park, and it includes almost all of the Julian Alps lying within Slovenia. The centrepiece of the park is, of course, Triglav (2864m) – Slovenia's highest mountain – but there are many other peaks here reaching above 2000m, as well as ravines, canyons, caves, rivers, streams, forests and alpine meadows.

Kranjska Gora to Soča Valley

One of the most spectacular – and easy – trips in Triglav National Park is simply to follow the paved road, open from May to October only, from Kranjska Gora via the Vršič Pass to Bovec, about 50km to the southwest. Between July and September, you can do the trip by bus. At other times, you'll need your own transport – be it a car or mountain bike.

The first stop from Kranjska Gora is **Jasna Lake** (Jezero Jasna), about 2km south of town. It's a beautiful, almost too-blue glacial lake with white sand around its rim and the little Pivnica River flowing alongside. Standing guard is a bronze statue of that irascible old goat **Zlatorog**, the mythical chamois (*gams* in Slovene) with the golden horns who once lived on Mt Triglav and guarded its treasure. Travellers might recognise Zlatorog's face; it's on the label of the country's best beer.

As you zigzag up to just over 1100m, you'll come to the **Russian Chapel** (Ruska Kapelica), a little wooden church erected on the site where more than 400 Russian prisoners of war were buried in an avalanche in March 1916 while building the road you are travelling on.

The climbing then begins in earnest as the road meanders past a couple of huts and corkscrews up the next few kilometres to **Vršič Pass** (1611m), about 13km from Kranjska Gora. The area was the scene of fierce fighting during WWI, and a high percentage of the dead lay where they fell (at 1525m there's a **military cemetery** to the east of the road). The Tičarjev Dom mountain hut is also east of the road. To the west is Mojstrovka (2366m), to the east Prisank (2547m) and to the south the valley of the Soča River points the way to Primorska. A hair-raising descent of about 10km ends just short of the **Julius Kugy Monument**. Kugy (1858–1944) was a pioneer climber and author whose books eulogise the beauty of the Julian Alps.

From here you can take a side trip of about 2.5km northwest along the **Soča Trail** (Soška Pot) to the **source of the Soča River** (Izvir Soče). Fed by an underground lake, the infant river bursts from a dark cave before dropping 15m to the rocky bed from where it begins its long journey to the Adriatic.

Not long after joining the main road again you'll pass the entrance to the **Alpinum Juliana**, a botanical garden established in 1926 and showcasing the flora of all of Slovenia's Alps (Julian, Kamnik-Savinja and Karavanke) as well as the Karst. The elongated mountain village of **Trenta** (population 115; elevation 662m) is about 4km to the south.

In lower Trenta the **Dom Trenta** (☎ 05-388 93 30; Trenta 31; ☼ 10am-6pm late Apr-Oct) contains the **Triglav National Park Information Centre** (☎ 04-578 0200; www.tnp.si) and the **Trenta Museum** (Trentarski Muzej; adult/child/student 900/600/550SIT), which focuses on the park's geology and natural history as well as the Trenta guides and pioneers of Slovenian alpinism.

The equally long village of **Soča** (population 144; elevation 480m) is another 8.5km downriver. The **Church of St Joseph** (Cerkev Sv Joža), from the early 18th century, has paintings by Tone Kralj (1900–75). Completed in 1944 as war still raged in Central Europe, one of the frescoes on the ceiling depicts Michael the Archangel struggling with Satan and the foes of humanity, Hitler and Mussolini.

CLIMBING TRIGLAV

Marked trails in the park – many of them under repair – lead to countless peaks and summits besides Triglav. Favourite climbs include Mangart (2678m) on the Italian border (the 12km road that descends to the Predel Pass is the highest road in Slovenia), the needlepoint of Jalovec (2645m) in the north, and the sharp ridge of Razor (2601m), southeast of Vršič.

To commune with nature in solitude, try climbing from Trenta. Because it's more difficult to reach from major population centres, the western approach to Triglav is quieter than the other routes. Get ready for a long climb starting from an altitude of just over 600m. From Trenta, an hour's hike along the Zajdnica Valley leads to the foot of Triglav's western face. Follow a long but relatively easy trail as it zigzags up the mountain to the Dolič saddle and the mountain hut **Tržaška Koča na Doliču** (☎ 04-574 4069) at 2151m. From here you can follow the normal route to the summit via **Dom Planika pod Triglavom** (☎ 04-574 4069) mountain hut at 2401m or take the slightly more difficult western ridge.

But the Triglav National Park is not only about climbing mountains. There are easy hikes through beautiful valleys, forests and meadows, too. Two excellent maps are the PZS 1:50,000 *Triglavski Narodni Park* and Freytag and Berndt's 1:50,000 *Julische Alpen Wanderkarte*. The new *Triglav National Park: Two Guides in One* (Založba Mladinska Knjiga), which comes as a 104-page booklet with a map, is also worth a look. Before setting out on a hike, it's wise to check with the Triglav National Park Information Centre (above) or local tourist offices for advice on current conditions. Mountaineering shops are another good source of information.

Bovec, the recreational centre of the Upper Soča Valley (Gornje Posočje), is 12km west of Soča.

SLEEPING & EATING

Gostišče Jasna (☎ 04-588 57 00; Vršiška c 41; meals from 1200SIT; ☺ 10am-10pm) This inn with a terrace overlooking Jasna Lake is a great place for a meal or a drink before pushing on for the Vršič Pass and beyond.

There are several mountain huts on or near the Vršič road. **Erjačeva Koča na Vršiču** (☎ 04-586 60 70, 050-610 031; Vršiška c 90) is at 1525m. **Tičarjev Dom na Vršiču** (☎ 04-586 60 70, 050-634 571; plan.drustvo@siol.net; Trenta 85; ☺ late Apr-late Oct) sits right on the pass.

Near the source of the Soča River at 886m is the **Koča pri Izviru Soče** (☎ 04-586 60 70, 041 603 190; plan.drustvo@siol.net; ☺ May-Oct).

Camping grounds abound in the park. In Trenta there's **Kamp Trenta** (☎ 041 615 966; Trenta 60a; per person 1100-1350SIT; ☺ May-Oct) and **Kamp Triglav** (☎ 041 388 93 11; Trenta 18; per person 1000SIT; ☺ Apr-Sep). The staff at the **Dom Trenta** (☎ 05-388 93 30) in Trenta can book private rooms (3500SIT per person) and apartments (apartment for four from 11,000SIT).

UPPER SOČA VALLEY
☎ 05
The bluer-than-blue water of the **Soča River** changes tone with the seasons, but is always surreally vivid. It has carved out one of the loveliest valleys in the Julian Alps.

GETTING THERE & AWAY
Public transport in the area is poor. Weekday buses from Bovec via Kobarid run five times daily to Nova Gorica (1710SIT, two hours) and thrice to Ljubljana (3150SIT, 3¾ hours), passing Most na Soči train station (for Bled and Bohinj). In July and August only, six daily buses cross the spectacular Vršič Pass to Kranjska Gora; from here hourly buses continue to Ljubljana.

Bovec
pop 1610
For alpine drama, the views are best around Bovec, above which towers Mt Kanin, Slovenia's highest ski area at 2587m. Although Bovec itself is no great beauty, it makes an ideal base for hiking, biking or climbing into the marvellous valley beyond and is nationally famous for extreme sports.

The compact village square (Trg Golobarskih Žrtev) has everything you need. There are cafés, a hotel, a very helpful **tourist office** (☎ 384 19 19; www.bovec.si; ☺ 9am-9pm Mon-Sat, 9am-1pm Sun summer, hr vary winter) and several adrenaline-rush adventure-sports companies: **Planet Sport** (☎ 040 639 433; www.drustvo-planet.si), **Sportmix** (☎ 389 61 60; www.sportmix.traftbovec.si), **Top Rafting** (☎ 041 620 636; www.top.si) and experienced, well-organised **Soča Rafting** (☎ 389 6200; www.SocaRafting.si).

Activities include:

Guided canyoning 9600SIT for two hours at Sušec.

Hydrospeed Like riding down a river on a boogie board; 7900SIT for 10km.

Kayaking Guided 10km paddle about 8400SIT per person, two-day training courses from €95, including equipment.

White-water rafting From 6200SIT to 10,000SIT depending on distance.

Save 10% to 15% with student cards, the TIC's 'Byways' booklet, or by simply avoiding midsummer and weekends. **Avantura** (☎ 041 718 317; www.bovec.net/avantura.html; Kot 9, Bovec) offers awesome tandem-jump paragliding (24,000SIT): in winter when the ski lifts operate you jump off the top of Mt Kanin!

Chalet-villages throughout the valley have private-room accommodation from €12 per person (plus various supplements). There is an extensive list of contacts at www.bovec.net but finding anything at all in August can be tough. The central **Alp Hotel** (☎ 388 63 70; www.bovec.net/hotelalp; Trg Golobarskih Žrtev 48; s/d €46/74.60) is smart and good value. Camping facilities are better in Kobarid, but camping ground **Polovnik** (☎ 041 641 898; www.kamp-polovnik.com; Ledina 8; camp sites from 1500SIT, showers 120SIT) is handily central.

Kobarid
pop 1240
Nearby Kobarid village (Caporetto in Italian) is quainter than Bovec, though the woodland scenery is somewhat tamer. On its main square is extreme-sports agency **XPoint** (☎ 388 53 08; www.xpoint.si; ☺ 8am-8pm daily Jun-Sep, Sat & Sun only Oct-May) and Internet-equipped **Bar Cinca Marinca** (Trg Svobode 10; per 30min 250SIT; ☺ 8am-11pm). Right in the town centre, the **tourist office** (☎ 389 00 00; www.kobarid.si) is within Kobarid's **museum** (adult/student 800/600SIT; ☺ 9am-6pm, to 7pm Apr-Sep), which is otherwise devoted mainly to the region's

WWI battles. These killed over 200,000 people and formed the backdrop to Ernest Hemingway's *Farewell to Arms*. The daring Austro-German breakthrough at Kobarid in October 1917 invented blitzkrieg. Remnant WWI troop emplacements as well as numerous Roman and 6th-century archaeological sites can be seen on an easy-to-follow, half-day hiking loop to the impressive **Slap Kozjak** (Kozjak Waterfalls).

Not far from Kobarid's central church, **Apartmaji-Sobe Ivančič** (☎ 389 10 07; apartma-ra@siol .net; Gregorčičeva 6C; s €18-30, d €30-50) is a popular central homestay. It's neat and clean, with bathrooms shared between pairs of cheaper rooms.

Lazar Kamp (☎ 388 53 33; www.lazar-sp.si; per person €6.50-9; ☼ Apr-Oct) is perched idyllically above the Soča River, 1.7km southeast of Kobarid, halfway to Slap Kozjak. Probably Slovenia's finest camping ground, the multilingual owners are conscientious and hospitable. Their wild west–style saloon-café serves delicious *palačinka* crepes. Go on, try the 'bear's blood'!

The renowned **Restaurant Kotlar** (mains 1500-3000SIT; ☼ noon-11pm Thu-Mon) is also located on Kobarid's main square.

NOVA GORICA/GORIZIA

Nova Gorica, a green but dull casino- and border-town, was torn from Italian-held old Gorizia after WWII. Today the two towns lie side-by-side on each side of the border. Nova Gorica is useful mainly as a money-saving public transport route between Italy's budget airline-served western cities of Trieste and Treviso and Slovenia's Julian Alps. Part of the mini-'Berlin Wall' dividing the cities was pulled down to great fanfare in 2004, leaving the anomalous Piazza Transalpina straddling the border right behind Nova Gorica station. At the piazza there's no fence and (usually) no guards, so in reality there's rarely anything to physically stop you wandering across to the Italian side, where the frequent Italian bus 1 will pick you up and conveniently whisk you to Gorizia station. Bizarrely, however, this is NOT a legal border crossing, and it won't be until Slovenia joins the Schengen Convention in October 2007. Meanwhile EU (plus Icelandic, Norwegian and Swiss) citizens may use a less direct shuttle bus (€1, 25 minutes, almost hourly)

between the two train stations, or cross on foot at the **Gabrielle border crossing** (☼ 8am-8pm Mon-Sat; no banks). Gabrielle is a two-minute stroll south of Nova Gorica train station, or 10 minutes southwest from the bus station: head straight down Erjavčeva which becomes Via San Gabriele in Italy. Continue five minutes to the five-way junction Piazza Medaglie d'Oro to pick up southbound Italian bus 1 for Gorizia station.

Other nationalities can't use the Gabrielle crossing. Instead they are expected to use the 24-hour Rožna Dolina–Cassa Rosa crossing (where there are banks with ATMs). This is reached by half-hourly buses (any number) from Nova Gorica bus station, or by walking 20 minutes south from the train station: follow the railway line through the cycle-tunnel, immediately thereafter cross the tracks on a footbridge and continue along Pinka Tomažiča and Pot na Pristavo. From Cassa Rosa take Italian bus 8 northbound along its convoluted route, which loops back to Gorizia bus/train stations.

There are banks with ATMs at Rožna Dolina and Nova Gorica bus station but not at Gabrielle, nor at the train station, which nonetheless does accept euros for tickets (at some 10% below market rates).

Nova Gorica's best-value place to stay is **Prenočišče Pertout** (☎ 303 21 94; www.prenociscepe tout.com; s/d 5000/7000SIT), a well-marked house just 50m east then north from the Rožna Dolina border crossing. It's surprisingly peaceful and comfortable.

Buses travel between Nova Gorica and Ljubljana (2380SIT, 2½ hours) approximately hourly via Postojna, and five times daily to Bovec via Kobarid.

Trains run to Bohinjski Bistrica (1190SIT, 1½ hours) and Bled or via Sežana and Divača to Postojna and Ljubljana.

KARST & COAST

Slovenia's 45km sliver of coastline has no beach worthy of the name, although that hasn't stopped Portorož becoming a major resort. The coast's real appeal lies in its charming old Venetian ports: Koper, Izola and picture-perfect Piran. En route from Ljubljana you'll cross Karst (Kras), Slovenia's west-central region, which is synonymous with eccentrically eroded limestone landscapes and riddled with magnificent caves. Slovenia's two most famous caves – theme park-style Postojna and quietly awesome Škocjan – couldn't be more different.

POSTOJNA

☎ 05 / pop 8500

Slovenia's foremost tourist attraction, **Postojna Cave** (☎ 700 01 00; www.postojnska-jama.si; adult/student/child 3690/2770/2390SIT) is a very obvious 2km stroll northwest of unremarkable Postojna town. Inside, impressive stalagmites and stalactites stretch almost endlessly in all directions, as do the chattering crowds who shuffle past them. A visit involves a 1.7km walk, with some gradients but no steps. It culminates in a quick encounter with a cute, endemic *Proteus anguinus* 'humanfish'. The very jolly highlight which both starts and finishes the tour is chugging between the limestone formations on an underground train. Dress warmly or hire a coat (700SIT): even on blistering summer days it's only 8°C to 10°C inside the cave, the train seats may be wet, and there's some wind chill on the open carriages.

Entry times are fixed. At a minimum there will be departures at 10am and 2pm daily plus at noon and 4pm on weekends. Frequency rises steadily towards summer, becoming hourly (from 9am to 6pm) between June and October.

Idyllic **Predjama** village is 9km northwest of Postojna. It consists of half a dozen houses, a rural inn, a mock-medieval jousting course and a remarkable **castle** (☎ 700 01 00; adult/student 1100/830SIT; 10am-4pm Jan-Mar & Nov-Dec, 10am-6pm Apr & Oct, 9am-7pm May-Sep) which appears to grow out of a yawning cave. Although a castle has stood on the site since 1202, the one you see today dates from the 16th century. Then – as now – the four-storey fortress looked unconquerable.

The castle's eight museum rooms contain little of interest, but it does have an eyrie-like hiding place at the top called **Erazem's Nook**, a drawbridge over a raging river, holes in the ceiling of the entrance tower for pouring boiling oil on intruders, a very dank dungeon and a 16th-century chest full of treasure (unearthed in the cellar in 1991).

Beneath the castle are stalactite-adorned **caves** (1100SIT, cave-castle combination ticket adult/student 2000/1500SIT), a 6km network of galleries spread over five levels. Much of it is open only to speleologists, but casual visitors can see about 900m-worth.

Sleeping & Eating

Dozens of Postojna houses rent rooms (single/double from 4500/7500SIT). Central **Kompas** (☎ 72 14 80; www.kompas-postojna.si; Titov trg; 8am-6pm Mon-Fri, 9am-3pm Sat) or the cave-side **tourist office** (www.postojna.si; 10am-4pm Sep-Apr, 9am-6pm May-Oct) can help.

Gostilna Požar (☎ 751 52 52; tw €46; closed Wed) Facing the cave-mouth castle in Predjama, this brilliantly situated inn has simple rooms with new bathrooms, and is above the village restaurant.

Hotel Kras (☎ 726 40 71; www.hotel-kras.com; Titov trg; s/d €33/47) This unlovely and somewhat tatty concrete box–style hotel is right on the central square, a 200m stroll north of the bus station.

Getting There & Away

Buses from Ljubljana to Koper, Piran or Novo Gorica all stop in Postojna (1¼ hours). The train is less useful as the station is 1km east of town near the bypass, ie 3km from the caves. There's no public transport except five local buses on school days from Postojna bus station to Bukovje village (390SIT). That's just 1.3km short of Predjama, a delightful, well-signposted walk.

CERKNICA

☎ 01 / pop 3550 / elev 559m

Cerknica is the largest town on a lake that isn't always a lake – one of Slovenia's most unusual natural phenomena. The town itself is not particularly important as a destination, but it is close to the 'intermittent' Lake Cerknica, the country park around Rakov Škocjan Gorge, Mt Snežnik and Snežnik Castle.

Orientation & Information

Cerknica lies about 3km north of Lake Cerknica. C 4 Maja is the main street in the centre of town. The bus station is on Čabranska ul, about 100m to the southwest and behind the post office. The **tourist office** (☎ 709 36 36; vlasta.kolenc@postojna.si; C 4 Maja 51; 7.30am-3pm Mon-Fri) is on the ground floor of the Notranjska Ecology Centre (Notranjski Ekološki Center).

SLOVENIA

Sights

LAKE CERKNICA

Since ancient times periodic Lake Cerknica has baffled and perplexed people, including the Greek geographer and historian Strabo (63 BC–AD 24), who called the mysterious body of water Lacus Lugeus (Mourning Lake). It wasn't until Valvasor (a 17th-century historian who published the first major study of Slovenia) explained how the water system worked that it was fully understood.

Cerknica is a *polje*, a field above a collapsed karst cavern full of sinkholes, potholes, siphons and underground tunnels that can stay dry for much of the year but then floods. From the south, the *polje* is fed by a disappearing river, the Stržen, and to the east and west it collects water underground from the Bloke Plateau and the Javornik Mountains. During rainy periods in the autumn and spring, all this water comes rushing into the *polje*. Springs emerge and the water begins to percolate between the rocks. The sinkholes and siphons cannot handle the outflow underground, and the *polje* becomes Lake Cerknica – sometimes in less than a day.

The surface area of Lake Cerknica can reach almost 40 sq km, but it is never more than a few metres deep. During dry periods (usually July to September or later), farmers drive cattle down to the *polje*.

The lake really begins at the village of Dolenje Jezero (population 225), about 2.5km south of Cerknica, where you will find the **Lake House Museum** (Muzej Jezerski Hram; ☎ 709 40 53; www.jezerski-hram.si; adult/child 550/450SIT, multimedia 200/150SIT; ☼ demonstration 3pm Sat & Sun), with a 5m by 3m, 1:2500 scale working model of Lake Cerknica, showing how the underground hydrological system works. There's also an ethnological collection and multimedia presentation.

RAKOV ŠKOCJAN

Protected Rakov Škocjan is a gorge 6km west of Cerknica. The Rak River, en route to join the Pivka River at Planina Cave, has sculpted 2.5km of hollows, caves, springs and **Veliki** and **Mali Naravni Most**, the Big and Little Natural Bridges. There are several hiking trails through and around the gorge.

From Rakek train station (right), you can reach the gorge on foot in about an hour.

Activities

The **Cerknica Mountain Trail** heads southwest from Cerknica to thickly forested **Veliki Javornik** (1269m). From here you can take a side trip of about two hours to the gorge at Rakov Škocjan. The trail then skirts the southern shore of Lake Cerknica and carries on north to **Križna Gora** (856m) and its nearby cave. It continues northwest to **Slivnica** (1114m), home of the witch Uršula and other sorcerers, where you will find a 32-bed mountain hut, **Dom na Slivnici** (☎ 709 41 40; ☼ daily May-Sep, Sat & Sun Oct-Apr). The next day you walk north to **Stražišče** (955m) and then back to Cerknica.

Festivals & Events

Cerknica is famous for its **Carnival** (Pustni Karneval) that takes place four days before Ash Wednesday (late February/early March) when merrymakers wearing masks of Uršula, who makes her home on Mt Slivnica, and other legendary characters parade up and down C 4 Maja while being provoked by upstarts with pitchforks.

Sleeping & Eating

Telič Vilma (☎ 709 70 90; drago.telic@siol.net; Brestova 9; s/d 5500/8500SIT) This small B&B on the eastern edge of town with two double rooms with shared bathroom and toilet has stunning views over the lake.

Valvasorjev Hram (☎ 709 37 88; Partizanska c 1; meals from 1500SIT; ☼ 8am-11pm) Serves pizza and has its own wine cellar.

You'll find a central supermarket (it's divided into two buildings) – a large **Mercator** (C 4 Maja 64; ☼ 7am-8pm Mon-Fri, 7am-1pm Sat, 8am-noon Sun) and another **Mercator** (C 4 Maja 64; ☼ 7am-9pm Mon-Sat, 8am-noon Sun) – diagonally opposite the tourist office.

Getting There & Away

Buses run between nine and 12 times a day to/from Ljubljana, and about half a dozen go to Lož, Rakek and Stari trg pri Ložu. Other destinations include Postojna (five during school term). Two or three buses a day cross the Croatian border to Previd.

Rakek, about 5km northwest of Cerknica, is on the rail line that connects Ljubljana with Sežana. About 10 trains a day to/from the capital stop at Rakek. Heading south, all stop at Postojna and Pivka, but only about half continue to Divača and Sežana.

SNEŽNIK CASTLE

☎ 01 / elev 593m

Just south of the village of Kozarišče (population 240), in the secluded Lož Valley (Loška Dolina) 21km southeast of Cerknica, stands 16th-century Renaissance **Snežnik Castle** (Grad Snežnik; ☎ 705 78 14; adult/student & child 700/600SIT; ⏰ 10am-1pm & 3-6pm Wed-Fri, 10am-6pm Sat & Sun mid-Apr–Oct). It is one of the loveliest and best-preserved fortresses in Slovenia. The entrance to the castle, which is surrounded by a large and protected park, is through a double barbican with a drawbridge and moat. The **exhibits** in the main building are the chattels and furnishings (notice the room done up in Egyptian handicrafts) of the Schönburg-Waldenburg family, who used what they called Schneeberg as a summer residence and hunting lodge until WWII. The castle also contains an **art gallery**.

Adjacent to the castle, a 19th-century dairy building houses the **Dormouse Collection** (Polharska Zbirka; ☎ 705 76 37; Kozarišče 70; 10am-1pm & 2-5pm Wed-Fri, 10am-1pm & 2-7pm Sat & Sun). The dormouse (*glis glis*) or loir (*polh*) is a tree-dwelling nocturnal rodent, not unlike a squirrel, which grows to about 30cm and sleeps through several months of the year. It is a favourite food in Notranjska, and the hunting and eating of it is associated with a lot of tradition. The fur is used to make the *polhovka*, the distinctive fur cap worn by Božiček, Slovenia's version of Santa Claus, and dormouse *mast* (fat) is a much-prized machine oil. According to popular belief, the dormouse is shepherded by Lucifer himself and thus deserves its fate in the cooking pot.

Križna Cave, about 7km north of Snežnik Castle and a kilometre or so after you turn off the main road from Cerknica, is one of the most magnificent water caves in the world. It is 8.5km long and counts 22 underground lakes filled with green and blue water as well as a unique 'forest' of ice stalagmites near the entrance. The dry part of the cave, which includes a short boat ride, can be toured (1100SIT) at 3pm on Sunday from May to October in an hour. To go as far as the Kalvarija chamber by rubber raft via 13 lakes (5500SIT to 7000SIT), you must contact the guide, **Alojz Troha** (☎ 041 632 153) in Bloška Polica (house No 7) in advance. It's a four-hour tour if you elect to do the entire cave, and the price includes all equipment.

A stage of the E6 European Hiking Trail leads from near Snežnik Castle for about 15km to **Snežnik** (1796m), whose peak remains snowcapped until well into the spring. It is the highest non-Alpine mountain in Slovenia. There is accommodation at the hut **Koča Draga Karolina na Velikem Snežniku** (☎ 041 333 198; pd.sneznik@email.si; ⏰ Sat & Sun May-Jul, Sep & Oct, daily Aug).

Festivals & Events

The big occasion in these parts is **Dormouse Hunting Night** (Polharska Noč). It's held on the first Saturday after 25 September during the brief period when it's open season for trapping the incredible edible dormouse.

Getting There & Away

Snežnik's isolation makes it tough to reach by public transport. Without a car, bicycle or horse, you'll have to take a bus from Cerknica to Stari trg pri Ložu (up to six a day) and walk 4km.

ŠKOCJAN CAVES & DIVAČA

☎ 05

The perky church tower of a tiny, red-roofed hamlet pokes jauntily through fluffy forests. Just beneath, the limestone earth cracks like broken eggshells, releasing the turbulent Reka River from the immense **Škocjan Caves** (www.park-skocjanske-jame.si; adult/student 2500/1800SIT). Harder to reach and much less commercialised than Postojna, these caves have been declared a Unesco World Heritage site. With relatively few stalactites, the attraction here is the sheer depth of the awesome underground chasm, which you cross by a dizzying little footbridge. To see this you must join a shepherded two-hour walking tour, involving hundreds of steps and ending with a rickety funicular ride. Year-round departures are assured at 10am and 1pm daily plus 3pm Sundays. June to September they leave additionally at 11.30am, 2pm, 3pm, 4pm and 5pm daily. Unlike Postojna the caves warm up somewhat in summer so there's no need for unseasonable coats.

The nearest town with accommodation is Divača, 4km to the northwest. The best place is **Gostilna Malovec** (☎ 763 12 25; Kraška 30a; s/d €20/40), 500m northeast of the train station. On the way, you'll pass the modest **Gostilna Risnik** (☎ 763 00 08; Kraška 24; s/tw 3500/7000SIT) over a bar 200m from the train station.

Ljubljana-Koper buses and trains stop at Divača half an hour after Postojna. Kindly staff at the train station often give visitors a photocopied route map for walking to the caves. Alternatively, stay on the bus a couple of minutes longer and get dropped off at a signposted junction just 1.6km from the caves. Timetables rarely mesh with cave-visit times, but you can make pleasant short hikes around the cave's visitor centre, where there's a bar and restaurant for those conserving their energy.

LIPICA
☎ 05 / pop 130

Since the 18th century, Lipica has been breeding snow-white Lipizzaner horses for the world-famous Imperial Spanish Riding School in Vienna. The village is basically just a hotel complex and the **Stud Farm** (☎ 739 15 80; www.lipica.org; tours per adult/student from 1500/800SIT), which offers equestrian fans a variety of rides, lessons and tours (hourly from 11am to 3pm, finishing later in summer). For comprehensive timetables and prices check the website carefully. The **Hotel Maestoso** (www.lipica.org; s/tw low season €50/78, mid-season €58/90, high season €65/100) has excellently appointed rooms looking over the golf course-like landscape. For cheaper places drive 3km west to Basovizza in Italy.

Divača to Lipica is only 10km but there's no viable public transport. With your own wheels stop halfway there in the village of **Lokev**, where the intriguing 1485 **Tabor tower** houses a cheap bar and a little **armaments museum** (☎ 767 01 07; ☼ 9am-noon & 2-6pm Wed-Fri), just off (and easily visible from) the main Divača–Lipica road.

KOPER
☎ 05 / pop 24,000

As you swing around it on the motorway, Koper appears to be a sprawling, industrial town dominated by container-port cranes. Yet its central core is delightfully quiet, quaint and much less touristy than nearby Piran. Also, being a working city, its accommodation is not quite as stretched as Piran's in summer.

Koper grew rich as a key Venetian salt-trading port. Known then as Capodistria, it was capital of Istria under the 15th- and 16th-century Venetian Republic. At that time it was an island commanding a U-shaped bay of saline ponds, something hard to imagine now, given the centuries of land reclamation that have joined it very firmly to the mainland.

Orientation
The joint bus and train station (bicycle hire available) is 1.4km southeast of central Titov trg. To walk into town, just head towards the cathedral's Moroccan-style bell tower; alternatively, take Bus 1, 2 or 3 to the Muda Gate. Pristaniška and Vojkovo nab mark what was once the southern coast of the medieval island.

Information
Banka Koper (Kidričeva 14; ☼ 8.30am-noon & 3-5pm Mon-Fri, 8.30am-noon Sat) Changes money.
Hospital (☎ 664 71 00; Dellavallejeva 3; ☼ 24hr)
Libris (www.libris.si in Slovene; Prešernov trg 9; ☼ 8am-7pm Mon-Fri, 9am-1pm Sat) Bookshop with postcards.
Maki Currency Exchange Bureau (Pristaniška ul; ☼ 7.30am-7.30pm Mon-Fri, 7.30am-1pm Sat) Compare rates with Ilirika across the road.
Net Bar (Vojkovo nab 33; ☼ 6am-11pm Mon-Fri, 8am-11pm Sat, noon-11pm Sun) Twenty minutes free Internet access when you buy a drink (beers 330SIT).
Pina (☎ 630 03 20; Kidričeva 43; per min adult/student 15/5SIT; ☼ 9am-8pm) Internet.
TIC (☎ 664 62 30; www.turizemvkopru.com; Praetorian Palace, Titov trg 3; ☼ 9am-5pm Mon-Fri, to 1pm Sat Jun-Sep, 9am-9pm Mon-Sat, to noon Sun Jul & Aug) The TIC's useful tourist map includes potted histories of key buildings.

Sights
The greatest attraction of Koper is simply purposeless wandering. You change centuries abruptly passing through the 1516 **Muda Gate**. Continue north past the 1666 **Da Ponte Fountain** (Prešernov trg) and up Čevljarska ul, the petite commercial artery, to reach Titov trg. This fine central square is dominated by the 1480 **tower** attached to the part-Gothic, part-Renaissance **Cathedral of St Lazarus**. The renovated 15th-century **Praetorian Palace** (Titov trg 3; admission free; ☼ 9.30am-2pm & 3.30-7pm) contains the city hall and an old pharmacy which is now a museum, as well as the tourist office.

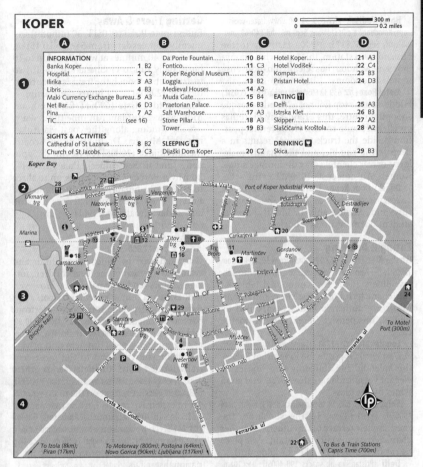

KOPER

0 — 300 m
0 — 0.2 miles

	A		B		C		D
INFORMATION		Da Ponte Fountain	10 B4	Hotel Koper	21 A3
Banka Koper	1 B2	Fontico	11 C3	Hotel Vodišek	22 C4
Hospital	2 C2	Koper Regional Museum	12 B2	Kompas	23 B3
Ilirika	3 A3	Loggia	13 B2	Pristan Hotel	24 D3
Libris	4 B3	Medieval Houses	14 A2		
Maki Currency Exchange Bureau	5 A3	Muda Gate	15 B4	**EATING**	
Net Bar	6 D3	Praetorian Palace	16 B3	Delfi	25 A3
Pina	7 A2	Salt Warehouse	17 A3	Istrska Klet	26 B3
TIC	(see 16)	Stone Pillar	18 A3	Skipper	27 A2
		Tower	19 B3	Slaščičarna Kroštola	28 A2
SIGHTS & ACTIVITIES		**SLEEPING**		**DRINKING**	
Cathedral of St Lazarus	8 B2	Dijaški Dom Koper	20 C2	Skica	29 B3
Church of St Jacobs	9 C3				

Koper Bay

Port of Koper Industrial Area

To Izola (8km);
Piran (17km)

To Motorway (800m); Postojna (64km);
Novo Gorica (90km); Ljubljana (117km)

To Bus & Train Stations
Capris Time (700m)

To Motel
Port (300m)

Several more fine façades face Trg Brolo, a wide, peacefully Mediterranean square. One such is the shield-dotted **Fontico** that started life as a 1392 grain warehouse. Beside this, with a small, simple campanile, is the 14th-century stone **Church of St Jacobs** (Martinčev trg).

The **Koper Regional Museum** (☎ 663 65 70; Kidričeva 19; adult/student 350/250SIT; ☾ 10am-6pm Mon-Fri, 9am-1pm Sat & Sun Sep-Jun, 9am-1pm & 6-9pm Tue-Sun Jul & Aug) is within the Belgramoni-Tacco mansion and features an Italianate sculpture garden. Kidričeva also has a few appealing **medieval houses** with beamed overhangs. It leads west into Carpacciov trg, the former fish market with a 15th-century **salt warehouse**, a 1571 **stone pillar**, a pub and a couple of street cafés.

Sleeping

The station-based **Capris Time** (☎ 631 15 55; www .capristime-sp.si; Kolodvorska 11; d Sep-Jun from €28, Jul & Aug from €32; ☾ 8am-4pm Mon-Fri) agency arranges private rooms with discounts for three-day stays. Similarly priced rooms are offered by **Kompas** (☎ 627 15 81; Pristaniška 17; ☾ 8am-7pm Mon-Fri, 8am-1pm Sat).

Hotel Koper (☎ 610 05 00; www.terme-catez.si; Pristaniška 3; s/d €55/102; ✖) This very smartly renovated business hotel is Koper's most central.

Pristan Hotel (☎ 614 40 00; fax 614 40 40; Ferrarska 30; s/d 13200/19,800SIT; ✖ ▯) Yet another hotel catering to the business traveller, with starkly modern rooms and suites that include a computer.

Hotel Vodišek (☎ 639 36 68; www.hotel-vodisek .com; Kolodvorska c 2; s/d early Sep–mid-Jul €40/60, mid-Jul–early Sep €56.80/85; P) Halfway to the bus and train station, this somewhat anonymous new hotel has clean, no-nonsense motel-style rooms.

Motel Port (☎ 639 32 60; Ankaranska 7; r 11,000SIT) Hidden on the top floor of a Mondrianesque shopping centre, this brand-new place has excellent ensuite rooms. However, its position beside the truck terminal results in a deep traffic rumble, and the mainly male, lorry-driver clientele may discourage single women. Air-con costs 1000SIT extra.

Dijaški Dom Koper (☎ 662 62 50; www.d-dom .kp.edus.si; Cankarjeva 5; dm 3500SIT; Jul-Aug) In July and August this brilliantly central student dorm becomes a hostel.

Eating & Drinking

Istrska Klet (☎ 627 67 29; Župančičeva 39; meals from 1200SIT; 7am-9pm) Squeeze together with fellow diners at the two communal tables of this characterful old wine cellar-restaurant. Meals are authentic and accompanied by typical, inexpensive Teran wine from the cask.

Loggia café (☎ 627 41 71; wine per glass from 250SIT; 7am-10pm) Opposite the Praetorian Palace, this splendid 1463 building now houses an elegant yet affordable café with several good wines by the glass.

Skipper (☎ 626 18 10; Kopališko nab 3; meals from 1900SIT; 9am-10pm) In the sunshine, the marina-view terrace of this otherwise rather characterless, upstairs restaurant is *the* place to eat fresh fish (7700SIT per kilogram).

Delfi (Pristaniška ul; snacks 190-400SIT; 10am-10pm) Good-value *burek* (a pie made with various fillings and filo pastry) and pizza slices that you can eat on a fairly pleasant terrace. There are other bars and eateries in adjoining units.

Slaščičarna Kroštola (ice-cream cones 160SIT; 8am-9pm) Perched on Koper's pitifully small pebble beach, the Kroštola is the best positioned of several alluring ice-cream parlour cafés.

Skica (☎ 627 2242; Čevljarska 29; 7.30am-midnight Mon-Sat, noon-11pm Sun) This rough-edged, thoroughly local bar has a little photo-gallery and a taste for blues music, and serves screwdrivers made with freshly squeezed oranges. Squint and you'll see Janis Joplin.

Getting There & Away

Buses run to Piran (610SIT, 30 minutes) frequently on weekdays from 5am to 10.15pm, and every 40 minutes at weekends. Up to 10 buses daily run to Ljubljana (2620SIT, two to 2½ hours), though the train is more comfortable (2040SIT, 2¼ hours, four daily).

Buses to Trieste (690SIT/€3, one hour, Monday to Saturday) run nine times daily, usually winding along the coast via Ankaran and Muggia. Destinations in Croatia include Rijeka (2000SIT,), Rovinj (3.55pm daily June to September), Pula (2700SIT, 2pm) via Poreč (1700SIT) plus up to three to Poreč only, notably at 7.30am Monday to Friday. There are summer ferries to Istria and Zadar, Croatia (see p404).

IZOLA
☎ 05 / pop 11,000

Overshadowed by much nicer Piran and swamped by vacationing local children, foreign visitors tend to bypass Izola. However, it does have a minor Venetian charm, a few narrow old alleys, and some nice waterfront bars and restaurants. The **TIC** (☎ 640 10 50; Sončno nabrežje 4; 10am-5pm Mon-Fri Oct-May, 9.30am-noon & 2-6pm daily June-Sep) can help find private rooms or you can head to the most centrally located hotel, the **Hotel Marina** (☎ 660 41 00; www.belvedere.si; Veliki trg 11; s 12,000-19,000SIT, d 13,400-20,600SIT P) right on the main square. More expensive rooms have sea views. Out in Izola's industrial suburbs, **Ambasada Gavioli** (☎ 641 82 12; www.ambasada-gavioli.com; Industrija c; Sat & party nights from midnight) is Slovenia's top rave club, featuring a procession of international star DJs.

Regular Koper–Piran bendy-buses drive via Izola.

PIRAN
☎ 05 / pop 4400

Little Piran (Pirano in Italian) is as picturesque a port as you can imagine, especially when viewed at sunset from the saw-toothed 16th-century walls that guard its hilly western flank. In summer the town gets pretty overrun by tourists, but in April or October it's hard not to fall in love with the winding Venetian-Gothic alleyways and tempting fish restaurants. The name derives from *pyr* (Greek for fire), referring to the Punta lighthouse at the tip of the town's peninsula. Since misty antiquity, this lighthouse has helped ships reach the great salt-port at Koper.

Orientation

Buses from everywhere except Portorož arrive at the bus station, just a 300m stroll along the harbourside Cankarjevo nab from central Tartinijev trg. Be warned that a car

is an encumbrance not a help in Piran. Vehicles are stopped at a tollgate 200m south of the bus station where the sensible choice is to use the huge Fornače car park. You could take a ticket and drive on in to the centre but old Piran is so small, parking is so limited and its alleyways so narrow (mostly footpaths) that you're likely to regret it.

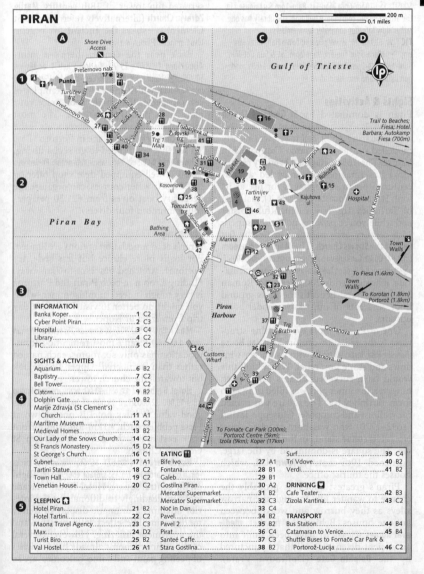

SLOVENIA

Information

Banka Koper (Tartinijev trg; ☾ 8.30am-noon & 3-5pm Mon-Fri, 8.30am-noon Sat) Money exchange and ATM.

Cyber Point Piran (☎ 671 00 24; Županičičeva 14; per hr 1000SIT; ☾ 9am-noon & 6-8pm Mon-Fri) Student centre and Internet connection.

Hospital (☎ 677 33 20; Cankarjevo 9; ☾ 24hr)

Library (☎ 671 08 70; Tartinijev trg; membership 500SIT; ☾ 10am-6pm Mon-Fri, 8am-1pm Sat) Housed in the attractive old courthouse building, the library has one rather slow Internet computer for members.

TIC (☎ 673 02 20; www.piran.si; Town Hall, Tartinijev trg; ☾ 10am-5pm Tue-Fri, 9am-2pm Sat & Sun Oct-May, 9am-1pm & 3-9pm daily Jun-Sep) Has maps, accommodation listings and excursion ideas.

Sights & Activities

Piran is dominated by **St George's Church** (Adamičeva 2; ☾ temporarily closed for renovation) whose soaring 1609 **bell tower** was clearly modelled on the San Marco Campanile in Venice. The 1650 octagonal **baptistry** *(krstilnica)* has imaginatively recycled a 2nd-century Roman sarcophagus for use as its font. **St Francis Monastery** (Bolniška 20), just west of Tartinijev trg, has a delightful cloister and while you're passing, notice the superb 15th-century arch painting in nearby **Our Lady of the Snows Church**. The **Maritime Museum** (☎ 671 00 40; Cankarjevo nab 3; adult/student 600/500SIT; ☾ 9am-noon & 3-6pm Tue-Sun) is in a fine marina-side mansion with 2000-year-old Roman amphorae (jars) beneath the glass ground floor, and lots of impressive model boats upstairs.

One of Piran's most eye-catching structures is the red 15th-century **Venetian House** (Beneške Hiša; Tartinijev trg 4), with its tracery windows and stone lion relief. When built this would have surveyed Piran's inner port; however, the inner port was filled in 1894 to form Tartinijev trg. The square was named for violinist and composer Giuseppe Tartini (1692–1770) who was born at what's now No 7. His **statue** stands in the square's middle. The square is dominated by the large, porticoed 19th-century **Town Hall**, which houses the tourist office.

Piran's greatest appeal is probably the chance to wander idly through the narrow alleys as they burrow and weave between antique houses. Behind the market, **medieval homes** (Obzidna ul) have been built into an ancient defensive wall that's punctured by the **Dolphin Gate** (Dolfinova Vrata).

The anachronistically named Trg 1 Maja (1st May Sq) may sound like a socialist parade ground but in fact it's one of Piran's cutest squares, with a 19th-century, statue-guarded **cistern** pool in the middle.

Punta, the historical 'nose' of Piran, still has a **lighthouse**, but today's is small and modern. Just behind it, however, the round, serrated-top tower of 18th-century **Marije Zdravja Church** (alternatively referred to as St Clement's) evokes the ancient *pyr* beacon that made Piran's name.

Back near the centre, there's a mini-**Aquarium** (☎ 673 25 72; Kidričevo nab 4; admission 500SIT; ☾ 10am-noon & 2-7pm Sep–mid-Jun, 9am-10pm mid-Jun–Aug) which shows living examples of several species that might soon grace your plate in a nearby restaurant. The most unusual underwater sight hereabouts is the wreck of a WWII seaplane in Portorož Bay. To see that you'll need to go scuba diving. **Subnet** (☎ 041 590 746; www.sub-net.si; Prešernovo nab 24), a well-equipped dive shop offering PADI open-water courses, can organise the necessary boat dives from €21.50 per person (minimum four divers).

Sleeping

Piran's accommodation options are limited. For loads more choice but less style, try Portorož, stretched out 2km to 7km away. Finding a room in both Piran and Portorož is very tough indeed in midsummer, when you might do better to visit Piran as a day trip from Izola or Koper.

Max (☎ 041 692 928; IX Korpusa 26; www.maxpiran .com; d €60-70) Piran's most romantic accommodation has only six rooms, each named rather than numbered. Upper floors look out towards the church tower.

Hotel Barbara (☎ 690 40 00; www.metropolgroup .si; s 15,000-22,000SIT; d 19,000-27,200SIT; ☒) This good-value holiday hotel is one of two at Fiesa pebble-beach, a 1km-long shore-front walk east along the north coast from St George's Church.

Hotel Tartini (☎ 671 16 66; www.hotel-tartini -piran.com; Tartinijev trg 15; s/d/apt €66/96/178) Right on the central square, Hotel Tartini's façade looks misleadingly traditional, yet the interior attempts a dramatic display of trendy modernism. The effect is impressive and the apartment amazing. However, several of the ordinary rooms already have touches of peeling paint and some 'balconies' are so minuscule they barely exist. Add a supplement of €5 for rooms with views.

Hotel Piran (☎ 676 21 00; www.hoteli-piran.si; Stjenkova 1; s from €53-68, d from €82-108; ❄ ▣) Smart, business-standard accommodation in the town centre's ugliest building. More expensive rooms have sea views and air-con but everyone gets Internet and wi-fi access.

Val Hostel (☎ 673 25 55; www.hostel-val.com; Gregorčičeva 38A; dm IYHA member €18-23, nonmember €20-24) Book well ahead for this superbly central hostel-*penzion* with shared bathrooms. There's a €2 surcharge for one-night stays.

Autokamp Fiesa (☎ 674 62 30; camp sites per person low/high season €7.50/8.35; ☉ May-Sep) This insecure handkerchief of grass behind a grotty caravan park is nonetheless packed full in summer, being just 1km from Piran, near Hotel Barbara.

Private rooms are available through **Maona travel agency** (☎ 674 03 63; www.maona.si; Cankarjevo nab 7; ☉ 9am-7pm Mon-Sat, 10am-2pm some Sun) starting at €19/31 a single/double in high season plus an additional 50% for stays shorter than three days. **Turist Biro** (☎ 673 25 09; www.turistbiro-ag.si; Tomažičev trg) lists similarly priced rooms but asks a €14 reservation fee.

Eating & Drinking

One of Piran's attractions is its plethora of fish restaurants, though don't expect any bargains. Virtually all charge around 1300SIT to 1500SIT for a plate of grilled squid, from 8000SIT per kilogram for fish and 400SIT to 500SIT for potatoes. Almost all open from 11am to 10pm or later in summer.

Galeb (☎ 673 32 25; Pusterla 5; ☉ 11am-3pm & 6-11.30pm Wed-Mon) Many visitors adore Galeb's 'family atmosphere' and the homestyle Slovenian food is equally popular.

Santeé Caffe (Cankarjevo nab; sandwiches 300-500SIT; ☉ 7am-midnight) This café has sandwiches and salads, and walls painted in colours as vivid as its excellent ice creams.

Pavel 2 (☎ 674 71 02; Kosovelova 1) It's marginally the suavest of the main sea-facing row of restaurants that includes the essentially similar Gostilna Piran, Bife Ivo, Pavel and Tri Vdove.

Inland you might prefer the characterful atmosphere of **Stara Gostilna** (☎ 041 641 020; Savurdrijska 2), the cistern-facing setting of **Fontana** (☎ 673 12 00; Trg 1 Maja), or smart little **Verdi** (☎ 673 27 37; Verdijeva ul), which on

summer days spills out onto the nearby square of Savudrijska ul.

Dining is marginally cheaper at **Pirat** (☎ 673 14 81; Cankarjevo nab) and **Surf** (☎ 673 11 75; Grudnova ul) towards the bus station. The latter has outdoor tables shaded by a rare little patch of greenery, and medium pizzas from 800SIT. The Hotel Piran restaurant does 1100SIT lunch deals. Hop on the No 1 shuttle bus to Portorož-Lucija for Mexican or Chinese food.

Piran has two Mercator supermarkets at Levstikova 6 and Bratsva trg 1, but minimart **Noč in Dan** (Cankarjevo nab; ☉ 6am-midnight) opens longer.

Cafe Teater (Kidričevo nab) Behind the Aquarium, atmospheric but expensive Cafe Teater is Piran's top pub and has a lively terrace.

Zizola Kantina (Tartinijev trg; ☉ 9am-midnight) An appealing nautically-themed bar, with tables right on the main square.

Getting There & Away

From the bus station buses run every 20 to 40 minutes to Koper (610SIT) via Izola, five per day head to Trieste (1290SIT, 1¾ hours, Monday to Saturday) and up to eight to Ljubljana (2720SIT, 2½ to three hours) via Divača and Postojna.

From Tartinijev trg, minibuses shuttle to Portorož-Lucija (minibus 1, 400SIT) and Portorož via Strunjan (minibus 3). There's also a free shuttle to the car park, but it's generally more comfortable and often quicker to walk. Piran and Izola dispatch catamarans to Venice at least once a week.

PORTOROŽ

☎ 05 / pop 13,000

In a long arc of woodland-backed bay, Slovenia's big hotel-resort town of Portorož (Portorose) is not unpleasant, but it's not much of an attraction either. The only beaches are pay-to-enter handkerchiefs of imported sand; if you want seaside fun you'd be better off continuing on to Croatia. Nonetheless, its vast assortment of accommodation makes Portorož a useful fall back if everything's full in nearby Piran. Greater Portorož stretches in a 5km-long arc, technically consisting of four subdistricts. From west (Piran side) to east there are Bernardin, Korotan, Portorož Centre and Lucija, though there's no noticeable boundaries between these districts. All are linked by the

5km-long curve of Obala, the main avenue and nearest road to the shore.

Full accommodation listings are available at the **tourist information office** (☎ 674 22 20; www .portoroz.si; Obala 16; ☒ 10am-5pm Sep-Jun, 9am-1.30pm & 3-9.30pm Jul & Aug) or from Piran TIC (p368). Handily close to Piran, the unusually up-market, summer-only **Hotel Riviera** and **Hotel Slovenija** (☎ 692 00 00; www.hoteli-morje.si; Obala 33; s €83-119, d €110-163; P ☒ ☒) are two sister hotels joined at the hip and are good choices if you want to stay someplace central. The renovated Riviera has 176 rooms, three fabulous swimming pools and the Wai Thai spa. Both have four stars. **Prenočišča Korotan** (☎ 674 54 00; www.prenocisca-korotan.vsk-sdp.si; Obala 11, Korotan; d €89.60; ☒ Jul & Aug; ☒) has ensuite rooms and its Internet computers are open to nonguests year-round.

There are dozens of decent pizzerias all along Obala. In the Grand Hotel Metropol, **San Lorenzo** (☎ 690 10 00; Obala 77; meals around 3500SIT) is arguably Portorož's best. For a change, try the very atmospheric Mexican taverna **Papa Chico** (☎ 677 93 10; Obala 26; meals from 2000SIT; ☒ 11am-midnight).

Every 20 minutes shuttle bus 1 from Piran trundles right along Obala to Lucija, passing the Prenočišča Korotan. From Bernardin and Korotan you could even walk into Piran in around 45 minutes, though the roads are unpleasantly busy.

SEČOVLJE
☎ 05 / pop 200

About 7km southeast of Portorož, in no-man's-land between the Slovenian and Croatian borders, is the fascinating **Sečovlje Salt-making Museum** (☎ 671 00 40; adult/student 600/500SIT; ☒ 9am-6pm Apr-May & Sep-Oct, 9am-8pm Jun-Aug). In one restored house there's an interesting little exhibition of salt-makers' equipment and lifestyles. Poignantly, many of the antique-looking photos were taken a mere 45 years ago. However, 'museum' is a misleading term, as the main attraction is the eerily desolate landscape sparsely dotted with abandoned old salt-diggers' homes amid a paddy-like patchwork of saltpans. Salt production here, at Koper and at Strunjan (between Piran and Izola) was once the region's economic *raison d'être*. What may look like simple square evaporation ponds are in fact the fruit of exceedingly complex engineering. Working entirely on wind and

tidal power, these were the ultimate examples of ecoenergy efficiency. Don't stand in the mud or you'll destroy a painstakingly cultivated 'skin' of protective algae which keeps the salt white. The dedicated staff laboriously maintain the delicate pools and still produce salt, which you can buy in souvenir burlap minisacks.

If you don't have your own vehicle or bicycle, the only practical way to visit Sečovlje is a 9.30am boat ride from Piran (2600SIT return, including admission). The main problem with this is that you're locked into a whole-day excursion, since boats don't usually return to pick you up until 4pm. Realistically an hour or so would be ample to get the idea.

EASTERN SLOVENIA

The rolling vineyard hills of eastern Slovenia are attractive but much less dramatic than the Julian Alps. If you're taking a bus from Ljubljana to Zagreb (Croatia), look left immediately after leaving Novo Mesto bus station (you'll stop briefly at the station) for picturesque views of Novo Mesto's old-town core rising directly across the Krka River. Travelling by car it would be nicer to drive via charming Kamnik then cross-country via chocolate-box villages like Motnik, big but pleasant Celje and the tiny but elegant spa-village Rogaška Slatina.

If you're heading by train to Vienna via Graz (Austria) it saves money to stop in lively Maribor; international tickets are very expensive per kilometre, so doing as much travelling as possible on domestic trains saves cash. While there, consider visiting postcard-perfect Ptuj.

KAMNIK
☎ 02 / pop 11,500

Magnificent views from the central ruins of Kamnik's **old castle** (*stari grad*) make for awesome photos, thanks to the perfect conjugation of red-tiled roofs, church towers and a dramatically close horizon of jostling snow-streaked peaks. Otherwise the town's charm is focused around its mostly pedestrianised main street, the very attractive Šutna ul/Glavny trg, along which are several appealing **galleries** and cafés. As this is all just two minutes' walk west of the bus station, Kamnik makes an easy half-day excursion from Ljubljana, 23km south.

Buses from Ljubljana (580SIT, 45 minutes) run almost every 30 minutes on weekdays. If you take the hourly train (470SIT, 45 minutes, hourly to 8.15pm), hop off at derelict-looking Kamnik Mesto, one stop after the main Kamnik station. The old castle is barely 100m east.

CELJE
☎ 03 / pop 40,000

While probably not worth a special detour, Celje has a long history, Roman remains and many elements of charm. A quick stopover is easy: all Ljubljana–Maribor trains stop here. Walk west out of the train station along grand, pedestrianised Krekov trg, which becomes Prešernova at the halfway bend. After 700m you'll reach the imposing **Narodni Dom**, in the side of which is the **tourist information office** (☎ 426 57 66; www.celje .si; Trg celjskih knezov 9; 8am-4pm Mon-Fri), handy for maps and inspiration. A short dogleg south and east from here is an arcaded palace containing the interesting **Pokrajinski Museum** (www2.arnes.si/~pokmuzce/index1.htm in Slovene; Muzejski trg; admission 800SIT; 10am-6pm Tue-Sun). Far and away its greatest attraction is a truly magnificent 17th-century trompe l'oeil ceiling, the Celje Ceiling (Celjski strop), 'discovered' in 1926.

West of the museum, attractive, time-warp Glavni trg has some pleasant terrace cafés and a **plague pillar**. Swerve round **St Daniel's Church** (Slomškov trg) and south down Savinjska to a fine riverside **viewpoint** (Savinjsko nab). You'll spot **St Cecilia's Church** (Maistrova ul) directly across the water, up a curious covered stairway. Harder to make out to its west is a reconstructed 2nd-century **Temple of Hercules**. Very obvious on a hill top high above to the southeast is the impressive if awkward-to-reach **Celje Castle**. From the viewpoint, walk five minutes northeast to return to the train station, passing medieval water- and defence-towers that incorporate recycled Roman stone blocks.

Trains to Ljubljana (1580SIT, 1½ hours) depart up to 28 times daily.

Around Celje
ŠEMPETER
☎ 03 / pop 1945 / elev 257m

Twelve kilometres west of Celje and accessible by bus and train, Šempeter is the site of a **Roman necropolis** (Rimska Nekropola; ☎ 700 20 56; www.td-sempeter.si; Ob Rimski Nekropoli 2; adult/child 700/500SIT; 10am-6pm Apr-Sep, 10am-4pm Sat & Sun Oct) reconstructed between 1952 and 1966. The burial ground contains four complete tombs and scores of columns, stelae and fragments carved with portraits, mythological creatures and scenes from daily life. They have been divided into about two dozen groups linked by footpaths.

If you get hungry, **Gostišče Štorman** (☎ 703 83 00; Šempeter 5a; meals from 3500SIT; 7am-midnight), one of the first private restaurants to open in Slovenia under the former regime, is about 2km east of the site on the road to Celje.

LOGARSKA DOLINA
☎ 03 / pop 95 / elev to 1200m

Logarska Dolina is about 40km northwest of Celje, near the Austrian border. Most of the glacial 'Forester Valley' – about 7.5km long and no more than 500m wide – has been a country park of 2438 hectares since 1987. This 'pearl of the Alpine region' with more than 30 natural attractions, such as caves, springs, peaks and waterfalls, is a wonderful place to spend a few days hiking and exploring.

Information
Tourist office (☎ 838 90 04; www.logarska-dolina.si; Logarska Dolina 9; 9am-1pm Apr-Sep) In a small kiosk in the Plesnik Hotel car park.

Sights & Activities
Logarska Dolina Country Park (Krajinski Park Logarska Dolina) is open year-round, but from April to September (and at weekends only in October) cars and motorcycles entering the park must pay 1000SIT and 700SIT respectively; pedestrians and cyclists get in free. A road goes past a chapel and through the woods to **Rinka Waterfall** (Slap Rinka), but there are plenty of trails to explore and up to 20 other waterfalls in the area.

The bottom of the Rinka Waterfall is a 10-minute walk from the end of the valley road. The climb to the top takes about 20 minutes. It's not very difficult, but it can get slippery. From the top to the west you can see three peaks reaching higher than 2200m: Kranjska Rinka, Koroška Rinka and Štajerska Rinka. Until 1918 they formed the triple border of Carniola (Kranjska), Carinthia (Koroška) and Styria (Štajerska).

Opposite the mountain hut of Dom Planincev is a trail leading to **Sušica Waterfall** and **Klemenča Cave**.

Another magnificent and much less explored valley, the 6km-long **Matkov Kot**, runs parallel to Logarska Dolina and the border with Austria. You can reach here by road by turning west as you leave Logarska Dolina. There are several farmhouses with accommodation in the valley.

The tourist office can organise any number of activities: from **horse riding** and **coach rides** (for up to five people) to **paragliding**, guided **mountaineering** and **rock climbing**. It also hires **mountain bikes**.

Sleeping & Eating

Plesnik Hotel (☎ 839 23 00; www.plesnik.si; Logarska Dolina 10; s €60, d €76-81; P) A 30-room hotel in the centre of the valley with a pool, sauna, a fine restaurant (open 7am to 9pm) and lovely public area.

Juvanija farmhouse (☎ 838 90 80; juvanija@email.si; Logarska Dolina 8; per person €19) Just inside the entrance to the park, this farmhouse has four rooms.

Lenar farmhouse (☎ 838 90 06; logarska@siol.net; Logarska Dolina 11; per person €19) Another farmhouse with four rooms, a couple of kilometres further south.

Dom Planincev (☎ 584 70 06, 031 269 785; Logarska Dolina 15a; per person €15) This mountain hut 2.5km from Rinka has a relaxed, rustic feel to it.

Getting There & Away

From Mozirje, there is an hourly bus service to Celje on weekdays but only two on Saturday. There are five to eight buses a day to Gornji Grad, five (one on Sunday) to Solčava and six (one on Sunday) to Velenje. One bus a day on weekdays from May to September makes its way from Celje to Logarska Dolina and the Rinka Waterfall car park.

From Gornji Grad, buses go to Ljubljana (four a day on weekdays, one on Saturday and Sunday), Celje (six a day), Kamnik (five, with one or two at the weekend), Ljubno (three, with one at the weekend) and Mozirje (one during the week). There's a 7.51am bus on Sunday to Logarska Dolina from June to September only.

PODSREDA CASTLE

☎ 03 / elev 475m

Perched on a hill south of the village of Podsreda (population 210), the **castle** (Grad Podsreda; ☎ 800 71 00; Podsreda 45; adult/child 600/500SIT; 10am-6pm Tue-Sun May-Oct, to 4pm Tue-Sun Mar & Apr) looks pretty much the way it did when it was built as Hörberg in about 1200. A barbican on the southern side, with walls three metres thick, leads to a central courtyard. The rooms in the castle wings, some with beamed ceilings and ancient chandeliers, now contain a rather dull glassworks exhibit (crystal from Rogaška Slatina, vials from the Olimje pharmacy, green Pohorje glass). However, the tiny Romanesque chapel is worth the visit, and there's a wonderful collection of prints of Štajerska's castles and monasteries taken from *Topographii Ducatus Stiria* (1681) by Georg Mattäus Vischer (1628–96). There's also a medieval kitchen and a dungeon hidden beneath a staircase. The view from the castle windows of the Kozjansko countryside and the pilgrimage church on **Svete Gore** (386m) above Bistrica ob Sotli are superb.

A rough, winding 5km-long road leads to the castle, but you can also reach it via a relatively steep 2km trail from Stari Trg, less than 1km southeast of Podsreda village. If you've built up an appetite climbing up and down those hills, there's a small *gostilna* called **Pri Martinu** (☎ 580 61 20; Podsreda 47; meals 1700SIT) in the village, which has a vine-covered terrace and also rents rooms (3000SIT per person).

Getting to Podsreda is tricky if you don't have your own wheels. The only option is to catch the one daily bus to Kozje from Celje and there wait for the one headed for Bistrica ob Sotli, which passes through Podsreda village.

ROGAŠKA SLATINA

Slovenia's oldest health retreat defies easy description. It's simultaneously grand yet rural, stylish yet ugly, bustling yet tranquil. For locals, the overwhelming attraction is magnesium-rich Donat-Mg spring water, which is sold expensively in bottles throughout Slovenia, but can be drunk direct from the spring here. Well almost. Don't imagine a limpid forest pool – someone's built a multistorey 1970s glass monstrosity on top of the **spring** (admission 300SIT). However, this eyesore is in a beautifully manicured park, and in front of it, facing the lawns of Zdravilški trg, the Grand Hotel looks something like a golden-yellow Buckingham Palace and has a vast chandeliered ballroom to match. At the other (southern) end of Zdravilški trg is the **tourist office** (☎ 581 44 14; www.rogaska-slatina.si; ◷ 9am-4pm Mon-Fri, to noon Sat), bus station, and the Escheresque **Hotel Slovenija**, with columns supporting nothing in particular. There are plenty more hotels (see www.terme-rogaska.si), all aimed at cure seekers who spend a week or so mooching about in dressing gowns, sipping the miracle waters – hot, cold, fizzy or flat – from curious tall, narrow glasses.

Of course, the pure air and simple living are probably as healthy as the sip-sipping. This then casts the brilliant 1904 Art Nouveau tavern **Tempel** (◷ 8am-1am Mon-Thu, to 3am Fri & Sat) in the devil's role of temptress. Water or beer? Choose both – a half litre of Donat-Mg supposedly prevents even the most well-earned hangover after a night on the tiles. You'll find Tempel in a park just off Kidrčeva (the main Celje road), where it bypasses the southern end of Zdravilška trg by a hundred metres or so.

Rogaška Slatina's also famous for colourful glassware, notably displayed in the Hotel Donat, on the way to its inhouse casino.

The tourist office may be able to arrange private accommodation.

The **Grand Hotel Rogaška** (☎ 811 20 00; www .terme-rogaska.com; Zdravilški trg 10; s/d from €90/190), **Styria and Strossmayer Hotels** (s/d from €58/100; P × ☒) – three interconnected hotels on the eastern side of Zdravilški trg, with more than 400 beds between them – are the crème de la crème of accommodation in Rogaška Slatina. The three-star Styria and Strossmayer date from the mid-19th century and the spectacular Grand, with four stars, from 1913.

The only convenient public transport access is from Celje; buses (800SIT, 40 minutes) run up to twice hourly on weekdays. Also from Celje, Rogatec-bound trains (620SIT, 50 minutes, five daily) stop 300m south of Rogaška Slatina bus station.

DOLENJSKE TOPLICE
☎ 07 / pop 750 / elev 179m
Within easy striking distance of Novo Mesto (13km to the northeast), this thermal resort is the oldest and one of the few real spa towns in Slovenia. Located in the karst valley of the Krka River below the wooded slopes of Kočevski Rog, Dolenjske Toplice is an excellent place in which to hike, cycle, fish or simply relax.

The first spa opened here in 1658, and Strascha Töplitz, as it was then called (after the nearby town of Straža), became a great favourite of Austrians from around the late 19th century up to WWI. The complex was used as a Partisan hospital during WWII.

Orientation & Information
Dolenjske Toplice lies about 1.5km south of the Krka River on a stream called the Sušica. Everything of importance is on or just off the main street, Zdravilíški trg. Buses stop just south of and opposite the post office. Contact the **tourist office** (☎ 384 51 88; www.do lenjske-toplice.si; Zdravilíški trg 8; ◷ 10am-5pm Mon-Fri, 10am-noon & 3-6pm Sat, 10am-noon Sun) for information about the region and its activities and the **spa** (www.krka-zdravilisca.si) for information about the health and wellness treatments.

Activities
HIKING
A number of walks and bike paths of less than 5km can be made from Dolenjske Toplice, or you might consider hiking in the virgin forests of Kočevski Rog.

Marked paths listed on the free pamphlet *Dolenjske Toplice Cycle and Footpaths* include a 3.5km archaeological walk west to Cvinger (263m), where Hallstatt tombs and iron foundries have been unearthed. Nature-lovers may be interested in the nature trail in the forest just west of Podturn (2km), which also takes in a small cave and the ruins of Rožek Castle.

THERMAL SPAS
Taking the waters is the *sine qua non* of Dolenjske Toplice: the warm mineral water (36° to 38°C) gushing from 1000m below the two covered thermal pools at the Vital Hotel is ideal for ailments such as rheumatism and can avert backache. The health resort also offers any number of other types of therapy, from underwater massage to aromatherapy.

The indoor and outdoor thermal pools in the Lagoon section of the **Balnea Wellness Centre** (◷ 9am-8pm Sun-Thu, 9am-11pm Fri & Sat)

SLOVENIA

are 300m north of the hotels, reached via a lovely park. The unusual carved wooden statues here recall the traditional occupations of this area: logging and woodcarving. In the Oasis section of the centre are saunas and steam baths; Aura has massage and treatments.

OTHER ACTIVITIES
The **tennis courts** on the hill northwest of the camping ground can be hired by nonguests (€15 per hour). Hotel guests can use them for free until 2pm.

Horse riding is available at the **Urbančič farmhouse** (☎ 306 53 36, 040 608 969; Kočevske Poljane 13; per hr €12; ☺ by arrangement) in Ločevske Poljane, 4km to the southwest. Horse-drawn carriages (€30 per hour) for four people can be hired from **Milan Novak** (☎ 041 590 877; Gregorčičeva 52).

Sleeping
Vital & Kristal Hotels (☎ 391 94 00; www.krka -zdravilisca.si; Zdraviliški trg 11; s/d 14,700/28,500SIT; ℗ ✿ ✆) The health resort's two four-star hotels share the same facilities, including two indoor thermal pools, two saunas and a fitness centre. Both offer discounted weekend and week-long packages.

Gostišče Rača (☎ 306 55 10; www.gostinstvo -luzar.si; Maksa Henigmana 15; d/apt €42/46-55; ✿) This renovated village house to the east of the centre has two-, three- and four-bed rooms with bathroom and TV that are cheaper for long stays.

Gostišče Pri Tomljetu (☎ 306 50 23, 031 643 345; Zdraviliški trg 24; s/d/tr 2750/5000/7500SIT) None of the eight rooms in this guesthouse behind the Balnea complex has its own bathroom, but each has a sink, and cooking facilities are available.

Eating
The health resort's main restaurant is the ornately decorated dining room of the Kristal Hotel, where most guests on half or full board take their meals.

Gostilna Rog (☎ 391 94 00; Zdraviliški trg 22; meals from 2300SIT; ☺ 9am-10pm Mon-Sat, to 7pm Sun) On the edge of the park, the 'Horn' serves traditional Slovenian dishes and has folk music from 8pm on Friday and Saturday.

Gostišče Rača (☎ 306 55 10; Maksa Henigmana 15; meals 1500SIT; ☺ 8am-11pm Mon-Thu, 8am-midnight Fri & Sat, 10am-11pm Sun Jul & Aug, 8am-10pm Mon-Thu,

8am-11pm Fri & Sat, 10am-10pm Sun Sep-Jun) This B&B does double duty as a restaurant and is a popular place for pizza and pasta.

Getting There & Around
There are hourly buses to Novo Mesto between 6am and 9.05pm Monday to Saturday and one on Sunday at 9.46am. There's a weekday bus at 10.29am and one on Saturday and Sunday at 5.04pm to Ljubljana via Žužemberk.

MARIBOR
☎ 02 / pop 116,000
Slovenia's light-industrial second city has no unmissable 'sights', but oozes with charm thanks to its delightful, patchily grand Old Town. Pedestrianised central streets buzz with cafés and student life and in late June and early July the old, riverside 'Lent' district hosts a major arts festival (check with the TIC for details). From the train station and nearby bus station, follow Partizanska c as it curls some 700m westwards to reach Grajski trg, where the nicest area of town begins with a somewhat dishevelled castle museum and the Orel Hotel.

Information
You'll find ATMs all over town and in the bus and train stations.
Hospital (☎ 228 62 00; Talcev 9; ☺ 24hr)
KIT/Kibla (☎ 252 44 40; Glavny trg 14; per 30min 150SIT; ☺ 9am-10pm Mon-Fri, to 2pm Sat) Central, fast and modern Internet access.
Nova KBM (46 Partizanska c; ☺ 8am-1pm & 2-5pm Mon-Fri) Changes travellers cheques.
Post office (Slomškov trg; ☺ 8am-7pm Mon-Fri, to 1pm Sat) This architectural masterpiece is painted goose-dropping green and draped with statues. Like other branches at Partizanska c 54 and Partizanska c 1, it changes money.
TIC (☎ 234 66 11; www.maribor-tourism.si; Partinzanska c 47; ☺ 9am-6pm Mon-Fri, to 1pm Sat) Helpful, especially for motorists seeking vinska cestas (wine routes). The office is handily opposite the train station.

Sights
The centre of the Old Town, **Grajski trg**, is graced with a 17th-century **Column of St Florian**, dedicated to the patron of fire-fighting.

Maribor Castle (Mariborski Grad; Grajski trg 2; adult/child 600/300SIT; ☺ 9am-5pm Tue-Sat, 9am-2pm Sun), on the square's northeastern corner,

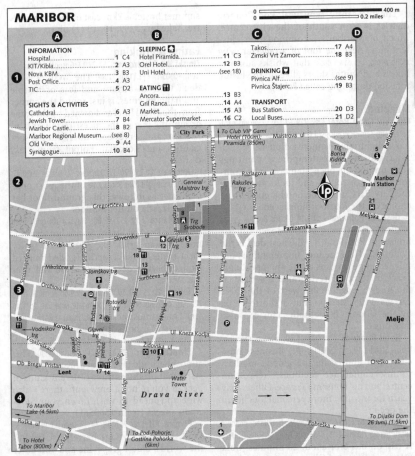

MARIBOR

INFORMATION
Hospital..............................1 C4
KIT/Kibla............................2 A3
Nova KBM...........................3 B3
Post Office..........................4 A3
TIC......................................5 D2

SIGHTS & ACTIVITIES
Cathedral............................6 A3
Jewish Tower.......................7 B4
Maribor Castle.....................8 B2
Maribor Regional Museum......(see 8)
Old Vine..............................9 A4
Synagogue.........................10 B4

SLEEPING
Hotel Piramida....................11 C3
Orel Hotel...........................12 B3
Uni Hotel.........................(see 18)

EATING
Ancora................................13 B3
Gril Ranca...........................14 A4
Market................................15 A3
Mercator Supermarket.........16 C2

Takos..................................17 A4
Zimski Vrt Zamorc...............18 B3

DRINKING
Pivnica Alf.......................(see 9)
Pivnica Štajerc....................19 B3

TRANSPORT
Bus Station.........................20 D3
Local Buses.........................21 D2

is a successor to the Piramida fortress of medieval times. The 15th-century castle contains a **Festival Hall** (Viteška Dvorana) with a remarkably disproportionate ceiling painting, the baroque **Loretska Chapel** and a magnificent **rococo staircase** (1759), with pink walls, stucco work and figures arrayed on the banisters.

The castle also contains the **Maribor Regional Museum** (Pokrajinski Muzej Maribor; ☎ 228 35 51; www.pmuzej-mb.si), with one of the richest collections in Slovenia, closed for renovation at the time of writing, but there are occasional temporary exhibits.

Two café-packed blocks southwest of Grajski trg, the **cathedral** (Slomškov trg) sits in an oasis of fountain-cooled calm. Follow little Poštna south from here into photogenic but traffic-divided **Glavny trg**. A block further south down alleys Mesarski or Splavarski Prehod is the Drava River's northern bank. Here you'll find the **Old Vine** (Stara Trta; Vojašniška 8), the world's oldest living grapevine, which has been trained along an old riverfront house. It has been a source of famous Maribor wine for over 400 years.

To the west of the water tower a set of steps lead to **Židovska** (Jewish St), the centre of the Jewish district in the Middle Ages. The 15th-century **synagogue** (☎ 252 78 36; Židovska 4; ☒ 7.30am-2.30pm Mon-Fri) has been renovated, and the square **Jewish Tower** (Židovski Stolp; Židovska 6) is now a **photo gallery** (☎ 251 24 90; ☒ 10am-7pm Mon-Fri, to 1pm Sat).

The pleasantly semirural Pod-Pohorje district is 6km south of the city centre. Much of Maribor's accommodation clusters here, near the foot of a **cable car** (www.pohorje.org; ☉ dawn-dusk) that whisks summer hikers and winter skiers alike up the lushly forested dumpling called **Pohorje**.

Sleeping

Club VIP Garni Hotel (☎ 229 62 00; www.vip-garni hotel.com; Tomišičeva 10; s/d €40/60) This new B&B has delightfully distinctive flourishes such as a gallery of contemporary paintings surrounding an open staircase. The comfortably retro rooms and its location near the City Park make the hotel a good-value choice on the Maribor hotel scene.

Gostilna Pohorka (☎ 614 01 10; Begova 2; s/d 5000/7000SIT) Among some dozen guesthouses in Pod-Pohorje, the best deal is the Podhorka. Here are four unpretentious but fully equipped rooms above an appealingly peaceful terraced restaurant. It's right at the forest's edge, 900m west of the cable car via Villa Merano, but a shorter walk by the woodland footpath. You can also take bus 6.

Hotel Piramida (☎ 233 44 00; www.termemb.si; Heroja Šlandra 10; s/d €90/114; **P**) Business travellers will appreciate the glossy, modern rooms, conference facilities, 'relaxation centre' and no-nonsense service. Others may yearn for warmer, more personal touches in the décor.

Hotel Tabor (☎ 421 64 10; www.hoteltabor.podhost nik.si; Heroja Zidanška 18; s/d from 7900/12,500SIT; **P**) A trip on bus 6 or about 20 minutes' walk (1km) southwest of Glavny trg (via Gorkega ul), this is the most central of several no-frills motel-style places dotted about the suburbs. All of these have parking, and similar price ranges, and most tend to put functional cleanliness over charm; ask at the TIC for details.

Uni Hotel (☎ 250 67 00; uni.hotel@termemb.si; Gosposka ul; beds €20) This fantastically central new hostel is only open to IYHA members and membership cards are not sold here. Check-in and reservations (highly advisable) are via the much better-known **Orel Hotel** (☎ 250 67 00; www.termemb.si; Grajski trg; s/d Sep-Jun €48/70, Jul & Aug €60/86) in the block behind (east). The price includes breakfast.

Dijaški Dom 26 Junij (☎ 480 17 10; Železnikova 12; dm €9; ☉ Jul & Aug) This typical student dorm/ summer hostel is 2km east of the town centre. Take bus 3, 99, 10, 10 (1) or 16.

Eating & Drinking

Zimski Vrt Zamorc (☎ 251 27 17; Gosposka 30; meals from 4000SIT; ☉ 11am-11pm) The 'Winter Garden', with an atrium and lots of marble and hanging vines, is just round the corner from the Orel Hotel and owned by the same group. It's one of the nicest restaurants in Maribor and serves both international specialities and Slovenian hotpot (*zamorček*) dishes.

Ancora (☎ 250 20 33; Jurčičeva 7; pizzas 1000SIT; ☉ 6am-midnight Mon-Sat) One of the most popular eateries in town, this ground-floor bar has a pizzeria on the 1st floor.

Gril Ranca (☎ 252 55 00; Dravska 10; grills from 1050SIT; ☉ 8am-11pm Mon-Sat) Simple but scrumptious Balkan grills like *pljeskavica* (spicy meat patties) and *ćevapčići* (grilled minced lamb or beef) are served up as you look over the Drava.

Takos (☎ 252 71 50; Mesarski Prehod 3; meals from 2200SIT, cocktails 600SIT; ☉ 9am-late Mon-Sat, to 1pm Sun) This atmospheric Mexican restaurant becomes Maribor's top nightspot after the 11pm happy hour on Friday and Saturday.

Pivnica Štajerc (☎ 234 42 34; Vetrinjska 30) This atmospheric old tavern has a brewery downstairs that produces three different kinds of beer. If you're not a brew-buff, there's also wine and mead to wash down your Slovenian snacks (from 1500SIT).

Pivnica Alf (☎ 251 48 44; Splavarski Prehod 5) Walk through a giant barrel just behind the world's oldest grapevine and you enter what seems to be the world's oldest pub, with beamed ceilings and ancient smoke-stained walls.

There's a **market** (Vodnikov trg; ☉ 6.30am-3pm Mon-Sat, to 12.30pm Sun) selling produce just north of the former Minorite monastery. There's a **Mercator supermarket** (☉ 7am-8pm Mon-Fri, 7am-6pm Sat, 8am-11am Sun) at Partizanska c 7, and cheap *burek* stands outside the train station.

Getting There & Away

Buses run to Ljubljana (2780SIT to 2950SIT depending on routing, up to 10 daily), Ptuj (970SIT, at least hourly Monday to Saturday, five on Sunday), Rogaška Slatina (four daily weekdays) and to various German cities.

Up to 18 direct trains daily link Maribor to Ljubljana (1710SIT, 2¾ hours). ICS trains are faster and more expensive.

Getting Around
Maribor's bus system is extensive. Single rides cost 240SIT if you pay on board. Purchased ahead, a return ticket costs 330SIT. Most useful routes start near the train station, including bus 6 to Pod-Pohorje, which terminates at the cable car.

PTUJ
☎ 02 / pop 19,100
Rising gently above a wide, almost flat valley, the compact Old Town of Ptuj (Roman Poetovio) forms a symphony of red-tile roofs viewed most photogenically from across the Drava River. It culminates in a well-proportioned castle containing the fine **Regional Museum** (www.pok-muzej-ptuj.si/english/ptgrad.htm; adult/child 600/300SIT; ☒ 10am-5pm, later in summer). For 10 days around Mardi Gras (usually in February) international crowds arrive to spot the shaggy Kurent straw men at Slovenia's foremost carnival. Kurent are traditional figures in Slovene lore that are analogous to a Dionysios or Shiva. The **tourist office** (☎ 779 60 11; www.ptuj-tourism.si; Slovenski trg 3; ☒ 8am-5pm Mon-Fri, to noon Sat) faces a **medieval tower** in the old centre. To reach it walk south from the bus and train stations, turn west passing the Hotel Poetovio (which stocks free maps), the classic **Haloze Wine Cellars** (☎ 787 98 10; tour-tastings 1500-1800SIT; ☒ by appointment) and the street cafés of Lacova ul, Mestni trg and Morkova ul.

West of the centre along grand Prešernov ul, the 18th-century **Mala Grad** (Small Castle; Prešernova 33-35) now houses a library with Internet connection.

Sleeping & Eating
Krapša Guesthouse (☎ 787 75 70; rozalija_k@hotmail.com; Maistrova 19; per person €17; ☒) All but two rooms of this utterly delightful homestay are bright, brand new and with en suite. It's in a quiet setting between cherry trees at the dead end of a 900m (as yet) unpaved track that starts west of castle hill. There are no single or short-stay supplements and the friendly hosts are as effervescent as their homemade wines.
Garni Hotel Mitra (☎ 787 74 55; www.hotelptuj.com; Prešernova 6; s/d/apt 11,000/13,500/18,000SIT)

This superbly central hotel has a colourful antique façade, but rooms have somewhat less panache than the artistic stairways would suggest.
Terme Ptuj (☎ 782 72 11; www.terme-ptuj.si; per person Jun-Aug/off-peak €12.10/10.30; ☒ 20 Apr-10 Oct, check-in 5-8pm) This small, starkly unshaded camping ground, attached to a spa/swimming pool complex on the Drava's southern bank, is about 1.4km from the Old Town via a footbridge.
Ribič (☎ 771 46 71; Dravska 9; set meals 2200-3600SIT; ☒ 10am-11pm) This old house with a great riverside terrace is the ideal spot for a fish feast. Try the tasty and healthy trout with courgettes. Vegetarian plates are also available.

There's an **open-air market** (Novi trg; ☒ 7am-3pm) for self-caterers.

Getting There & Away
Buses to Maribor (970SIT, 40 minutes) run at least hourly on weekdays but are very infrequent on Sunday. There are only five buses per week to Rogaška Slatina but if you're driving there's a delightful country road via Breg and Rogatec. The latter has a sweet little open-air museum of rural architecture. Two daily trains from Ljubljana (2½ hours) stop en route to Budapest (six hours) departing Ptuj at 9.44am, or 4.16pm (by InterCity train).

SLOVENIA DIRECTORY

ACCOMMODATION
Accommodation listings in this guide have been ordered by preference.

Slovenia's small but growing handful of youth hostels includes Ljubljana's unbelievably trendy Celica. However, many other hostels are moonlighting college dorms which only accept travellers in July and August. Thank goodness they do open then: in midsummer almost all other accommodation substantially raises prices and it can be hard to find a room at any price. Unless stated, hostel rooms share bathrooms. A hostel bed typically costs from €12 to €20.

Guesthouses (penzion, gostišče or prenočišča) are often cosy and better value than full-blown hotels, some of which are ugly if well-renovated Communist-era

PRACTICALITIES

■ The system used for weights and measures is metric.

■ The video system is PAL, which is incompatible with the North American and Japanese NTSC standard, and the SECAM system used in France.

■ Electrical supply is 220V to 240V/50Hz to 60Hz. Slovenia uses the standard European round-pronged plugs.

■ Take a look through any of the following English-language publications: *Slovenia Times*, a free newspaper that comes out every three weeks or so; *Slovenija*, a glossy quarterly with a heavy focus on culture; and *Ljubljana Life*, an excellent free bimonthly magazine.

■ Listen to the nightly news bulletin broadcast in English year-round at 10.30pm on *Radio Slovenija 1* (88.5, 90.0, 90.9, 91.8, 92.0, 92.9, 94.1, 96.4 MHz FM & 918 kHz AM).

Frankensteins. Nonetheless it can be difficult to find a double room for under €50. Beware that locally listed rates are usually quoted per person assuming double occupancy. The 150SIT to 200SIT per person tourist tax and a hefty single-occupancy supplement often lurk in the footnotes. This chapter quotes the total you'll pay. Unless otherwise indicated, room rates include ensuite toilet, shower with towels and soap, and a ham and cheese breakfast.

Tourist information offices can help you access extensive networks of private rooms, apartments and tourist farms or can recommend private agencies who will. Such accommodation can appear misleadingly cheap if you carelessly overlook the 30% to 50% surcharge levied on one- or two-night stays (this book incorporates them). Also beware that many such properties are in outlying villages with minimal public transport, and that the cheapest one-star category rooms with shared bathroom are actually very rare, so you'll often pay well above the quoted minimum. Depending on the season you might save a little money by going directly to any house with a sign reading *sobe* (rooms).

Camping grounds generally charge per person, whether you're camping or caravanning. Rates usually include hot showers. Almost all grounds close November to April. Camping 'rough' is illegal, and this is enforced, especially around Bled.

ACTIVITIES

Slovenia is a very well-organised outdoor-activities paradise.

Extreme Sports

Several areas specialise in adrenaline-rush activities, the greatest range being available at Bovec, famous for white-water rafting, hydrospeed, kayaking, and especially for canyoning – ie slithering down gullies and waterfalls in a neoprene wetsuit with the very important aid of a well-trained guide. Bovec is also a great place for paragliding; in winter you ascend Mt Kanin via ski lifts and then jump off. Gliding costs are remarkably reasonable from Lesce near Bled. Scuba diving from Piran is also good value.

Hiking

Hiking is extremely popular, with much of the capital's population heading for Triglav National Park at weekends. There are around 7000km of marked paths, and in summer 165 mountain huts offer comfortable trailside refuge (see the boxed text, p358). Several shorter treks are helpfully outlined in the Sunflower Guide *Slovenia* (www.sunflowerbooks.co.uk), which has excellent map-text correlation.

Skiing

Skiing is a Slovenian passion, with slopes particularly crowded at New Year and early in February. Maribor's **Pohorje** (www.pohorje .org) is a popular choice. Although relatively low (1347m) it's easily accessible, with very varied downhill pistes and relatively short lift queues. Enjoyable Pohorje **torch parties** (☎ 041 775 175; mopa@siol.net; 3700SIT plus ski lift) are organised, where partygoers ascend the slope at night with a glass of bubbly, ski with flaming torches to a barbecue, and hope that the shots of blueberry hooch don't stop them from skiing back again.

Kranjska Gora (1600m) has some challenging runs; the world record for ski-jumping was set at nearby Planica. Above Bohinj, Vogel (1922m) is particularly scenic, as is Kanin (2300m), above Bovec; Kanin has snow as late as May. Cerkno (1291m, www .cerkno.si in Slovene) is popular with snow-boarders. Being relatively close to Ljubljana, Krvavec (1970m), northeast of Kranj, can have particularly long lift queues. See www .sloveniatourism.si/skiing for information.

Other
The Soča River near Kobarid and the Sava in Bohinj are great for fly-fishing (season April to October). Licences (€58 per day, catch-and-release €48) are sold at TICs and hotels. Bohinj lake-fishing licences are somewhat cheaper (€45, March to September).

Mountain bikes are available for hire at Bovec, Bled and Bohinj travel agencies. However, the hire 'season' is usually limited to May through to October.

In late October there's a Ljubljana mara-thon (http://maraton.slo-timing.com/).

Spa cures (www.terme-giz.si) are very popu-lar. Most towns have a spa complex and hotels often offer free or bargain-rate entry to their guests. The most celebrated spa re-sort is Rogaška Slatina.

BUSINESS HOURS
Virtually all businesses post their open-ing times *(delovni čas)* on the door. Many shops close Saturday afternoon. Sunday are still 'holy': although a handful of grocery stores open, including some branches of the ubiquitous Mercator chain, on Sunday most shopping areas are as lively as Cher-nobyl. Museums often close on Monday. Banks often take lengthy lunch breaks and some open Saturday morning.

Restaurants typically open until at least 10pm, bars until midnight, though they may have longer hours at the weekend and shorter on Sunday.

The closer winter approaches the earlier many attractions close and the fewer visits they allow. This leads to intricately complex tables of opening times that are beyond the scope of this book to reproduce in detail. Fortunately, most attractions have websites and leaflets displaying complete schedules in their full glory.

EMBASSIES & CONSULATES
Slovenian Embassies & Consulates
Slovenian representations abroad are fully listed on www.gov.si/mzz/eng and include:

Australia (☎ 02-624 34830; vca@mzz-dkp.gov.si; level 6, St George's Bldg, 60 Marcus Clarke St, Canberra ACT 2601)
Austria (☎ 01-586 13 09; Nibelungengasse 13, Vienna; ✆ 9-11am Mon-Fri)
Belgium (☎ 02-646 90 99; Ave Louise 179, Brussels)
Bosnia & Hercegovina (☎ 033-271 250; Bentbasa 7, Sarajevo)
Canada (☎ 613-565 5781; 150 Metcalfe St, Suite 2101, Ottawa)
Croatia (☎ 01-63 11 000; Savska c 41, Zagreb; ✆ 9am-noon Mon-Fri)
Czech Republic (☎ 02-33 08 12 11; Pod Hradbami 15, Prague; ✆ 9am-noon Mon, Wed & Fri)
France (☎ 01 44 96 50 71; 28 rue Bois-le-Vent, Paris)
Germany (☎ 030-206 1450; Hausvogteiplatz 3-4, Berlin)
Hungary (☎ 01-438 5600; Cseppkő ut 68, Budapest; ✆ 9am-noon Mon-Fri)
Ireland (☎ 01-670 5240; Morrison Chambers, 32 Nassau St, Dublin)
Netherlands (☎ 070-310 86 90; Anna Paulownastraat 11, Den Haag)
New Zealand (☎ 04-567 0027; PO Box 30247, Eastern Hutt Rd, Pormare, Lower Hutt, Wellington)
UK (☎ 020-7222 5400; 10 Little College St, London SW1; ✆ 9am-2pm Mon-Fri)
USA (☎ 202-667 5363; 1525 New Hampshire Ave NW, Washington DC)

Embassies & Consulates in Slovenia
Among the embassies and consulates in Ljubljana (☎ 01) are:
Australia (☎ 425 42 52; Trg Republike 3/XII)
Belgium (☎ 200 60 10; Trg Republike 3/XII)
Bosnia & Hercegovina (☎ 432 4042; Kolarjeva 26) North of the centre.
Canada (☎ 430 35 70; Miklošičeva c 19)
Croatia (☎ 425 62 20; Gruberjevo nab 6) Southwest of the centre.
France (☎ 479 04 00; Barjanska 1)
Germany (☎ 479 03 00; Prešernova c 27)
Hungary (☎ 512 18 82; Konrada Babnika 5) Northwest of the centre.
Ireland (☎ 300 89 70; Poljanski nasip 6)
Netherlands (☎ 420 14 61; Poljanski nasip 6)
New Zealand (☎ 580 30 55; Verovškova 57) North of the centre.
Romania (☎ 505 82 94; Podlimbarskega 43) Northwest of the centre.
South Africa (☎ 200 63 00; Pražakova 4)
UK (☎ 200 39 10; Trg Republike XII)
USA (☎ 200 55 00; Prešernova c 31)

FESTIVALS & EVENTS

Shaggy Kurent straw men make Ptuj carnival the place to be at Mardi Gras, though the Julian Alps villages have several lesser-known equivalents. On 30 April villages hold bonfires and 'tree raising' nights. Throughout the summer there are dozens of musical and cultural events, notably in Ljubljana, Piran and Koper. For lots more information consult www.slovenia-tourism.si.

GAY & LESBIAN TRAVELLERS

The typical Slovene personality, rather like the Dutch, is quietly conservative but deeply self-confident, remarkably broadminded and particularly tolerant. **Roza Klub** (☎ 01-430 47 40; Kersnikova 4, Ljubljana) is composed of gay and lesbian branches of the Student Cultural Centre (ŠKUC).

The **GALfon** (☎ 01-432 40 89; ☉ 7-10pm) is a hotline and source of general information for gays and lesbians. The websites of **Slovenian Queer Resources Directory** (www.ljudmila.org/siqrd) and **Out In Slovenia** (www.outinslovenija.com) are extensive and partially in English.

HOLIDAYS

New Year 1 and 2 January. For a week hotel prices go mad especially in ski resorts.
Prešren Day of Culture 8 February
Easter Monday March/April
Insurrection Day 27 April. Commemorates the insurrection against WWII Nazi occupation.

Labour Days 1 and 2 May. Villagers light bonfires on the night of 30 April, and indulge in 'tree raising', a local semisport where competitors take a tree trunk and have to raise it vertically.
National Day 25 June
Assumption 15 August. Around this date virtually all accommodation will be booked solid.
Reformation Day 31 October
All Saints' Day 1 November
Christmas 25 December
Independence Day 26 December

INTERNET ACCESS

You'll find Internet access in most cities and towns but so-called Internet cafés rarely have more than one or two terminals. In some places you may have to resort to the local library, school or university. Note that Slovene keyboards are neither qwerty nor azerty but qwertz, reversing the y and z keys. Otherwise the follow the Anglophone norm.

INTERNET RESOURCES

The website www.slovenia-tourism.si is tremendously useful. Most Slovenian towns have very good websites often accessed by typing www.townname.si or www.townname-tourism.si. Specially good are www.ljubljana-tourism.si and www.maribor-tourism.si. For a particularly interesting series of Slovenian links, try www.carantha.net or www.matkurja.com/eng.

ADDRESSES & PLACE NAMES

Streets in Slovenian towns and cities are well signposted, although the numbering system can be a bit confusing with odd and even numbers sometimes running on the same sides of streets and squares.

In small towns and villages, streets are not named and houses are just given numbers. Thus Ribčev Laz 13 is house No 13 in the village of Ribčev Laz on Lake Bohinj. As Slovenian villages are frequently made up of one road with houses clustered on or just off it, this is seldom confusing.

Places with double-barrelled names such as Novo Mesto (New Town) and Črna Gora (Black Hill) start the second word in lower case (Novo mesto, Črna gora) in Slovene, almost as if the names were Newtown and Blackhill. This is the correct Slovene orthography, but we have opted to go with the English-language way of doing it to avoid confusion.

Slovene frequently uses the possessive case in street names. Thus a road named after the poet Ivan Cankar is Cankarjeva ul (although you won't see 'ul' used in this chapter; it's implied, so if it's not a trg or a cesta ('c'), it's a ulica) and a square honouring France Prešeren is Prešernov trg. Also, when nouns are turned into adjectives they often become unrecognisable to a foreigner. The town is 'Bled', for example, but 'Lake Bled' is Blejsko Jezero. A street leading to a castle (grad) is usually called Grajska ul; a road going in the direction of Trieste (Trst) is Tržaška c. The words 'pri', 'pod' and 'na' in place names mean 'at the', 'below the' and 'on the' respectively.

LANGUAGE

Closely related to Croatian and Serbian, Slovene (*Slovensko*) sounds like Russian soaked in wine and honey. On toilets, M (Moški) indicates men, and Ž (Ženske) women. Slovene for 'no smoking' may raise a giggle if you speak Slovak, in which language the same phrase means 'no farting'. Virtually everyone in Slovenia speaks at least one other language; restaurant menus and ATMs are commonly in Slovene, Italian, German and English. See the language chapter (p419) for key phrases and words.

MONEY

Until 2007 Slovenia's legal currency will remain the tolar (SIT) but euros are already very widely accepted. Exchanging cash is simple at banks, major post offices, travel agencies and *menjalnica* (exchange bureaus). Prices listed in this chapter are in euros or tolar, depending on which currency was quoted by the business reviewed. Travellers cheques are less convenient. Major credit and debit cards are accepted almost everywhere and ATMs are astonishingly ubiquitous. Slovenian and Italian prices are similar, and you'll find Slovenia considerably more expensive than Hungary or the Czech Republic.

POST

An international airmail stamp costs 107SIT. Poste restante is free: address mail to, and pick it up at, Slovenska c 32, 1101 Ljubljana.

TELEPHONE

Public telephones require a phonecard (*telefonska kartica*), available at post offices and most newsstands. The cheapest card (700SIT, 25-unit) gives about four minutes' calling time to other European countries. Most locals have a mobile phone. Some businesses quote only a mobile number, identifiable by codes 030, 031, 040 and 041.

EMERGENCY NUMBERS

- Ambulance ☎ 112
- Fire Brigade ☎ 112
- Police ☎ 113

TOILETS

Toilets are generally free in restaurants but occasionally you'll incur a 50SIT charge at bus stations.

TOURIST INFORMATION

The superhelpful **Slovenian Tourist Board** (www .slovenia-tourism.si) has dozens of Tourist Information Centres (TICs) in Slovenia and branches in nine cities abroad; see website for details. Request its free *Guide to Slovenia's Byways*, which contains tokens for 5-15% savings on various hotels, activities and sights, including the Škocjan Caves.

VISAS

Passport holders from Australia, Canada, Iceland, Israel, Japan, Norway, New Zealand, Switzerland, the USA and EU countries can stay 90 days without visas. South Koreans get 15 days. Most other citizens, including South Africans, must apply for a visa (multiple entry €35) at a Slovenian embassy or consulate before arriving in Slovenia. Note that there is no consulate in South Africa. You'll need travel insurance, passport photocopies and hotel bookings plus one photo. Same-day processing is possible in Zagreb (Croatia) but elsewhere it takes from three working days (London) to a week (Budapest).

EU and Swiss citizens can enter using a national identity card for 30-day stays.

WOMEN TRAVELLERS

Crime is low and harassment rare, but in emergencies contact the **women's crisis helpline** (☎ 080 11 55). Normally someone there will speak English.

TRANSPORT IN SLOVENIA

GETTING THERE & AWAY

This section covers how to get to and from Slovenia from other countries in the Western Balkans. Information about points of entry to the Western Balkan countries is covered in the Transport chapter (p402).

Air

Slovenia's only international airport is **Brnik** (code LJU; www.lju-airport.si) near Kranj, some

---

DEPARTURE TAX

A departure tax of 3600SIT is collected from everyone leaving Slovenia by air. This is usually included in the ticket price, but it's always best to check.

23km north of Ljubljana. From here the national carrier, **Adria Airways** (airline code JP; ☎ 01-239 10 10; www.adria-airways.com), has regular direct flights to Prishtina, Podgorica, Skopje and Sarajevo. **Maribor Airport** (code MPX; www.maribor-airport.si) handles charter flights and freight only.

Land

Whether by train or bus, chances are that you'll reach other Western Balkan countries via Croatia.

BUS

International bus destinations from Ljubljana include Sarajevo (9250SIT, 10 hours, 7.15pm Monday, Wednesday and Friday), Split (7150SIT, 10½ hours, daily), Rijeka (2990SIT, 2½ hours), and Zagreb (3340SIT, three hours, four daily) via attractive Novo Mesto.

CAR & MOTORCYCLE

Slovenia maintains about 150 border crossings with Italy, Austria, Hungary and Croatia, but not all are open to citizens of third countries. On country maps and atlases, those marked with a circle and a line are international ones; those with just a circle are local ones. Although it is a member of the EU, Slovenia will not be part of the Schengen border plan until 2006 at the earliest. The 670km border it shares with Croatia will then become the 'last frontier' of the EU.

International vehicle insurance is compulsory in Slovenia. If your car is registered in the EU, you are covered, and Slovenia has concluded special agreements with certain other countries, including Croatia. Other motorists must buy a Green Card valid for Slovenia at the border (€42 for 15 days, €60 for a month).

TRAIN

In addition to international lines (see p408), there are daily trains from Ljubljana to Zagreb, Croatia (2781SIT, 2½ hours, eight daily), Rijeka (2759SIT, 2½ hours, one daily via Opatija) and Pula (4259SIT, five hours, one daily, summer only).

Seat reservations, often compulsory, cost 300SIT extra.

Sea

The **Marina** (www.losinjska-plovidba.hr) sails from the port of Koper to Pula, Mali Lošinj and Zadar (€25.50, 13 hours) in Croatia once a week from mid-June to early September.

GETTING AROUND

Trains are usually cheaper but less frequent than buses. Beware: frequency on both drops off very significantly on weekends and in school holidays.

Bus

In recent years, bus service in Slovenia has gone from the sublime to the silly, particularly in the eastern part of the country. Bus departures have been halved (or worse), many stations are deserted and everyone seems to be behind their own wheel. Nowadays it would be very difficult to tour Slovenia exclusively by public bus but, in some areas, you don't have a choice. Bus is the only practical way to reach Bled, the Julian Alps and much of Dolenjska, Koroška and Notranjska.

You can buy your ticket at the bus station (*avtobusna postaja*) or simply pay the driver as you board. In Ljubljana you should book your seat one day in advance if you're travelling on Friday or to destinations in the mountains or on the coast on a public holiday. Bus services are severely restricted on Sunday and holidays (less so on Saturday). Many routes are serviced by more than one bus company. If you buy a return ticket you'll be limited to returning with the same company, which could mean a long wait. The 10% discount some companies offer for a return ticket may not be worth it.

Some bus stations have a left-luggage office (*garderoba*) and charge 350SIT per piece per hour. They often keep banker's hours; if it's an option, a better bet is to leave your things at the train station, which is usually nearby and keeps longer hours. If your bag has to go in the luggage compartment below the bus, it will cost 360SIT extra.

Bicycle

Cycling is a popular leisure pastime in Slovenia, and bikes can be carried free of charge in the baggage compartments of InterCity (IC) and regional trains. On buses, you can put your bike in the luggage compartment, space permitting. Cycling is permitted on all roads except motorways. Many towns and cities, including Ljubljana, Maribor, Celje, Ptuj and Kranj, have bicycle lanes and special traffic lights.

Car & Motorcycle

AUTOMOBILE ASSOCIATIONS

Slovenia's national automobile club is the Avto-Moto Zveza Slovenije (AMZS). For emergency roadside assistance, motorists should call it on ☎ 19 87 or ☎ 01-530 53 53. For information on road and traffic conditions, contact the **AMZS** (☎ 530 53 00; www.amzs.si; Dunajska c 128) in Ljubljana. All accidents should be reported to the **police** (☎ 113) immediately.

DRIVING LICENCE

If you don't hold a European driving licence and plan to drive in Slovenia, obtain an International Driving Permit from your local automobile association before you leave – you'll need a passport photo and a valid licence. They are usually inexpensive and valid for one year only.

FUEL & SPARE PARTS

Petrol stations, which accept most credit cards, are usually open from about 7am to 8pm Monday to Saturday, though larger towns have 24-hour services on the outskirts. Unleaded 95-octane petrol *(bencin)* costs about 225SIT per litre.

HIRE

Hiring a car is recommended, and can even save you money as you can access cheaper out-of-centre hotels and farm or village homestays. Daily rates usually start at €45, including unlimited mileage, collision-damage waiver and theft protection. At the time of research, **Hertz** (☎ 01-234 46 46; www .hertz.si), beside Ljubljana bus station, offered a tiny Smart at €40.

INSURANCE

International vehicle insurance is compulsory in Slovenia. If your car is registered in the EU, you are covered, and Slovenia has concluded special agreements with certain other countries, including Croatia. Other motorists must buy a Green Card valid for Slovenia at the border (€150 for 15 days, €218 for a month).

ROAD CONDITIONS

Roads in Slovenia are generally good (if a bit narrow at times) and well maintained. Driving in the alps can be hair-raising, with a gradient of up to 18% at the Korensko Sedlo Pass into Austria, and a series of 49 hairpin bends on the road over the Vršič Pass. Many mountain roads are closed in winter and early spring. Motorways and highways are very well signposted, but secondary and tertiary roads are not always; be sure to have a good map at the ready.

No less than US$4 billion has been invested in the expansion of Slovenia's motorways. There are two main motorway corridors – between Maribor and the coast and from the Karavanke Tunnel into Austria to Zagreb in Croatia – intersecting the Ljubljana ring road, with a branch from Postojna to Nova Gorica. Motorways are numbered from A1 to A10 (for *avtocesta*), and a toll is payable (eg 490SIT from Ljubljana to Postojna, 1160SIT to Maribor).

Major international roads are preceded by an 'E'. The most important of these are the E70 to Zagreb via Novo Mesto, the E61 to Villach via Jesenice and the Karavanke Tunnel, and the E57 from Celje to Graz via Maribor. National highways contain a single digit and link cities. Secondary and tertiary roads have two sets of numbers separated by a hyphen; the first number indicates the highway that the road runs into. Thus road 10-5 from Nova Gorica and Ajdovščina joins the A10 motorway at Razdrto.

ROAD RULES

You must drive on the right. Speed limits for cars and motorcycles are 50km/h in towns and villages, 90km/h on secondary and tertiary roads, 100km/h on highways and 130km/h on motorways.

The use of seat belts is compulsory, and motorcyclists must wear helmets. Another law taken very seriously is the one requiring all motorists to illuminate their headlights throughout the day. The permitted blood-alcohol level for drivers is 0.5g/kg.

Hitching

Hitchhiking is fairly common and perfectly legal, except on motorways and a few major highways. Even young women hitch in Slovenia, but it's never totally safe and Lonely Planet doesn't recommend it.

Train

Slovenske Železnice (Slovenian Railways; ☎ 01-291 33 32 from 5am-10pm; www.slo-zeleznice.si) has a useful online timetable. Buy tickets before boarding

or you'll incur a 500SIT supplement, except for IC trains where the surcharge can run up to 1000SIT. Note that the fast IC trains are more expensive than the local variety.

A useful and very scenic rail line from Bled Jezero station via Bohinjska Bistrica (Bohinj) cuts under roadless mountains to Most na Soči (for Kobarid), then down the Soča Valley to Nova Gorica. Cars are carried through the tunnel section on special Avtovlak trains.

Regional Directory

CONTENTS

The regional directory gives a general overview of conditions and information that apply to the whole of the Western Balkans. Given the diversity of the region, this has meant some generalisation, so for specifics on any given topic see the relevant directory for the country you require information on.

ACCOMMODATION

As a rule, for each accommodation listing we have used the currency in which the hotel, hostel or guesthouse quotes their prices. This means that for some hotels we give hotel prices in local currency, others are listed in euros or US dollars. In this book the accommodation suggestions and reviews are listed in three broad categories: budget, midrange and top end. These vary quite a lot across the region (Slovenia being in a very different class economically from Albania), so they are ordered according to local price ranges, not by some regional

standard. Within the budget, midrange and top-end categories the reviews are ordered from what we thought was the best down to what's still good, just not (in our opinion) quite as good. This is of course a highly subjective ordering, so just because Slava's place is listed before Mira's place doesn't necessarily mean there's a huge difference – it's just that Slava's might have had a minor advantage like a bigger bathroom or being a bit closer to the centre of town.

In most of the Western Balkans the cheapest places to rest your head are camping grounds, followed by hostels and student accommodation. Guesthouses, *pensions*, private rooms and cheap hotels are also good value. Self-catering flats in the city and cottages in the countryside are worth considering if you're in a group, especially if you plan to stay put for a while.

During peak holiday periods, accommodation can be hard to find; unless you're camping, it's advisable to book ahead where possible. Even some camping grounds can fill up, particularly popular ones near large towns and cities.

Hostels and cheap hotels in popular tourist destinations such as Dubrovnik, Hvar and Ljubljana can fill up very quickly – especially the well-run ones in desirable neighbourhoods. It's a good idea to make reservations as many weeks ahead as possible, at least for the first night or two. A two- or three-minute international phone call to book a bed or room is a more sensible use of time than wasting your first day in a city searching for a place to stay.

If you arrive in a country by air, there is often an accommodation-booking desk at the airport, although it rarely covers the lower strata of hotels. Tourist offices often have extensive accommodation lists, and the more helpful ones will go out of their way to find you something suitable.

Camping

The cheapest way to go is camping, and there are lots of camping grounds throughout most of the region. Many are large sites intended for motorists, though they're often easily accessible by public transport and there's almost always space for backpackers with tents. Many camping grounds rent small on-site cabins, bungalows or caravans for double or triple the regular camping fee. In the most popular resorts the bungalows will probably be full in July and August.

The standard of camping grounds varies quite a lot. They're crowded in Slovenia, and variable in Serbia and Montenegro and Macedonia. Albania has no camping grounds outside of some old communist-era workers' holiday camps in the south. Croatia's coast has nudist camping grounds galore (signposted 'FKK', the German acronym for 'naturist'); they're excellent places to stay because of the secluded locations – if you don't mind letting it all hang out.

Camping grounds may be open from April to October, May to September, or perhaps only June to August, depending on the category of the facility, the location and demand. A few private camping grounds are open year-round. You are sometimes allowed to build a campfire (ask first). Camping in the wild is usually illegal; ask locals about the situation before you pitch your tent on a beach or in an open field.

Guesthouses & Pensions

Small private *pensions* are very common in the Western Balkans. Priced somewhere between hotels and private rooms, *pensions* typically have fewer than a dozen rooms and sometimes a small restaurant or bar on the premises. You'll get more personal service at a *pension* than you would at a hotel, though perhaps at the expense of a teensy bit of privacy. Call ahead to check prices and ask about reservations – someone will usually speak some halting English or German.

Homestays & Private Rooms

Homestays are often the best and most authentic way to see daily life in the region. Make sure you bring some small gifts for your hosts – it's a deeply ingrained cultural tradition.

In most countries, travel agencies can arrange accommodation in private rooms at local homes. People will sometimes approach you at train or bus stations offering a private room or a hostel bed. This can be good or bad – it's impossible to generalise. Just make sure it's not in a mangy concrete apartment block next to an industrial estate

(unless you relish this sort of thing) and that you negotiate a clear price. Obviously, if you are staying with strangers like this, you shouldn't leave your valuables behind when you go out.

You don't have to go through an agency or an intermediary on the street for a room. Any house, cottage or farmhouse with *Zimmer frei, sobe* or *soba* displayed outside is advertising the availability of private rooms (these examples are in German, Slovene and Macedonian); just knock on the door and ask if any are available.

Hostels

Hostels offer the cheapest (secure) roof over your head in the Western Balkans, and you don't have to be a youngster to take advantage of them. Most hostels are part of the national Youth Hostel Association (YHA), which is affiliated with the Hostelling International (HI) organisation.

Hostels affiliated with HI can be found in most of the countries and regions of the Western Balkans – Kosovo and Albania being the exceptions, though Tirana should have one soon. A hostel card is seldom required, though you sometimes get a small discount if you have one. If you don't have a valid HI membership card, you can buy one at some hostels.

To join the HI, you can ask at any hostel or contact your local or national hostelling office. There's a very useful website at www.iyhf.org, with links to most HI sites.

At a hostel, you get a bed for the night plus use of the communal facilities, often including a kitchen where you can prepare your own meals. You may be required to have a sleeping sheet – simply using your sleeping bag is often not allowed. If you don't have a sleeping sheet, you can sometimes hire one for a small fee.

There are many available hostel guides with listings, including the bible, HI's *Europe*. Many hostels accept reservations by phone, fax or email, but not always during peak periods (though they might hold a bed for a couple of hours if you call from the train or bus station). You can also book hostels through national hostel offices.

Hotels

At the bottom of the bracket, cheap hotels may be no more expensive than private rooms or guesthouses, while at the other extreme they extend to five-star hotels. Categorisation varies from country to country and the hotels recommended in this book try to accommodate every budget. We have provided a combination of budget, mid-range and top-end accommodation in each city or town. Where the choice is between a cheap and cheerful guesthouse and a mouldering Stalinist-style Hotel Turizmi, we recommend the guesthouse. There are quite a few communist-era hotels and holiday resorts across the region, and while many are now in private hands they sometimes haven't had any maintenance done since Tito or Hoxha died and went to meet Marx. We generally don't list them unless they're the only option, though they are quite an experience.

Single rooms can be hard to find in the region, where you are generally charged by the room and not by the number of people in it; many local people still refuse to believe that anyone would actually take to the road alone. The cheapest rooms sometimes have a washbasin but no bathroom, which means you'll have to go down the corridor to use the toilet and shower. Breakfast may be included in the price of a room or be extra – and mandatory.

University Accommodation

Some universities rent out space in student halls during July and August. This is quite popular in Croatia and Slovenia. Accommodation will sometimes be in single rooms (but is more commonly in doubles or triples), and cooking facilities may be available. Inquire at the college or university, at student information services or at local tourist offices.

ACTIVITIES
Canoeing & Kayaking

Special kayaking and canoeing tours are offered in Croatia, especially around the Elafiti and Kornati Islands (see p220 for details on how to get to these islands). Kayaking is really only in its infancy further south in Montenegro and Albania.

Cycling

The hills and mountains of the Western Balkans can be heavy going, but this is offset by the abundance of things to see.

Physical fitness is *not* a major prerequisite for cycling on the plains of Slavonia and northern Serbia but the wind might slow you down. Most airlines will allow you to put a bicycle in the hold for a surprisingly small fee.

See p405 for more information on bicycle touring, and the individual destination sections for rental outfits.

Diving

The sparkling waters and varied marine life of the Adriatic support a thriving diving industry, in Croatia in particular. Cave diving is a Croatian speciality, and most of the coastal resorts have dive shops. There is also scuba diving at Piran in Slovenia.

Hiking

There's excellent hiking in the Western Balkans, with trails through forests, mountains and national parks. Public transport will often take you to the trailheads, and chalets or mountain huts offer dormitory accommodation and basic meals. The most popular hiking destination is the Julian Alps of Slovenia, but there are many other hiking areas that are less well known, including the Paklenica and Risnjak National Parks in Croatia. The three national parks of Macedonia and its spectacular gorges at Lake Matka near Skopje are some more options. Mt Tomorri National Park in Albania really is a hiking frontier. The best months for hiking are from June to September, especially late August and early September when the summer crowds will have disappeared.

Skiing

The region's premier skiing area is Slovenia's Julian Alps, though there are a dozen or so lesser-known ski resorts around the Western Balkans. The skiing season generally lasts from early December to late March, though at higher altitudes it may extend an extra month either way. Snow conditions can vary greatly from year to year and region to region, but January and February tend to be the best (and busiest) months. Sarajevo hosted the Winter Olympics in 1984, and the ski resorts of Jahorina and Bjelašnica are open again for business. Macedonia's Mavrovo ski resort is also building a name for itself. Serbia has ski resorts at Kopaonik and Zlatibor, while

Montenegro's candidate for the next skiing discovery is at Durmitor.

Yachting

The most famous yachting area is the passage between the long rugged islands off Croatia's Dalmatian coast. Yacht tours and rentals are available, although this is certainly not for anyone on a budget.

White-Water Rafting

Rafting is possible from March to October on a growing number of scenic rivers, including the Una River near Bihać in Bosnia, the Tara River in Montenegro's World Heritage–listed Durmitor National Park and the Soča River in Slovenia. Even Albania is starting to get in on the action.

BUSINESS HOURS

The Western Balkans tends to have similar working patterns to Western Europe and North America. Saturdays and Sundays are usually days off, although only banks and offices are shut – most shops, restaurants and cafés are open everyday of the week. Even the regions where Muslim culture predominates tend to take Sunday off rather than Friday (the Muslim day of prayer).

Banks are usually open from 9am to 5pm Monday to Friday, often with an hour or two off for lunch. During the hot summer months, some enterprises will shut for two or three hours in the early afternoon, reopening at 3pm or 4pm and working into the evening when it's cooler. See the directory of whichever country you are in for more specific detail.

CHILDREN

Travelling with the kids can add a new dimension to a trip to the Western Balkans, but successful travel with young children requires planning and effort. It might be best to avoid the high summer, as the sometimes extreme heat can make the little darlings very uncomfortable (and grumpy). Don't try to overdo things, and try to include the kids in the activities as well. Dragging children around too many churches and museums can be a deadening experience for everyone. Most car-rental firms have children's safety seats for hire at a small cost, but it is important that you book them in advance. The same goes for high chairs

and cots (cribs): they're standard in many restaurants and hotels but numbers are limited. The choice of baby food, infant formulas, soy and cow's milk, disposable nappies (diapers) and the like can be as great in local supermarkets as it is back home, but the opening hours may be quite different to what you are used to. Don't get caught out on the weekend.

CLIMATE CHARTS

The weather in the Western Balkans can be fairly extreme at times, but never enough to prevent travel. It's a fascinating place to visit any time of year – even during the icy winter. July and August can be uncomfortably hot, particularly in the cities, but this is the time when the alpine areas such as the Julian Alps and the mountains of western Macedonia are at their best, not to mention the beaches. All in all, May, June and September are the best times to visit from

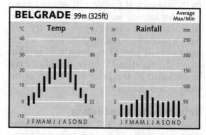

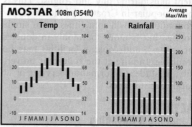

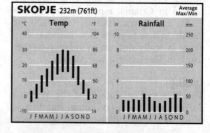

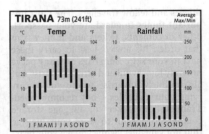

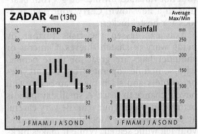

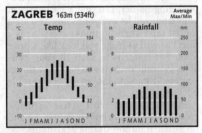

a climatic point of view, as nowhere will be too warm or too cool.

CUSTOMS

The usual allowances for tobacco (200 to 250 cigarettes), alcohol (2L of wine, 1L of spirits) and perfume (50g) apply to duty-free goods purchased at airports or on ferries. It's fair to say that on the tobacco quota in particular you can usually take more – the locals understand how expensive cigarettes are in the wider world. Customs checks are pretty cursory and you probably won't even have to open your bags, but don't be lulled into a false sense of security. There may also be restrictions on the import/export of local currency, although the amounts allowed these days are actually quite large.

While there's no problem with bringing in and taking out personal effects, be aware that antiques, books printed before 1945, crystal glass, gemstones and precious metals (gold, silver, platinum), securities and valuable works of art may still have to be declared in writing or even accompanied by a 'museum certificate' (available from the place of purchase) in many countries.

DANGERS & ANNOYANCES

The Western Balkans is generally slightly safer than the developed world. Putting aside the lurid horrors of the recent wars, personal safety is better than in the big cities of Western Europe, North America or Australia, and personal safety is what affects travellers the most. If you know how to handle yourself in the metropolises of the developed world, your street smarts should see you through the region without any problems. At the risk of sounding like a nanny, you're going to be less of a target if you dress in a similar style to the locals, don't flash around expensive cameras and jewellery, and don't stagger home through dark streets alone after a night out. There is, of course, a Mafia/underworld scene in the Western Balkans, but you really have to go looking for trouble to find it – they have bigger things on their mind. However, you may still find that your friends and relatives will be worried that the past wars mean anarchy today. The best way to allay these fears is to let them know where you are and how to get in touch, and to contact them regularly via phone or email.

Some locals will regale you with tales of how dangerous their city is and recount various cases of muggings and break-ins. Mostly they're comparing the present situation with that under communism when the crime rate was almost zero (or at least that's what the newspapers said). Bosnia and Kosovo have a unique form of danger: land mines – see those destinations for details. The regions where Muslim culture predominates (Kosovo, Albania and parts of Bosnia, Serbia and Macedonia) have less of a heavy drinking culture and less street crime. Something like 50% of street crime and violence is alcohol related.

Most of the countries in the region have relatively high rates of traffic accidents because of cavalier driving habits, badly maintained vehicles and extra road hazards such as wandering livestock. See p405 for more information, and the country chapters for local peculiarities.

Low-level corruption is disappearing fast as the back-scratching system so common during the communist regimes claims its rightful place in the dustbin of history, so do *not* pay bribes to persons in official positions, such as police, border guards, train conductors or ticket inspectors. Threatening to call your embassy is always a good move; if the situation is brought to the attention of the officer's superiors, they will, unsurprisingly, get in trouble.

Don't worry at all if you're taken to the police station for questioning as senior officers will eventually let you go (assuming, of course, you haven't committed a real crime). If you do have to pay a fine or supplementary charge, insist on a proper receipt before turning over any money. In all of this, try to maintain your cool, as any threats from you will only make matters worse.

Drugs

Always treat drugs with a great deal of caution. There are drugs available in the region, but none of them are legal. The local penalties are severe and prison conditions are not good.

Scams

A word of warning about credit cards: fraudulent shopkeepers have been known to make several charge-slip imprints with your credit card when you're not looking and then simply copy your signature from the authorised slip. There have also been reports of unscrupulous people making quick and very high-tech duplicates of credit- or debit-card information with a machine. If your card leaves your possession for longer than you think necessary, consider cancelling it.

Now that local currencies have reached convertibility, the days of getting five times the official rate for cash on the streets of Belgrade and Tirana are well and truly over. Essentially there is no longer a black market in currencies in any of these countries except for Albania; elsewhere anyone offering such a deal is your average garden-variety thief.

Theft

Theft can be a problem in the Western Balkans, and the threat comes from both local thieves and fellow travellers. The most important things to guard are your passport, other documents, tickets and money – in that order. It's always best to carry these next to your skin. Bum bags or fanny packs not only look awful and scream 'tourist' but also publicly advertise where you're carrying your valuables – not recommended. Train-station lockers or luggage-storage counters are useful to store your luggage (but not valuables) while you get your bearings in a new town. Carry your own padlock for hostel lockers.

You can lessen the risks further by being wary of snatch thieves. Cameras or shoulder bags are great for these people, who sometimes operate from motorcycles or scooters and slash the strap before you have a chance to react. A small day-pack is better, but watch your rear. Be very careful at cafés and bars; loop the strap around your leg while seated. While it makes pickpocketing harder, carrying a backpack on your front will let everyone know you are a tourist (and one who thinks everyone is a thief) as well as make you look like a prize idiot. Far better is to keep all your valuables in inside pockets and only have things you could stand to lose in easily accessible pockets.

Pickpockets are most active in dense crowds, especially in busy train stations and on public transport during peak hours.

Be careful even in hotels; don't leave valuables lying around in your room.

Parked cars containing luggage or other bags are prime targets for petty criminals in most cities, and cars with foreign number plates and/or rental-agency stickers attract particular attention. While driving in cities, beware of snatch thieves when you pull up at the lights – keep doors locked and windows rolled up.

In case of theft or loss, always report the incident to the police and ask for a written statement. Otherwise your travel-insurance company won't pay up.

Violence

Though it's unlikely that travellers will encounter any violence, skinheads and neo-Nazis have singled out local Roma as scapegoats. Avoid especially run-down areas in cities and *never* fight back. These people can be extremely dangerous.

DISABLED TRAVELLERS

The Western Balkans can be unpredictable when it comes to facilities for the disabled. The general pattern seems to be that the further south you go, the harder it gets. Slovenian hotels and restaurants (particularly upmarket ones) are often ready to cater for disabled travellers, while Albania's ripped-up pavements are hard enough for the able-bodied. The golden rule is never to expect much and you won't be disappointed, which is not exactly encouraging. Most major museums and sites have disabled access, although there are exceptions. Hotels outside the top bracket and public transport are still universally poor, and it's fair to say that access for the disabled has not been a regional priority in the past decade.

If you have a physical disability, get in touch with your national support organisation (preferably the travel officer if there is one) and ask about the countries you plan to visit. They often have complete libraries devoted to travel, with useful things like access guides, and they can put you in touch with travel agencies who specialise in tours for the disabled. The **Royal Association for Disability & Rehabilitation** (RADAR; ☎ 020-7250 3222 in UK; www.radar.org.uk; 12 City Forum, 250 City Rd, London EC1V 8AF) is a very helpful association with a number of publications for the disabled on sale.

DISCOUNT CARDS
Camping Card International

The Camping Card International (CCI) is a camping ground ID valid for a year that can be used instead of a passport when checking in to camping grounds, and includes third-party insurance. As a result, many camping grounds will offer a small discount (usually 5% to 10%) if you have one. CCIs are issued by automobile associations, camping federations and, sometimes, on the spot at camping grounds. See www.campingcardinternational.org for a list of national bodies that issue the cards. The CCI can also sometimes serve as a guarantee, so that you don't have to leave your passport at reception.

Hostel Cards

A hostelling card is useful, if not mandatory, for staying at hostels. Most hostels don't require that you be a hostelling association member, but they sometimes charge less if you have a card. Some hostels will issue one on the spot or after a few days' stay, though this might cost a bit more than getting one at home.

International Student, Youth & Teacher Cards

An International Student Identity Card (ISIC), a plastic ID-style card with your photograph, provides discounts on many forms of transport (including airlines and local transport), cheap or free admission to museums and sights, and inexpensive meals in some student cafeterias and restaurants. If you're under 26 but not a student, you are eligible to apply for an International Youth Travel Card (IYTC, formerly GO25), issued by the Federation of International Youth Travel Organisations, or the Euro26 card (the latter card may not be recognised in Albania and Serbia and Montenegro). Both go under different names in different countries and give much the same discounts and benefits as an ISIC. An International Teacher Identity Card (ITIC) identifies the holder as an instructor and offers similar deals. All these cards are issued by student unions, hostelling organisations or youth-oriented travel agencies.

Senior Cards

Many attractions offer reduced-price admission for people over 60 or 65 (sometimes as low as 55 for women). Make sure you bring proof of age. For a fee of around €20, European residents aged 60 and over can get a Railplus Card as an add-on to their national rail senior pass. This card entitles the holder to train-fare reductions of around 25%.

In your home country, a lower age may already entitle you to all sorts of interesting travel packages and discounts (on car hire, for instance) through organisations and travel agents that cater for senior travellers. Start hunting at your local senior citizens' advice bureau.

EMBASSIES & CONSULATES

It's important to realise what your embassy can and cannot do to help if you get into trouble while abroad. Generally speaking, it won't be much help in emergencies if

REGIONAL DIRECTORY

the trouble you're in is remotely your own fault. You are bound by the laws of the country you are visiting.

In genuine emergencies you might get some assistance, but only if other channels have been exhausted. For example, if you need to get home urgently, a free ticket back is exceedingly unlikely – the embassy would expect you to have insurance. If you have all your money and documents stolen, it might assist with getting a new passport, but a loan for onward travel is almost always out of the question.

See the individual country chapters for the addresses of embassies and consulates both in the Western Balkans and in your home country.

GAY & LESBIAN TRAVELLERS

While no longer illegal in any of the countries of the Western Balkans, homosexuality is still not completely socially acceptable, so it pays to be careful about public displays of affection. The most progressive attitudes towards gay life and gay travellers can be found in Slovenia, Croatia and Belgrade (Serbia). The majority of local gay men and women are reluctant to admit their sexual orientation, outside of a small but thriving bar and club scene in Zagreb (Croatia), Ljubljana (Slovenia) and Belgrade in particular. The gay scene in Tirana (Albania), Skopje (Macedonia) and Sarajevo (Bosnia) is deep underground, and outside of the large population centres, gay and lesbian life is almost nonexistent.

Good resources for gay travellers include websites such as www.queeria.org.yu (for Serbia and Montenegro), www.touristinfo .gay.hr (for Croatia), www.ljudmila.org/siq rd/guide.php (for Slovenia) and international sites such as www.gaydar.com and www.gay.com. Listings are given wherever possible in the individual country sections.

HOLIDAYS

The Western Balkans' school calendar is nothing unusual – children get the summer months off (usually July and August) as well as breaks for Easter and Christmas. These dates are generally followed even in countries with a large Muslim population, such as Bosnia and Hercegovina and Albania. See the relevant country's directory for details of local holidays and festivals.

The Muslim regions of the Western Balkans celebrate two major festivals or *bajrams*: the end of Ramadan and the Feast of the Sacrifice. Muslim religious holidays follow the lunar calendar, which is 11 or 12 days shorter than the Gregorian calendar, so the dates of the *bajrams* fall 11 or 12 days earlier each (Gregorian) year. To make it even more interesting, the exact dates depend on the sighting of the new moon. In some cases, an imam from one town will spot a sliver of the moon a day earlier or later than his colleagues, so the local faithful will celebrate on a different day, which means the dates below are only approximate.

Year	End of Ramadan	Feast of the Sacrifice
2006	24 October	31 December
2007	13 October	20 December
2008	1 October	8 December

INSURANCE

It is important to be insured against theft, loss and medical problems in the Western Balkans. If your finances are limited and you're planning a low-cost trip in the region, it is tempting to take your chances with no insurance, but the consequences if something does go wrong can be disastrous. The policies written by STA Travel and other student travel organisations are usually good value. Some policies offer lower and higher medical expense options; the higher ones are chiefly for countries like the USA that have extremely expensive medical costs. There are a wide variety of policies available, so check the fine print.

Some insurance policies will specifically exclude 'dangerous activities', which can include scuba diving, motorcycling, horse riding, skiing and even short treks. Some even exclude entire countries (eg Bosnia and Hercegovina or Serbia and Montenegro). It pays to compare the fine print.

You may prefer a policy that pays doctors or hospitals directly rather than requiring you to pay on the spot and claim later. If you have to claim later make sure you keep all documentation. Some policies ask you to call back (reverse charges) to a centre in your home country where an immediate assessment of your problem is made. Check that the policy covers ambulances and an emergency flight home. For more information on health insurance, see p410.

For details on car insurance, see p406.

INTERNET ACCESS

Practically every decent-sized town has Internet access. The connections may be slow, Internet 'cafés' may not serve coffee or other drinks, and sometimes you'll be limited to a monitor in a dark, smelly, smoky room full of teenage boys playing war games or looking up morally suspect websites – but one way or another you'll never be far from your email account. The hourly rates are generally quite low. Indeed, in some more developed cities, Internet cafés can be a social hub and a great way of meeting locals as well as travellers. Make sure you have a web-based email account so you can pick up email on the road without your own laptop. In the less developed corners of the region you may find that while Internet cafés do exist, their connections can be down for days at a time.

If you're travelling with a notebook or hand-held computer, be aware that your modem may not work once you leave your home country. The safest option is to buy a reputable 'global' modem before you leave home, or buy a local PC-card modem if you're spending an extended time in any one country. Wi-fi spots are beginning to appear in some hotels and trendy cafés in the region. For more information on travelling with a portable computer, see www.teleadapt.com.

MONEY

The main problem you'll face as you travel around the region is constant currency changes as you flit between the denar, dinar, lek, convertible mark, kuna, tolar and euro. Most of the local currencies are impossible to change once you're outside the particular country (with the partial exception of the Slovenian tolar), so remember to spend them all or change them into euros before you head onwards. There is no longer any particular desire for 'hard' currency (long gone are the days where hoteliers would slash the rates if you paid in US dollars) and the convertibility of all currencies makes them stable and reliable ways to carry cash.

ATMs & Credit Cards

All the countries and territories of the Western Balkans have plenty of ATMs in cities, major regional centres and tourist spots. Albania was the last country to adopt ATMs. The irritation of trying to change travellers cheques at the weekend and rip-off *bureaux de change* is history.

As purchase tools, credit cards are still not as commonly used as in Western Europe but they're gaining ground, especially Amex, Visa and MasterCard. You'll be able to use them at upmarket restaurants, shops, hotels, car-hire firms, travel agencies and many petrol stations, though cash is still preferred.

Cash or debit cards, which you use at home to withdraw money directly from your bank account or savings account, can be used throughout the Western Balkans at those ATMs linked to international networks like Cirrus and Maestro. Some local ATMs aren't linked to these networks, and some suggest they are but never seem to work. Don't panic, just go looking for another bank. The major advantage of using ATMs is that you don't pay commission charges to exchange money and the exchange rate is usually at a better interbank rate than that offered for travellers cheques or cash exchanges.

Charge cards like Amex, and to a lesser extent Diners Club, have offices in most countries and they can generally replace a lost card within 24 hours. That's because they treat you as a customer of the company rather than of the bank that issued the card. Their major drawback is that they're not widely accepted off the beaten track. Charge cards may also be hooked up to some ATM networks. Credit and credit/debit cards like Visa and MasterCard are more widely accepted because they tend to charge merchants lower commissions.

If you choose to rely on plastic, go for two different cards; this allows one to be used as backup in the case of loss. Better still is a combination of credit card, travellers cheques and cash so you have something to fall back on if an ATM swallows your card or the banks in the area won't accept it (a not uncommon and always inexplicable occurrence).

Cash

This is, of course, the easiest way to carry money, but obviously if you lose it, that's it. The most favoured currency throughout the Western Balkans is the euro. In Montenegro and Kosovo the euro is to all intents the official currency. The US dollar and the British pound are also accepted, though pounds can sometimes only be exchanged in major cities. It is also possible to exchange virtually any other major world currency in big cities, but you are inevitably at the mercy of the exchange office and its rates. It's best to change your money into euro before you leave home and you'll have no problems whatsoever.

Moneychangers

Shop around, never stop at the first place you see, and if you happen to be in a tourist area you can rest assured you'll be offered lower rates everywhere. Some airports, such as Nënë Tereza airport in Albania, also offer rather unfavourable rates. Before handing over any cash always check the commission and rate.

Tipping

Throughout the Western Balkans you tip by rounding up restaurant bills and taxi fares to the next whole figure. In some countries restaurants will already have added a service charge to your bill, so you don't have to round it up much (if at all). A tip of 10% is quite sufficient if you feel you have been well attended. Waiters in any place catering mostly to foreign tourists will usually expect such a tip. If 'rounding up' means you're only giving honest waiters a couple of cents, add a few more coins to keep them happy.

Travellers Cheques

The main idea of using travellers cheques rather than cash is the protection they offer from theft, though they have lost their once enormous popularity as more and more travellers withdraw cash through ATMs as they go along. This means that travellers cheques are becoming increasingly unfamiliar to bank staff, and are becoming more and more of a hassle to change. With travellers cheques you also generally do worse on fees, commissions and exchange rates than you do by using an ATM.

Banks usually charge from 1% to 2% commission to change travellers cheques. Their opening hours are sometimes limited. In the individual chapters, we recommend the most efficient banks of each country. Before signing a travellers cheque always check the commission and rate.

Amex and Thomas Cook representatives cash their own travellers cheques without commission, but both give poor rates of exchange. If you're changing more than US$20, you're usually better off going to a bank and paying the standard 1% to 2% commission to change there.

Western Union

If it all goes horribly wrong and everything gets stolen don't despair. While it's a horrid (and highly unusual) situation, as long as you know the phone number of a friend or relative back home, they will be able to wire money to you anywhere in the region via Western Union. We don't bother listing WU representatives in this guide, as there are literally thousands of them catering to locals working overseas and sending money home. Just look for the distinctive yellow and black sign, and if you're somewhere remote, ask the person sending you the money to ask WU for the nearest office to you. The sender will be given a code that they then communicate to you and you take to the nearest office, along with your passport, to receive your cash.

PHOTOGRAPHY & VIDEO

Film and camera equipment are available everywhere, but shops in the bigger cities have a wider choice. The region was once notorious for its photographic restrictions – taking shots of anything 'strategic' such as bridges or train stations was strictly forbidden. These days local officials are much less paranoid (at least the Albanian security forces won't send you to work in the chrome mines for the rest of your truncated life), but you need to use common sense when it comes to this issue. It is never a good idea to photograph military installations, for example (unless, of course, you really are spying). This is particularly true in Kosovo – the US army at Camp Bondsteel won't look on happy snaps too favourably. It is also sometimes risky (and in questionable taste) to photograph wardamaged areas. Photographing images of poverty and urban decay might also offend people. Extend the usual courtesies before taking close-up photos of people – generally people are happy to pose if you ask, and it's a good way to break the ice. If you want to give people a souvenir, having a Polaroid-style camera that pops out a photo instantly is much easier than taking down an address and remembering to post them a copy later.

In most countries, it is easy to obtain video cartridges in large towns and cities, but make sure you buy the correct format. It is usually worth buying at least a few cartridges duty-free at the start of your trip.

Be aware that museums often demand that you buy permission to photograph or video their displays, and it's often quite expensive, especially for video cameras. Do this when you buy your tickets, if you think you will, as you'll have to retrace your steps if you don't.

Anyone using a digital camera should check that you have enough memory to store your snaps – two 128MB cards will probably be enough. If you do run out of memory space your best bet is to burn your photos onto a CD. Increasing numbers of processing labs now offer this service. While it is possible to track down repair shops if you have a film camera that goes bung, there's not much you can do if a digital camera starts to malfunction, except wait until you get home and send it to the manufacturer's service centre.

To download your pics at an Internet café you'll need a USB cable and a card reader. Some places provide a USB on request but be warned that many of the bigger chain cafés don't let you plug your gear into their computers, meaning that it's back to plan A – the CD.

POST

Details of post offices are given in the information sections of each city or town in the individual country chapters, and postage costs given in the country directory. Both efficiency and cost vary enormously. There seem to be no set rules, but Slovenia and Croatia are likely to be faster, more reliable and more expensive than the rest of the region. The other former Yugoslav countries and territories are pretty good, but Albania is a step behind the rest of the region

Poste restante (having letters sent to you care of local post offices) is unreliable, not to mention an increasingly unnecessary

communication method in the 21st century. If you desperately need something posted to you, do your research: find a friend of a friend who could receive the mail at their address, or ask nicely at a hotel you plan to stay at.

To send a parcel from the Western Balkans you usually have to take it unwrapped to a main post office. Parcels weighing over 2kg often must be taken to a special customs post office. They will usually wrap the parcels for you. They may ask to see your passport and note the number on the form. If you don't have a return address within the country put your name care of any large tourist hotel to satisfy them.

SOLO TRAVELLERS

Travelling alone can be a fantastic experience. You can do exactly what you want to do, see what you want to see and travel at your own pace. You are also more likely to meet locals and socialise with people you'd otherwise never speak to. When you meet up with other solo travellers it's amazing how quickly you can click with certain people and become travelling companions for a day, a week or however long you're on the same trail. But it can also be lonely and less fun when things get frustrating or don't work out. However, backpacking and hostel culture is very adapted to people travelling alone and hostels are great places to meet others. The best advice for solo travellers therefore is to head for your nearest hostel if you feel like some company. All the capitals have expat bars (usually the ubiquitous Irish pubs) if you are missing some convivial company. The Western Balkans is a terrific place for solo travellers because there's such a good mix of places with a developed hostel and tourism scene as well as lots of lesser-known sights and delights which you can soak up in happy isolation.

TELEPHONE

Telephone service has improved throughout the Western Balkans in a very short time. Cities throughout the region have a huge number of call centres, increasingly the domain of entrepreneurs who offer discounted rates. Many Internet cafés offer cheap overseas phone calls – the quality can be a bit variable but at such low prices, you can't complain too much. There are also state-run call centres, which are often in the same building as the main post office. Here you can often make your call from one of the booths inside an enclosed area, paying the cashier as you leave. Public telephones are almost always found at post offices.

Mobile Phones

The expansion of mobile phones has been nothing short of breathtaking in the region and this can be great for travellers. All the mobile phone networks in the region use the GSM standard. If you plan to spend more than a week or so in one country, seriously consider buying a SIM card to slip into your phone (check before you leave with your provider at home that your handset has not been blocked). SIM cards can cost as little as €10 and can be topped up with cards available at supermarkets and any mobile phone dealers. Alternatively, if you have roaming, your phone will usually switch automatically over to a local network. This can be expensive if you use the phone a great deal, but can be very useful for ad hoc use on the road.

Phone Codes

Every country's international dialling code and international access code is given in the Fast Facts section at the beginning of each chapter. To call abroad you simply dial the international access code for the country you are calling from.

Every town has its local code within the country listed directly underneath its chapter heading. To make a domestic call to another city in the same country in the Western Balkans dial the area code with the initial zero and the number.

Phonecards

Local telephone cards, available from post offices, telephone centres, newsstands or retail outlets, are popular everywhere in the region. In fact, in many countries they have become the norm.

There's a wide range of local and international phonecards. For local calls you're usually better off with a local phonecard.

TIME

The Western Balkans lies within one time zone: central European time (GMT+1). This means it's in the same time zone as Italy, Austria and Hungary, but if you are entering the region from Greece, Bulgaria or Romania you need to put your clock back one hour. Greenwich Mean Time (GMT) is five hours ahead of New York, eight hours ahead of Los Angeles and 10 hours behind Sydney. See World Time Zones (p425) for more information. All countries employ daylight savings. Clocks are put forward an hour usually on the last Sunday in March. They are set back one hour on the last Sunday in September.

TOURIST INFORMATION

The quality and presence of tourist information across the Western Balkans varies enormously. While Slovenia and Croatia have successfully developed a network of excellent Tourist Information Centres (TICs), the rest of the region is lagging behind. However, things look set to improve and even Albania should have a TIC in Tirana by the time the next edition of this book is published. Montenegro, Serbia and Macedonia fall in a middle category of places actively trying to encourage tourism, but whose efforts remain rather obscure at the moment. See individual country directories for more specific information.

VISAS & DOCUMENTS
Passport

Your most important travel document is your passport, which should remain valid until well after you return home. If it's just about to expire, renew it before you travel. Some countries insist your passport remain valid for a specified period (usually three to six months) beyond the expected date of your departure from that country. In practice, this is rarely checked.

Once you start travelling, carry your passport (or a copy of it) at all times and guard it carefully. Some countries have laws requiring you to carry official documentation at all times. This is because the Western Balkans has become an important transit route for illegal immigrants into the EU, and the bureaucrats of Brussels are putting a lot of heat on regional governments to crack down on this. The hassles created by losing your passport can be considerably reduced if you have a record of its number and issue date or, even better, photocopies

THE VISA GAME

Citizens of the EU, US, Canada, Australia and New Zealand won't need visas in advance for any country in the Western Balkans (except Macedonia, where Canadians and Australians are required to have one; Australians can get a visa on arrival at Skopje's Petrovec airport, but not at any land border). In Albania, you are required to buy a tourist visa (€10) on arrival at a border, a port or the airport. Albania also has an exit charge of €10, so in effect a visit to Albania costs €20: €10 to get in, €10 to get out. However, visa regulations do change, so you should check with the individual embassies or a reputable travel agency before travelling. See individual country directories for more detail.

of the relevant data pages. A photocopy of your birth certificate can also be useful.

Camping grounds and hotels sometimes insist that you hand over your passport for the duration of your stay, which is very inconvenient, but a driving licence or Camping Card International (CCI) usually solves the problem.

Visas

A visa is a stamp in your passport or a separate piece of paper permitting you to enter the country in question and stay for a specified period of time. Often you can get the visa at the border or at the airport on arrival, but not always, especially if you're travelling by train or bus and the procedure is likely to hold up others. Check first with the embassies or consulates of the countries you plan to visit; otherwise you could find yourself stranded at the border. With a valid passport and visa (if required) you'll be able to visit all Western Balkans countries for up to three months. You are also required to have some sort of onward or return ticket and/or 'sufficient means of support', which in practice is rarely checked unless you turn up at a border or airport immigration control looking like you've been sleeping in a dumpster for a week. Appearances do make a difference, even if it's the least dirty T-shirt you can find.

For those who do require visas, it's important to remember that these will have a 'use-by' date, and you'll be refused entry after that period has elapsed.

Consulates sometimes issue visas on the spot, although some levy a 50% to 100% surcharge for 'express service'. If there's a choice between getting a visa in advance and on the border, go for the former option if you have the time. They're sometimes cheaper in your home country and this can save bureaucratic procedure. In the Western Balkans, the only embassy most people will have to visit is a Macedonian one, and then only if you're Canadian or Australian. Macedonian embassies generally accept visa applications in the morning, do the paperwork and have passports ready to be collected in the afternoon.

Decide in advance if you want a tourist or transit visa. Transit visas, usually valid for just 48 or 72 hours, are often cheaper and issued faster, but it's usually not possible to extend a transit visa or change it to a tourist visa.

The visa form may instruct you to report to police within 48 hours of arrival. If you're staying at a hotel or other official accommodation (camping ground, hostel, private room arranged by a travel agency etc), this will be taken care of for you by the travel agency, hotel or camping ground. If you're staying with friends or relatives, or in a private room arranged on the street or at the train station, you're supposed to register with the police yourself. During the communist days these regulations were strictly enforced, but things are pretty casual in most countries nowadays. However, consult the visa section in the relevant country's directory for full information.

WOMEN TRAVELLERS

Travel for women in the Western Balkans is not particularly challenging if you follow the usual precautions: keep your street smarts about you, remember that flirting may be interpreted as serious angling for sex, and try to maintain a sense of the ridiculous. There's really no way to explain how some women sail through the region without any irritations while others receive regular unwanted attention, but it just seems to happen like that. As long as you dress and behave sensibly when it's warranted, you shouldn't have any serious problems.

In general terms, the degree of difficulty for women travellers in the Western Balkans is a bit higher than Western Europe but much lower than Turkey or Morocco. There is also a certain amount of regional variation. The most culturally conservative part of the region regarding the place of women in society is probably Kosovo, followed by the Muslim areas of Macedonia and Serbia, and then Albania and Bosnia. Women travelling with a male companion in these regions might find that a mysterious cloak of invisibility descends around them. People will address your companion and seemingly not acknowledge you – this isn't out of rudeness but out of a rather quaint code of respect and politeness. It is not necessary to wear a headscarf anywhere besides a mosque or Muslim shrine.

These regions don't have the heavy male drinking culture that prevails in non-Muslim parts of the region, which cuts down on the blindly enthusiastic suitors. Of course, there's also a huge difference between urban and rural attitudes towards female travellers. Bars and restaurants with a regular foreign clientele in Prishtina are quite used to solo women customers, but dropping into a men-only café in the backwoods of Serbia may well bring some disapproving stares. In rural areas it pays to follow local customs such as sitting next to another woman on buses, minivans and trains, and sitting closer to the front than to the back. Hopefully the more women that travel, whether alone, in pairs or in groups, the less unwanted attention lone female travellers in the region will attract.

Despite feminism's advances in many countries in the region, women remain underrepresented in positions of power, in both governmental and corporate spheres. At the risk of generalising, women in the Western Balkans still prefer to wield influence rather than the levers of power themselves.

Transport in Western Balkans

THINGS CHANGE

The information in this chapter is particularly vulnerable to change. Check directly with the airline or a travel agent to make sure you understand how a fare (and ticket) works and be aware of the security requirements for international travel. Shop carefully. The details given in this chapter should be regarded as pointers and are not a substitute for your own careful, up-to-date research.

GETTING THERE & AWAY

This section covers getting to and from the countries of the Western Balkans from outside the region. For information about getting from, say, Croatia to Slovenia and back again, consult the Transport sections at the end of those chapters.

Most of the countries of the Western Balkans aren't served by low-cost 'no frills' airlines, the exception being Slovenia. Flights within the region tend to be expensive and not terribly competitive with buses or trains. Flights from Western Balkans coun-

tries to non-EU countries (eg Romania) are fiercely expensive. But public transport on the ground is cheap and plentiful, though generally the conditions of buses are reminiscent of the 1980s at best and rattling 1950s country buses at worst.

The Western Balkans has flocks of flights to the rest of Europe, but not so many further afield. With severe competition between long-haul airlines and the explosion in no-frills carriers in Europe and the USA, there are plenty of cheap tickets available to gateway cities. Most people arriving from outside Europe will probably end up travelling through Western Europe, simply because the best fares and most frequent connections go through a number of Western European gateway cities. Some travellers choose to reach the region by train – a far more exciting and atmospheric way to enter than flying. There are lots of bus connections from neighbouring countries, as well as many services to Austria, Switzerland and Germany, where generations of people from the Western Balkans have gone to work.

There are many ferry services linking Slovenia, Croatia, Montenegro and Albania with Italy, plus a couple of short rides connecting Greece and Albania.

ENTRY REQUIREMENTS

You won't be surprised to learn that all countries require visitors to have valid passports with at least six months' validity. EU travellers from countries that issue national identity cards can visit Slovenia with just their identity card. Visitors from most countries can visit most of the countries and territories in the region for up to 90 days without needing to get a visa in advance, and entry is usually free. The main exception to the freebie rule is Albania, where visas from all entry points cost €10 for everybody. Check the Visa section in the directory of each country chapter for more information.

AIR

All of the capitals and quite a few regional cities are served by a range of European airlines, though Slovenia's Ljubljana airport is the only one in the region served by low-cost carriers such as easyJet. Broadly speaking, the less touristy the country or region the more expensive the flight, so flying into Prishtina (Kosovo) and Tirana (Albania) is poor value compared to landing in Ljubljana (Slovenia), Zagreb (Croatia) or Belgrade (Serbia). For departure taxes out of particular countries, check the Transport section of the country chapter. Travellers from anywhere outside of Europe should look at getting a flight on a busy route to Western Europe and then a connecting flight into the region. Airlines such as Austrian Airlines, Swiss International Air Lines and Lufthansa may have deals where you fly from North America or Australia and get a flight to the Western Balkans for free. These airlines may also offer open-jaw tickets, where you can fly into, say, Ljubljana and out of Belgrade, which saves a bit of backtracking.

Airports & Airlines

The Western Balkans has six major airports and a host of smaller ones. The biggest in the region are in Belgrade and Zagreb, though Ljubljana punches above its weight as well. See the country chapters for more information about the airports in each country. The following are airlines that fly to and from the Western Balkans.

Ada Air (airline code ZY; www.adaair.com; hub Tirana)

Adria Airways (airline code JP; www.adria-airways.com; hub Ljubljana)

Aer Lingus (airline code EI; www.aerlingus.com; hub Dublin)

Aeroflot (airline code SU; www.aeroflot.com; hub Moscow Sheremetyevo)

Air Baltic (airline code BT; www.airbaltic.com; hub Riga)

Air France (airline code AF; www.airfrance.com; hub Paris)

Air India (airline code AI; www.airindia.com; hub New Delhi/Mumbai)

Albanian Airlines (airline code LV; www.flyalbanian .com; hub Tirana)

Albatros Airways (airline code 4H; www.albatrosair ways.net; hub Tirana)

Alitalia (airline code AZ; www.alitalia.it; hub Rome)

Austrian Airlines (airline code OS; www.aua.com; hub Vienna)

British Airways (airline code BA; www.britishairways .com; hub London Heathrow)

Croatia Airlines (airline code OU; www.croatiaairlines .hr; hub Zagreb)

ČSA (Czech Airlines; airline code OK; www.csa.cz; hub Prague)

EasyJet (airline code EZY; www.easyjet.com; hub London Luton)

Emirates (airline code EK; www.ekgroup.com; hub Dubai)

Hemus Air (airline code DU; www.hemusair.bg; hub Sofia)

JAT (airline code JU; www.jat.com; hub Belgrade)

KLM (airline code KL; www.klm.com; hub Amsterdam)

Kosova Airlines (airline code KOS; www.kosovaairlines .com in Albanian; hub Prishtina)

LOT Polish Airlines (airline code LOT; www.lot.com; hub Warsaw)

Lufthansa (airline code LH; www.lufthansa.com; hub Frankfurt)

Macedonian Airlines (MAT; airline code IN; www .mat.com.mk; hub Skopje)

Malév Hungarian Airlines (airline code MA; www .malev.hu; hub Budapest)

Montenegro Airlines (airline code YM; www.monte negro-airlines.com; hub Podgorica)

Olympic Airways (airline code OA; www.olympicairlines .com; hub Athens)

Royal Jordanian (airline code RJ; www.rja.com.jo; hub Amman)

TRAVELLING TO WESTERN BALKANS ON THE CHEAP

If saving money is more important than saving time, then consider a cheap flight to Western Europe and then a low-cost carrier to Slovenia or to the edge of the region, then travelling overland by bus, train or boat. It can work out very reasonably if you fly from London, Amsterdam or Paris to Austria, Hungary, Italy's Adriatic coast (eg Bari, Brindisi or Ancona) or to Thessaloniki or Corfu in Greece. Lots of Italian Adriatic ports have ferries to Slovenia, Croatia, Montenegro and Albania, and there are ferries from Corfu to Albania as well. Austria, Hungary, Greece and northern Italy also offer many routes into the region by bus and train.

For cheap flights to the edge of the Western Balkans and into Ljubljana, check with budget airlines such as **Ryanair** (www.ryanair.com), **easyJet** (www.easyjet.com), **Air Berlin** (www.airberlin.com), **Germania Express** (www.gexx.de), **Wizz Air** (www.wizzair.com), **bmi baby** (www.bmibaby.com) and **SkyEurope Airlines** (www.skyeurope.com) for their cheapest deals.

Ryanair (airline code FR; www.ryanair.com;
hub London Stansted)
SAS Scandinavian Airlines (airline code SK;
www.scandinavian.net; hub Copenhagen)
Scandjet (airline code FLY; www.scandjet.se;
hub Gothenburg)
SkyEurope Airlines (airline code NE; www.skyeurope
.com; hub Warsaw/Bratislava/Budapest)
SN Brussels Airlines (airline code SN; www.flysn.com;
hub Brussels)
Swiss International Air Lines (airline code LX;
www.swiss.com; hub Zurich)
Turkish Airlines (airline code TK; www.turkishairlines
.com; hub Istanbul)

Tickets

In times past there wasn't much to gain by
buying tickets directly from an airline – discounted tickets were released to selected
travel agencies and specialist discount agencies, and these were usually the cheapest
deals going. While this is still the case for
long-haul flights, shorter European routes
are now routinely sold at decent prices by
the airlines themselves. If dealing with the
expanding number of no-frills carriers, this
is often the only way to purchase tickets.

It's often easiest and cheapest to book
airline tickets online. Even scheduled flights
on commercial airlines can be profitably
booked online through a number of websites, see right. Shop around but always
make sure that the price you are quoted
includes the relevant taxes, as these can
make the difference between a good price
and a great price. For recommended travel
agencies in the Western Balkans, see the
Information sections for each capital city.

Albania

Albania is served by a small but steadily
growing number of airlines, including its
first home-grown budget carrier, Albatros
Airways. Tirana's Nënë Tereza airport is
the only international gateway. The oldest local airline is Albanian Airlines, which
connects Tirana to Frankfurt, Rome and
Istanbul. Ada Air flies to regional destinations such as Thessaloniki, Athens, Bari and
Sofia, while the new budget carrier Albatros
Airways flies to eight cities in Italy for as
low as €60 one way. Major foreign airlines
flying to Albania include Austrian Airlines
from Vienna, Alitalia from Rome, Olympic
Airways from Athens and Turkish Airlines

ONLINE TICKETS

Some recommended websites to book air
tickets include those listed below. They
usually levy a booking fee on any flights
bought, but even if you don't buy through
them, their software can be very useful for
checking that the flight prices offered to
you by other travel agents are the best
ones available.

- www.ebookers.com
- www.flybudget.com
- www.itasoftware.com
- www.opodo.com
- www.statravel.com

---

from Istanbul, and British Airways from
London Gatwick (starting March 2006). A
budget flight to Bari or Brindisi on Italy's
Adriatic coast followed by a ferry to the Albanian ports of Vlora or Durrësi combines
good value with a certain romanticism.

Bosnia & Hercegovina

Sarajevo is served by Austrian Airlines,
Lufthansa, Swiss International Air Lines and
Adria Airways, who pick up at interconti-
nental hubs such as Frankfurt, Vienna and
Zurich. No discount airlines fly into Bos-
nia and Hercegovina, but cheap flights to
Dubrovnik, Zagreb or Split in Croatia and a
bus trip into the country is a possibility.

Croatia

Zagreb is connected to most European capitals as well as Frankfurt, Munich, Istanbul
and Tel Aviv. Elsewhere in the country there
are these scheduled flights: Dubrovnik has
direct flights to Frankfurt, Glasgow, London,
Manchester and Vienna; Split has flights
to London, Lyon, Manchester, Munich,
Nottingham, Rome and Rotterdam; Rijeka
has flights to London; and Pula has a direct
flight to Manchester. Some of the flights to
coastal cities are in the summer only.

Macedonia

Macedonia has two international airports,
at Skopje and Ohrid. Skopje's Petrovec
airport is served by a smallish number of
airlines. Macedonian Airlines (MAT) has
direct flights to Skopje from Amsterdam,

Vienna, Rome, Zurich and Düsseldorf. Malév Hungarian Airlines flies from Budapest, ČSA (Czech Airlines) from Prague, Alitalia from Milan, Austrian Airlines from Vienna and Turkish Airlines from Istanbul. Ohrid airport has weekly flights from Vienna and Zurich year-round and extra services in summer.

Serbia & Montenegro
Connections from Belgrade throughout Europe include Amsterdam, Athens, Copenhagen, Düsseldorf, Frankfurt, London, Milan, Munich, Paris, Rome and Zürich. There are also flights to Cairo. The city is well served by regional airlines that pick up at intercontinental hubs, so travellers from Australia and New Zealand can fly to Dubai and pick up a JAT flight to Belgrade or fly with Lufthansa via Frankfurt or Austrian Airlines via Vienna. Travellers from North America are most likely to pick up connecting flights in London or Frankfurt. Malév Hungarian Airlines flies to Montenegro from Budapest, while Prishtina has quite good connections to London, Frankfurt, Istanbul and Vienna.

Slovenia
For a little country, Slovenia's Brnik airport is surprisingly well connected throughout Europe, notably on Adria Airways, which serves Amsterdam, Brussels, Copenhagen, Dublin, Frankfurt, Istanbul, London, Manchester, Munich, Vienna and Zürich direct. EasyJet has low-cost flights from London Stansted. Ryanair serves several airports just across the Italian and Austrian borders, such as Trieste and Graz.

LAND
For details of overland transport in and out of individual countries refer to the Transport sections in the country chapters. With the advent of the EU, border crossing in the region has never been simpler. The region can be entered from all sides with no problems at all. Some of the major routes are from Italy and Austria into Slovenia, into Serbia from Hungary and into Macedonia from Greece.

Austria
Austria has been a popular destination for guest workers from the Western Balkans for decades, and there are lots of bus and train services heading south into the region. Eurolines (www.eurolines.com) runs buses from Vienna to Zagreb (€29, six hours, two daily), Rijeka (€47, 8¼ hours), Split (€51, 15 hours) and Zadar (€43, 13 hours).

To reach Slovenia, there are buses from Graz to Slovenska Bistrica (€21, 2¼ hours), Rogaška Slatina (€27, three hours) and Ljubljana (€29, 4½ hours).

The *Ljubljana* express travels daily from Vienna to Rijeka (€65, 11½ hours) through Graz, Maribor, Ljubljana (€52, 6¼ hours) and Koper while the EuroCity *Croatia* travels from Vienna to Zagreb (€60, 6½ hours) stopping in Graz and Maribor and going on to Split. There is also a daily train from Vienna to Belgrade (€65, 11 hours).

Bulgaria
There's a daily train from Sofia to Belgrade (€12 to €18, 11 hours). There are four buses a day between Sofia and Skopje (€10, six hours) in Macedonia.

Germany
Deutsche Touring (a division of Eurolines) handles bus connections between German and Croatian cities. As there are too many to list here, it's best to consult www.deutsche-touring.de.

Greece
To Albania there are several daily buses from Thessaloniki (€35, 10 hours) and Athens (€50, 24 hours) to Tirana. There are also buses from Ioannina to Saranda (€6, 1½ hours) and Gjirokastra (€6, 1½ hours), and to Korça from Kastoria and Thessaloniki (€20, five hours).

The unneighbourly Greek policy towards Macedonia means that there are no regular buses between Greece and Macedonia. In the summer holiday season there are sometimes minibus services between Skopje and Thessaloniki (€15 to €20, four hours). But there are two daily trains between Thessaloniki and Skopje (€11, six hours).

To Belgrade there is one daily service from Thessaloniki (€30 to €41, 16 hours).

Hungary
By train there is a daily service from Budapest to Belgrade (€37, seven hours), as well as two daily trains from Szeged in south-

ern Hungary to Subotica (€2.50, 1¾ hours) in Serbia's northern Vojvodina region. There is also a daily bus from Budapest to Subotica (€14, four hours). The four daily trains between Budapest and Zagreb (€35, 6½ hours) also stop in Nagykanizsa, the first main junction inside Hungary. There are three daily Budapest–Ljubljana trains (€60, 8¾ hours) that stop at Maribor, Ptuj and Celje.

There are big discounts on return train fares from Hungary to the Western Balkans – up to 65% to Slovenia and Croatia and 40% to Serbia and Montenegro.

Italy
Monday to Saturday there are roughly hourly buses from Trieste in Italy to Koper (Capodistria in Italian; €3, one hour) and about six go on to Piran. There are also four daily buses direct from Trieste to Piran (€5, 1½ hours), and one direct Trieste–Ljubljana service (€10, three hours) at 6.25am.

Trieste is well connected with the Croatian coast. There are four daily buses to Pula (€14, 3¾ hours), three of which stop at Poreč (Parenzo in Italian) and Rovinj (Rovigno in Italian). There are six buses a day to Rijeka (€7.50, 2½ hours) that stop in Opatija (€7, two hours). There are fewer buses on Sunday. To Dalmatia there's a daily bus that leaves at 5.30pm and stops at Rijeka, Zadar (€32, 7½ hours), Split (€36, 10½ hours) and Dubrovnik (€64, 15 hours).

There's also a bus from Venice and Mestre from Monday to Saturday that stops in Rovinj (€21, three hours) and Pula (€23, 3½ hours). Plus there's a weekly bus in the summer from Milan to Pula (€49, 8½ hours).

Train routes include three daily from Venice to Ljubljana (€32, four to 5½ hours) via Trieste, and a direct morning train from Venice to Zagreb (€41, 6½ hours).

Romania
By train there is a daily service between Belgrade and Bucharest (€27 to €38, 14 hours). Unfortunately there don't seem to be any regular bus services between Serbia and Romania.

RIVER
There are no regular passenger ferries along the Serbian stretch of the Danube (Croatia also has a frontier on the river, but again

there are no regular services). After being closed by the NATO bombing campaign in 1999, the Danube has been open to traffic all the way from Germany to the Black Sea since 2002. There are international tourist cruises on the Danube but they're generally quite expensive. The **Danube Tourist Commission** (www.danube-river.org) is a great source of information on travelling on Eastern Europe's greatest inland waterway, and has lots of links to river cruise companies.

SEA
There is a dazzling array of ferries between Italy and Slovenia, Croatia, Montenegro and Albania, as well as a charming little jaunt between Corfu in Greece and southern Albania. Schedules change almost as frequently as the weather, but broadly speaking there are more boats across the Adriatic between May and October, and less from October until the end of April.

Italy
This is one of the most popular ways to get to the Balkans. Catching cheap flights to Ancona, Venice, Brindisi or Bari and then taking the ferry can often work out cheaper than a direct flight to Tirana or Split. Regular boats from several companies connect Italy with Albania, Croatia and Montenegro.

ALBANIA
A service run by **Adriatica di Navigazione** (www.adriatica.it) operates to Durrësi from Bari (€60, nine hours) daily. Cars cost €90.

Agemar (www.agemar.it) runs a car ferry three times a week to Durrësi from Trieste (€80, 22 hours) and three times a week to Durrësi from Ancona (€85, 17 hours). Cars cost €110 for both routes.

Skenderbeg Lines (www.skenderbeglines.com) runs daily except Sunday between Brindisi and Vlora (€40, 4½ hours).

Agoudimos Line (www.agoudimos-lines.com) also has daily services, except Sunday, between Brindisi and Vlora (€40, seven hours). It has three ferries a week between Bari and Durrësi (€60, nine hours).

CROATIA
Agestea (www.agestea.com), **Azzurraline** (www.azzurraline.com) and **Jadrolinija** (www.jadrolinija.hr), Croatia's national boat line, have ferries between Dubrovnik and Bari (€42 for reclining seat,

eight to nine hours) but only Jadrolinija runs them all year.

Enermar (www.enermar.it) runs a car ferry from Venice to Split (€45, 11 hours) from May to September. **Jadrolinija** (www.jadrolinija .hr), **SEM** (www.sem-marina.hr) and **Tirrenia Navigazione** (www.tirrenia.it) run car ferries from Ancona to Split (€42, 10 hours) and Zadar (€39.50, eight hours) that stop at Stari Grad (Hvar) and Korcula in the summer. **SNAV** (www.snav.it) has a fast car ferry from Pescara and Ancona to Split and from Pescara to Hvar in the summer for about the same price. **Losinska Plovidba** (www.losinjska-plovidba.hr) connects Koper, Slovenia with Pula (€10, 4½ hours), Mali Lošinj (on Lošinj Island; €20, 8½ hours) and Zadar (€25.50, 12½ hours), starting in late spring. **Miatours** (www .miatours.hr) runs passenger boats connecting Ancona with Zadar (€60, 3½ hours) and Hvar (€100, five hours) in summer. **Sanmar** (www.sanmar.it) has summer ferries from Pescara, Italy to Hvar (5½ hours) and Split (€64 to €84, seven hours). **Tirrenia Navigazione** (www.tirrenia.it) runs between Trieste and ports on Croatia's Istrian Peninsula, including Poreč and Rovinj, starting in late spring. **Venezia Lines** (www.venezialines.com) runs weekly and twice weekly passenger boats from Venice to Pula (three hours), Rovinj (2½ to four hours), Umag (just below the Slovenian border on the Istrian Peninsula, close to Koper; 2½ hours), Poreč (2½ hours), Rabac (between Pula and Rijeka on the Istrian Peninsula, very close to Labin; four hours) and Mali Lošinj (four hours) as well as from Rimini to Pula (2½ hours). It is about the same amount of time from Trieste to these destinations. Prices ranges from €43 to €63. The service runs from May to early October.

MONTENEGRO
Adriatica di Navigazione (www.adriatica.it) connects Ancona and Bar every Thursday (€60, 16 hours).

Montenegro Lines (www.montenegrolines.net) sails from Bari to Bar three times a week (€44, 10 hours) and once a week from Ancona to Bar (€77, 16 hours).

Greece
Finikas Lines (finikaslines@yahoo.com) has two ferries a day between Corfu and Saranda (€15, 90 minutes). From June to August the company also has boats between Himara and Corfu, usually two times a week, depending on demand.

Petrakis Lines (petrakis@hol.gr) has a daily hydrofoil between Corfu and Saranda (€15, 35 minutes).

GETTING AROUND

This section covers getting between the different countries of the Western Balkans.

AIR
The major Western Balkans cities are connected by a schedule of regular flights but tend to be fairly pricey. It costs around €150 to fly from Zagreb to Skopje, for example. Unless you are in a big hurry, taking the train is always a cheaper and more interesting option. The major regional air hubs are Zagreb, Ljubljana and Belgrade. Flights to the smaller cities such as Prishtina and Ohrid are even more expensive compared to land travel. Flights within particular countries aren't all that common, given the small size of the countries; the only route commonly used by visitors is within Croatia, from Zagreb to Dubrovnik. All of the airlines based in the region tend to be fairly small, and receive moderately good ratings for punctuality and service. See the country chapters for more details.

Airlines in Western Balkans
Adria Airways (airline code JP; ☎ 386 1-36 91 010; www.adria-airways.com; hub Ljubljana) Flies to Ohrid, Prishtina, Podgorica, Sarajevo, Skopje, Split, Tirana and Zagreb.

Albanian Airlines (airline code LV; ☎ 355 4-235 162; www.flyalbanian.com; hub Tirana) Flies to Prishtina.

Croatia Airlines (airline code OU; ☎ 385 1-48 72 727; www.croatiaairlines.hr; hub Zagreb) Flies to Bol (the main town on Brač Island in Croatia), Dubrovnik, Osijek, Pula, Rijeka, Sarajevo, Skopje, Split and Zadar.

JAT (airline code JU; ☎ 381 11-311 2123; www.jat.com; hub Belgrade) Flies to Banja Luka, Ljubljana, Podgorica, Sarajevo, Skopje, Tirana and Tivat (Montenegro).

Macedonian Airlines (MAT; airline code IN; ☎ 389 2-329 23 33; www.mat.com.mk; hub Skopje) Flies to Belgrade, Banja Luka and Ljubljana.

Montenegro Airlines (airline code YM; ☎ 381 81-664 411; www.montenegro-airlines.com; hub Podgorica) Flies to Belgrade and Ljubljana.

BICYCLE

Touring the region by bicycle varies quite a bit from country to country. Slovenia has a good setup for cycling as the roads are good and drivers are fairly sensitive to cyclists. Albania, at the other extreme, marries average to very bad road conditions with a populace of inexperienced drivers. The other countries and regions fall between these two extremes, though Croatia is pretty decent while Kosovo isn't so great. See under Bicycle in the Transport sections of the country chapters for more information on local conditions.

The key to a successful bike trip is to travel light, and don't overdo it on the first few days. Even for the shortest and most basic trip it's worth carrying the tools necessary for repairing a puncture. You might want to consider packing spare brake and gear cables, spanners, Allen keys, spare spokes and strong adhesive tape. At the risk of stating the bleeding obvious, none of the above are much use unless you know how to do basic repairs. Maintenance is also important (and obvious): check over your bike thoroughly each morning and again at night when the day's touring is over. Take a good lock and always use it when you leave your bike unattended.

The wearing of helmets is not compulsory but is certainly advised.

A seasoned cyclist can average about 80km a day but this depends on the terrain and how much weight is being carried. Again don't overdo it – there's no point burning yourself out during the initial stages.

If you want to bring your own bike, you should be able to take it on the plane. You can either take it apart and pack all the pieces in a bike bag or box, or simply wheel it to the check-in desk, where it should be treated as a piece of check-in luggage. You may have to remove the pedals and turn the handlebars sideways so that it takes up less space in the aircraft's hold; check all this with the airline before you pay for your ticket. If your bicycle and other luggage exceed your weight allowance, ask about alternatives or you may find yourself being charged a ransom for excess baggage.

Within Europe, bikes can usually be transported as luggage subject to a fairly small supplementary fee.

BUS

Buses are a viable alternative to the rail network in the Western Balkans, but generally buses tend to be best for shorter hops such as getting around cities and reaching remote rural villages. They are often the only option in mountainous regions. The ticketing system varies in each country, but advance reservations are rarely necessary. It's always safest to buy your ticket in advance at the station, but on long-distance buses you often just pay upon boarding.

See the individual country chapters for more details about long-distance buses.

CAR & MOTORCYCLE

Travelling by car or motorcycle gives you an immense amount of freedom and is generally worry-free in most of the Western Balkans, though travelling by car can be tricky between EU and non-EU countries. Driving in Albania is particularly troublesome, and we wouldn't dare suggest it was a fun, safe and easy thing to do. But while Enver Hoxha was covering Albania in concrete bunkers, Tito was building a fairly decent highway system in Yugoslavia, and driving in the former Yugoslav countries and regions is fairly easy. Some insurance packages (especially those covering rental cars) do not include all European countries; for example hiring a car in Italy and driving it to Croatia will cause problems unless you have the correct insurance stamp (ask the agency to insure you for wherever you plan to travel). Cars can be inconvenient in city centres when you have to negotiate strange one-way systems or find somewhere to park in a confusing concrete jungle. Local parking habits are quite carefree in the southern part of the Western Balkans in particular, so it's possible you can be blocked in by someone double-parking next to you. Also, theft from vehicles can be a problem. Every country except Albania has a national automobile association which can help with on-road mishaps, maps and more.

UK motoring organisations such as the **RAC** (www.rac.co.uk) and the **Automobile Association** (www.theaa.com) have excellent information on their websites on driving tips and conditions for all the countries of the Western Balkans.

Driving Licence

Proof of ownership of a private vehicle should always be carried (a Vehicle Registration Document for British-registered cars) when touring Europe. An EU driving licence is acceptable for driving throughout most of the Western Balkans, as are North American and Australian licences. But to be on the safe side – or if you have any other type of licence – you should obtain an International Driving Permit (IDP) from your national motoring organisation.

Fuel & Spare Parts

Finding the right type of fuel is no longer a problem in the Western Balkans. Fuel prices vary from country to country and may bear little relation to the general cost of living. Savings can be made if you check prices at a few service stations en route.

Unleaded petrol of 95 or 98 octane is widely available throughout the region. As usual, unleaded fuel is slightly cheaper than super (premium grade) and diesel is about 40% cheaper than unleaded. Petrol stations seem to be placed somewhat erratically. Several may be within a few kilometres of each other and then there may not be any for incredibly long stretches. Make sure you fill up your tank wherever possible – especially if you are travelling off the main highways.

Hire

Hiring a car is quite straightforward. The big international firms will give you reliable service and a good standard of vehicle. Prebooked rates are generally lower than walk-in rates at rental offices, but either way you'll pay about 20% to 40% more than in Western Europe. However, renting from small local companies is nearly always cheaper.

You should be able to make advance reservations online. Check out the following websites:

Avis (www.avis.com)
Budget (www.budget.com)
Europcar (www.europcar.com)
Hertz (www.hertz.com)

If you're coming from North America, Australia or New Zealand, ask your airline if it has any special deals for rental cars in Europe. You can often find very competitive rates.

Although local companies not connected with any chain will usually offer lower prices than the multinationals, when comparing rates beware of printed tariffs intended only for local residents, which may be lower than the prices foreigners are charged. If in doubt, ask. The big chain companies sometimes offer the flexibility of allowing you to pick up the vehicle from one place and drop it off at another at no additional charge.

Minimum age requirements vary from country to country and from one company to another. Generally the rule is that you need to have held a full licence for a minimum of one year. You also generally need a major credit card, though a large wad of cash as a deposit can also be persuasive.

Insurance

Third-party motor insurance is compulsory throughout Europe. For non-EU countries make sure you check the requirements with your insurer. For further advice and more information contact the **Association of British Insurers** (www.abi.org.uk).

In general you should get your insurer to issue a Green Card (which may cost extra), an internationally recognised proof of insurance, and check that it lists all the countries you intend to visit. You'll need this in the event of an accident outside the country where the vehicle is insured. The European Accident Statement (known as the 'Constat Amiable' in France) is available from your insurance company and is copied so that each party at an accident can record information for insurance purposes. The Association of British Insurers has more details. Never sign accident statements you cannot understand or read – insist on a translation and sign that only if it's acceptable.

If the Green Card doesn't list one of the countries you're visiting and your insurer cannot (or will not) add it, you will have to take out separate third-party cover at the border of the country in question. Generally this is only a problem if you plan to drive across to Bulgaria or into Albania.

Taking out a European vehicle breakdown assistance policy, such as the Five Star Service with AA (☎ 0870 550 0600 in UK; www.theaa .com) or the Eurocover Motoring Assistance with RAC (☎ 0800 550 055 in UK; www.rac.co.uk), is a good investment. Non-Europeans might find it cheaper to arrange for international coverage with their own national motoring organisation before leaving home. Ask your motoring organisation for details about free and reciprocal services offered by affiliated organisations around Europe.

Every vehicle travelling across an international border should display a sticker that shows the country of registration. It's compulsory to carry a warning triangle almost everywhere in Europe, which must be displayed in the event of a breakdown. Recommended accessories are a first-aid kit (this is compulsory in Croatia, Macedonia, Slovenia and Serbia and Montenegro) and a spare bulb kit (compulsory in Macedonia). Contact the RAC or the AA for more information.

Road Rules

Motoring organisations are able to supply their members with country-by-country information on motoring regulations, or they may produce motoring guidebooks for general sale.

Driving at night can be particularly hazardous in rural areas as the roads are often narrow and winding, and you may encounter horse-drawn vehicles, cyclists, pedestrians and domestic animals. In the event of an accident you're supposed to notify the police and file an insurance claim. If your car has significant body damage from a previous accident, point this out to customs upon arrival and have it noted somewhere, as damaged vehicles may only be allowed to leave the country with police permission.

Standard international road signs are used throughout all of the Western Balkans, though they may appear sporadically in Albania. You drive on the right-hand side of the road throughout the region and overtake on the left. Keep right except when overtaking, and use your indicators for any change of lane and when pulling away from the kerb. You're not allowed to overtake more than one car at a time, whether they are moving or stationary (eg pulled up at a traffic light).

Speed limits are posted, and are generally 110km/h or 120km/h on motorways (freeways), 100km/h on highways, 80km/h on secondary and tertiary roads and 50km/h or 60km/h in built-up areas. Motorcycles are usually limited to 90km/h on motorways. In towns you may only sound the horn to avoid an accident.

Everywhere in the Western Balkans the use of seat belts is mandatory and motorcyclists (and their passengers) must wear a helmet. In some countries, children under 12 and intoxicated passengers are not allowed in the front seat. Driving after drinking *any* alcohol is a serious offence – most Western Balkan countries have a 0% blood-alcohol concentration (BAC) limit.

HITCHING

Hitching is never entirely safe, and we wouldn't recommend it. There's always a risk when you catch a ride with strangers. It's safer to travel in pairs and to let someone know where you're planning to go. Once you've flagged down a vehicle, its safer if you sit next to a door you can open. Ask the driver where they are going before you say where you are going. Trust your instincts if you feel uncomfortable about getting in, and at the first sign of trouble do insist on getting out. You can find information on ride sharing and hooking up with drivers on websites such as www.hitchhikers.org and www.bugeurope.com.

LOCAL TRANSPORT
Boat

On Croatia's coast the national Jadrolinija car ferries operate year-round on the Bari–Rijeka–Dubrovnik coastal route, stopping at Zadar, Split and several islands. The ferries are more comfortable than buses on the same route, but also more expensive. Local ferries connect the bigger offshore islands with the mainland and with each other. Some of the ferries only operate a few times a day, and once they're full the remaining motorists must sit and wait for the next service. Montenegro and Albania do not have regular coastal ferry services, though in Albania it is sometimes possible to catch a ferry between Himara and Saranda on the Ionian Sea coast from June to August.

Minibus

The shared minibus or *furgon* is a quick but slightly cramped form of both intercity and city transport, particularly in Albania. They leave when full, and you pay when you're on board. They will stop frequently to let passengers on and off. *Furgons* often have very limited space for luggage, which is when you'll thank yourself for packing light.

TRAIN

Trains are the most atmospheric, comfortable and fun way to make long overland journeys in the Western Balkans. All major cities besides Tirana and Prishtina are on the rail network. The train line between Serbia and Montenegro is particularly spectacular, and is highly recommended. Overnight trains also have the benefit of saving you a night's accommodation, and it's a great way to meet locals.

When you travel overnight you'll get a bed reservation included in the price of your ticket, although you may have to pay a few euros extra for the bedding once on board. Each wagon is administered by a steward or stewardess who will look after your ticket and who will make sure that you get off at the correct stop – crucial, if you arrive during the small hours. Each wagon has a toilet and washbasin at either end, although their state of cleanliness can vary massively. Be aware that toilets may be closed while the train is at a station.

If you plan to travel extensively by train, it might be worth getting hold of the *Thomas Cook European Timetable*, which gives a complete listing of train schedules and indicates where supplements apply or where reservations are necessary. It is updated monthly and is available from **Thomas Cook** (www.thomascook.com) outlets in the UK, and from **Forsyth Travel Library** (☎ 800-367 7984; www.forsyth.com) in the USA. In Australia, look for it in a Thomas Cook outlet or one of the bigger bookstores, which can order in copies if they don't have any in stock. If you intend to stick to one or a handful of countries it might be worthwhile getting hold of the national timetable(s) published by the state railway(s). A particularly useful online resource for timetables in the Western Balkans is the DeutcheBahn website at www.bahn.de (in German). Train fares and schedules in US and Canadian dollars for the most popular routes in Europe, including information on rail and youth passes, can be found on www.raileurope.com. For fares in UK pounds go to www.raileurope.co.uk.

Classes

Throughout the Western Balkans there exists a similar system of classes on trains as there is in Western Europe. Short trips, or longer ones that don't involve sleeping on the train, are usually seated like a normal train: benches (on suburban trains) or aeroplane-style seats (on smarter intercity services).

There are generally three classes of sleeping accommodation on trains; some countries have a different name for them, but for the sake of simplicity, we'll call them 3rd, 2nd and 1st class.

Third-class accommodation is not available everywhere, but it's the cheapest way to sleep, although you may feel your privacy has been slightly invaded. The accommodation consists of six berths in each compartment.

Second class has four berths in a closed compartment. If there are two of you, you will share your accommodation with two strangers. However, if there are three of you, you'll often not be joined by anyone.

First class is a treat, although you are paying for space rather than décor or unsurly service in most countries. Here you'll find two berths in a compartment, usually adorned with plastic flowers to remind you what you've paid for.

Costs

While it's reasonable, train travel is pricier than bus travel in some countries. First-class tickets are double the price of 2nd-class tickets, which are in turn approximately twice the price of 3rd-class tickets.

Reservations

It is always advisable to buy a ticket in advance. Seat reservations are also advisable but only necessary if the timetable specifies one is required. Out of season, reservations can be made pretty much up to an hour before departure, but never count on this. On busy routes and during the summer, always try to reserve a seat several days in advance. For peace of mind, you may prefer to book tickets via travel agencies before you leave home, although this will be more expensive than booking on arrival in the Western Balkans.

Train Passes

INTERRAIL

These passes are available to European residents of more than six months' standing (passport identification is required). Terms and conditions vary slightly from country to country, but when travelling in the country where you bought the pass, there is only a discount of about 50% on normal fares. The InterRail pass is split into zones – somewhat inconveniently, the countries of the Western Balkans are divided into three different zones: Slovenia is in Zone G with Italy, Greece and Turkey; Croatia and Bosnia and Hercegovina are in Zone D with Hungary, Slovakia, the Czech Republic and Poland; Macedonia and Serbia and Montenegro are in Zone H with Bulgaria and Romania. This makes InterRail rather expensive for travel across the entire region. Albania is not covered by any InterRail pass.

The normal InterRail pass is for people under 26, though travellers 26 and over can get the InterRail 26+ version. The price for any single zone is €195/286 for those aged under 26/26 and over for 16 days of travel. Two-zone passes are valid for 22 days and cost €275/396, and the all-zone Global Pass is €385/546 for one month of travel.

BALKAN FLEXIPASS

The Balkan Flexipass offered by **Rail Europe** (www.raileurope.com) covers rail travel in Macedonia and Serbia and Montenegro, as well as Bulgaria, Romania, Greece and Turkey. It covers travel in 1st class only, and costs from US$189 for five days' travel in one month to US$397 for 15 days' travel in one month. There are special flexipasses for certain age groups. For people under 26 or over 60, five days' travel in one month costs US$112/152, and 15 days' travel in one month costs US$238/318.

Health

CONTENTS

Travel health depends on your predeparture preparations, your health care while travelling and how you handle any medical problem that does develop. The Western Balkans is generally an exceptionally safe place in terms of staying healthy, with no tropical diseases and an extensive, if sometimes basic, healthcare system.

Prevention is the key to staying healthy while abroad. A little planning, particularly for pre-existing illnesses, will save trouble later: see your dentist before a long trip, carry spare contact lenses or glasses, and take your optical prescription with you.

BEFORE YOU GO

Bring medications in their original, clearly labelled containers, along with a signed and dated letter from your physician describing your medical conditions and medications, including generic names. If carrying syringes, be sure to have a physician's letter documenting their medical necessity.

INSURANCE

If you're an EU citizen, an E111 form, available from health centres, covers you for most medical care. E111 will not cover you for nonemergencies or emergency repatriation home. If you do need health insurance, strongly consider a policy that covers you

---

> **TRAVEL HEALTH WEBSITES**
>
> It's usually a good idea to consult your government's travel health website before departure, if one is available.
>
> **Australia** www.dfat.gov.au/travel/
> **Canada** www.travelhealth.gc.ca
> **UK** www.doh.gov.uk/traveladvice/
> **US** www.cdc.gov/travel/

---

for the worst possible scenario, such as an accident requiring emergency flight home. Find out if your insurance plan will make payments directly to providers or reimburse you later for overseas health expenditures. The former option is preferable.

RECOMMENDED VACCINATIONS

The World Health Organisation (WHO) recommends that all travellers should be covered for diphtheria, tetanus, measles, mumps, rubella and polio, regardless of their destination. Since most vaccines don't produce immunity until at least two weeks after they're given, visit a physician at least six weeks before departure.

INTERNET RESOURCES

The WHO's useful publication *International Travel and Health* is revised annually and is available on line at www.who.int/ith/. Some other useful websites include www.mdtravel health.com (travel health recommendations for every country, updated daily), www.fit fortravel.scot.nhs.uk (general travel advice for the layperson), www.ageconcern.org.uk (advice on travel for the elderly) and www.mariestopes.org.uk (information on women's health and contraception).

IN WESTERN BALKANS

AVAILABILITY & COST OF HEALTH CARE

Good basic health care is readily available and for minor illnesses pharmacists can give advice and sell over-the-counter medication. They can also advise when more specialised help is required and point you in the right direction. The standard of dental care is usually good.

Medical care is not always readily available outside of major cities but embassies, consulates and five-star hotels can usually recommend doctors or clinics.

INFECTIOUS DISEASES
Poliomyelitis
Poliomyelitis is spread through contaminated food and water, and its vaccine is one of those given in childhood and should be boosted every 10 years, either orally (a drop on the tongue) or as an injection.

Rabies
Spread through bites or licks on broken skin from an infected animal, rabies is always fatal unless treated promptly. Animal handlers should be vaccinated, as should those travelling to remote areas where a reliable source of postbite vaccine is not available within 24 hours. Three injections are needed over a month. If you have not been vaccinated, you will need a course of five injections starting 24 hours or as soon as possible after the injury. If you have been vaccinated, you will need fewer injections and have more time to seek medical help.

Tickborne Encephalitis
Spread by tick bites, tickborne encephalitis is a risk in Croatia and Slovenia in the summer months. It is a serious infection of the brain and vaccination is advised for those in risk areas who are unable to avoid tick bites (such as campers, forestry workers and walkers). Two doses of vaccine will give a year's protection, three doses up to three years'.

Typhoid & Hepatitis A
Both of these diseases are spread through contaminated food (particularly shellfish) and water. Typhoid can cause septicaemia; hepatitis A causes liver inflammation and jaundice. Neither is usually fatal. Typhoid vaccine (typhim Vi, typherix) will give protection for three years. In some countries, the oral vaccine Vivotif is also available. Hepatitis A vaccine (Avaxim, VAQTA, Havrix) is given as an injection; a single dose gives protection for up to a year, and a booster gives 10 years' protection. Hepatitis A and typhoid vaccines can also be given as a single dose vaccine, hepatyrix or viatim.

TRAVELLER'S DIARRHOEA
To prevent diarrhoea, avoid tap water unless it has been boiled, filtered or chemically disinfected (with iodine tablets) and steer clear of ice. Only eat fresh fruits or vegetables if cooked or peeled; be wary of dairy products that might contain unpasteurised milk. Eat food which is heated through and avoid buffet-style meals. If a restaurant is full of locals the food is probably safe.

If you develop diarrhoea, be sure to drink plenty of fluids, preferably an oral rehydration solution (eg dioralyte). If you start having more than four or five stools a day, you should take an antibiotic (usually a quinolone drug) and an antidiarrhoeal agent (such as loperamide). If diarrhoea is bloody, persists for more than 72 hours or is accompanied by fever, shaking, chills or severe abdominal pain you should seek medical attention.

ENVIRONMENTAL HAZARDS
Heat Exhaustion
Heat exhaustion occurs following excessive fluid loss with inadequate replacement of fluids and salt. Symptoms include headache, dizziness and tiredness. Dehydration is already happening by the time you feel thirsty – drink sufficient water to produce pale, diluted urine. To treat heat exhaustion, replace lost fluids by drinking water and/or fruit juice, and cool the body with cold water and fans. Treat salt loss with salty fluids such as soup or Bovril, or add a little more table salt to foods than usual.

Insect Bites & Stings
Mosquitoes are found in most parts of Europe. They may not carry malaria but can cause irritation and infected bites. Use a DEET-based insect repellent.

Bees and wasps only cause real problems to those with a severe allergy (anaphylaxis). If you have a severe allergy to bee or wasp stings carry an 'epipen' or similar adrenaline injection.

Sandflies are found around the Mediterranean beaches. Usually, they cause only a nasty itchy bite, but they can carry a rare skin disorder called cutaneous leishmaniasis.

Water
Tap water is generally safe to drink in the main cities and resorts. Do not drink water from rivers or lakes as it may contain

HEALTH

bacteria or viruses that can cause diarrhoea or vomiting.

TRAVELLING WITH CHILDREN

All travellers with children should know how to treat minor ailments and when to seek medical treatment. Make sure the children are up to date with routine vaccinations, and discuss possible travel vaccines well before departure as some are not suitable for children less than one year old.

WOMEN'S HEALTH

Travelling during pregnancy is possible, but there are important things to consider.

Always have a medical check up before planning your trip. The most risky times for travel are during the first 12 weeks of pregnancy and after 30 weeks. Antenatal facilities vary greatly between countries and you should think carefully before travelling to a country with poor medical facilities or where there are major cultural and language differences from home.

SEXUAL HEALTH

Emergency contraception is most effective if taken within 24 hours after unprotected sex. Safe condoms are available throughout the region.

Language

CONTENTS

This language guide offers basic vocabulary to help you get around the Western Balkans. For more extensive coverage of the languages included in this guide, pick up a copy of Lonely Planet's *Eastern Europe Phrasebook*.

Some of the languages in this chapter use polite and informal modes of address (when shown, the informal is indicated by the abbreviation 'inf'). Use the polite form when addressing older people, officials or service staff.

ALBANIAN

PRONUNCIATION

Written Albanian is phonetically consistent and pronunciation shouldn't pose too many problems for English speakers. Each vowel in a diphthong is pronounced and the **rr** is trilled. However, Albanian possesses certain letters that exist in English but are rendered differently.

ë	often silent; at the beginning of a word it's like the 'a' in 'ago'
c	as the 'ts' in 'bits'
ç	as the 'ch' in 'church'
dh	as the 'th' in 'this'
gj	as the 'gy' in 'hogyard'
j	as the 'y' in 'yellow'
q	between 'ch' and 'ky', similar to the 'cu' in 'cure'
th	as in 'thistle'
x	as the 'dz' in 'adze'
xh	as the 'j' in 'jewel'

ACCOMMODATION

hotel	*hotel*
camping ground	*kamp pushimi*

EMERGENCIES – ALBANIAN

Help!	*Ndihmë!*
Call a doctor!	*Thirrni doktorin!*
Call the police!	*Thirrni policinë!*
Go away!	*Zhduku!/Largohuni!*
I'm lost.	*Kam humbur rrugë.*

Do you have any rooms available?	*A keni ndonjë dhomë të lirë?*
a single room	*një dhomë më një krevat*
a double room	*një dhomë më dy krevat*
How much is it per night/person?	*Sa kushton për një natë/njeri?*
Does it include breakfast?	*A e përfshin edhe mëngjesin?*

CONVERSATION & ESSENTIALS

Hello.	*Tungjatjeta/Allo.*
Goodbye.	*Lamtumirë.*
	Mirupafshim. (inf)
Yes.	*Po.*
No.	*Jo.*
Please.	*Ju lutem.*
Thank you.	*Ju falem nderit.*
That's fine.	*Eshtë e mirë.*
You're welcome.	*S'ka përse.*
Excuse me.	*Me falni.* (to get past)
	Më vjen keq. (before a request)
I'm sorry.	*Më falni, ju lutem.*
Do you speak English?	*A flisni anglisht?*
How much is it?	*Sa kushton?*
What's your name?	*Si quheni ju lutem?*
My name is ...	*Unë quhem .../Mua më quajnë ...*

SHOPPING & SERVICES

a bank	*një bankë*
chemist/pharmacy	*farmaci*
the ... embassy	*... ambasadën*
the market	*pazarin*
newsagency	*agjensia e lajmeve*
the post office	*postën*
the telephone centre	*centralin telefonik*
the tourist office	*zyrën e informimeve turistike*
What time does it open/close?	*Në ç'ore hapet/mbyllet?*

TIME, DAYS & NUMBERS

What time is it?	*Sa është ora?*
today	*sot*

LANGUAGE

SIGNS – ALBANIAN	
Hyrje	Entrance
Dalje	Exit
Informim	Information
Hapur	Open
Mbyllur	Closed
E Ndaluar	Prohibited
Policia	Police
Stacioni I Policisë	Police Station
Nevojtorja	Toilets
Burra	Men
Gra	Women

tomorrow	nesër
yesterday	dje
in the morning	në mëngjes
in the afternoon	pas dreke

Monday	e hënë
Tuesday	e martë
Wednesday	e mërkurë
Thursday	e ënjte
Friday	e premte
Saturday	e shtunë
Sunday	e diel

1	një
2	dy
3	tre
4	katër
5	pesë
6	gjashtë
7	shtatë
8	tetë
9	nëntë
10	dhjetë
100	njëqind
1000	njëmijë

TRANSPORT

What time does the ... leave/arrive?	Në ç'orë niset/arrin ...?
boat	barka/lundra
bus	autobusi
tram	tramvaji
train	treni

I'd like ...	Dëshiroj ...
a one-way ticket	një biletë vajtje
a return ticket	një biletë kthimi

(1st/2nd) class	klas (i parë/i dytë)
timetable	orar
bus stop	stacion autobusi

Directions

Where is ...?	Ku është ...?
Go straight ahead.	Shko drejt.
Turn left.	Kthehu majtas.
Turn right.	Kthehu djathtas.
near/far	afër/larg

BOSNIAN, CROATIAN & SERBIAN

WHO SPEAKS WHAT WHERE?

From a linguistic perspective, the differences between Bosnian, Croatian and Serbian are slight (they are all classed as Southern Slavonic languages), and the three are mutually intelligible. From a cultural perspective, the story is significantly different, with distinctions based on religion, ethnicity and geography all contributing to create a heady mix of official and preferred languages and writing systems. In effect, the resolution of the Balkan conflict meant that each new nation had a strong desire to reflect their independence through the recognition of their own official languages.

Croatia is perhaps the simplest to classify: the official language is Croatian and the official writing system is the Roman alphabet. Serbia is also fairly straightforward, with Serbian the official language title, but both Cyrillic and Roman alphabets recognised as official writing systems (and both in common use in schools and the media). Things become considerably more complicated in Bosnia and Hercegovina, however, where all three languages share official status. Bosnian itself is almost identical to Croatian (with a few lexical variations). It's spoken by the Muslim community (Bosniaks) and is written in the Roman alphabet. Croatian is spoken by the Bosnian Croats; it too is written in the Roman alphabet. Serbian (the Bosnian variety of which also sounds more like Croatian in pronunciation than Serbian) is spoken by the Bosnian Serbs and is written in the Cyrillic alphabet. So simple!

PRONUNCIATION

The writing systems of these languages are phonetically consistent: every letter within a word is pronounced and its sound will not vary from word to word. With regard to the position of stress, only one rule can be given: the last syllable of a word is never stressed. In most cases the accent falls on the first vowel in the word.

It's worth familiarising yourself with the Serbian Cyrillic alphabet (see p417). Bosnian and Croatian use a Roman alphabet and many letters are pronounced as in English – the following are some of the departures from the English alphabet and its pronunciation.

c	as the 'ts' in 'cats'
ć	as the 'tch' sound in 'future'
č	as the 'ch' in 'chop'
đ	as the 'dy' sound in 'verdure'
dž	as the 'j' in 'just'
j	as the 'y' in 'young'
lj	as the 'lli' in 'million'
nj	as the 'ny' in 'canyon'
š	as the 'sh' in 'hush'
ž	as the 's' in 'pleasure'

The principal difference between Serbian and Bosnian/Croatian is in the pronunciation of the vowel 'e' in certain words. A long **e** in Serbian becomes 'ije' in Bosnian/Croatian, eg *reka/rijeka* (river), and a short **e** in Serbian becomes 'je' in Bosnian/Croatian, eg *pesma, pjesma* (song). Sometimes, however, the vowel **e** is the same in both languages, as in *selo* (village). This chapter uses Bosnian/Croatian pronunciation for both languages. Any variation in vocabulary between the languages is indicated in the following phrase list by 'B/C/S' for Bosnian/Croatian/Serbian.

ACCOMMODATION
hotel
hotel   хотел
guesthouse
privatno prenoćište   приватно преноћиште
youth hostel
omladinsko prenoćište   омладинско преноћиште
camping ground
kamping   кампинг

Do you have any rooms available?
Imate li slobodne sobe?
Имате ли слободне собе?
How much is it per night/per person?
Koliko košta za jednu noć/po osobi?
Колико кошта за једну ноћ/по особи?

Does it include breakfast?
Da li je u cijenu uključen i doručak?
Да ли је у цену укључен и доручак?

I'd like ...
Želim ...   Желим ...
  a single room
  sobu sa jednim krevetom   собу са једним креветом
  a double room
  sobu sa duplim krevetom   собу са дуплим креветом

CONVERSATION & ESSENTIALS
Hello.
Bog (C)/Zdravo. (B/S)   Здраво.
Goodbye.
Zbogom (C)/
Doviđenja. (B, S)   Довиђења.
Yes.
Da.   Да.
No.
Ne.   Не.
Please.
Molim.   Молим.
Thank you.
Hvala.   Хвала.
That's fine/You're welcome.
U redu je/   У реду је/
Nema na čemu.   Нема на чему.
Excuse me.
Pardon.   Пардон.
Sorry.
Oprostite.   Опростите.
Do you speak English?
Govorite li engleski?   Говорите ли енглески?
What's your name?
Kako se zovete?   Како се зовете?

My name is ...
Zovem se ...   Зовем се ...

SHOPPING & SERVICES
I'm looking for ...
Tražim ...
Тражим ...
   a bank
   banku   банку
   the ... embassy
   ... ambasadu   ... амбасаду
   the market
   tržnicu (C)
   pijacu (B&S)   пијацу
   the post office
   poštu   пошту
   the telephone centre
   telefonsku centralu   телефонску централу
   the tourist office
   turistički biro   туристички биро

How much is it ...?
Koliko košta ...?   Колико кошта ...?

TIME, DAYS & NUMBERS
What time is it?	Koliko je sati?	Колико је сати?
today	danas	данас
tomorrow	sutra	сутра
yesterday	jučer	јуче
in the morning	ujutro	ујутро
in the afternoon	popodne	поподне

Monday	ponedeljak	понедељак
Tuesday	utorak	уторак
Wednesday	srijeda	среда
Thursday	četvrtak	четвртак
Friday	petak	петак
Saturday	subota	субота
Sunday	nedjelja	недеља

1	један	jedan
2	два	dva
3	три	tri
4	четири	četiri
5	пет	pet
6	шест	šest
7	седам	sedam
8	осам	osam
9	девет	devet
10	десет	deset
100	сто	sto
1000	хиљада	hiljada (B&S)/
		tisuću (C)

TRANSPORT
What time does the ... leave/arrive?
Kada ... polazi/dolazi?
Када ... полази/долази?
   boat
   brod   брод
   city bus
   gradski autobus   градски аутобус
   intercity bus
   međugradski autobus   међуградски аутобус
   train
   vlak (C)/voz (B&S)   воз
   tram
   tramvaj   трамвај

one-way ticket
   kartu u jednom pravcu   карту у једном правцу
return ticket
   povratnu kartu   повратну карту
1st class
   prvu klasu   прву класу
2nd class
   drugu klasu   другу класу

Where is the bus/tram stop?
Gdje je autobuska/tramvajska postaja?
Где је аутобуска/трамвајска станица?
Can you show me (on the map)?
Možete li mi pokazati (na karti)?
Можете ли ми показати (на карти)?

Directions
Go straight ahead.
Idite pravo naprijed.   Идите право напред.
Turn left.
Skrenite lijevo   Скрените лево

WAXING CYRILLICAL

The following list shows the letters of the Macedonian and Serbian Cyrillic alphabets. The letters are common to both languages unless otherwise specified.

CYRILLIC	SOUND	PRONUNCIATION
А а	a	short as the 'u' in 'cut'
		long as in 'father'
Б б	b	as in 'but'
В в	v	as in 'van'
Г г	g	as in 'go'
Д д	d	as the 'd' in 'dog'
Ѓ ѓ	j	as in 'judge'
(Macedonian only)		
Ђ ђ	j	as in 'judge'
(Serbian only)		
Е е	e	short as in 'bet'
		long as in 'there'
Ж ж	zh	as the 's' in 'measure'
З з	z	as in 'zoo'
Ѕ ѕ	dz	as the 'ds' in 'suds'
(Macedonian only)		
И и	i	short as in 'bit'
		long as in 'marine'
Ј ј	y	as in 'young'
К к	k	as in 'kind'
Л л	l	as in 'lamp'

CYRILLIC	SOUND	PRONUNCIATION
Љ љ	ly	as the 'lli' in 'million'
М м	m	as in 'mat'
Н н	n	as in 'not'
Њ њ	ny	as the 'ny' in 'canyon'
О о	o	short as in 'hot'
		long as in 'for'
П п	p	as in 'pick'
Р р	r	as in 'rub' (but rolled)
С с	s	as in 'sing'
Т т	t	as in 'ten'
Ќ ќ	ch	as in 'check'
(Macedonian only)		
Ћ ћ	ch	as in 'check'
(Serbian only)		
У у	u	as in 'rule'
Ф ф	f	as in 'fan'
Х х	h	as in 'hot'
Ц ц	ts	as in 'tsar'
Ч ч	ch	as in 'check'
Џ џ	j	as the 'j' in 'judge'
Ш ш	sh	as in 'shop'

Turn right.
Skrenite desno.   Скрените десно.
near/far
blizu/daleko   близу/далеко

MACEDONIAN

It's well worth familiarising yourself with the Macedonian Cyrillic alphabet (above). In the pronunciation guides included with the following phrase list, stress within words is marked as italic.

ACCOMMODATION
hotel
хотел   ho·tel
guesthouse
приватно сметување   pri·vat·no sme·tu·van·ye
youth hostel
младинско   mla·din·sko
преноќиште   pre·no·chish·te
camping ground
кампинг   kam·ping

Do you have any rooms available?
Да ли имате слободни соби?
da li i·ma·te slo·bod·ni so·bi?

How much is it per night/per person?
Која е цената по ноќ/по особа?
ko·ya e tse·na·ta po noch/po o·so·ba?
Does it include breakfast?
Да ли е вклучен појадок?
da li e vklyu·chen po·ya·dok?
a single room
соба со еден кревет
so·ba so e·den kre·vet
a double room
соба со брачен кревет
so·ba so bra·chen kre·vet
for one/two nights
за една/два вечери
za ed·na/dva ve·che·ri

CONVERSATION & ESSENTIALS
Hello.
Здраво.   zdra·vo
Goodbye.
Приатно.   pri·a·tno
Yes.
Да.   da
No.
Не.   ne
Excuse me.
Извинете.   iz·vi·ne·te
Please.
Молам.   mo·lam

Thank you.

Благодарам.   bla·*go*·da·ram

You're welcome.

Нема зошто/   *ne*·ma *zosh*·to/

Мило ми е.   *mi*·lo mi e

Sorry.

Опростете ве молам.   o·*pro*·ste·te ve *mo*·lam

Do you speak English?

Зборувате ли   zbo·*ru*·va·te li

англиски?   *ang*·li·ski?

What's your name?

Како се викате?   *ka*·ko se *vi*·ka·te?

My name is ...

Jac се викам ...   yas se *vi*·kam ...

SHOPPING & SERVICES

bank

банка   *ban*·ka

chemist/pharmacy

аптека   *ap*·te·ka

the embassy

амбасадата   am·ba·*sa*·da·ta

my hotel

мојот хотел   *mo*·yot *ho*·tel

the market

пазарот   *pa*·za·rot

newsagents

киоск за весници   *ki*·osk za *ves*·ni·tsi

the post office

поштата   *posh*·ta·ta

stationers

книжарница   kni·*zhar*·ni·tsa

the telephone centre

телефонската   te·le·*fon*·ska·ta

централа   *tsen*·tra·la

the tourist office

туристичкото биро   tu·ris·*tich*·ko·to *bi*·ro

How much is it?

Колку чини тоа?   *kol*·ku *chi*·ni *to*·a?

What time does it open/close?

Кога се отвора/затвора?   *ko*·ga se *ot*·vo·ra/*zat*·vo·ra?

TIME, DAYS & NUMBERS

What time is it?

Колку е часот?   *kol*·ku e *cha*·sot?

today	денес	*de*·nes
tomorrow	утре	*u*·tre
yesterday	вчера	*vche*·ra
morning	утро	*u*·tro
afternoon	попладне	po·*plad*·ne

EMERGENCIES – MACEDONIAN

Help!

Помош!   *po*·mosh!

Call a doctor!

Повикајте лекар!   po·*vi*·kay·te *le*·kar!

Call the police!

Викнете полиција!   *vik*·ne·te po·*li*·tsi·ya!

Go away!

Одете си!   o·*de*·te si!

I'm lost.

Jac загинав.   jas *za*·gi·nav

Monday	понеделник	po·*ne*·del·nik
Tuesday	вторник	*vtor*·nik
Wednesday	среда	*sre*·da
Thursday	четврток	*chet*·vrtok
Friday	петок	*pe*·tok
Saturday	сабота	*sa*·bo·ta
Sunday	недела	*ne*·de·la

0	нула	*nu*·la
1	еден	*e*·den
2	два	dva
3	три	tri
4	четири	*che*·ti·ri
5	пет	pet
6	шест	shest
7	седум	*se*·dum
8	осум	*o*·sum
9	девет	*de*·vet
10	десет	*de*·set
100	сто	sto
1000	илада	*i*·la·da

TRANSPORT

What time does the next ... leave/arrive?

Кога доаѓа/заминува идниот ...?

ko·ga *do*·a·ja/za·*mi*·nu·va *id*·ni·ot ...?

boat

брод   brod

city bus

автобус градски   *av*·to·bus *grad*·ski

intercity bus

автобус меѓуградски   *av*·to·bus me·*ju*·grad·ski

train

воз   voz

tram

трамвај   *tram*·vay

I'd like ...

Сакам ...   *sa*·kam ...

a one-way ticket

билет во еден правец   *bi*·let vo *e*·den *pra*·vets

SIGNS – MACEDONIAN	
Влез	Entrance
Излез	Exit
Отворено	Open
Затворено	Closed
Информации	Information
Полиција	Police
Полициска Станица	Police Station
Забрането	Prohibited
Клозети	Toilets
Машки	Men
Женски	Women

a return ticket
повратен билет · *pov*·ra·ten *bi*·let
1st class
прва класа · *pr*·va *kla*·sa
2nd class
втора класа · *vto*·ra *kla*·sa

timetable
возен ред · *vo*·zen red
bus stop
автобуска станица · av·*to*·bus·ka *sta*·ni·tsa
train station
железничка станица · zhe·*lez*·nich·ka *sta*·ni·tsa

I'd like to hire a car/bicycle.
Сакам да изнајмам кола/точак.
sa·kam da *iz*·nay·mam *ko*·la/*to*·chak

Directions
Where is ...?
Каде је ...? · *ka*·de ye ...?
Go straight ahead.
Одете право напред. · o·*de*·te *pra*·vo *na*·pred
Turn left/right.
Свртете лево/десно. · svr·*te*·te *le*·vo/*des*·no
near/far
блиску/далеку · *blis*·ku/*da*·le·ku

SLOVENE

PRONUNCIATION

Slovene pronunciation isn't difficult. The alphabet consists of 25 letters, most of which are very similar to English. It doesn't have the letters 'q', 'w', 'x' and 'y', but you will find ê, é, ó, ò, č, š and ž. Each letter represents only one sound, with very few exceptions. The letters **l** and **v** are both pronounced like the English 'w' when they occur at the end of syllables and before vowels. Though words like *trn* (thorn) look unpronounceable, most Slovenes (depending on dialect) add a short vowel like an 'a' or the German 'ö' in front of the 'r' to give a Scot's pronunciation of 'tern' or 'tarn'. Here is a list of letters specific to Slovene:

c	as the 'ts' in 'its'
č	as the 'ch' in 'church'
ê	as the 'a' in 'apple'
e	as the 'a' in 'ago' (when unstressed)
é	as the 'ay' in 'day'
j	as the 'y' in 'yellow'
ó	as the 'o' in 'more'
ò	as the 'o' in 'soft'
r	a rolled 'r' sound
š	as the 'sh' in 'ship'
u	as the 'oo' in 'good'
ž	as the 's' in 'treasure'

ACCOMMODATION
hotel · *hotel*
guesthouse · *gostišče*
camping ground · *kamping*

Do you have a ...? · *Ali imate prosto ...?*
bed · *posteljo*
cheap room · *poceni sobo*
single room · *enoposteljno sobo*
double room · *dvoposteljno sobo*

How much is it ...? · *Koliko stane ...?*
per night/person · *za eno noč/osebo*
for one/two nights · *za eno noč/za dve noči*

Is breakfast included? · *Ali je zajtrk vključen?*

CONVERSATION & ESSENTIALS
Good day/Hello. · *Dober dan.*
Hi. · *Pozdravljen.* (inf)
Goodbye. · *Nasvidenje.*
Yes. · *Da/Ja.* (inf)
No. · *Ne.*
Please. · *Prosim.*
Thank you (very much). · *Hvala (lepa).*
You're welcome. · *Prosim/Ni za kaj!*
Excuse me. · *Oprostite.*
What's your name? · *Kako vam je ime?*
My name is ... · *Jaz sem ...*
Where are you from? · *Od kod ste?*
I'm from ... · *Sem iz ...*

EMERGENCIES – SLOVENE	
Help!	Na pomoč!
Call a doctor!	Pokličite zdravnika!
Call the police!	Pokličite policijo!
Go away!	Pojdite stran!

SHOPPING & SERVICES

Where is the/a ...?	Kje je ...?
bank/exchange	banka/menjalnica
embassy	konzulat/ambasada
post office	pošta
telephone centre	telefonska centrala
tourist office	turistični informacijski urad

TIME, DAYS & NUMBERS

today	danes
tonight	nocoj
tomorrow	jutri
in the morning	zjutraj
in the evening	zvečer

Monday	ponedeljek
Tuesday	torek
Wednesday	sreda
Thursday	četrtek
Friday	petek
Saturday	sobota
Sunday	nedelja

1	ena
2	dve
3	tri
4	štiri
5	pet
6	šest
7	sedem
8	osem
9	devet
10	deset
100	sto
1000	tisoč

TRANSPORT

What time does the ... leave/arrive?	Kdaj odpelje/pripelje ...?
boat/ferry	ladja/trajekt
bus	avtobus
train	vlak

timetable	spored
train station	železniška postaja
bus station	avtobusno postajališče
one-way (ticket)	enosmerna (vozovnica)
return (ticket)	povratna (vozovnica)

Directions

Where is ...?	Kje je ...?
Can you show me on the map?	A mi lahko pokažete na mapi?
How do I get to ...?	Kako pridem do ...?
Is it near/far?	Ali je blizu/daleč?
(Go) straight ahead.	(Pojdite) naravnost naprej.
(Turn) left/right.	(Obrnite) levo/desno.

SIGNS – SLOVENE	
Vhod	Entrance
Izhod	Exit
Informacije	Information
Odprto	Open
Zaprto	Closed
Prepovedano	Prohibited
Stranišče	Toilets

LANGUAGE

Glossary

You may encounter some of the following words during your time in Albania (Alb), Bosnia and Hercegovina (B&H), Croatia (Cro), Macedonia (Mac), Serbia and Montenegro (S&M) and Slovenia (Slo). Some words of indeterminate Slavic origin are marked as (Sla).

acropolis – Classical Greek term for the 'upper town', often with a castle and temples
amam (Mac) – derived from the Turkish word *hammam*, meaning public baths
an (Mac) – derived from the Turkish word *han*, meaning inn

bairam or bajram – a Turkish word meaning feast, also used for the major Muslim religious festivals in the Western Balkans.
ban (Cro) – term for a duke or viceroy
bb (Sla) – *bez broja*, literally 'without a number', used in street addresses
Bektashi – a Muslim sect or Dervish order who revere the Prophet Mohammed's son-in-law, Ali
besa (Alb) – sacred oath, often in relation to a blood feud
bey – Turkish term for a governor or lord
bez broja (Sla) – see *bb*
bezistan, bezisten – Turkish term for a covered market, often connected financially and/or physically to a mosque
Bogumils – a heretical sect of the medieval Christian church in Bosnia and Hercegovina
bura – cold northeasterly wind in winter
buregdz/vinica (B&H) – a bakery selling *burek*
burek, byrek – a pie made with various fillings and filo pastry
burekdžinica (Mac) – a bakery selling *burek*

campanile – bell tower
čaršija (Sla) – Slavic word from Turkish term for a market
ćevabdžinica (B&H/Sla) – a shop selling *ćevapčići*
ćevap, ćevapčići (Sla) – grilled minced lamb or beef
convertible mark (B&H) – the currency of Bosnia and Hercegovina
Crna Gora – Montenegrin name for Montenegro

Dalmatia – the half of Croatia bordering the Adriatic Sea
denar – Macedonia's currency
djamija (Mac) – a main mosque, from the Arabic word *jami* meaning Friday; a mosque where Friday sermons are heard
dnevna karta (Cro) – 'day ticket' for public transport
dolazak (Cro) – arrival, as in train arrival time
domaća rakija (Sla) – homemade spirits

fis (Alb) – clan
FKK – 'Freie Körper Kultur', a German phrase meaning 'free body culture', or wear as little as you want. This acronym denotes nudist beaches in Croatia.
furgon (Alb) – a minivan which takes paying passengers on a fixed route
FYROM – Former Yugoslav Republic of Macedonia, a name used by the UN for Macedonia because of Greek protests, much resented in Macedonia

garderoba (Sla) – left-luggage office
Gheg (Alb) – dialect of northern Albania and Kosovo
gostilna (Slo) – traditional inn serving food
gostionica (Sla) – guesthouse, inn
gostišče (Slo) – guesthouse, inn

hammam – Turkish word for public baths
han – Turkish word for an inn
HDZ (Cro) – Hrvatska Demokratska Zajednica or Croatian Democratic Union, a Croatian political party
Helveti – a Muslim sect or brotherhood of Dervishes
Hrvatska (Cro) – the Croatian name for Croatia

iconostasis – in Orthodox churches, a wall highly decorated with icons separating the congregation from the inner sanctum
Illyrians – early, pre-Slavic inhabitants of the Western Balkans

Jadrolinija (Cro) – Croatia's national coastal ferry company

kabas (Alb) – instrumental Albanian polyphonic music
kafana (S&M) – café
kajmak (Sla) – devastatingly rich cream dish
kale – a Turkish word for a fortress
kanun (Alb) – a canon of traditional Albanian law and customs
Karad/-ord/-e – 19th-century Serbian royal family
karst – limestone
kavana (Cro) – café
kebapčići – a shop selling kebabs, grilled Turkish-style meat dishes
KFOR – Kosovo Force, the NATO-led international peacekeeping force in Kosovo
klapa (Cro) – Croatian a capella music
Knez (Slo) – Grand Duke
konoba (Cro) – small family-run bistro
krstilnica (Slo) – a baptistery or place for baptisms
kuna (Cro) – Croatian currency

lek (Alb) – Albanian currency

maestral – warm wind which blows over the Mediterranean from the Sahara

mafil (Alb) – an indoor balcony where women can watch guests in the guest room

manastir (Sla) – monastery or convent

minaret – the tower on a mosque from which the call to prayer *(azan)* is broadcast

musaka (Sla) – same as Greek moussaka, a baked dish made of layers of meat, potato and eggplant

NDH (Cro) – Nezavisna Država Hrvastka, Independent State of Croatia, the Fascist puppet state which nominally ruled half of the Western Balkans during WWII

ne vozi nedjeljom ni praznikom (Sla) – term in ferry schedules meaning no services on holidays or Sundays.

Nevruz – ancient spring festival of Persian origin, celebrated as a holiday by Bektashi followers

odlazak (Sla) – departure, as in departure time of a train

pasha – a Turkish term for a military governor

pivo (Sla) – beer

plaža (Sla) – beach

polazak (Sla) – arrival, as in arrival time of a train

polje (Sla) – field or plain

poslovni (Sla) – express, as in express train

qilim (Alb) – a woven rug or kilim

raki (Alb) – distilled spirits

rakija (Sla) – distilled spirits

ražnjiči (Sla) – shish kebab

restauracija (Sla) – restaurant

restavracija (Slo) – restaurant

ris (Sla) – lynx

Roma – name for the Romany-speaking communities of the Western Balkans, sometimes called Gypsies

rruga (Alb) – street

RS – Republika Srpska (Serb Republic), the Serbian entity in Bosnia and Hercegovina

salata (Sla) – salad

šar planinec (Mac) – famously protective Macedonian sheep dog

sevdah (B&H) – traditional Bosnian folk music, sometimes dubbed the 'Bosnian blues'

SFOR – Stabilisation Force, the NATO-led international peacekeeping effort in Bosnia and Hercegovina

sheshi (Alb) – square or plaza

Shqipëria (Alb) – the Albanian name for Albania

Sigurimi (Alb) – Albanian Communist-era secret police

skara (Mac) – barbecued meat, ubiquitous menu item in Macedonia

Slavonia – the inland half of Croatia, between Hungary and Bosnia and Hercegovina

slivovka (Slo) – a potent spirit made from plums

šljivovica (Sla) – a potent spirit made from plums

sobe, soba (Sla) – rooms, meaning rooms for rent

sofra – a large metal plate for serving food, from the Turkish word for dinner table

solata (Slo) – salad

stanica (Mac) – a bus station or train station

stelae – Roman funerary stones, a kind of gravestone

stećci (B&H) – medieval tombstones in Bosnia and Hercegovina

sveti (Sla) – saint and/or holy, eg Sveti Jovan (St John) or Sveti Bogorodica (Holy Mother of God)

tartufe (Sla) – truffle, underground fungus adored by gourmets

tekija (Sla) – shrine and/or place of worship for Muslim sects such as the Bektashi

tekke – see *tekija*

teqe (Alb) – see *tekija*

Tosk (Alb) – dialect of southern Albania

Trg (Sla) – square or plaza

Trgovski Centar (Mac) – shopping centre

turbe – Muslim gravestones and/or tombs

turbofolk – an unholy mix of folk tunes 'updated' with Europop music

UÇK (Alb) – Ushtria Çlirimtare Kombetare, National Liberation Army, an ethnic Albanian rebel group active in Kosovo and Macedonia in the late 1990s

ulica (Sla) – street, abbreviated to 'ul'

UNMIK – United Nations Mission in Kosovo, the interim government of this territory

Unprofor – United Nations Protective Force, the UN force which tried to intervene in the Bosnia and Hercegovina war of the early 1990s

Ustaša (s), **Ustaše** (pl) – brutal Croatian fascist party installed in power by the Nazis during WWII

Vlach – a rural community, traditionally shepherds, who speak a Latin-derived language called Aromanian

vladika (S&M) – title of a Montenegrin prince-bishop

VMRO (Mac) – Vnatresno-Makedonska Revolucionerna Organizacija, Internal Macedonian Revolutionary Organisation, early Macedonian liberation movement

Vojvodina – the part of Serbia north of the Danube River

vozi svaki dan (Cro) – means 'service every day' in ferry schedules

xhamia (Alb) – mosque

xhiro (Alb) – Albania's highly social evening stroll

Zimmer frei – German word for room, meaning rooms for rent

Behind the Scenes

THIS BOOK
The authoring of this first edition of *Western Balkans* was coordinated by Richard Plunkett. Vesna Maric and Jeanne Oliver wrote regional chapters. Dr Caroline Evans wrote the health chapter. FAMA International provided content from its *Sarajevo Survival Guide*.

THANKS from the Authors
Richard Plunkett I would like to thank everyone at the Stephen Centre in Tirana, Martin from the AYHA, the guys at Outdoor Albania, Martin Heusinger in Berati, Gan Fujii in Gjirokastra, Avrec Bujari, Michael Gold and Anita Begova in Skopje, Mirjana Davidovska, Graham Seed and especially Slavian Stefanovski in Ohrid. Thanks to Frederik for sharing the road trip – if you hadn't pointed out the times I was driving on the wrong side of the road I may not be here to write this. Cheers to Tim Seaward for engaging in a great Sonic Youth vs Joy Division debate in Skopje. Thanks also to Fiona Christie for her help – her skilful use of carrot and stick got me over the line. I'd also like to thank Greg Burgess at Deakin University for his assistance back in Melbourne, and most of all I should thank the bestest thing that ever happened to me, Rebecca Ryan.

Vesna Maric I wish to thank Rafael for his support and care. *Hvala mami i Tončiju.* Thanks to Gabriel, for once again ploughing through my text. Thanks to my cousins Bojan and Dado and all my Belgrade relatives, my Mostar posse and Ersan in particular.

Thanks very much to Čika Tomica in Sutomore for his hospitality and supplies of pomegranate juice. And, of course, big thanks to my editor Fiona Christie for her kindness and patience, and to all the Lonely Planet team. A big *zivjeli* for my sister who was so brave.

Jeanne Oliver So many people in Croatia and Slovenia helped my research that it would be impossible to name them all. However, I would particularly like to thank Vinko Bartolac in Plitvice, Nena Komarice of the Croatian National Tourist Office in New York, Andrea Petrov in Zagreb, Jagoda Bracanović in Hvar, Ratko Ojdanić in Korčula, Maja Milovčić in Dubrovnik, Samo Gardener in Bohinj, and Vanja in Bled.

CREDITS
Commissioning Editor Fiona Christie
Coordinating Editors Suzannah Shwer, Charlotte Orr
Coordinating Cartographer Jolyon Philcox
Coordinating Layout Designer Vicki Beale
Managing Cartographer Mark Griffiths
Assisting Editors Elizabeth Swan, Margedd Heliosz, Tom Smallman, Kim Noble, Paul Harding, Kate Evans
Assisting Cartographers Helen Rowley
Colour Designer David Kemp
Project Manager Ray Thomson
Language Content Coordinator Quentin Frayne

Thanks to: Brigitte Ellemor, Adriana Mammarella, Kate McDonald, Sally Darmody, Rebecca Lalor, Nick Stebbing, Jennifer Garrett, Tashi Wheeler, Celia Wood

---

THE LONELY PLANET STORY
The story begins with a classic travel adventure: Tony and Maureen Wheeler's 1972 journey across Europe and Asia to Australia. There was no useful information about the overland trail then, so Tony and Maureen published the first Lonely Planet guidebook to meet a growing need.

From a kitchen table, Lonely Planet has grown to become the largest independent travel publisher in the world, with offices in Melbourne (Australia), Oakland (USA) and London (UK). Today Lonely Planet guidebooks cover the globe. There is an ever-growing list of books and information in a variety of media. Some things haven't changed. The main aim is still to make it possible for adventurous travellers to get out there – to explore and better understand the world.

At Lonely Planet we believe travellers can make a positive contribution to the countries they visit – if they respect their host communities and spend their money wisely. Every year 5% of company profit is donated to charities around the world.

ACKNOWLEDGMENTS

Many thanks to FAMA International for the use of content from the *Sarajevo Survival Guide* in the Bosnia chapter.

Map data contained in colour highlights map, and globe on back cover © Mountain High Maps 1993 Digital Wisdom, Inc.

SEND US YOUR FEEDBACK

We love to hear from travellers – your comments keep us on our toes and help make our books better. Our well-travelled team reads every word on what you loved or loathed about this book. Although we cannot reply individually to postal submissions, we always guarantee that your feedback goes straight to the appropriate authors, in time for the next edition. Each person who sends us information is thanked in the next edition – and the most useful submissions are rewarded with a free book.

To send us your updates – and find out about Lonely Planet events, newsletters and travel news – visit our award-winning website: **www.lonelyplanet.com/feedback**.

Note: we may edit, reproduce and incorporate your comments in Lonely Planet products such as guidebooks, websites and digital products, so let us know if you don't want your comments reproduced or your name acknowledged. For a copy of our privacy policy visit www.lonelyplanet.com/privacy.

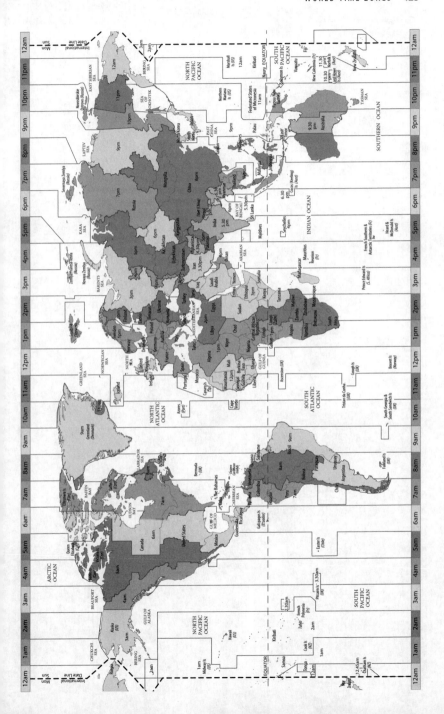

Index

INDEX

000 Map pages
000 Location of colour photographs

INDEX

INDEX

MAP LEGEND

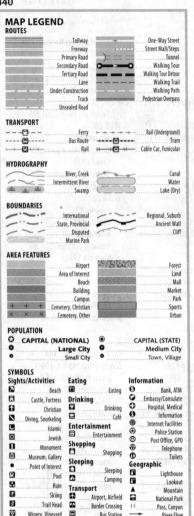

ROUTES

Tollway	One-Way Street
Freeway	Street Mall/Steps
Primary Road	Tunnel
Secondary Road	Walking Tour
Tertiary Road	Walking Tour Detour
Lane	Walking Trail
Under Construction	Walking Path
Track	Pedestrian Overpass
Unsealed Road	

TRANSPORT

Ferry	Rail (Underground)
Bus Route	Tram
Rail	Cable Car, Funicular

HYDROGRAPHY

River, Creek	Canal
Intermittent River	Water
Swamp	Lake (Dry)

BOUNDARIES

International	Regional, Suburb
State, Provincial	Ancient Wall
Disputed	Cliff
Marine Park	

AREA FEATURES

Airport	Forest
Area of Interest	Land
Beach	Mall
Building	Market
Campus	Park
Cemetery, Christian	Sports
Cemetery, Other	Urban

POPULATION

CAPITAL (NATIONAL)	CAPITAL (STATE)
Large City	Medium City
Small City	Town, Village

SYMBOLS

Sights/Activities
- Beach
- Castle, Fortress
- Christian
- Diving, Snorkeling
- Islamic
- Jewish
- Monument
- Museum, Gallery
- Point of Interest
- Pool
- Ruin
- Skiing
- Trail Head
- Winery, Vineyard
- Zoo, Bird Sanctuary

Eating
- Eating

Drinking
- Drinking
- Café

Entertainment
- Entertainment

Shopping
- Shopping

Sleeping
- Sleeping
- Camping

Transport
- Airport, Airfield
- Border Crossing
- Bus Station
- Parking Area

Information
- Bank, ATM
- Embassy/Consulate
- Hospital, Medical
- Information
- Internet Facilities
- Police Station
- Post Office, GPO
- Telephone
- Toilets

Geographic
- Lighthouse
- Lookout
- Mountain
- National Park
- Pass, Canyon
- River Flow
- Waterfall

LONELY PLANET OFFICES

Australia
Head Office
Locked Bag 1, Footscray, Victoria 3011
☎ 03 8379 8000, fax 03 8379 8111
talk2us@lonelyplanet.com.au

USA
150 Linden St, Oakland, CA 94607
☎ 510 893 8555, toll free 800 275 8555
fax 510 893 8572, info@lonelyplanet.com

UK
72–82 Rosebery Ave,
Clerkenwell, London EC1R 4RW
☎ 020 7841 9000, fax 020 7841 9001
go@lonelyplanet.co.uk

Published by Lonely Planet Publications Pty Ltd
ABN 36 005 607 983

© Lonely Planet 2006

© photographers as indicated 2006

Cover photographs: The World Heritage-listed Old Bridge in Mostar, Bosnia and Hercegovina, J Banks/Travel-Images.com (front); Lake Ohrid, Macedonia, Paul David Hellander/Lonely Planet Images (back). Many of the images in this guide are available for licensing from Lonely Planet Images: www.lonelyplanetimages.com

Printed through Colorcraft Ltd, Hong Kong.
Printed in China